SECOND EDITION

THE McGraw-Hill GUIDE

Writing for College, Writing for Life

DUANE ROEN
Arizona State University

GREGORY R. GLAU
Northern Arizona University

BARRY M. MAID
Arizona State University

For Northern Arizona University

Learning Solutions

Boston Burr Ridge, IL Dubuque, IA New York San Francisco St. Louis
Bangkok Bogotá Caracas Lisbon London Madrid
Mexico City Milan New Delhi Seoul Singapore Sydney Taipei Toronto

The McGraw-Hill Companies

The McGraw-Hill Guide: Writing for College, Writing for Life, Second Edition
For Northern Arizona University

This book is a McGraw-Hill Learning Solutions textbook and contains select material from *The McGraw-Hill Guide: Writing for College, Writing for Life*, Second Edition by Duane Roen, Gregory Glau, and Barry Maid. Copyright © 2011 by The McGraw-Hill Companies, Inc. Reprinted with permission of the publisher. Many custom published texts are modified versions or adaptations of our best-selling textbooks. Some adaptations are printed in black and white to keep prices at a minimum, while others are in color.

2 3 4 5 6 7 8 9 0 CCI CCI 13 12 11

ISBN-13: 978-0-07-743830-2
ISBN-10: 0-07-743830-2

Learning Solutions Representative: James Doepke
Production Editor: Kelly Heinrichs
Printer/Binder: Commercial Communications, Inc.

Brief Contents

Contents

"When I think about setting my goals, I think about my audience, my purpose, the rhetorical situation, my voice and tone, and the context, medium, and genre."

PART TWO Using What You Have Learned to Share Information 46

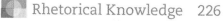

11 Writing to Solve Problems 358

PART FOUR Strategies for Effective Communication 407

hen I think t achieving als, I think t invention trategies to where I can good ideas, ether I will to conduct arch, how I ld organize ideas, how y peers can me improve writing, and ich writing nventions I o check my writing."

[W]hen I think about assessing my goals, I think about whether I attained the outcomes I hoped for and how my [a]udience responded to my writing."

To our students and colleagues, who offered us inspiration for this project.

D. R., G. G., and B. M.

To Maureen, an accomplished writer.

D. R.

For Courtney, with all my love. Thanks for sharing your life with me.

G. G.

For Claire, whose support helped me through.

B. M.

About the Authors

Duane Roen is Professor of English and Head of Humanities in the School of Letters and Sciences at Arizona State University, where he has also served as Director of Composition and Director of the Center for Learning and Teaching Excellence. Prior to that, he directed the Writing Program at Syracuse University, as well as the graduate program in Rhetoric, Composition, and the Teaching of English at the University of Arizona. Early in his career, he taught high school English in New Richmond, Wisconsin, before completing a doctorate at the University of Minnesota. In addition to more than 200 articles, chapters, and conference papers, Duane has published numerous books including *Composing Our Lives in Rhetoric and Composition: Stories about the Growth of a Discipline* (with Theresa Enos and Stuart Brown), *A Sense of Audience in Written Discourse* (with Gesa Kirsch), and *Views from the Center: The CCCC Chairs' Addresses, 1977–2005,* among others. Duane is Secretary of the Conference on College Composition and Communication (CCCC) and Vice President of the Council of Writing Program Administrators (WPA). Duane's interest in family history has motivated him to construct a database that lists more than 32,000 of his ancestors and to collaborate with his wife, Maureen, to write more than 15,000 pages of journal entries about their two children, Nick and Hanna.

Gregory R. Glau is Director of the University Writing Program at Northern Arizona University. Previously, he was Director of Writing Programs at Arizona State University. Greg received his MA in Rhetoric and Composition from Northern Arizona University, and his PhD in Rhetoric, Composition, and the Teaching of English from the University of Arizona. With Linda Adler-Kassner of Eastern Michigan University, Greg is co-editor of the *Bedford Bibliography for Teachers of Basic Writing* (2001; 2nd ed., 2005); the third edition is in press (co-edited with Chitralekha Duttagupta of Utah Valley University). Greg also is co-author of *Scenarios for Writing* (Mayfield/McGraw-Hill, 2001). Greg has published in the *Journal of Basic Writing, WPA: Writing Program Administration, Rhetoric Review, English Journal, The Writing Instructor, IDEAS Plus,* and *Arizona English Bulletin*. Greg regularly presents at CCCC and has presented at WPA, MLA, RMMLA, the Western States Composition Conference, NCTE, and others. He (with Duane Roen and Barry Maid) is past managing editor of *WPA: Writing Program Administration.*

Barry M. Maid is Professor and Head of Multimedia Writing and Technical Communication at Arizona State University, where he led the development of a new program in Multimedia Writing and Technical Communication. He has spent most of his career in some form of writing program administration. Before coming to ASU, he taught at the University of Arkansas at Little Rock where, among other duties, he directed the Writing Center and the First Year Composition Program, chaired the Department of English, and helped create the Department of Rhetoric and Writing. He has written or co-authored chapters for more than a dozen books. His work has also appeared in *Kairos, Computers and Composition,* and the *Writing Lab Newsletter,* among other technology-oriented publications. More recently, Barry has co-authored articles on information literacy for library journals. His professional interests remain primarily in computers and writing, writing program administration (especially program assessment), and partnerships between academia and industry. Barry enjoys long road trips. Over the past several years, he has driven along the Pacific Coast Highway from Los Angeles to Oregon, through national parks in Utah, Arizona, Montana, and Wyoming, and through much of the Carolinas and Tennessee.

Preface

Becoming a writer is a lifelong journey. While this journey often begins in the classroom, it is one that continues and changes in an individual's professional, civic, and personal life. As a fully integrated print and digital solution for the composition classroom with Web-optimized content, search, and peer review capability, *The McGraw-Hill Guide* will equip students with the knowledge and tools to adapt to their changing needs as writers. To meet this objective, "*The Guide*" shows students how to set, achieve, and assess the attainment of their writing goals as part of their journey to become better writers.

Why a Goal-Setting Approach?

The Guide is structured to help students set writing goals, use effective composing strategies to achieve those goals, and assess the results.

In our lengthy careers as writing program administrators and instructors, we have discovered that students are most successful when they have a clear idea about their writing goals. Consequently, we structured *The McGraw-Hill Guide* to help students set goals for their writing, use effective composing strategies to achieve those goals, and assess their progress toward achieving them. By understanding these goals, and the processes by which they can accomplish them, students are empowered to take ownership of their writing and their development as writers. In the short term, once they understand the underlying principles on which their writing is assessed—by doing it themselves—the grades they receive from their instructors no longer seem arbitrary or mystifying. In the long term, students develop the strategies they need to support their writing development when they leave the classroom.

Goals Based on the WPA Learning Outcomes

The student writing goals in *The McGraw-Hill Guide* are drawn from the learning outcomes established by the National Council of Writing Program Administrators because we know how important they have been in shaping discussions about writing curricula in the United States and other countries. These learning outcomes demonstrate the value of the full range of skills and knowledge that writers need to develop: rhetorical knowledge; critical thinking, reading, and writing; composing processes; and knowledge of conventions.

The McGraw-Hill Guide reaches out to students and shows how a goals-oriented approach to writing can be adapted to any writing situation. Effective writers today have a wide range of choices to make to accomplish the goals of any particular writing task. ***The McGraw-Hill Guide*** helps students make these choices by asking three questions:

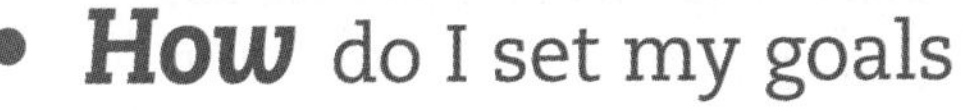

- ***How*** do I set my goals
- ***How*** do I achieve my goals?
- ***How*** do I assess my goals?

The McGraw-Hill Guide shows students how a goals-oriented approach to writing can be adapted to any writing situation.

The McGraw-Hill Guide is a first: it is the first rhetoric developed specifically with the WPA outcomes in mind and it is the first product of its kind that has been fully optimized for the Web, with online content designed for screen reading delivered in an easy-to-use platform that provides in depth peer review, ePortfolio, and assessment management. These tools and more allow *The Guide* to be used as either a hybrid (print + digital) or fully online text, helping students achieve better outcomes while also helping instructors teach them and foster student success.

How do I set my goals?

Effective writers set goals that address the particular situation—the purpose, context, and audience—in which they are writing. With *The McGraw-Hill Guide*, instructors can help students understand and set their writing goals using the assignment chapters in Parts Two and Three (Chapters 4–11). Each of these chapters focuses on a key purpose for which students need to write, provides detailed scenarios in which to situate their writing, and helps them to adapt their goals accordingly. Every chapter of the guide can be assigned and customized online—using only the material needed for any particular assignment. By following the unique structure of *The Guide*, students will be encouraged to:

Preview each chapter.

Each assignment chapter begins with an outline that shows students how that chapter will help them to set, achieve, and assess their writing goals.

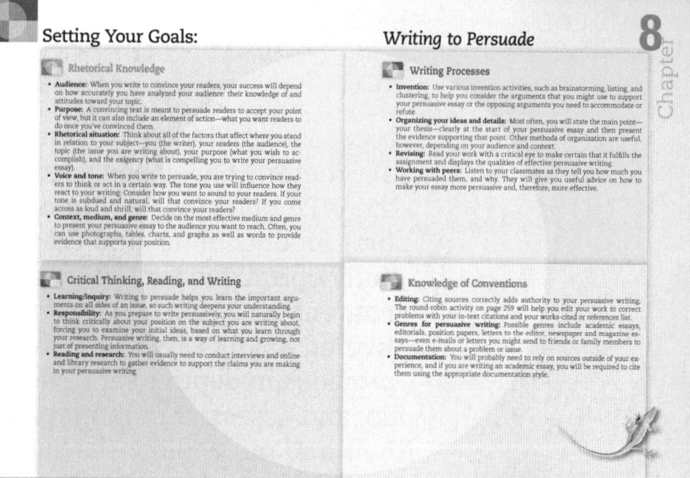

Setting Your Goals: *Writing to Persuade*

Chapter 8

Rhetorical Knowledge

- **Audience:** When you write to convince your readers, your success will depend on how accurately you have analyzed your audience: their knowledge of and attitudes toward your topic.
- **Purpose:** A convincing text is meant to persuade readers to accept your point of view, but it can also include an element of action—what you want readers to do once you've convinced them.
- **Rhetorical situation:** Think about all of the factors that affect where you stand in relation to your subject—you (the writer), your readers (the audience), the topic (the issue you are writing about), your purpose (what you wish to accomplish), and the exigency (what is compelling you to write your persuasive essay).
- **Voice and tone:** When you write to persuade, you are trying to convince readers to think or act in a certain way. The tone you use will influence how they react to your writing. Consider how you want to sound to your readers. If your tone is subdued and natural, will that convince your readers? If you come across as loud and shrill, will that convince your readers?
- **Context, medium, and genre:** Decide on the most effective medium and genre to present your persuasive essay to the audience you want to reach. Often, you can use photographs, tables, charts, and graphs as well as words to provide evidence that supports your position.

Writing Processes

- **Invention:** Use various invention activities, such as brainstorming, listing, and clustering, to help you consider the arguments that you might use to support your persuasive essay or the opposing arguments you need to accommodate or refute.
- **Organizing your ideas and details:** Most often, you will state the main point—your thesis—clearly at the start of your persuasive essay and then present the evidence supporting that point. Other methods of organization are useful, however, depending on your audience and context.
- **Revising:** Read your work with a critical eye to make certain that it fulfills the assignment and displays the qualities of effective persuasive writing.
- **Working with peers:** Listen to your classmates as they tell you how much you have persuaded them, and why. They will give you useful advice on how to make your essay more persuasive and, therefore, more effective.

Critical Thinking, Reading, and Writing

- **Learning/inquiry:** Writing to persuade helps you learn the important arguments on all sides of an issue, so such writing deepens your understanding.
- **Responsibility:** As you prepare to write persuasively, you will naturally begin to think critically about your position on the subject you are writing about, forcing you to examine your initial ideas, based on what you learn through your research. Persuasive writing, then, is a way of learning and growing, not just of presenting information.
- **Reading and research:** You will usually need to conduct interviews and online and library research to gather evidence to support the claims you are making in your persuasive writing.

Knowledge of Conventions

- **Editing:** Citing sources correctly adds authority to your persuasive writing. The round-robin activity on page 259 will help you edit your work to correct problems with your in-text citations and your works-cited or references list.
- **Genres for persuasive writing:** Possible genres include academic essays, editorials, position papers, letters to the editor, newspaper and magazine essays—even e-mails or letters you might send to friends or family members to persuade them about a problem or issue.
- **Documentation:** You will probably need to rely on sources outside of your experience, and if you are writing an academic essay, you will be required to cite them using the appropriate documentation style.

Consider their writing goals.

The *Setting Your Goals* feature, located near the beginning of these chapters, introduces the foundational concepts that will guide students' writing—rhetorical knowledge, critical thinking, writing processes, and knowledge of conventions. Based on the WPA outcomes, these goals encourage students to create a framework for their writing assignments based on sound rhetorical principles.

▶▶▶ Scenarios for Writing | Assignment Options

Your instructor may ask you to complete one or both of the following assignments that call for persuasive writing. Each of these assignments is in the form of a *scenario,* which gives you a sense of who your audience is and what you need to accomplish with your persuasive writing.

Starting on page 243, you will find guidelines for completing whatever scenario you decide—or are asked—to complete.

▶ Writing for College

SCENARIO 1 **Academic Argument about a Controversial Issue**

What controversial issues have you learned about in other college classes? Here are some possibilities:

- Political science: In what ways did the ethical issues some senators and members of the House of Representatives faced immediately before the 2006 election affect the results of that election?
- Business ethics: How effective is the threat of criminal punishment in preventing insider trading of stocks?
- Psychology: How should the courts use the concept of insanity to determine culpability in criminal cases?

Writing Assignment: Select a controversial issue or problem from one of your classes, and compose a paper convincing readers in that class that your position on the issue is valid.

▶ Writing for Life

SCENARIO 2 **Civic Writing: An Editorial about a Campus-Community Problem**

Every college campus has problems, ranging from scarce parking to overcrowded computer labs, to too much vehicle traffic, to too little community involvement. Many of these problems, such as too much traffic, extend into the neighborhoods near the campus.

Consider contexts.

Although most students have an immediate need to improve their academic writing, they will see the benefits of learning to write more clearly if they examine literacy practices in the other areas of their lives as well. Recognizing that writing is a lifelong journey, *The McGraw-Hill Guide* gives students and instructors the option—and the flexibility—of responding to writing scenarios based on academic, professional, civic, and personal contexts. Customizable assessment rubrics are available online for each assignment, giving instructors the ability to clearly show students how writing in different contexts can impact one's goals.

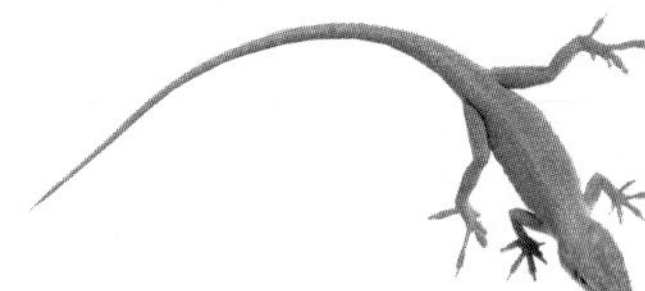

Know the qualities of effective writing.

Students are given clear guidelines and advice on writing throughout the text. "Learning the Qualities of Effective Writing" sections outline the characteristics of writing to meet the purpose discussed in the chapter. Online, more than two hundred brief "Ask the Author" videos allow students to get help on frequently asked questions whenever they need it.

Learning the Qualities of Effective Persuasive Writing

Much of the writing that you do is intended to convince someone to agree with you about something, typically about an issue. An **issue** is a subject or problem area that people care about and about which they hold differing views. Issues of current concern in the United States include tax cuts, campaign finance reform, and school vouchers. Subjects about which people tend to agree—for example, the importance of education in general—are not usually worth writing arguments about.

Persuasive writing that achieves the goal of convincing readers has the following qualities:

- Presentation of the issue. Present your issue in a way that will grab your readers' attention and help them understand that the issue exists and that they should be concerned about it. For example, if you are attempting to convince buyers to purchase cell phones with antivirus protection, you first need to demonstrate the prevalence of cell phone viruses. Another way to present the issue is to share an anecdote about it or to offer some statistics that clearly demonstrate the existence and danger of viruses.
- A clearly stated, arguable claim. A **claim** is the assertion you are making about the issue. Your claim should be clear, of course; a confusing claim will not convince readers. Any claim worth writing about also

How do I achieve my goals?

After presenting the qualities of effective writing related to a particular purpose, each assignment chapter (4–11) then illustrates the steps of the writing process with clear examples of a student writer adapting to a specific writing situation. Designed to emphasize their goals as writers, each assignment chapter helps students to:

View writing as a process.

Because students respond best to examples of student work, the "Writing Processes" section of each assignment chapter follows a student writer through the composing process from invention through drafting and revising. Excerpts from the student's writing, along with a final draft, provide a model for every step in the writing process. Online animations further illustrate how these pieces of writing evolve and take shape over the course of the writing process.

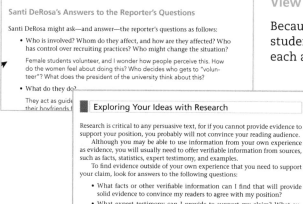

Santi DeRosa's Answers to the Reporter's Questions

Santi DeRosa might ask—and answer—the reporter's questions as follows:

- Who is involved? Whom do they affect, and how are they affected? Who has control over recruiting practices? Who might change the situation?

  Female students volunteer, and I wonder how people perceive this. How do the women feel about doing this? Who decides who gets to "volunteer"? What does the president of the university think about this?

- What do they do?

  They act as guide
  their boyfriends f

Exploring Your Ideas with Research

Research is critical to any persuasive text, for if you cannot provide evidence to support your position, you probably will not convince your reading audience.

Although you may be able to use information from your own experience as evidence, you will usually need to offer verifiable information from sources, such as facts, statistics, expert testimony, and examples.

To find evidence outside of your own experience that you need to support your claim, look for answers to the following questions:

- What facts or other verifiable information can I find that will provide solid evidence to convince my readers to agree with my position?
- What expert testimony can I provide to support my claim? What authorities on my issue might I interview?
- What statistical data support my position?

Integrate research.

A section on "Synthesizing and Integrating Sources into Your Draft" appears in each of Chapters 4–11. Complementing the two chapters on research, these sections outline the steps for integrating a range of secondary materials and provides specific examples from the student paper.

In this brief draft, note how Santi DeRosa incorporates information and examples from his life, as well as from outside sources. As he wrote, DeRosa did not worry about grammar, punctuation, and mechanics; instead, he concentrated on getting his main ideas on paper.

The Objectification of Woman. Who's Fault Is it?
Santi DeRosa

Are women being objectified by a university that has a responsibility to treat women with equality and not as second class citizens?

I say yes. All you need to do is look at the athletics department to see the way women are treated. What I don't understand is that in the year 2003, women are still allowing themselves to be used in such a way

In the past week I have read a couple of news articles from the campus newspaper that got me a little perplexed. Maybe it's the fact that I have a son the age of the female students in the articles. Or, maybe it's the fact that
d nieces that I respect as people and as
se of right and wrong.
icle, "Risky behavior not policed in univer-
igh school football players that visit the

Synthesizing and Integrating Sources: Incorporating Partial Quotes in Your Sentences

Conducting research provides you with lots of quotations, which means you have to determine how to incorporate those quotations into your text. One way to use quotations, whether they come from someone you interviewed or from someone you read, is to incorporate what they said into your sentences. Sometimes when writers use a quotation, the sequence is (1) who I spoke with and (2) what she or he told me:

> I interviewed Joy Watson and she said, "The recycling program is working."

Now, there is nothing wrong with that approach to using a quotation, but sometimes you want to integrate a quotation, or a part of quotation, into your sentences. The key to doing so is to select the most important part of the quotation and use that inside your sentence, which means you surround it with your own words. If you want to include an entire quotation in one of your sentences, be sure not only to introduce the quotation but also to follow up with your own words, after the quotation.

Use Visuals Effectively.

Because many writing situations today require visual as well as verbal texts, *Visualizing Variations* encourages students to consider how they can use visuals, such as Web sites, posters, graphs, and photos, in their writing. To bring the discussion of visuals together, Chapter 18 provides an overview on using design and visuals in one's writing.

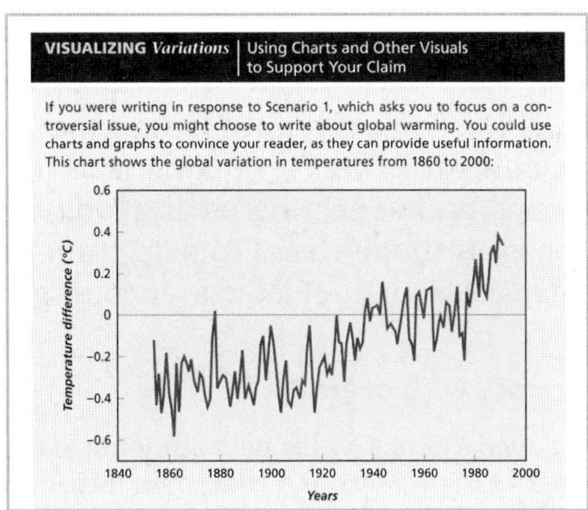

VISUALIZING Variations | Using Charts and Other Visuals to Support Your Claim
If you were writing in response to Scenario 1, which asks you to focus on a controversial issue, you might choose to write about global warming. You could use charts and graphs to convince your reader, as they can provide useful information. This chart shows the global variation in temperatures from 1860 to 2000:
Temperature difference (°C)
0.6
0.4
0.2
0
−0.2
−0.4
−0.6
1840
1860
1880
1900
1920
1940
1960
1980
2000
Years

Choose the Appropriate Genre.

Ways of Writing tables present examples of different genres relevant to the chapter topic and describe their advantages and limitations. "Genres Up Close" provides a closer look at one genre relevant to the chapter's writing purpose. Genres covered include a literacy narrative, a profile, and a poster. An example of the genre follows each of these sections. Additional genre descriptions are available online.

Ways of Writing to Explore

Genres for Your College Classes	Sample Situation	Advantages of the Genre	Limitations of the Genre
Academic essay	For your creative nonfiction class, you are asked to construct an essay exploring the writing styles of several authors you have read and studied.	Your exploration, using the conventions of an academic essay will help you better understand the details of the writing styles of the authors you've studied.	An exploration often leads to more questions, which can be unsettling to a writer.
Internet exploration	Your writing professor has asked you to explore the Internet for reliable and relevant Web sites pertaining to your research topic and then post their links with a summary on a discussion board for the class.	This will help you understand what electronic resources are available, as well as the range of quality.	Depending on your topic, there may be too much information to search through.
Exploratory paper	Your computer science instructor asks you to write an exploratory paper that proposes at least three viable solutions to a networking p	This activity will require that you envision multiple solutions rather than just one.	It can be difficult to write fairly about solutions you don't think will work.
Letter	You want to your school n explores the proposed cha parking and ment in the d		
Oral presentation	For your art c to construct a		

GENRES *Up Close* **Writing a Profile**

Because people are so curious about other people, they love to write and talk about them. To satisfy that craving, readers can find plenty of venues that offer profiles. Profiles of famous and not-so-famous people appear in magazines such as *People* and *Rolling Stone*, radio news shows such as *All Things Considered* on National Public Radio, television shows such as *E! News*, and especially online social networking sites such as MySpace and Facebook. The social networking sites are especially popular because they allow ordinary people to read profiles of other ordinary people. A recent Web search on the term "Facebook," for example, yielded more than half a billion sites. That is astounding, considering that Earth's population was approximately 6.7 billion at the time.

Although profiles often focus on people, they also can describe organizations, places, and events. Profiles have distinctive features. They tend to:

- Be brief. A profile may take no more than a few pages or computer screens.
- Focus on a short period of time. A profile may cover the time needed for a single event, such a two-hour dinner with friends, a day of shopping, or a weekend of camping at a state park.
- Provide some insight into the subject. A profile takes readers behind the scenes to reveal details that are not widely known.

As you consider the following Web page describing the Peace Corps, think about how it exemplifies the characteristics of a profile.

How do I assess my goals?

The McGraw-Hill Guide gives students experience evaluating the work of their peers and responding to others' evaluations of their own work through Writer's Workshop exercises and online peer reviewing tools. Then, by reflecting on the writing process, students assess themselves. To help students assess whether they have achieved their goals, *The McGraw-Hill Guide* encourages students to:

Collaborate with peers.

Writer's Workshop activities help students learn to examine the work of their peers and their own writing with a critical eye. These collaborative activities teach students to work constructively in groups to review each others' writing and provide critical first readings that eventually will help them to assess their own work.

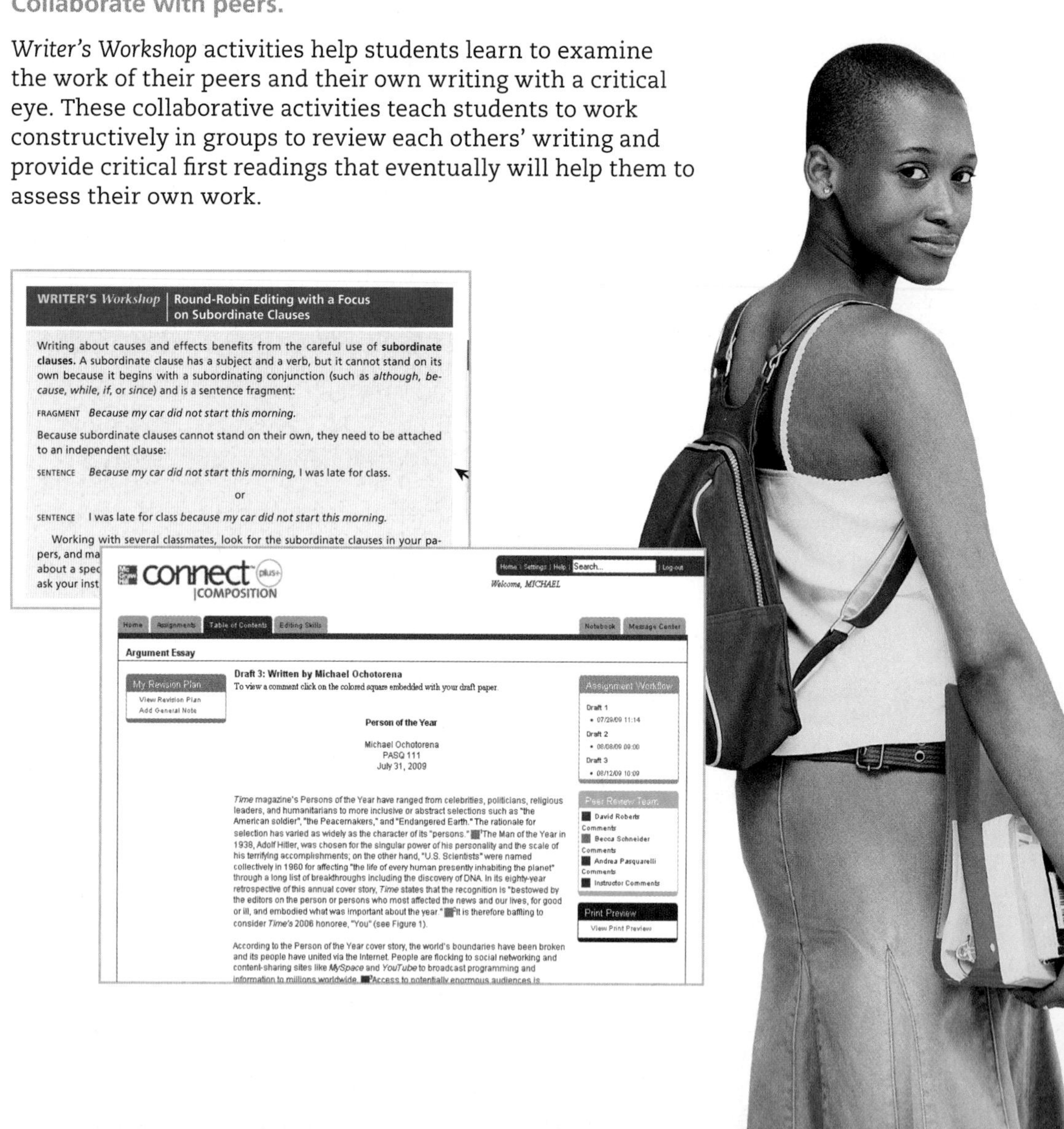

WRITER'S *Workshop* | Round-Robin Editing with a Focus on Subordinate Clauses

Writing about causes and effects benefits from the careful use of **subordinate clauses.** A subordinate clause has a subject and a verb, but it cannot stand on its own because it begins with a subordinating conjunction (such as *although, because, while, if,* or *since*) and is a sentence fragment:

FRAGMENT *Because my car did not start this morning.*

Because subordinate clauses cannot stand on their own, they need to be attached to an independent clause:

SENTENCE *Because my car did not start this morning,* I was late for class.

or

SENTENCE I was late for class *because my car did not start this morning.*

Working with several classmates, look for the subordinate clauses in your papers, and ma
about a spec
ask your inst

connect plus+
COMPOSITION
Home | Settings | Help Search... | Log out
Welcome, MICHAEL
Home
Assignments
Table of Contents
Editing Skills
Notebook
Message Center
Argument Essay
My Revision Plan
View Revision Plan
Add General Note
Draft 3: Written by Michael Ochotorena
To view a comment click on the colored square embedded with your draft paper.
Person of the Year
Michael Ochotorena
PASQ 111
July 31, 2009
Time magazine's Persons of the Year have ranged from celebrities, politicians, religious leaders, and humanitarians to more inclusive or abstract selections such as "the American soldier", "the Peacemakers," and "Endangered Earth." The rationale for selection has varied as widely as the character of its "persons." The Man of the Year in 1938, Adolf Hitler, was chosen for the singular power of his personality and the scale of his terrifying accomplishments; on the other hand, "U.S. Scientists" were named collectively in 1960 for affecting "the life of every human presently inhabiting the planet" through a long list of breakthroughs including the discovery of DNA. In its eighty-year retrospective of this annual cover story, Time states that the recognition is "bestowed by the editors on the person or persons who most affected the news and our lives, for good or ill, and embodied what was important about the year." It is therefore baffling to consider Time's 2006 honoree, "You" (see Figure 1).
According to the Person of the Year cover story, the world's boundaries have been broken and its people have united via the Internet. People are flocking to social networking and content-sharing sites like MySpace and YouTube to broadcast programming and information to millions worldwide.
Assignment Workflow
Draft 1
07/29/09 11:14
Draft 2
08/08/09 09:00
Draft 3
08/12/09 10:09
Peer Review Team
David Roberts Comments
Becca Schneider Comments
Andrea Pasquarelli Comments
Instructor Comments
Print Preview
View Print Preview

Online, *The Guide* provides several powerful tools for students to improve their writing skills, better understand their readers, assess the impact of their writing, and organize their revisions to address the needs of their audience. In particular, *The Guide's* digital peer review system allows students not only to see and consider the comments of others, but also to reflect on their work and create a roadmap for revision based on the feedback they receive. Instructors can use the technology to arrange peer groups in view of particular class dynamics and improve the peer group experience.

Self-Assessment: Reflecting on Your Goals

Now that you have constructed a piece of writing designed to convince your readers, review your learning goals, which you and your classmates may have considered at the beginning of this chapter (pages 224–225). Then reflect on all the thinking and writing that you have done in constructing your persuasive paper. To help reflect on the learning goals that you have achieved, respond in writing to the following questions:

Rhetorical Knowledge

- *Audience:* What have you learned about addressing an audience in persuasive writing?
- *Purpose:* What have you learned about the purposes for constructing an effective persuasive text?
- *Rhetorical situation:* How did the writing context affect your persuasive text?
- *Voice and tone:* How would you describe your voice in this essay? Your tone? How do they contribute to the effectiveness of your persuasive essay?
- *Context, medium, and genre:* How did your context determine the medium and genre you chose, and how did those decisions affect your writing?

Critical Thinking, Reading, and Writing

- *Learning/inquiry:* How did you decide what to focus on for your persuasive text? Describe the process you went through to focus on a main idea, or thesis.
- *Responsibility:* How did you fulfill your responsibilities to your readers?
- *Reading and research:* What did you learn about persuasive writing from the reading selections in this chapter? What research did you conduct? How sufficient was the research you did?
- *Skills:* As a result of writing this paper, how have you become a more critical thinker, reader, and writer? What skills do you hope to develop further?

Reflect on the writing process.

Each chapter concludes with questions to guide self-assessment, prompting students to consider how their work on the chapter's assignment has helped them progress toward attaining the goals for the chapter and build their knowledge of themselves as writers and thinkers. The self-assessment is organized around the four writing goals that students were asked to use to create their writing goals at the start of the chapter—rhetorical knowledge; critical thinking, reading, and writing; composing processes; and conventions.

Address course outcomes.

The Guide's powerful, customizable assessment tools provide instructors with a way to communicate assessment criteria for each class or across the entire writing program, so that students clearly understand the outcomes of the course as well as the grading rubrics used to assess their writing. These tools allow instructors to define learning outcomes for the course and create rubrics to assess students' writing holistically or in the context of outcomes for each writing assignment. Powerful reporting tools give instructors opportunities to generate assessment data for individual students, one or more sections of the course, or all sections to evaluate the success of their entire writing program.

Tegrity

Tegrity Campus is a service that makes class time available all the time by automatically capturing every lecture in a searchable format for students to review when they study and complete assignments. With a simple one-click, start-and-stop process, you capture all computer screens and corresponding audio. Students replay any part of any class with easy-to-use browser-based viewing on a PC or Mac.

Educators know that the more students can see, hear, and experience class resources, the better they learn. With Tegrity Campus, students quickly recall key moments by using Tegrity Campus's unique search feature. This search helps students efficiently find what they need, when they need it, across an entire semester of class recordings. Help turn all your students' study time into learning moments immediately supported by your lecture.

To learn more about Tegrity watch a two-minute Flash demo at http://tegritycampus.mhhe.com.

CourseSmart

Learn Smart. Choose Smart.

CourseSmart is a new way to find and buy eTextbooks. At CourseSmart you can save up to 50% off the cost of a print textbook, reduce your impact on the environment, and gain access to powerful web tools for learning. CourseSmart has the largest selection of eTextbooks available anywhere, offering thousands of the most commonly adopted textbooks from a wide variety of higher education publishers. CourseSmart eTextbooks are available in one standard online reader with full text search, notes and highlighting, and email tools for sharing notes between classmates. For further details, go to www.coursesmart.com.

Instructor's Resource Manual

Written by the authors of *The McGraw-Hill Guide*, this in-depth resource includes advice and companion instruction by three of the discipline's preeminent rhetoricians. This incredible resource features suggested assignment sequences, assignment rubrics, sample syllabi, in-class activities, and discussion topics. Instructors may gain access to the IRM at www.mhhe.com/mhguide2e.

Acknowledgments

On a personal level, we'd like to thank our colleagues at Arizona State University and at Northern Arizona University, who've heard us talking about the project (probably more than they'd wished to!), offered constant support, and gave us good advice: Demetria Baker, O. M. "Skip" Brack, Fred Corey, Barbara D'Angelo, Frank D'Angelo, Emily Davalos, Chitralekha Duttagupta, Ben Fasano, Janice Frangella, Maureen Goggin, Sonia Gracia-Grondin, Scott Guenthner, Barbara Hanks, Jeremy Helm, Glenn Irvin, Ruth Johnston, Cindy Lucas, Keith Miller, Neal Lester, Silvia Llamas-Flores, Ian Moulton, Patricia Murphy, Camille Newton, Sherry Rankins-Robertson, Dave Schwalm, Linda Searcy, Craig Thatcher, Cynthia Villegas, Andra Williams, Brooke Wonders, and Allen Woodman. Duane would like especially to thank Hanna and Maureen Roen.

A number of people have made important contributions to this text and its media components. Cynthia Jeney of Missouri Western State University contributed most of the TechNotes, for which we thank her. Charlotte Smith of Adirondack Community College helped us locate reading selections, and Joanna Imm, Julie McBurney, and Judy Voss all provided editorial suggestions and guidance at various stages. Video producers Peter Berkow and Bruce Coykendahl have worked tirelessly on the videos that are part of the *McGraw-Hill Guide Online* and the Faculty Development Web site. Debora Person of the University of Wyoming provided expert commentary on the sections on library and Internet research, for which we thank her.

At McGraw-Hill, we were fortunate to have some of the best in the business helping us with this project, including Steve Debow, president of the Humanities, Social Science, and Languages group; Mike Ryan, editor in chief; Sharon Loeb, director of marketing; Allison Jones, our tireless and creative marketing manager; and Ray Kelley, Paula Radosevich, Byron Hopkins, and Audra Bussey, our terrific field publishers. Sherree D'Amico, our senior sales representative, and Mina Mathies, our regional manager, have both provided us with valuable advice. Paul Banks, media development editor, has worked tirelessly on the *The McGraw-Hill Guide Online* and has provided us with useful comments on the text. Allister Fein oversaw the beautiful design of the text, Tom Briggs copy edited the text, Jennifer Blankenship and Natalia Peschiera handled the photo research, and Regina Ernst was responsible for seeing the text through production. We owe special thanks to Lisa Moore, now the publisher for history, arts, and the humanities, who originally helped us develop the concept and signed the project, and to Chris Bennem, senior sponsoring editor, who has guided us "editorially" in a thoughtful and kind manner. We also owe a special thanks to Carla Samodulski, senior development editor, who is quite simply the best developmental editor in the business—and to Cara Labell, who served cheerfully and professionally as the developmental editor for this second edition, and Judith Kromm, who worked with us as we moved through final editing and production. Thanks Lisa, Chris, Carla, Cara, and Judith.

Finally, we are indebted to all our fellow fellow Freshman Composition instructors whose valuable advice helped shape the second edition.

McGraw-Hill Assessment Research in Composition (MARC) Partners

McGraw-Hill is honored to partner with these five higher education institutions to conduct research on the ways in which pedagogical tools can constructively impact student performance in writing.

Collin College

Martha Tolleson
Sonja Andrus
Lauryn Angel-Cann
Betty Battacchi
Tammy Brightwell
Cathy Cloud
David Flanagin
Margaret Gonzalez
Susan Grimland
Lisa Kirby
Sarah Moore
Dana Moran
Beth Morley
Gordon O'Neal
Ray Slavens
Clay Stevens
John Wu

Johnson & Wales University—Providence

Donna Thomsen
Eileen Medeiros
Terry Novak

Northern Arizona University

Jacquelyn Belknap
Valerie Robin
Nicholas Tambakeras

Richland College

Paula Eschliman
Anthony Armstrong
Suzie Baker
Sarah Bowman
Debra Frazier

University of Texas—El Paso

Beth Brunk-Chavez
Christie Daniels
Judith Fourzan
Maggie Smith
Adam Webb
Judika Webb

The McGraw-Hill Guide Founder's Circle, *The McGraw-Hill Guide* Board of Advisors and Connect™ Composition and Writing Board of Advisors

McGraw-Hill is grateful to the members of these advisory boards for their ongoing availability to participate in reviews, focus groups and one-on-one consultations. We have great respect for all their contributions.

Aims Community College
Heidi Marie Magoon Connor
Auburn University
Michelle Sidler
Collin County Community College
Sonja Andrus, Kelly Martin
Daytona State College
Heather Eaton
Delgado Community College
Cathy Gorvine
Florida Gulf Coast University
Randall McClure
Fort Hays State University
John Ross
Fort Sumter Community College
Melanie Wagner
Guilford Technical College
Carolyn Schneider
Indian River State College
Sarah Mallonee
Johnson & Wales University–Miami
James Anderson

Johnson & Wales University–Providence
Donna Thomsen
Louisiana State University
Irv Peckham
Loyola Marymount University
K.J. Peters
Mesa Community College
Shelley Rodrigo
Nicholls State University
Keri Turner
North Carolina A&T State University
Jason DePolo
Oklahoma City Community College
Kim Jameson
Community College–Meramec
Richard Peraud, Deborah Hyland
University of Alabama
Steffen Guenzel
University of California–Irvine
Lynda Haas
University of West Georgia
Brandy James
Utah Valley University
Gae Lynn Henderson
Volunteer State Community College
Shellie Michael
Waubonsee Community College
Sarah Quirk
Wayne County Community College
Stacha Floyd
Western Kentucky University
Judith Szerdaelyi

Reviewers

***The McGraw-Hill Guide* was developed in large measure through the guidance of more than one hundred and forty instructors.**

Abraham Baldwin Agricultural College
Erin Campbell, Bobbie Robinson
Alamance Community College
Anne Helms
Arapahoe Community College
Tami Comstock-Peavy, Lindsay Lewan, Jamey Trotter
Arizona State University–Downtown
Regina Clemens Fox
Arizona State University–Tempe
Nicole Khoury
Atlanta Metropolitan College
Kokila Ravi
Bismarck State College
Jane Schreck
Bradley University
Edith Baker
Brigham Young University
Joyce Adams
Cardinal Stritch University
Karen Bilda
Cedar Valley College
Rebekah Rios Harris
Cerritos College
Jack Swanson
Chemeketa Community College
Eva Payne
Cincinnati State Technical and Community College
Robert Jakubovic, Andrea Leslie
College of Coastal Georgia
Meribeth Fell
College of DuPage
Helen Szymanski
College of Southern Nevada
Levia DiNardo Hayes, Sherry Rosenthal, Bradley Waltman
Collin Community College
Sonja Andrus, Kelly Martin
Cowley College
Marlys Cervantes, Julie Kratt
Cuyahoga Community College
Ben Davis, Jr.
Davidson County Community College
Dottie Burkhart
Dillard University
Gayle Duskin
Dona Anna Community College
Greg Hammond
East Carolina University
Wendy Sharer
Eastern Illinois University
Christopher Wixson
Eastern Washington University
Polly Buckingham
Edmonds Community College
Greg Van Belle
El Paso Community College
Theodore Johnston, Tony Procell, Mauricio Rodriguez, Kelli Wood

Emporia State University
Rachelle Smith

Finger Lakes Community College
Sandra Camillo, Deborah Ferrell

Florida International University
Kimberley Harrison

Fort Sumter Community College
Melanie Wagner

Front Range Community College
Donna Craine, Mary Lee Geary, Mark Saunders

Georgia Perimeter College
Kari Miller

Gordon College
Lori Ambacher

Guilford Technical Community College
Jo Ann Buck, Carolyn Schneider

Harrisburg Area Community College
Geraldine Gutwein

Holmes Community College
Billy Wilson

Indiana University–Purdue University–Fort Wayne
Stevens Amidon

Indiana University–Purdue University–Indianapolis
Scott Weeden, Anne Williams

J Sargeant Reynolds Community College
Ashley Bourne, Martha K. Leighty, Miles McCrimmon

Jackson Community College
Gary Cale

John Tyler Community College
Patrick Tompkins

Johnson & Wales University–Denver
Velda Iverson

Johnson & Wales University–Miami
James Anderson

Johnson & Wales University–Providence
William Lenox, Eileen Medeiros, Terry Novak, Donna Thomsen

Johnson County Community College
Mary Pat McQueeney, Jim McWard

Kansas City Kansas Community College
Adam Hadley, James Krajewski

Lake-Sumter Community College
Patricia Campbell, Jacklyn Pierce, Melanie Wagner

Longview Community College–Lees Summit
Dawnielle Robinson-Walker

Lorain County Community College
Suzanne Owens

Loyola University of Chicago
Angela Adams

McLennan Community College
Linda Cook

Mesa Community College
Shelley Rodrigo

Metropolitan Community College–Omaha
Kym Snelling, Janice Vierk

Montana State University
Doug Downs

New Mexico State University
Marc Scott

Nicholls State University
Keri Turner

North Carolina State University
Susan Miller-Cochran

North Dakota State University
Kevin Brooks

Northwest Arkansas Community College
Mary Hubbard, Timothy McGinn

Northern Virginia Community College
Shonette Grant

Oakton Community College
Mike McNett

Ohio University
Heather McFall

Oklahoma City Community College
Kim Jameson

Owens Community College
Jen Hazel, Deborah Richey

Pellissippi State Technical Community College
Keith Norris

Pima Community College
Shawn Hellman

Polk Community College
Rebecca Heintz

Prince Georges Community College
Wendy Perkins

Purdue University–Calumet
Lizbeth Bryant

Richland College
Paula Eschliman

Samford University
Charlotte Brammer, Billye Currie, David Dedo, Kathy Parnell

South Plains College
Linda McGann

Southern Illinois University–Edwardsville
Matthew Johnson

St. Louis Community College–Florissant Valley
James Sodon

St. Louis Community College–Meramec
Michael Burke, Richard Peraud

Tarrant County College
Dixil Rodriguez

Texas Christian University
Charlotte Hogg

Thomas Nelson Community College
Jaqueline Blackwell

Triton College
William Nedrow

University of Alabama–Birmingham
Peggy Jolly, Rita Treutel

University of Alabama–Tuscaloosa
Karen Gardiner, Steffen Guenzel, Jessica Kidd, Maryann Whitaker

University of Colorado at Colorado Springs
Debra Dew

University of Houston
Elizabeth Kessler

University of Illinois at Urbana–Champaign
Jessica Bannon, Hannah Bellwoar

University of Montana
Amy Ratto-Parks, Kathleen Ryan

University of North Carolina–Wilmington
Anthony Atkins

University of North Texas
Kathryn Raign

University of Rhode Island
Michael Pennell

University of South Florida–St. Petersburg
Morgan Gresham

University of Texas–Arlington
Margaret Lowry

University of Texas–El Paso
Beth Brunk-Chavez

University of Wisconsin–River Falls
Kathleen Hunzer, Steven Luebke

Utah State University
Brock Dethier

Utah Valley University
Gae Lyn Henderson

Waubonsee Community College
Jeanne McDonald, Sarah Quirk

Western Michigan University
Jonathan Bush

Wilkes Community College
Lisa Muir, Julie Mullis

Wright State University
Peggy Lindsey

Symposium Attendees

As part of its ongoing research in composition and in the design and administration of writing programs, McGraw-Hill conducts several symposia annually for instructors from across the country. These events offer a forum for instructors to exchange ideas and experiences with colleagues they might not have met otherwise. The feedback McGraw-Hill has received has been invaluable and has contributed directly to the development of *The McGraw-Hill Guide*. This list includes symposium participants in 2008 and 2009.

Alamance Community College
Anne Helms

Amarillo College
Dan Ferguson

Angelina College
Howard Cox

Arapahoe Community College
Lindsay Lewan

Baltimore City Community College
Paul Long

Bismarck State College
Jane Schreck

Bowling Green State University
Dawn Hubbell-Staeble

Cardinal Stritch University
Karen Bilda

Cedar Valley College
Rebekah Rios-Harris

Clark Atlanta University
Constance Chapman

College of DuPage
Beverly Reed

College of Southern Nevada
Shelley Kelly

Collin County Community College–Plano
Martha Tolleson

Community College of Baltimore
Evan Balkan

College of Southern Nevada
Jennifer Nelson

Delaware State University
Renee Young

East Carolina University
Wendy Sharer

Eastern Washington University
Polly Buckingham

Edmonds Community College
Hayden Bixby Nichols, Greg Van Belle

Florida Community College
Heidi Marshall

Georgia Perimeter College
Carol Warren

Greenville Technical College
April Childress

Guilford Technical Community College
Jo Ann Buck, Carolyn Schneider

Holmes Community College
Mary Brantley

Husson University
Stephanie Gross

Illinois State University
Bob Broad

Indiana University Purdue University–Fort Wayne
Stuart Blythe

Indiana University Purdue University–Indianapolis
Melvin Wininger

Indiana University Southeast
Charlotte Reynolds

J. Sargeant Reynolds Community College
Miles McCrimmon

Johnson County Community College
Matthew Schmeer

Johnson & Wales University–Miami
James Anderson

Joliet Junior College
Tamara Brattoli

Lamar University
Nancy Staub

Lorain County Community College
Suzanne Owens

Madisonville Community College
Greg Jewell

Marshalltown Community College
Connie Adair

Metropolitan Community College–Omaha
Kymberly Snelling, Janice Vierk

New Mexico State University
Marc Scott

North Carolina State University–Raleigh
Susan Miller-Cochran

North Dakota State University
Amy Taggart

Ohio University
Jennie Nelson

Purdue University–Calumet-Hammond
Lizbeth Bryant

Purdue University–West Lafayette
Samantha Blackmon

San Jacinto College–Pasadena
Sherrin Frances

Southeast Community College
Carolee Ritter

South Plains College
Linda McGann, Gary Poffenbarger

South Suburban College
Susan Sebok

Southern University–Baton Rouge
Kendric Coleman

St. Louis Community College–Meramec
Richard Peraud

Tarrant County College–Northwest
Dixil Rodriguez

Texas A&M University
Joanna Gibson

Texas Women's University
Lori Doddy

Triton College
Lesa Hildebrand

University of California–Irvine
Lynda Haas

University of Central Florida
Lindee Owens

University of Louisiana–Lafayette
Monica Busby

University of Montana
Amy Ratto-Parks, Kathleen Ryan

University of New Orleans
Kim McDonald

University of North Carolina–Wilmington
Tony Atkins

University of Rhode Island–Kingston
Ronald Schwegler

University of South Florida
Elizabeth Metzger

University of Texas–Dallas
John Gooch

University of Texas–El Paso
Beth Brunk-Chavez, Judith Fourzan

University of Toledo
Patricia Reid

University of Wisconsin–River Falls
Kathleen Hunzer, Steven Luebke

Weatherford College
Adrienne Treinies

Wharton County Junior College
Mary Otto Lang, Jennifer Mooney

Wilkes Community College
Julie Mullis

Design Reviewers

Alamance Community College
Anne Helms

Arapahoe Community College
Tami Comstock-Peavy

Cardinal Stritch University
Karen Bilda

Cincinnati State Technical and Community College
Robert Jakubovic, Andrea Leslie

Eastern Washington University
Polly Buckingham

Harrisburg Area Community College
Geraldine Gutwein

Indiana University Purdue University–Indianapolis
Scott Weeden

Jackson Community College
Gary Cale

Johnson & Wales University–Providence
Eileen Medeiros

Lake Sumter Community College
Patricia Campbell

Metropolitan Community College–Omaha
Janice Vierk

Montana State University
Doug Downs

St. Louis University
Janice McIntire-Strasburg

Southern Illinois University–Edwardsville
Matthew Johnson

University of Alabama–Tuscaloosa
Steffen Guenzel, Jessica Kidd, Maryann Whitaker

University of North Carolina–Wilmington
Anthony Atkins

University of Texas–El Paso
Beth Brunk-Chavez

University of Wisconsin–River Falls
Steven Luebke

Utah State University
Brock Dethier

User Diarists

Lake–Sumter Community College
Jacklyn Pierce

St. Louis Community College–Meramec
Deborah Hyland

Focus Group Participants

Arapahoe Community College
Lindsay Lewan

Arizona State University–Downtown
Regina Clemens Fox

Arizona State University–Tempe
Nicole Khoury

Brigham Young University
Joyce Adams

Front Range Community College
Mary Lee Geary, Mark Saunders

Pima Community College
Shawn Hellman

University of Alabama–Tuscaloosa
Karen Gardiner

University of Colorado–Colorado Springs
Debra Dew

University of Texas–Arlington
Margaret Lowry

WPA Outcomes Statement for First-Year Composition

Adopted by the Council of Writing Program Administrators (WPA), April 2000

For further information about the development of the Outcomes Statement, please see
http://comppile.tamucc.edu/WPAoutcomes/continue.html

For further information about the Council of Writing Program Administrators, please see
http://www.wpacouncil.org

A version of this statement was published in *WPA: Writing Program Administration* 23.1/2 (fall/winter 1999): 59–66.

Introduction

This statement describes the common knowledge, skills, and attitudes sought by first-year composition programs in American postsecondary education. To some extent, we seek to regularize what can be expected to be taught in first-year composition; to this end the document is not merely a compilation or summary of what currently takes place. Rather, the following statement articulates what composition teachers nationwide have learned from practice, research, and theory. This document intentionally defines only "outcomes," or types of results, and not "standards," or precise levels of achievement. The setting of standards should be left to specific institutions or specific groups of institutions.

Learning to write is a complex process, both individual and social, that takes place over time with continued practice and informed guidance. Therefore, it is important that teachers, administrators, and a concerned public do not imagine that these outcomes can be taught in reduced or simple ways. Helping students demonstrate these outcomes requires expert understanding of how students actually learn to write. For this reason we expect the primary audience for this document to be well-prepared college writing teachers and college writing program administrators. In some places, we have chosen to write in their professional language. Among such readers, terms such as "rhetorical" and "genre" convey a rich meaning that is not easily simplified. While we have also aimed at writing a document that the general public can understand, in limited cases we have aimed first at communicating effectively with expert writing teachers and writing program administrators.

These statements describe only what we expect to find at the end of first-year composition, at most schools a required general education course or sequence of courses. As writers move beyond first-year composition, their writing abilities do not merely improve. Rather, students' abilities not only diversify along disciplinary and professional lines but also move into whole new levels where expected outcomes expand, multiply, and diverge. For this reason, each statement of outcomes for first-year composition is followed by suggestions for further work that builds on these outcomes.

Rhetorical Knowledge

By the end of first-year composition, students should

- Focus on a purpose
- Respond to the needs of different audiences
- Respond appropriately to different kinds of rhetorical situations
- Use conventions of format and structure appropriate to the rhetorical situation
- Adopt appropriate voice, tone, and level of formality
- Understand how genres shape reading and writing
- Write in several genres

Faculty in all programs and departments can build on this preparation by helping students learn

- The main features of writing in their fields
- The main uses of writing in their fields
- The expectations of readers in their fields

Critical Thinking, Reading, and Writing

By the end of first-year composition, students should

- Use writing and reading for inquiry, learning, thinking, and communicating
- Understand a writing assignment as a series of tasks, including finding, evaluating, analyzing, and synthesizing appropriate primary and secondary sources
- Integrate their own ideas with those of others
- Understand the relationships among language, knowledge, and power

Faculty in all programs and departments can build on this preparation by helping students learn

- The uses of writing as a critical thinking method
- The interactions among critical thinking, critical reading, and writing
- The relationships among language, knowledge, and power in their fields

Processes

By the end of first-year composition, students should

- Be aware that it usually takes multiple drafts to create and complete a successful text
- Develop flexible strategies for generating, revising, editing, and proofreading
- Understand writing as an open process that permits writers to use later invention and re-thinking to revise their work
- Understand the collaborative and social aspects of writing processes
- Learn to critique their own and others' works
- Learn to balance the advantages of relying on others with the responsibility of doing their part
- Use a variety of technologies to address a range of audiences

Faculty in all programs and departments can build on this preparation by helping students learn

- To build final results in stages
- To review work-in-progress in collaborative peer groups for purposes other than editing
- To save extensive editing for later parts of the writing process
- To apply the technologies commonly used to research and communicate within their fields

Knowledge of Conventions

By the end of first-year composition, students should

- Learn common formats for different kinds of texts
- Develop knowledge of genre conventions ranging from structure and paragraphing to tone and mechanics
- Practice appropriate means of documenting their work
- Control such surface features as syntax, grammar, punctuation, and spelling

Faculty in all programs and departments can build on this preparation by helping students learn

- The conventions of usage, specialized vocabulary, format, and documentation in their fields
- Strategies through which better control of conventions can be achieved

Composing in Electronic Environments

Writing in the 21st century involves the use of digital technologies for several purposes, from drafting to peer reviewing to editing. Although the *kinds* of composing processes and texts expected from students vary across programs and institutions, there are nonetheless common expectations.

By the end of first-year composition, students should

- Use electronic environments for drafting, reviewing, revising, editing, and sharing texts
- Locate, evaluate, organize, and use research material collected from electronic sources, including scholarly library databases; other official databases (e.g., federal government databases); and informal electronic networks and internet sources
- Understand and exploit the differences in the rhetorical strategies and in the affordances available for both print and electronic composing processes and texts

Faculty in all programs and departments can build on this preparation by helping students learn

- How to engage in the electronic research and composing processes common in their fields
- How to disseminate texts in both print and electronic forms in their fields

Chapter 1

Writing Goals and Objectives for College and for Life

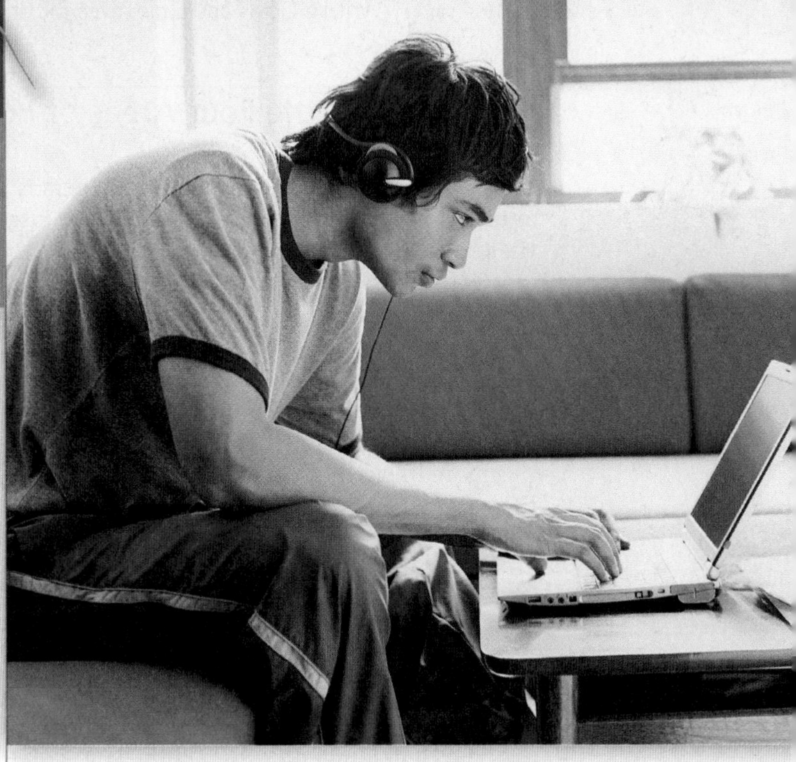

Whenever you write, you strive to fulfill a goal. In school, you write papers and essay exam answers to demonstrate what you have learned and to communicate your ideas to others. Outside of school, you use writing to perform your duties in the workplace, to make your voice heard in your community, and to communicate with friends and family. Most discourse has a goal or **purpose:** to explain, to inform, to persuade, and so on.

Whatever the purpose, effective writers achieve their objectives. **Rhetoric** is the use of words—either spoken or written—as well as visuals to achieve some goal. Each chapter in this book has a *rhetorical* focus on what you as a writer want your writing to *accomplish.*

The first decision a writer makes is rhetorical: What would you like this writing to *do* for a particular group of readers—your **audience**—at a particular place and time? Once you have determined your goals, you are prepared to decide how much and what kinds of information your audience needs to know and what will be convincing to this audience. You also decide how to collect this information and how to present it in an appropriate format. This rhetorical approach applies to writing that you do in various settings—not just in the classroom.

This chapter provides the context for the exploration of writing in subsequent chapters. Here we look at writing in the four areas of life, the course learning goals, the concept of becoming a self-reflective writer, and issues surrounding writing in the twenty-first century.

Writing in the Four Areas of Your Life

The ability to write effective college papers is an important goal of this course and this text. Writing skills are vital not just in college, however, but also in the professional, civic, and personal parts of your life.

Consider how you plan to spend the twenty-four hours in each day for the next week, the next month, the next year, the next four years, the next decade, and the next six decades. If you are like most students, during the next few years, you will devote much of your time to your academic studies. When you finish your academic studies, your time commitments will probably change. Although it is possible that you may still be a student half a decade from now, it is more likely that you will devote more time to the other three parts of your life—especially to your professional life.

Writing as a College Student

See Chapter 3 for writing-to-learn strategies.

You will be expected to do a great deal of writing in college because writing is a powerful tool both for learning and for demonstrating learning. Students who use writing to explore course material generally learn more—and get higher grades—than students who do not. The reason for this enhanced performance is fairly simple: Writing is an effective way to become more involved with your course material.

Writing as a Professional

Almost all jobs require some writing; some require a great deal of it. Furthermore, employers frequently list writing as one of the most important skills in job candidates.

Surveys of employers consistently confirm the importance of writing in the work world: Employers want to hire people who can write and speak clearly and effectively, think critically, solve problems efficiently, work well in teams, and use technology thoughtfully. The most competitive job seekers are those who begin honing these skills early.

Writing as a Citizen

As Thomas Jefferson frequently noted, democracies—and societies in general—work most effectively when citizens are well educated and involved. If you have strong feelings about certain issues and want to have a voice in how your society functions, you need to participate in your community. You can get involved by volunteering your time. Another important way to make your voice heard in a representative democracy is to write. You can write to elected officials at the local, state, and federal levels to let them know what you think about an issue and why you think the way that you do. In the civic part of your life, you often will work with others—neighbors or other citizens who are involved and interested in solving problems that affect them, their neighborhood, and their community.

Writing Activity

Balancing the Four Areas of Life

Working with two or three of your classmates, answer the following questions about the bar graph shown in Figure 1.1. Compare and discuss your responses. Your instructor may ask your group to share its findings with the rest of the class.

- Which bar graph (1, 2, 3, or 4) comes closest to representing the current balance in your life?
- Which bar graph comes closest to representing what you consider the ideal balance for someone enrolled full-time in college? For someone enrolled part-time? For a student with family responsibilities and/or a part-time or full-time job?
- Which bar graph best represents the balance that you would like to achieve a decade from now? Two decades from now? Five decades from now?

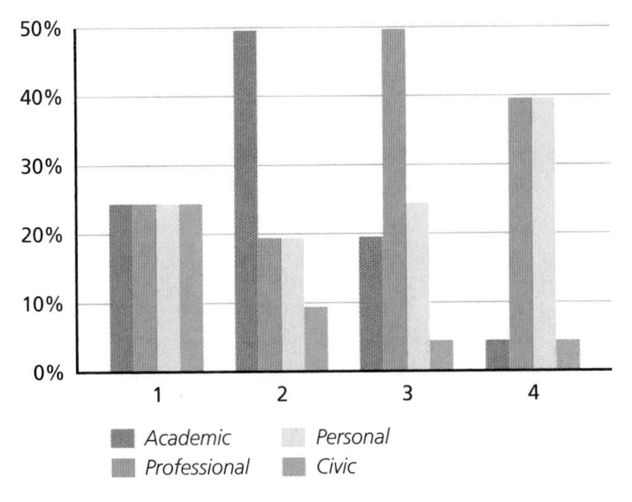

FIGURE 1.1 Balancing the Four Areas of Life

Writing as a Family Member or Friend

Even though writing in the academic, professional, and civic areas of life is important, the writing that you do in your personal life is probably the most important of all. We write to the people who are significant to us—whether on paper or in cyberspace—to accomplish life's daily tasks and to fulfill our needs.

Writing in the Four Areas in This Course

Because the academic, professional, civic, and personal parts of our lives are all important, this book offers numerous opportunities to write in all four areas. In each chapter in Parts 2 and 3, you have the option of writing in response to an academic or other type of situation. In addition, the writing assignments in Parts 2 and 3 are built around **scenarios**—simulated but realistic writing situations. For each scenario assignment, you will have a specific purpose for writing and a specific audience you are writing to.

Learning Goals in This Course

Whether you are writing for an academic, a professional, a civic, or a personal audience and purpose, you will need to draw on the same set of writing skills. Your work in this course will help you to learn and apply these skills to specific writing situations. To achieve this end, throughout the text we have incorporated the learning goals developed by the Council of Writing Program Administrators (WPA), a national organization of instructors who direct composition courses. The goals are organized into four broad areas: rhetorical knowledge and analysis; critical thinking, reading, and writing; writing processes; knowledge of conventions; and composing in electronic environments.

connect
mhconnectcomposition.com
Writing Tutorial QL1001

Rhetorical Knowledge

Rhetorical knowledge includes an understanding of

- Audience
- Purpose
- Rhetorical situation
- Writer's voice and tone
- Context, medium, and genre

AUDIENCE

To write for others successfully, you need to tailor your writing to their expectations and needs. You need to focus on where there is a meeting of minds—yours and theirs—and where there is not. For example, if you were to write the following grocery list and take it to the store, you would probably know precisely what you had in mind.

Grocery List
cereal
milk
coffee
bread
paper

If you were sick, however, and had to rely on a close family member to do your grocery shopping for you, you might have to revise the list by adding a few more details.

Version of the Grocery List for a Family Member
Cereal
1% milk
Coffee beans
Multigrain bread
Sunday paper

If you handed the list to a neighbor, though, you would probably have to add much more specific information.

Version of the Grocery List for a Neighbor
Grape Nuts Flakes
1% milk (half gallon)
whole-bean Starbuck's Sumatra extra-bold coffee
Grandma Sycamore's multigrain bread
the New York Times

In each case, you would adjust your list for the person who would be acting on the information. When you share a great deal of experience with your reader, you can leave gaps in information without causing serious problems. The fewer experiences you have in common with your audience, however, the more you need to fill in those gaps as you draft and revise, rather than after you have finished writing.

PURPOSE

In this book Chapters 3–12 focus on common rhetorical purposes for writing: to learn, to share experiences, to explore, to inform, to analyze, to convince, to evaluate, to examine causes and effects, to solve problems, and to respond to creative works. In Chapter 3 you will have opportunities to experiment with many forms of writing to learn, which will serve you in this course, as well as your other courses. In Chapters 4–11, you will have opportunities to engage with those purposes in some detail.

RHETORICAL SITUATION

Writing is done for a particular purpose, in response to the needs of a specific audience. In other words, writers write in response to a **rhetorical situation.** A rhetorical situation consists of the following elements:

- Writer
- Purpose
- Audience
- Topic
- Context/occasion

Although each rhetorical situation is unique, there are general types of situations that require writers to use the appropriate conventions of format and structure. For example, if you are writing a lab report for a biology course, your instructor will expect you to structure your report in a certain way and to use a neutral, informative tone. If you are proposing a solution to a problem in your community, your readers will expect you first to describe the problem and then to explain how your solution can be implemented, using a reasonable, even-handed tone and giving some attention to possible objections to your proposal.

WRITER'S VOICE AND TONE

A writer's **voice** is the personality or image that is revealed in the writer's text—the impression made on the reader. To establish a distinctive voice, a writer thoughtfully and consistently makes decisions about such elements as diction (word choice), syntax (sentence structure), and punctuation. For instance, think about a good friend whose use of a particular word or phrase clearly identifies that friend.

Tone is the writer's attitude toward the topic, the audience, and other people. Tone can reveal the extent to which a writer is ironic, respectful/disrespectful, patient/impatient, supportive/unsupportive, angry, happy, irritated, ironic, accommodating/unaccommodating, and the like. For example, when Jay Leno hosted *The Tonight Show,* he sometimes commented on the attire of individual members of the audience. Leno would say something like, "I see that you took extra time getting dressed for the show," to an audience member wearing cutoff blue jeans, a torn T-shirt, and flip-flops. Everyone knows that his tone is ironic; he clearly meant the opposite of what he was saying. He was doing so for humorous effect, and he always got a big laugh when he made such comments.

CONTEXT, MEDIUM, AND GENRE

The context for writing affects the writer's choice of medium and genre. For example, if an executive needs to announce a company's plan for furloughs (required time off without pay) to thousands of employees in several cities,

How would your writing change if you were writing (a) a friend who is still in high school about your new roommate, and (b) a housing administrator to request a housing change?

the executive probably would choose to send a memo (the genre) via e-mail (the medium). This genre and this medium make sense in this context because companies often use memos for such announcements. Further, the medium of e-mail is cost effective.

Context: Throughout this book you will have opportunities to write in a variety of **contexts,** or the circumstances that surround your writing, in all four arenas of life—the academic, the professional, the civic, and the personal. These opportunities appear in scenarios describing various rhetorical situations that give rise to writing. Consider what you would write if you were in the following rhetorical situations:

1. You want to convince the financial aid officer at your college that you need a scholarship to stay in school next semester.
2. After a disagreement with your spouse/fiancé/girlfriend/boyfriend, you want to write a letter to apologize for having said something that you regret.
3. After a disagreement with your supervisor at work, you want to write a letter to apologize for having said something that you regret.

As you contemplate these rhetorical situations, consider how the purpose, audience, topic, and context/occasion might alter what you will write. For instance, how does writing an apology to a love interest (no. 2 above) differ from writing an apology to your supervisor (no. 3 above)? In this case the purpose is the same, but the audiences differ.

Medium: A medium is a physical or electronic means of communication. **Media** include books, pamphlets, newspapers, magazines, CDs, DVDs, and the World Wide Web. As you develop projects for Chapters 4–11, you will be encouraged to use various media to communicate with your audience. Although you may want to use what feels most comfortable, you may also want to use media that you have not used before.

Genre: *Genre* is a French word meaning "kind" or "type." Although people frequently use the word *genre* to refer to kinds of texts, such as a letter, a formal paper, a report, or a memo, there is great variation in precisely how people use the word. People often use *genre* to refer to the **content** of texts. For example, Shakespearean plays are labeled tragedies, comedies, or histories. If a friend tells you that she saw a film version of a Shakespearean tragedy last night, you could guess fairly accurately that she saw characters die as a result of foul deeds. Likewise, if another friend said that she had read résumés all morning, you would know that she was reading about people's educational and work backgrounds.

Now consider how the concept of genre can become muddied. If a friend said that she saw a film in which lots of people died as a result of foul deeds, you might guess that she saw a tragedy (a genre) such as *Hamlet* or *Romeo and Juliet* or a horror movie such as *Scream 3* or *Day of the Dead.* However, your friend may have been watching Comedy Central, where she saw *Scary Movie 4,* a humorous parody (another genre) of horror films.

Genre also refers to different **forms** of texts. For example, think again about the friend who said that she had read résumés all morning. Résumés have not only standard content (educational and work background) but also a generally standard format; that is, you can recognize a résumé at a distance—even if it is so far away that you cannot read any of the words on the page.

From a rhetorical standpoint, you select the format or overall structure of the piece of writing you are constructing. For example, a letter will have a salutation, a body, and a signature, although the structure of the body of that letter could vary widely—it could be organized in paragraphs or as a list, for instance.

The point is that content can come in many kinds of packages. For example, in writing to convince people to wear seat belts, you could use any of the following: an academic paper, a flyer, a poster, or a Web site in which you present an argument in support of wearing seat belts; a poem, short story, play, or song about someone who died because he neglected to use a seat belt; an obituary; or a newspaper story.

You may choose from a wide variety of **genres** for writing projects in Chapters 4–11. In each of these assigned chapters, you will find information about genres that are commonly used for that rhetorical purpose. For example, in Chapter 8, "Writing to Convince," you will find information about editorials, position papers, job references, and advertisements. In writing, *genre* means that you follow the conventions of a kind of writing and provide, generally, what readers expect from that genre. A paper for one of your college classes will generally be more formal and detailed than an e-mail you might write to your classmates asking them to vote in an upcoming election.

Rhetorical Analysis

A **rhetorical analysis** can include any of the previously mentioned features of rhetorical situations: audience, rhetorical appeals, purpose, voice and tone, context, format, and genre. A rhetorical analysis is an examination of the relative effectiveness of a particular text written for a particular audience for a particular purpose. Although you may not realize it, the average person does many rhetorical analyses each day. For example, when someone says, "I don't think so," "yeah, right," or, "whatever," in response to a statement, the person is questioning the credibility—the ethos—of the speaker or the accuracy of the information—the logos. Although formal rhetorical analyses are more elaborate than this example suggests, the principle is the same.

For more information on rhetorical analysis, see Chapter 2.

Throughout this book, you will have opportunities to engage in rhetorical analysis. For example, at the end of each reading in Chapters 4–11, you will have an opportunity to write brief rhetorical analyses of those texts.

Critical Thinking, Reading, and Writing

To get the most out of your reading and to accomplish your goals as a writer, you need to develop and use critical thinking skills. In Chapter 2 we offer some informal reading and writing activities that promote critical thinking. Although these activities will help you read more thoughtfully, many of them are also tools for generating ideas and material for the more formal writing tasks you will do in all four parts of your life.

In general, you engage in **critical thinking** when you examine an idea from many perspectives—seeing it in new ways. For example, when you write a formal argument, you will need to address others' objections to your ideas if you hope to persuade your audience to accept your point. You can also apply critical thinking to understand the relationships among language, knowledge, and power. That is, language often has a greater effect when it is used by people in positions of social, political, or economic power. When used effectively, language is often far more powerful than physical weapons. Modern civilizations have written constitutions and written laws derived from those constitutions. The most politically and economically powerful people in societies tend to be those who use critical thinking and language most effectively to present their ideas.

Writing Processes

Although writing processes vary from writer to writer and from situation to situation, effective writers generally go through the following activities:

connect
mhconnectcomposition.com
Writing Tutorial: Writing Process QL1002

- Generating initial ideas
- Relating those ideas to the writing situation or assignment
- Conducting research to find support for their ideas

- Organizing ideas and support and writing an initial draft
- Revising and shaping the paper, frequently with the advice of other readers
- Editing and polishing the paper

The order of these processes can vary, and often you will need to return to a previous step. For example, while drafting you may discover that you need to find more support for one of your ideas; while revising you may find a better way to organize your ideas.

When writers revise, they add or delete words, phrases, sentences, or even whole paragraphs, and they often modify their ideas. After they have revised multiple times, they then edit, attending to word choice, punctuation, grammar, usage, and spelling—the "surface features" of written texts. Writers also revise and edit texts to meet the needs of particular readers.

Effective writers also ask others to help them generate and refine their ideas and polish their prose. Published writers in academic, civic, and professional fields rely heavily on others as they work, often showing one another drafts of their writing before submitting a manuscript to publishers.

Because effective writers get help from others, this book provides many opportunities for you and your classmates—your **peers**—to help one another. One key to working productively with others is to understand that they bring different backgrounds, experiences, knowledge, and perspectives to the writing task, so it is critical to treat what others think and say with respect, no matter how much you agree or disagree with them. You should also remember when working with others that the suggestions and comments they make are about your *text,* not about you.

Writing Activity

Assessing Your Strengths and Weaknesses

In no more than two pages, assess your current strengths and weaknesses in each of the four goal areas: rhetorical knowledge and analysis; critical thinking, reading, and writing; writing processes; and knowledge of conventions. Share your self-assessment with two or three classmates.

Knowledge of Conventions

Conventions are the table manners of writing. Sometimes they matter; other times they do not. Writing for yourself to learn course material is like eating breakfast alone at home. In this situation, table manners are not very important. When you are having dinner with your employer or the president of your college, though, table manners do matter. The same principle applies when you write for readers. Effective writers know which writing conventions to use in particular settings.

To make their writing more appealing to readers, writers need to master many conventions: spelling, punctuation, sentence structure, and word choice. While some conventions are considered signs of the writer's respect for readers (correctly spelling someone's name, for instance), other conventions, such as punctuation, organization, tone, the use of headers and white space, and documentation style, help your readers understand what you are saying.

Becoming a Self-Reflective Writer

By evaluating your strengths and weaknesses in each of the four learning outcomes, you have taken a step toward becoming a more reflective—and therefore a more successful—writer. Throughout this course, you will continue to build on this foundation. Toward the end of each chapter in Parts 2 and 3, you will be asked to reflect on the work you did for that chapter. Reflecting—in writing—on your own writing activities helps you learn what worked (and perhaps what did not work). That kind of activity will help you remember the best aspects of your process the next time you face a similar writing task.

GENRES *Up Close* Writing a Reflection

Reflection is an important form of thinking and writing. **Reflection** is an opportunity to think about something—to consider its importance, value, or applicability. It is a process that may enhance performance in learning a skill or acquiring knowledge. A reflection includes two components:

- A description of what is being reflected on. For example, if you reflect on a lab experiment, you first need to describe the experiment. If you reflect on what you learned from reading a novel, you first need to summarize the novel. Such descriptions or summaries help assure that your readers understand the object of your reflection. They also help you focus your attention on the object of your reflection.
- A thoughtful consideration of the object. For example, you could ask the following kinds of questions:
    - Why is this concept important? How can I apply it?
    - What have I learned from this experience?
    - What do I know about ________? What do I still need to learn about ________?
    - What do my readers know about ________? What do they not know about ________? What do they need to know about ________?
    - Why am I engaged in this activity?

In this book you will be asked to engage in many forms of reflection. The following example is an excerpt from a reflection by student writer Santi DeRosa, whose paper appears on pages 259–263. Notice how DeRosa addresses his knowledge and skills, as well as connections between the academic and personal arenas of his life:

> I could be more passionate about this paper than the previous paper I wrote. Then, I wanted to kind of distance myself from the topics that were assigned to us, but this time, I was really involved. This topic made me upset (and my readers can probably tell!).

GENRES UP CLOSE

STUDENT WRITING EXAMPLES

Brainstorming (pp. 158, 332)
Freewriting (pp. 114, 245, 383)
Criteria (p. 290)
Listing (p. 72)
Answers to Reporter's Questions (p. 244)
Organization (pp. 75, 164)
Clustering (pp. 114, 289)
Concept Mapping (p. 335)
Interviewing (p. 203)
Research (pp. 115, 160, 205, 246, 292, 384)
Reflection (p. 12)

When I started defining the issue, I was more involved in the topic. However, this paper was more difficult to organize than the first one. When I read the article about what happens during recruiting at my school, I was surprised and angry. Having these emotions made it easier to write the paper—I guess that they'd add to what my teacher called an "emotional appeal." During my research, I found that there are many ways in which women are objectified, and there are many ways to define "objectification."

I enjoyed writing this paper because it allowed me to explore my own feelings as well. Each time I revised the paper, I found that I had more to say. Because of peer review and input—as well as input from my wife (who is my best critic), I was able to organize the paper and develop the ideas more fully. I hope that it reads well.

My skills are getting better, but I feel that I still have much to do. Writing this paper also allowed me to consider the women in my life and get a better understanding of what makes them the way they are.

I also think that this persuasive essay might make a real difference to people, at colleges, if they read it and understand my point and then see if their school has a similar program. . . .

Writing in the Twenty-First Century

Regardless of whether they are writing for an academic, a professional, a civic, or a personal purpose, writers today have more responsibilities than ever before because online technology makes writing available to a wide spectrum of readers. Writers who are careless in representing themselves or who use technology negligently can live to regret their lack of caution. Wise writers ask themselves the following question before publishing any of their writing electronically: What would the consequences be if this piece of writing were to appear on the front page of a local or national newspaper, a radio show, a television news program, the homepage of a Web site or a blog?

Writing Responsibly

The Greek philosopher and rhetorician Aristotle suggested that a writer's or speaker's *ethos,* his or her credibility, is one of the ways people are persuaded: readers believe you because of who you are, how you portray yourself, how you present your information, what logic you use, and what language you employ. How a writer presents him- or herself establishes that *ethos*.

Not only do writers need to present their arguments accurately and fairly, but they also need to be aware of how they "sound" to their readers. You present a positive image of yourself to readers through the persona you create by the words you use. If you call opponents names and use incendiary language to describe the issue you are writing about, you will come across less convincingly than if you are logical and well prepared and provide solid evidence to support your case, with citations for all of your sources.

Composing in Electronic Environments

Aristotle said that effective communicators use "the available means of persuasion." Effective communicators throughout history have used available technologies—such as clay tablets, pencils, and typewriters—for writing and speaking. In the twenty-first century, those technologies include a variety of digital tools—computers, diverse software, and the World Wide Web.

As you make decisions about writing for various audiences and purposes in the four areas of your life, you will also need to make decisions about how and when to use various kinds of technology. Recently, researchers, educators, and others have been focusing on the ways in which digital technologies are affecting—positively or negatively—how people write. For our purposes, **technology** is a system or practice that extends human capabilities. The system of writing that we use is actually a technology for extending human thought across time and space. Other technologies facilitate the act of writing. For example, a person can write by using an index finger to inscribe letters on sand or even soft clay tablets. With your fingernails, you can inscribe less pliable surfaces such as soft wood or a wax tablet. The point, of course, is that writers have always used the most effective technologies available.

A generation ago it was relatively difficult to integrate words and pictures because the technology for doing so was expensive and time-consuming. However, it is now relatively easy to mix words, still pictures, video segments, audio segments, and Web links in a single digital text. These capabilities have enabled writers to become more imaginative as they compose, but these capabilities have also given writers many more choices to make. Throughout this text, you will be encouraged to make informed choices about the most appropriate technology for your audience and purpose. Chapter 17 offers additional advice on choosing a medium, genre, and technology for your written communication.

Digital Literacy

Sharing Digital Literacy

You and your classmates can help each other get more out of the writing technologies that are available on your campus. Offer to show your friends or the members of your study group shortcuts and tools in programs you are familiar with. Don't be shy about asking friends and classmates for tips and tricks they've picked up while writing their papers with computer software. You can use your own computing knowledge as "social collateral" in classes where students use computers to complete assignments, because some students will be more comfortable than others with the available software. For example, you might show your classmates how to use some of the formatting tools in the word processor and ask others to show you how to use slide show presentation, spreadsheet, or sound file mixing software.

Writing Activity

Assessing Your Uses of Technology

Think about the ways in which you have used digital technologies in the past year. In the grid below, list a few tasks that you have done with technology. Compare your list with those of several classmates.

Technological Tool	Academic Situation	Professional, Civic, or Personal Situation
• E-mail • Word-processing software • Web browser (e.g., Mozilla Firefox, Internet Explorer) • Web site composing tools (e.g., *Dreamweaver*) • Web logs (blogs) • Other		

Chapter

2

Reading Critically for College and for Life

In Chapter 1, we considered how writing skills will serve you in the academic, professional, civic, and personal areas of your life. This chapter focuses on an activity that reinforces and helps you improve your writing skills: **reading.** When we read, we make meaning out of words on a page or computer screen. We also "read" photographs and other visual images. Actually, then, reading is the active process of constructing meaning.

In this chapter, we ask you to consider how you now read different kinds of material and give you some helpful reading strategies. Specifically, the chapter presents prereading strategies, strategies for reading actively, and postreading strategies. All of these strategies will help you better understand what you read and use that information to make your own writing more effective.

In your college classes, you will be asked to read (and write) about all kinds of print and digital texts for all kinds of purposes. More often than not, you will use some of what you read in the papers that you write for your college classes. The connection between what you read and how you use that material in your writing requires you to read *critically.*

What does it mean to *read critically*? One thing *reading* critically does not mean is to be "nit-picky" or negative. Rather, when you read a text *critically*, you question what you read, make connections to other things you have read and to your own experiences, and think about how the information in the text might help you as you develop your own writing. To read critically means to read *thoughtfully*, to keep in mind what you already know, and to *actively* interact with the text. Critical readers underline, make notes, and ask questions as they read.

Why Read Critically? Integrating Sources into Your Own Writing

Why do you suppose that your teacher asks you to read critically and thoughtfully? In addition to reading to understand the information, a key reason to read critically and thoughtfully is so that you will be able to put the information and concepts you read about into your own writing, to support your own ideas.

There is an added bonus to reading critically: It helps you understand the ways the writing you read "works"—what makes that writing effective (or not), how that writing connects to and impacts (or not) readers, and so on. As you read and learn to understand how the writing your teachers ask you to read *functions,* you will be able to construct more effective texts.

In your college classes, you will be asked to read *a lot.* Understanding what you read and relating what you read to what you already know is what college is about. As you read for your college classes, consider how you might use that information in your own class papers or examinations. For example, if you know your philosophy instructor will ask you to construct a paper in which you outline and explain "philosophy of the mind," you should look for both of those terms and anything that connects them as you read. Ask yourself:

- What is the main point, the thesis? How does it relate to what I already know? To what I'm reading for this class?
- How are the main terms defined? How do the author's definitions compare to what I think the terms mean? What terms or concepts are not explained (and so I'll need to look them up)?
- How effective is the supporting evidence the author supplies?
- What did the author leave out? How does that affect his or her argument?
- What information in this text will help me construct my own paper?

You *use* what you learned from your reading by integrating those ideas into your own writing, by citing and paraphrasing the concepts you glean from your reading. You can read about using quotations in your own writing on pages 118–119. Pages 164–165 discuss how to paraphrase and attribute those ideas correctly.

Writing Activity

How Do You Read?

Take a few minutes to answer the following questions:

- What kinds of books or magazines do you like to read? Newspapers? Web sites? Blogs?
- How does the way you read a text online differ from the way you read an article from a print magazine or newspaper?
- How do you read your college textbooks? How do the strategies you use to read a text for one course differ from those you use to read texts for another course?
- What strategies do you use to read long, complex nonfiction texts?
- What strategies do you use to help you understand and remember what you have read?

Share your answers with several classmates. How do your responses compare with theirs? What strategies do they use that might be helpful to you?

Using Prereading Strategies

When you write something, you have a purpose in mind. As we noted in Chapter 1, the reason for writing is your **rhetorical purpose**—what you are hoping to accomplish. Likewise, before you read, think about your rhetorical purpose: What are you trying to accomplish by reading? Are you reading to be entertained, to learn new information, to understand a complex subject in more detail, or for some other reason? If you consciously think about *why* you are reading, as well as *how* you plan to read a particular piece of writing, you will have a strategy you can follow as you begin reading.

Before you start to read any written work, take a few minutes to preview its content and design. Look for the following elements:

- The title of the work, or of the particular section you are about to read
- Headings that serve as an outline of the text
- Boxes that highlight certain kinds of information
- Charts, maps, photographs, or drawings
- Numbered or bulleted lists (such as this one) that set off certain information

Think about what you bring to your reading task: In what ways does the text seem similar to or different from others of this type or on this topic that you have already read? What can you bring to the new reading that you have learned from your past experiences? If you are actively involved in the reading process and if you think of reading rhetorically—that is, if you think about what you want to get from the reading—then you will start with a useful map for any text you read.

Next, skim the text by reading the first and last sections or paragraphs, as well as any elements that are highlighted in some way, such as boxes, section titles, headings, or terms or phrases in bold or italic type. Sometimes a box or highlighted section at the beginning of an article—often called an **abstract**—will give you a quick summary of what is ahead.

As a final step before you start to read, consider again what you are hoping to accomplish by reading this particular text. Ask yourself:

- What information have I noticed that might help me with my writing task?
- How have I reacted so far to what I have seen in the text?
- What questions do I have?
- What in this text seems to relate to other texts that I have read?

Reading Actively

Now that previewing has given you a sense of what the text is about, you are ready to read actively. Here are some questions to ask yourself as you read:

- What is the writer's thesis or main point? What evidence does the writer provide to support that point? Does the writer offer statistics, facts, expert opinion, or anecdotes (stories)?
- How reliable is the information in this text? How conscientiously does the writer indicate the sources of his or her data, facts, or examples? How reliable do these sources seem?
- What else do you know about this topic? How can you relate your previous knowledge to what this writer is saying? In what ways do you agree or disagree with the point the writer is making?
- Has the writer included examples that clarify the text? Are there photographs, drawings, or diagrams that help you understand the writer's main points? Graphs or charts that illustrate data or other statistical information? In what way(s) do the examples and visuals help you better understand the text? What information do they give you that the written text does not provide? What is the emotional impact of the photographs or other visuals?
- What information or evidence is not in this text? (Your past experience and reading will help you here.) Why do you think that the author might have left it out?
- If what you are reading is an argument, how effectively does the writer acknowledge or outline other points of view on the issue at hand?

For more on strategies for argument, including dealing with opposing views, see Chapter 14.

By asking questions like these, you can use strategies such as annotating, performing a rhetorical analysis, reading visuals, and reading Web pages to read actively.

Writing Activity

Annotating "The Ethics of 'Stealing' a WiFi Connection"

"The Ethics of 'Stealing' a WiFi Connection" discusses a growing issue: Who "owns" the right to Internet access that comes from a person's or business's network? Annotate the rest of Eric Bangeman's comments (see Figure 2.1). As you work, keep in mind your own responses to his comments.

Your instructor may want you to share your annotations with several of your classmates, noting places where your responses are similar and where they may differ.

Annotating Effectively

When you **annotate,** you interact actively with the text as you read. To annotate a reading, make the following kinds of notes (Figure 2.1):

- Underline the main point or thesis of the reading, or otherwise mark it as the key point.
- Underline key supporting points, and indicate in the margins next to the corresponding paragraphs why you think each point is important.
- List any questions you have.
- Respond to the text with your own remarks.

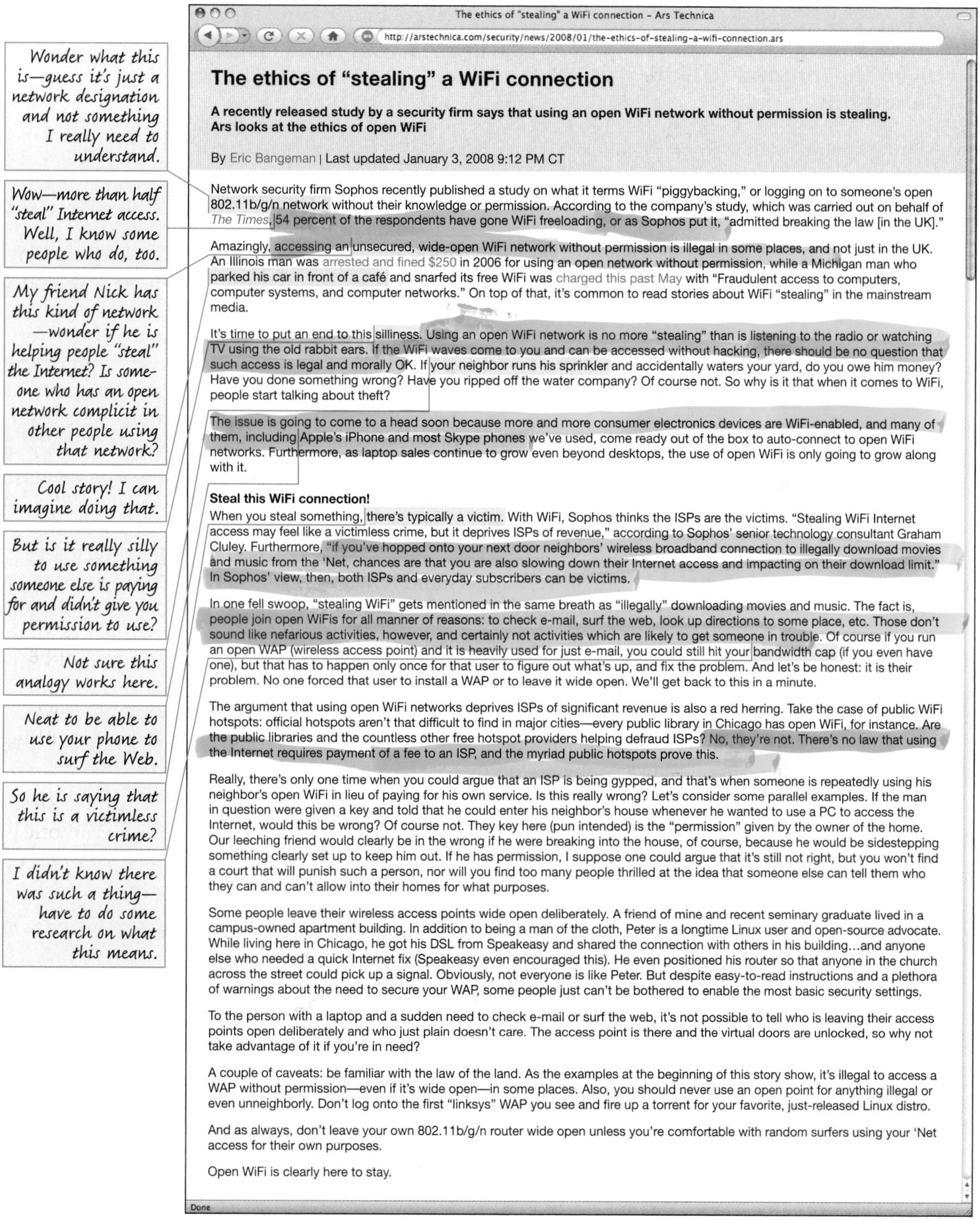

Wonder what this is—guess it's just a network designation and not something I really need to understand.

Wow—more than half "steal" Internet access. Well, I know some people who do, too.

My friend Nick has this kind of network—wonder if he is helping people "steal" the Internet? Is someone who has an open network complicit in other people using that network?

Cool story! I can imagine doing that.

But is it really silly to use something someone else is paying for and didn't give you permission to use?

Not sure this analogy works here.

Neat to be able to use your phone to surf the Web.

So he is saying that this is a victimless crime?

I didn't know there was such a thing—have to do some research on what this means.

The ethics of "stealing" a WiFi connection - Ars Technica

http://arstechnica.com/security/news/2008/01/the-ethics-of-stealing-a-wifi-connection.ars

The ethics of "stealing" a WiFi connection

A recently released study by a security firm says that using an open WiFi network without permission is stealing. Ars looks at the ethics of open WiFi

By Eric Bangeman | Last updated January 3, 2008 9:12 PM CT

Network security firm Sophos recently published a study on what it terms WiFi "piggybacking," or logging on to someone's open 802.11b/g/n network without their knowledge or permission. According to the company's study, which was carried out on behalf of *The Times*, 54 percent of the respondents have gone WiFi freeloading, or as Sophos put it, "admitted breaking the law [in the UK]."

Amazingly, accessing an unsecured, wide-open WiFi network without permission is illegal in some places, and not just in the UK. An Illinois man was arrested and fined $250 in 2006 for using an open network without permission, while a Michigan man who parked his car in front of a café and snarfed its free WiFi was charged this past May with "Fraudulent access to computers, computer systems, and computer networks." On top of that, it's common to read stories about WiFi "stealing" in the mainstream media.

It's time to put an end to this silliness. Using an open WiFi network is no more "stealing" than is listening to the radio or watching TV using the old rabbit ears. If the WiFi waves come to you and can be accessed without hacking, there should be no question that such access is legal and morally OK. If your neighbor runs his sprinkler and accidentally waters your yard, do you owe him money? Have you done something wrong? Have you ripped off the water company? Of course not. So why is it that when it comes to WiFi, people start talking about theft?

The issue is going to come to a head soon because more and more consumer electronics devices are WiFi-enabled, and many of them, including Apple's iPhone and most Skype phones we've used, come ready out of the box to auto-connect to open WiFi networks. Furthermore, as laptop sales continue to grow even beyond desktops, the use of open WiFi is only going to grow along with it.

Steal this WiFi connection!

When you steal something, there's typically a victim. With WiFi, Sophos thinks the ISPs are the victims. "Stealing WiFi Internet access may feel like a victimless crime, but it deprives ISPs of revenue," according to Sophos' senior technology consultant Graham Cluley. Furthermore, "if you've hopped onto your next door neighbors' wireless broadband connection to illegally download movies and music from the 'Net, chances are that you are also slowing down their Internet access and impacting on their download limit." In Sophos' view, then, both ISPs and everyday subscribers can be victims.

In one fell swoop, "stealing WiFi" gets mentioned in the same breath as "illegally" downloading movies and music. The fact is, people join open WiFis for all manner of reasons: to check e-mail, surf the web, look up directions to some place, etc. Those don't sound like nefarious activities, however, and certainly not activities which are likely to get someone in trouble. Of course if you run an open WAP (wireless access point) and it is heavily used for just e-mail, you could still hit your bandwidth cap (if you even have one), but that has to happen only once for that user to figure out what's up, and fix the problem. And let's be honest: it is their problem. No one forced that user to install a WAP or to leave it wide open. We'll get back to this in a minute.

The argument that using open WiFi networks deprives ISPs of significant revenue is also a red herring. Take the case of public WiFi hotspots: official hotspots aren't that difficult to find in major cities—every public library in Chicago has open WiFi, for instance. Are the public libraries and the countless other free hotspot providers helping defraud ISPs? No, they're not. There's no law that using the Internet requires payment of a fee to an ISP, and the myriad public hotspots prove this.

Really, there's only one time when you could argue that an ISP is being gypped, and that's when someone is repeatedly using his neighbor's open WiFi in lieu of paying for his own service. Is this really wrong? Let's consider some parallel examples. If the man in question were given a key and told that he could enter his neighbor's house whenever he wanted to use a PC to access the Internet, would this be wrong? Of course not. They key here (pun intended) is the "permission" given by the owner of the home. Our leeching friend would clearly be in the wrong if he were breaking into the house, of course, because he would be sidestepping something clearly set up to keep him out. If he has permission, I suppose one could argue that it's still not right, but you won't find a court that will punish such a person, nor will you find too many people thrilled at the idea that someone else can tell them who they can and can't allow into their homes for what purposes.

Some people leave their wireless access points wide open deliberately. A friend of mine and recent seminary graduate lived in a campus-owned apartment building. In addition to being a man of the cloth, Peter is a longtime Linux user and open-source advocate. While living here in Chicago, he got his DSL from Speakeasy and shared the connection with others in his building...and anyone else who needed a quick Internet fix (Speakeasy even encouraged this). He even positioned his router so that anyone in the church across the street could pick up a signal. Obviously, not everyone is like Peter. But despite easy-to-read instructions and a plethora of warnings about the need to secure your WAP, some people just can't be bothered to enable the most basic security settings.

To the person with a laptop and a sudden need to check e-mail or surf the web, it's not possible to tell who is leaving their access points open deliberately and who just plain doesn't care. The access point is there and the virtual doors are unlocked, so why not take advantage of it if you're in need?

A couple of caveats: be familiar with the law of the land. As the examples at the beginning of this story show, it's illegal to access a WAP without permission—even if it's wide open—in some places. Also, you should never use an open point for anything illegal or even unneighborly. Don't log onto the first "linksys" WAP you see and fire up a torrent for your favorite, just-released Linux distro.

And as always, don't leave your own 802.11b/g/n router wide open unless you're comfortable with random surfers using your 'Net access for their own purposes.

Open WiFi is clearly here to stay.

Done

FIGURE 2.1 Example of Annotations on a Page

- Jot down key terms and their definitions.
- Mark sections that summarize material as "summary" (see the example in Figure 2.1).

> **Digital Literacy**
>
> **Using the Internet to Find Definitions**
>
> Are you faced with one of those jargon-filled college reading assignments? When the glossary at the back of the book just isn't enough, try searching the Web for definitions. A number of good dictionaries and glossaries are available online. One strategy is to use a Web search engine to find definitions of complex terms. For example, if you're looking for a working definition of *existentialism,* type "define: existentialism" (without quotation marks) into a search engine's search box. Often your top results will include dictionary sites, academic Web sites, and technical sites that have developed working glossaries for students, experts, and professionals.

Constructing a Rhetorical Analysis

When you *analyze* something, you mentally "take it apart" to determine how the various parts or aspects function and relate to the whole. If you were to analyze, say, the winning team in last year's Super Bowl or World Series, you would examine the various aspects that make that team the very best (perhaps the coaching, the players, and/or the game plan) to determine how the various parts of that team work together to make it the best team. (For more on analysis, see pages 180–221.)

A rhetorical analysis is a way of looking at something, often a text, from a *rhetorical standpoint.* The purpose of examining a text from a rhetorical perspective and then constructing a rhetorical analysis of that text is to help you understand how the text functions: how each aspect of that text works to fulfill its purpose. So, if a text is trying to persuade you of something, you should examine how the various parts of that text work to *persuade.* If a text is intended to be informational (a newspaper article, for example), then you should read through the text looking for how that text informs.

A rhetorical analysis includes a search for and identification of what are called *rhetorical appeals:* the aspects of a piece of writing that influence the reader because of the credibility of the author (*ethos*), an appeal to logic (*logos*), and/or an appeal to the emotions of the audience (*pathos*). The relationships among *ethos, logos,* and *pathos* can be represented as a triangle in which the author is related to an appeal to *ethos,* the audience or reader to the appeal of *pathos,* and the purpose of the text to the appeal of *logos:*

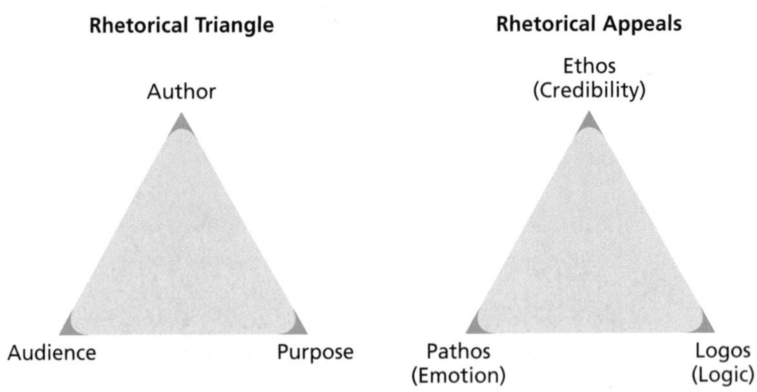

(For more on the rhetorical triangle, see page 460.)

GENRES *Up Close* Writing a Rhetorical Analysis

The purpose of a rhetorical analysis is to examine an item—most often a text—to determine how the parts or aspects of the text function together to accomplish the author's purpose. Rhetorical analysis, then, is really a critical reading.

One way to understand how to use a rhetorical approach is to consider an advertisement. How does a specific advertisement work to convince the audience? Most often, an advertisement is intended to convince a reader to buy a product. Consider the advertisement for Levi's Copper Jeans shown in Figure 2.2. Do you notice the shiny

GENRES UP CLOSE

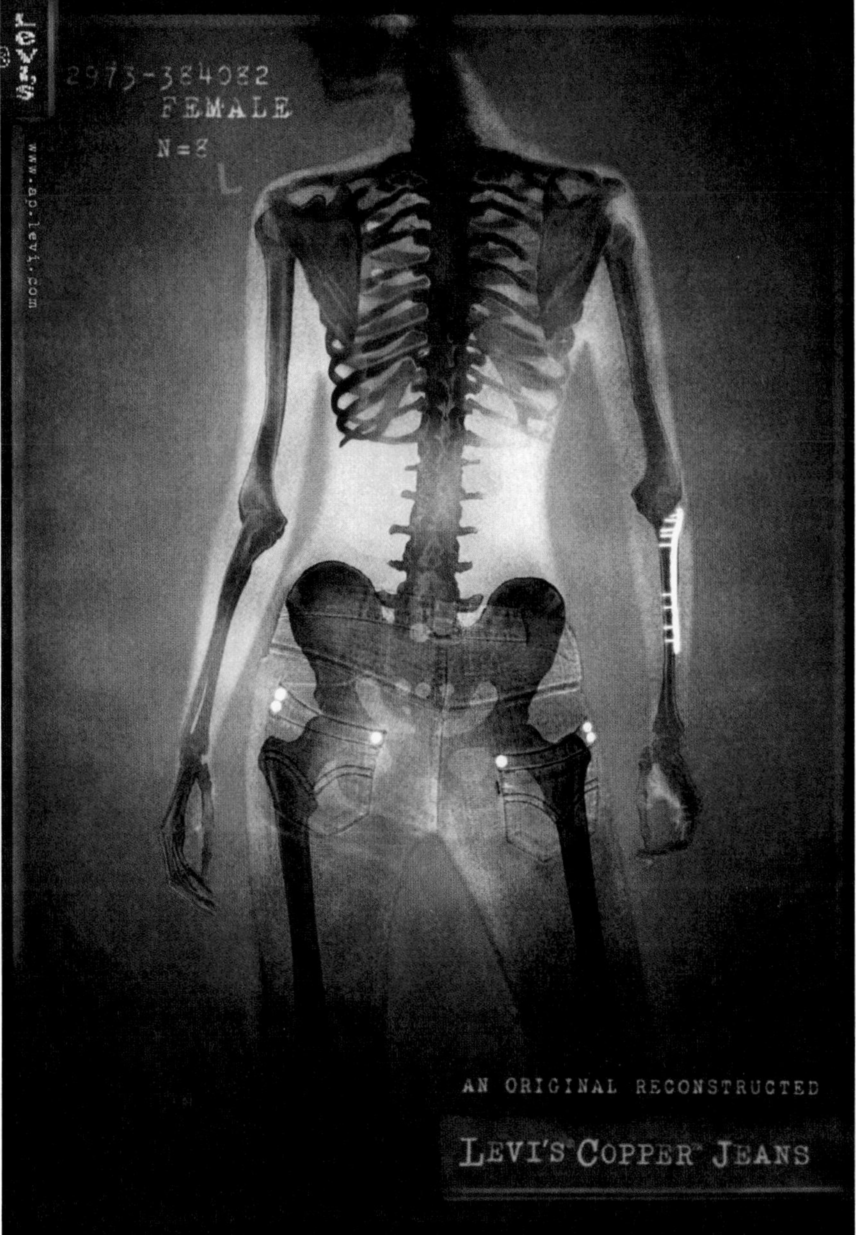

FIGURE 2.2 Advertisement for Levi's Copper Jeans

white areas in the ad? And the words "original" and "reconstructed"? And the copper-colored background, which reinforces the name of the product?

Could the ad be suggesting that the copper rivets used in the manufacturing of Levi's Copper Jeans are strong, like the metal used to surgically reconstruct (there is that word again) a broken arm? If so, what kind of rhetorical appeal is the ad making?

How do you interpret the use of the word "original" in this advertisement? Is the ad suggesting that only "original" people wear Levi jeans? That these jeans make you, somehow, original? If so, what kind of rhetorical appeal is the ad making?

Could the skeletal figure have been used to suggest that real "original" people wear these jeans, especially those engaged in dangerous activities (like extreme sports, which might account for her broken arm). If so, what kind of rhetorical appeal is the ad making?

In a rhetorical analysis, you generally will:

- Contextualize a piece of writing (author, audience, and purpose).
- Identify the structure of the piece (chronological, cause/effect, problem/solution, topical, and so on).
- Identify the rhetorical appeals of the piece (*ethos, logos, pathos*).

Ethos appeals to one's beliefs, ethics, and credibility, and to the trustworthiness of the speaker/author. When you read a text to identify the writer's *ethos,* look for the following characteristics:

- Language appropriate to the audience and subject
- A sincere, fair presentation of the argument
- Grammatical sentences
- A level of vocabulary appropriate for the purpose and formality

When you read a text to identify the rhetorical appeal of *logos,* look for the following characteristics:

- Denotative meanings or reasons (literal, dictionary definitions rather than metaphorical or connotative meanings)
- Factual data and statistics
- Quotations
- Citations from authorities and experts

When you read a text to identify the rhetorical appeal of *pathos,* look for the following characteristics:

- Vivid, concrete language
- Emotionally loaded language
- Connotative meanings (beyond the basic meaning)
- Emotional examples

- Narratives of emotional events
- Figurative language

(For more on rhetorical appeals, see pages 458–460.)

Here are some questions you might consider when you read a text, questions that will help you pinpoint the rhetorical appeals:

- Who is the intended audience? How do you identify the audience?
- What do you see as the writer's purpose? To explain? Inform? Anger? Persuade? Amuse? Motivate? Sadden? Ridicule? Is there more than one purpose? Does the purpose shift at all throughout the text?
- Can you identify the rhetorical appeals of this piece of writing (*ethos, logos, pathos*)? What would you add or omit to make the rhetorical appeals more effective?
- How does the writer develop his or her ideas? Narration? Description? Definition? Comparison? Cause and effect? Examples?
- What is the tone of the text? Do you react at an emotional level to the text? Does this reaction change at all throughout the text?
- How does the writer arrange his or her ideas? What are the patterns of arrangement?
- Does the writer use dialogue? Quotations? To what effect?
- How does the writer use diction? Is it formal? Informal? Technical? Jargon? Slang? Is the language connotative? Denotative? Is the language emotionally evocative? Does the language change throughout the piece? How does the language contribute to the writer's aim?

Writing Activity

Writing a Rhetorical Analysis

Apply the first three questions to the advertisement for Levi's Copper Jeans. Share your responses with several of your classmates. How are those responses similar? How different?

Reading Visuals

As a college student, you will most often be asked to read words on paper, but you can usually apply the same strategies you use to read sentences and paragraphs critically to other types of texts as well. You might think that visuals are easier to read than written text, but this assumption is not accurate. In fact, you often have to pay more attention to visual images, not only because they are sometimes subtler than written text but also because you are not accustomed to reading them critically.

While the process of understanding photographs, bar and line graphs, diagrams, and other visuals may seem different from that of reading and understanding textual information, you are essentially doing the same kind of work. When you read a text, you translate letters, words, and sentences into concepts and ideas; when you read a visual image, you do the same kind of translation. Just as you read a local newspaper or other printed text for information, you also read the photographs in the newspaper or the images on your television or computer screen to be informed.

Writing Activity

Reading Text and Visuals in an Advertisement

Select a full-page advertisement from a newspaper or magazine, and read both the written text and the visual elements carefully, keeping in mind that nothing in an advertisement is left to chance. Each element, from the kind and size of the typeface, to the colors, to the illustrations or photographs, has been discussed and modified many times as the advertisement was developed and tested. On a separate piece of paper, jot down answers to the following questions:

- What is this advertiser trying to sell?
- What kinds of evidence does the advertisement use to convince you to buy the product or service?
- Does the advertiser use the rhetorical appeal of *ethos* (see page 22), and if so, how?
- Does the advertiser use the rhetorical appeal of *logos* (see page 22), and if so, in what way?
- In what ways does the advertisement appeal to your emotions (the rhetorical appeal of *pathos*—see page 22)?
- What strategies does the advertiser employ to convince you of the credibility of the ad's message?
- How effective is this advertisement? Why?
- How might the various elements of the advertisement—colors, photos or other visuals, background, text—be changed to make the ad more, or less, effective?
- How much does the advertisement help potential buyers make informed decisions about this product?

If your instructor asks you to do so, share your advertisements and notes with several of your classmates. What similarities did you find in the advertisements that you selected? In what ways did the advertisements make use of visuals? What were the most effective elements of the advertisements?

As you read visuals, here are some questions to consider:

- How can you use words to tell what the visual shows?
- If the visual is combined with written text, what does the visual add to the verbal text? What would be lost if the visual were not there?
- Why do you think that the writer chose this particular format—photo, line drawing, chart, graph—for the visual?
- If you were choosing or designing a visual to illustrate this point, what would it look like?
- How accurately does the visual illustrate the point?
- What emotions does the visual evoke?

Reading Web Sites

Today many of us read Web sites, which can include not only text, with type in different colors and various sizes, but also photographs or other visual elements, videos that we can click on to view, and music. To read Web sites actively and critically, you need to examine the information on your screen just as carefully as you would a page of printed text or a visual in a magazine or newspaper. Because there are more aspects of the text to examine and consider, however, and also because it is often more difficult to establish where a text on the Web comes from, active reading becomes even more important. Consider the following additional questions when you are reading a Web page:

- The uniform resource locator (URL) of a site, its address, can give you clues about its origin and purpose. For any page you visit, consider what the URL tells you about the page, especially the last three letters—*edu* (educational), *gov* (U.S. government), *org* (nonprofit organization), or *com* (commercial). What difference does it make who sponsors the site?
- How reputable is the person or agency that is providing the information on this page? You can check the person's or agency's reputation by doing a Web search (in Google, Bing, or Yahoo!, for instance).
- What clues do you see as to the motives of the person or agency that is providing this information? Is there a link to an explanation of the purpose of the site? Usually, such explanations are labeled something like "About [name of organization or person]."
- How current is the information on this page? Can you find a date that indicates when the page was last updated?
- Can you identify any of the rhetorical appeals (*ethos, logos, pathos*)?
- How does the structure of the Web site impact its message?
- If there are links on the page, how helpful is the description of each link? Are the links working, or do they lead to dead ends?

For further details about evaluating information on the Web, see Chapter 19, "Finding and Evaluating Sources."

Writing Activity

Reading Web Pages: What You Can See

Using the questions on page 25, read the following Web page. Respond in writing to as many of the questions as you can. Compare your responses with those of your classmates.

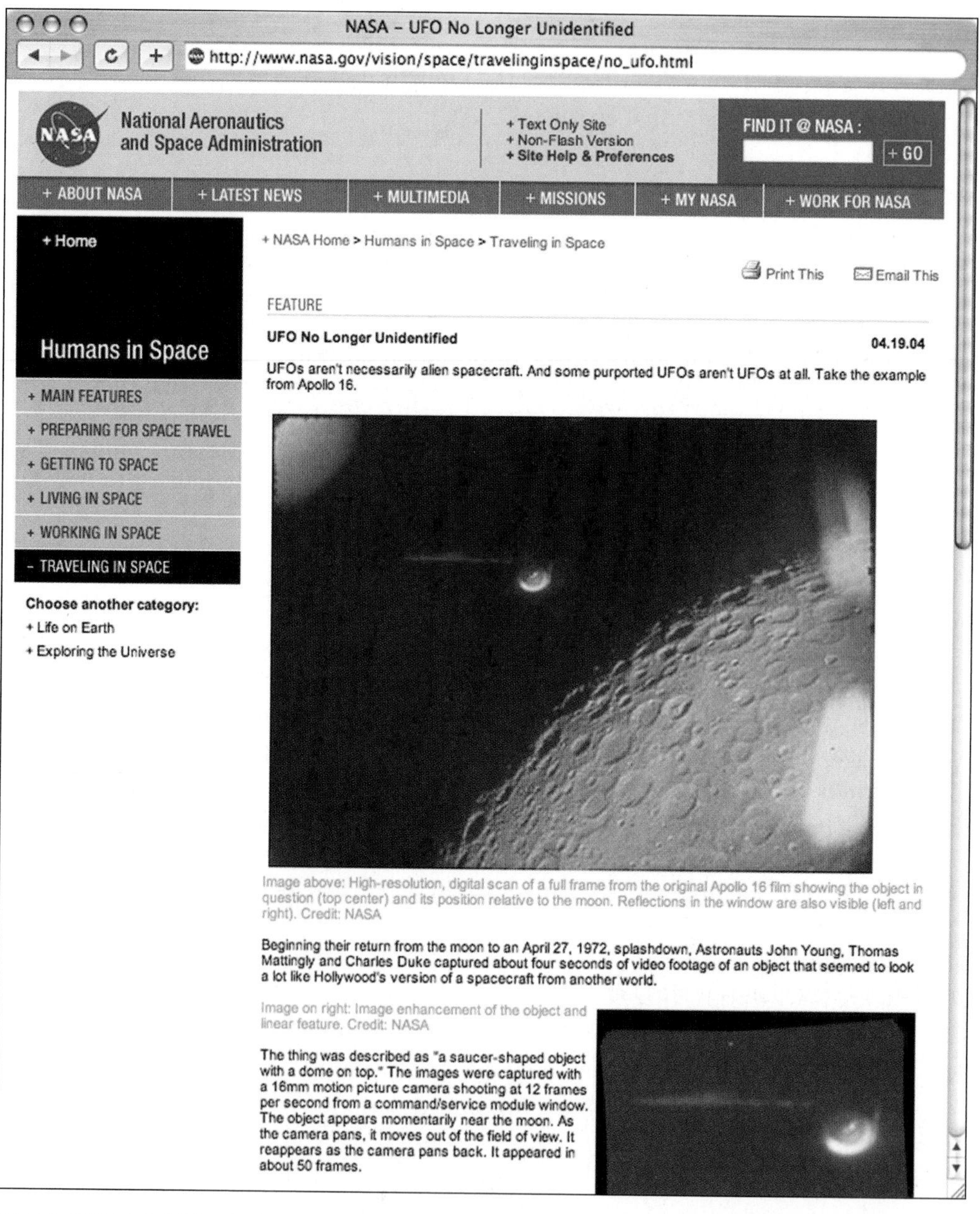

Using Postreading Strategies

After you have read an essay or other text actively and annotated it, spend a bit of time thinking about what you have learned from it and even writing in response to it. Review your annotations and answer the following questions:

- What is the main point or idea you learned from working through this text?
- What did you learn that surprises or interests you?
- How does the information in this text agree with or contradict information on this topic you have already read or learned from your own experience?
- What questions do you still have about this text?
- Where can you find answers to those questions?
- What in this reading might be useful in your own writing?

One useful method for storing and keeping track of what you have learned from your reading is to keep a writer's journal. A journal is a handy and accessible place to write down the information and ideas you gather, as well as your reactions to and insights about the texts you read. Other effective postreading strategies include writing summaries, synthesizing information, and using your reading in your writing.

Starting Your Writer's/Research Journal

A writer's journal is a place where you keep track of the notes, annotations, and summaries that you make from your reading. Because any writing project longer than a page or two demands more information than you can usually store in your memory, it is vital to keep a written record of information that you discover. You can use the entries in your journal as the basis for group discussions as well as for writing tasks.

The information that you include in your journal can vary based on the needs of the project you are working on. The format and design will also vary to suit your purpose. In other words, your rhetorical situation will have an impact not only on the material you collect, the notes that you take, and the summaries and syntheses that you write (see pages 28–31), but also on the physical makeup of your journal. If you are working on a project that requires a large number of illustrations, for example, you will need to include space in your journal to store them.

It is usually a good idea to keep a journal of some sort for *each* writing project you are working on. Consider the following questions for each journal:

- What kinds of information (data, charts, anecdotes, photos, illustrations, and so on) should you collect for this project?

- What information will help you get your message across to your intended audience?
- What information might you jot down that may lead to more complex ideas? Why would more complexity be desirable?
- What questions do you have and how might you go about finding answers to those questions?
- What kinds of illustrations might help you *show* what you mean?

For more on taking notes from and properly citing sources, see Chapter 20.

As you write in your journal, you should note where ideas or quotations come from in the original texts, so that you will be able to properly cite them in your own writing. Get in the habit of noting the information you will need to cite your source, including the page number an idea or quotation comes from.

connect™
mhconnectcomposition.com
Summarizing QL2001

Writing Effective Summaries

After they have read and annotated a text, many readers find that summarizing it also helps them to understand it better. A **summary** is a concise restatement of the most important information in a text—its main point and major supporting points.

Writing Activity

Reading a Text Critically

Assume that for your business ethics class, you have been asked to read the following column "Downloading Music: Harmful to the Artist, the Recording Company, or Neither?" by Carlton Vogt, who wrote the piece for *InfoWorld*. Based on what you have learned in this chapter, consider how you should go about reading this text. Use the critical reading skills you have learned to do the following:

- Explain what you already knew about this topic just from the title.
- In a brief paragraph, explain what you did before you read this text. Did you skim it?
- Annotate the first paragraph.
- Jot down your answers to the following postreading questions, using no more than two sentences for each response.
  - What was your initial reaction and response to this text?
  - What is the main idea you learned from working through this text?
  - Did you learn anything that surprises or interests you?
  - In what ways does the information in this text reinforce or contradict other texts you have read or what you know from your own experience?
  - What questions do you still have about this text?

(continued)

Reading a Text Critically *(continued)*

InfoWorld

http://www.infoworld.com/articles/op/xml/01/05/04/010504opethics.html

Ethics Matters *by Carlton Vogt*

Downloading music: harmful to the artist, the recording company, or neither?

I may be the best person to talk about Napster—or the worst. You can see where this is going already. I don't buy a lot of CDs. In fact, I can't remember the last time I bought one. I don't download music from the Internet. And I don't write or perform music. So I'm either completely neutral or totally out of the loop.

That's the nice way of putting it. Some readers, responding to recent columns, put it less charitably. Their verdict: I haven't thought about it enough, I'm totally clueless, or I'm an idiot. All of these were comments about my position on Napster, which is puzzling, because I haven't taken one. However, these readers pointed out to me that the situation is perfectly clear:

1. Downloading music is not stealing.
2. Downloading music is definitely stealing.
3. Downloading music is wrong, but not stealing.
4. Downloading music is neither wrong nor stealing.

How could I be so dense? There were several variations on these themes. Some thought you could rip music off a purchased CD to use on other devices. Others thought you could share certain tracks—but not the whole CD—with intimate friends (although they didn't say what level of intimacy you need to have achieved first). A few argued that the music industry was so evil that anything you can do to use music for free is totally justified.

And, in typical fashion, many were convinced that their opinions were not only correct, but also self-evident. So I'm glad we've cleared that up.

A few argued the fine points of copyright law, but the connection between law and ethics is, at best, tenuous—and the subject of a future column—so I usually hesitate to look to the law for the proper ethical answer.

But let's take my CD-buying experience as an entry point. What sometimes happens is that I go to the store, look at a CD that strikes my fancy, find four out of 12 tracks that I find appealing, and put the CD back. Is the recording company better off or worse off that I've not bought the album? I suppose you could say it's worse off, although I could argue that it's neither, because its position hasn't changed from before I looked at the album. However, it has lost a potential customer. Have I done anything wrong? No. I have no obligation to make the company better off by buying the album.

How about the artist? Again worse off—and on two counts. Not only has the artist not gotten whatever royalty would come from the sale of the CD, but also I haven't heard the music. And isn't the whole point of performing so that people will hear what you do?

I'm a writer, and I get paid for it. InfoWorld puts my column on its Web site. On one level I'm satisfied; I've got my money. However, if the Web site traffic maven were to come and tell me that my column got only two page hits, I would be devastated. I would be more devastated if InfoWorld didn't come through with the paycheck, but not having anyone read the column hurts a lot too.

Getting back to music, suppose I download the four CD tracks I like from the Internet? Is the record company better or worse off? It's not worse off, because I wasn't going to buy the CD anyway. It may be better off, because I just may buy the next CD the artist puts out if I like this one. Or I may tell someone about it, who might then go out and buy the CD.

How about the artist? The artist is definitely not worse off, because I wasn't going to buy the CD anyway. So he or she isn't losing anything. But, in the sense of having someone appreciate the performance, the artist is definitely better off. There may be some artists who don't care at all about audience appreciation, but if all a performer is interested in is the money, I suspect I wouldn't even be downloading the music.

So putting aside legal considerations, the ethical question at hand is, "Have I harmed anyone?" That is, have I set back any of their important interests without justification? Because I have no obligation to buy a CD, if I don't want one, it's hard to say that I have harmed either the artist or the recording company by not buying the CD. And in downloading the music, I may have advanced at least one of the artist's interests because I am listening to the music.

On the other hand, if I am downloading or sharing the music to avoid otherwise buying the CD, then you could say that I was harming both the artist and the recording company because I was depriving them of income they otherwise would have had—my money. And that makes all the difference.

The fly in the ointment lies in who determines whether or not I would have bought the CD. You certainly don't know and neither does the recording company. I may think I know, but we have a remarkable ability to deceive ourselves, especially when self interest is involved.

Carlton Vogt is a former InfoWorld editor.

Done

Writing Activity

Summarizing "Downloading Music: Harmful to the Artist, the Recording Company, or Neither?"

In no more than one page, summarize "Downloading Music: Harmful to the Artist, the Recording Company, or Neither?" (page 29). If your instructor asks you to, share your summary with several of your classmates.

Writing a Summary: To write an effective summary, start by listing the main points of the text, in effect outlining what you are reading. Remember, however, that a summary is more than just a list; a summary provides a brief narrative structure that connects these main ideas.

STEPS FOR WRITING A SUMMARY

1. Read the text relatively quickly to get a general sense of what it is saying.
2. Read the text again. Mark or highlight a sentence that expresses the main point of each paragraph, and paraphrase that point—put it entirely into your own words—in the margin.
3. For a longer text, label the major sections. If the writer has provided subheadings, use them as they are or paraphrase them. If not, write subheadings.
4. After considering what you have done in the first three steps, write a statement that captures the writer's main point or thesis.
5. Working backward from step 4, craft a paragraph—in your own words—that captures the gist of what the writer is saying.

Synthesizing Information in Readings

Synthesis calls for the thoughtful combination or integration of ideas and information with your point of view.

Suppose that you would like to see a particular movie this Saturday. You hope to convince a group of your friends to accompany you. You have read several reviews of the film, you know other work by the director, and you have even read the novel on which this movie is based. At the same time, simply sending your friends all the information you have about the film might overwhelm them. Unless you effectively structure what you have to say, one piece of information may contradict some other point that you want to make.

To organize your information, you could focus on what you see as the most compelling reasons your friends should see the film: the novel the film is based on, along with the director of the movie. You would then provide information on the following:

- How interesting the novel is, with specific examples to show what you mean
- How effectively the novel has been translated to film, using reviews or other information about the film as evidence
- Other films by the same director that you know your friends like

When you synthesize effectively, you take the jumble of facts, data, information, and other knowledge you have on hand and put it into an understandable format that fulfills the purpose you want to accomplish. And, of course, when you cite reviewers' opinions (in the hope of convincing your friends which movie to see), you will need to indicate where the comments came from—to properly attribute what the reviewers had to say and to lend their authority to your argument. Failure to properly attribute ideas to original sources constitutes plagiarism.

For more on avoiding plagiarism, see Chapter 20.

As we have noted, to fully understand information and then be able to synthesize it effectively, you must read critically, questioning, challenging, and engaging the text as you work through it. One strategy that will help you improve your critical thinking and reading is to work with others. When you work with your classmates, you hear their perspectives and ideas and have the opportunity to consider various points of view. Working with others also helps you learn to construct the most effective questions to ask, to help you become an active reader.

Using Your Reading in Your Writing

Information that you find in your reading can be used in many ways in your writing. If you have annotated the texts that your instructor asked you to read for a writing project in this course or another course, you can often use those annotations in your own writing. Likewise, if you have summarized sources for a research project, you can refer to and use those summaries to spot the important points of each text you have read, and then use relevant information as evidence to support your main idea. If you have found statistical information in graphical form, or photographs, drawings, maps, or other illustrations, these too can become part of your text. Of course, it is always important to

Writing Activity

Synthesizing Information

Using what you have learned from this chapter on critical reading and synthesizing information, reread "The Ethics of 'Stealing' a WiFi Connection" (page 19) and "Downloading Music: Harmful to the Artist, the Recording Company, or Neither?" (page 29). Both readings involve ethical issues: Synthesize the issues outlined in these readings in no more than two pages. Remember that a synthesis is a thoughtful integration of your readings with your own point of view. Where do you stand on these ethical dilemmas? What else have you read in your college classes that relates to these ethical situations?

indicate where you found information, whose ideas you use in your text, and where statistical information came from in order to establish your credibility and avoid *plagiarizing*—representing the words or ideas of others as your own ideas or words.

In the chapters in Parts 2 and 3 of this book, you will read various selections. As you read these texts or conduct library and/or Web research to find support for your writing, you will find it helpful to use the reading strategies described in this chapter.

hapter 3

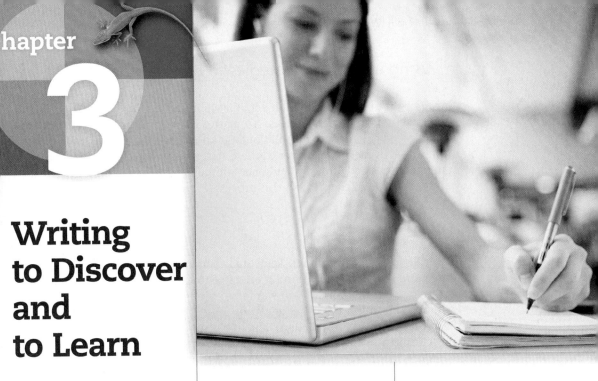

Writing to Discover and to Learn

Most of the chapters in this book focus on learning to write for an audience—to accomplish a purpose involving other people. This chapter, though, provides some tried-and-true strategies for using writing to discover ideas and to learn—to accomplish a purpose for yourself. As you probably are finding out as you do more of it, writing is a way of learning, of figuring out what you know and understand about a subject and, in the process, of coming to know and understand it better.

This chapter introduces strategies to help you to learn and to prepare for writing assignments. These tools can be used in academic, professional, civic, or personal settings. As discussed in Chapter 2, writing about what you read for your classes can help you learn that information better, not just by rewriting to summarize your notes, but by jotting down your questions and comments, reflecting on what you have read, and noting how any new ideas and information relate to other ideas and information. In your professional life, consider how writing about what was useful in a recent business meeting, what problems came up, and what issues did not get solved might help you conduct more effective and efficient meetings in the future.

In almost any situation, writing (immediately afterward) about what you *learned* from an experience will prepare you for similar situations you might face in the future. If you get into the habit of writing about the events and issues in your life, you likely will come to a more thoughtful and thorough understanding of those events and issues.

The strategies that follow are tools that writers have used to figure out what they have learned and what they still need to know.

Using Invention Strategies to Discover Ideas

As you begin to explore your subject, it is a good idea to use more than one invention activity to generate ideas. No matter what your purpose is for writing, you will need to generate information and knowledge about your topic through invention activities. Whichever of these strategies you use, a helpful accompanying activity is creating an audience profile. The "Genres Up Close" feature walks you through the steps of this process.

Listing

Listing involves jotting down keywords that will remind you of ideas as you write more later. You might find it effective to establish categories within your lists to jog your memory. If you wanted to propose a solution to a problem, for example, you might organize keywords under "history of the problem," "how the problem affects my readers," "possible solutions," "failed solutions," and "objections to a solution."

Freewriting

When you freewrite, you simply write for a set time—perhaps five or ten minutes. You jot down, or type, everything that comes to mind, even if you cannot think of anything (in that case, you might write, "I can't think of anything to write," until your ideas start to flow).

Questioning

One way to generate information and ideas is to ask questions about your topic, audience, and purpose:

- What am I trying to accomplish in this paper?
- What do I already know about my topic?
- What might my readers already know?
- What would readers need to know to understand my point?
- What kind(s) of information (for example, graphs, tables, or lists) might be useful to *show* my readers (rather than just to tell them)?
- What kinds of details and explanation can I provide?
- Where might I learn more about this subject (in the library, on the Internet, by interviewing people)?

Answering the Questions *Who? What? Where? When? Why?* and *How?*

You can expand the questioning approach (above) by spending a few minutes jotting down answers to the reporter's questions: *who, what, where, when, why,* and *how.* You may find that your answers lead to still more questions:

- Whom does this subject affect? In what ways?
- Who is involved in making a decision about this subject?
- Who is my audience?
- What am I trying to get my audience to do?
- What can't I ask my readers to do?
- What is important here?
- What are the historical aspects of this topic?
- Where does all of this take place?
- When might something happen to affect this situation?
- When would I like something to happen?
- Why should my readers care about my paper?
- Why is this topic important?
- Why will ______ happen?
- How does the context—the "where"—affect the situation?
- How might ______ happen?
- How might ______ react to the topic I am writing about?

Brainstorming

connect
mhconnectcomposition.com
Prewriting (brainstorming) QL3001

When you brainstorm, you record on paper or on-screen the information you already know about the topic you are exploring. Once you have written down several possible topics or ideas or possible ways to focus your paper, you may have an easier time finding the one that seems most promising.

Clustering

connect
mhconnectcomposition.com
Prewriting (clustering) QL3002

Clustering is especially useful for figuring out possible cause-and-effect relationships. For more on clustering and an example, see page 43.

GENRES UP CLOSE

GENRES *Up Close* Writing an Audience Profile

An audience profile is a genre that helps writers understand their audience's needs as part of the rhetorical situation. While understanding an audience's needs is only one part of the rhetorical situation, the more writers know about their audience, the better they are positioned to achieve their purpose and to present their information in the most effective fashion. In fact, one of the first things experienced writers do when they start a writing project is to identify and analyze their audience. For example, determining whether the audience is knowledgeable about the topic can help writers determine what level of detail and sophistication of language is most appropriate. The more writers know about their target audience, the more they can tailor the argument for the maximum impact on the audience. An informative pamphlet on the needs of children with autism in schools might have different information if the pamphlet were intended for parents and relatives of children with autism, for parents of children in classes with children with autism, or for school personnel.

When profiling their audience, writers ask themselves the following questions:

- Who is my audience?
- Does this writing task have only one audience, or are there multiple audiences?
- If there is more than one audience, how does each one differ from the others?
- What does my audience already know?
    - Are they experts in the field?
    - Are they knowledgeable laypeople?
    - Will I need to adjust my language and level of detail to meet my audience's needs?
- What does my audience need to know?
- Why is this information important to this audience?
- How do I expect my audience to use this information?

Here is a sample format you might use for an audience profile.

Main Audience

- What are their defining characteristics?

Secondary Audiences

- What are their defining characteristics?
- How do they differ from the main audience?

Audience's Knowledge of the Field

- What background (experience/education) do they have?
- What are their assumptions about the information?
- Does their cultural context affect their view of the information? How?

What the Audience Needs to Know

- Why is this important to the audience?
- How should I expect the audience to use this information?

Whether your instructor asks you to write an audience profile as a formal writing assignment or not, being able to informally profile an audience for every writing assignment you do is a valuable skill.

Keeping Notebooks and Journals

Writers and learners frequently maintain notebooks and journals because these forms of informal writing are useful places for recording and/or exploring ideas. Leonardo da Vinci, for example, kept notebooks for years, compiling 1,566 pages of ideas in words and images.

Double-Entry Notebook

One useful type of notebook is what composition scholar Anne Berthoff calls a **dialectical notebook** or **journal.** In a dialectical notebook, you write notes on one page and then write your questions and comments about those notes on the facing page. The **double-entry notebook,** which is a type of dialectical notebook, can be easily adapted to many contexts. The double-entry notebook has two columns. The left column is used to present whatever kind of information is appropriate to the context. Thus, in this column, you might record lecture, lab, field, or reading notes; list the steps in a math problem; construct a timeline; or list events in chronological order. The right column is used to respond to, comment on, question, and apply the information in the left column.

For instance, Judy Bowden was enrolled in an art history course. To understand some of the artwork that she was studying in the course, Bowden frequently used the double-entry notebook. Because her journal was electronic, she could download

Writing Activity

Your Dialectical Notebook

Select one of your college classes and go over your notes for the most recent week of classes. Construct a dialectical notebook that outlines your notes and also your reactions to, comments on, and questions about those notes.

public-domain artwork from the Web and paste it into the left column of her notebook. In the right column, she wrote about the work. Here is an example from Bowden's notebook.

Artwork	My Thoughts
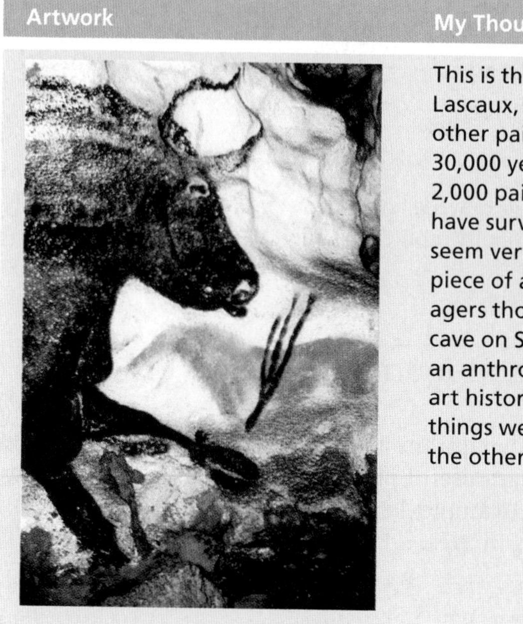	This is the *Black Bull* cave painting from Lascaux, France. It's amazing that this and other paintings in the cave are 10,000 to 30,000 years old. It's also amazing that 2,000 paintings and drawings in the cave have survived for so long. The details seem very sophisticated for such an old piece of art. I wonder what the four teenagers thought when they discovered the cave on September 12, 1940. If I were in an anthropology course instead of an art history course, I wonder what other things we'd learn about this painting and the others.

Field Notebook

Field notebooks are useful for students who are doing field research. A field notebook can take many forms, depending on the observations that you are making. For instance, Lindsay Hanson was enrolled in a summer session biology course for nonmajors. One of the requirements of the course was to pick a natural habitat and observe some life-forms in that habitat. Lindsay chose to do some bird-watching in a marsh near her campus. She decided to set up her field notebook in columns with headings.

For more on field research, see Chapter 19.

Date and Time	Location	Common Name	Scientific Name	Sex	Comments
6/6/07 6:20 p.m.	west shore of Widespread	red-winged blackbird	Agelaius phoeniceus	♂	The bird was sitting on the top of a weed, which was swaying in the breeze. Partly cloudy, 61°, windy
6/6/07 6:35 p.m.	south shore of Widespread	yellow-shafted flicker	Colaptes auratus	♀	The bird took off from some 8″–10″ grass. Partly cloudy, 61°

Writing Activity

Writing Your Own Field Notebook

If you have a class that requires fieldwork, construct a field notebook that includes drawings or other images and your notes on your field research. If you do not have a class that requires field research, spend an hour at some place on your campus, observing and making notes on what you see in a field notebook. Use these reporter's questions to guide you:

- Who is there? What are they doing? How are they dressed? What are they carrying or working with?
- What does the place look like? Can you take photos or make drawings? What sounds and smells are in this place?
- Where is this place? How does it connect or relate to other places on campus?
- When did you visit? Why? What makes that time different from another time when you might observe this place?
- Why did you select this particular spot? What other places did you consider? Why?

connect
mhconnectcomposition.com
Paraphrasing while taking notes QL3003

connect
mhconnectcomposition.com
Note taking overview QL3004

Rewriting Your Class Notes

Whether you use a double-entry notebook or some other method, make rewriting your class notes part of your own "homework" assignment each day:

- Put them into a readable and organized form.
- Think of questions about the information that had not occurred to you when you were taking the notes during class.
- Discover areas of interest that you want to find out more about.

Think of the "re" in the word *rewriting* and what it means: to resee, to reenvision, to reconsider, perhaps even to reorganize. When you rewrite your in-class notes, use the writing as a way to help you learn, not just by transcribing your notes, but by reconsidering them and asking questions, by reseeing what you wrote (and jotting down connections you make with other ideas and texts), and by reorganizing them so they make more sense than they might have made in class.

Digital Literacy

Communicating with Study Groups and Partners

When you take a college class, remember that your classmates can be a valuable resource. Create communication spaces on the Internet for study groups or for just yourself and one study partner. Exchange contact information with classmates, and use it. Remember, though, that if you post text or images straight from sources (such as textbooks or reference works), you must cite them properly. With copyrighted work, you must obtain permission from the source before posting that person's intellectual property on a public site. Better yet, if resources are available on legitimate Web sites, send or post a link to that site, making it available for your study partners.

After each college class meeting, convert your in-class notes to e-notes in a computer document. Doing so encourages you to reread your notes and put them into a more readable form. Just reading them over again helps cement the ideas in your memory—and writing them down again helps you remember them, too. Also, your notes will be easier to read when exam time comes around. Finally, your notes will be searchable, and you can copy and paste them, as needed, into your college papers.

Minute Paper

A minute paper is a quick, useful way to reflect on a class lecture or discussion, a chance to jot down—in a minute or two—your answers to two questions:

For more on e-mail, instant messaging, and blogs, see Chapter 17.

- What is the most important thing that I learned in class today?
- What is the most important question that I have about today's class lecture/discussion?

For example, Conner Ames, who was enrolled in a general studies course in sociology, responded at the end of a particular class as follows:

1. Today we learned that group behavior often is different from individual behavior: people will act differently in groups than they might act alone. This is especially true for male adolescents when a group interacts with other male adolescent groups.
2. What are more of the real-life implications of group behavior (and I also want to know more about *why* young males like me act as they do when they're in a group)?

Muddiest Point

As its name suggests, the muddiest-point strategy involves jotting down a concept or idea that is unclear or confusing and, if possible, exploring it through writing. This does not mean looking up the definition of a concept, but instead writing about it to clarify your thinking.

Your muddiest point may come from a paragraph in a chapter that you are reading for a course, or it may come from a class lecture or discussion. In many instances, you may be able to work through your confusion by writing. At the very least, you will crystallize the issue and provide yourself with a reminder to raise a question during the next class meeting, in an office-hour visit, in an e-mail to the professor, or on the online discussion board for the course.

Preconception Check

A *preconception* is something you think you know about a subject before you learn more about it in class, through your reading, and from other sources of information. One strategy for overcoming preconceptions is to become aware of them. For instance, Tom Ambrose was enrolled in an astronomy course. As he read a chapter about the solar system, he encountered a subsection titled "Why Are There Seasons on Earth?" Before he read the subsection, he realized that he had some preconceptions about why the seasons occur. He wrote the following in his learning journal for that course:

> I think that Earth has the four seasons because of the elliptical path of the planet as it orbits the Sun. When that path takes us farthest from the Sun (December–March), we have winter. When the path takes us closest to the Sun (June–August), we have summer.

This short explanation may seem trivial, but it served to make Ambrose more attuned to the explanation in his astronomy textbook. When he read that the seasons are caused by Earth's tilt on its axis, he was better prepared to process that information. He noted:

> When I read the chapter, I realized the problem with my preconception. If the elliptical path of Earth's orbit were the cause of the seasons, then the whole planet would have summer in June–August. I forgot that when it's summer in the northern hemisphere it's winter in the southern hemisphere.

Paraphrasing

One strategy you can use to make the material more understandable is to **paraphrase** it—to restate it in your own words. If you have ever tried to teach something to someone, you know that the act of teaching—explaining, demonstrating, answering questions—often aids your understanding of the subject or concept. This is the rationale behind paraphrasing—by explaining something in your own words, you come to understand it better.

Jack Johnson was taking an introductory physics course for nonmajors. Early in the course, the instructor mentioned "Ockham's razor" but did not define it. Using a popular search engine to investigate the term, Johnson found that it is defined as the principle of economy or of parsimony. After reading several Web sites, Johnson felt he understood the term and wrote the following in his course journal:

> In a nutshell, Ockham's razor means this: if two theories have equal explanatory power, choose the simpler one. That is, keep it simple, Stupid—K.I.S.S. In my geology class we discussed the Grand Canyon, and I kind of now see

how the simplest answer to its formation—a river and other natural weather conditions, acting over a long period of time—actually makes the most sense. If I try to get too complicated about something, I need to remember Ockham's razor: if two or more ideas seem to explain something, the simpler is probably the better answer.

For more on paraphrasing, see Chapter 20.

Organizing and Synthesizing Information

Finding and collecting information is part of learning, but effective learners need to organize and synthesize information to make it usable. As you conduct research and locate information that might be useful for your writing, do the following:

- Organize what you learn in a logical manner. Often an effective way to organize your notes is to put them into a digital document; you can then use its search function to locate particular words or phrases.
- Organize your notes by putting them into a spreadsheet like Excel. If you format the spreadsheet cells to "wrap text," you create a database of notes.
- As you take notes, synthesize the information: Condense it into a brief form, where the important aspects are listed, along with the reference, so you can easily locate the complete information.

For more on summary and synthesis, see pages 28–31.

Invented Interview/Unsent Letter

In an invented interview, you are the interviewer. The interviewee could be a person or a character whom you are studying or a person associated with a concept that you are studying. If you *really* could interview someone for a college class, what would you ask that person? What issues or concepts would you focus on? It is often useful to put your questions into an unsent-letter format so that you have a specific audience you are writing to as you generate interview questions.

Here are some sample questions:

- In a geometry course, you might interview Pythagoras to ask him about the process that led to his development of the Pythagorean theorem.
- In an entrepreneurship course, you might interview Bill Gates to ask him what drove him to found Microsoft.
- In an anthropology course, you might interview a group of Cro-Magnons to ask about their interactions with Neanderthals.
- In a United States history course, you might ask President Harry Truman why he decided to drop atomic bombs on two Japanese cities in 1945.

Taking this concept of an invented interview further, you can conduct research to determine how your questions might have been answered if you had been able to conduct such an interview.

The key to writing such interviews is that you need to move beyond the limits of your initial response to an event or a person. Use the interview as an opportunity to explore a topic from an intellectual as well as an emotional perspective.

Using Charts and Visuals to Discover and to Learn

Just as charts, graphs, tables, photographs, and other visuals help readers understand what you write about, using visuals is often a way for writers to explore ideas and really see and understand what they are writing about.

Clustering and Concept Mapping

Concept maps, or *clustering,* can help us to visualize abstract ideas and also to understand relationships among ideas. Figure 3.1 shows how student writer Santi DeRosa might have developed a cluster map to help him get started with his paper about how female students help recruit male athletes for his school. According to an article in the campus newspaper, women serve as campus guides when potential athletes visit the school. When he read the article, DeRosa had concerns about the ethics of this practice, so he decided to respond by writing an essay on the issue (you can read his complete essay in Chapter 8).

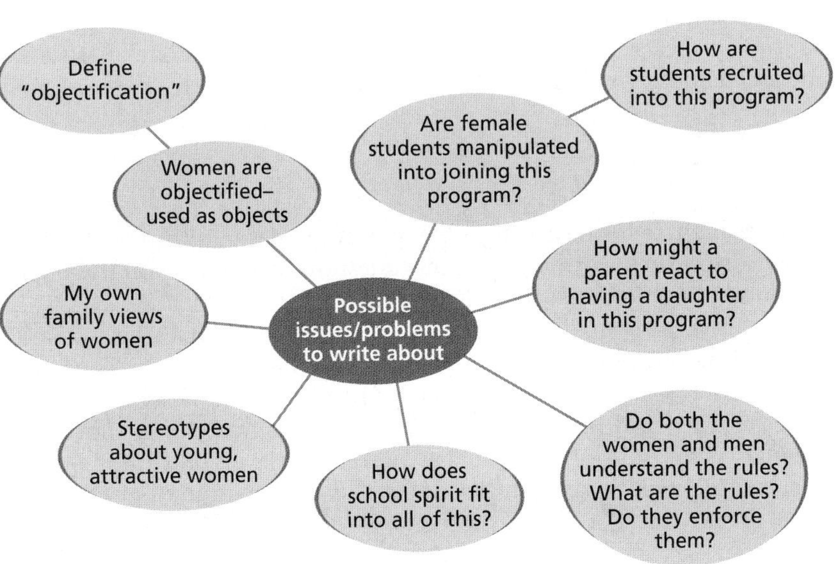

FIGURE 3.1 A Possible Cluster Map on the Topic of Recruiting Practices

Process Flowchart

A process flowchart is another visually useful tool for converting information from verbal to visual form. A flowchart allows you to translate several paragraphs of information into a clear, succinct visual that can make difficult concepts easier to understand. Rather than focusing on relationships in a system (how ideas or concepts might connect to one another), a flowchart indicates how things *move* through a system.

In his political science course, Brian Flores studied the process by which a bill moves through the U.S. House of Representatives. After reading a few pages on the process, Brian converted the material into the flowchart shown in Figure 3.2.

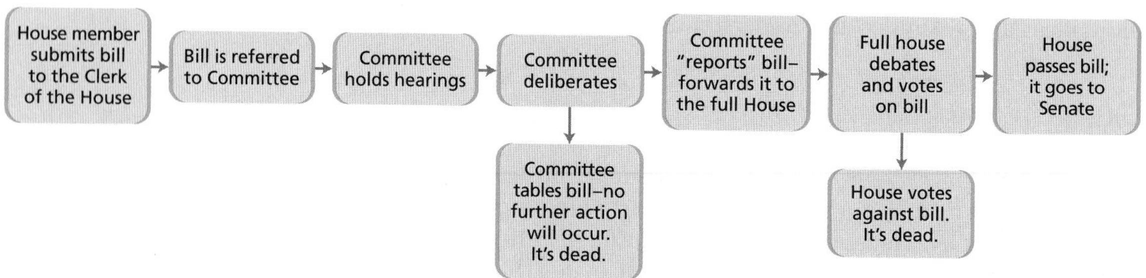

FIGURE 3.2 Following a Bill through the U.S. House of Representatives

Digital Literacy

Teaching Yourself by Teaching Others

One way to learn material more thoroughly is to help someone else learn about it. Create a Web site for yourself or someone else (a former teacher, a sibling, a club you belong to). Use your new knowledge to create links, text, and connections that will help others learn more about the topic.

Studying for Exams

If you study for tests strategically, you can usually anticipate the questions that will be asked and review the course material more efficiently.

Test Questions

One way to prepare for tests is to write questions that you think your instructor may pose on them. Anticipating test questions also gives you the opportunity to anticipate your answers, thus simulating the test itself.

If you are writing questions to prepare for a test, the first step is to ask the instructor about the kinds of questions that you should anticipate. Your instructor will probably indicate the formats that the questions will be in—for example, whether they will be multiple-choice, true/false, matching, short answer, and/or essay questions—and might also indicate the levels of thinking they will require: comprehension, application, analysis, synthesis, and/or evaluation.

One of the most effective strategies for writing test questions is to go through your class notes and reading notes, marking sections that you think are likely to be covered on the test. Then, as soon as possible after class or after reading the textbook, write a few questions and think about the answers. If you write some questions each week, you will learn much more than if you wait until just before the test, and you will cover the material more thoroughly.

For advice on creating an effective Web site, see the Online Appendix.

For advice on taking essay examinations, see Appendix B.

Mnemonic Play

Although in many courses you will learn course material without having to memorize facts, there may be times when you need to develop memory aids for some material. Here is an example that may already be familiar to you. Erin Wilson was enrolled in a general science course for nonmajors. To help her remember the order of the planets in the solar system (before Pluto's status as a planet was changed), she used the sentence "My very educated mother just served us nine pizzas." That is, the order, beginning with the planet closest to the sun, is Mercury, Venus, Earth, Mars, Jupiter, Saturn, Uranus, Neptune, Pluto.

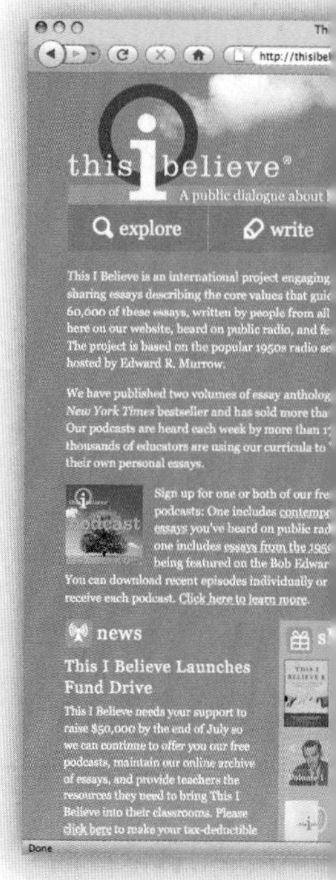

Writing to Share Experience

In "A Priceless Lesson in Humility," a story that appears on the Web site for This I Believe (www.thisibelieve.org), Felipe Morales, a network engineer, shares an experience that caused him to learn something about himself:

> A few years ago, I took a sightseeing trip to Washington D.C. I saw many of our nation's treasures, and I also saw a lot of our fellow citizens on the street—unfortunate ones, like panhandlers and homeless folks.
>
> Standing outside the Ronald Reagan Center, I heard a voice say, "Can you help me?" When I turned around, I saw an elderly blind woman with her hand extended. In a natural reflex, I reached in to my pocket, pulled out all my loose change and placed it on her hand without even looking at her. I was annoyed at being bothered by a beggar.
>
> But the blind woman smiled and said, "I don't want your money. I just need help finding the post office."
>
> In an instant, I realized what I had done. I acted with prejudice—I judged another person simply for what I as sumed she had to be.
>
> I hated what I saw in myself. This incident reawakened my core belief. I reaffirmed that I believe in humility, even though I'd l it for a moment.
>
> The thing I had forgot ten about myself is that I a an immigrant. I left Hondu ras and arrived in the U.S. the age of 15. I started my new life with two suitcases my brother and sister, and strong no-nonsense mothe Through the years, I have been a dishwasher, roofer, cashier, mechanic, pizza de livery driver among many other humble jobs, and eve

tually I became a network engineer.

In my own life, I have experienced many open acts of prejudice. I remember a time at age 17, I was a busboy and I heard a father tell his little boy that if he did not do well in school, he would end up like me. I have also witnessed the same treatment of family and friends, so I know what it's like, and I should have known better.

But now, living in my American middle-class lifestyle, it is too easy to forget my past, to forget who I am, where I have been, and lose sight of where I want to be going. That blind woman on the streets of Washington, D.C., cured me of my self-induced blindness. She reminded me of my belief in humility and to always keep my eyes and heart open.

By the way, I helped that lady to the post office. And in writing this essay, I hope to thank her for the priceless lesson.

In telling this story on the Web, Felipe Morales was engaging in a common activity—sharing a meaningful experience with other people. On any given day, you share your experiences in a variety of ways. At breakfast you might tell your roommate about the nightmare that awakened you at 3:00 in the morning, or at dinner you might tell your family about the argument that you had with your supervisor at work. In your academic life, you might have written an autobiography for your college application packet. In your professional life, you will need to narrate your experiences in résumés and letters of application. In your civic life, you may decide to appear before the city council to describe how the lack of a streetlight at a busy intersection led to an automobile accident.

Writing about your experiences helps you as a writer because the act of writing requires reflection, which is a powerful tool for gaining insight into and understanding about life. Also, when you share your experiences with others, you are offering others insight into what has worked well—and not so well—in your life.

Setting Your Goals:

Rhetorical Knowledge

- **Audience:** Readers may or may not know you or the people you are writing about personally, but you will want to make your experience relevant to them.
- **Purpose:** You may want to entertain readers and possibly to inform and/or persuade them.
- **Rhetorical situation:** Consider the constellation of factors affecting what you write—you (the writer), your readers (the audience), the topic (the experience that you're writing about), your purpose (what you wish to accomplish), and the exigency (what is compelling you to write).
- **Voice and tone:** You have a *stance*—or attitude—toward the experience you are sharing and the people you are writing about. You may be amused, sarcastic, neutral, or regretful, among many possibilities.
- **Context, medium, and genre:** Your writing context, the medium you are writing in (whether print or electronic), and the genre you have chosen all affect your writing decisions.

Critical Thinking, Reading, and Writing

- **Learning/inquiry:** Learn the features of writing to share experiences so that you can do so effectively in any writing situation.
- **Responsibility:** Represent your experiences accurately, with sensitivity to the needs of others.
- **Reading and research:** Draw on your own memories, memories of relatives and friends, photographs and documents, and ideas you develop from your reading.

Writing about Experiences

Chapter 4

Writing Processes

- **Invention:** Choose invention strategies that will help you recall details about your experience or experiences.
- **Organizing your ideas and details:** You will usually be organizing a series of events.
- **Revising:** Read your work with a critical eye, to make certain that it fulfills the assignment and displays the qualities of this kind of writing.
- **Working with peers:** Classmates and others will offer you comments on and questions about your work.

Knowledge of Conventions

- **Editing:** When writers share experiences, they tend to use dialogue to report what they said and what others said to them. The round-robin activity in this chapter (on page 82) addresses the conventions for punctuating dialogue.
- **Genres for sharing experiences:** Genres include personal essay, memoir, autobiography, literacy narrative, magazine or newspaper essay, blog, letter, and accident report.
- **Documentation:** If you have relied on sources outside of your experience, cite them using the appropriate documentation style.

mhconnectcomposition.com

Writing to Share Experiences Tutorial QL4001

Rhetorical Knowledge

When you write about your experiences in a private journal, you can write whatever and however you wish. When you write for other people, though, you need to make conscious choices about your audience; purpose; voice and tone; and context, medium, and genre. You need to consider what your audience may already know about the experience that you are sharing and what your purpose is in sharing this experience with this particular audience. You also need to think about how much of your attitude toward this topic and your audience you want to reveal. Further, the effectiveness of your narrative will be influenced by the medium and genre you choose.

Writing to Share Experiences in Your College Classes

Throughout your college career, you will be called on to share your experiences in writing. Such writing can help you learn more effectively because it encourages you to reflect on your academic experiences. Further, much academic writing takes the form of **narratives**—stories about the physical or human world. For example, one of the best-known philosophers in history, Plato, used stories as powerful teaching tools. In the *Republic,* Plato tells "The Allegory of the Cave" to illustrate what it's like to think like a philosopher.

In your own academic life—your life in college—you may be asked to share experiences in the following ways:

- A math instructor may ask you to write about some experience in which you used a math principle or procedure to solve a problem in your everyday life.
- A music instructor may ask you to attend a concert and then write about the experience.
- An education instructor might assign you to observe a classroom and write about your observations.

Writing to Share Experiences for Life

As humans we tend to organize our lives as ongoing narratives. While your life is one long narrative, within it are thousands of shorter narratives. Those are the kinds of events you will most likely focus on when you write to record and share experiences in the professional, civic, and personal parts of your life.

Curt Schilling, one of the most successful Major League Baseball pitchers of the 1990s and early 2000s, partially attributes that success to his ritual of recording his experience with every batter that he faced and noting the effectiveness of each pitch. You can follow Schilling's example by using writing to record and analyze your **professional** experiences so that you can learn from them.

To participate effectively in **civic** life, writers also need to share their experiences. For democratic institutions to function effectively, citizens need to be involved with their government, especially at the local level.

In **personal** settings, you have many opportunities to record and share experiences every day. For example, at the wedding of two friends, you may be asked to tell the story of how you introduced them in high school.

"Ways of Writing to Share Experiences" provides examples of genres you may use in your writing. The genres of writing you will be assigned will vary by the experiences you are sharing and your specific audience for those experiences.

Scenarios for Writing | Assignment Options

connect
mhconnectcomposition.com

Writer's Workshop: Applying Goals to Writing That Shapes Experiences QL4002

Your instructor may ask you to complete one or both of the following assignments that call for you to write about your experiences. Each assignment is in the form of a *scenario,* a brief story that provides some context for your writing. The scenario gives you a sense of who your audience is and what you need to accomplish with your writing.

Starting on page 70, you will find guidelines for completing the assignment. Additional scenarios for college and life may be found online.

Writing for College

SCENARIO 1 A Memoir about the Impact of a Teacher

Throughout your formal education, you have studied with dozens of teachers. Some of them have been especially influential in helping you learn to succeed in academic settings—and, of course, their influence may have spilled over into the other three parts of your life. You may have chosen your future profession because of a specific teacher's influence.

Writing Assignment: The word *memoir* comes from the French word *mémoire,* which in turn comes from from the Latin word *memoria,* meaning "memory" or "reminiscence." A memoir focuses on how a person remembers

Ways of Writing to Share Experiences

Genres for Your College Classes	Sample Situation	Advantages of the Genre	Limitations of the Genre
Academic essay	Your sociology professor asks you to construct an academic essay in which you share your family's holiday traditions.	This essay will help you understand how your traditions are unique and/or part of a larger culture	It may be difficult to identify how your traditions are the same or different as those practiced by others in a short paper.
I-Search essay	In your technology and society class, you are asked to relate how you use the internet to connect with friends and family.	An I-Search essay allows you to examine and explain your experiences with technology.	Because this assignment focuses on your experiences, it may be difficult to present that personal search in a formal assignment.
Academic reflection	After writing an extended argument for your economics class, your professor asks you to reflect on your writing process and explain what you might do differently next time.	This essay will help you understand your writing process and determine how to improve future performance.	You may have to provide evidence from your own writing and research, which may feel awkward.
Oral/visual presentation	Your humanities professor asks you to profile, in an oral and visual presentation, a period of Greek art.	Perhaps each member of the class will present on a different topic. This gives you the chance to teach them what you learned.	Because presentation time is limited, you will need to be selective and brief.
Project report	Your business professor asks you to write about your experience of working in a group on a marketing project.	This assignment will help you reflect on the group experience as well as your strengths and weaknesses as a collaborator.	You may feel you can't be honest about the group members who didn't work well with others.
Literacy narrative	Your writing teacher asks you to write about your earliest memories of learning to write.	A literacy narrative can provide insights into your current writing practices.	You may have only vague recollections of early writing experiences.
Genres for Life	**Sample Situation**	**Advantages of the Genre**	**Limitations of the Genre**
Letter to the editor	You want to construct a letter to the editor of your local paper, outlining your experiences with a local non-profit agency.	A letter to the editor allows you to encourage others in your community to become involved with the agency.	Space is limited, and not everyone reads the local paper or all parts of it. It might not be selected for publication.
Memo	You want to let the president of your firm know of a recent experience you had with a training company that your business uses.	A memo allows you to convey information quickly and professionally.	A memo forces you to write concisely and specifically about your experiences. You might need more space.
Blog	You want to construct a blog about being a student at your university.	A blog is an easy and simple way for you to convey information to a wide audience.	Someone will need to monitor the blog for inappropriate comments.
Web page	You want to construct a Web page to describe your experience with a local nature trail.	Your Web page will give all readers the same information at the same time; you can update it when necessary.	You may not have the technical skills to construct an interactive Web site.
Poster	You want to construct a poster for a self-help fitness program, focusing on the notion of "I did it—so can you!"	A poster allows you to share your experience with the program clearly and concisely, yet with sufficient detail. The poster's visual impact should engage your audience.	If what your poster presents is too concise, readers will not believe that "they can do it too."

his or her life. Although the terms *memoir* and *autobiography* are sometimes used interchangeably, the genre of memoir is usually considered to be a subclass of autobiography. While an autobiography usually encompasses a person's full life, a memoir usually focuses on memorable moments and episodes from a person's life.

Keeping in mind the qualities of a memoir, write about a teacher who was especially influential in your academic life. Your memoir can be designed for a general academic audience, or it can be designed for a specific course in a specific discipline. As you remember and discuss in writing how this teacher influenced you as a student, include specific examples that show that influence.

SCENARIO 2 A Literacy Narrative about an Effective Writing Experience

This scenario asks you to construct a *literacy narrative,* an account of a situation in which your writing *worked*—it did what you wanted it to do. This could have been a letter to your parents where you spelled out why you needed something, and they provided it for you. Or perhaps you could tell about a piece of writing that changed a friend's mind about an important issue he or she was grappling with.

Writing Assignment: Write a narrative account of a time when you constructed a piece of writing that did what you wanted it to do. Explain how you went about constructing the text: your audience, your approach, the information you included (and left out), the form of your text, and so on. Unlike a rhetorical analysis (see pages 21–23), in which you explain how the various aspects of a text worked together, a literacy narrative is about your own writing process and how you went about constructing that text.

Writing for Life

SCENARIO 3 Professional Writing: A Letter to a Prospective Employer

In this scenario, focus on a recent experience that you have had as an employee or a volunteer. Consider how that experience has made you think about your future. For example, when one of the authors of this book was in college, he worked the graveyard shift (11:00 p.m. to 7:00 a.m.) in a plastics factory. As he operated the machines each night, he was reminded that he wanted a job—a career—that would allow him to work directly with people, a job that would allow him to feel the satisfaction derived from helping people achieve their goals.

connect
mhconnectcomposition.com
Additional Scenarios QL4003

Writing Assignment: Write a letter to a prospective employer narrating some experience that you have had as an employee, volunteer, or student. Indicate how that experience has prepared or inspired you for future work.

connect
mhconnectcomposition.com
Business letter overview QL4004

Rhetorical Considerations in Sharing Your Experiences

Before you begin the process of writing in response to one of the scenarios presented above, take a few minutes to consider the following aspects of your writing situation.

- **Audience:** Who is your primary audience? Who else might be interested in this subject? Why?
- **Purpose:** Your narrative could have several interrelated purposes. For example, if you are writing in response to Scenario 1, your narrative can serve both to entertain your audience by sharing your experience with them and to thank or honor others who contributed to your academic development.
- **Voice, tone, and point of view:** Depending on the assignment, you may or may not be a major character in your narrative. If you are relating a story in which you are a participant, you have two roles: You are its writer, and you are also a major character in it. If you are not a participant, you will use the third-person point of view. Your attitude toward your characters will help determine the tone of your narrative. For example, your tone could be humorous, such as in "On Becoming a Writer" by Russell Baker (pages 66–68), or more straightforward and serious. What other attitudes could influence your tone?
- **Context, medium, and genre:** You will need to understand the situation that creates the occasion to write. Keeping the context of the assignment in mind, decide on a medium and a genre for your writing. How will your writing be used? If you are writing for an audience beyond the classroom, consider what will be the most effective way to present your information to this audience.

Critical Thinking, Reading, and Writing

Before you begin writing to share your own experiences, read one or more examples to get a feel for writing about experiences. You might also consider how visuals could enhance your writing, as well as the kinds of sources you might consult.

Writing about experiences has several qualities—a clear sense of purpose, a significant point, a lively narrative, and an honest representation. The writer also has a responsibility to respect the privacy of anyone who appears in a narrative. The reading selections and the visual text that appear in this section exemplify these qualities. Further, they may serve to stimulate your own inquiry and writing.

Learning the Qualities of Effective Writing about Experiences

Successful writing about experiences—often called *narrative writing*—engages your readers and keeps them interested. One of the best ways to engage readers when narrating your experiences is to incorporate real dialogue. Other strategies include providing telling details and description. The old advice to "show, don't tell" is especially important when writing about experiences.

Even when you are sharing experiences that seem self-evidently fascinating, you need to have a reason for writing about those experiences. In other words, you need to make a point.

Readers expect the following qualities in writing that shares experience:

- **A clear sense of purpose.** When you write about your experiences, provide readers with clues that will help them understand why you are sharing this narrative. Your tone is one important clue. The explanation and reflection that you include is another clue. If you are simply recording the event so that others can experience it vicariously, for example, you might include very little explanation or reflection. If, however, you want readers to learn something from your experience, or you are trying to convince them of something, you will probably use part of your paper to reflect on the significance of your experience.
- **A significant point.** Just as you need to have a clear purpose for what you are writing, you also need to use the experience to say something significant. Writers sometimes use their experiences to make a sweeping, clichéd point, such as "if I had known then what I know now," which usually leads to boring, obvious writing. Points have significance for readers when they are fresh and—often—unexpected.

  One way to show significance is to explain—with examples—how the event you are telling about affected you. You may or may not express your point in a thesis statement, however. Many writers who share their experiences use language, tone, and details to make their points implicitly.
- **A lively narrative.** Although your writing may include other elements, such as reflection, the foundation for writing about experience is a lively narrative. A narrative must answer the following questions: *Who? What? Where? When? Why?* and *How?* To answer these questions, you can use the following conventions of narrative writing:
  - *Dialogue:* Natural-sounding dialogue helps make a piece of writing immediate and lively. Dialogue—what people have to say—brings a narrative to life. Dialogue also can reveal something about the character of the people in your narrative.
  - *Vivid description:* Detailed descriptions of the people, or *characters,* mentioned in the narrative, the place where it occurs, and the actions that

For more on narration and description, see Chapter 13.

take place all help involve the reader in your story. Describing people, places, actions, and objects so that your readers can relate to them will help make your narrative memorable.

- *Point of view:* Although you will most often relate personal stories from your own point of view (first-person perspective, usually told using the pronouns *I* and *me*), it may be more interesting or effective to tell the story from a third-person perspective—perhaps from the point of view of another participant in the event (called the "third-person limited perspective") or from the point of view of an observer who knows what each participant is doing and thinking (called the "third-person omniscient perspective").
- *A climax or crisis:* Effective narrative *leads* to something: a point the writer wants to make or a concept the writer wants the reader to understand. By constructing your narrative to lead readers to your main idea or point, you keep them interested throughout your narrative. Sometimes, to build suspense, your narrative can lead up to a crisis, which may or may not have already been resolved.

- **An honest representation.** As you share your experiences, it's important to represent them to readers as accurately as possible. Although you can present your own perspective on any situation, it is usually important to present events without unnecessary embellishments, unless you are exaggerating for an obviously humorous purpose. Usually, you are not trying to convince readers to change their ways with this kind of writing, but to honestly relate your experiences so readers can understand their significance.

Reading, Inquiry, and Research: Learning from Narratives That Share Experiences

The selections that follow are examples of writing that share experiences. As you go through each of the selections your instructor asks you to read, consider the following questions:

- How does the author make his or her experiences understandable and indicate their significance?
- What qualities of writing that shares experiences does each selection exemplify?
- How can you use the techniques of sharing experiences exemplified in the selection in your writing?

TANYA BARRIENTOS

Se Habla Español

MEMOIR

Tanya Maria Barrientos has written for the *Philadelphia Inquirer* for more than twenty years. Barrientos was born in Guatemala and raised in El Paso, Texas. Her first novel, *Frontera Street,* was published in 2002, and her second, *Family Resemblance,* was published in 2003. Her column "Unconventional Wisdom" runs every week in the *Inquirer.* This essay originally appeared in the collection *Border-Line Personalities: A New Generation of Latinas Dish on Sex, Sass & Cultural Shifting.* We selected this reading because we see increasingly more students with linguistic backgrounds similar to Barrientos'. As you read her essay, compare your language background to hers.

1 The man on the other end of the phone line is telling me the classes I've called about are first-rate: native speakers in charge, no more than six students per group.

2 "Conbersaychunal," he says, allowing the fat vowels of his accented English to collide with the sawed-off consonants.

3 I tell him that will be fine, that I'm familiar with the conversational setup, and yes, I've studied a bit of Spanish in the past. He asks for my name and I supply it, rolling the double *r* in Barrientos like a pro. That's when I hear the silent snag, the momentary hesitation I've come to expect at this part of the exchange. Should I go into it again? Should I explain, the way I have to half a dozen others, that I am Guatemalan by birth but pura gringa by circumstance? Do I add the humble little laugh I usually attach to the end of my sentence to let him know that of course I see the irony in the situation?

4 This will be the sixth time I've signed up to learn the language my parents speak to each other. It will be the sixth time I've bought workbooks and notebooks and textbooks listing 501 conjugated verbs in alphabetical order, with the hope that the subjunctive tense will finally take root in my mind.

5 In class, I will sit across a table from the "native speaker," who won't question why the Irish-American lawyer, or the ad executive of Polish descent, has enrolled but, with a telling glance, will wonder what to make of me.

6 Look, I'll want to say (but never do). Forget the dark skin. Ignore the obsidian eyes. Pretend I'm a pink-cheeked, blue-eyed blonde whose name tag says Shannon. Because that is what a person who doesn't innately know the difference between corre, corra, and corrí is supposed to look like, isn't it? She certainly isn't supposed to be earth-toned or be from my kind of background. If she happens to be named García or López, it's probably through marriage, or because an ancestor at the very root of her family trekked across the American line three or four generations ago.

7 I, on the other hand, came to the United States at age three, in 1963, with my family and stopped speaking Spanish immediately.

College-educated and seamlessly bilingual when they settled in West Texas, my parents (a psychology professor and an artist) embraced the notion of the American melting pot wholeheartedly. They declared that their two children would speak nothing but inglés. They'd read in English, write in English, and fit into Anglo society beautifully. If they could speak the red, white, and blue without a hint of an accent, my mother and father believed, people would be forced to look beyond the obvious and see the all-American kids hidden inside the ethnic wrapping. 8

It sounds politically incorrect now. But America was not a hyphenated nation back then. People who called themselves Mexican-Americans or Afro-Americans were considered dangerous radicals, while law-abiding citizens were expected to drop their cultural baggage at the border and erase any lingering ethnic traits. Role models like Vikki Carr, Linda Ronstadt, and Raquel Welch[1] had done it and become stars. So why shouldn't we? 9

To be honest, for most of my childhood I liked being the brown girl who defied expectations. When I was seven, my mother returned my older brother and me to elementary school one week after the school year had already begun. We'd been on vacation in Washington, D.C., visiting the Smithsonian, the Capitol, and the home of Edgar Allan Poe. In the Volkswagen, on the way home, I'd memorized "The Raven," and I'd recite it with melodramatic flair to any poor soul duped into sitting through my performance. At the school's office, the registrar frowned when we arrived. 10

"You people. Your children are always behind, and you have the nerve to bring them in late?" 11

"My children," my mother answered in a clear, curt tone, "will be at the top of their classes in two weeks." 12

The registrar filed our cards, shaking her head. 13

I did not live in a neighborhood with other Latinos, and the public school I attended attracted very few. I saw the world through the clear, cruel vision of a child. To me, speaking Spanish translated into being poor. It meant waiting tables and cleaning hotel rooms. It meant being left off the cheerleading squad and receiving a condescending smile from the guidance counselor when you said you planned on becoming a lawyer or a doctor. My best friends' names were Heidi and Leslie and Kim. They told me I didn't seem "Mexican" to them, and I took it as a compliment. I enjoyed looking into the faces of Latino store clerks and waitresses and, yes, even our maid, and saying "yo no hablo español." It made me feel superior. It made me feel American. It made me feel white. 14

It didn't matter that my parents spoke Spanish and were successful. They came from a different country, where everyone looked alike. In America, fitting in with the gringos was key. I didn't want to be a Latina 15

[1]Three popular entertainers of Hispanic orgin.

anything. I thought that if I stayed away from Spanish, the label would stay away from me.

When I was sixteen, I told my father how much I hated being called Mexican—not only because I wasn't, but also because the word was hurled as an insult. He cringed and then he made a radical plan. That summer, instead of sending me to the dance camp in Aspen that I wanted to attend, he pointed me toward Mexico City and the Ballet Nacional. 16

"I want you to see how beautiful Mexico is," he said. "That way when anybody calls you Mexican, you will hold your head up." 17

I went, reluctantly, and found out he was right. I loved the music, the art, the architecture. He'd planted the seed of pride, but it would take years for me to figure out how to nurture it. 18

Back at home, my parents continued to speak only English to their kids while speaking Spanish to each other. 19

My father enjoyed listening to the nightly Mexican newscast on television, so I came to understand lots of the Spanish I heard. Not by design, but by osmosis. So, by the time I graduated from college, I'd become an odd Hispanic hybrid—an English-only Latina who could comprehend Spanish spoken at any speed but was reluctant to utter a word of it. Then came the backlash. In the two decades I'd worked hard to isolate myself from the stereotype I'd constructed in my own head, society shifted. The nation had changed its views on ethnic identity. 20

College professors had started teaching history through African-American and Native American eyes. Children were being told to forget about the melting pot and picture America as a multicolored quilt instead. 21

Hyphens suddenly had muscle, and I was left wondering where I fit in. The Spanish language was supposedly the glue that held the new Latino-American community together. But in my case it was what kept me apart. I felt awkward among groups whose conversations flowed in and out of Spanish. I'd be asked a question in Spanish and I'd have to answer in English, knowing that raised a mountain of questions. I wanted to call myself Latina, to finally take pride, but it felt like a lie. So I set out to learn the language that people assumed I already knew. 22

After my first set of lessons, which I took in a class provided by the newspaper where I worked in Dallas, I could function in the present tense. "Hola Paco, ¿qué tal? ¿Qué color es tu cuaderno? El mío es azul."[2] My vocabulary built quickly, but when I spoke my tongue felt thick inside my mouth, and if I needed to deal with anything in the future or the past I was sunk. I suggested to my parents that when I telephoned we should converse only in Spanish, so I could practice. But that only lasted a few short weeks. Our relationship was built in English and the essence of it got lost in the translation. 23

---

[2]Hello Paco. What's happening? What color is your notebook? Mine is blue.

By my mid-twenties I had finally come around to understanding that being a proud Latina meant showing the world how diverse the culture can be. As a newspaper reporter, I met Cubans and Puerto Ricans and brown-skinned New Mexicans who could trace their families all the way back to the conquistadores. I interviewed writers and teachers and migrant workers, and I convinced editors to put their stories into print. Not just for the readers' sake, but for my own. I wanted to know what other Latinos had to say about their assimilation into American culture, and whether speaking Spanish somehow defined them. What I learned was that they considered Spanish their common denominator, linking them to one another as well as to their pasts. With that in mind, I traveled to Guatemala to see the place where I was born, and basked in the comfort of recognizing my own features in the faces of strangers. I felt connected, but I still wondered if without flawless Spanish I could ever fill the Latino bill. 24

I enrolled in a three-month submersion program in Mexico and emerged able to speak like a sixth-grader with a solid C average. I could read Gabriel García Márquez with a Spanish-English dictionary at my elbow, and I could follow ninety percent of the melodrama on any given telenovela. 25

But I still didn't feel genuine. My childhood experiences were different from most of the Latinos I met. I had no quinceañera, no abuelita teaching me to cook tamales, no radio in the house playing rancheras. I had ballet lessons, a high school trip to Europe, and a tight circle of Jewish friends. I'd never met another Latina like me, and I began to doubt that they existed. 26

Since then, I've hired tutors and bought tapes to improve my Spanish. Now I can recite Lorca. I can handle the past as well as the future tenses. But the irregular verbs and the subjunctive tense continue to elude me. 27

My Anglo friends call me bilingual because I can help them make hotel reservations over the telephone or pose a simple question to the women taking care of their children. But true speakers discover my limitations the moment I stumble over a difficult construction, and that is when I get the look. The one that raises the wall between us. The one that makes me think I'll never really belong. Spanish has become a pedigree, a litmus test showing how far from your roots you've strayed. Of course, the same people who would hold my bad Spanish grammar against me wouldn't blink at an Anglo tripping over a Spanish phrase. In fact, they'd probably be flattered that the white man or woman was giving their language a shot. They'd embrace the effort. But when I fumble, I immediately lose the privilege of calling myself a full-fledged Latina. Broken Spanish doesn't count, except to set me apart from "authentic" Latinas forever. 28

My bilingual friends say I make too much of it. They tell me that my Guatemalan heritage and unmistakable Mayan features are enough to legitimize my membership in the Latino-American club. After all, not all Poles speak Polish. Not all Italians speak Italian. And as this nation grows 29 more and more Hispanic, not all Latinos will share one language. But I don't believe them. I think they say those things to spare my feelings.

30 There must be other Latinas like me. But I haven't met any. Or, I should say, I haven't met any who have fessed up. Maybe they are secretly struggling to fit in, the same way I am. Maybe they are hiring tutors and listening to tapes behind the locked doors of their living rooms, just like me. I wish we all had the courage to come out of our hiding places and claim our rightful spot in the broad Latino spectrum. Without being called hopeless gringas. Without having to offer apologies or show remorse.

31 If it will help, I will go first.

32 Aquí estoy.[3]

33 Spanish-challenged and pura Latina.

[3] I am here.

QUESTIONS FOR WRITING AND DISCUSSION: LEARNING OUTCOMES

Rhetorical Knowledge: The Writer's Situation and Rhetoric

1. **Audience:** For whom do you suppose Barrientos is writing about these experiences?
2. **Purpose:** What do you see as Barrientos's purpose in writing this essay?
3. **Voice and tone:** Barrientos has specific attitudes toward her subject matter. What parts of her essay can you cite to show what her attitudes are?
4. **Responsibility:** How reliable does Barrientos seem in the way that she presents factual information? What specific details in her essay seem most credible? Why?
5. **Context, format, and genre:** Although Barrientos presents her experiences as true, she still relates them almost in the form of a story. How effective is this strategy for writing about such experiences? How does Barrientos use dialogue in her autobiographical narrative to represent the views of participants?

Critical Thinking: The Writer's Ideas and Your Personal Response

6. Barrientos says that her parents "declared that their two children will speak nothing but inglés." What were their motives for saying that? What do you think about that declaration?
7. In many ways, this essay is about how Barrientos is trying to fit into American culture and society. Where have you tried to fit in, and what have your struggles been?

Composing Processes and Knowledge of Conventions: The Writer's Strategies

8. Barrientos tells of her experiences in the first person. How would it alter the effectiveness and interest of this essay if it had been written in the third person? Why?
9. Barrientos now and then writes in Spanish. How do the Spanish sentences affect her essay?

Inquiry and Research: Ideas for Further Exploration

10. Interview several family members about their language background and experiences. In a brief paper, explain how their experiences compare to those related by Barrientos.

SUKI KIM

MEMOIR

Facing Poverty with a Rich Girl's Habits

Suki Kim is the author of the novel *The Interpreter.* She was born in South Korea in 1970 and came to the United States in 1983. She lives in the East Village in New York City. We included Kim's essay in this textbook because it is a compelling story, and like Barrientos (page 57), Kim discusses how language affects and determines how she might "fit in."

Queens in the early 80's struck me as the Wild West. Our first home there was the upstairs of a two-family brownstone in Woodside. It was a crammed, ugly place, I thought, because in South Korea I had been raised in a hilltop mansion with an orchard and a pond and peacocks until I entered the seventh grade, when my millionaire father lost everything overnight. Gone in an instant was my small world, made possible by my father's shipping company, mining business and hotels. Because bankruptcy was punishable by a jail term, we fled, penniless, to America. 1

The ugly house was owned by a Korean family that ran a dry cleaner in Harlem. Their sons, Andy and Billy, became my first playmates in America, though playmate was a loose term, largely because they spoke English and I didn't. The first English word I learned at the junior high near Queens Boulevard was F.O.B., short for "fresh off the boat." It was a mystery why some kids called me that when I'd actually flown Korean Air to Kennedy Airport. 2

At 13, I took public transportation to school for the first time instead of being driven by a chauffeur. I had never done homework without a governess helping me. I also noticed that things became seriously messy if no maids were around. Each week, I found it humiliating to wheel our dirty clothes to a bleak place called Laundromat. 3

One new fact that took more time to absorb was that I was now Asian, a term that I had heard mentioned only in a social studies class. In Korea, yellow was the color of the forsythia that bloomed every spring along the fence that separated our estate from the houses down the hill. I certainly never thought of my skin as being the same shade. 4

Unlike students in Korean schools, who were taught to bow to teachers at every turn, no one batted an eye when a teacher entered a classroom. Once I saw a teacher struggle to pronounce foreign-sounding names from the attendance list while a boy in the front row French-kissed a girl wearing skintight turquoise Jordache jeans. In Korea, we wore slippers to keep the school floor clean, but here the walls were covered with graffiti, and some mornings, policemen guarded the gate and checked bags. 5

My consolation was the English as a Second Language class where I could speak Korean with others like me. Yet it did not take me long to realize that the other students and I had little in common. The wealthier Korean immigrants had settled in Westchester or Manhattan, where their children attended private schools. In Queens, most of my E.S.L. classmates came from poor families who had escaped Korea's rigid class hierarchy, one dictated by education level, family background and financial status. 6

Immigration is meant to be the great equalizer, yet it is not easy to eradicate the class divisions of the old country. What I recall, at 13, is an acute awareness of the distance between me and my fellow F.O.B.'s, and another, more palpable one between those of us in E.S.L. and the occasional English-speaking Korean-American kids, who avoided us as though we brought them certain undefined shame. It was not until years later that I learned that we were, in fact, separated from them by generations. 7

We who sat huddled in that E.S.L. class grew up to represent the so-called 1.5 generation. Many of us came to America in our teens, already rooted in Korean ways and language. We often clashed with the first generation, whose minimal command of English traps them in a time-warped immigrant ghetto, but we identified even less with the second generation, who, with their Asian-American angst and anchorman English, struck us as even more foreign than the rest of America. 8

Even today, we, the 1.5 generation, can just about maneuver our anchor. We hip-hop to Usher with as much enthusiasm as we have for belting out Korean pop songs at a karaoke. We celebrate the lunar Korean thanksgiving as well as the American one, although our choice of food would most likely be the moon-shaped rice cake instead of turkey. We appreciate eggs Benedict for brunch, but on hung-over mornings, we cannot do without a bowl of thick ox-bone soup and a plate of fresh kimchi. We are 100 percent American on paper but not quite in our soul. 9

In Queens of the early 80's, I did not yet understand the layers of division that existed within an immigrant group. I preferred my Hello Kitty backpack to the ones with pictures of the Menudo boys, and I cried for weeks because my parents would not let me get my ears pierced. I watched reruns of "Three's Company" in an attempt to learn English, thinking the whole time that John Ritter was running a firm called Three's. I stayed up until dawn to make sense of "Great Expectations," flipping through the dictionary for the definition of words like "Pip." 10

More brutal than learning English was facing poverty with a rich girl's habits and memory. In my neighborhood, a girl who grew up with a governess and a chauffeur belonged to a fairy tale. This was no Paris Hilton's "Simple Life," but the beginning of my sobering, often-terrifying, never simple American journey. I soon discovered that I had no choice but to ad- 11 just. I had watched my glamorous mother, not long ago a society lady who lunched, taking on a job as a fish filleter at a market.

Before the year was over, my parents moved us out of the neighborhood in search of better jobs, housing and education. As for the family who owned the house in Woodside, I did not see any of them again until the fall of 2001, when Billy walked into the Family Assistance Center at Pier 94, where I was volunteering as an interpreter. He was looking for his brother, Andy, who had been working on the 93rd floor when the first plane crashed into the north tower. 12

QUESTIONS FOR WRITING AND DISCUSSION: LEARNING OUTCOMES

Rhetorical Knowledge: The Writer's Situation and Rhetoric

1. **Audience:** Who is the primary audience for this autobiographical essay? What makes you think that?
2. **Purpose:** Why has Kim chosen to write about this particular set of experiences?
3. **Voice and tone:** What is Kim's attitude toward her readers? What is her attitude toward her subject? What cues in her writing make you think this?
4. **Responsibility:** What evidence can you find in this essay to suggest that Kim has responsibly portrayed her family to readers?
5. **Context, format, and genre:** Kim's autobiographical essay did not include photos other than the one that appears at the beginning of the essay. If she were to make this essay available in an online environment, where she could easily include photos, what photos would you most like her to add? To what extent does Kim's essay follow the chronological organizational pattern typical of autobiographical essays?

Critical Thinking: The Writer's Ideas and Your Personal Response

6. What is your response to Kim's mentioning in the first paragraph that "bankruptcy was punishable by a jail term" in South Korea?
7. At the end of paragraph 2, Kim notes that she did not understand why other children called her "fresh off the boat" because she had flown to Kennedy Airport. What does this observation say about her use of the English language when she first arrived in the United States?

Composing Processes and Knowledge of Conventions: The Writer's Strategies

8. In autobiographical essays, one convention is to use past-tense verbs to narrate past events. How well does Kim follow this convention? Point to several examples to support your judgment.
9. Only once in this autobiographical essay does Kim quote other people—"fresh off the boat" in paragraph 2. She does not include any dialogue in the essay. Where might she have included dialogue?

Inquiry and Research: Ideas for Further Exploration

10. In paragraphs 8 and 9, Kim refers to the "1.5 generation." The 1.5 generation includes people who emigrate from another country before or during adolescence. Such immigrants bring with them some cultural features from their home countries, but they are young enough to adapt relatively easily to the new culture. Conduct a Web search to read more about the term "1.5 generation." How does it differ from "first-generation" and "second-generation" immigrants?

As illustrated by "Ways of Writing to Share Experiences" (page 52), experiences can be shared through many genres. The "Genres Up Close" feature explores doing so through a literacy narrative.

GENRES *Up Close* Writing a Literacy Narrative

The literacy narrative has been a popular genre for decades, but it has become increasingly so in recent years. Readers are curious about how others, especially famous writers, have developed their writing and reading skills. When reporters and talk-show hosts interview well-known writers, they frequently ask about the writers' experiences with reading and writing, particularly early in life.

When writers craft literacy narratives, they often do the following:

- **Narrate their experiences with using language—reading and writing in particular situations.** As you craft a literacy narrative, think about those moments when you were most aware that you were using language as a reader and/or writer.
- **Critically reflect on their experiences with using language.** As you craft a literacy narrative, think about the effects of particular experiences with reading and writing. For example, if your first-grade teacher congratulated you for reading a book when you when you were six years old, how did that positive reinforcement affect your reading after that moment?
- **Think about how they developed agency as readers and writers.** That is, what has reading and writing allowed them to do in life? As you craft a literacy narrative, think about the ways that reading and writing have helped you to achieve certain goals. Think about how reading and writing have helped you to make a difference in the world.
- **Define "literacy" broadly.** As you consider your literacy experiences, be inclusive. In addition to reading and writing with words, how have you developed other similar or related skills? For example, what are your experiences with visual images? What are your experiences with information literacy (finding, evaluating, and using information)?

To explain how they became literate people, writers may use dialogue to tell part of their literacy narratives. Another common practice in literacy narratives is to describe the emotions that the writer felt at a particular moment. Sharing these emotions can help readers understand the impact of the event. Of course, strong positive emotions can motivate people to keep doing something. In the selection by Russell Baker, "On Becoming a Writer," notice how Baker uses both of these conventions to convey how he developed his lifelong commitment to writing.

RUSSELL BAKER

LITERACY NARRATIVE

Born in Virginia in 1925, Russell Baker began his professional writing career with the *Baltimore Sun* in 1947, after attending Johns Hopkins University. In 1973 he won a Pulitzer for commentary for his nationally syndicated column, "Observer," which he wrote for the *New York Times* from 1962 to 1998. Baker is the author of a Pulitzer Prize–winning memoir *Growing Up* (1982) and *Looking Back: Heroes, Rascals, and Other Icons of the American Imagination* (2002) and has edited numerous books. Baker's writing regularly appears in the *New York Times Magazine, Sports Illustrated,* and *McCalls.* The following selection is excerpted from *Growing Up.* Russell Baker's literacy narrative focuses on his dream of becoming a writer. As you read his piece, think about your own dreams. How can college help you achieve those dreams?

On Becoming a Writer

The only thing that truly interested me was writing, and I knew that sixteen-year-olds did not come out of high school and become writers. I thought of writing as something to be done only by the rich. It was so obviously not real work, not a job at which you could earn a living. Still, I had begun to think of myself as a writer. It was the only thing for which I seemed to have the smallest talent, and, silly though it sounded when I told people I'd like to be a writer, it gave me a way of thinking about myself which satisfied my need to have an identity. 1

The notion of becoming a writer had flickered off and on in my head since the Belleville days, but it wasn't until my third year in high school that the possibility took hold. Until then I'd been bored by everything associated with English courses. I found English grammar dull and baffling. I hated the assignments to turn out "compositions," and went at them like heavy labor, turning out leaden, lackluster paragraphs that were agonies for teachers to read and for me to write. The classics thrust on me to read seemed as deadening as chloroform. 2

When our class was assigned to Mr. Fleagle for third-year English I anticipated another grim year in that dreariest of subjects. Mr. Fleagle was notorious among City students for dullness and inability to inspire. He was said to be stuffy, dull, and hopelessly out of date. To me he looked to be sixty or seventy and prim to a fault. He wore primly severe eyeglasses, his wavy hair was primly cut and primly combed. He wore prim vested suits with neckties blocked primly against the collar buttons of his primly starched white shirts. He had a primly pointed jaw, a primly straight nose, and a prim manner of speaking that was so correct, so gentlemanly, that he seemed a comic antique. 3

I anticipated a listless, unfruitful year with Mr. Fleagle and for a long time was not disappointed. We read *Macbeth*. Mr. Fleagle loved *Macbeth* and 4 wanted us to love it too, but he lacked the gift of infecting others with his own passion. He tried to convey the murderous ferocity of Lady Macbeth one day by reading aloud the passage that concludes

> . . . I have given suck, and know
> How tender 'tis to love the babe that milks me.
> I would, while it was smiling in my face,
> Have plucked my nipple from his boneless gums. . . .

The idea of prim Mr. Fleagle plucking his nipple from boneless gums was too much for the class. We burst into gasps of irrepressible snickering. Mr. Fleagle stopped.

"There is nothing funny, boys, about giving suck to a babe. It is the— the very essence of motherhood, don't you see." 5

He constantly sprinkled his sentences with "don't you see." It wasn't a question but an exclamation of mild surprise at our ignorance. "Your pronoun needs an antecedent, don't you see," he would say, very primly. "The purpose of the Porter's scene, boys, is to provide comic relief from the horror, don't you see." 6

Late in the year we tackled the informal essay. "The essay, don't you see, is the . . ." My mind went numb. Of all forms of writing, none seemed so boring as the essay. Naturally we would have to write informal essays. Mr. Fleagle distributed a homework sheet offering us a choice of topics. None was quite so simple-minded as "What I Did on My Summer Vacation," but most seemed to be almost as dull. I took the list home and dawdled until the night before the essay was due. Sprawled on the sofa, I finally faced up to the grim task, took the list out of my notebook, and scanned it. The topic on which my eye stopped was "The Art of Eating Spaghetti." 7

This title produced an extraordinary sequence of mental images. Surging up out of the depths of memory came a vivid recollection of a night in Belleville when all of us were seated around the supper table—Uncle Allen, my mother, Uncle Charlie, Doris, Uncle Hal—and Aunt Pat served spaghetti for supper. Spaghetti was an exotic treat in those days. Neither Doris nor I had ever eaten spaghetti, and none of the adults had enough experience to be good at it. All the good humor of Uncle Allen's house reawoke in my mind as I recalled the laughing arguments we had that night about the socially respectable method for moving spaghetti from plate to mouth. 8

Suddenly I wanted to write about that, about the warmth and good feeling of it, but I wanted to put it down simply for my own joy, not for Mr. Fleagle. It was a moment I wanted to recapture and hold for myself. I wanted to relive the pleasure of an evening at New Street. To write it as I wanted, however, would violate all the rules of formal composition I'd learned in school, and Mr. Fleagle would surely give it a failing grade. Never mind. I 9 would write something else for Mr. Fleagle after I had written this thing for myself.

When I finished it the night was half gone and there was no time 10
left to compose a proper, respectable essay for Mr. Fleagle. There was no
choice next morning but to turn in my private reminiscence of Belleville.
Two days passed before Mr. Fleagle returned the graded papers, and he returned everyone's but mine. I was bracing myself for a command to report
to Mr. Fleagle immediately after school for discipline when I saw him lift
my paper from his desk and rap for the class's attention.

Because this piece of dialogue includes the title of his essay, Baker uses both double and single quotation marks.

"Now, boys," he said, "I want to read you an essay. This is titled 'The 11
Art of Eating Spaghetti'."

And he started to read. My words! He was reading *my words* out loud to 12
the entire class. What's more, the entire class was listening. Listening at-
tentively. Then somebody laughed, then the entire class was laughing, and
not in contempt and ridicule, but with openhearted enjoyment. Even Mr.
Fleagle stopped two or three times to repress a small prim smile.

By sharing his emotions, Baker helps readers understand the impact the event had on him. With the clause "I had discovered a calling," he indicates the formation of a lifelong commitment to writing.

I did my best to avoid showing pleasure, but what I was feeling was 13
pure ecstasy at this startling demonstration that my words had the power
to make people laugh. In the eleventh grade, at the eleventh hour as it
were, I had discovered a calling. It was the happiest moment of my entire
school career. When Mr. Fleagle finished he put the final seal on my happi-
ness by saying, "Now that, boys, is an essay, don't you see. It's—don't you
see—it's of the very essence of the essay, don't you see. Congratulations,
Mr. Baker."

For the first time, light shone on a possibility. It wasn't a very hearten- 14
ing possibility, to be sure. Writing couldn't lead to a job after high school,
and it was hardly honest work, but Mr. Fleagle had opened a door for me.
After that I ranked Mr. Fleagle among the finest teachers in the school.

QUESTIONS FOR WRITING AND DISCUSSION: LEARNING OUTCOMES

Rhetorical Knowledge: The Writer's Situation and Rhetoric

1. **Audience:** Who is Baker's primary audience for this piece of writing? What makes you think that?
2. **Purpose:** What is Baker's purpose in telling this story about becoming a writer?
3. **Voice and tone:** What is Baker's attitude toward his topic and his audience? How do you know that.
4. **Responsibility:** What has Baker done in this essay to be a responsible writer?
5. **Context, format, and genre:** Even though this piece is excerpted from Baker's book-length memoir, *Growing Up,* what makes it work as a stand-alone essay? How has Baker used dialogue in this autobiographical narrative?

Critical Thinking: The Writer's Ideas and Your Personal Response

6. How do Baker's experiences in high school English compare with your experiences?
7. How does Baker help readers understand what it means to become a writer?

Composing Processes and Knowledge of Conventions: The Writer's Strategies

8. Why do you think Baker uses dialogue in describing Mr. Fleagle's class rather than simply summarizing or paraphrasing what Fleagle said?
9. Baker is well known for his use of precise language, carefully selecting just the right words to express what he means. Where is that care most evident in this essay?

Inquiry and Research: Ideas for Further Exploration

10. In *Growing Up,* Baker narrates many other stories from his life. In your school library, or online, read more stories about Baker's life. Find one that you consider to be especially compelling. What are the qualities or features of that story that you can use in your writing?

Digital Literacy **Organizing Your Files**

Are your files stored in folders (directories) on your computer? If so, have you ever lost track of where you've stored a song, video, project, or paper on your computer? Before it happens again, take some time to organize your folders and files.

Start by looking at the names of all of the folders you've already created. Did you use some principle for naming and organizing them? Are they alphabetized? Named according to project or media type (such as music or video)? Or are the names more or less random? See if you can find relationships among the names of your folders, and look for ways to group folders and files and store them together in one folder. Establish a separate folder for each course you are taking.

Taking a little time to organize your files and folders now can save you time and prevent confusion when you need to locate specific documents.

Writing Processes

In the pages that follow, you will engage in various writing processes to help you generate ideas and draft, revise, and edit your writing. These processes are *recursive,* which means that you will probably revisit each activity numerous times as you work. As you work on the assignment scenario that you have chosen, keep these processes and the qualities of effective writing about experiences in mind (pages 55–56).

If you are considering several possible topics, store your notes in a separate computer document for each topic. Once you determine which topic you will write about, it will be easy to access and use those notes. As you work on your project, make certain that you save your computer files frequently. Also, savvy writers back up their computer files in two or more places—on an internal or external hard drive of the computer, on a USB flash drive, and/or on a rewritable CD or DVD.

Digital Literacy

Using Technology to Unjam Writer's Block

You can use technology to "unjam" writer's block! Some writers find it hard to get started when faced with a new task. You can download some images related to your topic, play a video from a popular Web site, or even use Twitter® or texting to brainstorm with friends and classmates while you're getting started.

Invention: Getting Started

As you begin to explore your subject, it is helpful to use more than one invention activity to come up with ideas. Especially when you are writing to share experiences, the more detail that you generate about the experience through invention, the better you will be able to convey the experience and its meaning to your readers. As you begin the process, consider the following questions:

- What do I already know about the experience that I am writing about?
- What feelings, attitudes, or notions do I already have about this experience?

- What questions can I ask about the experience? That is, what gaps do I have in my memory of it or knowledge about it that might help me understand what information a reader might need?
- Who would know about my experience (a relative or friend)? What questions might I ask that person in an interview?
- What do I know about my audience? What don't I know that I should know? Why might they be interested in reading my text?
- What might my audience already know about my subject? Why might they care about it?
- To what extent will sensory details—color, shape, smell, taste—help my reader understand my topic? Why?
- What visuals might I use to help my readers understand my experience?

For more on descriptive writing, see Chapter 13.

Completing invention activities such as the ones suggested in the first writing activity should yield a wealth of information that you can draw on for your first draft. (Doing your invention work in electronic form, rather than on paper, lets you easily use that work when you construct a draft.) As with any kind of writing, invention activities improve with peer feedback and suggestions. Consider sharing the invention work you have done so far with several classmates or friends in order to understand your rhetorical situation more clearly and to generate more useful information.

For help with strategies for discovery and learning, see Chapter 3.

Writing Activity

Listing, Questioning, and Freewriting

Get started with your paper by using listing, questioning, and freewriting. First, list key words that will remind you of ideas and organize them in related categories, such as location, images, and sounds. Second, generate basic details of the event using the five questions commonly asked by reporters:

- *Who* are the participants in this event, and what information about those participants will help me share my experience?
- *What* are the participants doing and what are they saying?
- *Where* did the event occur?
- *When* did the event occur, and what is the significance of when it happened?
- *Why* did the participants do what they did? What motivated their actions?

Finally, use freewriting (see page 34) to get your ideas down on paper. (For an example of freewriting, see page 114.)

Finally, if you already keep a journal, you might skim through it to find ideas for your writing. If you don't already keep a journal, you might do so while you are getting started on this writing project.

Jessica Hemauer's Listing

For help with listing, questioning, and freewriting, as well as other strategies for discovery and learning, see Chapter 3.

EXAMPLES OF INVENTION

Brainstorming (pp. 158, 332)
Freewriting (pp. 114, 245, 383)
Criteria (p. 290)
Listing (p. 72)
Answers to Reporter's Questions (p. 244)
Organization (pp. 75, 164)
Clustering (pp. 114, 289)
Concept Mapping (p. 335)
Interviewing (p. 203)
Research (pp. 115, 160, 205, 246, 292, 384)
Reflection (p. 12)

For a memoir about her experience growing up on a farm, Jessica Hemauer, a student in a first-year composition course, generated the following list:

small town
farm chores—endless
Dad worked hard; we did too
coffee
siblings
Orange, multi-stained carpet
Oversized, cluttered table
Stuffed, pine shelves
Steep, creaky stairs
Bathroom
Basement
Loud, plastic runners covering the multi-stained orange carpet
Warm, rustic steel woodstove

Blinds
Navy blue, understuffed, corduroy sofa that has one cushion burnt b/c it was too close to the woodstove
White, clean carpet
Clean table set for 2
Neatly lined bookshelves
Round staircase with a wood banister

Exploring Your Ideas with Research

For more on conducting interviews, see Chapter 19.

Depending on the scenario you are responding to, you may need to interview family members or friends about the experiences you are exploring. Be sure to record their stories carefully; their recollections will enliven your text. Ask them for remembered dialogue—what people said—as those remembered sentences will help you show (rather than just tell) the experience you are writing about.

You may also find it useful to go back through old family files, letters, documents, and photo albums—all wonderful sources of information. See the "Visualizing Variations" box for more on generating ideas from photographs and documents.

Use an electronic journal to record images, URLs, and other electronic pieces of information that you find as you are conducting your research. Such an e-journal makes it easy for you to add those e-documents once you start drafting your paper.

A WRITER'S *Responsibility* | Sharing Experiences Responsibly

When you share your experiences with other people, make careful decisions about what to reveal about yourself. As you write, decide how to fulfill your responsibilities not only to your readers but also to those people who are characters in your narratives.

For instance, if you are testifying in a criminal or civil trial, you have an ethical and legal responsibility to narrate your experience as truthfully as possible. If you agree to serve as a reference for a colleague who is searching for a job, you have a responsibility to portray your experiences with that person accurately because the potential employer will rely on that person to perform the job well.

You also have another responsibility: If you write about criminal activity, your teacher or your classmates may feel compelled to report that activity to authorities. For certain kinds of criminal behavior—domestic violence or sexual abuse, for instance—state law may require your teacher to report the activity to the police.

Organizing Your Ideas and Details

Once you have generated ideas and details about your subject using invention activities and, if necessary, research, consider how you might organize this material. The questions that you need to ask yourself when deciding on your organization are all rhetorical:

- Who is your audience?
- Why might they be interested in your narrative—and how can you make them interested?
- What is your purpose for writing—that is, what do you want your readers to understand about you or the event you are narrating?

The answers to these questions can help you decide what to emphasize, which in turn will help you choose an organizational strategy.

It is usually helpful to try *several* organizational strategies in early drafts because seeing your words on paper—in various ways—will help you decide what strategy will work best for you. Most often, writing about experiences is sequential: The writer starts at some specific point in the past and then moves to a later time or to the present.

An alternative would be to use the narrative technique known as **flashback.** In a flashback, commonly used in film, something that happened in the past is shown "just the way it happened," and then the narrator returns to the present to reflect on the event's significance.

VISUALIZING *Variations* | Using Photos and Documents as Sources

If you are writing in response to Scenario 1 (page 51), you may be able to use photographs and documents to help you generate ideas and recall or reconstruct events.

The photograph at right is of the mother and son of one of the authors of this book. Consider these questions:

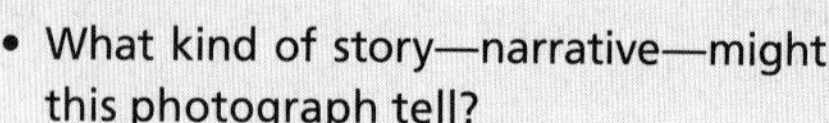

- What kind of story—narrative—might this photograph tell?
- What might this grandmother say if she were to write about this experience?

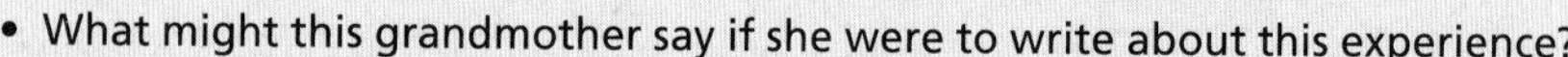

- What can you infer about this experience from the photograph? Is this perhaps the first time this grandmother has fed her new grandson? Is she singing or talking to him? How is he responding?
- Does this photograph speak to a larger theme about how fragile people are when they are young? About the relationship between the young and the old?

The photograph at left, taken in Wisconsin circa 1955, includes one of the authors of this book and his siblings. Use the following questions to speculate about this photograph or a similar one from your past:

- On what day of the week do you think the photograph was taken? What evidence supports that assumption?
- During what time of year was the photograph taken? Why do you think that?
- What do the expressions on the children's faces tell you about the situation?

In addition to photographs, you might have a letter, diary, or other document that you or your relatives or ancestors wrote that can give you insight into your experience or their experiences. Use the following questions to generate more ideas about this assignment:

- When and where was the document written? What was the writer's purpose in writing it? How can you tell?
- What does the document reveal about the writer's experiences or about your experiences at the time?
- How significant does the experience seem? In what ways did the experience in the document change the writer's, or your, life?

Consider including a copy of the photograph or a selection of photographs and quoting from the document in your final paper.

Here are three possible organizational structures that you might use for a piece of writing that shares experiences:

Options FOR Organization
Options for Organizing a Narrative

Chronological Approach	Flashback Approach	Crisis Approach
• Narrate the experience from beginning to end—straightforward chronology • Relate key details surrounding the event or experience. • Note the impact of the experience on your life or the lives of others who were part of the experience. • Reflect on the significance of the experience. (optional)	• Begin in the present. • Flash back to the events and experiences you want to share and relate them in sequence. • Relate key details surrounding the events. • Look back on those events and experiences in terms of the impact they had on your life or the lives of others. • Reflect on the significance of the experiences. (optional)	• Begin with the crisis point in the event or experience. • Go back to the beginning and tell the story to the end. • Relate key details surrounding the event or experience. • Reflect on the significance of the event and experience. (optional)

Jessica Hemauer's Organization

Jessica Hemauer looked over her invention material and then put together a rough outline for her draft. She decided to use the third approach, beginning at the crisis point:

Begin as a 10-year-old girl—waking up to feed calves
Describe daily family routine
Good feelings about being in charge when feeding calves
Describe parents
  Impact of their relationship on me
School WAS social life
  Being a farm girl made me different
  How I didn't fit in
Playing basketball in 8th grade
  Started to feel included—but worked harder than others
  Falling asleep in class
THE FAMILY MEETING
Freed from farmwork and being involved
Why I'm still different and that's ok.

EXAMPLES OF INVENTION

Brainstorming (pp. 158, 332)
Freewriting (pp. 114, 245, 383)
Criteria (p. 290)
Listing (p. 72)
Answers to Reporter's Questions (p. 244)
Organization (pp. 75, 164)
Clustering (pp. 114, 289)
Concept Mapping (p. 335)
Interviewing (p. 203)
Research (pp. 115, 160, 205, 246, 292, 384)
Reflection (p. 12)

mhconnectcomposition.com

Drafting and Revising QL4006

Constructing a Complete Draft

Once you have chosen the organizational approach that works most effectively for your audience and purpose, you are ready to construct the rest of your draft. Before you begin your draft, review all your invention material to see what needs to be included and what might be left out. To make these decisions, consider your purpose for sharing this experience with others: What is the significance of the experience? How can you help readers see the significance?

You will also want to discover the method of writing a first draft that works best for you. Some writers prefer drafting large chunks at once. Others prefer drafting small pieces over time. Remember that you do not have to compose your essay in a linear way—from beginning to end. You might find it easiest to jump in somewhere in the middle.

INTEGRATING SOURCES

Synthesizing and Integrating Sources into Your Draft: Including Others' Perspectives in Narratives

When writers share experiences in first-person narratives, they primarily offer their own perspectives on events because they often are the leading characters in the narratives. However, most narratives also include other individuals who interact with the narrator. Writers can reconstruct interactions with other people by describing actions and by including dialogue. Although describing actions helps readers see what happened, those descriptions limit the perspective to that of the writer/narrator. Because multiple perspectives help readers see the story from several vantage points, effective writers often include dialogue—either by quoting it or by summarizing it.

In "Farm Girl," which appears on pages 83–87 of this chapter, writer Jessica Hemauer includes dialogue with some of the other people in her story. For example, in paragraph 17, Hemauer reconstructs the conversation with Ms. Cain, her teacher:

> One time my teacher, Ms. Cain, comes over to my wooden desk, where my head is resting on top of a math textbook. She taps her knuckles on the hollow wood and says, "Jessica, are you okay? Do you need to go to the health room?" Raising my head, embarrassed that she caught me sleeping, I say quickly, "No, Ms. Cain, I'm fine. I'm sorry for being rude and causing a disruption. I promise to be more attentive."

Although Hemauer could have described the dialogue by writing that her teacher asked if she was okay, she instead makes the teacher's concern more concrete by quoting the teacher's words.

When you use dialogue to present others' perspectives in your narratives, you can follow these guidelines:

1. If you have easy access to people whom you are quoting, ask them if the dialogue accurately reflects what they said and what they thought at the time.
2. Follow punctuation conventions for dialogue. See page 82.

Parts of a Complete Draft

connect
mhconnectcomposition.com
Introductory paragraph overview QL4007

Introduction: One of the qualities of a successful narrative is that it grabs and holds readers' attention. A number of strategies for beginning your narrative can help get your readers interested, including the following:

- **Start your narrative with a surprising event or piece of dialogue.** Tanya Barrientos (her essay appears on pages 57–61) starts her essay by telling of a phone conversation and then adds a word readers may not know or expect: "*Conbersaychunal.*"
- **Start with interesting details** to draw the reader in through sensual, descriptive words and phrases.
- **Start with a comment that might startle your readers.**

For more on introductions, see Chapter 13.

Body: The main part, or body, of your narrative is the place to tell your story. Use dialogue and descriptive details to develop the story and reveal the character of the people in your narrative. To hold your readers' interest, build your narrative to a crisis or climax, unless you are writing for an informative purpose and are required to maintain a neutral tone (or unless you are beginning with the crisis point of the narrative—see page 75). Choose the verb tense that will best serve the purpose of your narrative. If you use past-tense verbs to narrate the experience, you remind readers that the event happened in the past and that you have had time to reflect on it. If you use present-tense verbs, you make the story seem as if it is happening now, and you will seem to reveal its significance to yourself and to your readers at the same time. Also, you might consider using photographs to complement your words.

connect
mhconnectcomposition.com
Concluding paragraph overview QL4008

Conclusion: Your conclusion should tie things together for your readers by explaining or suggesting the significance of the experience or experiences you have shared. Here are some strategies for concluding a paper in which you have shared experiences:

- Review the subject's most important aspects.
- Explain the subject's significance.
- Suggest avenues for a reader's further inquiry.
- Refer back to the introduction of your narrative.

For more on conclusion, see Chapter 13

Title: Rather than thinking of a title before you start writing, it is often more useful to construct a first draft and then consider possible titles. As with the introduction, an effective title for a narrative intrigues readers and makes them want to read the text.

Writing Activity

Constructing a Full Draft

Using the writing you did when selecting an organizational approach, write a complete draft of your paper that shares an experience.

A Portion of Jessica Hemauer's First Draft

After deciding on her organizational approach, Jessica Hemauer wrote the first draft of her essay about growing up on a farm. The following is a portion of her first draft. Like all first drafts, it includes problems with grammar, spelling, and punctuation. (The numbers in circles refer to peer comments—see page 80.)

Farm Girl

Jessica Hemauer

BEEP! BEEP! BEEP! It's 5:00 a.m. My eyes are heavy with sleep and struggle to open. I think to myself, "A typical ten-year-old child does not have to wake up at five in the morning to do chores!" I hit the snooze button with disappointment, hoping desperately that the cows would for once, feed and milk themselves. Seconds away from falling back into a deep sleep, I hear the heavy footsteps of what could only be my father coming near my bedroom door. They stop and my door opens with a creak. "Jessica, are you awake yet?" my father asks. Without a word, knowing from the past that an argument doesn't get me anywhere, I stagger out of my warm twin bed, trudging dejectedly past the figure at the narrow doorway. I continue down the hall toward the small bathroom to find my sisters, Angie and Melissa, and my brother Nick already awake.➊

We all proceed with our usual morning routine, which consists of washing our faces, brushing our teeth and taking turns on the white porcelain throne. In the lower level of the old farmhouse our outside clothes await. My mother made it a rule to keep them there so that they wouldn't stink up the rest of the house. As soon as you opened the door to the basement, you can smell the putrid aroma of cows that has seeped from our clothing into the damp cool air.➋ We took our turns going down the steep, narrow steps, using the walls on either side for extra guidance. As we dressed not a single word was spoken because we all felt the same way, "I hate this!" Although most of the time our choice of vocabulary was much more creative. . . .

While Melissa and my father milked the 100 cows, Nick and Angie fed the cows, and I went to feed the newborn calves.➌ Being the youngest in the family, this was my favorite chore because I rarely had the chance to look after someone or feel like I was taking care of them. I have always had older siblings who looked after me, watching every step I took, being sure that I didn't get into trouble. When feeding the calves, I was finally the one in charge. It was a nice feeling, being on the opposite end of the spectrum. They were my responsibility. I was in charge of them and caring for them during feeding time every morning and evening. Little did I know at that time, this was the beginning of a lifetime of responsibilities. . . .

. . . Typically, we would finish with the chores and return to the house around 7:30 in the morning.

When we made our way back to the farmhouse, we draped our clothes on a folding chair next to the washing machine in the basement and crawled up the stairs. The delicious smell of smoked bacon and cheese omelets grew more intense with each step. As our stomachs ached with hunger, we took turns in the shower, cleaning ourselves as fast as possible in order to get to the breakfast table. My brother would be the first to the table because as we all know, girls take longer to get ready than boys. My father would eat and be back outside on the farm by the time my sisters or I would run by the kitchen grabbing a glass of fresh squeezed orange juice and a piece of toast as we yelled frantically at the bus, "Wait!" It seemed our daily lives operated in shifts, not like a real family.❹ . . .

When I finally arrived at school I had already been up for four hours doing chores on the farm in the bitter cold. The other kids in my private grade school just rolled out of their beds inside their subdivision homes an hour before the bell rang. The school day always went by fast.❺ While my other classmates were thinking about what television show they were going to watch after school, I was thinking about the chores that await me once I get off the yellow school bus. . . .

Revising

mhconnectcomposition.com

Revising and Editing overview (also Drafting) QL4009

Finishing a complete draft may give you a justified sense of accomplishment. However, you still need to revise and then edit the draft. It is helpful to let your draft sit for a while after you have finished it. When you return to it, you are much more likely to find sections that need to be revised: places where details need to be added, other places where details may need to be removed, and still others where some of your words or sentences need to be shifted from one place to another.

Technology can help you revise and edit your writing more easily. Use your word processor's track-changes tool to try out changes. After you have had time to think about the possible changes, you can "accept" or "reject" them. If your classmates are offering feedback on your draft, they can also use track changes, the comment tool, or the peer-commenting feature of the software. Friends or family members may also be willing to read your draft and offer useful suggestions.

WRITER'S *Workshop* | Responding to Full Drafts

Working with one or two classmates, read each other's paper and offer comments and questions that will help each of you see your paper's strengths and weaknesses. Consider the following questions as you do:

- What is your first impression of this draft? How effectively does the title draw you into the narrative? What do you like about the draft?
- How well does the introduction work? What is effective about it? What suggestions can you make on how to improve the introduction?
- What significant point is the writer making about the experience he or she is relating? How might the writer be able to make that point more clearly?
- Why is the writer relating this experience? What in this piece of writing helps you see why the experience was important to the writer?
- How lively is the narrative? Where has the writer gone beyond simply telling readers about the experience to showing it? How might the writer use more dialogue?
- How has the writer used description to make people, places, and scenes vivid for readers? Where is more description needed?
- How effectively does the story build in terms of reaching a climax, holding the readers' attention throughout, and making logical sense in how one action follows another?
- Has the writer honestly explained the experience? If not, why do you question it?
- What could be added or changed to make the conclusion more effective? How well does it bring the narrative to a satisfying conclusion?

Student Comments on Jessica Hemauer's Draft

Here are some comments that student reviewers made about Jessica Hemauer's draft, keyed to the first draft on pages 78–79:

1. "I really liked the description of you getting up early and getting ready. I could almost feel the cold and smell the farm smells."
2. "I like how the real details (like all of the smells) help me 'be there' with you."
3. "I think you're writing this because you want to tell people that all those awful farm chores really helped you."
4. "I think your point was that all the time you wanted to fit in, and then when you could do things normal kids do, you found out you were different anyway."
5. "I'd like to hear more about school and the people there."

As with the comments you will receive from your teacher and classmates, Jessica had to determine which comments and suggestions made sense—and then to revise her paper accordingly.

Responding to Readers' Comments

After receiving feedback from peers, teachers, writing tutors, and others, writers have to determine what to do with that feedback.

Consider carefully what your readers tell you. Some might not understand your point, or they may misunderstand something you wrote. It is up to you either to accept or to ignore their comments and suggestions. Others may offer perspectives that you may not have. You may find that comments from more than one reader contradict each other. In that case, use your own judgment to decide which reader's comments are on the right track.

Jessica Hemauer's readers had the following reactions:

- Two readers liked some of the descriptive passages in the paper. Hemauer needed to consider whether more description could be added because this strategy had been effective.
- One reader outlined what seemed to be the point, or thesis, of Hemauer's paper. When you get such feedback on your papers, make sure that the reader does understand and reiterate your point. If the reader does not get your point, then perhaps you are not being clear and explicit enough.

In the final version of her paper, on pages 83–87, you can see how Jessica Hemauer responded to these comments, as well as to her own review of her first draft.

Knowledge of Conventions

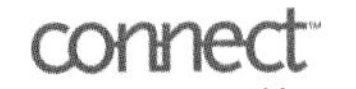

mhconnectcomposition.com

Using commas with coordinate adjectives QL4011

When effective writers edit their work, they attend to the conventions that will help readers understand their ideas. These include genre conventions, documentation, format, usage, grammar, punctuation, and mechanics. By attending to these conventions in your writing, you make reading a more pleasant experience for readers.

Editing

After you revise, you need to go through one more important step: editing and polishing. When you edit and polish your writing, you make changes to your sentence structures and word choices to improve your style and to make your writing clearer and more concise. You also check your work to make sure it adheres to conventions of grammar, usage, punctuation, mechanics, and spelling.

Because it is sometimes difficult to identify small problems in a piece of writing you have been mulling over for some time, it often helps to distance yourself from the text before your last reading so you can approach the draft with fresh eyes. Some people like to put the text aside for a day or so; others try reading aloud; and some even read from the last sentence to the first so that the content, and their familiarity with it, does not cause them to overlook an error. Because checking conventions is easier said than done, though, we strongly recommend that you ask classmates, friends, and tutors to read your work to find sentence problems that you do not see.

To assist you with editing, we offer here a round-robin editing activity focused on punctuating dialogue, which is a common concern in writing to share experiences.

ROUND-ROBIN EDITING WITH A FOCUS ON

WRITER'S *Workshop* | Round-Robin Editing with a Focus on Punctuating Dialogue

When writers share their experiences, they often use dialogue to make the scenes and events vivid for readers, but writers who use dialogue need to be aware of the conventions for punctuating it.

All dialogue needs to be enclosed in quotation marks to set it off from the rest of the text. If the dialogue is presented within a sentence, the phrase that introduces the dialogue ends with a comma and then the dialogue begins with a quotation mark:

> Embarrassed that she caught me sleeping, I said quickly, "No, Ms. Cain. I'm fine."

Note that if the dialogue is not introduced within a sentence, it usually starts a new paragraph that begins with a quotation mark.

Periods and commas go inside the quotation marks, but question marks and exclamation points go either inside or outside of the quotation marks, depending on whether they are part of the quotation itself.

> "Jessica, are you awake yet?" my father asks.

> "It was terrible! Coach was in such a bad mood!"

Work with two peers to edit one another's papers for problems in punctuating dialogue. Compare notes to see if you have any questions about the conventions for punctuating dialogue. If you are uncertain about a rule, consult reading selections in this book with punctuated dialogue, such as "On Becoming a Writer" (pages 66–68) or "Se Habla Español" (pages 57–61); check the rules in a grammar handbook; or ask your instructor for assistance.

Genres, Documentation, and Format

If you are writing an academic paper, follow the conventions for the discipline in which you are writing and the requirements of your instructor. If you have chosen to write a letter to a prospective employer, you should also follow the conventions of a business letter.

A Writer Shares Her Experiences: Jessica Hemauer's Final Draft

The final draft of Jessica Hemauer's essay "Farm Girl" follows. As you read Hemauer's essay, think about what makes it an effective example of writing about experiences. Following the essay, you'll find some specific questions to consider.

JESSICA HEMAUER

Farm Girl

MEMOIR

1 BEEP! BEEP! BEEP! It's 5:00 a.m. My eyes are heavy with sleep and struggle to open. I think to myself, "A typical ten-year-old child does not have to wake up at five in the morning to do chores!"

2 I hit the snooze button, hoping desperately that the cows will, for once, feed and milk themselves. Seconds away from falling back into a deep sleep, I hear my father's heavy footsteps outside my bedroom door. They stop and my door opens with a creak. "Jessica, are you awake yet?" my father asks. Without a word, knowing from past experience that an argument won't get me anywhere, I stagger out of my warm twin bed, trudging dejectedly past the figure at the narrow doorway. I continue down the hall toward the small bathroom to find my sisters, Angie and Melissa, and my brother, Nick, already awake.

3 We all proceed with our usual morning routine, which consists of washing our faces, brushing our teeth, and taking turns on the white porcelain throne. In the lower level of the old farmhouse, our outside clothes await. My mother makes it a rule to keep them there so that they won't stink up the rest of the house. As soon as we open the door to the basement, we can smell the putrid aroma of cows that has seeped from our clothing into the damp cool air. We take our turns going down the steep, narrow steps, using the walls on either side for extra guidance. As we dress, not a single word is spoken because we all feel the same way, "I hate this!" However, most of the time our choice of vocabulary is much more creative.

One of Hemauer's peer readers wrote the following comment:

I like how the real details (like all of the smells) help me "be there" with you.

Notice the sensory details in this paragraph.

4 Nick opens the basement door leading outside to the barn. There is a brisk and bitter wind accompanied by icy snowflakes that feel like needles digging into our faces. We don't turn back. We desperately want

to, but we know my father is patiently waiting for us to help him milk and feed the cows before school starts at 8:30 a.m. We lift our scarves and pull down our hats so only our squinted eyes show. We lower our bodies to dodge the fierce winds and trudge a half mile to the red barn, which is somehow standing sturdily in the dreadful blizzard.

When we finally reach the barn, Nick, leading the pack, grabs the handle of the heavy wooden door and props it open for my sisters and me to pass through. Nick goes immediately to help my father herd the cows and get them into their proper stalls to be milked. Meanwhile, my sisters and I go to the milk house to sanitize the milking machines, prepare all the milking equipment, and set up a station with towels and charts of the cows that are being medicated. 5

While Melissa and my father milk the one hundred cows, Nick and Angie feed them, and I feed the newborn calves. Because I am the youngest in the family, this is my favorite chore because I rarely have the chance to look after someone or feel like I am taking care of him or her. I have always had older siblings who look after me, watching every step I take, making sure that I don't get into trouble. We all work together—that's critical. When I feed the calves, I am finally the one in charge. It is a nice feeling, being on the opposite end of the spectrum. They are my responsibility. Little do I realize it, but this is the beginning of a lifetime of responsibilities. 6

After the calves are fed, other chores have to be done. Cleaning out various huts and pens and laying down fresh straw are a part of our daily duties. This is the worst of the jobs I have to do. It is so dusty that I can hardly breathe at times, but we all know it has to be done so there is no sense complaining. My brother, sisters, and I work together to get the chores done as quickly as possible. Typically, we finish with the chores and return to the house around 7:30 in the morning. 7

Again, note the sensory details in Hemauer's paper: the smells, being hungry, fresh OJ, and so on.

We make our way back to the farmhouse, drape our clothes on a folding chair next to the washing machine in the basement, and crawl up the stairs. The delicious smell of smoked bacon and cheese omelets grows more intense with each step. Our stomachs aching with hunger, we take turns in the shower, cleaning ourselves as fast as possible in order to get to the breakfast table. My father eats quickly and is back outside on the farm by the time my sisters or I run by the kitchen, grabbing a glass of fresh squeezed orange juice and a piece of toast as we yell frantically at the bus, "Wait!" It seems our daily lives operate in shifts, not like a real family. 8

When I finally arrive at school, I have already been up for four hours doing chores on the farm in the bitter cold. The other kids in my private grade school have just rolled out of their beds inside their subdivision homes an hour before the bell rang. The school day always goes by fast. While my other classmates are thinking about what television show they 9 are going to watch after school, I am thinking about the chores that await me once I get off the yellow school bus.

School has always been my social life. I want to join teams or different 10
clubs, but I always have to consider how my chores on the farm will get done, which makes it difficult for me to get involved. If I join a team that practices after school, I can't participate. If I join a club that meets before school, I can't attend the meetings. Being a farm girl means that I can't be like the other kids in my class. Not being able to participate in school activities like my friends makes me feel left out and depressed. The topic of conversation at the lunch table never involves me.

"Hey, Carrie, how was basketball practice last night?" Susan asks as 11
she pulls out a chair from the lunch table and sets her plastic tray down next to the tall, broad, blond-haired girl.

Hemauer uses dialogue to engage her readers in the human interaction of her experience. Dialogue is an effective tool for making the experience more concrete.

"It was terrible! Coach was in such a bad mood!" Carrie shoves a hand- 12
ful of French fries into her mouth, spilling catsup down the front of her white tee shirt without noticing. "He made us run sprints for every shot we missed. And Kelly was missing all her shots last night. I'm so sore today."

Carrie starts rubbing her legs when she notices the streak of catsup 13
on her shirt. She begins to wipe it off with one of her napkins, with little success.

One peer reviewer made this suggestion:

I'd like to hear more about school and the people there.

"Hey, Carrie, how was the student council meeting this morning? Did 14
you decide if we're going to have a formal dance this winter?"

"Yeah, we're having it on the Saturday before Christmas. Are you go- 15
ing to come?"

I sit listening in silence. The twenty-minute lunch period always feels 16
like eternity. While everyone around me continues talking and laughing, I sit there next to them silently eating my French fries, listening carefully, trying to laugh at the right times.

Note the details and specific examples that Hemauer provides to really show what she means (rather than just telling).

In eighth grade I really want to play basketball, and after begging and 17
pleading with my parents, they finally say I can join the team as long as I continue to help with chores in the morning before school and after practice. I quickly agree. I become the basketball team's starting point guard. I am thrilled to be on a team, and I finally feel like I am starting to have a life like the other kids. Now I am included in the conversations at lunch, and I feel like a part of the group. I never tell anyone that I have to go home after practice and work on the farm, or that I wake up every morning at five to help with chores. None of my friends, teachers, or coaches know. I don't think they would care and I don't want them to know that I am different.

In high school I become more involved with the school. Coincidently, 18
my father's farm continues to grow. We are now up to two hundred cows, and my dad still wants to expand the farm. During my freshman year I

continue to work on the farm before and after school, making sure that I can still play on the basketball team. A few times a teacher catches me with my eyes closed during class. One time my teacher, Ms. Cain, comes over to my wooden desk, where my head is resting on top of a math textbook. She taps her knuckles on the hollow wood and says, "Jessica, are you okay? Do you need to go to the health room?" Raising my head, embarrassed that she caught me sleeping, I say quickly, "No, Ms. Cain, I'm fine. I'm sorry for being rude and causing a disruption. I promise to be more attentive."

Shortly after freshman year, my father arranges a meeting with my 19
entire family. He explains that he wants our farm to continue to grow, and this means that he needs more help on the farm than his children can provide. In fact, he says that he would rather not have us work on the farm anymore, unless we want to. He would rather have us be more involved in school and go on to college. After this meeting, I feel happy and relieved, and I can tell my father is relieved too. He knows that my siblings and I have sacrificed our school activities and social lives to help with the family business, and I know that this is his way of saying thank you.

From this moment on, I become more involved with my school. I join 20
the homecoming club, audition for musicals and plays, serve as the president of the student council as well as president of my class. I also become more social with my friends. I even take on a waitressing job at a resort in a neighboring town. During all these activities, I always notice that I stick out from the group. In school people come up to me and ask how I manage my time so well, without getting stressed out. When I'm with a group of my friends, I always seem to be more mature than they are, leading the group while others try to follow in my footsteps. When it comes to my job, I am always on time, never calling in sick and never complaining about a task I have been asked to do.

One night after work, I sit down in front of the full-length mirror in 21
my bedroom and start thinking about the past years. I had believed that joining various clubs and social activities would make me fit in with my peers. But in fact, it has not. I still stick out. And the more I think about it, the more I realize why. My life growing up has been much different from the lives of my peers. From an early age, I had to learn how to manage my time so that I could do my chores and attend school. When I started to play basketball, I had to manage my time even more carefully. I have always had a challenging amount of responsibility, and I have learned to complete tasks in a timely fashion. The work that I had to do on the farm was far from glamorous. I have done some of the worst jobs conceivable, so I have a higher tolerance for work than most people. Though I hated it growing up, working on the farm has taught me many lessons about life, and it has shaped me into the individual I am today.

Each day of my life there are times when I reflect back to working on the farm. And every day people notice that I am different from the rest of my peers. At school, teachers and organization leaders are impressed by my time management skills and the amount of responsibility I take on. At work, my boss continues to ask me where he can find some more hard working people. I simply tell him, "Try hiring some farm girls. I hear they turn out pretty good." 22

QUESTIONS FOR WRITING AND DISCUSSION: LEARNING OUTCOMES

Rhetorical Knowledge: The Writer's Situation and Rhetoric

1. **Purpose:** Why did Hemauer write this essay? How might different audiences see different purposes?
2. **Audience:** Who do you see as Hemauer's audience? What can you point to in the text that supports your claim?
3. **Voice and tone:** How does Hemauer establish her *ethos*—her credibility—in this essay?
4. **Responsibility:** What is Hemauer's responsibility to her readers? To the members of her family? How does she fulfill those responsibilities?
5. **Context, format, and genre:** Hemauer has written a personal essay. When writing in this genre, writers try to relate their own personal experiences to much broader, more general human experiences. How has Hemauer used her personal remembrances of growing up on a dairy farm to help her readers, whose own lives may have been very different from that of a midwestern farm girl, relate to the essay?

Critical Thinking: The Writer's Ideas and Your Personal Response

6. Even though you may have had a much different childhood from Hemauer's, can you relate to some of her experiences? What does she do to develop interest in the subject of her essay?
7. What do you see as the significance of Hemauer's story?

Composing Processes and Knowledge of Conventions: The Writer's Strategies

8. How do descriptive and narrative details function in the essay? Point to several places where Hemauer "shows" instead of "tells."
9. How does Hemauer use dialogue in the essay? What other methods does she use to show readers what her life as a farm girl was like?

Inquiry and Research: Ideas for Further Exploration

10. Search the Web to find other narratives—even blog entries—in which college students reflect on their life and work experiences. How do they compare to Hemauer's narrative about her farm-life experience?

 Self-Assessment: Reflecting on Your Goals

Now that you have constructed a piece of writing to share experiences, revisit your learning goals, which you and your classmates may have considered at the beginning of this chapter (see pages 48–49). Here are some questions to help you focus on what you have learned from this assignment. Respond to the questions in writing, and discuss your responses with classmates. If you are constructing a course portfolio, your responses to these questions can also serve as invention work for the portfolio.

Rhetorical Knowledge

- *Audience:* What did you learn about your audience as you wrote about your experience or experiences?
- *Purpose:* How successfully do you feel you fulfilled your purpose? Why?
- *Rhetorical situation:* What was your rhetorical situation? How have you responded to the rhetorical situation?
- *Voice and tone:* How did you reveal your personality? What tone did you use?
- *Context, medium, and genre:* What context were you writing in? What medium and genre did you choose, and how did those decisions affect your writing?

Critical Thinking, Reading, and Writing

- *Learning/inquiry:* What did you discover about writing about experiences while you were working on this assignment? What did you discover about yourself? About your experiences?
- *Responsibility:* How did you fulfill your responsibility to your readers? To the people you wrote about?
- *Reading and research:* Did you rely on your memories, or did you conduct additional research for this assignment? If so, what sources did you consult? How did you use them?

Writing Processes for Sharing Experiences

- *Invention:* What invention strategies were most useful to you?
- *Organizing your ideas and details:* What organization did you use? How successful was it?
- *Revising:* What one revision did you make that you are most satisfied with? What are the strongest and the weakest parts of the paper you wrote for this chapter? Why?
- *Working with peers:* How did your instructor or peer readers help you by making comments and suggestions about your writing? List some examples of useful comments that you received. How could you have made better use of the comments and suggestions you received?
- *Visuals:* Did you use photographs or other visuals to help you describe your experience or experiences? If so, what did you learn about incorporating these elements?
- *Writing habits:* What "writerly habits" have you developed, modified, or improved on as you constructed the Writing Assignment for this chapter?

Knowledge of Conventions

- *Editing:* What sentence problem did you find most frequently in your writing? How will you avoid that problem in future assignments?
- *Genre:* What conventions of the genre you were using, if any, gave you problems?
- *Documentation:* Did you use sources for your paper? If so, what documentation style did you use? What problems, if any, did you have with it?

connect
mhconnectcomposition.com
Jessica Hemauer Reflects on Her Writing QL4010

Refer to Chapter 1 (pages 11–12) for a sample reflection by a student.

Chapter 5

Writing to Explore

When you hear the word *exploration,* you may envision astronauts or explorers of earlier centuries, people who physically ventured to previously uncharted territory. When astronauts Neil Armstrong and Edwin E. "Buzz" Aldrin went to the moon in 1969, they were looking for answers to questions that humans have asked for thousands of years: What is the moon like? What is it composed of? What does Earth look like from the moon? More recently, the Hubble Space Telescope has enabled explorers to view remote parts of the universe such as the brilliant star cluster NGC 346. And today's space explorers are often not astronauts but robots—like the Mars Rover.

Although we commonly associate exploration with physical travel, there are many other kinds of explorations. Indeed, some of the most valuable explorations are those that take place in your own mind. Often,

B.

C.

through the act of writing, you can discover new ideas or new perspectives.

Playwright Edward Albee once noted, "I write to find out what I'm talking about." In addition to exploring what you already know, exploratory writing gives you the chance to ask questions and to consider what else you would like to find out.

Exploring various perspectives on issues, concepts, places, or people will help you to work your way through ideas and problems in college and in the professional, civic, and personal areas of your life.

In any exploration, you investigate a particular subject closely. You will often need to explore an idea or a concept—or a decision you need to make—in detail, from various perspectives, before you can really see and understand the overall situation.

Photo taken on July 20, 1969, by Neil A. Armstrong of Edwin E. "Buzz" ·lrin during the Apollo 11 mission to the moon.

The Mars Rover, one of two "robot geologists" that landed on the ·face of Mars in January 2004.

A view of the star cluster NGC 346 in the Small Magellanic Cloud, a ·ellite galaxy of the Milky Way, taken by the Hubble Space Telescope.

Setting Your Goals:

Rhetorical Knowledge

- **Audience:** Because you are learning as you write, you will often be the main audience. Who else can you visualize reading your work? What will that person or those people expect to find in it? How can you appeal to those readers as well?
- **Purpose:** Your purpose might be simply to learn more about the topic, but often exploratory writing leads to the unexpected and unfamiliar, so you need to be prepared to be surprised.
- **Rhetorical situation:** Consider the myriad of factors that affect what you write—you (the writer), your readers (the audience), the topic (the subject you are exploring), your purpose (what you wish to accomplish), and the exigency (what is compelling you to write). In an exploratory essay, you are writing to raise questions and to let them guide your inquiry; your readers are reading your text so that they can grapple with those same questions.
- **Voice and tone:** Generally, exploratory writing has an inquisitive tone. Of course, sometimes an exploratory essay can have a humorous tone.
- **Context, medium, and genre:** The genre you use to present your thinking is determined by your purpose: to explore. You will need to decide on the best medium and genre to use to present your exploration to the audience you want to reach.

Critical Thinking, Reading, and Writing

- **Learning/inquiry:** By reading and writing as an explorer, you gain a deeper understanding of diverse and complex perspectives.
- **Responsibility:** You have a responsibility to represent diverse perspectives honestly and accurately.
- **Reading and research:** Your research must be accurate and as complete as possible, to allow you to consider the widest possible array of perspectives.

Writing to Explore

5 Chapter

Writing Processes

- **Invention:** Choose invention strategies that will help you thoughtfully contemplate diverse perspectives.
- **Organizing your ideas and details:** Find the most effective way to present perspectives to your readers, so they can easily understand them.
- **Revising:** Read your work with a critical eye, to make certain that it fulfills the assignment and displays the qualities of effective exploratory writing.
- **Working with peers:** Your classmates will make suggestions that indicate parts of your text they find difficult to understand so you can clarify.

Knowledge of Conventions

- **Editing:** When you explore, you might tend to leave your thoughts—and sentences—incomplete. To help you avoid this pitfall, the round-robin activity in this chapter (on page 126) deals with sentence fragments.
- **Genres for exploratory writing:** Possible genres include exploratory essays, profiles, and more informal types of exploratory writing such as blogs, journals, and diaries.
- **Documentation:** If you have relied on sources outside of your own experience, you will need to cite them using the appropriate documentation style.

mhconnectcomposition.com

Writing to Explore Tutorial QL5001

Rhetorical Knowledge

When you write to explore, consider how your exploration will help you gain some greater understanding, how you can help your readers understand your topic in a new way, and why you want them to gain this understanding. You will also need to decide what medium and genre will help you communicate your exploration most effectively to your audience.

Writing to Explore in Your College Classes

Your college classes give you wonderful opportunities to explore your current interests and discover new ones. Taking a college class in almost any field allows you to begin exploring that field, reading its literature, and listening to and interacting with people who are experts in the field. Each class you take also gives you the opportunity to explore the subject area in writing. During your college career, you may write the following kinds of papers:

- In a history class, your instructor may encourage you to explore several perspectives on the Cuban Missile Crisis in 1962. Such an exploration might then lead to a writing project in which you argue that certain events and factors were the actual causes of this crisis.
- In a nutrition class, your instructor may ask you to explore several perspectives on vegetarian diets. Here, too, your exploration could lead to a paper in which you demonstrate specific effects of vegetarianism or in which you argue for or against such a diet.
- For a communication course, your instructor may ask you to explore whether there is evidence that men and women have different communication styles.

For information on writing a cause-and-effect analysis, see Chapter 10. For information on writing to convince, see Chapter 8.

For all of these writing situations, think about what you might need to do to communicate your ideas effectively: what information you might need to include, how you would describe your exploration, what visuals or examples you might use, and so on.

Writing to Explore for Life

Just as you will undoubtedly write to explore in your academic life, you are likely to use different kinds of exploratory writing in other areas of your life. In your professional life, creating scenarios may help you explore options and make difficult decisions. In your civic life, you may also have opportunities to use exploratory writing. You may enjoy keeping a journal of your personal life.

In much of the exploratory writing you will do in your *professional* life, you will find yourself exploring various options. To what extent will hiring Ms. X

Digital Literacy **Writing a Blog**

The ultimate form of writing to explore might be a personal or professional online journal, or *blog*. A blog (a shortening of "Web *log*") can be a fun place to explore issues and events of the day while developing your voice, style, and expressive self. If your teacher recommends blogging, a good place to get started with ideas for a blog might be Maggie Mason's book *No One Cares What You Had for Lunch: 100 Ideas for Your Blog* (Peachpit Press, 2006).

instead of Mr. Y make a difference to the business? A teacher might ask what effect one lesson plan would have on a group of students compared to a different lesson plan?

People working for the good of a community often deal with *best options*—solutions to problems for which there may not be a single perfect result but rather many possible outcomes. Therefore, those involved in *civic* life can find exploratory writing especially useful.

Your *personal* life offers many opportunities for exploratory writing. You may respond regularly to e-mails or notes from friends, family members, and classmates in which you explore the possibilities for a group gift for someone important to all of you, propose convenient times for getting together, or consider a new wireless carrier. You may keep a journal, where you can explore your thoughts, ideas, responses, and feelings privately.

The "Ways of Writing" feature (page 96) presents different genres that can be used when writing to explore in life.

For more on blogs, see Chapter 17.

▶▶▶ Scenarios for Writing | Assignment Options

connect
mhconnectcomposition.com
Writer's Workshop: Applying Learning Goals for Exploratory Writing QL5002

Your instructor may ask you to complete one of the following assignments that call for exploratory writing. Each assignment is in the form of a *scenario*, a brief story that provides some context for writing. The scenario gives you a sense of who your audience is and what you need to accomplish with your writing.

Starting on page 113, you will find guidelines for completing whatever assignment option you choose. Additional scenarios for college and life may be found online.

▶ Writing for College

SCENARIO 1 An Academic Paper Exploring a Career

For this scenario, assume you are taking a "career and life planning" class—a class devoted to helping college students decide what discipline they might like to major in. This class gives you the opportunity to explore different career paths, to learn what the educational requirements are for various majors,

Ways of Writing to Explore

Genres for Your College Classes	Sample Situation	Advantages of the Genre	Limitations of the Genre
Academic essay	For your creative nonfiction class, you are asked to construct an essay exploring the writing styles of several authors you have read and studied.	Your exploration, using the conventions of an academic essay will help you better understand the details of the writing styles of the authors you've studied.	An exploration often leads to more questions, which can be unsettling to a writer.
Internet exploration	Your writing professor has asked you to explore the Internet for reliable and relevant Web sites pertaining to your research topic and then post their links with a summary on a discussion board for the class.	This will help you understand what electronic resources are available, as well as the range of quality.	Depending on your topic, there may be too much information to search through.
Exploratory paper	Your computer science instructor asks you to write an exploratory paper that proposes at least three viable solutions to a networking problem.	This activity will require that you envision multiple solutions rather than just one.	It can be difficult to write fairly about solutions you don't think will work.
Letter	You want to write a letter to your school newspaper that explores the possibilities of a proposed change in campus parking and encourages involvement in the decision.	The school newspaper will allow you to engage the appropriate audience about an issue that matters to them.	A letter to the editor allows only limited space, and you cannot use visuals to show what you mean. It might not be published.
Oral presentation	For your art class, you are asked to construct an oral and visual presentation exploring the "local art scene" by showing and discussing visuals of works from local artists.	The visuals in your presentation will allow your audience to actually see some of the art you are discussing.	Sometimes it is hard to get really good photographs of sculptures and other works of art. Aspiring artists may also not grant you permission to photograph their work.
Genres for Life	**Sample Situation**	**Advantages of the Genre**	**Limitations of the Genre**
Poster	You decide to construct a poster titled "Exploring ________" to help viewers understand what a specific nonprofit organization does.	Your poster is a visual way to help readers explore the purpose of your nonprofit organization.	A poster restricts the amount of space you can use; illustrations are needed to catch the eye of passing viewers.
Blog	You and two neighbors want to construct a blog to help everyone in your neighborhood explore possible ways to improve the area.	A blog lets your neighborhood interact and share community information.	A blog must be monitored for potentially offensive comments; not everyone will feel comfortable blogging.
Wiki	For the business you work for, you construct a wiki asking everyone in your company to explore ways to serve the public more efficiently.	A wiki is an easy and uncomplicated way for everyone in your business to contribute their ideas while building on the ideas of others.	Someone will need to monitor the wiki for inappropriate entries and to collect suggestions.
Web page	You want to construct a Web page allowing members of your community to explore various options on new taxes for the community.	Your Web page can provide both text and graphs/charts, and link to related areas.	Readers cannot interact with a static Web page.
E-mail profile	Your family is planning a large family reunion; you construct an e-mail profile of some possible locations.	Your e-mail lets you explore potential locations with a large number or people.	An e-mail can get lengthy as family members respond; not everyone will feel comfortable using e-mail.

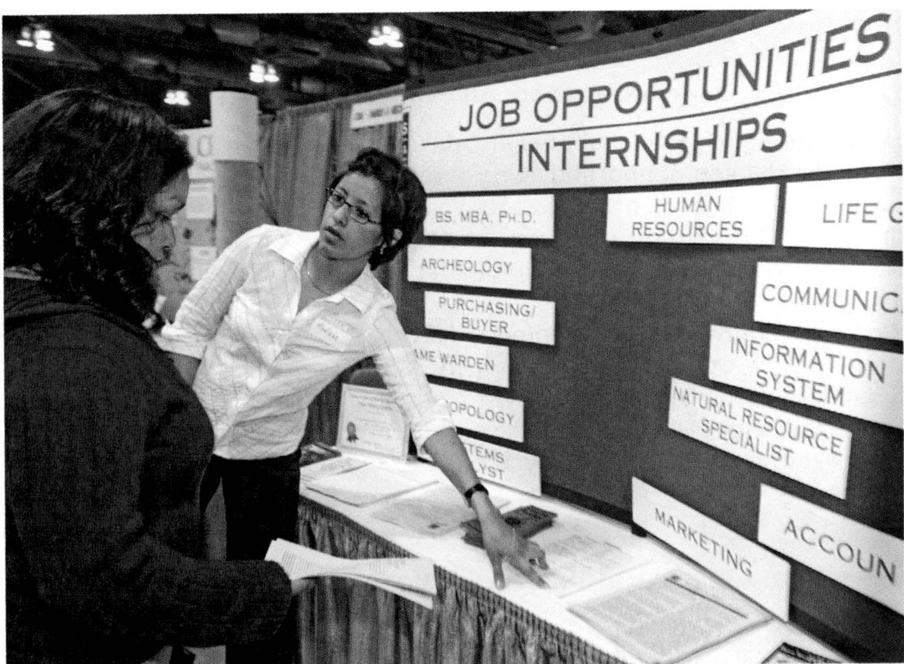

and to find out what job opportunities will be available and what salaries and other forms of compensation different jobs might offer.

Writing Assignment: Select one college major or career that you may be interested in pursuing, and construct an exploratory paper in which you consider the various aspects of that major or career from many angles, including the preparation you would need for it and the rewards and pitfalls you might encounter if you decide to pursue it. Asking and answering questions about the major or career you are considering will form the heart of your exploratory paper.

SCENARIO 2 **A Profile Exploring a Personal Interest**

In this writing option, you will explore a subject that interests you personally and write a profile of it. This assignment gives you the chance to explore something or someone you are interested in and would like to know more about.

Writing Assignment: Think of a subject that you would like to know more about—perhaps a type of music or musician, a sport, a popular singer or actor, a local hangout, a community center, or something completely different. This assignment offers you the opportunity to research and write about a topic you are interested in. Use this opportunity not only to learn about the subject but also to examine your perceptions of and reactions to it.

Writing for Life

SCENARIO 3 Personal Writing: An Exploration in a Letter to a Friend

Think of something you really believe in. You might want to discuss your views on raising children, supporting aging parents, choosing a simpler lifestyle, discovering some important truth about yourself, or some other quality or belief that makes you who you are. (Because religious beliefs are so personal, you may want to select a strongly held opinion that does not involve your religion.)

Writing Assignment: In a sentence or two, write something you believe in strongly. Now explore the basis for your belief. Consider what in your background, education, history, family, friendships, upbringing, and work experience has helped you come to the conclusions you have reached about the topic. Why do you believe what you do? Put your text into the form of a letter to a good friend.

connect
mhconnectcomposition.com
Additional Scenarios QL5003

Rhetorical Considerations for Exploratory Writing

- **Audience:** Although your instructor is one audience for this paper, you are also part of your audience—this assignment is designed to help you think through some possible educational and career choices, to explore an interest, or to explore some of your personal beliefs. Your classmates are also your audience, as some of them may also be considering these issues and ideas. They will learn from your research and perhaps ask questions and think of ideas they had not yet considered. Who else might be part of your audience?
- **Purpose:** Your purpose is to explore the various aspects of your topic in enough detail and depth to lead you to a greater understanding of it and what you believe about it.
- **Voice, tone, and point of view:** As you explore your topic, you will step back to consider whether any preconceptions you may have about it are accurate. Your stance should be objective, and you should be open to the different possibilities you will discover. The point of view you take should be one of questioning—what can you learn by exploring your topic?—but the tone you use can range from humorous to serious.
- **Context, medium, and genre:** Because you will be exploring an area you are already interested in, you will have the incentive to learn more as you research and write. The knowledge you gain may benefit you later. For example, you may be able to use the information you have acquired from this assignment to write a causal analysis or a proposal paper. If you are writing for an audience beyond the classroom, what will be the most effective way to present your information to this audience? You

For more on choosing a medium and genre, see Chapter 17 and the Online Appendix. For more on writing a causal analysis, see Chapter 10. For more on writing a proposal paper, see Chapter 11.

might write a letter to a friend, prepare a formal report for colleagues at work, or construct a Web site.

Critical Thinking, Reading, and Writing

Before you begin to write your exploratory paper, consider the qualities of successful exploratory writing. It also helps to read one or more examples of this type of writing. Finally, you might consider how visuals could enhance your exploratory writing, as well as the kinds of sources you will need to consult.

Unlike many other kinds of writing, where writers have a good idea of their intent, exploratory writing frees writers to take intellectual chances and to see where different possibilities may lead. Although effective exploratory writing involves taking intellectual risks and finding alternatives that you may not have thought of before, your writing will not be successful if you simply write anything you please. Effective exploratory writing is based on reasonable options and uses information culled from solid research.

Learning the Qualities of Effective Exploratory Writing

As you think about how you might construct an exploratory paper, consider that readers probably expect the unexpected from this kind of text. Effective exploratory writing will include the following qualities:

- **A focus on a concept or question.** Rather than focusing on a specific, narrowly provable thesis, exploratory writing is more open-ended. Writers are more than likely trying to answer a question, to lay the groundwork for a solution to a problem, or to redefine a concept. For instance, a writer might pose a question such as this one: "We had a large number of traffic fatalities in my city last year. What possible solutions might I explore?"
- **An inquisitive spirit.** Any explorer begins with an interest in finding out more about the subject. Ask questions that you want to answer, and let the answers lead you to further questions. Although you want to make sure your queries are grounded in reality, you should not feel constrained by conventional thinking. For instance, Albert Einstein used "thought experiments" to explore time and space in ways conventional experiments could not. As a result, he developed his revolutionary theory of relativity.
- **A consideration of the range of perspectives in a subject.** As you explore your subject, you need to be willing to see it from different vantage

points and to consider its positive and negative aspects. Effective exploratory writing looks at a topic from as many angles as possible. This can be difficult to do sometimes, as we often get locked into our own ways of thinking. In exploratory writing, however, it is vital to look at alternative views and to understand that others may have a different perspective from yours.

- **Expansive coverage of a subject.** Effective exploratory writing does not try to make a case or attempt to persuade you as writer or your reader of something. Rather, it examines all aspects of the topic, often developing a **profile** of its subject. You need to look at as much information about your subject as possible, while realizing that not all information is good or relevant. You will use your critical reading and thinking skills to help determine the reliability and relevance of the information you have gathered. Because exploratory writing is often inductive in nature, you might find it useful to organize your details in categories, using a cluster chart or listing.

For more on inductive thinking, see Chapter 14. For more on cluster charts and listing as strategies, see Chapter 3.

Reading, Inquiry, and Research: Learning from Texts That Explore

The following readings are examples of exploratory writing. Each offers perspectives on a subject. As you read each one, consider the following questions:

- What makes this reading an interesting and useful exploration?
- After reading the selection what else do you want to learn about the subject? Why?
- How can you use the writer's techniques of exploratory writing in your own writing?

KENNETH CHANG

PROFILE

Scientist at Work—Terence Tao: Journeys to the Distant Fields of Prime

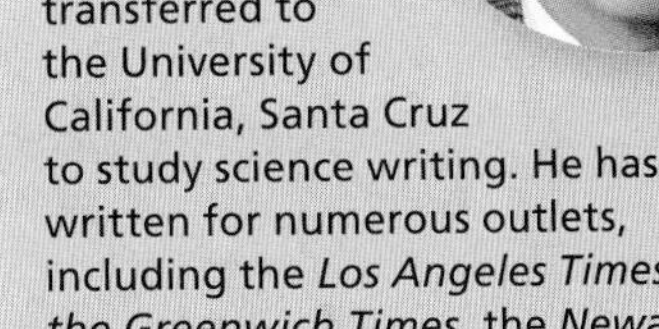

After working on his Ph.D. in physics at the University of Illinois for seven years, Kenneth Chang transferred to the University of California, Santa Cruz to study science writing. He has written for numerous outlets, including the *Los Angeles Times, the Greenwich Times*, the *Newark Star-Ledger,* and ABCNews.com. Since 2000, Kenneth Chang has regularly written science articles for the *New York Times.* A good example of a profile exploring the world of a mathematician, the following article was first published in the *New York Times* in March 2007. Some readers might assume that a profile of a mathematics professor is less interesting than other kinds of profiles. But we think Kenneth Tang's profile of Dr. Tao is fascinating. How does Tang make the profile interesting?

Four hundred people packed into an auditorium at U.C.L.A. in January to listen to a public lecture on prime numbers, one of the rare occasions that the topic has drawn a standing-room-only audience. 1

Another 35 people watched on a video screen in a classroom next door. Eighty people were turned away. 2

The speaker, Terence Tao, a professor of mathematics at the university, promised "a whirlwind tour, the equivalent to going through Paris and just seeing the Eiffel Tower and the Arc de Triomphe." 3

His words were polite, unassuming and tinged with the accent of Australia, his homeland. Even though prime numbers have been studied for 2,000 years, "There's still a lot that needs to be done," Dr. Tao said. "And it's still a very exciting field." 4

After Dr. Tao finished his one-hour talk, which was broadcast live on the Internet, several students came down to the front and asked for autographs. 5

Dr. Tao has drawn attention and curiosity throughout his life for his prodigious abilities. By age 2, he had learned to read. At 9, he attended college math classes. At 20, he finished his Ph.D. 6

Now 31, he has grown from prodigy to one of the world's top mathematicians, tackling an unusually broad range of problems, including ones involving prime numbers and the compression of images. Last summer, he won a Fields Medal, often considered the Nobel Prize of mathematics, and a MacArthur Fellowship, the "genius" award that comes with a half-million dollars and no strings. 7

"He's wonderful," said Charles Fefferman of Princeton University, himself a former child prodigy and a Fields Medalist. "He's as good as they come. There are a few in a generation, and he's one of the few." 8

Colleagues have teasingly called Dr. Tao a rock star and the Mozart of Math. Two museums in Australia have requested his photograph for their permanent exhibits. And he was a finalist for the 2007 Australian of the Year award. 9

"You start getting famous for being famous." Dr. Tao said. "The Paris 10
Hilton effect."

Not that any of that has noticeably affected him. His campus office is 11
adorned with a poster of "Ranma 1/2," a Japanese comic book. As he walks the halls of the math building, he might be wearing an Adidas sweatshirt, blue jeans and scruffy sneakers, looking much like one of his graduate students. He said he did not know how he would spend the MacArthur money, though he mentioned the mortgage on the house that he and his wife, Laura, an engineer at the NASA Jet Propulsion Laboratory, bought last year.

After a childhood in Adelaide, Australia, and graduate school at Prince- 12
ton, Dr. Tao has settled into sunny Southern California.

"I love it a lot," he said. But not necessarily for what the area offers. 13

"It's sort of the absence of things I like," he said. No snow to shovel, for 14
instance.

A deluge of media attention following his Fields Medal last summer 15
has slowed to a trickle, and Dr. Tao said he was happy that his fame might be fleeting so that he could again concentrate on math.

One area of his research—compressed sensing—could have real-world 16
use. Digital cameras use millions of sensors to record an image, and then a computer chip in the camera compresses the data.

"Compressed sensing is a different strategy," Dr. Tao said. "You also 17
compress the data, but you try to do it in a very dumb way, one that doesn't require much computer power at the sensor end."

With Emmanuel Candès, a professor of applied and computational 18
mathematics at the California Institute of Technology, Dr. Tao showed that even if most of the information were immediately discarded, the use of powerful algorithms could still reconstruct the original image.

By useful coincidence, Dr. Tao's son, William, and Dr. Candès's son 19
attended the same preschool, so dropping off their children turned into useful work time.

"We'd meet each other every morning at preschool," Dr. Tao said, "and 20
we'd catch up on what we had done."

The military is interested in using the work for reconnaissance: blan- 21
ket a battlefield with simple, cheap cameras that might each record a single pixel of data. Each camera would transmit the data to a central computer that, using the mathematical technique developed by Dr. Tao and Dr. Candès, would construct a comprehensive view. Engineers at Rice University have made a prototype of just such a camera.

Dr. Tao's best-known mathematical work involves prime numbers— 22
positive whole numbers that can be divided evenly only by themselves and 1. The first few prime numbers are 2, 3, 5, 7, 11 and 13 (1 is excluded).

As numbers get larger, prime numbers become sparser, but the Greek 23
mathematician Euclid proved sometime around 300 B.C. that there is nonetheless an infinite number of primes.

Many questions about prime numbers continue to elude answers. Euclid 24
also believed that there was an infinite number of "twin primes"—pairs of prime numbers separated by 2, like 3 and 5 or 11 and 13—but he was unable to prove his conjecture. Nor has anyone else in the succeeding 2,300 years.

A larger unknown question is whether hidden patterns exist in the 25
sequence of prime numbers or whether they appear randomly.

In 2004, Dr. Tao, along with Ben Green, a mathematician now at the 26
University of Cambridge in England, solved a problem related to the Twin Prime Conjecture by looking at prime number progressions—series of numbers equally spaced. (For example, 3, 7 and 11 constitute a progression of prime numbers with a spacing of 4; the next number in the sequence, 15, is not prime.) Dr. Tao and Dr. Green proved that it is always possible to find, somewhere in the infinity of integers, a progression of any length of equally spaced prime numbers.

"Terry has a style that very few have," Dr. Fefferman said. "When he 27
solves the problem, you think to yourself, 'This is so obvious and why didn't I see it? Why didn't the 100 distinguished people who thought about this before not think of it?'"

Dr. Tao's proficiency with numbers appeared at a very young age. "I 28
always liked numbers," he said.

A 2-year-old Terry Tao used toy blocks to show older children how to 29
count. He was quick with language and used the blocks to spell words like "dog" and "cat."

"He probably was quietly learning these things from watching 'Ses- 30
ame Street,'" said his father, Dr. Billy Tao, a pediatrician who immigrated to Australia from Hong Kong in 1972. "We basically used 'Sesame Street' as a babysitter."

The blocks had been bought as toys, not learning tools. "You expect 31
them to throw them around," said the elder Dr. Tao, whose accent swings between Australian and Chinese.

Terry's parents placed him in a private school when he was 3½. They 32
pulled him out six weeks later because he was not ready to spend that much time in a classroom, and the teacher was not ready to teach someone like him.

At age 5, he was enrolled in a public school, and his parents, admin- 33
istrators and teachers set up an individualized program for him. He proceeded through each subject at his own pace, quickly accelerating through several grades in math and science while remaining closer to his age group in other subjects. In English classes, for instance, he became flustered when he had to write essays.

“I never really got the hang of that,” he said. “These very vague, unde- 34
fined questions. I always liked situations where there were very clear rules
of what to do.”

Assigned to write a story about what was going on at home, Terry went 35
from room to room and made detailed lists of the contents.

When he was 7½, he began attending math classes at the local high 36
school.

Billy Tao knew the trajectories of child prodigies like Jay Luo, who grad- 37
uated with a mathematics degree from Boise State University in 1982 at
the age of 12, but who has since vanished from the world of mathematics.

“I initially thought Terry would be just like one of them, to graduate 38
as early as possible,” he said. But after talking to experts on education for
gifted children, he changed his mind.

“To get a degree at a young age, to be a record-breaker, means nothing,” 39
he said. “I had a pyramid model of knowledge, that is, a very broad base and
then the pyramid can go higher. If you just very quickly move up like a column, then you’re more likely to wobble at the top and then collapse.”

Billy Tao also arranged for math professors to mentor Terry. 40

A couple of years later, Terry was taking university-level math and 41
physics classes. He excelled in international math competitions. His parents decided not to push him into college full-time, so he split his time between high school and Flinders University, the local university in Adelaide.
He finally enrolled as a full-time college student at Flinders when he was
14, two years after he would have graduated had his parents pushed him
only according to his academic abilities.

The Taos had different challenges in raising their other two sons, al- 42
though all three excelled in math. Trevor, two years younger than Terry, is
autistic with top-level chess skills and the musical savant gift to play back
on the piano a musical piece—even one played by an entire orchestra—
after hearing it just once. He completed a Ph.D. in mathematics and now
works for the Defense Science and Technology Organization in Australia.

The youngest, Nigel, told his father that he was “not another Terry,” 43
and his parents let him learn at a less accelerated pace. Nigel, with degrees
in economics, math and computer science, now works as a computer engineer for Google Australia.

“All along, we tend to emphasize the joy of learning,” Billy Tao said. 44
“The fun is doing something, not winning something.”

Terry completed his undergraduate degree in two years, earned a mas- 45
ter’s degree a year after that, then moved to Princeton for his doctoral studies. While he said he never felt out of place in a class of much older students,
Princeton was where he finally felt he fit among a group of peers. He was
still younger, but was not necessarily the brightest student all the time.

His attitude toward math also matured. Until then, math had been 46
competitions, problem sets, exams. "That's more like a sprint," he said.

Dr. Tao recalled that as a child, "I remember having this vague idea 47
that what mathematicians did was that, some authority, someone gave
them problems to solve and they just sort of solved them."

In the real academic world, "Math research is more like a marathon," 48
he said.

As a parent and a professor, Dr. Tao now has to think about how to 49
teach math in addition to learning it.

An evening snack provided him an opportunity to question his son, 50
who is 4. If there are 10 cookies, how many does each of the five people in
the living room get?

William asked his father to tell him. "I don't know how many," Dr. Tao 51
replied. "You tell me."

With a little more prodding, William divided the cookies into five 52
stacks of two each.

Dr. Tao said a future project would be to try to teach more non- 53
mathematicians how to think mathematically—a skill that would be useful in everyday tasks like comparing mortgages.

"I believe you can teach this to almost anybody," he said. 54

But for now, his research is where his focus is. 55

"In many ways, my work is my hobby," he said. "I always wanted to 56
learn another language, but that's not going to happen for a while. Those
things can wait."

QUESTIONS FOR WRITING AND DISCUSSION: LEARNING OUTCOMES

Rhetorical Knowledge: The Writer's Situation and Rhetoric

1. **Audience:** Who is the audience for Chang's essay? What makes you think that?
2. **Purpose:** What is Chang's primary purpose for writing this profile of Terence Tao? How effectively does he fulfill that purpose? Why do you think that?
3. **Voice and tone:** What is Chang's tone in this profile?
4. **Responsibility:** How has Chang acted responsibly in writing this essay?
5. **Context, format, and genre:** Chang wrote this profile for the *New York Times,* a major daily newspaper. If he had written it for an academic journal, what might he have done differently? How does Chang take readers behind the scenes to reveal personal details about Tao?

Critical Thinking: The Writer's Ideas and Your Personal Response

6. What do you find most interesting in Chang's essay about Terence Tao? Why do you find this aspect of the essay interesting?
7. Why do you think Chang includes information about three areas of Tao's life—the academic, the professional, and the personal?

Composing Processes and Knowledge of Conventions: The Writer's Strategies

8. Why does Chang use so many quotations in the profile? Why do you think he uses quotations instead of paraphrases in particular places?
9. Because he is writing for a newspaper, Chang cites his sources within the body of his article rather than using a formal system of documentation. How do his sources lend credibility to his writing? What other sources of information might he have cited?

Inquiry and Research: Ideas for Further Exploration

10. Conduct research on some person whom you find interesting. Write a profile of that person.

JOHN LURZ

Professor, Demystify Yourself: Working Closely with Brilliance and Getting the Hang of It

PROFILE

John Lurz, a native of Baltimore, Maryland, majored in English at Princeton University. He was a columnist for the *Daily Princetonian* and *Princeton Alumni Weekly,* commonly called *PAW.* (The following piece appeared in PAW in 2002.) After finishing his undergraduate degree in 2003, he was awarded a Fulbright Scholarship to teach English in Eisenstadt, Austria. Following that, he worked for the Paul and Daisy Soros Fellowships for New Americans, an organization that supports immigrants in postgraduate study. As a doctoral student in English at the University of California, Berkeley, he won the Joel Fineman Prize for the best essay written by a first-year graduate student at the university. We selected Lurz's profile for several reasons, including his wonderful description of meeting someone who we think is more knowledgeable than we are (an experience most of us can relate to). We also appreciate his argument that professors are real people.

1 Dry mouth, sweaty palms, and a racing heartbeat accompanied me as I walked into my thesis adviser's office last week. It was our first meeting. I had a few rough ideas about a topic bouncing around in my head, but the sight of Princeton University Professor of English D. Vance Smith immediately ejected them from my mind like a pilot in a flight emergency. And it wasn't because Professor Smith is an intimidating figure. Far from it. He is a tall, reserved man who wears little round glasses. His goatee, neatly trimmed, is delicately scattered with gray. His gentle accent, though slight, reminds me he grew up in South Africa. No, it wasn't his actual appearance that emptied my mind, it was the need I felt to be as intelligent and as much of an expert as I envisioned Professor Smith to be.

2 That afternoon, I imagined him as a draconian task master ready to impatiently fling me out of his office for lacking a definite and completely formulated—not to mention brilliant—thesis topic. I imagined that an eminent and busy professor would not take any more time than completely necessary to work with a babbling, incoherent undergraduate.

3 Which was why his first question—"How was your summer?"—immediately startled me into a rambling chain of prattle about summer days spent hiking in New Hampshire. Did Professor Smith really care about my summer or was he just being polite, I wondered. When I finally remembered all the manners my parents taught me and asked him about his summer, he responded with tales of teaching and traveling with his family.

All of a sudden, words like "my wife" and "vacation" were coming out 4
of his mouth. Is Professor Smith a real person who has actual human relationships, I asked myself? Does he actually lead a life outside of being an articulate and accomplished Medievalist lecturing on Chaucer? Is he also a husband, friend and colleague who interacts with people the way

my friends and I do? As we talked, I began to realize the pigeonhole I'd put Professor Smith into was quite a narrow and limited view of him.

We continued chatting, talking about the classes I was taking and the 5 ones he was teaching, about my plans for next year, and about a friend of mine who is a former advisee of his. I suddenly felt the need to stop "wasting" his time and get to the point of the meeting. I thought that he must have more important things to do: maybe work on his own writing or prepare a lecture for the next day.

I began, almost in spite of myself, to repeat the rehearsed lines about 6 the relationship between memory and writing that I hoped I could develop into a viable thesis topic for my English degree. I'd written my junior paper on a theory of the novel in which memory played a crucial role and wanted to expand a bit on that. The way writing aids or harms the faculty of memory had interested me since I began aspiring to write my own fiction.

When Professor Smith began asking me questions about my ideas, I 7 felt threatened—did he not think they were smart ideas? Had I ruined my chance for impressing him? How could I salvage something of this meeting? I began to sweat more, and my heartbeat surged as I tried to think about his questions and respond with intelligent answers. Was I saying the right thing, I wondered? What did he think? Was he going to send me out of his office with a look of disdain and contempt?

And as I responded to his questions and he responded to my answers 8 with comments or more questions, I grew used to the dialectic, falling easily into the Socratic method. Teasing relevant ideas from my garbled words, Professor Smith formulated and repeated back to me in a more coherent and clear style what I had blathered to him. After a few minutes, we had a viable beginning point for a topic, were assembling a reading list, and we were both excited about the prospect of the work ahead. The idea had been mine from the start, but I just needed the help of Professor Smith to focus it into something about which I could write 80+ pages. He told me to email him sometime in the coming week and we could set up another appointment.

He told me, though, that I shouldn't hesitate to hound him for appoint- 9 ments and attention, admitting that he could be a bit absent-minded. At that moment I realized that professors are people too.

Professor Smith—as well as every other professor on our campus— 10 have [sic] real feelings, real relationships, and don't just exist as talking heads in front of a group of cowering undergrads. They aren't perfect; they have doubts; they aren't always sure of things. And sometimes they forget about their advisees.

It was undoubtedly an immature viewpoint that I held of my adviser 11 that probably hints at my own insecurities and self-confidence issues more than I'd like to acknowledge. Yet, from what I've heard from talking with my friends, I'm not the only one who thinks this way. It's not our job, though, to be perfect, brilliant academics; we're supposed to flounder around with ideas, and professors are supposed to help us. Professors enjoy taking time to work with students. If you've ever taught anything, you know the satisfaction that comes from that look of comprehension or from watching someone accomplish a goal you've helped them to achieve. It's important to remember that someone helped these professors to get where they are and that many times they are learning as much from you as you are from them. One day—be it tomorrow or further in the future, whether it be in academia, business, or any other field—you'll be helping and teaching someone too.

QUESTIONS FOR WRITING AND DISCUSSION: LEARNING OUTCOMES

Rhetorical Knowledge: The Writers' Situation and Rhetoric

1. **Audience:** What evidence in this piece indicates that Lurz is writing to college students? What evidence suggests a wider audience?
2. **Purpose:** Why is Lurz telling this story about his meeting with Professor Smith?
3. **Voice and tone:** How would you describe Lurz's attitude toward his readers? What evidence in the text supports your judgment?
4. **Responsibility:** How responsibly has Lurz portrayed Professor Smith to readers?
5. **Context, format and genre:** Why is this piece appropriate for an alumni magazine? How does Lurz take us behind the scenes to reveal information that is unavailable to people who have not met Professor Smith?

Critical Thinking: The Writer's Ideas and Your Personal Response

6. After reading this piece, what is your impression of Professor Smith? Why do you think that?
7. How does this piece affect your views of professors? Why?

Composing Processes and Knowledge of Conventions: The Writer's Strategies

8. Why does Lurz quote Professor Smith in this piece?
9. Why does Lurz include some physical description of Professor Smith?

Inquiry and Research: Ideas for Further Exploration

10. Conduct a Web search to find more information about Professor Smith. What information seems consistent with the details that Lurz offers?

GENRES UP CLOSE

GENRES *Up Close* Writing a Profile

Because people are so curious about other people, they love to write and talk about them. To satisfy that craving, readers can find plenty of venues that offer profiles. Profiles of famous and not-so-famous people appear in magazines such as *People* and *Rolling Stone,* radio news shows such as *All Things Considered* on National Public Radio, television shows such as *E! News,* and especially online social networking sites such as MySpace and Facebook. The social networking sites are especially popular because they allow ordinary people to read profiles of other ordinary people. A recent Web search on the term "Facebook," for example, yielded more than half a billion sites. That is astounding, considering that Earth's population was approximately 6.7 billion at the time.

Although profiles often focus on people, they also can describe organizations, places, and events. Profiles have distinctive features. They tend to:

- **Be brief.** A profile may take no more than a few pages or computer screens.
- **Focus on a short period of time.** A profile may cover the time needed for a single event, such a two-hour dinner with friends, a day of shopping, or a weekend of camping at a state park.
- **Provide some insight into the subject.** A profile takes readers behind the scenes to reveal details that are not widely known.

As you consider the following Web page describing the Peace Corps, think about how it exemplifies the characteristics of a profile.

Peace Corps Web Site—http://www.peacecorps.gov

PROFILE

President John F. Kennedy established the Peace Corps in 1961 to encourage people to serve the United States and the world. Since then, more than 190,000 Americans have served in 139 counties. As you explore the Peace Corps Web site, consider what the writers have done to make it more than simply informational. You may even decide to apply for a position.

QUESTIONS FOR WRITING AND DISCUSSION: LEARNING OUTCOMES

Rhetorical Knowledge: The Writer's Situation and Rhetoric

1. **Audience:** Who is the primary audience for the Peace Corps Web site?
2. **Purpose:** What are the major purposes of this Web site?
3. **Voice and tone:** Although we do not know who wrote the material for this Web site, what attitude toward viewers does the site convey?
4. **Responsibility:** In what ways does the homepage of the Web site suggest that the Peace Corps encourages responsible behavior?
5. **Context, format and genre:** What features of the Web site's homepage encourage readers to explore the Peace Corps? How would you characterize the links on the Peace Corps homepage?

Critical Thinking: The Writer's Ideas and Your Personal Response

6. Visit the Web site for the Peace Corps (www.peacecorps.gov), and click on some of the links to pages that provide answers to questions about the Peace Corps. Which information is most interesting? Why?
7. What are the most appealing features of the Peace Corps that you learned about from the organization's Web site?

Composing Processes and Knowledge of Conventions: The Writer's Strategy

8. Under the heading "About the Peace Corps" are some questions that serve as links to further information. Why did the writer(s) pose questions here?
9. Web sites often include photos or other visual elements. What is the function of the photos on the homepage of the Peace Corps Web site? (Note: If you click the refresh button on your browser while viewing the homepage, a new photo will appear.)

Inquiry and Research: Ideas for Further Exploration

10. Do a Web search on the phrase "Peace Corps." Visit several of the resulting sites to see how they portray the Peace Corps. How do some of these portrayals differ from the portrayal on the Peace Corps site?

Writing Processes

As you work on the assignment you have chosen, remember the qualities of an effective exploratory paper, which are listed on pages 90–100. Also remember that writing is recursive—you might start with an invention activity or two and then conduct some research, which leads to more invention work and then a first draft. But then you might need to do more invention work to help flesh out your draft and conduct more research to answer questions that come up as you explore your ideas further. And then you'll revise your draft and possibly find another gap or two. So while the activities listed below imply that writers proceed step-by-step, the actual process of writing is usually messier.

For a tip on organizing your computer files, see page 70.

As you work on your project, make sure that you save your computer files frequently because any work that you don't save could be lost. Savvy writers back up their computer files in two or more places—on an internal or external hard drive of the computer, on a USB flash drive, and on a rewritable CD or DVD, for example.

Invention: Getting Started

The invention activities below are strategies that you can use to get some sense of what you already know about a subject. Whatever invention method(s) you use (or that your instructor asks you to employ), try to answer questions such as these:

- What do I already know about my subject?
- What preconceptions—positive, negative, neutral—do I have?
- Why am I interested in exploring this subject?
- What questions about the subject would I most like answers to? Who might I be able to talk to about this subject?
- What do I know about my audience? What can I say to interest them in my subject?
- What might my audience already know about my subject? What questions might they have?
- What is my purpose in exploring this subject? What would I like the end result of my research and writing to be? More knowledge? Information that I might use to pursue some goal?

Doing your invention work in electronic form, rather than on paper, lets you easily use this early writing as you construct a draft.

As with any kind of writing, invention activities improve with peer feedback and suggestions. Consider sharing the invention work you have done so far with several classmates or friends in order to understand your rhetorical situation more clearly and to generate more useful information.

Writing Activity

Freewriting, Listing, and Clustering

Using the questions on page 113, freewrite for ten minutes, writing down everything you can think of about your subject. Even if you cannot think of anything to say, keep writing. Or list your ideas about the subject. Develop categories for your list to help you brainstorm.

Once you have gathered your ideas using one of the above methods, cluster them to determine how they relate to one another.

EXAMPLES OF INVENTION

Brainstorming (pp. 158, 332)
Freewriting (pp. 114, 245, 383)
Criteria (p. 290)
Listing (p. 72)
Answers to Reporter's Questions (p. 244)
Organization (pp. 75, 164)
Clustering (pp. 114, 289)
Concept Mapping (p. 335)
Interviewing (p. 203)
Research (pp. 115, 160, 205, 246, 292, 384)
Reflection (p. 12)

Rick Mohler's Freewriting and Clustering

Rick Mohler was taking a "career and life planning" class at his local community college, so he decided to respond to Scenario 1 on page 95. Rick was interested in a lot of areas—especially sports—but he was not quite sure what he might want to pursue as a career. Here is a portion of his freewriting, which reflects his questions and concerns about finding a career that he will enjoy:

> I think what I like most is sports—playing them, thinking about them, learning new rules and games. Football is my game! But I know I probably won't have a professional career—not many people make it to the NFL. I'm not a very fast runner. I can work at it and try, but I need some fallback position, if I'm not good enough. I can't think of anything, maybe an analyst? Sportswriter? Coach? Sports medicine? Photographer? Trainer? Do something with the physical aspect of football?
>
> But if I can't be an NFL player, what can I do? Do I want to stay with sports? What other careers besides being an athlete goes with sports, especially football? Careers in sports, jobs in sports, jobs about sports. Are there college classes I can take to lead me there?

Rick Mohler also used listing to explore his ideas about a career. (See Chapter 4, page 72, for an example of this strategy.) Then he combined ideas from his freewriting and list into a cluster.

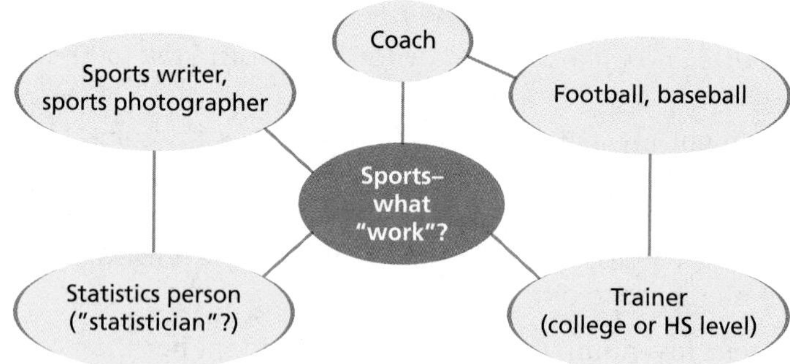

For help with locating sources of information, see Chapter 19; for help with taking notes and documenting your sources, see Chapter 20.

Exploring Your Ideas with Research

Although your opinions and ideas—and especially your questions—are central to any exploratory writing that you do, you need to answer the questions you raise as you explore your subject. Getting those answers usually requires research, which can include reading books and periodical articles at the library, reading articles in your local newspaper, interviewing people who know more than you do about your subject, and conducting searches online, among other means. The information that you discover through your research can help you respond to the questions that prompted your exploration.

Before you start your research, review your invention work to remind yourself of all that you know about your subject and the questions you have about it. Use the reporter's questions—*who, what, where, when, why,* and *how*—to get started. After you have decided what information you need, determine what kind of research will help you to gather that information. Then conduct research in the library and on the Internet.

You could conduct several kinds of research in response to the scenarios on pages 95–98. For Scenario 1, for example, in which you explore potential majors, you might visit the Web sites of various departments at your school to gather information about degree programs, courses offered, and careers of alumni. You might also visit the Web sites of companies that hire graduates in the fields that you are exploring. You could even search newspapers and the Internet to find job advertisements in those fields. You might interview graduating seniors to ask them about their experiences in the majors that you are exploring or people who hold the kinds of jobs that require those majors. Finally, you could search for and read blogs maintained by people who write about their professional fields and careers.

Digital Literacy

Using the Internet to Gain an International Perspective

Writing to explore is not about getting and giving information or simple answers. Exploration involves the hard work of experiencing and understanding *different perspectives.* A good way to learn about different or unusual perspectives is to read news reports from around the world, including those published in foreign newspapers and newsmagazines. Most major publications are now available in English translation. The following are some examples of Web sites maintained by foreign news organizations:

ABYZ News Links
http://www.abyznewslinks.com
French News
http://www.french-news.com/
Japan Times
http://www.japantimes.co.jp/
Pravda (Russia)
http://english.pravda.ru/
London Times (UK)
http://www.timesonline.co.uk/tol/news/

Rick Mohler's Research

Student writer Rick Mohler wanted to explore possible careers in the world of sports other than being an athlete. In addition to sitting at his computer and browsing the Web, he went to his college library and examined recent issues of his school newspaper, some magazines, and several books. To find helpful articles, he used the search term "sports—careers." He used the same search term to search his school's online library indexes. Based on what he read, he made some notes to himself in order to try to find some direction. Here are some of Mohler's notes:

1. Read through back issues of the campus newspaper—*College Press*—there were some interviews with several coaches, all from different sports. Interview them to find out more?

EXAMPLES OF INVENTION

Brainstorming (pp. 158, 332)
Freewriting (pp. 114, 245, 383)
Criteria (p. 290)
Listing (p. 72)
Answers to Reporter's Questions (p. 244)
Organization (pp. 75, 164)
Clustering (pp. 114, 289)
Concept Mapping (p. 335)
Interviewing (p. 203)
Research (pp. 115, 160, 205, 246, 292, 384)
Reflection (p. 12)

2. Also lots of photos of athletes. That might be an interesting career choice: sports photographer. Probably gets into the games free, too.
3. Someone has to write all those articles in *Sports Illustrated*. I wonder: how do you become a big-time sportswriter?

Writing Activity

Conducting Research

As you generate questions about your topic, consider where you might find the answers—books, journals, databases, the Internet, and so on. Begin to gather and read your sources. Manage your research by setting time (for example, two weeks) or quantity (say, ten sources) parameters to ensure that you meet your writing deadlines. Your teacher may specify the number and kinds of resources to focus on.

Reviewing Your Invention and Research

For more on developing a thesis, see Chapter 13.

After you have conducted your research, review your invention work and notes. At this point, you may be tempted to decide on a **thesis statement**—a statement that summarizes the main point of your exploration. Even though you might already have a general idea of the conclusion your research is leading you to, it is often hard to know for certain what your thesis will be. Your thesis should come *from* your exploration. It is best to decide on your thesis after you have done a lot of invention work (listing, brainstorming, clustering, and so on) and research, or even after you construct your first draft.

A WRITER'S *Responsibility* | Exploring Ideas

Writers who are considering and examining multiple viewpoints have a responsibility to their readers to present those viewpoints as accurately as possible. In exploratory writing, you can express your opinions, responses, and reflections, but you must be careful not to misrepresent the viewpoints of others. Because you may not feel comfortable, at least initially, with all the points of view you will be exploring, you need to make sure you are using reliable information that readers can verify themselves. You do not have to accept all of the perspectives you examine, but you do have an ethical responsibility to treat them all honestly and respectfully.

Your purpose is to open yourself and your readers to different possibilities. If you find yourself limiting the perspectives you explore because you feel uncomfortable with some of them, you are limiting your and your readers' options.

Organizing Your Ideas and Details

Because the purpose of writing an exploratory text is to examine an idea or concept from various perspectives, you will need to organize your thoughts in a useful manner. The questions that you need to ask yourself when deciding on your organization are all rhetorical:

- Who is your audience?
- Why might they be interested in your exploratory writing, or how can you make them interested in it? One way to emphasize the importance of your exploration to your audience is to show them why your subject is interesting to you.
- What is your purpose for writing—that is, why should your readers explore this topic with you?

Here is a brief outline of three possible organizational approaches to writing an exploratory paper:

Options FOR Organization

Options for Organizing an Exploratory Paper

Classify Ideas	Compare and Contrast Ideas	Relate Causes and Effect
Begin with your questions, perhaps from the least to the most important. Explain each question in detail and then provide possible answers. Look at each question in detail. You may find that classifying both questions and answers is a useful method of organization. Offer follow-up questions that may lead to further exploration. Perhaps conclude by suggesting that your exploration does not answer all the questions and that other, specified, questions now need to be asked.	Note how many possible perspectives there may be on your subject and how they relate to one another. Explore each perspective in detail. Recognize that, because you began by noting multiple perspectives, comparison and contrast might be a useful method of organization. Explore your topic through various lenses to come to a better understanding of your subject, especially in relation to the different points of view on it. Having presented multiple perspectives on your topic, indicate which conclusion your exploration has led you to.	Start from what happens first and move to later events. Explore and explain the various possible causes or effects. Use specific examples to show how one cause or effect logically leads to the next. This is a variation on a cause-and-effect paper. In an exploratory paper, you *consider* possible causes and effects; in a cause-and-effect paper, you *argue* that specific phenomena are causes or effects. Perhaps end your paper with what seems like the final effect—keeping the entire paper chronological.

connect
mhconnectcomposition.com
Drafting and Revising QL5005

Constructing a Complete Draft

Once you know your subject, have recorded your ideas down on paper or stored in a computer file, and have conducted research, you are ready to construct your initial draft. It is possible that you will find a suitable organizational approach before you begin drafting, but you may also find it—or decide to change it—as you are drafting or even after you have constructed a draft. Also, as you write the first version of your exploratory paper, do not worry about editing your work.

INTEGRATING SOURCES

Synthesizing and Integrating Sources into Your Draft: Quoting Information from Sources

Because effective writers use research to support claims, it is important to learn how to integrate sources in your own text. One way writers integrate sources is by incorporating direct quotations.

As mentioned in Chapter 20, there are a number of situations when using a direct quotation is most appropriate—for example, when you are quoting a primary source such as an interviewee. Generally, you will include a direct quotation—exactly what someone told you—when the comments are concise and support your own assertions. When someone you interview gives you an abundance of information, or if you interview a number of people, you may want to summarize their comments instead of using an exact quotation (for more on *summarizing,* see page 338; for more on *paraphrasing* someone's interview comments, see page 164).

Whether you directly quote or summarize what someone has said, you can help readers by introducing the information and documenting the source. Rather than simply inserting a quotation into a text and assuming the reader will understand why the quotation is there and how it relates to the point in the text, introduce the quotation and explain how that quotation connects to your claim.

For example, student writer Rick Mohler lets his readers know who John Wilson is when he introduces his quotation from Wilson. Note also that Mohler tells his reader what questions he asked Wilson:

> John Wilson, the spring workouts *College Press* writer, was kind enough to give me an interview. I asked him what kind of background an aspiring sportswriter needs. "It's not as easy as it sounds," Wilson told me. "I'm an English major, which really helps, and while that combined with my interest in and knowledge of sports is good, what's hard for me is the process of writing." (paragraph 7)
>
> I asked Wilson what he meant about writing and effort . . . (paragraph 8)

Here, Mohler manages to (1) tell us what he asked the interviewee, (2) provide the answer the person gave in that person's own words, and (3) transition to the next question he asked Wilson. Note also that once he completes his interview with Wilson, Mohler relates Wilson's comments to the purpose of his paper, writing that Mohler could see sportswriting "appealing to my competitive nature" (paragraph 9).

So, for your own citing, remember to:

- Introduce the quotation (never just plop it into your text).
- Accurately report and document the source of the quotation.
- Explain how the quotation relates to your claim.

If you have conducted research by interviewing numerous people, or if one person told you too much to directly quote, you probably need to summarize what you learned. Student writer Mohler summarizes his interview with Brad Taylor in paragraphs 11–14, which gives him the space to provide many details. Note that there are no direct quotations here; instead, Mohler summarizes what Taylor told him. Summarizing allows Mohler to give the reader much interesting information, including Taylor's football background, the writing he did in college, how that developed into newspaper work, and how he eventually became high school sports editor for that paper—a lot of information that works effectively because Mohler summarized it.

Parts of a Complete Draft

mhconnectcomposition.com

Introductory paragraph overview QL5006

Introduction: One of the qualities of successful exploratory writing is that it grabs and holds readers' attention. There are a number of strategies for beginning your paper that will help you hook your readers:

- **Take your readers on the journey.** Let your readers know from the beginning that this is an exploration. Let them be your travel companions. In "Scientist at Work—Terence Tao: Journeys to the Distant Fields of Prime," Kenneth Chang indicates that his essay will be a journey through his title and his opening anecdote, in which Tao promises an audience at a lecture "a whirlwind tour."
- **Ask one or more questions.** By asking questions, you present options and directions. Your exploratory writing will help you and your reader find solutions.
- **Set the stage by exploring and explaining your own feelings.** Outline your feelings, expectations, concerns, and so right off the bat, as John Lurz does in "Professor, Demystify Yourself."

Body: The body of your paper will lead you and your readers through your exploration process. You may choose one or several different kinds of organization. You might try classification, for example, where by grouping ideas in like categories, you discover similarities. However, comparison and contrast, where you discover both similarities and differences, might be more helpful. Or you might discover that cause and effect is the most powerful kind of organization for your paper.

Writing Activity

Constructing a Complete Draft

After selecting an organizational approach, write a complete draft of your paper that explores your topic. In exploratory writing, your thesis statement may not appear until after you have completed a first draft. Use as much detail as possible—the more you get down on paper initially, the easier it will be to flesh out and revise your paper later. Your first draft will likely to lead to additional questions and answers you will want to include in your revision(s).

Conclusion: Following your exploration, your conclusion should leave your readers feeling satisfied.

- If in your exploration you discover that there will be consequences if certain events occur, you may choose to present these final consequences.
- If you discover that your exploration has led to even more questions, you may simply state the new questions that need to be researched.
- If your exploration does lead you to a reasonable conclusion, state that conclusion, explaining to readers how you reached it.

Title: You might think that you need to craft a title before you start writing, but often it is more useful to get a first draft down on paper or into a computer file and then consider possible titles. For an exploratory paper, your title should indicate your subject and give your reader a reason to want to explore it with you. The titles "Professor, Demystify Yourself" and "Journeys to the Distant Fields of Prime," for example, indicate that their authors have a unique approach to their subjects.

connect
mhconnectcomposition.com
Concluding paragraph overview QL5007

Rick Mohler's First Draft: A Sporting Career?

After doing research and deciding on an organizational approach, Rick Mohler was ready to begin his first draft. As he wrote, he did not concern himself with grammar, punctuation, or mechanics, but instead tried to get his questions and answers and ideas on paper. Note that Mohler started his paper with a series of questions—one of the organizational methods described above. Note also that Mohler incorporated some of his research information into his paper. (The numbers in circles refer to peer comments—see pages 124–125.)

A Sporting Career?

Rick Mohler

If you ask most people about a career in sports, they'll usually say, "professional athlete," as that is the most visible (and well-paid) career option. But what about those of us who will never make a professional team? We may have enough desire, but what if we're not big enough, or fast enough, or have enough talent to "make the pros"? Are there other career options available to us and if so, what are they? How can we learn about them? What are some of the good things about those careers, and what are some of the bad things? What might their work entail? What are the opportunities for promotion? ❶

VISUALIZING *Variations* | Using Visuals to Make Your Exploration Clear

An appropriate image can add visual appeal to any exploratory writing. If you are exploring some personal interest, consider using a visual or visuals to show why you find your topic appealing. Suppose you collect state quarters, and, as your collection has grown, you have become more interested in the images on the backs of the quarters, the stories behind them, and the artists who designed them.

As you think about presenting your profile of quarter collecting to your readers, you decide which of the quarters' images will be most intriguing to them and which will best demonstrate your exploration. You might choose the Nevada quarter, for instance, released in 2006.

The image on the Nevada quarter tells a story about the state, but you need to do some exploration to discover what that story is. Your exploration might lead you to the Web site for the United States Mint (http://www.usmint.gov), where you find the story behind the "design of three galloping wild horses, sagebrush, the sun rising behind snow-capped mountains and the State's nickname, 'The Silver State,' inside a banner" and how it was chosen from five candidates.

Although you could certainly use words, the photo of the image will help readers see it more clearly. Using this image as an example, consider the best way to enhance your exploratory writing for your readers with an image or images. Use the following questions to guide you:

- What can an image or images add that the words alone cannot show?
- How can I use the image to surprise readers—to offer them something unexpected?
- Should the image(s) I use be in color or black-and-white? What would be most effective?
- What kinds of images would draw readers into my text and make them want to read and learn more?
- How can the image(s) I select help show my exploration?

Those are just a few of the questions that I will explore in this paper, as I'm one of the people described above—I'll never be big enough or fast enough to "make the pros," but I also want to pursue a career in sports.❷

My favorite sport is football—and it's also America's choice, especially NFL football. In addition to the players, what other careers might be associated with the NFL? A few come to mind, including coach, weight-trainer/

conditioning coach, publicity folks, and others. I want to explore two that interest me:

- Sportswriter
- Sports photographer ❸

One important part of either of these careers is that they are everywhere. Local newspapers as well as national television companies need them, so there are plenty of employment opportunities.

Since I've always been a pretty good writer, the idea of becoming a sportswriter strikes me as an interesting career. Last week's College Press, for example, carried seven sports-related articles, all written by student writers. Two touched on football, and perhaps the most interesting article was about spring workouts for our football players.

John Wilson, the spring workouts College Press writer, was kind enough to give me an interview. I asked him what kind of background you needed. "It's not as easy as it sounds," Wilson told me. "I'm an English major, which really helps, and while that combined with my interest and knowledge of sports is good, what's hard for me is the process of writing."

I asked John what he meant, and he said "it's just a lot of work. You have to go to the game and take notes. Then you interview some of the people involved—the coaches, the players, etc. Then you figure out some angle or slant that you want to focus on—one big play, or how a coach made a great call, or whatever. Then, finally, you have to write it all into a coherent form." I told John that the process he described was just what I was learning in my college writing class. He also told me that much of the writing has hard deadlines. You have to write fast as well as accurately. John said that he likes the challenge. I can see that appealing to my competitive nature.

Since I wanted to find out what a professional sportswriter might do John also suggested I email Brad Taylor, the high school sports editor of a large local newspaper.

My email correspondence and subsequent phone conversation with Brad Taylor proved even more interesting. Taylor explained to me the path he took to become a sportswriter. Like me, he had played football in high school but wasn't big enough or good enough to play in college. He was a history major in college but also wrote for the College Press, being sports editor his senior year. As much as he enjoyed working on the newspaper, he didn't think it was a real career. He expected to either go to law school or graduate school in history and become a history professor.

I was amazed to hear that he had been accepted by some really good law schools and grad schools but chose to start work on a masters degree instead. For a number of reasons, school wasn't as exciting as he thought it would be. On a whim, he went to the sports department of the large local paper. They asked if he had clippings. He brought them some of his college articles. They offered him a job as a stringer covering high school football.

Taylor told me that something clicked when he started covering high schools. He got a real thrill talking to the coaches and the players. Eventually, he dropped out of grad school when offered a full-time reporting job. Over time he became editor for all of high school sports. I could hear the excitement in his voice. It reminded me of the times in my old high school locker room.❹

Revising

Revising means re-seeing and re-thinking your exploratory text. The most effective way to revise your work is to read it as if you are reading it for the first time. Reading your work in this way is difficult to do, of course—which is why writers often put their work aside for a time. The more you can see your writing as if for the first time, the more you will respond to it as your real readers might, questioning and exploring it. As you reread the first draft of your exploratory writing, here are some questions to ask yourself:

- What are the most important questions, the ones I would really like to have answered? How well have I answered them?
- How well have I answered the questions that will help me understand every facet of my subject?
- How well do I understand the draft? What parts are confusing or need more information? What research might I need to conduct to further clarify my ideas?
- What information, if any, might I provide as a visual?

Technology can help you revise and, later, edit your writing more easily. Use your word processor's track-changes tool to try out revisions and editing changes. After you've had time to think about the possible changes, you can "accept" or "reject" them. Also, you can use your word processor's comment tool to write reminders to yourself when you get stuck with a revision or some editing task.

Because it is so difficult even for experienced writers to see their emerging writing with a fresh eye, it is almost always useful to ask classmates, friends, or family members to read and comment on drafts.

WRITER'S *Workshop* | Responding to Full Drafts

As you read and respond to your classmates' papers (and as they comment on yours), focus on the exploratory nature of this assignment, but from a reader's perspective. Be sure to ask questions of their writing and to respond to their ideas by exploring your reactions and responses to their thoughts.

Working in pairs or groups of three, read each others' papers, and then offer your classmates comments that will help them see both their papers' strengths and places where they need to develop their ideas further. Use the following questions to guide your responses to the writer's draft:

- What is your first impression? How interested are you in reading beyond the first paragraph? Why? Do you have any suggestions for improving the title?
- What do you like about the draft? Provide positive and encouraging feedback to the writer. How interesting, educational, or useful did you find this exploration? Why?
- What is the focus of the paper? How does the focus emerge as you read? How well do you understand how the writer comes to her or his conclusion?
- How easily can you follow the writer's thought process? Comment on how the writer's exploratory writing helps you better understand the questions or problems posed in the introduction.
- How thoroughly does the writer explore the subject? How might the writer explore it more fully?
- How viable are the differing perspectives? How appropriate are the writer's sources?
- Reread the conclusion: How logically does it follow from the rest of the paper? Were you surprised by the conclusion? What are other possible conclusions based on the information the writer has presented?
- What do you see as the main weaknesses of this paper? How might the writer improve the text?

Student Comments on Rick Mohler's First Draft

Rick Mohler got comments on his first draft from several readers. Below are comments on his draft, keyed to the first draft on pages 120–123.

1. "The above are really useful questions, but maybe you should kind of build up to the most important ones and leave the rest for the body of the paper. Another question I thought of is about how many possible careers in sports are there?"
2. "That's a really interesting point. Most sports fans think it's either the pros or nothing, so I like the way you're trying to be realistic and still come up with a career that lets you do what you like most."
3. "Why are you interested in these two careers? What about them attracts you? I really do not know what a person in either position does all day

long. Maybe to focus the paper a little more, you ought to focus on just one career?"

4 "This is a good story, but I'd like to see more in your conclusion. What's so good about your old locker room?"

Responding to Readers' Comments

Once they have received feedback on their writing from peers, teachers, friends, and others, writers have to figure out what to do with that feedback. You may decide to reject some comments, of course. Other comments, though, deserve your attention, as they are the words of real readers speaking to you about how to improve your text. You may find that comments from more than one reader contradict each other. In that case, use your own judgment to decide which reader's comments are on the right track.

In the final version of Rick Mohler's paper, on pages 127–129, you can see how he responded to his peers' comments, as well as to his own review of his first draft.

Knowledge of Conventions

When effective writers edit their work, they attend to the conventions that will help readers move through their writing effortlessly. By paying attention to these conventions in your writing, you make reading a more pleasant experience for readers.

Editing

mhconnectcomposition.com

Revising and Editing overview (also Drafting) QL5008

The last task in any writing project is editing—the final polishing of your document. When you edit and polish your writing, you make changes to your sentence structure and word choice to improve your style and to make your writing clearer and more concise. You also check your work to make sure it adheres to conventions of grammar, usage, punctuation, mechanics, and spelling, as well as genre conventions. Use the spell-check function of your word-processing program, but be sure to double-check your spelling personally. If you have used sources in your paper, make sure you are following the documentation style your instructor requires.

See Chapter 20 for more on documenting sources using MLA or APA style.

As with overall revision of your work, this final editing and polishing is most effective if you can put your text aside for a few days and come back to it with fresh eyes. Because checking conventions is easier said than done, though, we strongly recommend that you ask classmates, friends, and tutors to read your work to find sentence problems that you do not see.

To assist you with editing, we offer here a round-robin editing activity focused on sentence fragments, a common concern in all writing.

ROUND-ROBIN EDITING WITH A FOCUS ON

WRITER'S *Workshop* | Round-Robin Editing with a Focus on Fragments

Because exploratory writing often includes incomplete thoughts, writers sometimes inadvertently use sentence fragments to express their thinking. A sentence fragment is missing one or more of the following elements: a subject, a verb, or a complete thought. Some fragments lack a subject, a verb, or both:

FRAGMENT College sports are popular. *Generating lots of money for schools with successful teams.*

SENTENCE College sports are popular. They generate lots of money for schools with successful teams.

Other fragments have subjects and verbs, but they begin with a subordinating word like *because* or *although* and so are not complete thoughts:

FRAGMENT *Although I have played football in high school and college.* I'm not good enough to play on a professional team.

SENTENCE Although I have played football in high school and college, I'm not good enough to play on a professional team.

Work with two peers to look for sentence fragments. For each fragment, decide whether to connect it to a nearby sentence or to recast it into a complete sentence.

connect
mhconnectcomposition.com
Recognizing fragments QL5009

connect
mhconnectcomposition.com
Recognizing comma splices and run-ons QL5012

Genres, Documentation, and Format

For advice on writing in different genres, see the Online Appendix. For guidelines for formatting and documenting papers in MLA or APA style, see Chapter 20.

If you are writing an academic paper, follow the conventions for the discipline in which you are writing and the requirements of your instructor. However, if you are exploring potential majors (Scenario 1), you might choose to write a letter or an e-mail message to family members. If you are doing a personal exploration (Scenario 2), you might want to write a journal entry. If you have chosen to do a personal exploration, you might avoid writing a blog entry, because blogs can have thousands of readers—including potential employers.

If you have used material from outside sources, including visuals, give credit to those sources, using the documentation style required by the discipline you are working in and by your instructor.

A Writer Shares His Exploration: Rick Mohler's Final Draft

As you read the final version of Rick Mohler's exploratory paper, consider what makes it effective. Following the reading you will find some questions to help you conduct an exploration of this paper.

RICK MOHLER

A Sporting Career?

ANALYTICAL ESSAY

If you ask most people to name a career in sports, they'll usually say, "professional athlete," because that is the most visible (and well-paid) career option. But what about those of us who have the desire, but not the size, speed, or talent? Are there other career options available to us, and if so, what are they? 1

I'm one of those people. I doubt that I have the size or speed to make the pros, but I want a career in sports, as do many others. Perhaps my "wonderings" here can help others as they try to decide what career path they may want to follow. 2

My favorite sport is football—and it's also America's choice. While the players have the faces and names that fans recognize, they are only one part of the big picture that is NFL football. Many other people make the games happen, keep the players in good condition, and tell the rest of America all about the sport. Coaches, weight trainers and conditioning coaches, publicists, writers, and photographers all have a part to play in the game of football. 3

The career path that excites me most is being a sportswriter. The job has an artistic element that appeals to me. As a sportswriter, I wouldn't just describe what took place at a game or event—I would really try to paint a picture. Maybe someday I'll even be able to write something as famous as Grantland Rice's description of the Notre Dame football team: 4

> Outlined against a blue-gray October sky, the Four Horsemen rode again. In dramatic lore they are known as Famine, Pestilence, Destruction and Death. These are only aliases. Their real names are Stuhldreher, Miller, Crowley and Layden. They formed the crest of the South Bend cyclone before which another fighting Army football team was swept over the precipice at the Polo Grounds yesterday afternoon as 55,000 spectators peered down on the bewildering panorama spread on the green plain below.

Though not all sportswriters become as famous as Rice, they are everywhere. Local newspapers as well as national television networks need them, so there are plenty of employment opportunities. Just as most sports have both amateur and professional athletes, a sportswriter can start as an amateur and advance to the pros. It seems to make sense to begin working for a student newspaper, especially since I've always been a fairly good writer. 5

Last week's <u>College Press</u>, for example, included seven sports-related articles, all written by student writers. Two touched on football, and per- 6

One of Mohler's classmates made this comment on his paper:

Another question I thought of is about how many possible careers in sports are there?

Notice how he provides information to answer this peer-review question.

One of Mohler's classmates wrote this comment on an early draft:

Why are you interested in these two careers? What about them attracts you? I really do not know what a person in either position does all day long. Maybe to focus the paper a little more, you ought to focus on just one career.

Notice how Mohler does what his classmate suggested, focusing on one specific career path.

haps the most interesting article was about spring workouts for our football players.

Mohler uses direct quotations from his interviews to bring other people's perspectives into his work.

7 John Wilson, the spring workouts College Press writer, was kind enough to give me an interview. I asked him what kind of background an aspiring sportswriter needs. "It's not as easy as it sounds," Wilson told me. "I'm an English major, which really helps, and while that combined with my interest in and knowledge of sports is good, what's hard for me is the process of writing."

8 I asked Wilson what he meant about writing and effort, and he gave me a description of how he typically covers a game:

> It's just a lot of work. You have to go to the game and take notes. Then you interview some of the people involved—the coaches, the players, etc. Then you figure out some angle or slant that you want to focus on—one big play, or how a coach made a great call, or whatever. Then, finally, you have to write it all into a coherent form.

I told Wilson that the process he described was just what I was learning in my college writing class. "You have to write fast as well as accurately," Wilson said. He also told me that he likes the challenge. I can see that appealing to my competitive nature.

9 Because I wanted to find out what a professional sportswriter might do, Wilson also suggested I contact Brad Taylor, the high school sports editor of a large newspaper in my hometown.

10 My communications with Brad Taylor proved even more interesting. Taylor explained the path he took to become a sportswriter. Like me, he had played football in high school but wasn't good enough to play in college. He was a history major in college but also wrote for the College Press, becoming sports editor his senior year. As much as he enjoyed sportswriting, he didn't think it was a real career. He expected to go either to law school or graduate school in history and become a history professor.

Mohler ended his first version with the words "locker room," and a peer reviewer asked about his ending:

This is a good story, but I'd like to see more in your conclusion. What's so good about your old locker room?

Notice how Mohler has now added some information to answer his classmate's question.

11 Despite being accepted by some really good law schools and graduate schools, he chose to start work on a master's degree at a local college. For a number of reasons, school wasn't as exciting as he thought it would be. On a whim, he went to the sports department of the large local paper. They asked if he had clippings, and he brought some of his college articles. They offered him a job as a stringer covering high school football.

12 Taylor told me that something clicked when he started covering high schools. He got a real thrill talking to the coaches and the players.

13 Eventually, he dropped out of graduate school when offered a full-time reporting job. Over time he became editor for all of high school sports. I could hear the excitement in his voice. It reminded me of the times in my old high school locker room—the joy after winning and the disappointment after losing, the camaraderie among teammates, the team meetings

to discuss strategy. I wouldn't mind reliving that again—even if it's a vicarious experience.

This paper follows MLA guidelines for in-text citations and works cited. Note that URLs are optional.

Works Cited

Rice, Grantland. "The Four Horsemen." *University of Notre Dame Archives.* Web. 5 May 2003. <http://lamb.archives.nd.edu/rockne/rice.html>.

Taylor, Brad. Personal E-mail. 7 May 2003.

———. Personal Interview. 9 May 2003.

Wilson, John. Personal Interview. 30 Apr. 2003.

QUESTIONS FOR WRITING AND DISCUSSION: LEARNING OUTCOMES

Rhetorical Knowledge: The Writer's Situation and Rhetoric

1. **Audience:** Who is the intended audience for Mohler's essay? What in the essay makes you think so?
2. **Purpose:** What does Mohler hope will happen when people read his essay?
3. **Voice and tone:** How would you describe Mohler's tone in his essay?
4. **Responsibility:** How responsibly has Mohler reported information about being a sportswriter to you? To himself? Why do you think so?
5. **Context, format, and genre:** Mohler wrote this paper for a college course. If you were an editor for your local newspaper, would you consider hiring Mohler as a sportswriter? Why or why not? In an exploratory essay, the writer starts with a premise and then follows one or more lines of inquiry to discover something new. Do you think Mohler has adequately explored the possibility of a career in sportswriting? Why or why not?

Critical Thinking: The Writer's Ideas and Your Personal Response

6. What is the main point of Mohler's essay? How well does he focus the essay? How does he support his main idea? What questions do you still have about his subject?
7. How easily can you relate to what Mohler writes about? Why?

Composing Processes and Knowledge of Conventions: The Writer's Strategies

8. In what ways does Mohler establish his *ethos,* or his credibility, in this exploratory essay?
9. How effective are Mohler's introduction and conclusion? Why?

Inquiry and Research: Ideas for Further Exploration

10. In what other ways might Mohler have researched his choice? What sources might he have investigated?

 Self-Assessment: Reflecting on Your Goals

Now that you have constructed a piece of exploratory writing, go back and consider the goals at the beginning of this chapter (see pages 00–00). Reflecting on your writing process and the exploratory text you have constructed—and putting such reflections down *in writing*—is another kind of exploration: You are exploring, thinking about, and commenting on your own work as a writer. Answering the following questions will help you reflect on what you have learned from this assignment:

Rhetorical Knowledge

- *Audience:* What have you learned about addressing an audience in exploratory writing?
- *Purpose:* What have you learned about the purposes of exploratory writing?
- *Rhetorical situation:* How did the writing context affect your exploratory text?
- *Voice and tone:* How would you describe your voice in this project? Your tone? How do they contribute to the effectiveness of your exploratory essay?
- *Context, medium, and genre:* How did your context determine the medium and genre you chose, and how did those decisions affect your writing?

Critical Thinking, Reading, and Writing

- *Learning/inquiry:* How did you decide what to focus on in your exploratory writing? How did you judge what was most and least important in your exploratory writing?
- *Responsibility:* How did you fulfill your responsibility to your readers?
- *Reading and research:* What did you learn about exploratory writing from the reading selections you read for this chapter? What research did you conduct? How sufficient was the research you did?
- *Skills:* As a result of writing this exploration, how have you become a more critical thinker, reader, and writer? What critical thinking, reading, and writing skills do you hope to develop further in your next writing project? How will you work on them?

Writing Processes for Exploration

- *Invention:* What invention strategies were most useful to you? Why?
- *Organizing your ideas and details:* What organization did you use? How successful was it?
- *Revising:* What one revision did you make that you are most satisfied with? What are the strongest and the weakest parts of the paper or other piece of writing you wrote for this chapter? Why?

- *Working with peers:* How did your instructor or peer readers help you by making comments and suggestions about your writing? How could you have made better use of the comments and suggestions you received? How could your peer readers help you more on your next assignment? How might you help them more, in the future, with the comments and suggestions you make on their texts?
- *Visuals:* If you used photographs or other visuals to help present your exploration to readers, what did you learn about incorporating these elements?
- *Writing habits:* What "writerly habits" have you developed, modified, or improved on as you completed the writing assignment for this chapter?

For help with freewriting and clustering, as well as other strategies for discovery and learning, see Chapter 3.

Knowledge of Conventions

- *Editing:* What sentence problem did you find most frequently in your writing? How will you avoid that problem in future assignments?
- *Genre:* What conventions of the genre you were using, if any, gave you problems?
- *Documentation:* If you used sources for your paper, what documentation style did you use? What problems, if any, did you have with it?

Refer to Chapter 1 (pages 11–12) for a sample reflection by a student.

connect
mhconnectcomposition.com
Rick Mohler Reflects on His Writing QL5010

Writing to Inform

We all deal with *information* every day of our lives. We learn about facts, ideas, and ways of doing things, and then communicate such information to others through spoken or written words and, at times, graphic or other visual means.

Many newspaper articles are examples of informative writing. The headlines from the *New York Times* Online demonstrate that the primary goal of headline writers is simply to provide information. Readers don't expect headlines to contain elements of persuasion, argumentation, or evaluation. We could argue, of course, that any type of writing has elements of persuasion, and by selecting certain words and emphasizing particular facts, a writer will influence a reader's response. However, the goal of most informative writing, especially the informative writing you will do in college, *is* to be as neutral as possible, so it is the writer's responsibility to present information impartially.

As a college student, you read informative writing in your textbooks and other assigned reading, and are expected to write informative responses on tests and to provide information in the papers your teachers assign. While you may think that you encounter informative writing only in your textbooks and in newspapers or magazines, you can easily find examples of such

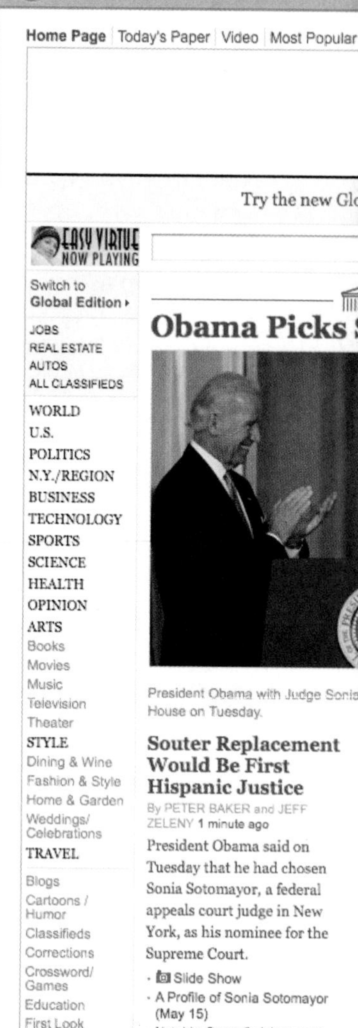
http

Home Page | Today's Paper | Video | Most Popular

Try the new Glo

EASY VIRTUE NOW PLAYING

Switch to Global Edition ›

JOBS
REAL ESTATE
AUTOS
ALL CLASSIFIEDS

WORLD
U.S.
POLITICS
N.Y./REGION
BUSINESS
TECHNOLOGY
SPORTS
SCIENCE
HEALTH
OPINION
ARTS
Books
Movies
Music
Television
Theater
STYLE
Dining & Wine
Fashion & Style
Home & Garden
Weddings/Celebrations
TRAVEL

Blogs
Cartoons / Humor
Classifieds
Corrections
Crossword/Games
Education
First Look
Learning Network
Multimedia
NYC Guide
Obituaries
Podcasts
Public Editor

Obama Picks

President Obama with Judge Sonia ... House on Tuesday.

Souter Replacement Would Be First Hispanic Justice

By PETER BAKER and JEFF ZELENY 1 minute ago

President Obama said on Tuesday that he had chosen Sonia Sotomayor, a federal appeals court judge in New York, as his nominee for the Supreme Court.

- Slide Show
- A Profile of Sonia Sotomayor (May 15)
- Notable Court Opinions and Articles by Sotomayor

Back Story With The Times's Neil A. Lewis

5:40

Post a Comment | Read (209)

Done

reading and writing in each area of your life. In your professional life, for example, you may need to read (or construct) a training manual, while in your civic life, you may be called on to write a voter guide about two candidates, presenting their positions without revealing your personal views.

:ing News, World News & Multimedia

Get Home Delivery | Log In | Register Now | TimesPeople

York Times

09 Last Update: 12:12 PM ET

: from a global perspective. Switch to Global Edition »

Try Our **EXTRA** Home Page

› Get Home Delivery | Personalize Your Weather

ng Intellect

zier Muhammad/The New York Times

ı R. Biden Jr. at the White

AGAZINE PREVIEW

'hat's a Liberal Justice ow?

JEFFREY ROSEN

President Obama wants to eate a progressive Supreme ourt for the 21st century, ere is a new school of legal ought to guide him.

Times Topics: Supreme Court

MENT

(Cardinal Spellman ment of pride and crossed. "

- Gypsy

OPINION »

Douthat: Liberated and Unhappy

In the 1960s, American women reported themselves happier, on average, than did men. Today, that gender gap has reversed.

- Herbert: Our Crumbling Foundation | Comments
- Brooks: Angels Rejoice
- Editorial: Global Trade
- Bolton: Test Ban Trouble
- Opinionator: North Korea
- Happy Days: Divine Mind

SCIENCE TIMES »

In Hot Pursuit of Fusion (or Folly)

In a colossus of light and mirrors, scientists dream of kindling the power of stars.

- Graphic: From Laser Light to a Miniature Star

HEALTH »

Texting May Be Harmful to Your Health

Nearly 80 messages a day, on average, take their toll in a range of ways.

MARKETS » At 12:20 PM ET

S.&P. 500	Dow	Nasdaq
905.09	8,442.99	1,741.86
+18.09	+165.67	+49.85
+2.04%	+2.00%	+2.95%

GET QUOTES My Portfolios »

Stock, ETFs, Funds | Go

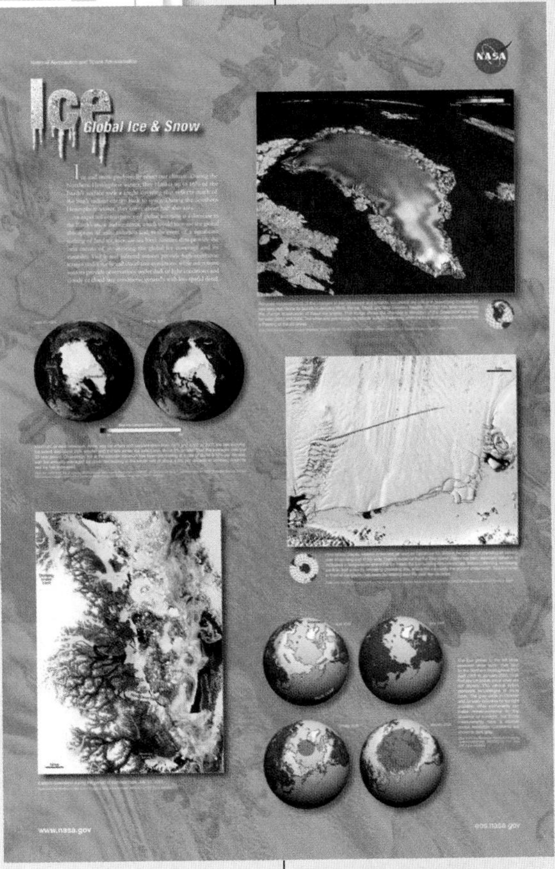

Setting Your Goals:

Rhetorical Knowledge

- **Audience:** Consider what your readers need to know—and how you can interest them in that information. What about your subject might your audience be *most* interested in? What information might readers consider unusual?
- **Purpose:** You want readers to understand the information you are sharing, so your writing must be clear. Considering what your audience might *do* with the information you provide will help you decide how best to provide the information to your readers.
- **Rhetorical situation:** In an informational essay, you are writing to share information; your readers are reading your text to learn about (and—you hope—to understand) that information.
- **Voice and tone:** Generally, informational writing has a neutral tone because you as the writer are trying, not to convince or explore, but rather to inform your readers. Of course, sometimes an informational essay can have a humorous tone.
- **Context, medium, and genre:** The genre you use to present your information is determined by your purpose: to inform. Decide on the best medium and genre to use to present your information to the audience you want to reach.

Critical Thinking, Reading, and Writing

- **Learning/inquiry:** Because you are helping your readers learn about the subject of your text, decide on the most important aspects of your topic and explain them in a clear, focused way.
- **Responsibility:** You have a responsibility to represent your information honestly and accurately.
- **Reading and research:** Your research must be accurate and as complete as possible, to allow you to present thoughtful, reliable information about your subject.

Writing to Inform

Chapter 6

Writing Processes

- **Invention:** Choose invention strategies that will help you generate and locate information about your topic.
- **Organizing your ideas and details:** Find the most effective way to present your information to your readers so they can easily understand it.
- **Revising:** Read your work with a critical eye, to make certain that it fulfills the assignment and displays the qualities of good informative writing.
- **Working with peers:** Your classmates will make suggestions that indicate the parts of your text they found difficult to understand so you can work to clarify.

Knowledge of Conventions

- **Editing:** Informative writing benefits from the correct use of modifiers, so the round-robin activity on page 172 focuses on avoiding misplaced or dangling modifiers.
- **Genres for informative writing:** Possible genres include newspaper or magazine articles, informative letters, informative essays, and Web documents.
- **Documentation:** If you have relied on sources outside of your experience, cite them using the appropriate documentation style.

mhconnectcomposition.com

Writing to Inform Tutorial QL6001

Rhetorical Knowledge

When you provide information to readers, you need to consider what your readers might already know about your topic, as well as what other information you have learned about through your research would be useful to them. You will also need to decide what medium and genre will help you communicate that information to your audience most effectively.

Writing to Inform in Your College Classes

Much of the writing you will do for your college classes will be informative, as will much of the reading you will do in your college textbooks. In your world history class, for example, you would expect your textbook to provide historically accurate information; the same is true for your biology book, your psychology text, and so on. The genre of a college textbook is, almost by definition, informative. The purpose of most of the reading you will do in college is to learn new information—and many writing assignments will require you to relate new facts and concepts to other facts and concepts you have already read and learned about, as in the following examples:

- Your psychology instructor may ask you to read several essays or books about recovered memory and to *synthesize* the information they contain—to explain to a reader the most important points made in each text and how the information in one text agrees or disagrees with the information in the others.
- Your art instructor may ask that you trace the development of a specific approach to art, providing examples and details that show its evolution over time.
- Your political science instructor may ask you to examine "presidential bloopers," where presidential candidates did or said something awkward—and explain in writing how those instances affected the next election.

The "Ways of Writing" feature presents different genres that can be used when writing to inform in your college classes.

Writing to Inform for Life

In addition to your academic work, you will also construct informative texts for the other areas of your life, including your professional career, your civic life, and your personal life.

Much of the writing done in professional settings is designed to inform and often to teach. Almost everyone who has had a job, for example, can relate to this situation. Consider what you know about this job, including everyday activities and interactions, the tools or equipment you use or used, and so on.

Now consider how you would explain the details of your job to someone who is going to take it over: What information would that person need to know to do your job effectively? How could you best relay that information to your replacement? What you have just considered are the details that make up a training manual, a type of informative writing that most businesses have in one form or another. On a more regular basis, health care workers such as nurses and lab technicians often write reports informing doctors of their findings.

Likewise, much civic writing is designed to provide information to residents, voters, neighbors, and other citizens to help them decide issues or take advantage of community resources and programs. Perhaps citizens are being encouraged to participate in a community program such as a citizen's watch campaign, a civic event that would almost certainly require informative writing.

You will also do a great deal of informative writing in your personal life, ranging from notes to family members to Facebook conversations with relatives and friends. While you may feel more comfortable jotting down information for your friends and family than you do for other audiences, you probably feel especially obligated to provide accurate and useful information because you care about your personal relationships.

The "Ways of Writing" feature presents different genres that can be used when writing to inform in life.

▶▶▶ Scenarios for Writing | Assignment Options

connect™
mhconnectcomposition.com
Writer's Workshop: Applying Learning Goals to Informative Writing QL6002

The following writing assignments call for you to construct informative texts. Each is in the form of a *scenario*, a brief story that provides some context for your writing. The scenario gives you a sense of who your audience is and what you need to accomplish. Starting on page 157, you will find guidelines for completing whatever assignment option you choose or that is assigned to you.

▶ Writing for College

SCENARIO 1 Informative Essay on Littering

Your sociology class has been focusing on student behavior. Just last week a classmate mentioned the problem of trash on campus: "Our campus is a big mess because students just don't care," she said. "They ignore the trash cans and recycling boxes and just toss their garbage everywhere!"

Although this scenario focuses on littering, if you prefer you may write about some other issue on your campus. Your task is not to propose a solution for the issue; rather, your task is to inform other members of the campus community that a problem exists.

Digital Literacy

Using a Camera When Making Observations

A digital camera or your cell phone camera can be an ideal tool for any assignment that asks you to make observations. Once you have transferred the photographs of your subject to your computer, it is easy to add them to your text. Be sure, though, to get written permission from anyone you photograph before using images of them in your work. If your instructor allows electronic submission of your work, you may wish to incorporate video and sound as well into your final project presentation.

Ways of Writing to Inform

Genres for Your College Classes	Sample Situation	Advantages of the Genre	Limitations of the Genre
Academic essay	Your sociology professor asks you to make observations about the group behavior of a campus organization (the volleyball team, the debating club, and so on.)	This project enables you to engage in primary research that you design; your readers can learn from your research findings.	It is difficult to be objective and present information in a neutral tone; you need to take lots of detailed notes to have sufficient research information.
Review of literature	Your economics teacher asks you to review the current literature on the causes of the Great Depression.	This project gives your reader a better understanding of the economies of the time period.	A limited number of texts can be examined, so your focus will be narrow. In many fields, the most current literature is seen as the most important.
Letter to your college newspaper	You want to write a letter to your school newspaper that informs students about an upcoming campus event sponsored by several student organizations.	Your letter will allow you to reach your intended audience and encourage them to attend.	There is limited space for your letter; you must provide all of the details so others will know what the event is, where it will be held, and when. It might not be published.
Profile	Your English professor asks you to make observations and construct a profile—a neutral description—about a place on your campus (the campus recreation center, for example).	You observe and take notes with lots of description, so your readers can "see" what the place looks like, who inhabits this place, what happens there, what the location is like, and so on.	The writer generally does not analyze why things happen in this place, so there is a limited understanding of why the place is as it is.
Narrated timeline	Your philosophy professor asks you to create a timeline of influential philosophers, showing when they lived and outlining their main ideas.	A timeline is a useful way to provide information, and is supplemented with text about the philosophers and their major ideas.	There is lots of ground to cover; it shouldn't be just a timeline showing when the philosophers lived. It will be difficult to describe complex thoughts and ideas and show relationships in limited space.
Genres for Life	**Sample Situation**	**Advantages of the Genre**	**Limitations of the Genre**
Brochure	You need to explain what a non-profit organization does, what services it provides, and so on.	A brochure can provide readers with a brief overview of the agency's mission and services.	There is limited space for presenting information about the agency's specific services.
Information-sharing blog	You would like to share information about candidates in a local election.	blog can be an easy way to update and share information with a wide audience.	Someone will need to monitor the comments or inappropriate posts. It should be updated often.
Fact sheet	You want to provide facts about a proposed tax increase for your neighbors, most of whom have children in the same school district as you.	A fact sheet allows you to objectively present the details so that your neighbors can make up their own minds.	It may be hard to remain neutral if you feel strongly one way or the other about the tax proposal.
Business comparison	The company you work for asks you to compare several locations for a possible expansion of the business.	By comparing and contrasting the details about each location, not advocating for one or the other, you let your readers make up their own minds.	With a vested interest in the decision, it is difficult to present information without making a recommendation.
Instructions	To help train new employees, you are asked to prepare a set of instructions for a specific task you do at work.	Step-by-step instructions will give enough detail for someone to understand and to complete the task.	It may be difficult to provide the right kind of detail—not too much and not too little.

Writing Assignment: Construct an informative paper, based on two sets of information: (1) your observations of the problem on campus, and (2) interviews you conduct with at least two of your classmates, asking them what their thoughts are on why some students don't use trash cans as they should, or on the alternate problem you have chosen to write about.

SCENARIO 2 A Review of Literature

This scenario asks you to examine and then construct a "review of literature"—basically, what others have said and written about a particular topic. In most of your college classes, it is critical to know what others have said about any topic you might want to write on, so that you will not have to "reinvent the wheel," so to speak. The only way to know what others have said is to read their work and see how it relates to other ideas on the same subject. And, of course, once you know what others have written about a topic, you can then add your own ideas and thoughts to the continuing discussion.

Writing Assignment: Select a topic that you would like to gather more information about, and construct an informative text that outlines what others have written about the topic. You will not be able to read everything, of course, so your teacher may outline how many items to read, what kind (such as essays, books, email lists, and blogs), and so on. Your text should outline the most important aspects of each item you are asked to read—essentially reviewing the literature for your readers, in a clear and accurate manner.

Writing for Life

SCENARIO 3 Civic Writing: Brochure for a Local Service Organization

Many colleges and universities, have a service-learning class or component of such a class. "Service-learning" opportunities include tutoring young children, helping with food banks, volunteering at rest homes, and other ways of serving the community in some manner. As the National Youth Leadership Council notes, service-learning can be conceptualized in this way:

> Picking up trash on a riverbank is *service.*
>
> Studying water samples under a microscope is *learning.*
>
> When science students collect and analyze water samples, document their results, and present findings to a local pollution control agency . . . that is *service-learning.* (www.nlc.org)

Writing Assignment: Select a local nonprofit service agency, and learn about services they provide to your community. Your research might include looking at the Web page for the agency, interviewing people who work there, examining any literature they provide, and volunteering with the agency (probably the best way to learn about it). Then construct a brochure for the agency that outlines the work it performs for the community. Think of this brochure as

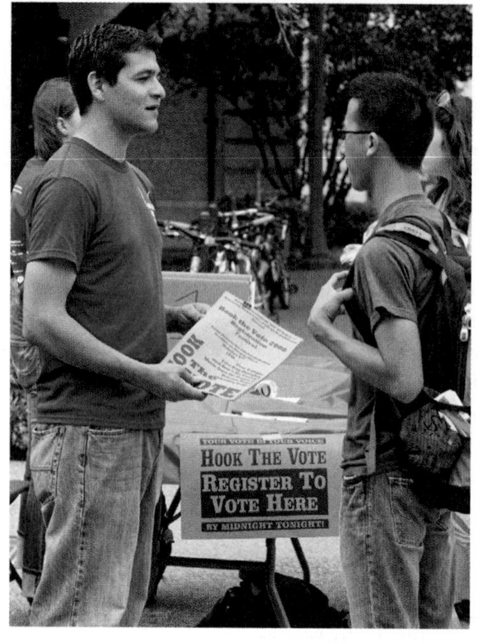

one the agency would actually provide and use. In other words, construct a brochure as if you actually worked for the agency and were asked to develop such a handout. (For more information on constructing a brochure, see "Visualizing Variations: Using a Web Site, Poster, or Brochure to Inform Your Readers," page 167.)

As with any writing assignment, consider who your audience might be and what they might already know about the agency. What else would you like them to know? What kind(s) of information would be useful to your audience? Are there photos or tables that might show what the agency does, how it spends any donations it receives, or something about the people who work there and the people the agency serves?

Rhetorical Considerations in Informative Writing

connect
mhconnectcomposition.com
Additional Scenarios QL6003

- **Audience:** Who is your primary audience? Who else might be interested in your subject? Why?
- **Purpose:** As noted in Chapter 3, writing can be a powerful tool for learning, so use the information you collect and write about as a way to increase your knowledge of your subject, as well as the knowledge of your readers. Bear in mind as you write that your purpose is not to convince readers to agree with an opinion you hold about your subject, but rather to inform them about it in neutral terms.
- **Voice, tone, and point of view:** If you have a limited knowledge of your topic, your stance, or attitude, will be that of an interested investigator, and your tone will usually be neutral. If you are writing about a topic that you know well, take care to keep any biases out of your writing. If you are writing about a problem, present all opinions about the problem fairly, including those you disagree with. Your point of view will usually be third person.
- **Context, medium, and genre:** Keeping the context of the assignment in mind, decide on a medium and genre for your writing. How will your writing be used? If you are writing for an audience beyond the classroom, consider what will be the most effective way to present your information to this audience.

For more on choosing a medium and genre, see Chapter 17 and the Online Appendix.

Critical Thinking, Reading, and Writing

Before you begin to write your informative paper, read examples of informative writing. You might also consider how visuals can inform readers, as well as the kinds of sources you will need to consult.

Writing to provide information has several qualities—a strong focus; relevant, useful information that is provided in an efficient manner; and clear, accurate explanations that enable readers to understand the information easily. The reading selections and the visual text that appear in the next sections will stimulate your inquiry and writing. Finally, informative writing almost always requires that you go beyond your current knowledge of a topic and conduct careful research.

Learning the Qualities of Effective Informative Writing

As you think about how you might compose an informative paper, consider what readers expect and need from an informative text. As a reader, you probably look for the following qualities in informative writing:

- **A focused subject.** In *The Elements of Style*, his classic book of advice to writers, author and humorist E. B. White suggests, "When you say something, make sure you have said it. The chances of your having said it are only fair." White's comment is especially applicable to informative writing. The best way to "make sure you have said" what you want to say is to have a clear focus. What information about your subject is the most important? If you could boil down your information into one sentence, what would it be? Condensing the important aspects of your information into a single sentence forces you to craft a thesis statement, which in turn helps you connect all your details and examples back to that main point.

For more on thesis statements, see Chapter 13.

- **Useful and relevant information.** People often read to gain information: They want to check on how their favorite sports team is doing, to find the best way to travel from one place to another, or to learn why high blood pressure is a health concern. How can you present your information so that readers understand what they might *do* with it and how it relates to their lives? Perhaps there is an unusual or a humorous angle on your subject that you can write about. And if you *synthesize* the information you have—explain the most important points made in each source you have consulted and how the information in one source agrees or disagrees with that in the other sources you have read—you will provide readers with a more thorough understanding of your subject.

For more on using examples and comparison and contrast, see Chapter 13. For more on conducting research and taking notes, see Chapters 19 and 20.

- **Clear explanations and accurate information.** Information needs to be presented clearly and accurately so it is understandable to readers who do not have background knowledge about your subject. Consider your information as if you knew nothing about the subject. Examples are almost always a useful way to help explain ideas and define terms. *Comparison and contrast* can be useful when you need to explain an unfamiliar subject—tell the reader what a subject is like and what it is not like. One strategy that will help you write clear, accurate papers is to take careful notes when you conduct research.

- **Efficiency.** Information should usually be presented concisely. To help readers grasp the information, you might want to provide them with a "road map," an outline of what you have in mind, at the beginning of the paper so they will know what to expect. Another way to present data efficiently is to "chunk" your writing—put it into sections, each dealing with a different aspect of the subject, making it easier for readers to understand. As you plan your paper, you should also consider whether it would be helpful to present your information in a table, graph, chart, or map. Consider how the title of your informative text not only will help your reader understand your focus but also will help to draw readers in, motivating them to read your paper.

For more on the use of visuals to enhance your explanations, see Chapter 18.

In an electronic form that you can copy and paste, you might jot down the main ideas from the qualities of effective informative writing above. Later, you can paste them into your working draft to remind you of the qualities that make an effective informative text.

Reading, Inquiry, and Research: Learning from Texts That Inform

The following reading selections are examples of informative writing. As you read, consider these questions:

- What makes this reading selection useful and interesting? What strategies does its author use to make the information understandable for readers?
- What parts of the reading could be improved by the use of charts, photographs, or tables? Why? How?
- How can you use the techniques of informative writing exemplified here in your writing?

CAROL EZZELL

Clocking Cultures

ARTICLE

Carol Ezzell has been a science writer since the early 1990s and currently works as a writer and an editor at *Scientific American*, specializing in biology and biomedicine. She has also worked for *Nature, Science News, BiolWorld,* and the *Journal of NIH Research.* An award-winning writer, Ezzell has been recognized for her science journalism by the National Association of Science Writers and the Pan American Health Organization. In 2000, she won a Science in Society Journalism award for her article "Care for a Dying Continent," about how AIDS has affected women and girls in Zimbabwe. This article was originally published in the September 2002 issue of *Scientific American.* We find that our students enjoy and learn from Ezzell's essay, and are sometimes surprised by the information it contains.

1 Show up an hour late in Brazil, and no one bats an eyelash. But keep someone in New York City waiting for five or 10 minutes, and you have some explaining to do. Time is elastic in many cultures but snaps taut in others. Indeed, the way members of a culture perceive and use time reflects their society's priorities and even their own worldview.

2 Social scientists have recorded wide differences in the pace of life in various countries and in how societies view time—whether as an arrow piercing the future or as a revolving wheel in which past, present and future cycle endlessly. Some cultures conflate time and space: the Australian Aborigines' concept of the "Dreamtime" encompasses not only a creation myth but a method of finding their way around the countryside. Interestingly, however, some views of time—such as the idea that it is acceptable for a more powerful person to keep someone of lower status waiting—cut across cultural differences and seem to be found universally.

3 The study of time and society can be divided into the pragmatic and the cosmological. On the practical side, in the 1950s anthropologist Edward T. Hall, Jr., wrote that the rules of social time constitute a "silent language" for a given culture. The rules might not always be made explicit, he stated, but they "exist in the air. . . . They are either familiar and comfortable or unfamiliar and wrong."

4 In 1955 he described in *Scientific American* how differing perceptions of time can lead to misunderstandings between people from separate cultures. "An ambassador who has been kept waiting for more than half an hour by a foreign visitor needs to understand that if his visitor 'just mutters an apology' this is not necessarily an insult," Hall wrote. The time system in the foreign country may be composed of different basic units, so that the visitor is not as late as he may appear to us. You must know the time system of the country to know at what point apologies are really due. . . . Different cultures simply place different values on the time units.

Most cultures around the world now have watches and calendars, 5
uniting the majority of the globe in the same general rhythm of time. But that doesn't mean we all march to the same beat. "One of the beauties of studying time is that it's a wonderful window on culture," says Robert V. Levine, a social psychologist at California State University at Fresno. "You get answers on what cultures value and believe in. You get a really good idea of what's important to people." Levine and his colleagues have conducted so-called pace-of-life studies in 31 countries. In *A Geography of Time*, published in 1997, Levine describes how he ranked the countries by using three measures: walking speed on urban sidewalks, how quickly postal clerks could fulfill a request for a common stamp, and the accuracy of public clocks. Based on these variables, he concluded that the five fastest-paced countries are Switzerland, Ireland, Germany, Japan and Italy; the five slowest are Syria, El Salvador, Brazil, Indonesia and Mexico. The U.S., at 16th, ranks near the middle. Kevin K. Birth, an anthropologist at Queens College, has examined time perceptions in Trinidad. Birth's 1999 book, *Any Time Is Trinidad Time: Social Meanings and Temporal Consciousness*, refers to a commonly used phrase to excuse lateness. In that country, Birth observes, "if you have a meeting at 6:00 at night, people show up at 6:45 or 7:00 and say, 'Any time is Trinidad time.'" When it comes to business, however, that loose approach to timeliness works only for the people with power. A boss can show up late and toss off "any time is Trinidad time," but underlings are expected to be more punctual. For them, the saying goes, "time is time." Birth adds that the tie between power and waiting time is true for many other cultures as well.

The nebulous nature of time makes it hard for anthropologists and 6
social psychologists to study. "You can't simply go into a society, walk up to some poor soul and say, 'Tell me about your notions of time,'" Birth says. "People don't really have an answer to that. You have to come up with other ways to find out."

Birth attempted to get at how Trinidadians value time by exploring 7
how closely their society links time and money. He surveyed rural residents and found that farmers—whose days are dictated by natural events, such as sunrise—did not recognize the phrases "time is money," "budget your time" or "time management," even though they had satellite TV and were familiar with Western popular culture. But tailors in the same areas were aware of such notions. Birth concluded that wage work altered the tailors' views of time. "The ideas of associating time with money are not found globally," he says, "but are attached to your job and the people you work with."

How people deal with time on a day-to-day basis often has nothing to 8
do with how they conceive of time as an abstract entity. "There's often a disjunction between how a culture views the mythology of time and how

they think about time in their daily lives," Birth asserts. "We don't think of Stephen Hawking's theories as we go about our daily lives."

Some cultures do not draw neat distinctions between the past, present 9
and future. Australian Aborigines, for instance, believe that their ancestors crawled out of the earth during the Dreamtime. The ancestors "sang" the world into existence as they moved about naming each feature and living thing, which brought them into being. Even today, an entity does not exist unless an Aborigine "sings" it.

Ziauddin Sardar, a British Muslim author and critic, has written about 10
time and Islamic cultures, particularly the fundamentalist sect Wahhabism. Muslims "always carry the past with them," claims Sardar, who is editor of the journal *Futures* and visiting professor of postcolonial studies at City University, London. "In Islam, time is a tapestry incorporating the past, present and future. The past is ever present." The followers of Wahhabism, which is practiced in Saudi Arabia and by Osama bin Laden, seek to re-create the idyllic days of the prophet Muhammad's life. "The worldly future dimension has been suppressed" by them, Sardar says. "They have romanticized a particular vision of the past. All they are doing is trying to replicate that past."

Sardar asserts that the West has "colonized" time by spreading the 11
expectation that life should become better as time passes: "If you colonize time, you also colonize the future. If you think of time as an arrow, of course you think of the future as progress, going in one direction. But different people may desire different futures."

QUESTIONS FOR WRITING AND DISCUSSION: LEARNING OUTCOMES

Rhetorical Knowledge: The Writer's Situation and Rhetoric

1. **Audience:** Who is the audience for Ezzell's essay? How can you tell?
2. **Purpose:** What realm (academic, professional, civic, or personal) does Ezzell's essay best fit into? Why?
3. **Voice and tone:** How would you describe Ezzell's tone in this essay? How does her tone contribute to her believability?
4. **Responsibility:** Ezzell discusses the notions of time across different cultures in her essay. How respectful of those cultures is she? Why do you think that?
5. **Context, format, and genre:** This essay was published during a time of worldwide fear of terrorism. How does that context affect your reading of this essay? The essay genre was developed to allow writers to discover other ways of seeing the world. How does Ezzell's essay display this feature of the genre?

Critical Thinking: The Writer's Ideas and Your Personal Response

6. What is the most interesting piece of information in Ezzell's article? Why? The least interesting? Why?
7. What is the main idea—or thesis—in Ezzell's essay? How well does Ezzell provide support for this idea? Why do you think that?

Composing Processes and Knowledge of Conventions: The Writer's Strategies

8. Ezzell uses information and quotations from experts throughout her essay. How does she present this information? What does the presence of these experts add to the essay?
9. Prepare a quick outline of this essay. What does this outline reveal about the way Ezzell has organized her information for readers?

Inquiry and Research: Ideas for Further Exploration

10. Prepare a list of questions that you still have about time and cultures. Interview several of your friends, asking them the questions that you have listed, and then explain, in no more than two pages, their answers to your questions.

KATIE HAFNER

Growing *Wikipedia* Revises Its "Anyone Can Edit" Policy

ARTICLE

1 *Wikipedia* is the online encyclopedia that "anyone can edit." Unless you want to edit the entries on Albert Einstein, human rights in China or Christina Aguilera.

2 *Wikipedia*'s come-one, come-all invitation to write and edit articles, and the surprisingly successful results, have captured the public imagination. But it is not the experiment in freewheeling collective creativity it might seem to be, because maintaining so much openness inevitably involves some tradeoffs.

3 At its core, *Wikipedia* is not just a reference work but also an online community that has built itself a bureaucracy of sorts—one that, in response to well-publicized problems with some entries, has recently grown more elaborate. It has a clear power structure that gives volunteer administrators the authority to exercise editorial control, delete unsuitable articles and protect those that are vulnerable to vandalism.

4 Those measures can put some entries outside of the "anyone can edit" realm. The list changes rapidly, but as of yesterday, the entries for Einstein and Ms. Aguilera were among 82 that administrators had "protected" from all editing, mostly because of repeated vandalism or disputes over what should be said. Another 179 entries—including those for George W. Bush, Islam and Adolf Hitler—were "semi-protected," open to editing only by people who had been registered at the site for at least four days. . . .

5 While these measures may appear to undermine the site's democratic principles, Jimmy Wales, *Wikipedia*'s founder, notes that protection is usually temporary and affects a tiny fraction of the 1.2 million entries on the English-language site.

"Protection is a tool for quality control, but it hardly defines *Wikipedia*," Mr. Wales said. "What does define *Wikipedia* is the volunteer community and the open participation." 6

From the start, Mr. Wales gave the site a clear mission: to offer free knowledge to everybody on the planet. At the same time, he put in place 7

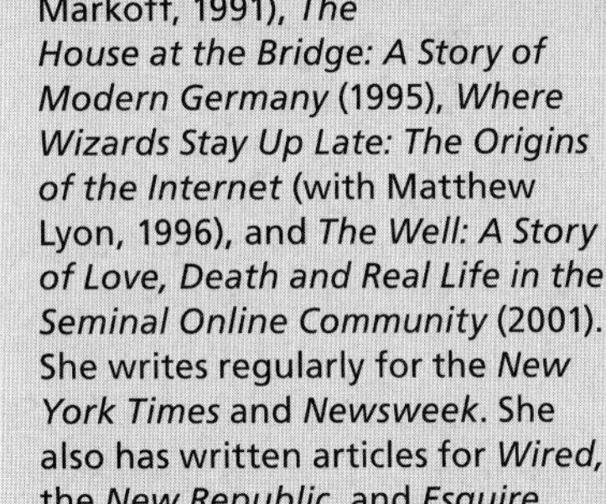

Katie Hafner has written widely about technology. Her books include *Cyberpunk: Outlaws and Hackers on the Computer Frontier* (with John Markoff, 1991), *The House at the Bridge: A Story of Modern Germany* (1995), *Where Wizards Stay Up Late: The Origins of the Internet* (with Matthew Lyon, 1996), and *The Well: A Story of Love, Death and Real Life in the Seminal Online Community* (2001). She writes regularly for the *New York Times* and *Newsweek*. She also has written articles for *Wired*, the *New Republic*, and *Esquire*. As a student, she studied German literature and culture. This article, published in the *New York Times* in 2006, concerns *Wikipedia*, the well-known online encyclopedia. As you read Hafner's article, think about your experience with conducting research—and how you decide what is correct and accurate information and what is not. Many of our students look at Wikipedia entries as starting points when they conduct research, but they often find that the information is very limited.

a set of rules and policies that he continues to promote, like the need to present information with a neutral point of view.

The system seems to be working. *Wikipedia* is now the Web's third-most-popular news and information source, beating the sites of CNN and Yahoo News, according to Nielsen *NetRatings*. 8

The bulk of the writing and editing on *Wikipedia* is done by a geographically diffuse group of 1,000 or so regulars, many of whom are administrators on the site. 9

"A lot of people think of *Wikipedia* as being 10 million people, each adding one sentence," Mr. Wales said. "But really the vast majority of work is done by this small core community." 10

The administrators are all volunteers, most of them in their 20's. They are in constant communication—in real-time online chats, on "talk" pages connected to each entry and via Internet mailing lists. The volunteers share the job of watching for vandalism, or what Mr. Wales called "drive-by nonsense." Customized software—written by volunteers—also monitors changes to articles. 11

Mr. Wales calls vandalism to the encyclopedia "a minimal problem, a dull roar in the background." Yet early this year, amid heightened publicity about false information on the site, the community decided to introduce semi-protection of some articles. The four-day waiting period is meant to function something like the one imposed on gun buyers. 12

Once the assaults have died down, the semi-protected page is often reset to "anyone can edit" mode. An entry on Bill Gates was semi-protected for just a few days in January, but some entries, like the article on President Bush, stay that way indefinitely. Other semi-protected subjects as of yesterday were Opus Dei, Tony Blair and sex. 13

To some critics, protection policies make a mockery of the "anyone can edit" notion. 14

"As *Wikipedia* has tried to improve its quality, it's beginning to look more and more like an editorial structure," said Nicholas Carr, a technology writer who recently criticized *Wikipedia* on his blog. "To say that great work can be created by an army of amateurs with very little control is a distortion of what *Wikipedia* really is." 15

But Mr. Wales dismissed such criticism, saying there had always been protections and filters on the site. 16

Wikipedia's defenders say it usually takes just a few days for all but the most determined vandals to retreat. 17

"A cooling-off period is a wonderful mediative technique," said Ross Mayfield, chief executive of a company called Socialtext that is based on the same editing technology that *Wikipedia* uses. 18

Full protection often results from a "revert war," in which users madly change the wording back and forth. In such cases, an administrator usu- 19 ally steps in and freezes the page until the warring parties can settle their differences in another venue, usually the talk page for the entry. The Christina Aguilera entry was frozen this week after fans of the singer fought back against one user's efforts to streamline it.

Much discussion of *Wikipedia* has focused on its accuracy. Last year, an article in the journal *Nature* concluded that the incidence of errors in *Wikipedia* was only slightly higher than in *Encyclopaedia Britannica*. Officials at *Britannica* angrily disputed the findings. 20

"To be able to do an encyclopedia without having the ability to differentiate between experts and the general public is very, very difficult," said Jorge Cauz, the president of *Britannica*, whose subscription-based online version receives a small fraction of the traffic that *Wikipedia* gets. 21

Intentional mischief can go undetected for long periods. In the article about John Seigenthaler Sr., who served in the Kennedy administration, a suggestion that he was involved in the assassinations of both John F. and Robert Kennedy was on the site for more than four months before Mr. Seigenthaler discovered it. He wrote an op-ed article in *USA Today* about the incident, calling *Wikipedia* "a flawed and irresponsible research tool." 22

Yet Wikipedians say that in general the accuracy of an article grows organically. At first, said Wayne Saewyc, a *Wikipedia* volunteer in Vancouver, British Columbia, "everything is edited mercilessly by idiots who do stupid and weird things to it." But as the article grows, and citations slowly accumulate, Mr. Saewyc said, the article becomes increasingly accurate. 23

Wikipedians often speak of how powerfully liberating their first contribution felt. Kathleen Walsh, 23, a recent college graduate who majored in music, recalled the first time she added to an article on the contrabassoon. 24

"I wrote a paragraph of text and there it was," recalled Ms. Walsh. "You write all these pages for college and no one ever sees it, and you write for *Wikipedia* and the whole world sees it, instantly." 25

Ms. Walsh is an administrator, a post that others nominated her for in recognition of her contributions to the site. She monitors a list of newly created pages, half of which, she said, end up being good candidates for deletion. Many are "nonsense pages created by kids, like 'Michael is a big dork,'" she said. 26

Ms. Walsh also serves on the 14-member arbitration committee, which she describes as "the last resort" for disputes on *Wikipedia*. 27

Like so many Web-based successes, *Wikipedia* started more or less by accident. 28

Six years ago, Mr. Wales, who built up a comfortable nest egg in a brief career as an options trader, started an online encyclopedia called Nupedia.com, with content to be written by experts. But after attracting only a few dozen articles, Mr. Wales started *Wikipedia* on the side. It grew exponentially. 29

For the first year or so, Mr. Wales paid the expenses out of his own 30
pocket. Now the Wikimedia Foundation, the nonprofit organization that supports *Wikipedia*, is financed primarily through donations, most in the $50 to $100 range.

As the donations have risen, so have the costs. The foundation's an- 31
nual budget doubled in the last year, to $1.5 million, and traffic has grown sharply. Search engines like Google, which often turn up *Wikipedia* entries at the top of their results, are a big contributor to the site's traffic, but it is increasingly a first stop for knowledge seekers.

Mr. Wales shares the work of running *Wikipedia* with the administra- 32
tors and four paid employees of the foundation. Although many decisions are made by consensus within the community, Mr. Wales steps in when an issue is especially contentious. "It's not always obvious when something becomes policy," he said. "One way is when I say it is."

Mr. Wales is a true believer in the power of wiki page-editing tech- 33
nology, which predates *Wikipedia*. In late 2004, Mr. Wales started Wikia, a commercial start-up financed by venture capital that lets people build Web sites based around a community of interest. Wiki 24, for instance, is an unofficial encyclopedia for the television show "24." Unlike *Wikipedia*, the site carries advertising.

Mr. Wales, 39, lives with his wife and daughter in St. Petersburg, Fla., 34
where the foundation is based. But Mr. Wales's main habitat these days, he said, is the inside of airplanes. He travels constantly, giving speeches to reverential audiences and visiting Wikipedians around the world.

Wikipedia has inspired its share of imitators. A group of scientists has 35
started the peer-reviewed *Encyclopedia of Earth*, and *Congresspedia* is a new encyclopedia with an article about each member of Congress.

But beyond the world of reference works, *Wikipedia* has become a sym- 36
bol of the potential of the Web.

"It can tell us a lot about the future of knowledge creation, which will 37
depend much less on individual heroism and more on collaboration," said Mitchell Kapor, a computer industry pioneer who is president of the Open Source Applications Foundation.

Zephyr Teachout, a lawyer in Burlington, Vt., who is involved with 38
Congresspedia, said *Wikipedia* was reminiscent of old-fashioned civic groups like the Grange, whose members took individual responsibility for the organization's livelihood.

"It blows open what's possible," said Ms. Teachout. "What I hope is that 39
these kinds of things lead to thousands of other experiments like this encyclopedia, which we never imagined could be produced in this way."

QUESTIONS FOR WRITING AND DISCUSSION: LEARNING OUTCOMES

Rhetorical Knowledge: The Writer's Situation and Rhetoric

1. **Audience:** How would you describe the audience that Hafner had in mind when she wrote this article?
2. **Purpose:** What purpose(s) would someone have for reading Hafner's article? In addition to its informative purpose, how is Hafner's writing also persuasive? How might it alter readers' perceptions of *Wikipedia*?
3. **Voice and tone:** How does Hafner establish her authority? To what extent do you believe what Hafner has to say? How does her tone contribute to her credibility? Why?
4. **Responsibility:** One important quality of any successful informative text is *clarity*, especially when the author is dealing with a complex subject. How does Hafner meet her obligation to her readers to be clear? Where might she have been clearer?
5. **Context, format, and genre:** Given Hafner's topic, it seems natural that her piece appeared in an online format, with hyperlinks, but it also appeared in the print edition of the *New York Times*. How does appearing in both print and online formats affect the credibility of Hafner's comments? Why? How does Hafner incorporate multiple perspectives in her essay?

Critical Thinking: The Writer's Ideas and Your Personal Response

6. What in Hafner's text do you want to learn more about? What questions do you still have?
7. Hafner addresses the delicate balance between the importance of accuracy and the advantages of openness—that anyone can contribute to *Wikipedia*. If you were an editor of *Wikipedia*, how would you maintain that balance?

Composing Processes and Knowledge of Conventions: The Writer's Strategies

8. Hafner covers a good deal of ground in this reading selection, yet she has a central idea. What is her central idea, or focus? How does she maintain it?
9. Because she is a journalist writing for a newspaper, Hafner cites her sources within the body of her article rather than using a formal system of documentation. How do her sources lend credibility to her writing? What other sources of information might she have cited?

Inquiry and Research: Ideas for Further Exploration

10. Research a concept or issue on the Web. Make a list of the information you collect that seems contradictory. How might you reconcile those inconsistencies, to figure out what *is* accurate?

GENRES *Up Close* Writing an Annotated Bibliography and a Review of Literature

As illustrated in "Ways of Writing to Inform" (page 138), information can be shared through many genres. Annotated bibliographies and reviews of literature are two such genres.

Annotated bibliographies and reviews of literature are two forms of research that describe what is already known about a topic. These two genres accomplish the same purpose, but in different levels of detail.

You may be asked to develop an annotated bibliography as part of a research paper or even as the first step in writing a research paper. Becoming proficient at writing annotated bibliographies will prepare you for writing reviews of literature, which require more detailed analysis and information.

An **annotated bibliography** provides the citation of a work and a brief summary or synopsis. A **review of literature**, or literature review, is a standard section in a scholarly research report that familiarizes readers with previous research related to the current study by summarizing findings. It provides the background and context for the paper, assuring readers that the current study is a logical next step in a line of research, that the current study is needed, and that the current study draws on the best practices used in previous research studies. You may be asked to write a review of literature in preparation for a research project. Further, as your research papers become more complex, they will often include a section devoted to this overview.

When constructing an annotated bibliography, a writer should:

- List the appropriate citation information.
- Briefly summarize the cited work.

Here is a typical annotated bibliography entry by student writer Larissa Venard:

> Holling, C. S., Meffe, Gary K. "Command and Control and the Pathology." *Conservation Biology* 10 (1996): 1–10.
>
> Describes solutions to natural resource management and suggests that rationing is not one of them. The authors believe that rationing can cause distress to both society and the economy as it decreases the need for and use of a resource, eliminating jobs. The solution proposed is a "golden rule" that is comprised of many different solutions to each natural resource, such as marking up the price on natural goods to match their value in the economy and society. Other suggestions that they propose are to eliminate fire relief from forestry areas that are prone to fire and instead designate them as wilderness and not allow people to build houses near them.

In writing a review of literature, a writer does much more. In addition to listing the citation, writers:

- **Describe the contributions of previous research.** As you describe these contributions, you should maintain a relatively tight focus. First, focus on those studies that will most inform the research that you may choose to do after completing your review of literature. Second, rather than summarizing everything in a selected research study, focus on those parts that will inform your own proposed research study. For example, if you want to study the history of injuries in high school football in your home state, you may opt to review similar studies in states that are like your state. Note that you will go into more depth and detail than you would in an annotated bibliography, which includes only a brief summary.

- **Critically analyze and evaluate previous studies.** As you consider previous studies, analyze and evaluate features that relate to your study because studies can vary in how well they follow standard methodology for gathering, coding, and analyzing data. For example, a study may include data on football injuries but not include more fine-grained information about the types and severity of injuries.
- **Explain how previous studies help readers understand the topic.** As you review existing research studies, explain to readers how those studies can be used to gain a particular understanding of your topic. That is, respond to this question: Individually and collectively, what do these studies tell us?
- **Describe relationships among previous studies.** Typically, research studies build on the results of previous studies. For example, one study might look at hand injuries in high school football. After that, researchers might build on that work by conducting more fine-grained research studies. So, a follow-up study might make distinctions between metacarpal bones and phalanges. If you were to review those two studies, you should note that the second one was informed by the previous study.
- **Explain and possibly reconcile conflicting results found in previous studies.** For example, if some studies indicate that leg fractures are the most serious football injuries in high school and other studies say that arm fractures are the most serious, how can you explain and reconcile those differences?

In the opening paragraphs of a review of literature, the writer typically outlines the topic area for the review and notes general trends in existing research on the topic. In the middle paragraphs of the review, the writer groups studies that are similar and then summarizes, analyzes, and evaluates individual studies and groups of studies. In the closing paragraphs of the review, the writer summarizes the major contributions of the previous studies; shows gaps, defects, contradictions, and discrepancies in the existing body of research; and suggests a need for the current study.

One common convention of reviews of literature is the use of specific cohesive devices (see Chapter 13, pages 681–684, "Using Strategies That Guide Readers") to show relationships between or among ideas in adjacent sentences. In the review of literature that follows, note the three cohesive devices we highlighted in the second paragraph. Consider how cohesive devices function to make connections between adjacent sentences and what would be the effect of deleting any of them. As you read the following review of literature, consider ways in which it displays the features of the genre. Note that the authors briefly review scholarship in areas related to their research, including the effects of layoffs on surviving employees, including workforce restructuring, employee cynicism following a layoff, post layoff job insecurity, and work effort, and point to common themes across these research streams. Because the full review of literature is too long to include here, we excerpt one section of the review—the authors' discussion of prior findings of research on workforce restructuring.

REVIEW OF LITERATURE

Pamela Brandes is associate professor of management in the Whitman School of Management at Syracuse University. Her research focuses on employee attitudes, corporate governance, and executive compensation. Her papers have appeared in prestigious journals such as *Organization Science, Academy of Management Review, Strategic Management Journal, Academy of Management Perspectives, Journal of Business Research, Group and Organization Management,* and *Human Resource Management Review.*

The Interactive Effects of Job Insecurity and Organizational Cynicism on Work Effort Following a Layoff

PAMELA BRANDES
Syracuse University
STEPHANIE L. CASTRO
Florida Atlantic University
MATRECIA S. L. JAMES
Jacksonville University
ARTHUR D. MARTINEZ
TIMOTHY A. MATHERLY
GERALD R. FERRIS
WAYNE A. HOCHWARTER
Florida State University

Workforce Restructuring

Describes the contributions of previous research.

1 Layoffs have become an endemic component of virtually all work contexts. Survivor reactions, which range from anger to relief (Mishra & Spreitzer, 1998; Robbins, 1999), are often associated with the observed layoff *process* (McKinley, Mone, & Barker, 1998; Edwards, Rust, McKinley, & Moon, 2003; Rust et al., 2005), most notably in the form of perceived fairness (Brockner, Tyler, & Cooper-Schneider, 1992; Brockner, Wiesenfeld, Reed, Grover, & Martin, 1993). For example, research has shown post-layoff fairness perceptions to be favorably associated with outcomes such as commitment, trust, satisfaction, and turnover intent (Brockner et al., 1997; Davy, Kinicki, & Scheck, 1997; Kernan & Hanges, 2002). Conversely, when downsizing activities are viewed as unjust or management fails to keep employees informed throughout the process, the integrity of the company is questioned (Paterson & Cary, 2002). These environments serve as breeding grounds for distrust that often continues well beyond the time of the restructuring (Mishra & Spreitzer, 1998).

In contrast to the counsel of 2
Brockner, Dewitt, Grover, and Reed (1990), and Wanberg, Bunce, and Gavin (1999), who suggested that managers display caring attitudes and provide explanations for lay-

offs, some restructurings have been done in ways that violate common decency (Folger & Skarlicki, 1998). In addition to incivility connected with the downsizing, employees are increasingly angered by how both organizations and senior executives are "rewarded" by layoffs. Kashefi and McKee (2002) found that layoff announcements were met with abnormally positive returns. For example, firms that combined downsizing with asset restructuring often demonstrate better stock outcomes and increased return on investment (Cascio, Young, & Morris, 1997) than those that do not. Finally, it was reported that executives at General Dynamics garnered bonuses equivalent to twice their yearly salary following an announced workforce reduction of over 12,000 workers (Robbins, 1999). According to Mirvis (1991, p. 2), "It has now reached the point where cynicism is chic and loyalty to the company is for saps and suckers."

3 Increasing numbers of restructurings, coupled with a lack of consideration, and excessive executive compensation following the layoff, have made organizations ideal contexts for studying post-layoff cynicism (Hochwarter, James, Johnson, & Ferris 2004). In fact, some scholars have gone so far as to suggest that management actions of the last 15 years have created a "legacy of cynicism and resistance following changes which have been driven or forced as inevitable or fashionable, and which have increased working pressures and stress without clear benefits" (Buchanan, Claydon, & Doyle, 1999, p. 20). Moreover, it appears that the legacy of layoffs will trickle down to the newest entrants into the workforce. Barling, Dupre, and Hepburn (1998) reported that parental job insecurity perceptions affected children's subsequent work beliefs, including the level of alienation and cynicism brought to the job. In short, the new generation of workers fosters cynical attitudes towards their employer even prior to starting their careers.

The use of cohesive devices, such as the ones marked here, is a common convention of reviews of literature. What is the purpose of these cohesive devices?

QUESTIONS FOR WRITING AND DISCUSSION: LEARNING OUTCOMES

Rhetorical Knowledge: The Writers' Situation and Rhetoric

1. **Audience:** Who is the primary audience for this review of literature? What have the authors done to make the review accessible to a wider audience?
2. **Purpose:** What are the authors trying to accomplish in this excerpt from their review of literature? How successful are they? What is the basis for your judgment?
3. **Voice and tone:** How have the authors established their credibility in this excerpt from their review of literature?
4. **Responsibility:** What evidence do you have that the authors have accurately surveyed previous studies?
5. **Context, Format, and Genre:** This excerpt is from an article that appears in *Journal of Leadership & Organizational Studies.* How does this context affect the format of the review of literature? Which features of a review of literature can you find in this excerpt?

Critical Thinking: The Writers' Ideas and Your Personal Response

6. Given what you know about corporate culture, to what extent to you agree with Mirvis, to whom the authors attribute this quotation: "It has now reached the point where cynicism is chic and loyalty to the company is for saps and suckers"? Why do you think that?
7. The authors note that "Barling, Dupre, and Hepburn (1998) reported that parental job insecurity perceptions affected children's subsequent work beliefs, including the level of alienation and cynicism brought to the job." Without revealing too much personal information about your family, discuss with peers the ways in which your parents' job perceptions have affected your beliefs about work.

Composing Processes and Knowledge of Conventions: The Writers' Strategies

8. Consult Chapter 20, "Synthesizing and Documenting Sources," to determine which style guide—MLA or APA—the authors are using. What evidence supports your conclusion?
9. At the end of the second paragraph, the authors quote a scholar named Mirvis. Using the guidelines for quoting, paraphrasing, and summarizing (see pages 562–566 in Chapter 20, "Synthesizing and Documenting Sources"), explain why the authors may have chosen to quote Mirvis, rather than paraphrasing or summarizing what Mirvis said.

Inquiry and Research: Ideas for Further Exploration

10. Do a Web search using the phrase "workforce restructuring" and the names of some of the authors cited in the review. How do the search results relate to the content of the review of literature?

Writing Processes

As you work on the assignment scenario you have chosen, keep in mind the qualities of an effective informative paper (see pages 141–142). Also remember that writing is more a recursive than a linear process. So while the activities listed below imply that writers go through them step-by-step, the actual process of writing is usually less straightforward. You will keep coming back to your earlier work, adding to it and modifying the information to be more accurate as you conduct more research and become more familiar with your topic.

As you work on your project, make certain that you save your computer files frequently, because any work that you do not save could be lost. Also, savvy writers back up their computer files in two or more places—on the hard drive of the computer, on a USB flash drive, and/or on a rewritable CD or DVD.

Invention: Getting Started

Use invention activities to explore the information that you want to include in your first draft. It is useful to keep a journal as you work on any writing project, for your journal is a place where you can record not just what you learn but also the questions that arise during your writing and research activities.

For more on using journals, see Chapters 2 and 3.

Try to answer these questions while you do your invention work:

- What do I already know about the topic that I am writing about?
- What feelings or attitudes do I have about this topic? How can I keep them out of my text so that my writing is as free of bias as possible?
- What questions can I ask about the topic?
- Where might I learn more about this subject (in the library, on the Web)? What verifiable information on my topic is available?
- Who would know about my topic? What questions might I ask that person in an interview?
- What do I know about my audience? What don't I know that I should know? Why might they be interested in reading my text?
- What might my audience already know about my subject? Why might they care about it?
- To what extent will sensory details—color, shape, smell, taste, and so on—help my reader understand my topic? Why?
- What visual aids might I use to better inform my readers?

For more on descriptive writing, see Chapter 13.

Doing your invention work in electronic form, rather than on paper, lets you easily use this early writing as you construct a draft.

As with any kind of writing, invention activities improve with peer feedback and suggestions. Consider sharing the invention work you have done so far with several classmates or friends in order to understand your rhetorical situation more clearly and to generate more useful information.

Writing Activity

Brainstorming

Working with the questions on the last page, spend a few minutes brainstorming—jotting down everything you can think of about your topic.

Craig Broadbent's Brainstorming

Craig Broadbent, a first-year student, chose to respond to Scenario 1 on page 137. Broadbent decided that he would brainstorm to get onto paper what he already knew about the litter issue on his campus before he interviewed his friends about it:

—I see stuff every day—newspapers, those extra advertising things they put into the paper, cups, plates, and—especially—cigarette butts.
—It's always worst around where ashtrays are—that's really weird.
—The paper stuff is always worst around where the newspapers are.
—Oh—they do put a box or some container next to the paper stands for students to toss those inserts, if they don't want to read them. Not sure why so many end up on the ground.
—Bad in the men's rooms, too, at times—towels on the floor almost always.
—Classrooms: stuff tacked or taped to the walls, old soda cups and crumpled-up hamburger wrappers and old napkins and candy wrappers . . .

EXAMPLES OF INVENTION

Brainstorming (pp. 158, 332)
Freewriting (pp. 114, 245, 383)
Criteria (290)
Listing (p. 72)
Answers to Reporter's Questions (p. 244)
Organization (pp. 75, 164)
Clustering (pp. 114, 289)
Concept Mapping (p. 335)
Interviewing (p. 203)
Research (pp. 115, 160, 205, 246, 292, 384)
Reflection (p. 12)

Craig also used freewriting and clustering to explore his topic. (See Chapter 5, page 114, for examples of these strategies.)

Exploring Your Ideas with Research

Although you can sometimes draw exclusively on your experience in a piece of informative writing, especially in personal writing contexts, in academic, professional, and civic writing situations, you will usually need to include information gained from outside research.

Assume, for example, that you would like to inform a group of your friends about a local homeless shelter. You would probably want to list the services the shelter provides, indicate the various ways people can become involved with the shelter, and cite financial data on what percentage of each cash donation goes to support the shelter's clients. To provide this information to your readers, you would need to conduct some form of research.

Research provides you with the statistical data, examples, and expert testimony that will enable you to give your audience enough information, and the right kind of information, on your topic. As with any other aspect of your writing, the kind and amount of research you will need to do will depend on

Digital Literacy

Using a Search Engine to Analyze a Potential Topic

The results of a general search for sources on your topic can let you know if your informative topic is unwieldy. If a search brings up thousands of Web sites with information about your topic, it is probably too broad. For example, when a search engine such as Google returns more than 2 million links for the topic "Avian influenza virus," you need to narrow the topic so that your ideas and research will be more focused. Adding search terms based on your specific interests and concerns can help narrow your exploratory Web search. (Tip: Separate your terms or phrases in the search window with quotation marks.) The terms "Avian influenza virus" plus "Michigan" plus "schools" narrow the search to 1,300 sites that are likely to give information about concerns in the Michigan schools about possible exposure to the Avian influenza virus—a more focused topic, but still fairly broad. Adding the term "Detroit" brings the total results down to 446, with the top-ten hits including government policy Web sites that contain documents a researcher can incorporate into a paper about local preparations for and prevention of an outbreak.

your rhetorical situation: who your audience is and what you are trying to accomplish. If you are writing a paper for a sociology course on aspects of male group behavior, you will need to locate articles in scholarly journals, as well as statistical data, which you could present in a chart. If you are writing about a problem in your community, you will need to read articles and government documents, and you might also interview government officials.

As you work on the scenario you have chosen (see pages 137–140), you could conduct several kinds of research. When you are researching a problem on campus or in your community, you will need to conduct interviews with students or residents affected by the problem. As an alternative, you might consider conducting a survey of a representative sample of students or community members. You will also need to observe the problem.

Gather, read, and take notes on your topic from outside sources. You might use an electronic journal to record images, URLs, and other electronic pieces of information that you find as you research. Such an e-journal makes it easy for you to add those e-documents once you start drafting your paper.

For help with locating sources of information, see Chapter 19; for help with documenting your sources, see Chapter 20.

Craig Broadbent's Research

For his informative paper on the litter problem on his campus, Craig Broadbent thought it would be useful to include data that show how long it takes certain waste products to decompose. By searching with the keywords "campus litter," using the search engine Dogpile, he found this table on a Web site maintained by the University of British Columbia.

For more on using search engines, see Chapter 19.

Rate of Biodegradability

Product	Time It Takes
Cotton rags	1–5 months
Paper	2–5 months
Rope	3–14 months
Orange peels	6 months
Wool socks	1–5 years
Cigarette butts	1–12 years
Plastic coated paper cartons	5 years
Plastic bags	10–20 years
Leather shoes	25–40 years
Nylon fabric	30–40 years
Tin cans	50–100 years
Aluminum cans	80–100 years
Plastic 6-pack holder rings	450 years
Glass bottles	1 million years
Plastic bottles	Never

Using the same search terms in Google, he found information he thought he might be able to use, which he copied into his research journal, carefully noting its source:

> **Hidden Litter Is a Problem**
> On Thursday, 06 February 2003, the Litter Patrol picked up a small area near the Computer Technology and Mathematics building on the beautiful SCC campus. I had noticed that this area contained hidden litter. The pick-up (which lasted almost an hour) yielded 423 cigarette butts and one wasted glove. [This area could not be cleaned using a litter picker-upper.]
>
> **Author:** G. D.Thurman [gdt@deru.com]
> **Created:** 07 Feb 2003
> **URL:** http://azlitter.org/adopt-a-campus/hiddenlitter.html
> **Last modified:** 02/11/2003 08:04:34

Reviewing Your Invention and Research

After you have conducted your research, review your invention work and notes, and think about the information you have collected from outside sources. At this time, you may be tempted to decide on a thesis statement—a statement that summarizes your main point. Even though you might already have a general idea of what you want your informative paper to focus on, until you get some of your ideas and research on paper, it is often hard to know what your thesis will be. Your thesis should come *from* the writing you do about your topic. Once you have done a lot of invention work (listing, brainstorming, clustering, and so on) and research, you may be ready to decide on your working thesis. Or you can wait until after you construct your first draft.

For more on deciding on a thesis, see Chapter 13.

Writing Activity

Using Your Invention and Research to Help Focus Your Ideas

To help develop your thesis, review your invention and research notes:

- Look for connections between the pieces of information you have gathered. By doing so, you are synthesizing the information from your sources. Craig Broadbent noticed several instances where the recycling program on his campus seemed invisible. This discovery became the main idea of his paper.
- Decide on the most important piece of information you have collected. One approach is to start your paper with this information. To emphasize the invisibility of recycling on his campus, Craig Broadbent starts his paper with "We seem to have a case of invisible blue barrels on campus—when was the last time you saw one and what is unusual or unique about it?"

Craig Broadbent's Review of His Research

Craig Broadbent wanted his paper to include some of the information about recycling that he learned from his research. He investigated the issue on his campus, he interviewed two of his classmates about it, and he did a brief search of back issues of the campus's newspaper, the *Campus Reporter,* for information about campus recycling. His review of his research helped him decide on an effective way to start his paper. Here are some of his notes:

1. Jim Roberts (roommate) told me that no one had mentioned the school's recycling program to him, at orientation or anywhere else.
2. Tracy Worsam (friend and classmate) told me that she'd even asked about the program at her orientation, and no one there seemed to know much about it, other than "we have some blue barrels around campus."
3. The last ten or twelve issues of the Campus Reporter had only one small advertisement and no articles about the program. Why so little? All of those things make me wonder if I should start with a question, perhaps like, "Why doesn't anyone on campus know about our recycling program?" And, maybe a title something like, "A big campus secret: Our blue barrels."
4. I also looked on the Web and found this, from the University of Nebraska at Lincoln. It's cute and might help make my point with a neat visual:

"Did You Know?" *The Garden.* 6 Sept. 2002. University of Nebraska–Lincoln. 3 June 2003. *<http://busfin.unl.edu/LS/litter/litter.html>*

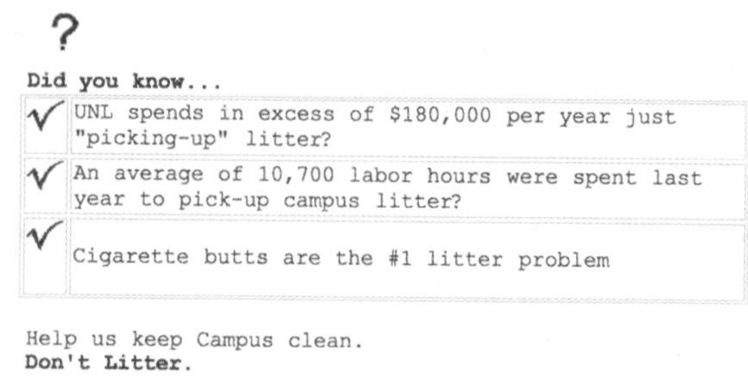

?

Did you know...

✓	UNL spends in excess of $180,000 per year just "picking-up" litter?
✓	An average of 10,700 labor hours were spent last year to pick-up campus litter?
✓	Cigarette butts are the #1 litter problem

Help us keep Campus clean.
Don't Litter.

from <http://busfin.unl.edu/LS/litter/litter.html>.
Downloaded 6/27/03.
From the University of Nebraska-Lincoln.

That would also be an interesting way to start my paper—with that little table and the "did you know?" drawing.

A WRITER'S *Responsibility* | Presenting Informative Writing Conscientiously

People often use information from their reading to help them make a decision, to support an idea in their writing, or to teach someone else. It is important, therefore, that you present accurate information and that you are aware of any biases, or preconceived ideas, you may bring to your writing about a topic—biases that might cause you to present that information in a way that is other than neutral. Ethical writers also take care to present reliable data. For example, you cannot say, "the majority of students who attend this college think that the school does a good job of recycling on campus," unless you have asked a sufficiently large and representative group of your schoolmates and are reasonably certain that you are presenting a true majority opinion.

Organizing Your Information and Research

Once you have some sense of what you would like your informative paper to include, consider how you might organize this material. The questions to ask yourself when deciding on your organization are all rhetorical:

- Who is your audience?
- Why might they be interested in your subject, or how can you make them interested in it? (One way to indicate why your subject is impor-

tant to your audience is to explain how your audience will be affected by it.)

- What is your purpose for writing—that is, what do you want to *inform* your readers about?
- What are the most important ideas, concepts, or statistics that you want your readers to learn about from your text?

The answers to these questions can help you decide what you need to emphasize, which in turn will help you choose an organization.

Here are three possible organizational approaches for writing an informative paper:

Options FOR Organization

Options for Organizing Informative Writing

Capture Your Readers' Attention	Question Your Readers	Create a Context
Start with an unusual or surprising piece of information about your subject.	Begin with a question to help readers see why they might want to read about your topic.	Set the stage. What is the situation that your readers may be interested in?
Present the information, starting from the least unusual or surprising idea and moving to the most.	Outline the information, starting with the least significant piece of information and working toward the most important.	Broaden your initial explanation with specific details, quotations, and examples so your reader can "see" what you are writing about.
Use specific examples, quotations, statistics, and so on to illustrate your topic.	Use specific examples, quotations, statistics, and so on to illustrate your topic.	Compare and contrast your subject with another one, to help readers understand the information.
End your paper by restating a unique or surprising aspect of your topic.	Conclude by answering the question that you started with.	Conclude your paper by reinforcing your reader's connection to your topic.

Craig Broadbent's Organization

Craig Broadbent reviewed his invention material and then put together a rough outline for his first draft. He decided to start with a question and to use the second approach described above.

> Set the stage, so to speak, by asking if readers know what the blue barrels are and how they work.
> State my purpose: informational.
> Explain recycling and how it works.
> Include tables, photos, charts to show my ideas.
> Explain the cost aspects of recycling.
> Let people know how to find out more information.

Constructing a Complete Draft

connect
mhconnectcomposition.com
Drafting and Revising QL6005

Once you have chosen the organizational approach that works best given your audience and purpose, you are ready to finish constructing your draft. Look back over the information you have generated through your invention activities and collected through your research, as well as any comments made by your classmates. You should also reexamine your focus or your thesis (if you have one) and decide whether you need to modify it. If you do not have a thesis yet, consider whether you are ready to develop a working thesis.

Remember that you will learn more about your subject as you write, and your ideas will probably change as you compose the first draft of your informative essay. Consider, too, what visual aids your readers might find useful.

Integrating Sources into Your Draft: Paraphrasing Information from Sources

One effective way to present information is to paraphrase it: to put that information into your own words. This is especially true for information from interviews. You will discover once you start interviewing people that interviewees, while providing much helpful information, often ramble. Paraphrasing can help you present only that information that is pertinent to your subject.

Look at the notes Craig Broadbent had from his interviews of students:

> Tracy Worsam:
> I've been active in recycling efforts both at my high school and in my church. I just assumed this university would have a full-scale program. So I asked a whole bunch of people at orientation about what this school did. One person, I'm not even sure who, just pointed and said "we have some blue barrels around campus." I was really disappointed.

Jim Roberts:
I'm kind of interested in recycling and all kinds of green activities. I was expecting to hear how I could help during orientation. Unless I missed it completely, no one mentioned recycling at all—neither during orientation nor since I've been here. You're the first person I've met who seems interested in it.

Group interview with James Wilson, Stacy Marble, and Sam Addams:

Marble—Yeah, we and a few other guys all rent rooms in that house.

Wilson—Those of us who live here try to keep the place neat—but, you know, it's really the landlord's job to clean up the front yard.

Addams—No kidding. We wake up on Saturday morning and there are all those beer cans and other litter in the front yard. We hate it.

Marble—We can't stay up all night to see who's trashing our yard.

Addams—No, but you know, maybe a webcam would be cool.

You can see that, although the interviews yield relevant information, they also contain much extraneous information. By paraphrasing, you can take only the relevant ideas you've gained from your interviews and state them in your own words. But remember: Even though the words are yours, you still need to cite where you found the ideas.

Notice how Craig Broadbent integrated parts of his interviews into his paper to get a clearer picture of how you might do so as well. Because one of the comments Broadbent received on his initial draft was, "The weakest part is the interview information, which made me want to read more of what other people had to say," he decided to include more paraphrase of his interview information his final draft. As he started working on his final draft, Broadbent noted that he had already paraphrased from the interviews he had done with two students, Jim Roberts and Tracy Worsam. In order to respond to the student comment on his draft, Broadbent kept the comments from Roberts and Worsam and added a sentence that paraphrased interviews with three other students—Wilson, Marble, and Addams: "They all told me that *they* never littered even though their yard was a mess" (Wilson, Marble, and Addams). Notice that this paraphrase gets to the heart of the matter while eliminating unrelated comments.

Parts of a Complete Draft

mhconnectcomposition.com

Introductory paragraph overview QL6006

Introduction: Successful informative writing grabs and holds readers' attention. The following strategies can help you hook your readers:

- **Define any important terms that the reader might not know.** Defining terms does not mean listing their dictionary definitions, but rather explaining those terms in the context of your explanation of your subject. For an especially effective opening, you might get readers' attention by defining a familiar term in an unexpected way.

- **Start your text with unusual or surprising information.**
- **Get down to business by bluntly stating your thesis.** A straightforward statement like "Denver's new sign code is causing businesses to lose money" often gets readers' attention. Journalists, who are trained to put the most important information up front, often use this approach.
- **Start with a provocative example or two.**

Body: Think of the body of your informative text as the place to provide all of the information that you want your readers to know and to understand. This is the section where you will present your data: quotations, graphs, tables, charts, and so on. The body of your paper is always the longest part, and, although you are not trying to prove anything in an informative essay, you are providing information to your readers, and most of it will appear in this section. After presenting different pieces of information, the body is where you will synthesize the information.

connect
mhconnectcomposition.com
Concluding paragraph overview QL6007

Conclusion: Your conclusion should tie your paper together for readers by explaining or suggesting the significance of the information you have given them: why it is useful or interesting to them. Here are some strategies for concluding an informative paper:

- **Summarize your main points.**
- **Explain the subject's most critical part.** Carol Ezzell uses a quotation from an expert to indicate what is most significant about her topic: "If you colonize time, you also colonize the future" (page 145).
- **Outline again the subject's most important aspects.**

Title: You might think that you need to craft a title before you start writing, but often it is more useful to get a first draft on paper or into a computer file and then consider possible titles. Your paper's title should indicate what your paper is about, but it should also capture your readers' interest and invite them to read your paper.

- **Use a title that readers will wonder about.** For example, "Clocking Cultures" makes readers wonder what this essay could be about.
- **Start with something current.** Katie Hafner titles her article, "Growing *Wikipedia* Revises Its 'Anyone Can Edit' Policy." Anyone familiar with *Wikipedia* will want to read more.

Writing Activity

Constructing a Full Draft

Using the writing you did when selecting an organizational approach, write a complete draft of your informative paper.

VISUALIZING *Variations* | Using a Web Site, Poster, or Brochure to Inform Your Readers

If you are working with Scenario 3, which calls for civic writing, one way to present your information to your readers would be to construct a Web site, poster, or brochure instead of a newspaper article.

The following Web site from EasyVoter.org is designed to provide information on issues that are important to California voters, as well as information on how to vote.

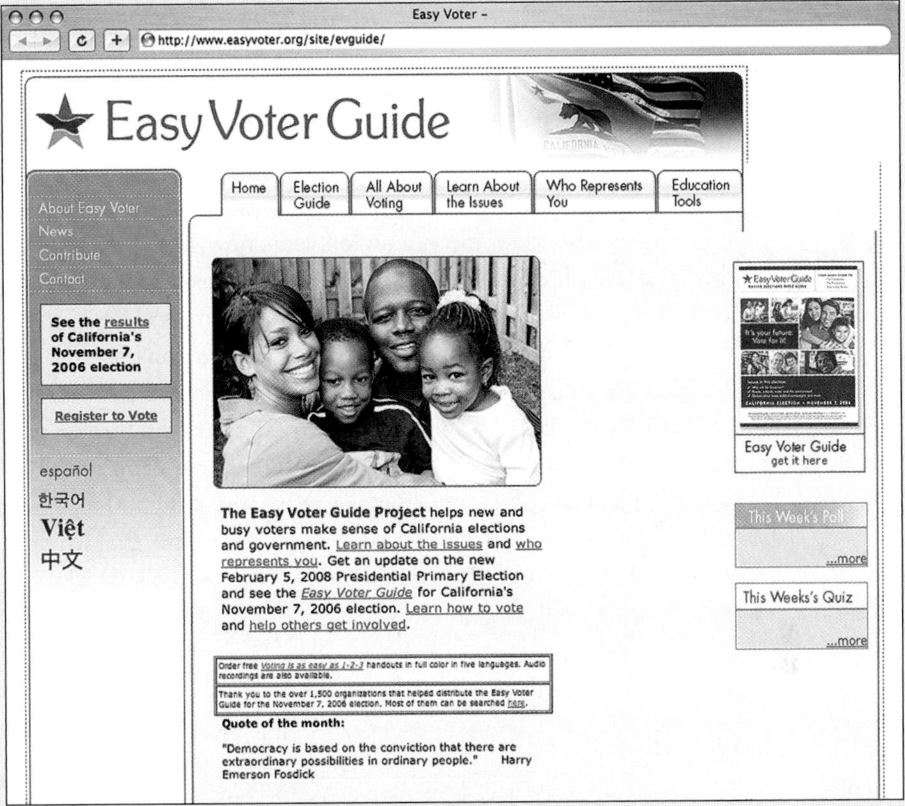

Using this Web site as an example, consider the most effective way to present the information you have researched to the voters in your area. Use the following questions to guide you:

- Who do you see as your audience for your document? What information do you already know about them?
- What is the most effective format for your information? Which format—a Web site, poster, or brochure—would be easiest for your audience to gain access to?
- Should you illustrate your Web site, poster, or brochure with tables or photos? Why?
- What kind(s) of charts would be effective? How might you test a chart to see if it would be useful to include in your document?
- If you decided to create a Web document, what hyperlinks would you want to include? How effective are the hyperlinks in this document? What makes them effective?

Craig Broadbent's First Draft

After deciding on an organizational approach, Craig Broadbent was ready to begin his first, or working, draft. As he wrote, he did not worry about grammar, punctuation, mechanics, or proper documentation style; instead, he concentrated on getting his main ideas on paper. Here is the first draft of his recycling paper. (The numbers in circles refer to peer comments—see page 000.)

Watch for the Blue Barrels

Craig Broadbent

Have you ever wondered what all of those blue barrels are, around campus . . . and if you know what they're for, do you wonder why students don't seem to use them?❶

Joan Meyers, who coordinates our campus recycling program, says that it has been around for more than ten years now, but receives little publicity (Meyers). My purpose here is to outline what we're doing here on campus, what the costs and income are from the program, and finally, based on several interviews, to suggest reasons why students don't use the blue barrels.

Our campus program not only keeps the campus cleaner, since items are collected in the blue barrels instead of perhaps being thrown on the ground, but also makes some $5,000 a year for the school (Meyers). Ms. Meyers also told me that our college could make as much as $30,000 a year from recycling, if we all recycled all the newspapers, cans, etc., that we now throw away. Here is some cost information from another college:❷

"Did You Know?" *The Garden.* 6 Sept. 2002. University of Nebraska–Lincoln. 27 June 2003. *<http://busfin.unl.edu/LS/litter/litter.html>*

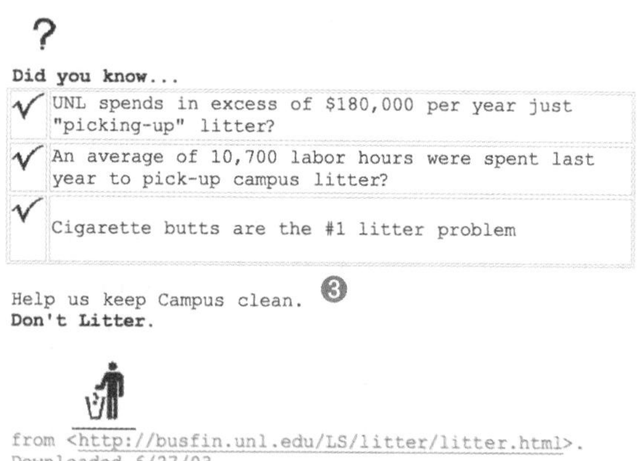

?

Did you know...

✓	UNL spends in excess of $180,000 per year just "picking-up" litter?
✓	An average of 10,700 labor hours were spent last year to pick-up campus litter?
✓	Cigarette butts are the #1 litter problem

Help us keep Campus clean. ❸
Don't Litter.

from <http://busfin.unl.edu/LS/litter/litter.html>.
Downloaded 6/27/03.
From the University of Nebraska-Lincoln.

Students, though, don't use the program, sometimes because they're not aware of it. Student Jim Roberts told me that at orientation or anywhere else no one had mentioned the school's recycling program to him (Roberts).

And Tracy Worsam even asked about the program at her orientation, and no one there seemed to know much about it, other than "we have some blue barrels around campus" (Worsam).❹

A search of several issues of the Campus Reporter perhaps explains why not many students are really aware of the blue barrel program. During the last few months, there has been only one small advertisement about the campus recycling program, and no articles about the program were published.

In order to know about and understand the recycling program, Meyers suggests that information be provided at all orientation meetings, and that weekly advertisements are run in the Campus Reporter (Meyers).❺

Revising

Revising means reviewing and re-thinking your informative text. The most effective way to revise your work is to read it as if you are reading it for the first time. Reading your own work in this way is difficult to do, of course—which is why writers often put their work aside for a time. The more you can see your writing as if for the first time, the more you will respond to it as your real readers might, questioning and probing and exploring it. As you reread the first draft of your informative writing, here are some questions to ask yourself:

- What else might my audience want or need to know about my subject?
- How else might I encourage my audience to learn more about my subject?
- What information did I find that I did not include in my paper? (Effective research always results in more information than you can include, so consider what you left out that you might include in your next draft.)
- Have I clearly explained any terms my readers might not know?
- Is it clear how I've formulated my synthesis from the information I've presented?
- Could some of my information be more effectively presented as a graph, a chart, or in a photograph?

Technology can help you revise and edit your writing more easily. Use your word processor's track-changes tool to try out revisions and editing changes. After you've had time to think about the possible changes, you can "accept" or "reject" them. Also, you can use your word processor's comment tool to write reminders to yourself when you get stuck with a revision or some editing task.

Because it is so difficult to see our own emerging writing with a fresh eye (even for experienced writers), it is almost always useful to ask classmates, friends, or family members to read and comment on drafts of your papers.

WRITER'S *Workshop* | Responding to Full Drafts

As you read and respond to your classmates' papers (and as they comment on yours), focus on the informative nature of this assignment, but from a reader's perspective. Be sure to ask questions of their writing and to respond to their ideas by exploring your reactions and responses to their thoughts.

Working in pairs or groups of three, read each others' drafts, and then offer your classmates comments that will help them see both their papers' strengths and places where they need to develop their ideas further. Use the following questions to guide your responses to the writer's draft:

- What is your first impression of this draft? How effectively does the title draw you into the paper? Why?
- What do you like about the draft? Provide positive and encouraging feedback to the writer.
- What is the writer's focus? If the paper loses focus, where does it do so?
- What part(s) of the text are especially informative? What information was interesting and/or new to you?
- Comment specifically on the introduction: What is effective about it? What suggestions can you make on how to improve it?
- What do you think is the author's thesis or main point? How could it be expressed or supported more effectively?
- In the main part of the paper, are there parts that are confusing? Where would you like more details or examples to help you see what the author means? What parts could use more explanation or definitions?
- How clear is the author's informative writing? If there are places that seem wordy or unclear, how might the author revise to address those problems?
- How accurate does the information seem? How does the author indicate the sources of statistics and other information that are not common knowledge?
- Reread the conclusion: How well does it tie everything together? To what extent does it make you want to learn more about this topic?
- What do you see as the main weaknesses of this paper? How might the writer improve the text?
- If you are working with a nontraditional text (a Web page, for example, or a brochure), what special attributes are present, and how effective are they?
- If there are visual aspects of the document, how effectively do they illustrate the point being made? How much do the visuals add to a reader's overall understanding of the information?

Student Comments on Craig Broadbent's Draft

Here are some comments that student reviewers made about Craig Broadbent's draft, keyed to the first draft on pages 168–169.

1. "I thought your introduction 'worked' and made me want to read more."
2. "It seems to me that the strongest parts of your paper are the examples, especially the little drawings and all the statistics."
3. "I'd like more tables and charts, if you have them—they help me see what you mean."
4. "The weakest part is the interview information, which made me want to read more of what other people had to say."
5. "Your conclusion was weak—maybe you could add what students ought to be doing now? Put another way, what do you want your readers to do with this (interesting) information?"

Responding to Readers' Comments

Once they have received feedback from peers, teachers, and others, writers have to decide what to do with that feedback. Because the text is *your* paper, you as the writer are responsible for dealing with reader responses to your work. You may decide to reject some comments, of course, and that decision is yours. Some of your readers might not understand your main point, or they may misunderstand something you wrote—so it is up to you either to accept or to ignore their comments and suggestions. Other comments, though, deserve your attention, as they are the words of real readers speaking to you about how to improve your text. You may find that comments from more than one reader contradict each other. In that case, use your own judgment to decide which reader's comments are on the right track.

Knowledge of Conventions

When effective writers edit their work, they attend to the conventions that will help readers—the table manners of writing. These include genre conventions, documentation, format, usage, grammar, punctuation, and mechanics. By attending to these conventions in your writing, you make reading your work a more pleasant experience.

Editing

mhconnectcomposition.com

Revising and Editing overview (also Drafting) QL6008

The last task in any writing project is editing. When you edit and polish your writing, you make changes to your sentence structure and word choice to improve your style and to make your writing clearer and more concise. You also check your work to make sure it adheres to conventions of grammar, usage, punctuation, mechanics, and spelling. Use the spell-check function of your

See Chapter 20 for more on documenting sources.

word-processing program, but be sure to double-check your spelling personally. If you have used sources in your paper, make sure you are following the documentation style your instructor requires.

As with overall revision of your work, this final editing and polishing is most effective if you can put your text aside for a few days and come back to it with fresh eyes. We strongly recommend that you ask classmates, friends, and tutors to read your work as well.

To assist you with editing, we offer here a round-robin editing activity focused on finding and correcting problems with modifiers.

ROUND-ROBIN EDITING WITH A FOCUS ON

WRITER'S *Workshop* | Round-Robin Editing with a Focus on Modifiers

Informative writing benefits from the careful use of **modifiers**—words or groups of words that describe or limit other words—such as adjectives, adverbs, infinitives, participles, prepositional phrases, and relative clauses. Working in small groups, read one another's papers, looking for two common problems: misplaced and dangling modifiers

When a modifier is misplaced, it is too far away from the word or phrase it is modifying, so that it appears to be modifying something else. To correct the problem, the modifier needs to be moved.

MISPLACED Student Jim Roberts told me ~~at orientation or anywhere else~~ no one had mentioned the school's recycling program to him ^ *at orientation or anywhere else*.

A modifier is dangling when the word or phrase it modifies does not appear in the sentence to all. You can correct the problem by adding the word or phrase.

DANGLING In order to know about the recyling program, ^ *students need to be provided with* ~~Meyers suggests that~~ information ~~be provided~~ at all orientation meetings ^ *according to Meyers*.

Compare notes to see if you have questions about modifiers, and consult a grammar handbook or ask your instructor for assistance.

connect
mhconnectcomposition.com
Correcting dangling modifiers QL6010

connect
mhconnectcomposition.com
Correcting mixed modifiers QL6011

Genres, Documentation, and Format

If you are writing an academic paper, follow the conventions for the discipline in which you are writing and the requirements of your instructor. If you are constructing a brochure for a local service organization (Scenario 3), refer to the guidelines presented in the "Visualizing Variations" section on page 167. If you have used material from outside sources, including visuals, give credit to those sources, using the documentation style required by the discipline you are working in and by your instructor.

For advice on writing in different genres, see the Online Appendix. For guidelines for formatting and documenting papers in MLA or APA style, see Chapter 20.

A Writer Informs His Readers: Craig Broadbent's Final Draft

The final draft of Craig Broadbent's essay "Watch for the Blue Barrels" follows. As you read Broadbent's essay, think about what makes it effective. Note, too, how he used the suggestions his classmates offered during peer review to make his informative paper more effective. Following the essay, you'll find some specific questions to consider.

CRAIG BROADBENT

INFORMATIVE ESSAY

Watch for the Blue Barrels

Have you ever wondered what all of those blue barrels that are scattered around campus are for . . . and if you know what they're for, do you wonder why students don't seem to use them? Those blue barrels are the heart of our campus-wide recycling program, and it is critical not only that students know what they are, but also that they <u>use</u> the barrels. 1

This is Broadbent's thesis sentence. Here he tells his readers that he will inform them about the campus recycling program and why they should take part.

Joan Meyers, who coordinates our campus recycling program, says that it has been in place for more than ten years now, but receives little publicity. My purpose here is to outline what we're doing about recycling on campus, to show what the costs and income are from the program, and finally, based on several interviews, to suggest the reasons that students don't use the blue barrels. 2

What is recycling and why should we care about it? Recycling is the reuse of some product. We all know that reusing plastic, aluminum cans, newspaper, glass, and other items by recycling them saves energy (and thus helps our air pollution problem) and can also save money. Recycling is environmentally sound—the more paper, plastic, and metal products that we can reuse, the less we have to make. That's the case even though things are usually not recycled into what they were to start with. That is, aluminum cans, Meyers told me, rarely are recycled to make more aluminum cans. But they <u>are</u> recycled and made into other products (frying pans, for instance). In addition to Meyers' examples, the United States Environmental Protection Agency mentions that there are more than 4500 products which are made from recycled material, including things such 3

One peer suggestion Broadbent received was the following:

I'd like more tables and charts, if you have them—they help me see what you mean.

To address this reader's concern, Broadbent added this paragraph and also Table 1.

as car bumpers, egg cartons, and carpets. Therefore, recycling saves trees and other natural resources.

Not only that, but if certain items are not recycled, they can be around forever. That is, if we don't recycle some household items, they never seem to "waste away." For example, the University of British Columbia reports that some items can last huge amounts of time: glass bottles last a million years and plastic bottles never go away, as shown in Table 1. 4

Table 1
Rates of Disintegration of Common Waste Products

Product	Time it takes
Paper	2–5 months
Orange Peels	6 months
Wool Socks	1–5 years
Cigarette butts	1–12 years
Plastic coated paper cartons	5 years
Plastic bags	10–20 years
Aluminum cans	80–100 years
Glass bottles	1 million years
Plastic bottles	Never

Source: "Facts about Litter." UBC Waste Management Litter Reduction Program. University of British Columbia. 23 June 2003 <http://www.recycle.ubc.ca/litter.html>.

Even seemingly minor items like cigarette butts can last as long as 12 years, and empty soda cans—unless they are recycled—can last for up to 100 years. 5

Joan Meyers notes that our recycling program not only keeps the campus cleaner, since items are collected in the blue barrels instead of perhaps being thrown on the ground, but it also generates some $5,000 a year in revenue for the school. Ms. Meyers also told me that our college could make as much as $30,000 a year from recycling if we all recycled all the newspapers, cans, and other waste that we now throw away. Figure 1 shows some cost information from the University of Nebraska at Lincoln. 6

Likewise, a 2003 study from MIT determined that "recycling 40 percent of MIT's trash would reduce the Institute's $1 million annual waste-management budget by about 10 percent. MIT's annual recycling rate for 2003 was 22 percent—double its rate in 2000" (Stauffer). It clearly appears that if colleges increase the scale of their recycling programs they will see increased revenue. 7

Students, though, don't use the program, sometimes because they're not aware of it. Student Jim Roberts told me that no one had mentioned the school's recycling program to him, at orientation or anywhere else. An- 8

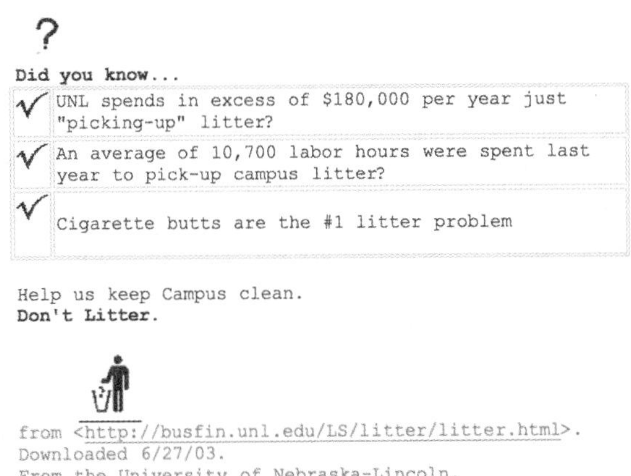
?

Did you know...

✓	UNL spends in excess of $180,000 per year just "picking-up" litter?
✓	An average of 10,700 labor hours were spent last year to pick-up campus litter?
✓	Cigarette butts are the #1 litter problem

Help us keep Campus clean.
Don't Litter.

from <http://busfin.unl.edu/LS/litter/litter.html>.
Downloaded 6/27/03.
From the University of Nebraska-Lincoln.

Figure 1 Revenue generated from recycling at the University of Nebraska–Lincoln Botanical Garden and Arboretum. "Did You Know?" *The Garden.* 6 Sept. 2002. University of Nebraska–Lincoln. 3 June 2003. <http://busfin.unl.edu/LS/litter/litter.html>.

other student, Tracy Worsam, even asked about the program at her orientation, but no one there seemed to know much about it, other than to say "we have some blue barrels around campus." Finally, I interviewed several students who live in that old house on the edge of campus. It's not really a fraternity but more of a boarding house. They all told me that *they* never littered, even though their yard was a mess (Wilson, Marble, and Addams). Maybe my interview with them—and the information I gave them about the blue barrel program—will help. Maybe if they understood recycling and had blue barrels in a convenient location, they would recycle plastic, paper, glass, and so on.

9 A search through several back issues of the *Campus Reporter* may explain why not many students are really aware of the blue barrel program. During the last few months, only one small advertisement about the campus recycling program has appeared in the *Reporter,* and no articles about the program were published.

10 Our campus is not the only one that has trouble getting students engaged with recycling. In a document, *Recycling and Beyond: A College Campus Primer,* written by Christine von Kolntz of the Medical University of South Carolina and Karyn Kaplan of the University of Oregon, they suggest the following in order to get students involved on campus:

> Student employees are an excellent resource on a college campus. Students also seek out volunteer and internship opportunities that will gain them academic credit. Campus recycling is a wealth of opportu-

Another comment Broadbent received from his peer review session pointed out a problem:

The weakest part is the interview information, which made me want to read more of what other people had to say.

Note how he has now included a good deal of information from the students he interviewed.

Broadbent's peer made this comment on his earlier draft:

Your conclusion was weak—maybe you could add what students ought to be doing now? Put another way, what do you want your readers to do with this (interesting) information?

Note how he now addresses what students can *do* to become more involved with their campus recycling program.

This paper follows MLA guidelines for in-text citations and works cited. Note that URLs are optional.

nities for engaging students in amazing projects. Some ways students can get involved include: working on PR campaigns, spearheading grassroots efforts to draw attention to an issue, assisting with event recycling efforts, performing research and analysis, doing surveys, and building educational displays. The possibilities are endless.

In order to know about and understand the recycling program, stu- 11
dents need to be provided with information at all orientation meetings, and weekly advertisements need to be run in the *Campus Reporter,* according to Joan Meyers. In the meantime, students who would like to learn more about the recycling program on campus, and how they can help, can contact Meyers at JoanMeyers@Ourcollege.edu.

Works Cited

"Did You Know?" *The Garden.* 6 Sept. 2002. University of Nebraska–Lincoln Botanical Garden and Arboretum. Web. 27 June 2003. <http://busfin.unl.edu/LS/litter/litter.html>.

Environmental Protection Agency. Web. 1 Oct. 2008. <http://web.mit.edu/newsoffice/2004/waste-0211.html>.

Meyers, Joan. Personal interview. 17 March 2004.

"Facts about Litter." UBC Waste Management Litter Reduction Program. University of British Columbia. Web. 23 June 2003. <http://www.recycle.ubc.ca/litter.html>.

Roberts, Jim. Personal interview. 15 March 2004.

Stauffer, Nancy. "Study Finds More Recycling Would Benefit Both Budget and Environment." Web. 1 Oct. 2008. <http://web.mit.edu/newsoffice/2004/waste-0211.html>.

von Kolntz, Christine, and Karyn Kaplan. *Recycling and Beyond: A College Campus Primer.* Web. 1 Oct. 2008. <http://www.uoregon.edu/~recycle/Book/index.htm>.

Wilson, James, Stacy Marble, and Sam Addams. Personal interview. 17 March 2004.

Worsam, Tracy. Personal interview. 15 March 2004.

QUESTIONS FOR WRITING AND DISCUSSION: LEARNING OUTCOMES

Rhetorical Knowledge: The Writer's Situation and Rhetoric

1. **Audience:** How effective is Broadbent at appealing to the audience that this information is intended for—students at a college or university? What can you point to in the article to demonstrate what you mean?
2. **Purpose:** In addition to its informative purpose, what other purposes does this paper have?
3. **Voice and tone:** What is Broadbent's attitude toward his subject? How does he indicate this attitude in his tone?
4. **Responsibility:** What can you point to in Broadbent's informational essay that gives the text its *ethos*? To what extent do you believe the information that Broadbent presents here? Why?
5. **Context, and format, and genre:** How has Broadbent's context—his college campus— affected his paper? How might he have written about the same subject differently in another context? The first sentence of Broadbent's essay directly engages the reader in a personal way that wouldn't be found in a formal report. Do you think Broadbent's informality here is appropriate for his audience? Will it succeed in getting his audience more fully engaged?

Critical Thinking: The Writer's Ideas and Your Personal Response

6. What ideas in Broadbent's essay seem the most important to you? Why?
7. How effectively does Broadbent inform the reader? What examples can you point to in the text that provide useful information?

Composing Processes and Knowledge of Conventions: The Writer's Strategies

8. How effective are the visuals that Broadbent includes? What is your opinion of the sources he uses? What other sources might he have consulted?
9. What is your opinion of Broadbent's conclusion?

Inquiry and Research: Ideas for Further Exploration

10. Go to your college's main Web page and search for "recycling." In no more than one page, outline what you learn.

Self-Assessment: Reflecting on Your Goals

Now that you have constructed a piece of informative writing, go back and consider your learning goals, which you and your classmates may have considered at the beginning of this chapter (see pages 134–35). Write notes on what you have learned from this assignment.

Rhetorical Knowledge

- *Audience:* What did you learn about your audience as you wrote your informative paper?
- *Purpose:* How successfully do you feel you fulfilled your informative purpose?
- *Rhetorical situation:* How did the writing context affect your informational text? How did your choice of topic affect the research you conducted and how you presented your information to your readers? What do you see as the strongest part of your paper? Why? The weakest? Why?
- *Voice and tone:* How would you describe your voice in this essay? Your tone? How do they contribute to the effectiveness of your informational essay?

Critical Thinking, Reading, and Writing

- *Learning/inquiry:* How did you decide what to focus on in your informative paper? Describe the process you went through to focus on a main idea, or thesis.
- *Responsibility:* How did you fulfill your responsibility to your readers?
- *Reading and research:* What did you learn about informative writing from the reading selections you read for this chapter? What research did you conduct? Why? What additional research might you have done?

Writing Processes for Informative Writing

- *Invention:* What invention strategies were most useful to you? Why?
- *Organizing your ideas and details:* What organization did you use? How successful was it? Why?
- *Revising:* What one revision did you make that you are most satisfied with? Why? If you could make an additional revision, what would it be?
- *Working with peers:* How did your instructor or peer readers help you by making comments and suggestions about your writing? How could you have more effectively used the comments and suggestions you received?
- *Visuals:* Did you use photographs or other visuals to help you inform your readers? If so, what did you learn about incorporating these elements?

- *Writing habits:* What "writerly habits" have you developed, modified, or improved on as you constructed the writing assignment for this chapter?

Knowledge of Conventions

- *Editing:* What sentence problem did you find most frequently in your writing? How will you avoid that problem in future assignments?
- *Genre:* What conventions of the genre you were using, if any, gave you problems?
- *Documentation:* Did you use sources for your paper? If so, what documentation style did you use? What problems, if any, did you have with it?

mhconnectcomposition.com

Craig Broadbent Reflects on His Writing QL6009

Refer to Chapter 1 (pages 11–12) for a sample reflection by a student.

Writing to Analyze

What are you afraid of?

To more clearly understand a subject such as the irrational fear of spiders or snakes, scientists analyze it, or break it down. An **analysis** examines an issue or topic by identifying the parts that make up the whole. You can gain a clearer understanding of your subject when you look closely at the individual pieces that constitute the whole. An analysis of a *phobia,* defined as an uncontrollable (and sometimes irrational) fear of some situation, object, or activity, would require you to examine the various aspects of that phobia.

Analyzing phobias is an area of study at colleges and universities. Here is an excerpt from an essay about anxiety disorders, which includes phobias, by a researcher at the University of Texas at Austin:

> Fear can be a good thing.
>
> Being afraid makes us heed severe weather warnings and keeps us from running across busy freeways. It is a survival mechanism for most, but for some people their fear has become consuming and out of control.
>
> Since 1988 Dr. Michael Telch and the Laboratory for the Study of Anxiety Disor- ders (LSAD) in the Depart- ment of Psychology at The University of Texas at Aust have been researching tre ments for anxiety-related disorders such as panic dis der, obsessive-compulsive order, social anxiety disorc and specific phobias, inclu ing claustrophobia, arachn phobia and cynophobia (d phobia).
>
> "Anxiety is part of bei a human being," Telch saic "The question is when doe it become a disorder? Mot Nature gave us an alarm system of anxiety and pan

to cope with threats. This signal system is critical to our survival. The bad news is that this mechanism is capable of sending a false alarm.

"It can become a disorder when the alarm is out of proportion to the threat," he added. "The hallmark is that the brain is receiving danger messages when the danger isn't there. While many people have these false alarms, it becomes a disorder when it interferes with daily functioning or when the response is above and beyond what is called for. Anxiety disorders are the largest—and one of the most treatable—classes of psychiatric disorders."

Rapid breathing, pounding heart and a desire to flee are typical—and reasonable—reactions to perceived danger, but for someone experiencing an anxiety disorder, these feelings become overwhelming. The fight or flight response kicks into overdrive when a person is experiencing the symptoms of an anxiety disorder. Research has shown that anxiety disorders in the U.S. cost more than $42 billion each year, about one third of the amount spent on mental health care in this country.

Although psychologists analyze subjects such as phobias to understand mental processes better, analysis can also be helpful in your everyday life. You have probably analyzed the college you are currently attending: examining its catalogue to consider the variety of courses offered, perhaps reading through faculty lists to consider whom you might be able to study with, and considering other factors. Using analysis in your writing can help you come to a deeper understanding of your subject and share that understanding with your readers.

Setting Your Goals:

Rhetorical Knowledge

- **Audience:** Determine who will benefit from your analysis. What do the audience members probably already know? What will you need to tell them?
- **Purpose:** When you analyze a complex situation, process, or relationship, you can help others understand the subject more thoroughly.
- **Rhetorical situation:** In an analysis, you break down your subject into parts or categories to help your reader understand it more clearly.
- **Voice and tone:** When you write an analysis, be detailed and thorough, but avoid an all-knowing attitude that might be interpreted as arrogant.
- **Context, medium, and genre:** Decide on the best medium and genre to use to present your analysis to the audience you want to reach.

Critical Thinking, Reading, and Writing

- **Learning/inquiry:** By reading and writing analytically, you gain a deeper understanding of issues and the ability to make more informed decisions.
- **Responsibility:** Effective analysis leads to critical thinking. When you engage in analysis, you see the nuances of all the potential relationships involved in your subject.
- **Reading and research:** Analysis can involve close observation as well as interviews and online and library research.

Writing to Analyze

Chapter 7

Writing Processes

- **Invention:** Use invention activities such as brainstorming, listing, and clustering to help you consider the parts of your subject and how they relate to one another.
- **Organizing your ideas and details:** If your subject is large, you might break it down into more understandable parts, or you might begin with individual parts and examine each one in detail.
- **Revising:** Read your work with a critical eye to make certain that it fulfills the assignment and displays the qualities of good analytical writing.
- **Working with peers:** Listen to your classmates to make sure that they understand your analysis.

Knowledge of Conventions

- **Editing:** The round-robin activity on page 216 will help you check your analysis for wordy sentences.
- **Genres for analytical writing:** Usually, analyses are written as formal documents, so most times your analysis will be a formal report or an academic essay.
- **Documentation:** If you have relied on sources outside of your own experience, cite them using the appropriate documentation style.

mhconnectcomposition.com

Writing to Analyze Tutorial QL7001

Rhetorical Knowledge

When you write an analysis, you need to consider how it will help your readers understand your topic in a new way and why you want them to gain this understanding. You will also need to decide what medium and genre will help you get your analysis across to your audience.

Writing to Analyze in Your College Classes

Although academic disciplines vary widely, all of them use the process of analysis, because when you analyze something, you almost always come to understand it more completely. In your college career, you may be asked to construct written analyses in many of your classes:

- In a chemistry class, you might be asked to break down an unknown compound to find what elements are present and write a lab report on your findings.
- In a literature class, you might be asked to analyze how an author develops the hero of a novel to be a sympathetic character.
- In an American history class, you may analyze what political circumstances led to the ratification of an amendment to the U.S. Constitution.

Performing an analysis usually requires you to make close observations or conduct research so that you will have a command of your subject. Writing an analysis forces you to put your understanding of that subject into your own words.

The "Ways of Writing" feature presents different genres that can be used when writing to analyze in your college classes.

Writing to Analyze for Life

In the professional, civic, and personal areas of your life, you also will construct analyses of various ideas, products, and situations.

The kind of analytical writing you do in your professional life will depend on your career, yet the odds are that at some point you will be asked to do an analysis and write a report on your findings. For example, a physician analyzes her patient's symptoms as she attempts to diagnose the illness and prescribe a cure. A food service manager might analyze the use of certain perishable foods in order to make sure the restaurant maintains a reasonable supply of fresh ingredients. The list of possibilities is endless, but it's clear the quality of your analytical thinking and writing will influence your ultimate success.

All too often the first impulse in civic life is emotional. You may get angry when the city council decides to demolish an old building, or you might enthusiastically support a local developer's plan to buy unused farmland. Despite your personal feelings on the issues, your voice will be taken much more seriously if you engage in a balanced, in-depth analysis.

Interestingly, in our personal lives, we often tend to analyze events or conversations after they have happened. You may have had a conversation with a close friend that left both of you feeling unhappy. After the encounter, you replay the conversation in your mind, trying to take apart what was said by whom

Ways of Writing to Analyze

Genres for Your College Classes	Sample Situation	Advantages of the Genre	Limitations of the Genre
Behavioral analysis	In your social psychology class, you are asked to construct a statistical analysis of the behavior in specific situations of male college students in groups, as compared to how they act individually in those same situations.	Your research and statistical analysis will provide your readers with useful information about behavior.	It is difficult to find enough reliable statistics for such an analysis; there sometimes are time constraints that limit your research.
Rhetorical analysis	Your writing professor asks you to analyze the rhetorical appeals on a Web site.	This analysis will help you to understand how a Web site appeals to its readers.	This is only one way to examine a Web site.
Nutrition analysis	In your health and nutrition class, your professor asks you to analyze several new diets.	You can provide useful information to readers.	Your analysis is not an evaluation of a diet, which often is what readers want.
Letter to your campus newspaper	Your ethics professor asks you to draft a letter to your college newspaper analyzing a campus problem.	Your college newspaper is a useful arena to publicize your analysis of the campus problem to the right audience.	A letter to the editor allows only limited space for your analysis. It might not be published.
Chemical analysis report	Your biology teacher asks you to construct a report on the toxicity of a specific group of chemicals when they are combined.	This report helps readers understand the interaction between chemicals. Such knowledge is critical whenever medicine is dispensed.	A specific report format will limit and control the information you can include in your analysis.
Visual analysis	Your writing teacher asks you to analyze the visual features of advertisements for cellular phones.	A visual analysis will help you to understand that visuals can have as much impact on an audience as text.	A focus on visual elements can divert attention from verbal content.
Genres for Life	**Sample Situation**	**Advantages of the Genre**	**Limitations of the Genre**
Brochure	As part of a neighborhood group, you construct a brochure, to analyze an issue for a school bond vote.	A brochure is a convenient format for distributing information.	A brochure offers limited space for your analysis of the school bond.
Web site	Your business offers a Web site that allows employees to input their salary, tax situation, and so on to help them determine the best way to invest their retirement funds.	This is an interactive venue for employees to analyze their possible investment scenarios.	Sometimes Web sites can be difficult to use and take time to update with new information.
Wiki	You want to create a wiki that allows members of your community to share their analyses of a local issue.	A wiki is an uncomplicated way for interested parties to share their analyses.	Wikis can become long and convoluted; someone needs to monitor activity.
Brand analysis	Your company asks you to analyze several potential new lines of merchandise.	Your analysis will provide sufficient information to help the company make good business decisions.	It can be difficult to find adequate information for such an analysis.
Letter	In a letter that you will never send, you analyze a problem in a relationship with a friend to avoid similar problems in the future.	A "letter to yourself" helps you to honestly understand a problem.	Because you do not plan to send the letter, you might not put much effort into writing it.

and figure out what went wrong. You may then write a note to the other person, explaining your analysis of the situation and what you propose to do to make amends. The "Ways of Writing" feature presents different genres that can be used when writing to analyze in life.

connect
mhconnectcomposition.com

Writer's Workshop: Applying Learning Goals to Analytical Writing QL7002

Scenarios for Writing | Assignment Options

Your instructor may ask you to complete one or more of the following analytical writing assignments. Each assignment is in the form of a *scenario*, a situation that provides some context for the analysis you will construct. The scenarios are designed to provide a sense of who your audience is and what you want to accomplish with your analytical writing, including your purpose; voice, tone, and point of view; context; and genre.

Starting on page 202, you will find guidelines for completing the assignment option that you choose or that is assigned to you.

Writing for College

SCENARIO 1 **Analysis of a Campus Issue**

Analysis helps people understand whether an idea is a good one or not, or whether a policy should be followed or not. For example, there was a discussion on our campus about giving the student government the responsibility to operate the student union. The university would allow the students to decide what restaurants and stores would operate in the building, how meeting rooms would be used, and other matters. Interested parties were considering whether this change would be beneficial. An analysis of the issues involved in a decision such as this one could help the decision makers understand what would be at stake, and they could then make an informed choice when they voted on the issue.

On your campus, there are many issues that you might analyze:

- Tuition increases: Tuition increases at one school declined over a period of five years—on a percentage basis—but the cumulative increase for the five years was about 44 percent.
- Extra fees: Why are they necessary? Where does that money go?
- Availability of professors during their office hours (and at other times).

Writing Assignment: Think about what is happening on your campus. Select a complex problem that affects you or others. Construct a report that analyzes the problem and offers insights about it.

SCENARIO 2 **A Visual Analysis**

Visuals are important and pervasive. Often, we see them in texts and use them in our own texts; sometimes, they stand alone. Visual elements of a text in-

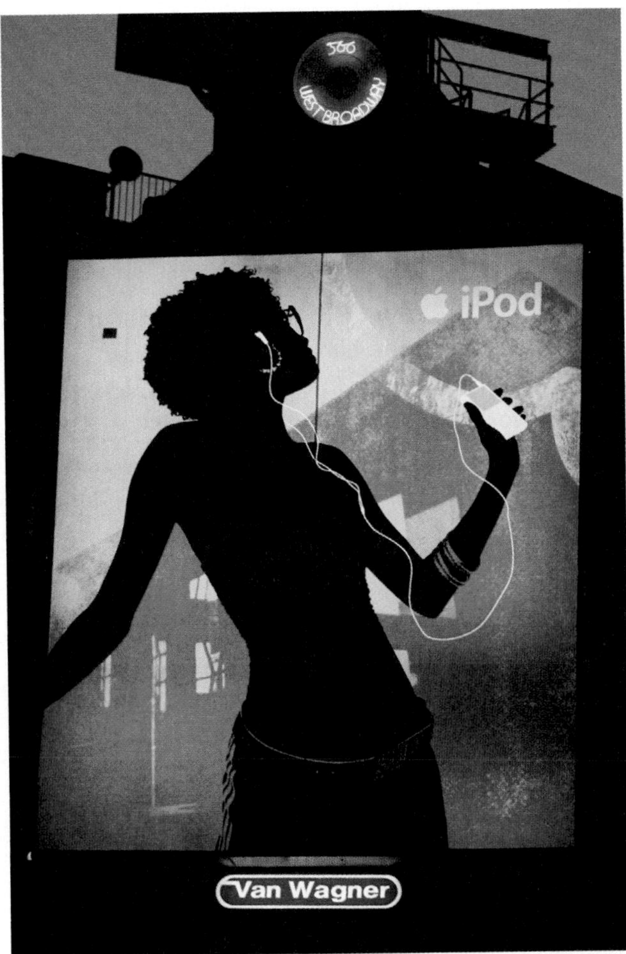

FIGURE 7.1 Billboard advertisement

clude not only photos, charts, and drawings but also the fonts used in that text. Here we will focus on an image.

You analyze an image in the same manner that you analyze a verbal text: What are the elements of the visual that make it work? How do those various aspects function together, complementing one another, to have the intended effect.

For practice, examine Figure 7.1, a billboard advertising a media player. Consider the elements that make up this ad and how they work together to tell a viewer about the product and to encourage that person to buy an iPod. See the "Genres Up Close" feature on page 198 for suggestions.

Writing Assignment: For this assignment, select a visual image (a Web page, a photograph, or a drawing), and analyze how the aspects of that image work together. In your essay, start by outlining what you think the image is trying to do. Your analysis, then, centers on how effectively the aspects of the image function together to create that effect.

Writing for Life

SCENARIO 3 Professional Writing: A Business Report Analyzing Part of Your Future Career

Think forward to the day when you are ready to apply for jobs in your chosen field. Select an image or advertisement related to your future career—the position you plan to seek after you graduate from college. You might select the following, for example:

- A movie advertisement, if you are planning to work as an actor, director, or screenwriter, or in another role in the film industry
- An advertisement for a product produced by or a service provided by the company you hope to work for
- An image from a company's annual report
- A company's logo
- A Web page from a nonprofit or government agency for which you hope to work

Writing Assignment: For this writing project, analyze the image or advertisement that you selected. Your task is not to evaluate the image or advertisement, but rather to analyze its various aspects (color, point of view, text, size, and shading) to understand how the image or advertisement works.

connect
mhconnectcomposition.com
Additional Scenarios QL7003

Rhetorical Considerations in Analytical Writing

- **Audience:** Although your teacher and classmates are the initial audience for your analysis, also consider a wider audience. What kinds of analysis will be most interesting to this group of readers?
- **Purpose:** By researching and analyzing the problem, issue, concept, options, or object, you will provide your readers with an analysis that will allow them to make more informed decisions. What kinds of information will you include in your analysis to support your purpose?
- **Voice, tone, and point of view:** You have probably chosen your topic because you have a personal interest in the subject. What preconceptions do you have? How can you avoid letting them oversimplify your analysis? How can you use voice and tone to establish credibility, so your readers believe your analysis?
- **Context, medium, and genre:** Keeping the context of the assignment in mind, decide on a medium and a genre for your writing. How will your analysis be used? Who might be interested in reading your analysis? If you are writing for an audience beyond the classroom, consider what will be the most effective way to present your analysis to this audience.

For more on choosing a medium and genre, see Chapter 17.

Critical Thinking, Reading, and Writing

Before you begin to write your analysis, consider the qualities of successful analytic writing. It also helps to read one or more examples of analysis to see these qualities in action. Finally, you might consider what visuals can add to an analysis, as well as the kinds of sources you will need to consult.

As we have seen, effective analytical writing focuses on a complex subject, thoroughly explains the parts of that subject and their relationship to one another, and is almost always based on research rather than on personal experience. An analysis is usually focused and straightforward, with insights and a conclusion that ties the aspects of your subject together for readers.

Learning the Qualities of Effective Analytical Writing

To help you and your readers better understand your subject, you need to make sure your analysis includes the following qualities:

- **A focus on a complex subject.** Any subject worth analyzing—a political position, a book, a war strategy—will consist of many parts or features, and these parts will interact with one another in complicated ways.
- **A thorough explanation of the parts and how they relate to one another.** Your first step will be to identify the component parts or aspects of your subject and then consider how those parts function separately and together. For a subject such as a new school tax bond, you might consider aspects like the following:
    - Benefits:
        - to the students
        - to the local tax base
        - to the teachers, administration, and support staff
    - Problems and costs:
        - costs in the form of debt that will need to be paid off
        - interest charges
    - What happens if the community does not fund the schools in this way?
        - Will school taxes need to be raised?
        - Will the quality of the school suffer?

  After you have identified the parts or aspects of your subject, you need to gain a thorough understanding of each one so that you can explain it to your readers.
- **Research-based rather than personal-based writing.** A formal analysis usually requires research. Your understanding of the subject is seldom

For more on conducting research, see Chapters 19 and 20.

enough to inform a thorough analysis. If you were analyzing the bond proposal, for example, you would need to read the entire proposal, interview the officials or citizen groups behind it, and examine recent school budgets.

- **A focused, straightforward presentation.** An effective analysis focuses on the subject's component parts, always working to show how they combine to make up the whole subject. All aspects of your text must focus on some central theme or idea that links all parts or aspects of the analysis.

  Like an informative text, an analysis is usually neutral in tone—the writer's primary purpose is, not to persuade, but rather to explain how the writer's subject functions.
- **Insights.** Taking something apart to analyze it provides insights into how each part functions, how each aspect relates to every other aspect and to the whole.
- **A conclusion that ties parts together.** In an analysis, your conclusion does much more than just state your major claim (as a *thesis statement* usually does). Although your paper serves to explain each aspect of the subject you are analyzing, in your conclusion, you have the opportunity to outline how those parts function together and also to explain whether you believe that those parts function together effectively or not.

For more on thesis statements, see Chapter 13.

Summarize each quality of an effective analysis in your own words, and then refer to that summary as you conduct research and write your paper.

Reading, Inquiry, and Research: Learning from Texts That Analyze

The reading selections that follow are examples of analytical writing. As you read the texts, ask yourself the following questions:

- What makes this analysis effective?
- What qualities of an effective analysis (see pages 189–190) do the selections exhibit?
- What parts of the analysis leave me with questions?
- How can I use these analytical techniques in my writing?

JAMES M. LANG

Putting In the Hours

OPINION PIECE

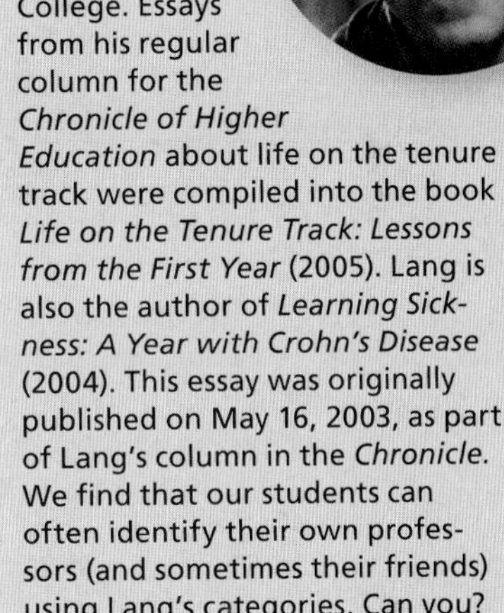

James M. Lang is a public speaker, workshop leader, and assistant professor of English at Assumption College. Essays from his regular column for the *Chronicle of Higher Education* about life on the tenure track were compiled into the book *Life on the Tenure Track: Lessons from the First Year* (2005). Lang is also the author of *Learning Sickness: A Year with Crohn's Disease* (2004). This essay was originally published on May 16, 2003, as part of Lang's column in the *Chronicle*. We find that our students can often identify their own professors (and sometimes their friends) using Lang's categories. Can you?

1 Most casual observers of the North American professor assume his natural habitat to be the classroom, where he engages in those behaviors commonly associated with his species: speaking to audiences of young people in a loud voice, marking with writing utensils on green or white boards, receiving and distributing pieces of paper.

2 But the casual observer may overlook that this species usually spends an equal, if not greater, part of his week in his den, holding what his institution terms "office hours." At small, liberal-arts colleges in New England, like the one where our observations have been centered, he and his colleagues are, in fact, required to hold 10 office hours each week—time set aside for advisees and students who want to consult with the professor outside of the normal classroom hours.

3 Working our way up and down the halls of one faculty office building, checking out the office-hour schedules posted below the nameplates, and observing the work and leisure habits of these specimens through their half-opened doors, we have been able to classify, according to their office-hour behavior, some subspecies of the North American professor.

4 The Early Bird: Whether he actually likes mornings or not, the Early Bird schedules all of his office hours before 10 a.m.—in other words, before most of his students have rolled out of bed. The Early Bird can be assured that he will have fewer office visits than his next-door neighbor, who has scheduled all of her hours after noon.

5 The Early Bird has done nothing technically wrong, of course; he probably keeps his office hours more regularly than most faculty members. But the Early Bird also knows exactly what he is doing. He doesn't particularly want students visiting during office hours, and he has found the best legal means of ensuring that they don't.

6 The Door Closer: The Door Closer knows that students are far more likely to knock on an open door than a closed one, so he wards off all but the most desperate and devoted of his students by keeping his door completely shut during office hours. For extra effect, he will lock it, forcing

students to realize that they are interrupting him by compelling him to walk to the door and open it.

We have actually observed students walk up to a professor's office, see the door closed, and walk away dispirited—only to watch the office's occupant emerge moments later, heading to the departmental office for a coffee refill. Like the Early Bird, the Door Closer has not violated the letter of his contract; he relies instead upon simple and subtle discouragement. 7

The Counselor: The Door Closer's antithesis, the Counselor props his door open as wide as it will allow, faces his desk towards the doorway, and peeks out expectantly at every passing footfall. The Counselor wants students to visit him in his office. The Counselor wants to know how they're doing. The students actually divulge this information to the Counselor: They tell him about their roommates, and their relationships, and their home lives. The Counselor loves it. 8

Other faculty members are baffled by the Counselor, and slightly suspicious of him. They suspect—and they are probably right—that their own names come up occasionally in the Counselor's office, and that the Counselor listens to student complaints about them with a sympathetic ear. 9

The Chatterer: Chatterers, whether they want students in their office or not, like to spend their office hours socializing. They stop in to visit other colleagues who are having office hours, they linger in the departmental office to check their mail or fill their coffee mug, and they welcome long lines at the copy machine. As a rule, nonchattering faculty members tend to appreciate Chatterers most at paper-grading time, when frequent interruptions to their work are happily tolerated. When they are trying to prepare for a class they have to teach in 30 minutes, the average faculty member sees his Chattering neighbor as a nuisance. 10

Most Chatterers are people who simply like to talk, and practice their chatting habits in other realms of their lives as incessantly as they do at the office. 11

We have noticed a subspecies of Chatterers, though: people who live by themselves, especially those newly arrived at the college, without much of a social network outside the campus. For this species, the time they spend in the office provides them with their primary socializing opportunity. Back in their apartments, it's a book or the television. During office hours they get to communicate with other members of their species. 12

The Fugitive: The counterpart to the lonely Chatterer, the Fugitive has a houseful of living creatures—spouses, children, dogs, cats, hermit crabs—and sees the office as his refuge from the chaos that constantly threatens to overwhelm his home life. Fugitives can best be recognized by their relaxed attitude during office hours. However much work they have to do at the office, it can't be any more stressful than what they have to deal with at home. Fugitives usually have at least one extremely comfort- 13 able chair in their office, and can occasionally be spotted sitting in that chair and staring off into space, just enjoying the peace and quiet.

In the interests of scientific objectivity, we should disclose that the author of this paper is a Fugitive. 14

He has a recliner purchased from the Salvation Army, and the most relaxing part of his day are those moments when he can balance a cup of tea on the armrest, kick off his shoes, and read the material he has assigned for class. He has a little refrigerator in his office, and he has expressed his desire to install a television/VCR as well. 15

"If you ever kick me out," he has been known to remark to his wife, with just a hint of hopefulness, when he has all three kids in the tub and the phone and the doorbell are ringing and the cats are scratching at the door, "I'll be able to move right into my office." 16

"Don't get your hopes up," she has been known to respond. 17

But the truth of the matter is, he is not always or exclusively a Fugitive. Sometimes he engages in behaviors associated with the Chatterer, and the Door Closer, and sometimes the Early Bird too (he draws the line at the Counselor—much as he loves his students, he does not want to hear about their latest relationship problems). 18

He holds one office hour on Friday morning from 8:30 to 9:30 a.m., before his first class. In an entire semester, he has had one visitor during that office hour, and she came under extreme duress, when all other options were exhausted. He counts three Chatterers in his department among his closest friends, so he often welcomes the opportunity to talk with them, even occasionally instigating such conversations. And he will close his door when he is having one of those weeks when the paper stack never seems to diminish, no matter how many he grades. So we have begun to suspect that these observations are perhaps more appropriately classified as behaviors rather than subspecies types. 19

Most North American professors do have a dominant behavior that characterizes their office-hour activity, but most also engage in multiple behaviors in the course of a single week. 20

Given the early and exploratory nature of these observations, we would welcome notes from fellow field researchers who have studied the office-hour habits of the North American professor, and have observed other forms of both common and unusual behaviors. 21

QUESTIONS FOR WRITING AND DISCUSSION: LEARNING OUTCOMES

Rhetorical Knowledge: The Writer's Situation and Rhetoric

1. **Audience:** The *Chronicle of Higher Education* is a weekly newspaper for college professors. How effectively does Lang understand and reach his audience? Who else—besides college teachers and students—might be interested in reading Lang's analysis?
2. **Purpose:** Why do you suppose Lang wrote this essay?
3. **Voice and tone:** What can you point to in Lang's tone that helps to establish his *ethos*?
4. **Responsibility:** What can you cite from the essay that shows how Lang was fulfilling his responsibilities as a writer when he wrote "Putting In the Hours"?
5. **Context, format, and genre:** Lang's essay appeared in a respected academic periodical, the *Chronicle of Higher Education*. Is his essay typical of the kind of writing you would expect in such a journal? Why? How does Lang twist the genre of the serious academic essay to make this a humorous piece?

Critical Thinking: The Writer's Ideas and Your Personal Response

6. What is your initial reaction to Lang's analysis? Do you find it humorous? Why?
7. How accurate are Lang's categories and subcategories? Why? Do you agree with his analysis? Why or why not?

Composing Processes and Knowledge of Conventions: The Writer's Strategies

8. Consider Lang's overall organization by making a sentence or scratch outline of it (outline the text by writing, in one sentence, what each paragraph has to say). How effective is his organization? Why? In what other way(s) might this essay be organized?
9. Lang starts his essay with this line: "Most casual observers of the North American professor assume his natural habitat to be the classroom . . ." (paragraph 1). What effect does Lang have by making his essay sound like an animal observation?

Inquiry and Research: Ideas for Further Exploration

10. Visit two of your professors in their offices. How do they compare to Lang's professors? Be specific in your description.

TAMARA DRAUT

All Work and No Play

ANALYTIC ESSAY

Tamara Draut is the director of the Economic Opportunity Program at Demos, a public policy center. She has written widely on economic security, and her op-ed pieces frequently appear in major newspapers. She is also a frequent guest commentator on television and radio talk shows. The following selection is an excerpt from her book *Strapped: Why America's 20- and 30-Somethings Can't Get Ahead* (2006). Many of our students work and can identify with Draut's essay. What monetary concerns do you have about your own education? How can those concerns be alleviated?

In the fall of 1997, Shaney, who is now 27, enrolled in the University of Arkansas. She chose the state college because it was close to home and the nearby private colleges were financially out of the question. Shaney's excellent grades in school scored her a $10,000 scholarship to help cover the cost of tuition for four years. The scholarship was an enormous relief for Shaney and her family. Neither of her parents had gone to college and they couldn't offer any financial support for her studies. With tuition covered by the scholarship, Shaney was confident she could earn enough for room and board through part-time jobs. She opted out of living in the dorms, choosing instead to get an apartment with a friend from high school. 1

Shaney worked a lot of hours during school, holding down two or three jobs at all times. During summers, Shaney was unable to capitalize on internship opportunities that would have helped her gain better work experience because the pay was too low and she had to continue to earn. She waited tables instead, trying to save as much money as she could before school started again in the fall. She regrets not being able to accept an internship that would have helped her build more impressive and relevant experience for her résumé. 2

Shaney's college days were a far cry from the keg parties and dorm room shenanigans that dominate our popular conception of college. Tuition increases made her scholarship money run out sooner than expected. Because Shaney was a French major, she opted to study abroad in France for a year, which she paid for with student loans. She also took out loans to deal with tuition increases. All told, Shaney left school with $25,000 in student loans. After working two or three jobs for the last four years, Shaney was looking forward to being done with school and having a regular nine-to-five job and her nights once again free. 3

For all of Shaney's hard work, she graduated into one of the worst job markets in recent history and has yet to find a job. Staring down the barrel of $25,000 in loans, Shaney is understandably worried about her financial future. She's begun to question the value of going to college and finds herself wondering whether it wasn't all a waste of time. 4

Stress-filled college days like Shaney's are much more common than they were twenty or thirty years ago. Full-time on-campus students work more hours at paying jobs while in college than did students in the 1970s or 1980s. According to an analysis of U.S. Department of Education survey data, today three quarters of full-time college students are holding down jobs. Like Shaney, nearly half of them work twenty-five hours or more a week. Working while going to school isn't inherently a bad thing—in fact, some studies show that working on-campus for fifteen hours or less per week can help foster better academic performance. On-campus jobs, which are often work-study slots, provide a chance for students to deepen their connections to the campus through contact with other students, faculty, and staff. The problem is that more and more students are working off-campus at multiple jobs and for longer hours. Students who work twenty-five hours or more a week are much more likely to report that work affected their grades and interfered with their class schedule. Grades suffer as studying time declines and so does the free time to participate in academic clubs and social activities. 5

Not everyone can handle the added stress of long work hours on top of college. Too often students give up under the pressure. As anyone who has made it past their first two years of college can attest, the second half is when college becomes really interesting; it's the whole four-year package that provides the analytical, problem-solving, and writing skills that distinguish a bachelor's degree from an associate's degree. But when an 18-year-old is borrowing $8,000 or more a year and working twenty-five hours a week to pay for college, it changes the equation. Under these conditions, a boring class is no longer just a snooze fest—it's an extremely *expensive* snooze fest. It's not surprising that under a debt-for-diploma and work till you drop environment, one third of students drop out after their first year of college. And first-generation college students are almost twice as likely as students with college-educated parents to drop out before their second year. 6

This is why the percentage of students who actually earn their bachelor's degree hasn't risen nearly as fast as enrollments would suggest. Just over half (53 percent) of all students who enroll in four-year colleges end up getting their bachelor's degrees within five years. Not surprisingly, there are wide disparities by class and race in who completes college. Within five years of entering college, 40 percent of students from the top socioeconomic quartile (25 percent) will earn a four-year degree as compared to only 6 percent of students in the lowest quartile. Over a quarter of white students who enter college will earn a bachelor's degree, whereas only about 15 percent of black and Hispanic college students will complete their degrees. 7

QUESTIONS FOR WRITING AND DISCUSSION: LEARNING OUTCOMES

Rhetorical Knowledge: The Writer's Situation and Rhetoric

1. **Audience:** From reading this short excerpt from *Strapped,* what inferences can you make about the intended audience for the book?
2. **Purpose:** What is Draut's purpose for analyzing the experiences of college students such as Shaney?
3. **Voice and tone:** How would you characterize Draut's tone in this piece? How does it affect her credibility?
4. **Responsibility:** Draut makes attending college appear to be fraught with financial worries. Is she merely being honest, or is she sensationalizing the situation? What makes you think so?
5. **Context, format, and genre:** This piece is an excerpt from a book. What clues from the piece, if any, that indicate this is an excerpt from a book, rather than a self-contained essay, are there? What insights does Draut's analysis offer?

Critical Thinking: The Writer's Ideas and Your Personal Response

6. As a college student, what is your initial reaction to Draut's analysis?
7. What point do you think Draut is trying to make here? What conclusions is Draut drawing from her analysis of the information she is presenting?

Composing Processes and Knowledge of Conventions: The Writer's Strategies

8. Draut begins this piece with an example of one student in financial straits because of student loans. She then generalizes to other groups and shows how financial problems can lead to dropping out. How effective do you find this method?
9. Draut uses many statistics, which she works into her text. How effective is this strategy?

Inquiry and Research: Ideas for Further Exploration

10. Find out the graduation rate for your college or university. Is your school doing anything to improve it? If so, what? If the problem is primarily financial, what, if anything, can an institution of higher education do to address it?

GENRES *Up Close* Writing a Visual Analysis

On any given day, you are likely to encounter hundreds or even thousands of texts with visuals such as photos, diagrams, charts, maps, and graphs. For example, advertisements with visual elements appear in magazines, newspapers, billboards, Web sites, and various other media. The visuals that you see each day are as rhetorical as the words that you read. Because these kinds of visual elements are pervasive and often persuasive, readers/viewers need skills for analyzing them. Writing visual analyses helps to develop these reading/viewing skills.

A visual analysis will usually include the following features:

- A copy of the image. Seeing the image will help the reader understand the analysis, and reading the analysis will help the reader gain new insights into the visual.
- A written description of the image. The description can help guide readers' attention to specific features.
- An analysis of what the visual image is communicating—the rhetorical features of the visual. As you craft your analysis, consider the material offered in Chapter 18, "Communicating with Design and Visuals." Also ask yourself the following kinds of questions:
  - What are the parts of the visual? How do the parts relate to the whole?
  - What story does the visual tells?
  - How do you react to the visual emotionally and/or intellectually?
  - What is the purpose of the visual?
  - How does the visual complement any verbal content in the text? (Most advertisements include both words and images.)
  - How is the visual placed in the text? Why do you think it is placed there?
  - How does this visual appeal to the intended audience? For example, a photo of Steve Lake (a catcher for the Chicago Cubs, Philadelphia Phillies, and St. Louis Cardinals in the 1980s and 1990s) playing in Game 7 of the 1987 World Series might appeal to a knowledgeable connoisseur of baseball, but it might not mean much to a casual fan of the game.
  - What would the text be like if the visual were missing?
  - What other visuals could work as well as, or even more effectively than, the current one? For example, a diagram might be more effective than a photo because a diagram can reveal more details.
  - What design principles (see Chapter 18) has the writer used in the visual?

JESSE HASSENGER

Irony As a Disguise

VISUAL ANALYSIS

Jesse Hassenger writes about popular culture for *PopMatters,* AMC's filmcritic.com, and *The L Magazine.* Favorite topics include animation, sketch comedy, and *Veronica Mars;* his essay on the latter was published in the anthology *Neptune Noir.* This analysis has not been published previously.

1 When faced with a barrage of competing advertisements, often ad-makers will disguise their images in order to better stand out. Upon first glance, this anti-drug ad looks like another sort entirely: the kind of retro enticement once found on the backs of comic books and youth-oriented magazines. Rather than an advertisement for weight-gain pills or a miracle diet, however, it recruits readers to become a professional "TV remote control operator," making hyperbolic claims about this dubious career path.

Even within this established framework, the central point may not be immediately clear to the reader—the piece could be construed as a public-service ad for any number of causes, such as encouraging exercise or discouraging the passive nature of TV watching. Those are both elements of the image, but it's only in the tagline at the bottom of the page that the ad's more specific goal becomes clear: "Hey, not trying to be your mom, but there aren't many jobs out there for potheads." 2

This is key to the ad's goal: to discourage drug use in a less hectoring tone than its audience may be accustomed to reading or hearing. The casual wording of that tagline—opening with "hey, not trying to be your mom"—seems designed to downplay the fact that the ad is, essentially, attempting to offer advice and guidance. This, combined with the humorous parody style of the ad, is arranged so that the reader might let his or her guard down and feel less resistant to the earnest and not necessarily "fashionable" message contained at its core. 3

Though the placement of its key, revealing tagline is subtle rather than attention-grabbing, the ad is actually quite text-heavy overall, using fonts, design, and fake-aging texture in place of too many images. Highlighting the flim-flam nature of its fake claim—that a fine living can be carved out from sitting on the couch and watching television—the ad's dominant images are a single greasy-looking fellow in a variety of ridiculous poses, with a few supporting images of a generic diploma and a hand holding a remote control. Though the text is enthusiastic, the spare and uninspiring (maybe even depressing) images signal the ad's irony. 4

The ad also uses its retro style to contribute to this sense of irony, since these types of ads are now recognized as silly and blatantly disingenuous. In fact, one potential problem with the ad would be if its target audience did not understand the reference to these kinds of old-timey huckster advertisements; the modern equivalent would likely be found in infomercial-style television spots, rather than a print source. However, the ad's sarcasm should be recognizable even without a familiarity with its inspiration, because of the prominent placement of the largest image, with the goofy-looking guy wielding two remotes. This image is the clearest immediate signal to readers that they are dealing with some kind of parody, and not a "real" advertisement—or rather, that the real advertisement will be revealed with closer attention. This sort of playful but decodable deception speaks to an image and advertising-saturated culture, where disguises can be the most efficient way to sneak a message across. 5

QUESTIONS FOR WRITING AND DISCUSSION: LEARNING OUTCOMES

Rhetorical Knowledge: The Writers' Situation and Rhetoric

1. **Audience:** What audience do you think Hassenger has in mind for this visual analysis? Why do you think that?
2. **Purpose:** What is Hassenger trying to accomplish in this visual analysis?
3. **Voice and Tone:** What is Hassenger's attitude toward his audience and the topic?
4. **Responsibility:** How seriously has Hassenger taken his responsibilities as a writer?
5. **Context and Format:** If Hassenger were to make this essay available in some other venue, such as a blog, how might he need to change the analysis?
6. **Genre:** A visual analysis usually includes the visual image, a description of the image, and some analysis of the image. To what extent does Hassenger's analysis do these three things?

Critical Thinking: The Writers' Ideas and Your Personal Response

7. To what extent do you agree with Hassenger's analysis? Why?

Composing Processes and Knowledge of Conventions

8. How has Hassenger organized his analysis? Why do you think that he organized it that way?

Inquiry and Research: Ideas for Further Exploration

9. Hassenger does not comment on the text in the middle of the ad elaborating on the advantages of being a TV remote control operator. What could be said about those words relative to the visual image?
10. Find other ads that include humor to stand out. How many of them use visuals, as Hassenger notes, to "signal to readers that they are dealing with some kind of parody, and not a 'real' advertisement - or rather, that the real advertisement will be revealed with closer attention"?

mhconnectcomposition.com

Writing to Analyze Animated Walkthrough QL7004

Writing Processes

As you work on the assignment you have chosen, remember the qualities of an effective analytical paper, which are listed on pages 189–190. Also remember that writing is recursive—you might start with an invention activity or two and then conduct some research, which leads to more invention work and then a first draft; but then you might need to do more invention work to help flesh out your draft and conduct more research to fill in gaps in information; and then you will revise your draft and possibly find another gap or two. . . . So while the activities listed below imply that writers go through them step-by-step, the actual process of writing is usually messier.

Invention: Getting Started

Try to answer these questions while you do your invention work:

- What do I already know about the subject that I am considering for my analysis?
- What insights do I already have to offer?
- Where might I learn more about the topic I am considering? What verifiable information am I likely to find?
- What do I know about my audience?
- What might my audience already know about this topic? How can I make my insights convincing for them?
- What questions do I need to answer before I can begin (and complete) my analysis?

Writing Activity

Freewriting, Listing, and Interviewing

Using the questions above, jot down (freewrite) everything you can think of about your subject in ten minutes. Even if you cannot think of anything to say, keep writing.

Next, place your ideas in a sequence—whether from smallest to largest or least to most important. A list helps you categorize each aspect of your subject for an analysis. Once you have put your information in a list, you can move each item around as you see fit.

Finally, ask others what they know about your subject—what they see as its component parts, what they think are its important aspects, and how they think those parts or aspects work together. A useful way to conduct such interviews is to center on the *who, what, where, when, why,* and *how* questions that a newspaper reporter generally asks.

Sarah Washington's Interviewing

Student writer Sarah Washington decided to respond to Scenario 1 (page 000) about a campus issue. When her instructor mentioned the issue of campus parking, Washington knew she had found her subject. In class, she used free-writing to get her initial ideas on paper and then decided to interview Michael Nguyen, who heads her college's Parking and Transit office. Here is a portion of that inteview:

Question: Can you tell me a little about who you are and what your background is?

Answer: I have a degree—believe it or not—in Public Parking, and I'd worked with two businesses before I came here. When I started here, I had to start at the bottom and slowly worked my way up and I've had this position for nearly five years.

Q: What exactly does Parking & Transit do? What does it cost to park on campus?

A: P&T has 4,500 parking spaces available—most are in paved lots, but we also handle the Elm Street garage, which has six levels of covered parking, and the garage on Maple with five levels. We handle the cleaning, the paving and repair work, selling parking permits to students and faculty, and so on. We also patrol the campus, giving parking tickets to anyone illegally parked.

Lately, we've spent a lot of time talking to dorm residents, to see how we might provide better and more parking for their use. But it's a battle—we only have so much space on campus, and we're growing every semester in terms of students. That's a good problem to have.

Parking costs for the covered garage are $250 a semester; for the surface lots it's $200 a semester. However, it costs us about $150 a semester to maintain a surface parking space, and about $200 a semester to maintain a garage space in the garage—so we really lose money.

Q: When does most of your work take place?

A: Well, we're really busy right before classes start, selling permits. But we also get busy at mid-term as the lots and garages are pretty dirty by then—lots of litter—so there's an ongoing cleaning program. And we're busy all the time patrolling—we give out a lot of parking tickets.

EXAMPLES OF INVENTION

Brainstorming (pp. 158, 332)
Freewriting (pp. 114, 245, 383)
Criteria (p. 290)
Listing (p. 72)
Answers to Reporter's Questions (p. 244)
Organization (pp. 75, 164)
Clustering (pp. 114, 289)
Concept Mapping (p. 335)
Interviewing (p. 203)
Research (pp. 115, 160, 205, 246, 292, 384)
Reflection (p. 12)

Exploring Your Ideas with Research

Before you begin your research, consider what your focal point should be. For example, you may want to research how electronic telecommunications such as cell phones and the Internet are helping families to keep in touch and to share more information. You may choose to focus on how college students who live away from home are keeping in touch with their parents. Look over your invention work to remind yourself of all that you know about your subject, as well as the questions you came up with about it. Use the reporter's questions of *who, what, where, when, why,* and *how* to get started on your research. After you have decided what information you need, determine what kind of research you need to conduct in order to gather that information. Use an electronic journal to record images, URLs, interview notes, and other electronic pieces of information that you find as you conduct your research.

Writing Activity

Conducting Research

Consider your subject for analysis and, in no more than two pages, outline a research plan. In your plan, indicate the following:

- What you already know about your subject
- What questions you still have
- Who or what sources might be able to answer your questions
- Who (roommates, college staff, professors) might be able to provide other perspectives on your subject
- Where you might look for further information (library, Web, primary documents, other sources)
- When you plan to conduct your research

Sarah Washington's Research

Sarah Washington began her invention and research on college parking by writing down what she already knew and the questions she still had. During the early stages of her invention work, she realized that she was having an emotional response to the issue of parking and really did not have good information about the reasons for the situation. She started her formal research by interviewing Michael Nguyen. She then interviewed others affected by college parking to find out what they thought about their situation, focusing on the reporter's *who, what, where, when, why,* and *how* questions; she also learned what other colleges do in terms of parking, examined how parking permits are issued, and determined whether the parking costs at her college are in line with what other, similar, colleges charge for parking.

After interviewing several people on campus, she made the following notes in her research journal.

There needs to be sufficient parking for all the students who live in campus housing who have or are allowed to have cars. Of course, this number could vary from semester to semester.

We have 4,500 parking places, in the garages and in surface lots (Nguyen interview).

There also needs to be sufficient parking for the staff who drive to work during regular business hours. Faculty needs are more difficult to determine. Their time on campus is inconsistent. While it is easy to know when they teach and hold office hours, other times (class preparation, grading, writing, researching in labs or the library, attending meetings, etc.) all vary from week to week. They need a parking spot, but they might not all be on campus at the same time. The trick is to figure out what pecentage is likely to be on campus.

Mr. Nguyen told me that there were 13,845 total students enrolled this semester. Of that total, 6,735 live on campus. 2,700 of the resident students have cars. There are 512 full-time faculty and 193 part-time faculty. In addition, there are 398 staff people who work at the university.

Commuter students—there are about 6,500 of them, according to Mr. Nguyen—may be the group whose parking needs are most difficult to determine. They often lead complicated lives balancing school, work, and family obligations. They come to campus for class, but also likely come to campus at other times to use the library and other campus facilities, or to take part in other activities. It's difficult to determine when they will be on campus. I should ask some commuter students in my English class when they actually *are* at school—in class or at the library or whatever—to get some sense of how much that group of students is on campus.

Finally, all campuses need to provide parking spaces for visitors. Again, the needs of visitors vary. They can be prospective students, businesspeople, government employees, or industry leaders who need to meet with the faculty or administration. Sometimes they are members of the general public who want or need to use university facilities that may be open. Who can I talk to about how many visitors we have, on average?

EXAMPLES OF INVENTION

Brainstorming (pp. 158, 332)
Freewriting (pp. 114, 245, 383)
Criteria (p. 290)
Listing (p. 72)
Answers to Reporter's Questions (p. 244)
Organization (pp. 75, 164)
Clustering (pp. 114, 289)
Concept Mapping (p. 335)
Interviewing (p. 203)
Research (pp. 115, 160, 205, 246, 292, 384)
Reflection (p. 12)

Reviewing Your Invention and Research

After you have conducted your research, review your invention work and notes, and think about the information you have collected from outside sources. You may be ready to decide on a working thesis statement—a statement that summarizes the main point of your analysis—at this point. Even though you might already have a general idea of the conclusion your analysis is leading you to, until you get some of your ideas and research down on paper, it is often difficult to know what your thesis will be. It is helpful to decide on your thesis after you have done your invention work (listing, brainstorming, and clustering, for example) and research.

For more on developing a thesis, see Chapter 13.

A WRITER'S *Responsibility* | Constructing Analytical Writing in the Sciences

Effective analytical writing is thorough, examining and explaining as many details as possible. If you are working in a field that has particular procedures in place, you have an obligation to follow the accepted procedures faithfully. For example, if you are working in a scientific field, you will need to document everything you do—from taking notes on your process, to constructing drawings that illustrate the process, to verifying measurements with specific instruments. You also must clearly and accurately present any statistical data, with all supporting evidence and detail, and you must explain relationships between variables in your experiment.

To construct an effective scientific analysis, follow the four-step **scientific method:**

1. Observe and describe a phenomenon or group of phenomena.
2. Formulate a hypothesis to explain the phenomena.
3. Use your hypothesis to predict the existence of other phenomena or to predict quantitatively the results of new observations.
4. Test your predictions by conducting experiments.

Source: The four steps are adapted from Frank Wolfs, "Appendix E: Introduction to the Scientific Method." http://teacher.nsrl.rochester.edu/phy_labs/AppendixE/AppendixE.html. Downloaded 12/13/03.

Organizing Your Information

When you have some sense of what your analysis will include, consider how you might organize this material. The questions to ask yourself when deciding on your organization are rhetorical:

- Who is your audience?
- Why might they be interested in your analysis, or how can you make them interested in it?
- What is your purpose for writing—that is, why do your readers need this analysis?
- What is the most important aspect of your subject?

For more on cause and effect, see Chapter 10; for more on classification, see Chapter 13.

The answers to these questions can help you decide what you need to emphasize, which in turn will help you choose an organization.

Here are three organizational structures that you might consider.

Options FOR Organization

Options for Organizing an Analysis

Defining Parts	Classification	Relating Causes and Effects
Explain why the subject you are analyzing is important to your readers.	Start with a question about your subject that readers probably do not know the answer to.	Begin with information about your subject that may surprise your readers.
Provide examples of how readers might be affected by the subject.	Explain why knowing the answer to this question will benefit your readers.	Explain how an analysis of your subject will lead to more surprises and better understanding.
Provide background information so readers can see the whole subject of your analysis.	Use the writing strategy of *classification* to explain your subject, labeling and explaining each aspect or part.	Use the writing strategy of *cause and effect* to show how each aspect or part of your subject causes or is affected by the other aspects or parts.
Use a strategy of *description* to explain each aspect or part of your subject.	Provide specific examples to illustrate each category.	Provide specific examples to show what you mean.
Provide examples to show what you mean.	Conclude by showing how the aspects or parts function together to make up the whole of your subject.	Conclude by outlining how parts of your subject function together.
Conclude by showing how each aspect or part works together.		

Constructing a Complete Draft

Once you have chosen the most effective organizational approach, you are ready to construct the rest of your draft. Consider how you might use the invention materials you generated and how you might integrate the research information you gathered.

As you write your first draft, remember the main point that you are trying to make (if you have decided on one). In an analysis, you will want to make sure that your discussion of the aspects of your subject helps to support what it is that you are trying to say about the whole.

There are many ways to write a first draft. It may seem to make the most sense to you to start at the first sentence and then move to the end; however, many writers, once they are comfortable with their organization, write individual pieces of their draft and then put them all together.

Synthesizing and Integrating Sources into Your Draft: Incorporating Numerical Data

connect
mhconnectcomposition.com
Drafting and Revising QL7005

When writers use numerical data, they do not need to put numbers in quotation marks because there is no other way to express numbers. However, if a writer uses the exact words of a source to comment on those data, then quotation marks are required. For example, in the essay "Campus Parking: Love It or Leave It" (pages 217–219), writer Sarah Washington includes numerical data, which she gathered from Michael Nguyen and from some offices at other universities. Notice that she reports the data without any commentary from Nguyen or anyone else. Therefore, readers can assume that the following section of her analytical essay includes the exact numbers that Nguyen provided, but that the words are Washington's:

INTEGRATING SOURCES

> When I interviewed Mr. Michael Nguyen, head of Parking and Transit, he gave me the following background information:
> —A total of 13,845 students are registered this semester.
> —Of those, 6,735 live on campus.
> —A total of 2,700 resident students (that is, student who live on campus) have cars.
> —There are 512 full-time faculty members; 193 part-time faculty.
> —There are 398 staff employees.

Even though Washington is not quoting Nguyen, she is crediting him as a source when she introduces the data with the sentence "When I interviewed Mr. Michael Nguyen, head of Parking and Transit, he gave me the following background information:" Of course, in her list of works cited at the end of the essay, Washington also includes information about the source:

> Nguyen, Michael. Personal interview. 2 November 2008.

When integrating numerical data into your writing projects, consider the following guidelines:

1. Double-check the source to make certain that you have reported the data accurately.
2. Do not place numbers in quotation marks unless you include commentary from the source.
3. Indicate the source in the body of your text and in your list of works cited or references.

Parts of a Complete Draft

connect
mhconnectcomposition.com
Introductory paragraph overview QL7006

Introduction: Regardless of your organizational approach, begin with a strong introduction that captures your readers' attention and introduces the subject you are analyzing. To do so, you might use one of the following strategies:

- **Explain (briefly) why an analysis of your subject might be of interest.** In "Putting In the Hours" (pages 191–193), James Lang suggests that it might be interesting to consider the behavior of his subject, the North American college professor.
- **Provide a brief outline of what most people know about your subject.**
- **Explain (briefly) why your analysis is important.** Just as Tamara Draut does in "All Work and No Play" (pages 195–196), you may want to look at how the problem affects one person and then generalize to show how it affects many people.
- **Provide a fact about the subject you are analyzing that will surprise or concern your readers.**

Body: You can use various writing strategies to effectively analyze your subject:

- **Classify and label each aspect of your subject.** In "Putting In the Hours", James Lang organizes his descriptions of professors and their offices by labeling them: the "Early Bird," the "Door Closer," the "Chatterer," and so on. He then describes each type.
- **Define the various parts of your subject—explaining what each is and how it relates to the other parts.** If you were to analyze a smart phone, for example, you would probably focus on the input options (keypad or touch screen), texting and phone capability, audio, video, and web-browsing capability.
- **Compare and contrast each aspect of your subject, so readers can see the differences and similarities.** For instance, you might compare the functional features of two PDAs.
- **Focus on the cause-and-effect relationship of each aspect of your subject,** to show how one aspect causes, or is caused by, one or more other aspects. This approach would work well if you were analyzing a complex machine such as a car or an airplane.

For more on classification, definition, comparison and contrast, and causal analysis, see Chapter 13.

Conclusion: In your conclusion, review the major parts or aspects of your subject, explaining the following:

- How they relate to one another
- How they function together
- How all of the aspects of your subject lead to the conclusion you have reached

connect
mhconnectcomposition.com
Concluding paragraph overview QL7007

Title: As you compose your analysis, a title may emerge, but often it will not occur to you until late in the process. Because an analysis is by definition complex, you may not be able to summarize your main ideas in your title, but it should be something that catches your readers' attention.

VISUALIZING *Variations* | Using Charts and Graphs to Make Your Analysis Clear

Changes in Tuition, 2004–2008

	Our College	Other Colleges
2004	4.00%	5.60%
2005	6.50%	7.70%
2006	4.70%	5.00%
2007	3.70%	6.10%
2008	5.20%	7.10%

You might discover that an effective way to show your analysis is by means of a chart or graph such as a flowchart, a pie chart, a bar graph, or a line graph. For example, the data at left focuses on the changes in tuition costs at a fictional college, in percentages, between 2004 and 2008:

If you wanted to show these data in a graph, you could present them in several ways. A line graph would look like this:

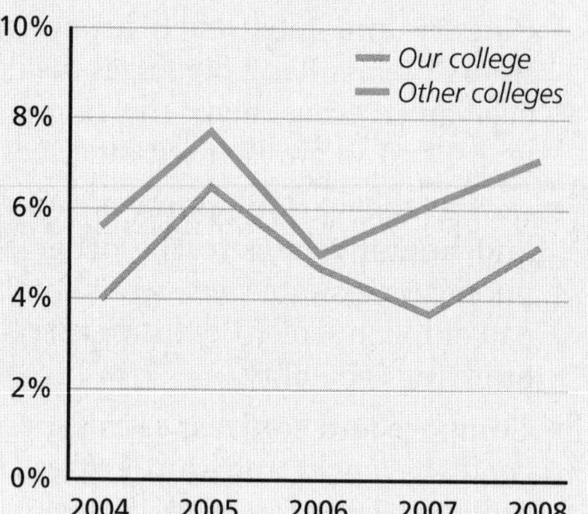

If you displayed the same data in a bar graph, the visual would look like this:

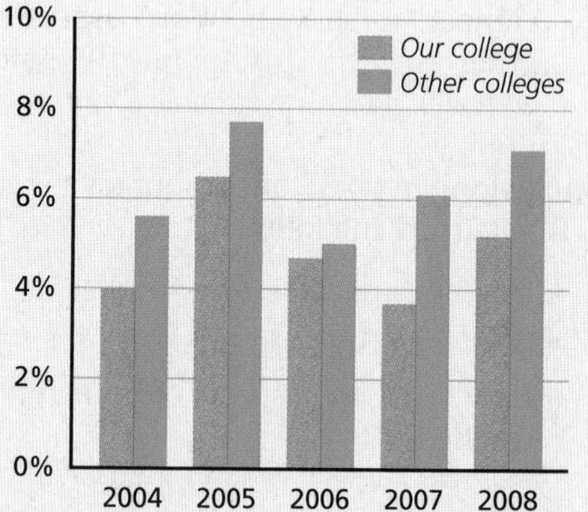

- What type of chart or graph most effectively shows and explains how your college's tuition has changed in relation to other colleges' tuition? Why?
- How would it affect your audience's understanding if you used more than one kind of chart or graph in your analysis?

Digital Literacy **Using Excel to Convert Data into Visuals**

If you are working with numbers and quantities for your analysis, consider using a spreadsheet program such as Microsoft Office Excel. The Excel program can quickly convert your data into tables, graphs, and charts. If you are taking a class that uses advanced spreadsheet software such as SPSS, you may want to use it for creating charts and graphs that illustrate data you are writing about.

Sarah Washington's First Draft

Sarah Washington decided to start her first draft with a portion of her original freewriting as an opening paragraph. Note also that she uses headings for her report, which is excerpted below.

Because this is a first draft, Washington did not worry about errors in usage, grammar, punctuation, or spelling. She concentrated on getting her ideas down. (The numbers in circles refer to peer comments—see page 215.)

Writing Activity

Constructing a Complete Draft

Using the writing you did when selecting an organizational approach, write a complete draft of your analytical paper. Remember that your analysis will likely evolve as you write.

Campus Parking: Love It or Leave It

Sarah Washington

Like many others, I've been frustrated by the parking situation since I first started school here. . . . Every year it seems as though the parking fees go up, and every year it seems as though it's harder to find a good parking spot.❶

I finally decided to do something about it. I started by going to the Student Government Office to see if they had information on why the parking was so bad on this campus and what they were planning to do about it. I was told the best person to talk with was Michael Nguyen, the head of our parking department.

Campus Data

I interviewed Mr. Nguyen and received the following background information:

There were 13,845 total students enrolled this semester. Of that total, 6,735 live on campus. 2,700 of the resident students have cars. There are 512 full-time faculty and 193 part-time faculty. In addition, there are 398 staff people who work at the university.❷

Analysis

Looking at those numbers, I was able to make the following quick determinations. If everyone drove themselves to campus and needed to be there at the same time, the campus would need 12,913 parking spots (the total of all the faculty and staff and students who are either nonresidential or have cars). That means the university would have to be looking at close to 13,000 parking spots, which is especially important because Nguyen told me that the campus presently has 4,500 parking spots.

My initial response was no wonder I always felt I could never find a parking spot.❸ However, I soon realized that even at 9:00 am on Monday not every one of those 13,000 people will be on campus and not everyone drives. I knew I had friends who lived in apartments close enough to campus that they walked to class. And, after talking to Nguyen, I realized that not only are all students not on campus at the same time, but all faculty aren't necessarily on campus at the same time either. In addition, some students, and to a lesser degree, faculty and staff, carpool. All of these variables act to reduce the number of parking spaces that is really needed.

We can get a better idea of how great the need really is by looking❹ at the following scenario. By looking at staff surveys done by the Parking Office, we learn that 15% of the staff either carpool or use some other means of transportation. That gives us around 340 spots that are necessary to support employees not counting the faculty.

If we then assume, at the busiest time of day, 60% of the full time faculty and 50% of the part time faculty need to be on campus, and they all drive their own vehicles and don't carpool, that will cause us to have an additional need of around 410 spots.

It may be more difficult to determine the real number of spots that students need. However, if we assume that at the time of highest traffic, 70% of students are there, we can see there will then be a need for approximately 4,500 student spaces—not counting the necessary 2,700 spaces by the resident halls.

Adding all of these numbers, we discover that the campus may need around 7,950 parking spots, or a little more than 61% of the initial estimate of more 13,000 spots. It also becomes evident that the campus really can use a lot more parking at peak periods—not my initial thought of 5,500 spots. . . .

Conclusion

I also became acutely aware that determining how many parking spots are needed is not an exact science. There are many variables and they may change from semester to semester. In addition to the raw numbers, I discovered that part of the problem exists as a result of the desirability of the lots. Everyone wants to be close to where they're going, but that "where" keeps changing. During the morning, students all want to park in the lots closer to the academic buildings where their classes were being held. Later in the day, more vehicles could be found in the lot that serves the student union and the library. One thing that might help is simply having students plan their days on campus a little better. For example, if they have classes in the morning and plan on staying on campus for most of the day, they might have a much easier time looking for a parking spot over by the library rather than the classroom buildings.❺

Revising

Many writers find that it is useful to let their work "sit" for a time—to put it aside for a day or two and then revise it. When you approach your work this way, you will find it easier to notice parts that are not explained in enough detail, or examples that are confusing, or places where an illustration or graph might show what you mean more clearly than the text does.

As you revise your early drafts, wait before doing any heavy editing. When you revise, you will probably change the content and structure of your paper, so time spent working to fix problems with sentence style or grammar, punctuation, or mechanics at this stage is often wasted.

When you reread the first draft of your analysis, here are some questions to ask yourself:

- What else might my audience want or need to know about my subject?
- How else might I interest my audience in my analysis of this subject?
- What did I find out about my subject that I did not include in my paper?
- Have I clearly explained any terms my readers might not know?
- Could some aspects of my analysis be better presented as a graph or chart?

Use your word processor's track-changes tool to try out revisions and editing changes. After you have had time to think about the possible changes, you can "accept" or "reject" them. Also, you can use your word processor's comment tool to write reminders to yourself.

Because it is so difficult to see emerging writing with a fresh eye (even for experienced writers), it is almost always useful to ask classmates, friends, or family members to read drafts of your papers and comment on them.

WRITER'S *Workshop* | Responding to Full Drafts

Working in pairs or groups of three, read one another's papers, and then offer your classmates comments that will help them see both their papers' strengths and places where they need to develop their ideas further. Use the following questions to guide your responses to the writer's draft:

- What is your first impression of this draft? How effectively does the title draw you into the paper? Why?
- What do you like about the draft?
- What is effective about the introduction? What suggestions can you make on how to improve it?
- How well do you understand what the author is trying to do in this paper? Does the paper wander a bit? Where? What questions are left unanswered?
- How has the writer demonstrated an awareness of readers' knowledge, needs, and/or expectations for the analysis?
- How effective is this paper as an analysis? How has the writer covered—or failed to cover—all of the parts or aspects of the subject adequately? What *other* aspects of the subject should be included?
- What is your opinion of the author's insight into the subject? How meaningful is it?
- What do you think is the author's thesis or main claim for the analysis? How could it be expressed or supported more effectively?
- In the main part of the paper, are there parts that are confusing or concepts that are unclear? Where would you like more details or examples to help you see what the author means?
- Is the writer's tone straightforward and neutral?
- What rhetorical appeals (*ethos, pathos, logos*) do you see in the text? How could they be used more effectively? (See page 12 in Chapter 1 and pages 458–460 in Chapter 14 for definitions of *ethos, pathos,* and *logos.*)
- How accurate and appropriate is the supporting evidence? Are there any questionable statistics, inaccurate facts, or questionable authorities. How clearly does the author indicate the sources for statistics and other supporting information?
- How well does the conclusion tie everything together?
- If there are visual aspects of the document, how effectively do they illustrate the point being made?
- What do you see as the main weaknesses of this paper? How might the writer might improve the text?

Student Comments on Sarah Washington's First Draft

Sarah Washington received comments on her first draft from several readers. Below are comments on her draft, keyed to the first draft on pages 211–213.

1. "Interesting introduction, but I'm not sure what the purpose of your paper is. Are you going to try to inform readers of parking problems or persuade us to do something?"
2. "These numbers are confusing like this—maybe put them into a list?"
3. "Also interesting, but you have a lot of your personal feelings in your paper. If I understood your paper's purpose, I'd know better whether it's appropriate for them to be in it."
4. "Who is 'we' here? I'm not sure why you're using 'we'—sounds strange."
5. "Now you're ending, and you're back to the number of parking spaces, without ever explaining what all that information about parking has to do with anything."

Responding to Readers' Comments

Once they have received feedback from peers, teachers, and others, writers have to decide how to deal with those comments and suggestions. It is important to consider carefully what your readers are saying to you. You may decide to reject some comments, of course, because they are not consistent with your goals for your paper. For example, some readers may disagree with your point of view or conclusion. You may find that comments from more than one reader contradict each other. In that case, use your own judgment to decide which reader's comments are on the right track.

In the final draft of Sarah Washington's paper, on pages 217–219, you can see how Washington responded to readers' comments, as well as to her own review of her first draft.

Knowledge of Conventions

When effective writers edit their work, they attend to the conventions that will help readers—the table manners of writing. These include genre conventions, documentation, format, usage, grammar, punctuation, and mechanics. By attending to these conventions in your writing, you make reading a more pleasant experience for readers.

connect
mhconnectcomposition.com
Revising and Editing overview (also Drafting) QL7008

Editing

The last task in any writing project is editing—the final polishing of your document. When you edit and polish your writing, you change your sentence structures and word choices to improve your style and to make your writing clearer and more concise. You also check your work to make sure it adheres to conventions of grammar, usage, punctuation, mechanics, and spelling. Use the spell-check function of your word-processing program, but be sure to double-check your spelling personally. If you have used sources in your paper, make sure you are following the documentation style your instructor requires.

See Chapter 20 for more on documenting sources.

As with overall revision of your work, this final editing and polishing is most effective if you can put your text aside for a time and come back to it with fresh eyes. Because checking conventions is easier said than done, though, we strongly recommend that you ask classmates, friends, and tutors to read your work as well.

To assist you with editing, we offer here a round-robin editing activity focused on finding and correcting problems with wordy sentences, a constant challenge for many writers.

ROUND-ROBIN EDITING WITH A FOCUS ON

Punctuating Dialogue (p. 82)
Fragments (p. 126)
Modifiers (p. 172)
Wordiness (p. 216)
Citing Sources (p. 259)
Careful Word Choice (p. 303)
Subordinate Clauses (p. 347)
Inclusive Language (p. 395)

WRITER'S *Workshop* | Round-Robin Editing with a Focus on Wordiness

Wordiness—using more words than necessary—is a common concern for writers and their readers. Wordy sentences take longer to read, and having a large number of them in your paper will increase your reader's workload and decrease your paper's effectiveness.

Work with two peers to edit one another's papers for wordiness. Ask yourself questions like "Is the writer repeating herself?" and "Has the writer included phrases that don't add meaning to the sentence?" Circle sentences that can be made more concise, and make suggestions on how to tighten them. Compare notes to see if you have any questions about wordiness, and ask your instructor for assistance.

connect
mhconnectcomposition.com
Correcting wordy sentences QL7010
Correcting missing words QL7011

Genres, Documentation, and Format

For advice on writing in different genres, see the Online Appendix. For guidelines for formatting and documenting papers in MLA or APA style, see Chapter 20.

If you are writing an academic paper, follow the conventions for the discipline in which you are writing and the requirements of your instructor. If you are constructing a formal business report for Scenario 3, follow the model for a business analysis report.

If you have used material from outside sources, including visuals, credit those sources, using the documentation style required by the discipline you are working in and by your instructor.

A Writer Shares Her Analysis: Sarah Washington's Final Draft

After meeting with peer reviewers, Sarah Washington continued to revise her paper and eventually constructed a finished draft. The final draft of "Campus Parking: Love It or Leave it" follows. As you read the essay, think about what makes it effective.

SARAH WASHINGTON

Campus Parking: Love It or Leave It

ANALYTICAL ESSAY

Like many others, I've been frustrated by the parking situation since I first started school here. While talking to other students, I've discovered that we're all not very happy about the parking. It's too expensive, and there are never enough spots. I've talked to other students who are juniors and seniors, and they say it's been like this since they started. Every year it seems as though the parking fees go up, and every year it seems as though it's harder to find a good parking spot. An analysis of the parking situation on campus will help anyone concerned with parking (and that includes most students) understand how parking "works" at our college. I am focusing my analysis on two aspects of campus parking: the number of spaces, including how many spaces are actually needed, and also the costs for parking on campus, especially compared to what other colleges charge. 1

One classmate wrote this comment on Washington's paper:

Interesting introduction, but I'm not sure what the purpose of your paper is. Are you going to try to inform readers of parking problems or persuade us to do something?

In her revision, Washington clearly indicates what she is trying to accomplish: to analyze the parking situation.

Campus Data

When I interviewed Mr. Michael Nguyen, head of Parking and Transit, he gave me the following background information: 2

A total of 13,845 students are registered this semester.
Of those, 6,735 live on campus.
A total of 2,700 resident students (that is, student who live on campus) have cars.
There are 512 full-time faculty members, 193 part-time faculty.
There are 398 staff employees.

Washington responded to one of her peer reviewers and placed this information in a list to make it more readable.

Analysis

Looking at the numbers Mr. Nguyen provided, I was able to make the following quick determinations. If everyone drove to campus and needed to be there at the same time, the campus would need 12,913 parking spots (the total of all the faculty, staff, and students who are either nonresiden- 3

In her earlier draft, Washington got this comment from one of her peer reviewers to this sentence from her first draft: "My initial response was no wonder I always felt I could never find a parking spot."

Also interesting but you have a lot of your personal feelings in your paper. If I understood your paper's purpose I'd know better whether it's appropriate for them to be in it.

Note that in her final version she has removed her personal comment as she continues to outline the details of her analysis.

A classmate asked this question and made this comment on Washington's draft:

Who is "we" here? I'm not sure why you're using "we" so much—sounds strange.

She revised her draft to remove the word *we*, which also helped to make her sentences more concise.

tial or have cars). That means the university would have to provide close to 13,000 parking spots, or around 5,500 additional spots. This is especially important because, according to Nguyen, the campus presently has 6,100 parking spots.

However, even at 9:00 a.m. on Monday not every one of those 13,000 people will be on campus, and not everyone who is on campus drives. I have friends who live in apartments close enough to campus to allow them to walk to class. And, after talking to Nguyen, I realized that not only are all students not on campus at the same time, but all faculty aren't necessarily on campus at the same time either. In addition, some students, and to a lesser degree, faculty and staff, carpool. All of these variables act to reduce the number of parking spaces really needed on campus. Clearly we need further analysis to understand the severity of the parking problem. 4

Staff surveys done by the Parking Office indicate that 15% of the staff either carpool or use some other means of transportation. Therefore, around 340 spots are necessary to support employees, not counting the faculty. If we then assume that, at the busiest time of day, 60% of the full-time faculty and 50% of the part-time faculty need to be on campus, and they all drive their own vehicles and don't carpool, then the campus will need around 410 additional spots. 5

It may be more difficult to determine the real number of spots that students need. However, assuming that at the time of highest traffic there are 70% of the nonresident students present on campus, and since many students live close enough to walk and are more likely to carpool, we can estimate that 70% of those students need parking. At these times, then, the campus will need approximately 4,500 student spaces—not counting the necessary 2,700 spaces by the resident halls. 6

Adding all of these numbers, we determine that the campus may need in the neighborhood of 7,950 parking spots, or a little more than 61% of the initial estimate of more 13,000 spots. It is evident that the campus really can use some more parking at peak periods, but only around 500 spots—not my initial estimate of 5,500 spots. 7

Parking Costs

This analysis reveals that the college is close to the number of parking spots it needs, but cost is another part of the whole campus parking picture. Parking on our campus—which for students runs $200 per semester, seems to be in the midrange. Some universities such as Iowa State University only charge students $100 per year to park (Iowa State University). However, the University of Washington charges students $1,140 for yearly parking (University of Washington). 8

Other schools charge varying amounts: 9

The University of Nebraska: "perimeter parking " is 238.50 per year while "reserved parking" is $670.50 per year. There are two other levels, $337.50 and $427.50 per year, in between (University of Nebraska).

The University of Texas at Austin: students can park in surface lots for $110 or $170 a year, but if they want garage parking, it runs from $677 to $743 per year (University of Texas).

Parking costs at our school, it appears, are not out of line with other colleges.

Conclusion

Determining how many parking spots are needed on a campus is not an 10
exact science. There are many variables involved and those variables may change from semester to semester. In addition to the raw numbers, I discovered that part of the problem with parking exists as a result of the desirability of the lots. Everyone wants to be close to where they're going, but that "where" keeps changing. During the morning, students all seem to want to park in the lots closer to the academic buildings where their classes are being held. Later in the day, more vehicles can be found in the lot that serves the student union and the library. Students can help the situation by simply planning their days on campus a little better. For example, if they have classes in the morning and plan on staying on campus for most of the day, they might have a much easier time finding a parking spot over by the library rather than in crowded lots near the classroom buildings. Where parking is concerned, a little strategy can go a long way.

Works Cited

Iowa State University Department of Public Safety. "2008–2009 Fees." Web. 13 November 2008. <http://www.dps.iastate.edu/wordpress/?page_id=79>.

Nguyen, Michael. Personal interview. 2 November 2008.

University of Nebraska–Lincoln Parking & Transit Services. "Permit Costs." Web. 13 November 2008. <http://parking.unl.edu/permits/cost.shtml>.

University of Texas at Austin. "Parking and Transportation Services." Web. 13 November 13, 2008. <http://www.utexas.edu/parking/parking/student/>.

University of Washington Facilities Services. "Commuter Services." Web. 13 November 2008. <http://www.washington.edu/commuterservices/parking/fees/index.php>.

In her first draft, Washington received this comment from a classmate:

Now you're ending, and you're back to the number of parking spaces, without ever explaining what all that information about parking has to do with anything.

Note how she now offers a more effective conclusion to her text.

Washington has provided a synthesis of the information she has analyzed.

This paper follows MLA guidelines for in-text citations and works cited. Note that URLs are optional.

QUESTIONS FOR WRITING AND DISCUSSION: LEARNING OUTCOMES

Rhetorical Knowledge: The Writer's Situation and Rhetoric

1. **Audience:** What audience does Washington have in mind for this essay? How can you tell?
2. **Purpose:** What can you point to in Washington's paper that indicates her purpose?
3. **Voice and tone:** How would you describe the tone Washington uses in her paper? Would a different tone (more strident, perhaps, or more subdued) have made her analysis more, or less, effective? Why?
4. **Responsibility:** How accurately does Washington represent statistical information? How credible is Washington's analysis? Why?
5. **Context, format, and genre:** Washington is writing as a college student concerned about parking on her campus. How does this context affect her use of language, appeals, and evidence in her analysis? Washington chose to write her analysis as an informal report. What impact does this genre have on you as a reader? Can you explain how by using this genre Washington's paper is more or less understandable than if she had chosen to just write an essay?

Critical Thinking: The Writer's Ideas and Your Personal Response

6. What is your initial response to Washington's analysis? What in her text causes your response?
7. To what extent does Washington's report give you insight into how parking might work at other public places serving large groups of drivers?

Composing Processes and Knowledge of Conventions: The Writer's Strategies

8. Construct a brief outline of Washington's analysis. How effective is her organization? Why?
9. How effectively does Washington use statistics or data to support her claims?

Inquiry and Research: Ideas for Further Exploration

10. At your library, find a journal or magazine that covers the area you think you want to major in, and locate an example of an analysis. In no more than two pages, explain why that text is or is not an effective analysis.

Self-Assessment: Reflecting on Your Goals

Now that you have constructed a piece of analytical writing, go back and consider your learning goals. Write notes on what you have learned from this assignment.

Rhetorical Knowledge

- *Audience:* What have you learned about addressing an audience in analytical writing?

- *Purpose:* What have you learned about the purposes for constructing an analysis?
- *Rhetorical situation:* How did the writing context affect your analytical text? How did your choice of topic affect the research you conducted and the way you presented your analysis to your readers? What do you see as the strongest part of your analysis? Why? The weakest? Why?
- *Voice and tone:* How would you describe your voice in this essay? Your tone? How do they contribute to the effectiveness of your analysis?

Critical Thinking, Reading, and Writing

- *Learning/inquiry:* What process did you go through to focus on a main idea, or thesis. How did you judge what was most and least important?
- *Responsibility:* How did you fulfill your responsibility to your readers?
- *Reading and research:* What did you learn about analytical writing from the reading selections you read for this chapter? What research did you conduct? How sufficient was the research you did?
- *Skills:* As a result of writing this analysis, how have you become a more critical thinker, reader, and writer?

Writing Processes

- *Invention:* What invention strategies were most useful to you?
- *Organizing your ideas and details:* What organization did you use? How successful was it?
- *Revising:* What one revision did you make that you are most satisfied with? Why? If you could make an additional revision, what would it be?
- *Working with peers:* How did your instructor or peer readers help you by making comments and suggestions about your writing? How could you have made better use of the comments and suggestions you received?
- *Visuals:* Did you use photographs or other visuals to help explain your analysis to readers? If so, what did you learn about incorporating them?
- *Writing habits:* What "writerly habits" have you developed, modified, or improved on as you completed the writing assignment for this chapter?

Knowledge of Conventions

- *Editing:* What sentence problem did you find most frequently in your writing? How will you avoid that problem in future assignments?
- *Genre:* What conventions of the genre you were using, if any, gave you problems?
- *Documentation:* Did you use sources for your paper? If so, what documentation style did you use? What problems, if any, did you have with it?

Refer to Chapter 1 (pages 11–12) for a sample reflection by a student.

Sarah Washington Reflects on Her Writing QL7009

Writing to Convince

Think of the last time you wrote something. Whether it was a formal academic paper, a letter, or an informal note such as a text message to a friend, your writing was most likely designed to convince someone about something—to persuade your reader that he or she should accept your particular point of view. In fact, most purposes for writing—to inform, to explain, to analyze—to some degree almost always involve persuasion.

You encounter **persuasive writing**—writing designed to convince readers to agree with the writer's position—many times a day. Notice, for example, the persuasive appeals in the advertisement here. The top line noting that Monte Alban is "The oldest city of the Americas" is an ethical appeal because it shows that the ad writers are knowledgeable about the area's history. The same holds true for the details that appear below the photograph. At the same time, these historical details

can be considered logical appeals because they are pieces of information. "Live the mystery" is, of course, an emotional appeal, as is the color photograph that showcases the breathtaking beauty of Monte Alban. How effectively does this advertisement convince you to visit this place?

Advertisements, of course, are clearly intended to convince the reader to buy something—a product or service or trip to Mexico. For most of the persuasive writing you will do, you will have a more limited audience than the audience for an advertisement or a newspaper editorial, but the strategies that you will use to assert your point of view and persuade readers are the same.

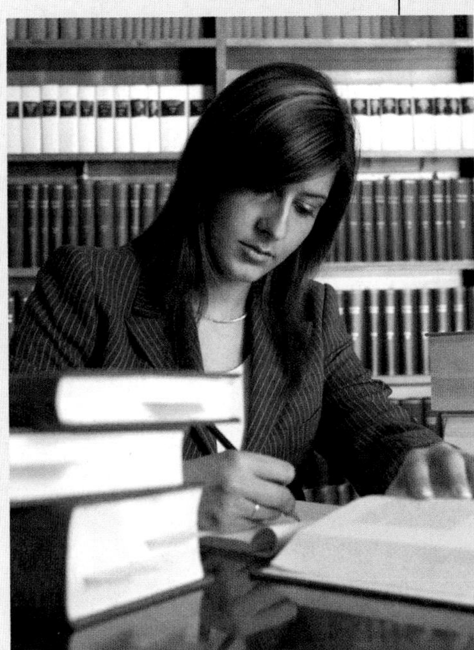

Setting Your Goals:

Rhetorical Knowledge

- **Audience:** When you write to convince your readers, your success will depend on how accurately you have analyzed your audience: their knowledge of and attitudes toward your topic.
- **Purpose:** A convincing text is meant to persuade readers to accept your point of view, but it can also include an element of action—what you want readers to do once you've convinced them.
- **Rhetorical situation:** Think about all of the factors that affect where you stand in relation to your subject—you (the writer), your readers (the audience), the topic (the issue you are writing about), your purpose (what you wish to accomplish), and the exigency (what is compelling you to write your persuasive essay).
- **Voice and tone:** When you write to persuade, you are trying to convince readers to think or act in a certain way. The tone you use will influence how they react to your writing: Consider how you want to sound to your readers. If your tone is subdued and natural, will that convince your readers? If you come across as loud and shrill, will that convince your readers?
- **Context, medium, and genre:** Decide on the most effective medium and genre to present your persuasive essay to the audience you want to reach. Often, you can use photographs, tables, charts, and graphs as well as words to provide evidence that supports your position.

Critical Thinking, Reading, and Writing

- **Learning/inquiry:** Writing to persuade helps you learn the important arguments on all sides of an issue, so such writing deepens your understanding.
- **Responsibility:** As you prepare to write persuasively, you will naturally begin to think critically about your position on the subject you are writing about, forcing you to examine your initial ideas, based on what you learn through your research. Persuasive writing, then, is a way of learning and growing, not just of presenting information.
- **Reading and research:** You will usually need to conduct interviews and online and library research to gather evidence to support the claims you are making in your persuasive writing.

Writing to Convince

8
Chapter

Writing Processes

- **Invention:** Use various invention activities, such as brainstorming, listing, and clustering, to help you consider the arguments that you might use to support your persuasive essay or the opposing arguments you need to accommodate or refute.
- **Organizing your ideas and details:** Most often, you will state the main point—your thesis—clearly at the start of your persuasive essay and then present the evidence supporting that point. Other methods of organization are useful, however, depending on your audience and context.
- **Revising:** Read your work with a critical eye to make certain that it fulfills the assignment and displays the qualities of effective persuasive writing.
- **Working with peers:** Listen to your classmates as they tell you how much you have persuaded them, and why. They will give you useful advice on how to make your essay more persuasive and, therefore, more effective.

Knowledge of Conventions

- **Editing:** Citing sources correctly adds authority to your persuasive writing. The round-robin activity on page 259 will help you edit your work to correct problems with your in-text citations and your works-cited or references list.
- **Genres for persuasive writing:** Possible genres include academic essays, editorials, position papers, letters to the editor, newspaper and magazine essays—even e-mails or letters you might send to friends or family members to persuade them about a problem or issue.
- **Documentation:** You will probably need to rely on sources outside of your experience, and if you are writing an academic essay, you will be required to cite them using the appropriate documentation style.

mhconnectcomposition.com

Writing to Convince Tutorial QL8001

Rhetorical Knowledge

When you write to persuade, you need to have a specific purpose in mind, a strong sense of your audience, and an idea of what might be an effective way to persuade that audience. You need to make a point and provide evidence to support that point, with the goal of persuading your readers to agree with your position.

Writing to Convince in Your College Classes

Many—if not most—of the papers you will be asked to write for your college classes will be persuasive. Although your college assignments will often specifically require that you inform or analyze, they will frequently include an element of persuasion. Here are some examples:

- In a literature course, your instructor might ask you to argue that the concept of the Oedipal complex is appropriate for analyzing Hamlet's behavior.
- Your sociology professor might ask you to develop and support a thesis about deviant behavior in prisons.
- Your mechanical engineering professor might ask you to argue for or against using a particular material in a specific situation.

Writing to Convince for Life

Although persuasive writing is common in college and university courses, it plays an even larger role in professional, civic, and personal settings. Consider these examples of professional writing:

- A product development team needs to convince company executives to manufacture a product it has designed and tested.
- A paralegal needs to ask fellow members of the local legal community to work *pro bono* (for free) for a specific group.
- A division manager needs to convince the human resources manager to hire a particular applicant.

Persuasive writing is also present in civic settings. Civic leaders and other participants in the political process—mayors, city council members, school board members, town supervisors, volunteers, and ordinary citizens—are all involved in persuasion. In fact, it is difficult to imagine a political process without persuasion as its major component. For instance, concerned citizens might write to their city council to argue that a stop light needs to be installed at an intersection where many accidents have occurred.

In personal settings, you constantly negotiate with those around you as you make life decisions, often working to convince others that your views and ideas are most effective. For example, you might write to persuade a family member to send you money for tuition. Or you might write to a friend or family member to encourage him or her to have a medical test if that person is having trouble making a decision.

The "Ways of Writing" feature presents different genres that can be used when writing to convince in life.

Ways of Writing to Convince

Genres for Your College Classes	Sample Situation	Advantages of this Genre	Limitations of the Genre
History essay	Your world history professor asks you to construct a paper in which you argue that specific events caused the Iraq war of 2003.	Your research will provide documented details of what led up to the war. It will help your readers understand the causal relationships.	Your essay may not give a broad enough overview to give readers an idea of how the war might have been prevented.
Letter to your campus newspaper	Your political science professor asks you to send a letter to your college newspaper, encouraging your classmates to change the form of student government.	Anything published in a college newspaper will have a wide audience of people who have an interest in campus affairs.	You will have to make your argument in a limited amount of space. It might not be published.
Editorial for your local newspaper	For your writing class, you are asked to construct an editorial responding to public criticism about your campus: Students driving fast through neighborhoods, loud parties at student-occupied apartment buildings, and so on.	Editorials are read by a local audience and are therefore useful for convincing local readers about an issue that is important to them.	You will have to make your argument in a limited amount of space and without visuals. It might not be published.
Oral presentation	Your environmental science professor asks you to prepare a ten-minute speech that convinces your classmates to attend a rally for a community clean-up.	Talking to your audience gives you the opportunity to engage them and gauge their involvement.	Some listeners will "tune out" so you have to work to keep their attention.
Genres for Life	**Sample Situation**	**Advantages of the Genre**	**Limitations of the Genre**
Brochure	With several of your neighbors, you want to construct a brochure that presents the benefits of raising taxes for your local schools.	A brochure can provide a quick overview of the arguments in favor of a tax increase.	Your argument must be presented in a limited amount of space.
Business letter	Your business is moving to a neighboring state, and you want as many employees as possible to make the move with your company.	A letter is a personalized way to explain the benefits of the new location.	Asking employees to make such a move is a difficult task; a letter might be too brief to be convincing.
Poster	To encourage people to attend an upcoming school event, you construct a poster that you will copy and place in various locations on campus.	A poster is a visual way to get readers interested. Posters can be placed in many places, ensuring exposure to your message.	A limited number of people will see and read the posters.
Web site	You want to create a Web site that will convince your community to vote for a mayoral candidate.	Your Web site can provide useful information for a particular demographic that is otherwise difficult to reach.	Some readers will only skim a Web site and not all have access.
Job application cover letter	You need to construct a cover letter in response to a job ad.	A cover letter lets you discuss and explain your background and experiences in a positive way, specific to the particular job.	Your background might not be a good match for the job forcing you to "stretch" in your letter.

mhconnectcomposition.com

Writer's Workshop: Applying Learning Goals to Persuasive Writing QL8002

Scenarios for Writing | Assignment Options

Your instructor may ask you to complete one or both of the following assignments that call for persuasive writing. Each of these assignments is in the form of a *scenario,* which gives you a sense of who your audience is and what you need to accomplish with your persuasive writing.

Starting on page 243, you will find guidelines for completing whatever scenario you decide—or are asked—to complete.

Writing for College

SCENARIO 1 Academic Argument about a Controversial Issue

What controversial issues have you learned about in other college classes? Here are some possibilities:

- Political science: In what ways did the ethical issues some senators and members of the House of Representatives faced immediately before the 2006 election affect the results of that election?
- Business ethics: How effective is the threat of criminal punishment in preventing insider trading of stocks?
- Psychology: How should the courts use the concept of insanity to determine culpability in criminal cases?

Writing Assignment: Select a controversial issue or problem from one of your classes, and compose a paper convincing readers in that class that your position on the issue is valid.

Writing for Life

SCENARIO 2 Civic Writing: An Editorial about a Campus–Community Problem

Every college campus has problems, ranging from scarce parking to overcrowded computer labs, to too much vehicle traffic, to too little community involvement. Many of these problems, such as too much traffic, extend into the neighborhoods near the campus.

Writing Assignment: Using the list of features of an editorial on page 239, write an editorial for your school newspaper in which you identify a campus problem that also affects the surrounding community and then persuade your readers that the problem exists and that it needs to be taken seriously. Although you need to do more than simply provide information about the problem (that is an informative paper, covered in Chapter 6), you do not need to suggest detailed solutions to the problem (that is a proposal, covered in

Chapter 11). Your goal is to convince your readers that your campus has a problem and that this problem has a negative impact on the surrounding neighborhoods.

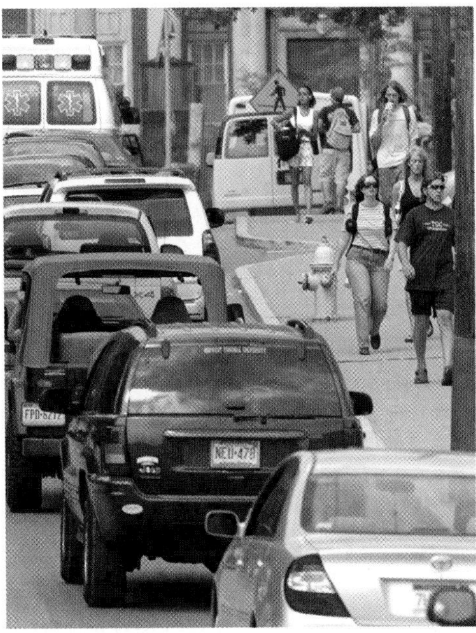

Insufficient parking is an issue at many college campuses, especially those located within cities.

Rhetorical Considerations in Persuasive Writing

- **Audience:** Although your instructor and classmates are your initial audience for this assignment, you might also consider other audiences for your persuasive writing. What would you like them to believe or do? How might they respond to your argument? How might you best convince them?
- **Purpose:** Your main purpose is to make your audience aware of the issue and to convince them that it is significant and that your position is the most reasonable one. How can you do this? You might also want to convince them to *do something* about it. What are different ways to accomplish this?
- **Voice, tone, and point of view:** Why are you interested in the issue? What are your attitudes toward the issue and the audience? How will you convey those attitudes to your audience?
- **Context, medium, and genre:** Although you are writing this persuasive paper to fulfill a college assignment, most issues worth writing about are important beyond the classroom. How might your views make a difference to your community? Keeping the context of the assignment in mind, decide on the most appropriate medium and genre for your writing. If you are writing for an audience beyond the classroom, consider what will be the most effective way to present your argument to this audience. You might write an e-mail message to a friend, prepare a memo for colleagues at work, or write a brochure or op-ed piece for members of your community.

connect
mhconnectcomposition.com
Additional Scenarios QL8003

For more on choosing a medium and genre, see Chapter 17.

Critical Thinking, Reading, and Writing

As we have seen, effective persuasive writing focuses on an issue and provides sufficient and compelling evidence to convince readers that the writer's position on that issue is correct, or at least worthy of respect. Before you begin to write your own persuasive paper, read one or more persuasive essays to get a feel for this kind of writing. Also consider how visuals could make your writing more convincing, as well as the kinds of sources you will need to consult.

For more on gathering and evaluating information from sources, see Chapter 19.

When you write to convince, you will often need to draw on material from other sources by conducting research. To research effectively, you must read the material critically and evaluate it carefully, to make certain that the evidence you are offering as proof adequately supports your claims. Of course, thinking critically also means that you need to consider other points of view about your issue and decide whether those views are compatible or in conflict with your own position.

Learning the Qualities of Effective Persuasive Writing

Much of the writing that you do is intended to convince someone to agree with you about something, typically about an issue. An **issue** is a subject or problem area that people care about and about which they hold differing views. Issues of current concern in the United States include tax cuts, campaign finance reform, and school vouchers. Subjects about which people tend to agree—for example, the importance of education in general—are not usually worth writing arguments about.

Persuasive writing that achieves the goal of convincing readers has the following qualities:

- **Presentation of the issue.** Present your issue in a way that will grab your readers' attention and help them understand that the issue exists and that they should be concerned about it. For example, if you are attempting to convince buyers to purchase cell phones with antivirus protection, you first need to demonstrate the prevalence of cell phone viruses. Another way to present the issue is to share an anecdote about it or to offer some statistics that clearly demonstrate the existence and danger of viruses.
- **A clearly stated, arguable claim.** A **claim** is the assertion you are making about the issue. Your claim should be clear, of course; a confusing claim will not convince readers. Any claim worth writing about also

Digital Literacy **Political-Discussion Posts**

One way to see argumentation and persuasion in action is to look at political-discussion posts on news Web sites. Choose a topic thread or news article, and, as you skim or read the posts, ask yourself three questions about each post: (1) How much credibility does the writer seem to have as a person (*ethos*)? (2) How does the writer use reason and logic to make his or her points (*logos*)? (3) What is your emotional reaction to the writer's remarks (*pathos*)? You can determine the weight a writer's comments probably carry with others by assessing that writer's credibility, reasoning, and emotional integrity. Be sure to assess the language writers use in response to each other as well.

needs to be arguable: a statement about which reasonable people may disagree. For example, "All cell phone users should purchase antivirus software" is an arguable claim; a reader could disagree by saying, "Cell phone viruses are not a major threat." However, no one would disagree with the statement "Computer viruses can be annoying and disruptive." Therefore, it is not arguable and so is not an effective claim for a piece of persuasive writing.

- **An awareness of audience.** Because your task as a writer is to convince other people, it is crucial to be aware of the needs, situations, and perspectives of your audience. In any audience, you can expect some members to be more open to your claim than others:
  - If someone already agrees with you, persuasion is unnecessary.
  - If someone mildly disagrees with you or is undecided, persuasion has a good chance of working.
  - If someone strongly disagrees with you, there is little chance that persuasion will work.
- **Convincing reasons.** Writers of convincing arguments offer support for what they are asking their reader to believe or to do. Think of the reasons you use to support your point as the other part of a *because* statement, with the claim being the first part. Here's an example: "Animal fur should not be used in clothing *because* synthetic fur is available and looks like real fur."
- **Sufficient evidence for each reason.** After considering the degree to which the audience agrees or disagrees with your claim, provide enough evidence, and the right kind(s) of evidence to convince your readers and, if applicable, persuade them to act accordingly. Evidence includes statistics, expert opinion, examples, and anecdotes (stories).
- **Appeals based on the writer's logic, emotion, and character.** Effective persuasive writers carefully decide when to use three kinds of appeals—*logos* (appeals based on logic), *pathos* (appeals to the audience's emotions), and *ethos* (appeals based on the writer's character or credibility). Appeals based on logic are generally the most effective. Emotional appeals can be effective with audience members who are predisposed to accept your claims. Appealing to an audience's emotions is risky, however, because critical thinkers will reject this type of appeal unless it is accompanied by logical and ethical appeals. Appeals based on the writer's authority and credibility—ethical appeals—can be powerful, especially when coupled with logical appeals.
- **An honest discussion of other views.** For any arguable claim or thesis, there will be at least one other point of view besides yours. To be effective, the writer of a persuasive text needs to acknowledge and deal with possible objections from the other side. You already make this kind of **counterargument** naturally. For example, when you are told that you "cannot register

For more on strategies for argument, including dealing with opposing views, see Chapter 14.

for this course because you have not completed the prerequisite," you probably already have an answer to that objection such as, "You're right, but I received approval from the dean because of my prior professional experience."

If you think that another perspective has merit, you should certainly *acknowledge* it and even *concede* that it is valid. Another possibility is a Rogerian approach (see Chapter 14), in which both sides negotiate a compromise position. Perhaps you can offer a compromise by incorporating aspects of the other perspective into your thesis. Of course, if other perspectives on your issue are without merit, you will need to *refute* them by indicating how they are inappropriate, inadequate, or ineffective.

- **A desired result.** The goal of persuasive writing is to convince readers to change their minds about an issue or at least to give your view serious consideration. Often the goal is to get your reader to act in some way—vote for a candidate, write a letter to the school board, or buy some product.

Reading, Inquiry, and Research: Learning from Texts That Persuade

The readings that follow are examples of persuasive writing. As you read the persuasive selections your instructor assigns, consider the following questions:

- What makes this selection convincing?
- To what extent am I convinced by the writer's reasons and evidence? Why?
- What parts of the selection could be improved? In what ways?
- How can I use the techniques of persuasive writing exemplified here in my writing?

MAUREEN DOWD

Our Own Warrior Princess

EDITORIAL

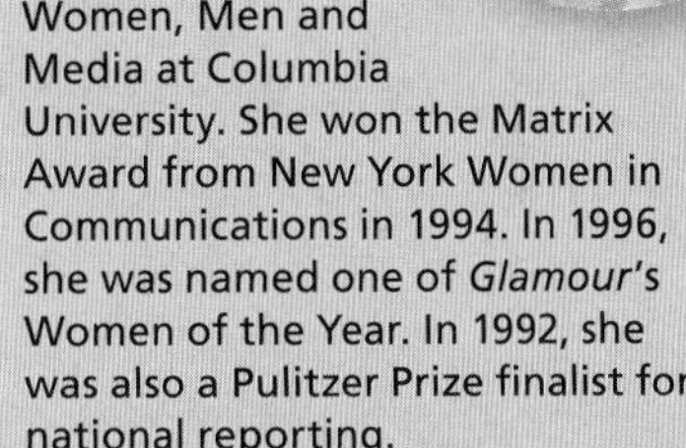

Maureen Dowd won the Pulitzer Prize for Commentary in 1999. In 1992, she received the Breakthrough Award from Women, Men and Media at Columbia University. She won the Matrix Award from New York Women in Communications in 1994. In 1996, she was named one of *Glamour*'s Women of the Year. In 1992, she was also a Pulitzer Prize finalist for national reporting.

In the following column, which first appeared in the *New York Times* on June 1, 2003, Dowd writes in a personal way about organ donation—telling the story of what her niece, Jennifer, did to help her brother, Michael. Although persuasive writing most often uses facts, statistics, and hard evidence to make its case, as you read Dowd's column, consider how effective she is in using emotional appeals to persuade you. Is Dowd's column persuasive enough for you to sign up to be an organ donor? Why?

1 Jennifer showed me her scar Friday. It's the most beautiful scar I've ever seen. A huge stapled gash on her stomach, shaped like the Mercedes logo. A red badge of courage. Jennifer is my niece, a 33-year-old lawyer. On Wednesday, she had half her liver taken out at Georgetown University Hospital to save the life of her uncle (my brother Michael), who had gotten hepatitis years ago from a tainted blood transfusion.

2 The complicated and risky operation for the two, side by side, went from 7:30 am. until after 10 pm. Then, when a Medivac helicopter arrived with a matching liver for another patient, the same team of doctors had to start on another emergency six-hour liver transplant.

3 The night nurse told Jennifer she was an oddity. "We don't see many live donors," she said. "Not many people are that generous."

4 Or brave. Jennifer's morphine drip wasn't attached properly the first night after the operation, and no one knew it. She felt pain, but didn't want to be a wimp by complaining too loudly. Instead, she was Reaganesque, cracking jokes and wondering where the cute doctors were.

5 She survived the first night after this excruciating operation au naturel, like Xena the Warrior Princess. If all goes well, her liver will grow whole again in several weeks, as will Michael's half.

6 Unlike her father, who charged people a nickel to see his appendix scar when he was 10, she let me look for free. As we sat in her room, watching Mariah Carey singing with a bare midriff on the "Today" show, I worried a little how she would take the disfigurement.

7 She's a fitness fanatic, who works as a personal trainer in her spare time. She's single, out in the cruel dating world. And we live in an airbrush culture, where women erase lines with Botox, wrinkles with lasers, and fat with liposuction. I told Jen scars are sexy; consider that great love scene in "Lethal Weapon 3" when Mel Gibson and Rene Russo, as police officers, compare scars.

Jennifer has every quality of heart, spirit, mind and body a woman could want. She's smart, funny, generous, loyal, principled, great looking and, obviously, adventurous. 8

"Write a column about me," she smiled, tubes coming out of every part of her body, as I left her room. 9

I knew what she meant. She didn't want me to write about her guts, but to encourage others to have the guts to donate organs. When she came to, she asked for the green ribbon pin that encourages organ donation. Her exquisite doll-like transplant surgeon, Dr. Amy Lu, in white coat and black high-heeled mules, still on the job after 21 hours in the operating room, removed her pin and gave it to Jennifer. 10

As Neal Conan said on NPR Thursday: "More than 80,000 Americans are on waiting lists for organ donations, and most will never get them. Thousands on those lists die every year. One big reason for the shortage is that families are reluctant to give up their relatives' organs. Even when people filled out a donor card or checked the organ donor box on their driver's license, family members often refuse. The need is so acute and so frustrating that more and more doctors are wondering whether financial incentives might persuade some families to change their minds and save lives." (Iran has wiped out its kidney transplant wait by offering rewards.) 11

As the New York Organ Donor Network Web site notes: "One donor can save up to eight lives through organ donation and improve dozens of lives through corneal, bone, skin and other tissue transplants. Across the U.S., 17 men, women and children of all races and ethnic backgrounds die every day for lack of a donated organ." 12

I'm one of the scaredy-cats who never checked the organ donation box or filled out the organ and tissue donor card. 13

Some people don't do it because they have irrational fears that doctors will be so eager to harvest their organs, they'll receive subpar care after an accident.

I had nutty fears, too, straight out of a Robin Cook medical thriller, that they might come and pluck out my eyes or grab my kidney before I was through with them. 14

On Friday, Michael's birthday, I got the card online, filled it out and stuck it in my wallet. If Jennifer is brave enough to do it alive, how can I be scared of doing it dead? 15

BRIAN J. G. PEREIRA, M.D.

Letter Responding to Dowd

LETTER TO THE EDITOR

To the Editor:

Re "Our Own Warrior Princess" (column, June 1):

1 Maureen Dowd's inspiring story of her niece's live liver donation points to an emerging trend in transplantation.

2 The year 2001 was the first in which there were more living donors than nonliving donors in the United States. Because of new techniques for kidney removal and the medical success of live liver transplantation, more people are considering saving lives through organ donation while they are alive.

3 A recent survey by the National Kidney Foundation found that one in four Americans would consider donating a kidney or a piece of their liver or lung to a complete stranger.

4 This is not just talk. The real numbers are encouraging. In 2002, 353 people became living liver donors, and 6,234 were live kidney donors.

5 While the need for organ donors continues to grow, people like Ms. Dowd's niece represent hope for a future when the transplant waiting list will cease to exist.

BRIAN J. G. PEREIRA, M.D.
Pres., National Kidney Foundation
Boston, June 2, 2003
New York Times

Brian Pereira is a professor of medicine at the Tufts University School of Medicine. Dr. Pereira is a nationally recognized expert on kidney disease and nephrology. He is the president of the National Kidney Foundation and chairman of the International Nephrology Network, and he has served on the editorial board of many scientific journals. Dr. Pereira also serves as a director of Kidney Care Partners, Wellbound Inc., and Satellite Health Care Inc.

This letter, in response to Dowd's essay, appeared in the *New York Times* a few days after Dowd's column was published. After reading Dowd's column and Pereira's response, would you ever consider being a *living* organ donor? Why?

QUESTIONS FOR WRITING AND DISCUSSION

Rhetorical Knowledge: The Writer's Situation and Rhetoric

1. **Audience:** How effective is Dowd in reaching the audience for whom this information is intended—someone reading the *New York Times* and perhaps interested in organ donation? What can you point to in Dowd's column to demonstrate what you mean?
2. **Purpose:** In what area of life (academic, professional, civic, personal) does "Our Own Warrior Princess" best fit? What is Dowd trying to convince the reader to believe or do? What can you point to in the column to support your opinion?
3. **Voice and tone:** What is Dowd's attitude toward people who don't offer to donate organs? How does she attempt to reach them?
4. **Responsibility:** Dowd's primary evidence consists of the story of her niece's sacrifice, which is an emotional appeal to her readers. How justified is Dowd's use of *pathos*—an appeal to readers' emotions? How effective is it? Why?
5. **Context, format, and genre:** Newspaper columns such as Dowd's have specific length limits (as compared to, say, an essay that might appear in a journal). How might such a form constrain Dowd? How might it benefit her? In a letter to the editor, the writer often focuses on how much he or she agrees or disagrees with an editorial. How does Dr. Pereira do that?

Critical Thinking: The Writer's Ideas and Your Personal Response

6. How has Dowd's column affected your views about becoming an organ donor?
7. Consider other persuasive writing that you have read. In what way(s) are they similar to or different from Dowd's column?

Composing Processes and Knowledge of Conventions: The Writer's Strategies

8. How does Dowd establish her *ethos* in this article? How does Pereira establish his *ethos* in his letter?
9. Dowd uses a personal story to make her point. How effective is this writing strategy? Why?

Inquiry and Research: Ideas for Further Exploration

10. What questions do you still have about organ donation? Where can you go to get answers to those questions?

Organ Donation

Although Allsup, Inc. is a corporation that assists people seeking Social Security benefits, it sometimes runs public-service campaigns, such as the one below for organ donation. Most readers would assume the mother in this photograph was donating an organ for her child. But what if it was the other way around? Would you support a child donating an organ to a parent? Why?

ADVERTISEMENT

You're donating more than an organ.
You're giving someone a second chance at life.

April is National Donate Life Month.

An estimated 77 people get organ transplants every day, yet more than 98,000 people are still waiting for organ, tissue, marrow and blood donors. During National Donate Life Month, we thank all those who have given the gift of life…and encourage everyone to register to become organ donors. This simple act today can give someone in need a lifetime of tomorrows.

www.allsup.com

QUESTIONS FOR WRITING AND DISCUSSION: LEARNING OUTCOMES

Rhetorical Knowledge: The Writer's Situation and Rhetoric

1. **Audience:** Who is the audience for this advertisement? What makes you think that?
2. **Purpose:** What language in the poster most clearly indicates the purpose of the advertisement?
3. **Voice and tone:** What attitude does Allsup have toward the audience?
4. **Responsibility:** To whom does Allsup seem to feel responsible?
5. **Context, format, and genre:** Why is it fitting that this advertisement include a chalkboard? Advertisements that appear on posters or in other venues frequently include visual elements such as photos. What does the photo add to this advertisement?

Critical Thinking: The Writer's Ideas and Your Personal Response

6. How persuasive do you find this advertisement? Why?
7. How do the persuasive features of this advertisement compare to those in Dowd's essay earlier in this chapter?

Composing Processes and Knowledge of Conventions: The Writer's Strategies

8. Why does the advertisement include the numerical information that appears at the bottom?
9. Why does the advertisement use the relatively informal contraction "You're" instead of the more formal "You are"?

Inquiry and Research: Ideas for Further Exploration

10. Conduct a Web search to find other advertisements for organ donation. How do their appeals (*ethos, logos, pathos*) compare to the appeals in this advertisement?

GENRES *Up Close* Writing an Editorial

Writers use a range of genres to convince in professional, civic, and personal situations that include editorials/opinion pieces, position papers, job reference letters, and business letters. For example, editorials are appropriate when you want to convince readers that you have a valid position on a controversial or debatable topic. An op-ed piece is one that appears on the page opposite the editorial page in a newspaper or magazine; thus "op-ed" is short for "opposite editorial." However, it can also mean "opinions and editorials."

Features of effective op-eds or editorial letters include the following:

- They usually respond to a previously published article in a newspaper.
- They are usually short (250–800 words).
- They include an opinion or stance.
- They make a point in the first few sentences.
- They indicate why the issue is important.
- They show respect for other points of view.
- They suggest or imply an action that readers can take.

As you read the following example of an editorial, consider in what ways Emrich's text matches the description above of an op-ed piece.

GENRES UP CLOSE

LIZ EMRICH

EDITORIAL

Slut-O-Ween

Liz Emrich lives in Virginia, where she writes a blog for Salon .Com. She has also worked as a lawyer. We chose this reading because it focuses on a provocative problem—one that many female students might personally relate to and have strong opinions about.

Responds to a previously published article.

Makes the main point in the first few sentences.

A recent discussion by Rob St. Amant about unfortunate Halloween costumes reminded me of one of my personal pet peeves about Halloween—the fact that it has now become the excuse that girls (and women) use to don outfits that in their normal lives would be considered way, way, WAY too risque. 1

Personally, I've never understood it. I'm perfectly happy to flaunt what I've got—to a point. The fact is that desire is always about what one doesn't have, which means that desire will always obsess more over what is suggested but cannot be seen than what is displayed openly. The obvious bid for sexual attention embodied by a tiny skirt and a plunging neckline and four inch stilettos to me seems overkill. 2

Grown women, of course, may do what they please. Frankly I think it's rather funny the way many of the women I know who would not be caught dead showing up in anything that even breathed a hint of cleavage during the rest of the year will gladly don an up-to-there skirt and fishnet stockings in order to walk the streets with their four year old, or to attend a party in the neighborhood. Sexual repression is very much alive and well here in suburbia. No one wants to be the "slutty mom" whose tops are cut too low, whose skirts are too tight, and who all the dads raise an eyebrow at and wonder if she's really as easy as her clothes are supposedly suggesting. Halloween seems to be the release valve for all those moms who 3

checked their sexuality at the door when they gave birth—their one opportunity to remind themselves of how hot they used to think they were.

Kids, however, are another story. Walk the aisles at Target, and even the costumes for little girls have a sexual element to them that I either blocked out or don't remember from my youth. Dressing up as a cat or a witch or a cowgirl isn't enough anymore. It must be a tarted-up version of the costume in question. Cat costumes must consist of clingy leotards. Cowgirls must have really short skirts. In fact, any costume involving a skirt must be horrifically, inappropriately short. 4

Of course, the current trend in Halloween costumes for girls is not the first or even the grossest incidence of inappropriate sexualization of small girls and young women. Girls at younger and younger ages are seeking to wear clothing that makes them look way too grown up. And in some respects, this is not new. Mothers have been trying to protect daughters from being "vulgar" in how they dress for generations. Parents have worried about daughters "growing up too fast" since the days when showing your ankles was considered akin to announcing yourself as a prostitute. And for almost as long, daughters have tried to wheedle their way out of these social constraints. 5

Indeed, owning your sexuality as a woman is an important part of gender equality. Certainly for generations women were told they were supposed to stay virginal until marriage, and couldn't even walk alone with a man without risking their reputation. And those are not days that should be looked on fondly. That some women still live that way in some parts of the world makes me shudder. And part of owning your sexuality is the ability to choose how you represent that sexuality to the world in how you dress—to play it up or down consistent with what the circumstances your preferences dictate. 6

But little girls are a whole other matter. Owning your sexuality is a responsibility, sort of like owning your own home, or owning your own car. If you don't know what you're doing with it, you run the risk of damaging something important, including yourself. This is not about prudishness. Every woman deserves a sex life that is healthy, vibrant, active and happy, that is as individual as the woman herself. 7

Indicates why the issue is important

An immature girl doesn't know what she's doing when she wears a sexy Halloween costume, a suggestive outfit of any sort. She has only the most shallow understanding of the role she is assuming, of the corresponding role she is tacitly suggesting. And even if you want to chalk it up to experimentation which is often the beginning of learning, there's a line, and crossing it should not be an unconscious act. And while one could dispute what is the appropriate age to start experimenting with this line, I think it's a pretty universal notion that the "tween" ages—9 to 12—is not 8

Includes an opinion or stance.

Usually short—this piece is just over 800 words.

Does not show respect for other points of view.

No real suggested action presented.

the appropriate age. And yet, this is precisely the age that you start seeing the "slut-o-ween" costumes emerge.

On one level, all of this makes me thankful that I have a son, and not a daughter. I do not envy my friends with daughters who are already clamoring for clothes that look way too grown up. For better or worse, boys do not use clothes to telegraph sexuality in the same way as women. But I do worry about teaching my son how to treat women. I don't want him to be the kind of man who sees women as objects. I don't want him to see a short skirt as an unconditional invitation. I want him to be as curious about what is under a girl's hat as what is under her skirt. I am still working out how to do this. 9

Slut-O-Ween does not help. 10

QUESTIONS FOR WRITING AND DISCUSSION: LEARNING OUTCOMES

Rhetorical Knowledge: The Writer's Situation and Rhetoric

1. **Audience:** What audience does Emrich have in mind for this essay?
2. **Purpose:** What is Emrich's purpose in writing this essay?
3. **Voice and tone:** What is Emrich's attitude toward her audience and the topic?
4. **Responsibility:** How does Emrich demonstrate that she takes seriously her responsibilities as a writer?
5. **Context, format, and genre:** This essay appeared on the Salon.Com Web site on October 19, twelve days before Halloween. If it were your choice, what date would you pick for such an essay? Why? What features indicate that "Slut-O-Ween" is an editorial?

Critical Thinking: The Writer's Ideas and Your Personal Response

6. To what extent do you agree with Emrich's position on this topic? Why?
7. What seem to be the principles underpinning Emrich's argument?

Composing Processes and Knowledge of Conventions: The Writer's Strategies

8. Emrich has invented a new term, "Slut-O-Ween." What is the effect of using this invented term rather than some existing word or phrase?
9. How has Emrich established her *ethos* as a credible person in this editorial piece?

Inquiry and Research: Ideas for Further Exploration

10. Conduct a Web search to see what language vendors use to describe the kinds of Halloween costumes that Emrich depicts. Does that language support Emrich's claims?

Writing Processes

As you work on the assignment that you have chosen, remember the qualities of an effective and convincing persuasive paper, listed on pages 230–232. Also remember that writing is recursive—you might start with an invention activity or two and then conduct some research, which leads to more invention work and then a first draft; but then you might need to do more invention work to come up with additional reasons and conduct more research to add more support or to refute an opposing argument; and then you will revise your draft and possibly find another gap or two. So, while the activities listed below imply that writers proceed step-by-step, the actual process of writing is usually messier: You will keep coming back to your earlier work, adding to it, modifying the information to be more accurate as you conduct additional research and become more familiar with your issue.

connect
mhconnectcomposition.com
Writing to Convince Animated Walkthrough QL8004

If you are considering several issues for your persuasive text, put your notes into a separate computer document for each one. Once you determine the focus of your paper, it will be easy to access and use the notes on that issue.

Invention: Getting Started

The invention activities below are strategies that you can use to help you get some sense of what you already know about the issue you have chosen. Whatever invention method(s) you use (or that your teacher asks you to use), try to answer questions such as these:

- What do I already know about this issue?
- What is my point of view on this issue?
- Where might I learn more about this issue? What verifiable information is available?
- What might my audience already know? What might their point of view be?
- What do I know about my audience? What don't I know that I should know?
- What questions do I have about the issue?
- What are some other views on this issue?

Doing your invention work in electronic form, rather than on paper, lets you easily use your invention work as you construct a draft.

For more on strategies for discovery and learning, see Chapter 3.

Writing Activity

Questioning and Freewriting

Spend a few minutes jotting down answers to the reporter's questions about your issue: *who, what, where, when, why,* and *how.* You may find that your answers to these questions lead to more questions, which will help you focus on further aspects of your subject to research.

Then, using the answers you noted above, freewrite about *one side* of your issue for ten minutes. Then freewrite about the *opposing side* of your issue, again for ten minutes. This activity will help you better understand and appreciate the arguments on both sides of your issue.

Student writer Santi DeRosa read an article in his college paper about how female students help recruit male athletes for his school. DeRosa had concerns about the ethics of this practice, so he decided to respond by writing an essay on the issue for his writing class.

EXAMPLES OF INVENTION

Brainstorming (pp. 158, 332)
Freewriting (pp. 114, 245, 383)
Criteria (p. 290)
Listing (p. 72)
Answers to Reporter's Questions (p. 244)
Organization (pp. 75, 164)
Clustering (pp. 114, 289)
Concept Mapping (p. 335)
Interviewing (p. 203)
Research (pp. 115, 160, 205, 246, 292, 384)
Reflection (p. 12)

Santi DeRosa's Answers to the Reporter's Questions

Santi DeRosa might ask—and answer—the reporter's questions as follows:

- Who is involved? Whom do they affect, and how are they affected? Who has control over recruiting practices? Who might change the situation?

  Female students volunteer, and I wonder how people perceive this. How do the women feel about doing this? Who decides who gets to "volunteer"? What does the president of the university think about this?

- What do they do?

  They act as guides and escorts. Nothing sexual—or is there? I wonder how their boyfriends feel about their participation.

- Where does the recruiting occur?

  Taking someone to a local fast-food restaurant seems pretty harmless, while visiting other places may not.

- When does the recruiting happen? What sequence of events is involved?

  I think that recruiting is in the fall, but I'm not certain. How do the people get matched up? Do they work (escort) in groups, and if not, is there a chaperone?

- Why does this happen? Why are these particular students involved?

  How well does this form of "recruiting" really work? Some young men might be influenced if attractive young women showed them around the campus and the city. Why do the young women volunteer? They must get some satisfaction—a sense of civic responsibility and pride in the school, which is a good thing.

- How do the female students act when they are with the athletes? React?

  I need to find out more about the logistics of these recruiting visits. Do NCAA rules and regulations apply? How are the female students trained for this work?

Santi DeRosa's Freewriting

DeRosa also used freewriting to explore his ideas. A portion of his freewriting appears here:

> Interesting that women are used to recruit male athletes here, and that they volunteer. Is this a good idea? Are the women being used and objectified? What if they want to do it? What if the whole process is pretty innocent? The newspaper sensationalized it, which bothers me. I can't think of what to write, I can't think—hey, do they use males to recruit female athletes? I need to find out about that. . . .

EXAMPLES OF INVENTION

Brainstorming (pp. 158, 332)
Freewriting (pp. 114, 245, 383)
Criteria (p. 290)
Listing (p. 72)
Answers to Reporter's Questions (p. 244)
Organization (pp. 75, 164)
Clustering (pp. 114, 289)
Concept Mapping (p. 335)
Interviewing (p. 203)
Research (pp. 115, 160, 205, 246, 292, 384)
Reflection (p. 12)

Exploring Your Ideas with Research

Research is critical to any persuasive text, for if you cannot provide evidence to support your position, you probably will not convince your reading audience.

Although you may be able to use information from your own experience as evidence, you will usually need to offer verifiable information from sources, such as facts, statistics, expert testimony, and examples.

To find evidence outside of your own experience that you need to support your claim, look for answers to the following questions:

For help with locating sources of information, see Chapter 19; for help with documenting your sources, see Chapter 20.

- What facts or other verifiable information can I find that will provide solid evidence to convince my readers to agree with my position?
- What expert testimony can I provide to support my claim? What authorities on my issue might I interview?
- What statistical data support my position?
- What are other people doing in response to this issue or problem?

The subject you focus on and the kind of essay you are constructing help to determine the research you conduct. For example, for the scenarios above, you could conduct several kinds of research:

- For Scenario 1 (page 228), which asks you to focus on a controversial issue, assume that you have decided to write about whether the threat of criminal punishment helps to prevent insider trading of stocks. What kinds of research might you conduct? At your library, a search of business publications such as the *Wall Street Journal, BusinessWeek,* and *Forbes* would be a good place to start. But you could also interview some local business executives to get their perspectives for your paper. And you could interview local law enforcement officials and attorneys to get their take on whether the threat of punishment helps stop insider trading.

- For Scenario 2 (page 228), where you focus on a problem in your campus community, that same kind of local research—interviewing your classmates, for example—will provide useful information for your paper. Consider the comments you could get, for instance, if you were writing about an issue involving your classrooms, such as the condition of the building or the time classes are scheduled, or a campus issue, such as campus safety, student fees, or athletics. Speaking with campus officials and administrators will also give you useful information for your paper. In addition, a search of the campus newspaper archives in your college's library may provide good background information on your issue.
- One way to learn about other perspectives on your subject is to read online blogs or join e-mail lists that focus on your topic. These ongoing electronic conversations often can provide multiple perspectives and ideas on the issue you are writing about—which then can help you with your own thinking and research.

Writing Activity

Conducting Research

Using the list of qualities of effective persuasive writing, go through your invention activity notes to find the questions you still have and want to ask. Now is the time to determine the best way/s to answer those questions. Would it be useful to:

- Conduct more library research in books?
- Interview people about your subject?
- Conduct more library research in journals?

Make a research plan. Where will you conduct your research, and when will you do so?

EXAMPLES OF INVENTION

Brainstorming (pp. 158, 332)
Freewriting (pp. 114, 245, 383)
Criteria (p. 290)
Listing (p. 72)
Answers to Reporter's Questions (p. 244)
Organization (pp. 75, 164)
Clustering (pp. 114, 289)
Concept Mapping (p. 335)
Interviewing (p. 203)
Research (pp. 115, 160, 205, 246, 292, 384)
Reflection (p. 12)

Student Example: An Excerpt from Santi DeRosa's Research

For my paper, I can use some of the details from the school newspaper's articles. Those articles offer a clear narrative account of recruiting activities. They also help to demonstrate that there is an issue.

I also found some information about the same kind of thing at Colorado State University (Lambert article).

I will need to research how to define the concept of "objectification," a term I've read about. I need to be clearer on this concept. I did check the *American Heritage Dictionary* through Dictionary.com and they had this great quotation under the word's definition that I could include in my paper:

> To present or regard as an object: "Because we have objectified animals, we are able to treat them impersonally" (Barry Lopez).

I like how that really connects to the point I'm trying to make in my paper.

Reviewing Your Invention and Research

After you have conducted your research, review your invention work and notes and the information you collected from outside sources. Once you have a general idea of the conclusion your research is leading you to, you can develop a "working" thesis statement: If you had to make a point now, based on what you have learned, what would it be? It is called a working thesis because your main point or thesis will inevitably change as you continue to conduct research and learn more. And, as you know, through the process of writing itself, you will learn about your topic, so give yourself permission to modify and develop this initial thesis statement as you draft and revise your text. Once you have written several drafts, received feedback on them, and revised them, you will be better able to determine what your final thesis statement should be.

For more on deciding on a thesis, see Chapter 13.

Writing Activity

Considering Your Research and Focusing Your Ideas

Using your research notes as a starting point, again use the reporter's questions of *who, what, where, when, why,* and *how* to get onto paper what you know about your issue. For example, if you were focusing on a campus-community problem, some of your research notes might look like these:

Who: Students and neighbors alike who are affected when lots of student cars are going through the neighborhood, often too fast, both when they come to campus and when they leave.

What: The biggest issues seem to be too many cars on neighborhood streets, too many of them speeding, and too many of them parking where they should not.

A WRITER'S *Responsibility* | Establishing and Maintaining Credibility

Dealing Fairly with Opposing Views

An ethical writer must deal with opposing views fairly and honestly. If you ignore or distort opposing views, readers will think you are either unaware, or dishonest, which will quickly weaken or destroy your *ethos*—your credibility. Ignoring the other side of an issue, the objections that others might have to your point of view, actually weakens your position, as your readers may be aware of the objections and wonder why you did not deal with these other perspectives.

And if you are going to be honest with your readers, you have an ethical obligation to note that there are arguments against your position. You don't necessarily have to write, "Here is another position that you may think is stronger than mine," but you do need to acknowledge that "other sides to this issue include XXX," and then explain why your position is still the stronger one.

Avoiding Logical Fallacies

Using faulty logic intentionally will weaken your credibility and annoy your audience. Using faulty logic unintentionally will indicate that you are not a critical thinker. If you include logical fallacies, which are flaws in reasoning, or *red herrings*, in which you use misleading evidence that serves only to distract your readers, you are not presenting an ethical text. That is, instead of writing to persuade, you are writing to mislead. See Chapter 14, pages 475–478 for more on avoiding logical fallacies.

Organizing Your Information

Because the purpose of writing a persuasive text is to convince your readers to accept your point of view, you will need to organize your reasons and evidence strategically. The questions that you need to ask yourself when deciding on your organization are all rhetorical:

- Who is your audience? What is your readers' position on your issue likely to be? If they are undecided, you might try a classical or an inductive approach, both of which are discussed below. If they are likely to hold an opposing view, then a refutation approach, also discussed below, may be the better choice.
- Why might they be interested in your persuasive writing, or how can you make them interested in it?
- What is your purpose for writing—that is, why do you want to convince readers of this position?

When you construct a persuasive paper, determine the most effective organizational approach for your purpose and audience. One method of organizing an argument, called the *classical scheme,* was first outlined by Aristotle nearly 2,400 years ago. If you are using the classical scheme, this is the sequence you will follow:

See more on Aristotelian organization on page 461 in Chapter 14.

> introduction → main claim → evidence supporting claim → discussion of other perspectives (acknowledging, conceding, and/or refuting them) → conclusion

Aristotle's approach is also called the **deductive method** because you state your claim and then help the reader understand, or deduce, how the evidence supports your claim. The advantage of this method is that you state your position and make your case early, before your reader starts thinking about other perspectives.

Another organizational approach is commonly known as the **inductive method.** When using this approach, you first present and explain all of your reasons and evidence, then draw your conclusion—your main claim. The advantage is that your reader may come to the same conclusion before you explicitly state your position and will therefore be more inclined to agree with your point of view.

Because persuasive writing must usually acknowledge and incorporate or refute opposing viewpoints, a third organizational method starts by presenting the views of the other side. In this method, you first deal with objections to your claim and then state your position and provide reasons and evidence to support it. This is an especially effective strategy if the opposing view or views are widely held.

Here are three organizational structures that you might consider for your persuasive paper.

Options FOR Organization

Organizing a Persuasive Paper

The Classical (Deductive) Approach	The Inductive Approach	The Refutation Approach
Introduce the issue and state your thesis. Explain the importance of the issue. Present your reasons and evidence—why readers should agree with you. Answer objections—either incorporating or refuting other points of view. Conclude—often with a call to action.	Introduce the issue. Offer reasons and evidence for your claim. Draw your conclusion—your main claim. Deal with other viewpoints either before or after presenting your claim. Conclude—often with a call to action.	Introduce the issue. List opposing views. Deal with each objection in turn. Introduce your position and explain why it makes sense, offering reasons and evidence. Conclude—often with a call to action.

Constructing a Complete Draft

connect
mhconnectcomposition.com
Drafting and Revising QL8005

Once you have chosen the best organizational approach for your audience and purpose, you are ready to construct your draft. After you have reviewed your invention writing and research notes, developed a working thesis, and carefully considered all of the reasons and evidence you generated, construct a complete first draft.

As you work, keep the following in mind:

- You may discover that you need to do more invention work and/or more research as you write.
- As you try out tentative claims and reasons, ask your classmates and other readers about the kinds of supporting evidence they consider convincing.
- Consider whether photographs or other visuals might help support your thesis.
- If you become tired and the quality of your thinking or your productivity is affected, take a break.

For more on choosing visuals, see Chapter 18.

INTEGRATING SOURCES

Synthesizing and Integrating Sources: Incorporating Partial Quotes in Your Sentences

Conducting research provides you with lots of quotations, which means you have to determine how to incorporate those quotations into your text. One way to use quotations, whether they come from someone you interviewed or from someone you read, is to incorporate what they said into your sentences. Sometimes when writers use a quotation, the sequence is (1) who I spoke with and (2) what she or he told me:

> I interviewed Joy Watson and she said, "The recycling program is working."

Now, there is nothing wrong with that approach to using a quotation, but sometimes you want to integrate a quotation, or a part of quotation, into your sentences. The key to doing so is to select the most important part of the quotation and use that inside your sentence, which means you surround it with your own words. If you want to include an entire quotation in one of your sentences, be sure not only to introduce the quotation but also to follow up with your own words, after the quotation.

For instance, student writer Santi DeRosa quotes Joe Watson from an article in the campus newspaper and then follows that quotation with a part of Watson's comments within his own sentence, a piece of Watson's quotation that DeRosa wanted to emphasize:

> The people interviewed for the article who support the "hostess" program defend it by saying that "the recruiters perform respectable duties during high school recruits' campus visits" (Watson 2). Does the responsibility of "performing respectable duties" end when they leave the campus for a party? (paragraph 5)

Here, student writer DeRosa first introduces a quotation in the traditional manner:

> The people interviewed for the article who support the "hostess" program defend it by saying that "the recruiters perform respectable duties during high school recruits' campus visits" (Watson 2).

He then goes on to use just a part of that quotation, a phrase he wants to emphasize for readers, inside his next sentence:

> Does the responsibility of "performing respectable duties" end when they leave the campus for a party? (paragraph 5)

Using only part of the quotation allows DeRosa to focus on a phrase that he thinks is important and that he wants the reader to pay special attention to.

For your own citing of quotations, remember the following:

1. Always introduce the quotation (never just put it into your text without some words of introduction).
2. Accurately report and document where the quotation came from.

If you want to use only part of a quotation, select the portion that is most important to the point you are trying to make, and surround that text with your own words.

Parts of a Complete Draft

Introduction: Regardless of your organizational approach, you need to have a strong introduction to capture your readers' attention and introduce the issue. To accomplish these two goals in an introduction, you might do one or more of the following:

Introductory paragraph overview QL8006

- **Share an anecdote that clearly exemplifies the issue.** Maureen Dowd begins her column on organ donation (page 233) with the story of her niece's bravery in choosing to donate part of her liver to her uncle.
- **Provide a brief history of the issue.**
- **Provide a fact or statistic about the issue that will surprise—and possibly concern—readers.** We probably all would agree that young

girls between ages 9 and 12 should not wear inappropriate costumes, so we might be shocked to read that Emrich's research shows that . . ." this is precisely the age that you start seeing the 'slut-o-ween' costumes emerge."

- **Explain (briefly) why your persuasive text is important.**
- **Ask an intriguing question about your subject.** Student writer Santi DeRosa opens his paper (page 259) by asking a key question:

> Are women at the university being treated as objects by the very university that has a responsibility to treat them with equality and dignity and not as second-class citizens?

For more on rhetorical appeals and argument strategies, see Chapter 14.

Body: You can use various writing strategies, including defining all terms your reader might not understand within the body of your text, to effectively persuade your reader. This is the area of your paper where you will provide supporting examples or evidence for each reason you offer, use visual aids (photographs, charts, tables) to support your position, and use rhetorical appeals—*ethos, logos, pathos* (page 20)—to help convince your readers.

connect
mhconnectcomposition.com
Concluding paragraph overview QL8007

Conclusion: In your conclusion, you need to restate or allude to your thesis and let your readers know what you would like them to do with the information they learned from your essay. Conclusions in persuasive writing often do the following:

- **Explain your main thesis or point—what you want to persuade your reader about.**
- **Summarize how each supporting point adds evidence to support your main point.** In a long, involved argument, a summary can help readers recall the main points that you are making.
- **Reach out to the audience.**
- **Include a "call to action."** Maureen Dowd ends "Our Own Warrior Princess" with a description of herself filling out an organ donor card and the strong implication that readers should do so as well.

Title: As you compose your persuasive writing, a title should emerge at some point—perhaps late in the process. The title should reflect the point you are trying to make, and it should catch your readers' attention and make them want to read your essay. It may be risky to state your major claim in the title: If you state a controversial claim in your title, you run the risk that some readers will choose not to read your argument. However, there are times when stating a bold claim in the title is appropriate—especially if readers may not have even considered the topic.

VISUALIZING *Variations* | Using Charts and Other Visuals to Support Your Claim

If you were writing in response to Scenario 1, which asks you to focus on a controversial issue, you might choose to write about global warming. You could use charts and graphs to convince your reader, as they can provide useful information. This chart shows the global variation in temperatures from 1860 to 2000:

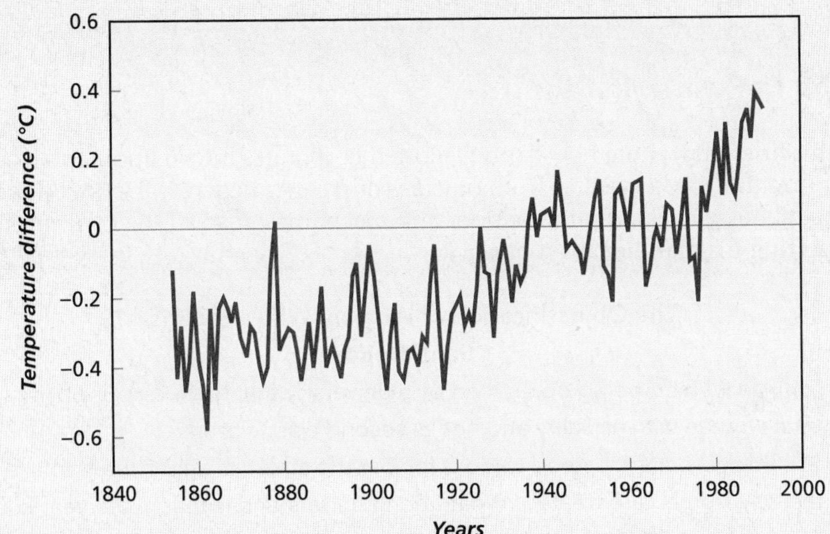

If you were to combine this chart with the following information from the same source, you would be providing your reader with a useful chart along with some specific data to explain it.

> The temperature values in the data set are provided as differences from a mean of 15 degrees C. These data have been analyzed by scientists to show a 0.5 degree C increase in global temperatures. However, this finding is under dispute because some claim that the amount of error in the data is too large to justify the conclusion. This data set has been created using the following steps:
>
> - Data were collected from land based stations, from ocean buoys, and from ships.
> - For each year, data have been averaged to come up with a yearly average.
> - Data are smoothed to accommodate historical changes that skew the data (e.g., weather stations near cities record artificially high temperatures because [cities] create what is called an "urban heat island effect").

The purpose of using visuals in your essays is to help support the point you are trying to make in your text in a way that will help readers not only understand but also be convinced by your argument.

Writing Activity

Constructing a Complete Draft

Using the writing you did when selecting an organizational approach for your persuasive paper, write a complete first draft of your paper. Remember that your argument will evolve as you write, so your ideas will most likely change as you draft.

Santi DeRosa's First Draft

In this brief draft, note how Santi DeRosa incorporates information and examples from his life, as well as from outside sources. As he wrote, DeRosa did not worry about grammar, punctuation, and mechanics; instead, he concentrated on getting his main ideas on paper.

The Objectification of Woman. Who's Fault Is it?
Santi DeRosa

Are women being objectified by a university that has a responsibility to treat women with equality and not as second class citizens?

I say yes. All you need to do is look at the athletics department to see the way women are treated. What I don't understand is that in the year 2003, women are still allowing themselves to be used in such a way

In the past week I have read a couple of news articles from the campus newspaper that got me a little perplexed. Maybe it's the fact that I have a son the age of the female students in the articles. Or, maybe it's the fact that I have a wife, a sister, a mother and nieces that I respect as people and as women. The articles upset my sense of right and wrong.

Joe Watson wrote the first article, "Risky behavior not policed in university recruiting" and explains how high school football players that visit the university for the purpose of being recruited are met by coeds, of which, thirty-five of the thirty-seven are females. Is this just a coincidence? No, I don't think so. It is no coincidence when schools from all over the country use the same practices to recruit high school players. The reporter took an informal survey of 117 Division 1-A football programs nationwide and found many with the same recruiter make-up. Louisiana State has 55 females; Alabama leads the way with 100 females. The university advertises every spring for new recruiters. Most come from sororities. The football coaches say they prefer using females because that's the way the other schools do it and the players coming to campus to be recruited would be uncomfortable if they were greeted by males, because they are used to female recruiters. I think that this is just an excuse to turn a blind eye to a potential problem. Most of the players who come to be recruited are 17 and 18 years old. There have been many reports of under-age drinking at local clubs and parties and sometimes sex according to some senior recruiters. The people interviewed for the article who are in support of the "hostess" program defend it by saying that "the recruiters perform respectable duties during high school recruits' campus visits." Does the responsibility of "performing respectable duties" end when they leave the campus for a party? I believe that Becky Stoltz, a fourth year recruiter said it best when interviewed, "It's a disaster waiting to happen."

The second news article I read was by Megan Rudebeck. The story titled "'Hot' recruiters draw prospects" seems to be defending the program. Ms. Rudebeck not only talked to the coaches that run the program; she spoke with recruiters and players as well. She almost had me convinced that I might have been over reacting. I started to think that here is a woman writing a story that seems to be in defense of the way the recruiting program works. Maybe I am reacting wrongly. That is until the last line of the story when she quotes Zach Krula, a freshman offensive lineman. Zach says, "We've got a lot of hot girls, we might as well utilize them." After a few minutes I started to think to myself, why isn't Ms. Rudebeck insulted by that comment? Is she, as well as the women that are part of the program, so brain-washed with the need to get quality players into the football program that they are willing to overlook the fact that they are being "utilized."

As ideas for further development, Santi made these notes at the end of his initial draft:

Short history of women's struggle for equality.
Use family stories to tell history of strong women?
Define the objectification of women.
Conclusion.

Revising

Once you have a full draft of your persuasive text, you still have much to do. First, however, you should set the draft aside so that you can gain some critical distance. You can then read it with fresh eyes. When you approach your work this way, you will find it easier to notice reasons that are irrelevant, evidence that is not fully developed, or places where a compelling visual might add to the impact of your argument.

As you work to revise your early drafts, do not be concerned about doing a great deal of heavy editing. When you revise, you will probably change the content and structure of your paper, so time spent fixing problems with sentence style or grammar, punctuation, or mechanics at this stage is often wasted.

When you reread the first draft of your persuasive writing, here are some questions to ask yourself:

- How clearly and persuasively am I making my point? Am I sure my readers can understand it? How easily will they be able to restate the thesis?
- How effectively does all of my evidence support that main point? (Sometimes it is easy to include evidence that seems persuasive but that does not support the point you are arguing for.)
- Are there other photographs, charts, or graphs that might help make my point?
- Are there parts of my paper that might confuse a reader? If so, how might I clarify them?
- Do I restate or allude to my main point at the end of my paper and also explain to the reader what I would like him or her to *do* (to vote, to write a letter to the editor, to *do* what I have been arguing for)?

Technology can help you revise and edit your writing more easily. Use your word processor's track-changes tool to try out revisions and editing changes. After you have had time to think about the possible changes, you can "accept" or "reject" them. Also, you can use your word processor's comment tool to write reminders to yourself when you get stuck with a revision or some editing task.

Because it is so difficult even for experienced writers to see their emerging writing with a fresh eye, it is almost always useful to ask classmates, friends, or family members to read and comment on drafts of your persuasive writing.

WRITER'S *Workshop* | Responding to Full Drafts

Working with one or two classmates, read each paper, and offer comments and questions that will help each of you see your papers' strengths and weaknesses. Consider the following questions as you do:

- What is your first impression of this draft? How effective is the title at drawing you in? Why? What are your overall suggestions for improvement? What part(s) of the text are especially persuasive? What reasons could use more support? Indicate what you like about the draft, and provide positive and encouraging feedback to the writer.
- How tight is the writer's focus? Does the paper wander a bit? If so, where?
- How effective is the introduction? What suggestions can you make to improve it?
- What is the author's thesis or main claim? How could it be expressed or supported more effectively?
- Are there parts that are confusing? Where would you like more details or examples to help clarify the writer's meaning?

(continued)

- How accurate and appropriate is the supporting evidence? How clearly does the author indicate the sources of statistics and other supporting evidence?
- Might visuals such as charts, tables, photographs, or cartoons make the text more convincing?
- How clearly and effectively does the writer present any opposing points of view? How effectively does the writer answer opposing viewpoints? How might the writer acknowledge, concede, and/or refute them more effectively?
- How well has the writer demonstrated an awareness of readers' knowledge, needs, and/or expectations? How might the writer demonstrate greater awareness?
- How carefully has the writer avoided logical fallacies?
- What could be added or changed to the conclusion to make it more effective? How well does it tie everything together? If action is called for, to what extent does it make you want to take action?

Notes on Santi DeRosa's First Draft, from a Conference with His Instructor

After writing his first draft, DeRosa met with his instructor, who thought his topic was promising but indicated that he needed more support on recruiting practices at his school and at other campuses. Together they brainstormed more ideas to develop his paper in more depth. The practice of using female students to help recruit male athletes led to these objections, which are more completely developed in DeRosa's final draft (see pages 259–263):

1. Using women for their bodies
2. Manipulation
3. A program that reinforces age-old notions of exploitation
4. Limits and defines women's roles
5. Under the guise of school spirit
6. Better add some more extensive research info

Responding to Readers' Comments

Once they have received feedback on their writing from peers, instructors, friends, and others, all writers have to figure out what to do with that feedback.

The first thing to do with any feedback is to consider carefully what your readers have said about your text. In his case, DeRosa arranged a conference with his writing teacher, who helped him brainstorm some specific objections to the recruiting program at his school to give his argument more depth.

As with all feedback, it is important to really listen to it and consider what your reader has to say. Then it is up to you, as the author, to decide how to come to terms with these suggestions. You may decide to reject some comments, of course; other comments, though, deserve your attention, as they are the words of real readers speaking to you about how to improve your text. It is especially important to deal with comments from readers indicating that they are unconvinced by your argument. You sometimes may find that comments from more than one reader contradict each other. In that case, you need to use your own judgment to decide which reader's comments are on the right track.

In the final version of his paper, you can see how Santi DeRosa responded to his instructor's comments, as well as to his own review of his first draft.

connect
mhconnectcomposition.com
Using commas with nonrestrictive words or word groups QL8010

Knowledge of Conventions

When effective writers edit their work, they attend to the conventions that will help readers process their work. These include genre conventions, documentation, format, usage, grammar, and mechanics. By attending to these conventions in your writing, you make reading a more pleasant experience for readers.

Editing

connect
mhconnectcomposition.com
Revising and Editing overview (also Drafting) QL8008

The last task in any writing project is editing—the final polishing of your document. When you edit and polish your writing, you make changes to your sentence structures and word choices to improve your style and to make your writing clearer and more concise. You also check your work to make sure it adheres to conventions of grammar, usage, punctuation, mechanics, and spelling. Use the spell-check function of your word-processing program, but be sure to double-check your spelling personally. If you have used sources in your paper, make sure you are following the documentation style your instructor requires.

As with overall revision of your work, this final editing and polishing is most effective if you can put your text aside for a few days and come back to it with fresh eyes. Because checking conventions is easier said than done, though, we strongly recommend that you ask classmates, friends, and tutors to read your work as well.

See Chapter 20 for more on documenting sources using MLA or APA style.

To assist you with editing, we offer here a round-robin editing activity focused on citing sources correctly.

WRITER'S *Workshop* | Round-Robin Editing with a Focus on Citing Sources

Working in small groups, look over both the in-text citations and the works-cited or references lists in your papers. For example, you might notice a problem with an in-text citation that is supposed to be in MLA style, such as this one:

> In the last line of the story, however, Rudebeck quotes Zach Krula, a freshman offensive lineman. Zach says, "We've got a lot of hot girls, we might as well utilize them" (Rudebeck 1).

In MLA style, it is not necessary to include the source's name in parentheses if the name has been given within the text.

As you work with your peers, consult Chapter 20 of this text, which provides guidelines for using MLA or APA style when citing sources.

ROUND-ROBIN EDITING WITH A FOCUS ON

Punctuating Dialogue (p. 82)
Fragments (p. 126)
Modifiers (p. 172)
Wordiness (p. 216)
Citing Sources (p. 259)
Careful Word Choice (p. 303)
Subordinate Clauses (p. 347)
Inclusive Language (p. 395)

connect
mhconnectcomposition.com

MLA Style: QL20006, QL20007

APA Style: QL20008, QL20009

Genres, Documentation, and Format

If you are writing an academic paper in response to Scenario 1, you will need to follow the conventions for the discipline in which you are writing and the requirements of your instructor. If you are writing an editorial for your college newspaper (Scenario 2), you should check the newspaper's editorial page or its Web site to see what the requirements are for length and format and what information you need to include when you submit the editorial.

A Writer Shares His Persuasive Writing: Santi DeRosa's Final Draft

Santi DeRosa continued to revise and edit his paper, and constructed a finished draft, which follows. As you read the essay, think about what makes it effective. Following the essay, you'll find some specific questions to consider.

SANTI DEROSA

PERSUASIVE ESSAY

The Objectification of Women: Whose Fault Is It?

1 Are women being treated as objects by the very university that has a responsibility to treat them with equality and dignity and not as second-class citizens? All anyone needs to do is look at the athletics department to see the way women are treated here. What I don't understand is why in the year 2003 women are still allowing themselves to be used in such a way.

DeRosa and his instructor brainstormed a number of objections to the recruiting practices for him to develop in his revised draft, including this one:

I need to develop the idea that these practices use women for their bodies.

Note how DeRosa develops this objection.

Here DeRosa paraphrases a newspaper article.

DeRosa and his instructor also came up with the following objection for him to develop:

The program reinforces age-old notions of prostitution.

Note how he adds details and specific examples to support this part of his persuasive text.

In the past week I have read two news articles in the campus newspaper about recruiting practices that made me a little perplexed. Maybe it's because I have a son the age of the female students in the articles, or maybe it's because I have a wife, a sister, a mother, and nieces whom I respect as people and as women, but these articles upset my sense of right and wrong. Objectification of women, sexual or otherwise, should never be allowed or condoned. 2

In the first article I read, "Risky Behavior Not Policed in Recruiting," reporter Joe Watson explains how high school football players who visit campus for the purpose of being recruited are met by coeds. Thirty-five of thirty-seven student recruiters are females. Is this just a coincidence? I don't think so. Schools from all over the country use the same practices to recruit high school players. Watson conducted an informal survey of 117 Division 1-A football programs nationwide and found many with similar proportions of female to male recruiters. Louisiana State has 55 females; Alabama leads the way with 100 females (1). 3

As Watson reports, the university advertises every spring for new recruiters. Most come from sororities. The football coaches say they prefer using women because that's the way the other schools do it. They maintain that the players coming to campus to be recruited would be uncomfortable if they were greeted by men because they are used to female recruiters. 4

This justification is just an excuse to ignore a potential problem. Most of the players who come to campus to be recruited are 17 and 18 years old. There have been many reports of under-age drinking at local clubs and parties and sometimes sex, according to some senior recruiters. The people interviewed for the article who support the "hostess" program defend it by saying that "the recruiters perform respectable duties during high school recruits' campus visits" (Watson 2). Does the responsibility of "performing respectable duties" end when they leave the campus for a party? I believe that Becky Stoltz, a fourth-year recruiter who was interviewed for the article said it best: "It's a disaster waiting to happen." Big problems have in fact already happened at the University of Colorado, where a recruiting aide was indicted for improper conduct after a three-month grand-jury investigation of illegal recruiting practices, including allegations of sexual assault (Lambert). 5

Over the last hundred years, women have traveled a rocky road to greater equality. At the turn of the twentieth century women didn't have many of the rights we take for granted today, such as the right to own property and the right to vote. By staying strong, working together, and maintaining their dignity, women eventually gained these rights for themselves and their daughters and granddaughters. 6

In my own family, my grandmother and great-grandmother took care of their family in Italy while my grandfather came to America to set up a 7 decent life for them. My grandmother held things together for six years until her husband was able to go back and get her. Although she did not have the same rights as a man of that time, she never gave up hope and never lost her pride. In this country she worked as a seamstress, as so many Italian women did, in order to help the family make it through bad times and to provide a better life for her children. My mother also worked a full-time job as a seamstress in a factory while taking care of her home and family, as women did in the 1950s and 1960s. However, women of that time were being taken for granted, and their roles had to change. Women wanted more, and through their strength of conviction, they got it—more equitable pay for their work. However, over the last forty years, the great strides women have made have been somewhat squandered. Women have made impressive gains in their professional lives, but they have also come to be seen, more and more, as objects.

The objectification of women in popular culture and sports is not new. 8
During the 1950s and 1960s, the advertising industry started to portray women in roles outside the kitchen, but it also created a perspective on women that objectified them. To consider women in terms of the way they look is objectification. Examples of this are common: (1) Female newscasters chosen for their appearance, (2) the Dallas Cowboy cheerleaders—and cheerleading squads for other teams, and (3) beautiful women appearing in advertisements for beer and automobiles.

Amanda Bonzo, in an opinion piece in the online journal *The Digital* 9
Collegian, writes the following about this process of objectification:

> In our society, a woman's body is objectified daily on television, music videos, advertisements. What do we do with objects? We buy, sell, trade them. . . . We tame them through rape and domestic abuse. Finally, we destroy them.

DeRosa effectively uses quotations to help make his point.

And Casey Jacketta, writing for the University of New Mexico's *Daily* 10
Lobo, notes the following:

> I was pleased that my favorite show, "Law and Order," was on. Then, as I kept watching, I realized that the assistant district attorney, played by Angie Harmon—a woman—didn't say a word in court. This troubled me, so I changed the channel to MTV. This upset me even more! All I saw was a bunch of barely clothed women shaking their bodies for the male singer's pleasure. (1)

We see what these writers are talking about daily in advertising and 11
in other media such as television, movies, and music. It is unfortunate that the sexual objectification of women sells products, and unless women understand that advertisers, filmmakers, college athletic departments, and others are taking advantage of them, this exploitation will never change.

Barbara Fredrickson and her colleagues explain that this process causes women to start to view themselves the way others view them; as a consequence, "[a] woman views her own body as an object (or each piece as a separate object)" (274).

Objectification is often disguised as free speech and free expression, 12
which are both noble principles, although they are often misused. What I don't understand is how any woman would allow herself to be used in this way. In the case of recruiters, objectification is disguised as school spirit.

In the second news article I read, "'Hot' Recruiters Draw Prospects," 13
Megan Rudebeck seems to be defending the program. Ms. Rudebeck not only talked to the coaches that run the program; she spoke with recruiters and players as well. She almost had me convinced that I might be overreacting. After all, here is a woman who is defending the way the recruiting program works. In the last line of the story, however, Rudebeck quotes Zach Krula, a freshman offensive lineman. Zach says, "We've got a lot of hot girls, we might as well utilize them" (1). That quotation made me wonder why Ms. Rudebeck wasn't insulted by that comment. Is she, as well as the women who are part of the program, so brainwashed by the need to get quality players onto the football team that they are willing to overlook the fact that they are being "utilize[d]"?

DeRosa also needed to develop this objection to the recruiting program:

It operates under the guise of school spirit.

He added information from another article (by Megan Rudebeck) that puts a positive spin on the practice DeRosa is criticizing and provides a defense of the program; he then refutes Rudebeck's argument.

The use of women as sexual objects in mass media advertising, televi- 14
sion, and music has made the practice so commonplace that we fail to see that it degrades our society. It amazes me that the women of the recruiting staff have not made the connection. It amazes me that Ms. Rudebeck and the coaching staff say they don't see what's going on, and that students, faculty, the alumni, and the administration buy into this degrading and potentially dangerous practice. I hope that a copy of Joe Watson's article makes it into the hands of each of the recruiter's parents and the Board of Regents. This practice is an insult to the women of the university, as well as to every woman in the last century who has sacrificed in order to achieve social equality.

Works Cited

This paper follows MLA guidelines for in-text citations and works cited.

Bonzo, Amanda. Letter. *The Digital Collegian*. 20 Nov. 2000. Web. 4 Feb. 2003 <http://www.collegian.psu.edu/archive/2000/11/11-20-00tdc/11-20-00dops-letter-1.asp>.

Fredrickson, Barbara L., Tomi-Ann Roberts, Stephanie M. Noll, Diane M. Quinn, and Jean M. Twenge. "That Swimsuit Becomes You: Sex Differences in Self-Objectification, Restrained Eating, and Math Performance." *Journal of Personality and Social Psychology*, 75 (1998): 269–84. Print.

Jacketta, Casey. "Women's Lib Has Not Ended Objectification." *Daily Lobo*. 25 Nov. 2002. Web. 3 Feb. 2003 <http://www.dailylobo.com/news/2002/11/25/Opinion/Column.Womens.Lib.Has.Not.Ended.Objectification-332561.shtml>.

Lambert, Liz. "Maxcey Indicted in CU Grand Jury Probe." Web. 6 Sept. 2004 <http://9news.com/cu/>.

Rudebeck, Megan. "'Hot' Recruiters Draw Prospects." *The State Press* Web. 18 Oct. 2002: 1–2. 3 Feb. 2003 <http://www.asuwebdevil.com/main.cfm?include=detail&storyid= 300645>

Watson, Joe. "Risky Behavior Not Policed in Football Recruiting." *The State Press*. 9 Dec. 2002: 1–2. Web. 3 Feb. 2003 <http://www.asuwebdevil.com/main.cfm?include=detail&storyid= 339775>.

QUESTIONS FOR WRITING AND DISCUSSION

Rhetorical Knowledge: The Writer's Situation and Rhetoric

1. **Audience:** What audience does DeRosa have in mind for this essay? How can you tell?
2. **Purpose:** What purpose(s) does DeRosa have for writing this essay? How well does he achieve his purpose(s)?
3. **Voice and tone:** How does DeRosa's voice and tone help to establish his ethos? Is his tone appropriate? Why or why not?
4. **Responsibility:** How effectively does DeRosa represent opposing views on the issue of using female students as recruiters? In what ways, if any, could he represent their views more fairly?
5. **Context, format, and genre:** DeRosa is writing as a student but also as a husband and father. How does this context affect his use of language, appeals, and evidence? DeRosa has written an academic essay that argues for a specific change. The markers of this genre are that the writer must convince the readers that a problem exists and then must convince them that the proposed solution is a good one. Does DeRosa convince you that a problem exists? Do you think his solution is a good one?

Critical Thinking: The Writer's Ideas and Your Personal Response

6. To what extent does DeRosa's text appeal to your emotions? In what way(s)?
7. What is DeRosa's main point, or claim? To what extent do you agree with it? Why?

Composing Processes and Knowledge of Conventions: The Writer's Strategies

8. How convincing is the evidence DeRosa supplies? What other evidence might he have used?
9. What organizational method does DeRosa use? How effective is it? What other method(s) might he have used?

Inquiry and Research: Ideas for Further Exploration

10. Conduct a search (at your school library or on the Web), focusing on the events that DeRosa describes in his family history (paragraph 7). What similarities can you find to the family story that DeRosa relates in his text?

Self-Assessment: Reflecting on Your Goals

Now that you have constructed a piece of writing designed to convince your readers, review your learning goals, which you and your classmates may have considered at the beginning of this chapter (pages 224–225). Then reflect on all the thinking and writing that you have done in constructing your persuasive paper. To help reflect on the learning goals that you have achieved, respond in writing to the following questions:

Rhetorical Knowledge

- *Audience:* What have you learned about addressing an audience in persuasive writing?
- *Purpose:* What have you learned about the purposes for constructing an effective persuasive text?
- *Rhetorical situation:* How did the writing context affect your persuasive text?
- *Voice and tone:* How would you describe your voice in this essay? Your tone? How do they contribute to the effectiveness of your persuasive essay?
- *Context, medium, and genre:* How did your context determine the medium and genre you chose, and how did those decisions affect your writing?

Critical Thinking, Reading, and Writing

- *Learning/inquiry:* How did you decide what to focus on for your persuasive text? Describe the process you went through to focus on a main idea, or thesis.
- *Responsibility:* How did you fulfill your responsibilities to your readers?
- *Reading and research:* What did you learn about persuasive writing from the reading selections in this chapter? What research did you conduct? How sufficient was the research you did?
- *Skills:* As a result of writing this paper, how have you become a more critical thinker, reader, and writer? What skills do you hope to develop further?

Writing Processes

- *Invention:* What invention strategies were most useful to you?
- *Organizing your ideas and details:* What organizational approach did you use? How successful was it?
- *Revising:* What one revision did you make that you are most satisfied with? If you could go back and make an additional revision, what would it be?
- *Working with peers:* How did your instructor and peer readers help you by making comments and suggestions about your writing? List some examples of how you revised your text based on comments from your instructor and your peer readers. How could you have made better use of the comments and suggestions you received? How could your peer readers help you more on your next assignment? How might you help them more, in the future, with the comments and suggestions you make on their texts?
- *Visuals:* Did you use photographs, charts, graphs, or other visuals to help you convince your readers? If so, what did you learn about incorporating these elements?
- *Writing habits:* What "writerly habits" have you developed, modified, or improved on as you constructed the writing assignment for this chapter? How will you change your future writing activities based on what you have learned about yourself?

Knowledge of Conventions

- *Editing:* What sentence problem did you find most frequently in your writing? How will you avoid that problem in future assignments?
- *Genre:* What conventions of the genre you were using, if any, gave you problems?
- *Documentation:* Did you use sources for your paper? If so, what documentation style did you use? What problems, if any, did you have with it?

If you are constructing a course portfolio, file your written reflections so that you can return to them when you next work on your portfolio. Refer to Chapter 1 (pages 11–12) for a sample reflection by a student.

Santi DeRosa Reflects on His Writing QL8009

Writing to Evaluate

In 1997, the American Film Institute (AFI) announced a list of the hundred greatest American films. The list was chosen by a panel of "leaders from across the film community." In 2007, the AFI updated this list, which now includes one film released since 2000: *Lord of the Rings: The Fellowship of the Ring. Citizen Kane,* however, retained its spot at the top of list. Following are the top twenty-five:

American Film Institute's Greatest Movies, 1–25

1. *Citizen Kane* (1941)
2. *The Godfather* (1972)
3. *Casablanca* (1942)
4. *Raging Bull* (1980)
5. *Singin' in the Rain* (1952)
6. *Gone with the Wind* (1939)
7. *Lawrence of Arabia* (1962)
8. *Schindler's List* (1993)
9. *Vertigo* (1958)
10. *The Wizard of Oz* (1939)
11. *City Lights* (1931)
12. *The Searchers* (1956)
13. *Star Wars* (1977)
14. *Psycho* (1960)
15. *2001: A Space Odyssey* (1968)
16. *Sunset Boulevard* (1950)
17. *The Graduate* (1967)
18. *The General* (1927)

TALKING ABOUT IT!
Terrific!
I love him!
He's a saint!
He's a genius!
RSON
ELLES
TIZEN
KANE
EVERETT SLOANE · RAY COLLINS · GEORGE COULOURIS

19. *On the Waterfront* (1954)
20. *It's a Wonderful Life* (1946)
21. *Chinatown* (1974)
22. *Some Like It Hot* (1959)
23. *The Grapes of Wrath* (1940)
24. *E.T.—The Extra-Terrestrial* (1982)
25. *To Kill a Mockingbird* (1962)

Whether you agree with these rankings or not, for the AFI to compile the list, people had to evaluate movies based on specific criteria.

Evaluations are part of everyday life. When you decide which classes to take, what to eat for breakfast, or which candidate to support, you decide which choice is best for you and act accordingly. As you think about the choices you confront in your life, consider why you make the ones that you do.

You make such decisions by evaluating your available choices based on certain **criteria,** or standards. For example, if you are evaluating a product, you may consider factors such as price, brand name, location, and size. Usually, you will base your evaluation on a combination of criteria—and you will inevitably weigh some criteria more heavily than others.

Whether you realize it or not, you have years of practice in judging the trustworthiness of others' evaluations and the relevance of the criteria they use. When a newspaper endorses a political candidate, your familiarity with the newspaper and its editorial policy influences your view of that endorsement. If you are a movie fan, you have probably already come to some conclusions about the excerpt from the AFI's evaluation of the "Greatest Movies" based on your agreement or disagreement with its list of films. Your experience with everyday evaluations will help you determine the criteria for the evaluations you write.

Setting Your Goals:

Rhetorical Knowledge

- **Audience:** Determine who will benefit from your evaluation. Who needs to make decisions about the subject of your evaluation? What do the audience members probably already know about your subject? What will you need to tell them?
- **Purpose:** When you evaluate, you make a judgment based on specific criteria. Your purpose is not simply to say, "I think the Toyota truck is better than the Chevy," but to convince your reader to agree.
- **Rhetorical situation:** Consider the many factors that affect where you stand in relation to your subject. If you have some personal interest in your evaluation, you will have a different stance than a more neutral party might.
- **Voice and tone:** When you construct an evaluation, you are trying to explain your reasoned judgment. If you come across as a know-it-all, your readers may lose interest or suspect your judgment.
- **Context, medium, and genre:** Decide on the best medium and genre to use to present your evaluation to the audience you want to reach.

Critical Thinking, Reading, and Writing

- **Learning/inquiry:** By observing, listening to, and/or reading about the subject of your evaluation, and then by writing about it, you gain a deeper understanding of its qualities and the ability to make more informed judgments about it.
- **Responsibility:** Effective evaluative writing leads naturally to critical thinking. When you engage in evaluating something, you have to consider all aspects of that item, not only to determine the criteria on which you will base your evaluation but also to construct a reasoned argument for your evaluation.
- **Reading and research:** To evaluate a subject, you need not only to examine it in detail but also to examine similar items.

Writing to Evaluate

Writing Processes

- **Invention:** Various invention activities can help you consider all aspects of the subject you are evaluating.
- **Organizing your ideas and details:** The act of evaluating necessarily means that you think about the various aspects of your subject. That process can help you organize your thinking, and later your writing, into categories, based on your criteria.
- **Revising:** Read your work with a critical eye to make certain that it fulfills the assignment and displays the qualities of effective evaluative writing.
- **Working with peers:** Listen to your classmates to make sure that they understand your evaluation.

Knowledge of Conventions

- **Editing:** Effective evaluations usually require careful word choice.
- **Genres for evaluative writing:** In many situations, your evaluation will be a formal report or an academic paper. Evaluations written about movies, restaurants, or other products or services are not quite as formal as college assignments, however.
- **Documentation:** If you relied on sources outside of your experience, cite them using the appropriate documentation style.

mhconnectcomposition.com

Writing to Evaluate Tutorial QL9001

Rhetorical Knowledge

When you write an evaluation, you need to consider the criteria on which you will base your evaluation as well as how you will develop those criteria. What aspects of the work, product, service, or idea should you examine for your evaluation? How can you best make an evaluative judgment about it? You will also need to decide what medium and genre will help you get your evaluation across to your audience most effectively.

Writing to Evaluate in Your College Classes

As a college student, you will be expected to read and write evaluations in many of your classes:

- Your political science instructor might ask you to rate the effectiveness of a political campaign.
- Your business and marketing instructor might ask you to evaluate several potential store locations.

In much of your academic writing, you will also have to evaluate the sources and evidence you select to support your thesis statements.

The "Ways of Writing" feature presents different genres that can be used when writing to evaluate in your college classes.

Writing to Evaluate for Life

In addition to the evaluations you will consider and write while in college, you will no doubt make evaluations every day in the professional, civic, and personal areas of your life.

In your professional life, your writing will often have an evaluative purpose. For example, if you have employees reporting to you, you will probably be asked to evaluate their job performances. You may consider criteria that include both verifiable information (does your employee arrive at work on time?) and opinions (is he or she an effective leader?). You will need to provide evidence to support your judgments while sufficiently explaining your opinions. A different kind of workplace evaluation might be one your supervisor asks you to write. A lab technician may be asked to test two different brands of instruments the lab is thinking of purchasing and then write an evaluative report on her findings.

In your civic life, you will often evaluate people and proposals, and then make decisions or recommendations. Suppose that a local power company is planning to expand a power plant in your neighborhood, and you are a member of a committee that is evaluating the impact of the expansion. Before drafting its report, your committee will need to establish appropriate criteria for evaluating the plant, including the impact that the plant will have on property values and rents, and the change it will cause in the local landscape.

Without realizing it, we often make evaluations when writing in our personal life. An e-mail to a relative may include comments about favorite restaurants, teachers, or newfound friends. On the one hand, we might feel more comfortable making evaluations for our friends and family. On the other, we may feel especially obligated to provide a useful evaluation because we care about the relationship.

The "Ways of Writing" feature presents different genres that can be used when writing to evaluate in life.

Scenarios for Writing | Assignment Options

Your instructor may ask you to complete one or both of the following writing assignments that call for evaluation. Each of these assignments is in the form of a *scenario*, which gives you a sense of who your audience is and what you need to accomplish with your evaluative writing.

Starting on page 288, you will find guidelines for completing whatever scenario you decide—or are asked—to complete. Additional scenarios for college and life are online.

connect
mhconnectcomposition.com
Writer's Workshop: Applying Learning Goals to Evaluative Writing QL9002

Writing for College

SCENARIO 1 Academic Evaluation: What Are the Rules?

You may currently live (or may previously have lived) in a communal setting such as a dormitory, a military barracks, a summer camp, or a house or apartment with roommates. In that setting, you are probably aware of rules and regulations, yet you may not have thought about whether they are fair or not, or even if there are punishments for not obeying the rules. Or you may be living with one or both of your parents, who probably insist on certain rules.

Consider questions such as these:

- Who controls what happens in the living quarters?
- What are the rules for living in the particular setting (communal or parental)? Are they fair and reasonable?
- Who is paying for the living quarters? Do they (should they) have total control of what happens in them? What, if any, restrictions are there?
- Should parents be allowed to place restrictions on college-age students who live at home? What rules would be reasonable?
- If an organization such as a college or the government controls the living quarters, can they monitor e-mail? Internet access?

Writing Assignment: Write an evaluation of the rules of the communal setting in which you currently live or once lived, or of your parent's or parents' rules. You will need to do some research on what the rules are and consider

Ways of Writing to Evaluate

Genres for Your College Classes	Sample Situation	Advantages of the Genre	Limitations of the Genre
Career assessment	In your career and life planning class, you are asked to construct an evaluation focusing on possible careers after you graduate: the kind of work, the pay, the job possibilities for the future, the qualifications, and so on.	This formal assignment insists that you explain your personal evaluative conclusions in a well-reasoned manner.	You might not have time to gather really meaningful data if you lack the time to interview people in those careers.
History essay	In your world history class, you are asked to evaluate whether one or more of several possible causes were the reason for an historical event.	This evaluation will require you to develop and apply valid criteria to reach a historical conclusion.	Historical events rarely occur in isolation, and no set of criteria will be all inclusive.
Letter to your campus newspaper	Your mathematics professor asks you to write a letter using statistics drawn from interviews to evaluate a specific aspect of campus life (dining, parking, and so on).	Anything published in a college newspaper will have a wide audience of people who have an interest in campus affairs.	A letter to the editor gives you limited space for your evaluation, and you may not have enough room to adequately make your case. It might not be published.
Business report	Your business instructor asks you to evaluate several marketing plans for a new product for college students	An evaluative report allows you to create criteria and then research what students might and might not purchase.	It does not allow for extraneous factors that may not be included in your research.
Genres for Life	**Sample Situation**	**Advantages of the Genre**	**Limitations of the Genre**
Brochure	As part of a community group, you want to publicize your evaluation of a sales tax increase that will be voted upon.	Your evaluation, often with illustrations and in a compact form, will provide readers with evaluative criteria in order to make a more informed decision.	A brochure provides limited space for your evaluation.
Letter	You are planning a family reunion, at which you expect nearly a hundred family members from around the country, and you want to evaluate possible locations.	A letter is an effective way to share information, and to explain the criteria on which you are basing your evaluation.	Letters and responses to letters are slow; sending the letter by email or posting it to a Web site is another option but that may exclude some family members.
Blog	You start a blog that evaluates software programs used for education.	A blog is an easy and uncomplicated way for you to share your evaluations with a wide and interested audience.	Blogs often need monitoring for improper comments; sometimes there is a lot of information generated that takes time to read through.
E-mail	You send an email to co-workers that evaluates several digital storage options for your company.	An email allows you to input links to the prospective companies' Web sites and ask for feedback.	Some people might feel they need more information than the email includes.
Performance review	You are required to submit a performance review for several employees whom you supervise.	Often there is a form which provides specific criteria on which you construct your evaluation.	Sometimes the criteria for an evaluation no longer fits the work the employee does; forms provide limited room for originality or extra comments and suggestions.

what you might use as criteria for evaluating them. Your audience will be your instructor and your classmates.

Writing for Life

SCENARIO 2 Personal Writing: Evaluating a Cultural Event or Performance

In your personal life, you attend any number of cultural events: museum exhibits, art shows (whether those of professional artists, photographers, or sculptors, or those of your friends), musical performances, plays, dance performances, and so on. Your college or university is a wonderful source of cultural events. How do you evaluate such cultural performances or events? On what criteria *should* they be evaluated? How much weight should you give one criterion in relation to others? How might your own criteria match up with those of other students who also attend the event or performance?

Writing Assignment: For this assignment, assume that your local newspaper or a local magazine has asked you to evaluate a recent cultural event or performance. In no more than 1,200 words, explain the evaluative criteria that you see as important, and then give your evaluation of that event or performance. Consider how you might use visuals to help illustrate your evaluation (for more on using visuals, see "Using Visuals to Support Your Evaluation" on page 298).

mhconnectcomposition.com

Additional Scenarios QL9003

Rhetorical Considerations in Evaluative Writing

Audience: Although your instructor and classmates are your initial audience for this assignment, who are other possible audiences? Consider whether the members of your audience will agree with you about the criteria for evaluating your subject, or whether you will need to convince them to accept your criteria.

Purpose: Your main purpose is to evaluate your subject in terms of the criteria you decide on. How will you persuade your audience to accept your judgment of it?

Voice, tone, and point of view: You have probably chosen your subject because you have a personal interest in it. What preconceptions about it do you have? How can you avoid letting them color your evaluation? How can you use voice and tone to establish credibility?

For more on choosing a medium and genre, see Chapter 17 and the Online Appendix.

Context, medium, and genre: Keeping the context of the assignment in mind, decide on a medium and genre for your evaluation. How will your evaluation be used? If you are writing for an audience beyond the classroom, consider what will be the most effective way to present your evaluation to this audience.

Critical Thinking, Reading, and Writing

Before you begin to write your evaluation, read one or more evaluations to get a feel for this kind of writing. You might also consider how visuals could enhance your evaluative writing, as well as the kinds of sources you may need to consult.

To write an effective, responsible evaluation, you need to understand your subject and the reasons for your evaluation of it. You will need to choose valid criteria, organize your writing logically, and present your evaluation in a way that fulfills your responsibility to your readers. To do this, you need to think critically about your own views, as well as those of any outside sources. Thinking critically does not necessarily mean that you will criticize, but rather that you will carefully consider which criteria are most and least important and how different aspects of your subject relate to each other.

Learning the Qualities of Effective Evaluative Writing

As we have seen, most writing is purposeful. Focusing on the outcome should be the starting point for everything you write, and for an evaluation, you want to make a reasoned, thoughtful, and justifiable judgment. You need to outline the criteria on which you will base your evaluation and then explain how the subject of your evaluation fits the criteria.

Evaluative writing that achieves its goal has the following qualities:

- **Clearly defined and explained criteria.** Readers expect an evaluation to be based on specific criteria that are germane to the item being evaluated. You would evaluate an array of backpacks in a sporting-goods store using different criteria from those you would use to evaluate, say, a television news program. Readers deserve to have the criteria you use defined in detail, so they can understand your reasoning.

  If you are evaluating a work of art, you should use—and explain—criteria appropriate for evaluating art—for example, aesthetic appeal, the impact the work has on the viewer, and how well it represents a specific genre.

- **Comparisons based on the criteria.** Especially when you are evaluating products or services, you will need to show how your subject can be measured against similar subjects and then explain this basis of comparison. You will compare like with like, showing how each aspect of the item you are evaluating rates in comparison with the same (or a similar) aspect of a similar item.

  You can make comparisons based on numerical information ("Tire brand C has a 50 percent longer tread life rating than Brand B, and twice as long as Brand A"). A table can help your readers see the basis of your claim.

Tire Brand	Tread Life Rating
Brand A	30,000 miles
Brand B	40,000 miles
Brand C	60,000 miles

Because this numerical information is verifiable and is not a matter of opinion, it can be persuasive evidence for your overall evaluation.

Finally, you can make comparisons based on more subjective criteria, such as your definition of "quality": You might note that a backpack "should have this kind of fabric, this type of zipper, a lifetime warranty, and straps made out of this material." Then you could go on to outline how each backpack matches (or perhaps does not match) each of your criteria.

When you compare, it is important not to slant your evaluation by leaving out negative information or highlighting only those details that make the product, service, or work you favor seem to be the best. Instead, explain and compare honestly so your readers can reach their own conclusions about the effectiveness of your evaluation. You may find that the item you judge to be best is weak when measured on the basis of one or more of your criteria. It is vital to your overall credibility to account for such shortcomings. Just because something is comparatively weak in one or more areas does not mean that it cannot still come out on top in your evaluation.

- **Evidence that supports your claims.** To accept your evaluation, readers need to understand that you are not just making assertions about your subject, but that you have evidence to support your claims. Evidence can include the following:
  - Testimony: "I've owned Ford automobiles for twenty years, and they've never let me down."
  - Statistical information: "A recent study by the National Highway Traffic Safety Administration found that nearly 50 percent of the 11,500 cars, pickup trucks, vans, and sport-utility vehicles the agency checked had at least one tire with half-worn tread. Another 10 percent had at least one bald tire" (*Consumer Reports*).
  - Detailed description: The more details you can provide, the easier it will be for a reader to understand what you mean.
- **An analysis and explanation of how any visual elements affect your evaluation.** When they evaluate textbooks, teachers often consider how the visual elements in the books might help students learn more effectively. If you were a science teacher, for example, you might focus on the photographs or drawings in the various books under consideration and cite examples from the texts in your evaluative comments.
- **A clearly stated judgment.** Readers can either agree or disagree with your conclusions, but if you have written a successful evaluation, they will understand how you arrived at your judgment.

Reading, Inquiry, and Research: Learning from Texts That Evaluate

The following reading selections are examples of evaluative writing. As you read through the selections, consider the following questions:

- How clearly are the evaluative criteria explained?
- To what extent do I agree with the evaluation? Why?
- How well do I understand why the writer evaluated this subject as he did? That is, how clearly has the writer explained his judgment?
- How familiar am I with the subject that is being evaluated?
- What else would I like to know about the subject being evaluated?
- How can I use the techniques of evaluative writing, as demonstrated here, in my own writing?

R. ALBERT MOHLER

Ranking the Presidents—A New Look at the Best and the Worst

OPINION PIECE

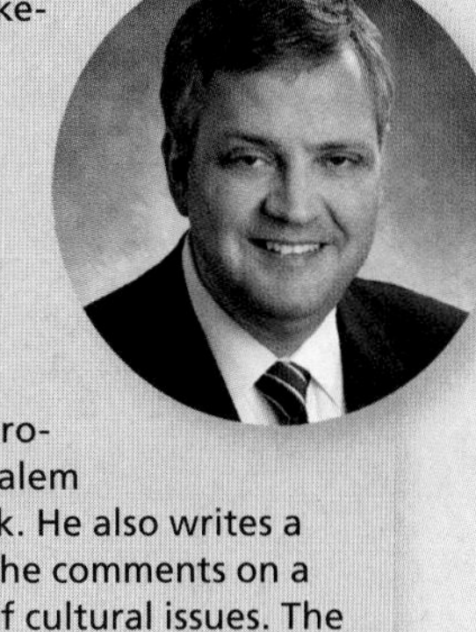

A native of Lakeland, Florida, Dr. R. Albert Mohler serves as president of the Southern Baptist Theological Seminary. He hosts a daily program on the Salem Radio Network. He also writes a blog in which he comments on a wide variety of cultural issues. The following blog entry appeared on June 9, 2004, shortly after the death of Ronald Reagan, fortieth president of the United States. Based on Mohler's ranking scale, where do you think our current president stands in comparison to his predecessors?

1 How would you rank America's presidents? That question is a matter of historical preoccupation for a large number of presidential historians, both amateur and professional. Various schemes for rating America's presidents have been attempted, but none so comprehensive as a recent project undertaken by *The Wall Street Journal* and The Federalist Society.

2 In October 2000, The Federalist Society and *The Wall Street Journal* gathered "an ideologically balanced" group of 132 academics teaching in the fields of law, history, and political science, and asked them to rate the presidents on a 5-point scale, "with 5 meaning highly superior and 1 meaning well below average." Seventy-eight scholars participated in the rankings, and they considered 39 of America's chief executives. Due to their brief terms in office, William Henry Harrison and James Garfield were left out of the rankings, and the survey was conducted before the election of George W. Bush. The remaining 39 presidents were ranked in terms of effectiveness in office and character in leadership. The results are both reassuring and surprising.

3 A comprehensive guide to the rankings can be found in *Presidential Leadership: Rating the Best and the Worst in the White House,* edited by James Taranto of *The Wall Street Journal* and Leonard Leo of The Federalist Society. This new book, released the very week of President Ronald W. Reagan's death, underlines the historical importance of those who held the nation's highest office.

4 In order to ensure ideological balance, the organizers chose scholars representing both the political left and the right. "Our goal was to present the opinions of experts, controlling for political orientation," commented James Lindgren, Professor of Law at Northwestern University. As such, this study sought to correct the imbalance represented by previous rankings undertaken by groups of mostly liberal scholars, or mostly conservative scholars, but not both together.

5 The scholars were asked to rate each president on a 5-point scale and then to identify the most overrated and underrated presidents. In the end, most of the presidents ranked somewhere in the midsection of the

rankings. "The plain fact is that over half of our presidents have been mediocrities," noted historian Robert Rutland.

6 Those presidents rated as "average" include William Taft, John Quincy Adams, George H. W. Bush, and Bill Clinton, among others. "Above average" presidents ranged from Grover Cleveland and John Adams to James Madison, Lyndon Johnson, and John F. Kennedy. Of course, the greatest interest is found at the top and bottom of the rankings.

7 Out of the 39 presidents, only three ranked as "great." George Washington, Abraham Lincoln, and Franklin Roosevelt stood head and shoulders over other presidents in these rankings. As Professor Lindgren remarked, "Being president is a tough job. Only one president in each century is rated high enough for us to call him 'great'."

8 Ranking as failures were Andrew Johnson, Franklin Pierce, Warren Harding, and James Buchanan. Those listed among the failures were judged by the scholars to have been incompetent chief executives whose inability in office threatened the very institution of the presidency. The Civil War, for example, erupted under the presidency of James Buchanan, whose vacillating personality led him to attempt a separation between the moral and legal aspects of slavery. "What is right and what is practicable are two different things," Buchanan argued. That logic led to civil war, and at the end of Buchanan's administration the very future of the republic was in doubt. As Christopher Buckley commented: "It's probably just as well that James Buchanan was our only bachelor president. There are no descendants bracing every morning on opening the paper to find another headline announcing: 'Buchanan Once Again Rated Worst President In History'." It is worth noting that presidential greatness is often inserted between mediocrity or worse. The presidents immediately preceding and succeeding Abraham Lincoln are both rated as failures, while Lincoln scored second place in the pantheon of presidents.

9 Listed in the "below average" rankings were presidents who, in the main, had lofty ambitions for themselves and the nation, but lacked the ability to fulfill those aspirations. Some, like Herbert Hoover and Jimmy Carter, were ranked in this category due to perceived lack of competence. Others, such as Richard Nixon and Ulysses Grant, find their place in this rank because of a devastating loss of character in themselves or their subordinates.

10 The "above average" presidents were characterized by acknowledged competence in office and boldness in leadership. Grover Cleveland reestablished a sense of integrity to the office of president, even as John Adams, James Madison, and James Monroe helped the young nation to assume its rightful place in the world. Presidents such as Lyndon Johnson and John Kennedy were ranked as "above average" due to the boldness of their domestic policies and their response to the critical issues of their times.

11 This sense of historical timing plays an important part in the ranking process. Those who achieved the "near great" ranking generally served in times of national trial. Harry Truman, Dwight Eisenhower, and Ronald Reagan led the nation during a time of war or international conflict and were largely identified with the issue of national defense in a time of crisis. Andrew Jackson redefined the presidency as a public office, embodying the national will. Thomas Jefferson, James Polk, and Theodore Roosevelt brought ambitious plans for national expansion to their administrations, redefining the nation and asserting American leadership in the world arena.

12 The three presidents ranked as the greatest stand in a unique place in the nation's history. The presidency was largely defined by George Washington, who in a very real sense was the singular individual around whom the framers of the constitution conceived the office. As Richard Brookhiser reflected, one of Washington's greatest acts of leadership was to stand at the inauguration of his successor, John Adams, demonstrating to the nation and the world that the presidency is not a monarchy. Abraham Lincoln [ranked at 4.87 compared to Washington's 4.93] is credited with saving the nation and preserving the union. More books have been written about Lincoln than about any other individual American. As historian Jay Winik judged Lincoln: "He instinctively understood the moral burdens he had to shoulder; he appreciated the high seriousness of the crisis; he grasped its tragic dimensions while never losing sight of the good that could somehow be made out of this awful conflict. And he did this with both a human empathy and a steely resolve that, even now, history has trouble fully sorting out or explaining."

13 Franklin D. Roosevelt places among the greats because of his inspiring and effective leadership during a time of incredible national crisis, with the nation's survival at stake due to both domestic and international challenges. Robert H. Bork presents an honest assessment of Roosevelt's leadership, noting his combination of enthusiasm for an activist government and his vision for America as a force for liberty in the international sphere. Though criticizing his record, Bork acknowledges that "Roosevelt's unwavering public optimism had sustained America through its trials." That was no small gift to the nation.

14 Ronald Reagan's place among the "near great" puts him in good company, between Harry Truman and Dwight Eisenhower. Harvard Professor Harvey C. Mansfield acknowledges the success of Reagan's domestic policies, but places his true greatness in the international arena. "Reagan's claim to presidential greatness is that by deliberate but energetic policy and with peaceful means, and against the advice of the experts and the obstruction of partisan opponents, he won the Cold War that America waged for 45 years against one of the three worst regimes known in human history."

15 *Presidential Leadership* is a fascinating volume sure to please and infuriate most readers at some point. The rankings pose an intellectual challenge

to the reader, even as the chapters on individual presidents offer thoughtful analysis and historical interpretation.

In his foreword, William J. Bennett offers a good framework for historical analysis and appreciation. "Our nation's presidents have their warts, to be sure. But they have far more than warts. Whatever is said of the worst of them, it must also be remembered that, at the very least, they submitted themselves—and their character—to public scrutiny and public service." 16

The office of President of the United States represents one of the central and essential institutions of American democracy. The very fact that each of these men held the nation's highest office ranks them as persons of worthwhile interest and reflection. Readers will make their own judgments about the rankings, but in a week that finds the nation mourning its beloved 40th president, this reminder of presidential significance is well timed, and well done. 17

QUESTIONS FOR WRITING AND DISCUSSION: LEARNING OUTCOMES

Rhetorical Knowledge: The Writer's Situation and Rhetoric

1. **Audience:** How wide of an audience does Mohler seem to be addressing in this blog?
2. **Purpose:** Why do you think that Mohler wrote this review of the 2000 project that ranked the presidents?
3. **Voice and tone:** To what extent does Mohler reveal his attitude toward the topic or the audience? Where does he do that?
4. **Responsibility:** What suggests to you that Mohler has accurately described the contents of the project that ranked the presidents?
5. **Context, format, and genre:** Mohler's review appears on Mohler's blog. What signs are there that this is the case? Reviews typically include some summary of the work being reviewed. To what extent and how effectively has Mohler done that?

Critical Thinking: The Writer's Ideas and Your Personal Response

6. What do you think about the particular rankings that Mohler includes in his commentary? Which ones do you agree with most? Why? Which ones do you agree with least? Why?
7. What do you think about the criteria that Mohler mentions at the end of the second paragraph—"effectiveness in office and character in leadership"?

Composing Processes and Knowledge of Conventions: The Writer's Strategies

8. How does Mohler establish his *ethos* in this commentary?
9. Why does Mohler use the quoted material that appears in his commentary?

Inquiry and Research: Ideas for Further Exploration

10. Conduct a Web search on the phrase "ranking presidents." How much disagreement do you find across various rankings? How can you explain those differences?

GENRES *Up Close* Writing a Review

Critical reviews play important roles in daily life. Before people go to such places as restaurants, movie theaters, concert halls, bookstores, or music stores, they often read reviews to help them make thoughtful decisions about how to spend their money. Before employers decide to hire job applicants, renew employees' contracts, or offer employees salary increases, they read reviews of those applicants and employees. Those reviews appear in such forms as letters of recommendation and annual performance evaluations.

Although many critical reviews appear in print (newspapers, magazines, letters, reports), many also appear in audio form on radio shows such as *All Things Considered* and *Weekend Edition* on National Public Radio. They also appear in video form on television shows such as *Countdown with Keith Olbermann* (MSNBC), *Anderson Cooper 360* (CNN), *The O'Reilly Factor* (Fox), and *E News* (E! TV). On the Internet, they can appear in written, audio, or video formats.

The critical review has some standard features:

- **A brief summary of what's being reviewed.** A summary helps readers make sense of the evaluation the reviewer is making. For example, if a reviewer says that the décor of a restaurant is unattractive, the reviewer needs to describe enough of that décor so that readers can understand what parts of the décor are unattractive. Such a summary also helps the reader decide how much the reviewer's tastes in décor are like the reader's. It may be that the reviewer does not like bright colors on walls, but some readers may love bright colors on walls. For some types of reviews, the reviewer needs to be careful not to provide too many details. For example, saying that a dating couple gets married at the end of a film could ruin the film for some people who had planned to see the movie.
- **An evaluation or critique.** The evaluation focuses on the features that matter most to readers. Of course, the focus will vary depending on what is being reviewed. For example, a movie review focuses on such features as acting, set design, sound track, special effects, character development, plot, directing, and editing. A restaurant review, however, focuses on such features as décor, atmosphere, service, cost, menu, and flavor.

In the reviews that follow, notice how the reviewers attend to these genre features. In the two film reviews, for example, look at what standard film elements they summarize and critique. Consider how the writers' choices of what they evaluate affects your impressions.

GENRES UP CLOSE

TY BURR

REVIEW

Star Trek

Ty Burr has written film reviews for the *Boston Globe* since 2002. He has also written arts reviews and other kinds of articles for numerous publications, including *Spin, Entertainment Weekly, New York Times*, and the *Boston Phoenix*. Burr is the author of several books: *The Best Old Movies for Families: A Guide to Watching Together, The Hundred Greatest Movies of All Time*, and *The Hundred Greatest Stars of All Time*. To what extent do you agree with Burr that the main characters in this version of Star Trek are "young" and "hopeful"?

About two-thirds of the way into the ridiculously satisfying new "Star Trek" movie, opening Thursday, there comes a brief shot of the crew on the bridge of the Federation Starship Enterprise. The film has been picking up familiar names as it goes, but you suddenly realize with a jolt that everyone, at last, is here: young, hopeful versions of Captain James T. Kirk (Chris Pine) and Mr. Spock (Zachary Quinto), communications officer Uhura (Zoe Saldana) and pilot Sulu (John Cho), Bones (Karl Urban) and Chekhov (Anton Yelchin) and Scotty (Simon Pegg). 1

It's a throwaway image, yet you feel the final pieces of the puzzle snap into place with a witty and intensely fond reverence. I just about wept with joy, and I'm not even a Trekkie. 2

Neither, apparently, is director J.J. Abrams, and that may have made the difference. "Star Trek"—a.k.a. "Star Trek XI," a.k.a. "Star Trek the Franchise Reboot"—approaches the late Gene Roddenberry's original science fiction world not on bended knee but with fresh eyes, a spring in its step, and the understanding that we know these people better than they know themselves. Indeed, much of the vast pleasure of this movie comes from characters suddenly discovering things about each other that we learned watching TV four decades ago. There are flaws to pick at in terms of story line and other matters, but that can wait until the glow has faded. In the pop high it delivers, this is the greatest prequel ever made. 3

Summarizes the history of the genre.

Summarizes the movie.

"Star Trek" isn't all fun and games. The universe has to be saved (again), and Spock has to undergo a personality crisis severe even by the standards of his half-human/half-Vulcan nature. A renegade Romulan named Captain Nero (played by Eric Bana with facial tattoos and a taste for waterboarding) has dropped in from decades into the future, and he's very, very angry about something the older Spock has done, or will do. Nero's first order of business is to attack a starship, in the process killing Kirk's father (Chris Hemsworth) just as Mother Kirk (Jennifer Morrison) is giving birth to our hero in an escape shuttle. 4

Provides an evaluation of the movie, specifically the character development.

Conceptually, this is a genius move: It establishes the entire movie as an alternate, parallel "Star Trek" universe in which Abrams and his screenwriters Roberto Orci and Alex Kurtzman can do as they wish, fanboys and the canon be damned. Kirk can grow up a rebellious hothead, only learning about his father through the paternal Captain Pike (Bruce Greenwood). Kirk and Spock can meet not on the bridge of the Enterprise but as clashing cadets in training school. ("Who was that pointy-eared bastard?" Kirk mutters.) Spock can even have a simmering relationship with Uhura that occasionally involves long, steamy kisses. Heresy! 5

But it works. As the characters scramble to deal with the Romulan threat—the baddies want to destroy the Federation's planets one by one, and they have the future tech to do it—their initial enmity is forged into camaraderie under heavy fire, and Abrams has a blast letting them get to know each other. Sulu and Kirk first connect while free-falling through space on their way to dismantling a Romulan megaweapon, and the ensuing fight with the enemy is outrageously choreographed, a ballet of high-impact fencing and brute force. 6

At the same time, Abrams respects the campy verities of the original show enough to include a third Enterprise crewmember on this mission—the guy I and my roommates used to call "Lunchmeat." Remember him? The extra you'd never seen before who beamed down with the leads solely because someone needed to bite it? The script calls him "Olson" (Greg Ellis), but, trust me, he's Lunchmeat, and the movie's the better for his brief appearance and spectacular demise. 7

The editing, cinematography, and special effects work are state-of-the-art, as you'd expect—extra praise goes to an astonishingly detailed sound mix—but so are the same aspects of "Wolverine," and that film's a joyless bore by comparison. What lifts the Abrams film into the ether is the rightness of its casting and playing, from Saldana's Uhuru, finally a major character after all these years, to Urban's loyal, dyspeptic McCoy, to Simon Pegg's grandly comic Scotty, the movie's most radical reimagining of a "Star Trek" regular. 8

That said, the appearance of Winona Ryder as Spock's human mother comes as a jolt, and in no known universe can I imagine Tyler Perry as a Federation elder. (Abrams is a fan, I guess.) Still, the movie's center holds. The classic lines get trotted out—"Ah'm givin' it all she's goot, Cap'n," "Dammit, man, I'm a doctor, not a physicist"—but the players bring an affection and depth to their parts that's bigger than mere nostalgia; when they color outside the lines, it's on purpose. And when Pine sits down in the captain's chair with the exact macho sprawl William Shatner employed in the original series, you almost want to applaud. 9

Do you have to be a hard-core fan to enjoy the movie? Not at all. "Star Trek" has been knocking around for so long that the basics have seeped 10 into the culture by osmosis. The director indulges himself with a monster that resembles his "Cloverfield" beastie, and there are in-jokes for followers of "Lost" and other Abrams projects, but he has made sure to tap into the longstanding emotion that surrounds the "Trek" mythos.

Above all, he understands the potency and pleasure of the Kirk/Spock relationship. There are certain pop duos that have become cultural institutions and about whom it's endlessly enjoyable to speculate. Who wouldn't want to have been there when Holmes met Watson or Butch met Sundance? (Or Oscar met Felix, or Jack Aubrey met Stephen Maturin; you could play this game forever.) Pine makes a fine, brash boy Kirk, but Quinto's Spock is something special—an eerily calm figure freighted with a heavier sadness than Roddenberry's original. The two ground each other and point toward all the stories yet to come. 11

Then, at a certain point, the movie's curtains part and Leonard Nimoy appears, playing an older, wiser, more fragile Spock. You're grateful for the continuity—his appearance carries much more emotion than you'd expect—and also thankful that this "Star Trek" stops there. One strutting ham of a Captain Kirk is enough, thanks. 12

The movie's not perfect. The final battle feels awfully "Star Wars"—later "Star Wars"—as does Scotty's sidekick, an Ewok knock-off in a lousy mask. Character, not plotting, is the film's strong suit, yet plotting takes over in the final half hour. Emotionally, though, "Star Trek" hits every one of its marks, functioning as a family reunion that extends across decades, entertainment mediums, even blurring the line between audience and show. Trading on affections sustained over 40 years of popular culture, "Star Trek" does what a franchise reboot rarely does. It reminds us why we loved these characters in the first place. 13

PETER BRADSHAW

Star Trek

REVIEW

1 You want "bromance"? I'll give you bromance—the greatest of them all. It's the bromance that flowers in this wildly exciting and enjoyable summer action movie, about the manly relationship between a mercurially talented starship commander and his mixed-race first officer, whose virile otherness is signalled by discreetly tapering pointy ears, eyebrows in a thick geometric frown and that extraordinary straight fringe, a hairdo he must maintain in front of the bathroom mirror every night with a ruler and pair of scissors.

Peter Bradshaw is a film critic for the *Guardian*. He has also written reviews for the *Daily Telegraph*, the *Observer*, and BBC News. What is your reaction to Bradshaw's term, "bromance"? Can you point to any personal instances of what he is discussing?

2 Why have we filmgoers wasted so much of our time and attention on all those other beta-male bondings and under-par buddy hookups when the greatest friendship of all was right there under our noses? The story of Kirk and Spock is brought thrillingly back to life by a new first generation: Chris Pine and Zachary Quinto, who give inspired, utterly unselfconscious and lovable performances, with power, passion and some cracking comic timing. It's a film in which my chief emotion was a kind of grinning embarrassment at enjoying it all quite so much.

This is Star Trek: The Early Years, the story of the Enterprise crew when they were teen- to twentysomethings with some serious cadet attitude. Their fledgling relationships are dramatised and interspersed with spectacular action sequences, juxtaposing the "nighttime" effect of deep space with the sunlit, parched alien planets on which the stars find themselves crash-landing. For people like me who grew up watching Star 3

Trek movies and feeling secretly shocked at how old Shatner, Nimoy et al. looked compared to their lithe selves on the TV show—well, this makes for an extra blast of pure energy.

Summarizes the movie.

4 Director J.J. Abrams and screenwriters Roberto Orci and Alex Kurtzman have found a cunning way of rewriting the backstory. Hateful Romulan Nero, played by Eric Bana, enraged by what he (wrongly) sees as Spock's destruction of his home planet, travels backwards in time with a mission to destroy the future authors of his people's misfortune. James T Kirk's father, who was originally to grow happily old, witnessing his son's glorious rise through the Star Fleet ranks, now dies in a Romulan attack, after he gets his pregnant wife to safety—and she excitingly gives birth to Jim in the escape module itself. And so we are given a new, parallel-universe early story of the Enterprise.

5 Without his dad's calming influence, Jim grows up a tearaway and a wrong 'un: there is a fantastic sequence in which he crashes his uncle's vintage sports car while pursued by a hi-tech robo-speed-cop. After being beaten senseless in a bar fight, Kirk is redemptively recruited to the fleet by a friend of his late father: wise Capt Christopher Pike (Bruce Greenwood). Meanwhile, the bookish and earnest young Spock (Quinto), is bullied by his Vulcan classmates for having a human mother—played by Winona Ryder—and made the subject of racist condescension by his Vulcan elders, who refer to his human ancestry as a disability. Incensed, Spock joins the human Starfleet and instantly becomes a star pupil.

6 In fact, it looks very much as if Spock, not Kirk, will be the star of the film as well, and the Kirk-Spock friendship is to ignite in rivalry and even violence. Spock has what first seems like the greater leadership potential, and to Jim's chagrin, the beautiful African-American crew-member Uhura (Zoe Saldana) seems to like Spock more. Spock also gets a powerfully surreal (and not entirely, ahem, logical) meeting with his older self: Leonard Nimoy contributes a performance of gentle, other-worldly dignity, and it is this older Spock, over the closing credits, who gets to recite the legendary words about the mission to seek out new life, new civilisations. The final words are, incidentally, politically corrected to "where no one has gone before".

Provides an evaluation of the movie, in comparison to the original *Star Trek* TV series.

7 What a treat it is to see the bridge of the USS Enterprise, box fresh and gleaming new: it is quite irrationally exciting to hear that strange, echoey-tweety heartbeat of the shipboard computer-system, the klaxon alarm in moments of peril, and the fsssht-fsssht of the automatic doors opening and closing. It is weird, in 2009, to see the 1960s UN-style ethos preserved, with the mini-skirt costumes for female personnel and toddler pyjama-tops for the guys. Then, as now, there's an American at the helm, but other nations, and present and former foes are generously represented: the Russian Chekhov (Anton Yelchin) and the Japanese Sulu, played by the Korean-

American actor John Cho. As in the 60s, however, Starfleet unfortunately feels no great conciliatory need to include anyone from the Middle East. Britain's Simon Pegg plays the engineer Scotty, and beings his own distinctive shtick to the part, and Karl Urban is Bones, the gruff medic—of all the current cast, he seems the one nearest in age to the original.

Unlike George Lucas's massively encumbered and obese Star Wars prequel-trilogy, this new Star Trek is fast-moving, funny, exciting warp-speed entertainment and, heaven help me, even quite moving—the kind of film that shows that, like it or not, commercial cinema can still deliver a sledgehammer punch. It sure didn't feel like a trek to me. 8

QUESTIONS FOR WRITING AND DISCUSSION: LEARNING OUTCOMES

Rhetorical Knowledge: The Writers' Situation and Rhetoric

1. **Audience:** Who is the intended audience for each review? To what extent are Burr and Bradshaw appealing to similar or different audiences? What makes you think so?
2. **Purpose:** How similar are Burr's and Bradshaw's purposes for writing their reviews?
3. **Voice and tone:** How do Burr and Bradshaw reveal their attitudes toward the film and toward their readers?
4. **Responsibility:** To what extent do Burr and Bradshaw seem responsible to their readers? How responsible should movie reviewers be to their readers? Why?
5. **Context and genre:** Consider how this film has been highly anticipated by a huge audience. How does that anticipation seem to affect both reviews? A movie review typically includes some plot summary to help readers who have not seen the film. How effectively has each reviewer summarized the plot of *Star Trek*?

Critical Thinking: The Writers' Ideas and Your Personal Response

6. What are the relative strengths and weaknesses of each review?
7. If you have seen *Star Trek,* on what points do you most agree and most disagree with Burr and/or with Bradshaw?

Composing Processes and Knowledge of Conventions: The Writers' Strategies

8. Compare the attention that Burr and Bradshaw pay to plot and characters. How do they differ?
9. How clearly do Burr and Bradshaw state their criteria for evaluating *Star Trek*?

Inquiry and Research: Ideas for Further Exploration

10. Conduct a Web search to find other reviews of *Star Trek*. How are those reviews similar to or different from the ones that Burr and Bradshaw wrote?

Writing Processes

connect
mhconnectcomposition.com
Writing to Evaluate Animated Walkthrough QL9004

As you work on the assignment that you have chosen, remember the qualities of an effective and convincing evaluative paper, which are listed on pages 274–276. Also remember that writing is recursive—you might start with an invention activity or two and then conduct some research, which leads to more invention work and then a first draft; but then you might need to do more invention work to help flesh out your evaluation and conduct more research to add more criteria or more support; and then you'll revise your draft and possibly find another gap or two. So, while the activities listed below imply that writers proceed step-by-step, as you write, you will keep coming back to your earlier work, modifying the criteria and strengthening the support for your claim.

Invention: Getting Started

For more on discovery and learning, see Chapter 3.

Invention activities can help you clarify what you might want to evaluate before you make your evaluation. Writers often find it useful to work through several invention activities for any particular writing task. Regardless of the invention activities you do, try to answer these questions while you work:

- What do I already know about the subject that I am thinking about evaluating?
- What makes each potential subject suitable for evaluation?
- What criteria can I establish for my evaluation? On what basis should I make my judgment? How can I compare it with similar items?
- What kinds of explanation can I provide about each of my criteria?
- Where might I learn more about the subject?
- What verifiable information about my subject is available?
- Are any of my criteria potentially just a matter of opinion, and if so, how might I explain them?
- What might my audience already know about my subject? What do I know about my audience? What don't I know that I should know?

Writing Activity

Clustering

Clustering is an invention technique that can help you focus on a subject to evaluate and come up with criteria for your evaluation. Working with the questions here, spend a few minutes jotting down everything you can think of about the subject or subjects you want to evaluate or discussing them with classmates. Don't worry about putting this information into sentences or paragraphs; simply record it using any words that come to mind. Or try freewriting, which is writing continuously.

Once you have some ideas, you can then use clustering to see relationships between or among them. Put the subject you are focusing on into a circle in the center of a piece of paper, and spend a few minutes creating a cluster of your ideas about the subject.

Annlee Lawrence's Clustering

Annlee Lawrence decided to write an evaluation of meals at some local fast-food restaurants. To get started, Lawrence brainstormed her initial thoughts, which turned out to be a series of questions. She continued her invention work by doing some freewriting and then clustering her ideas. Below is an example of a cluster Lawrence might have done for her evaluation of fast-food restaurants.

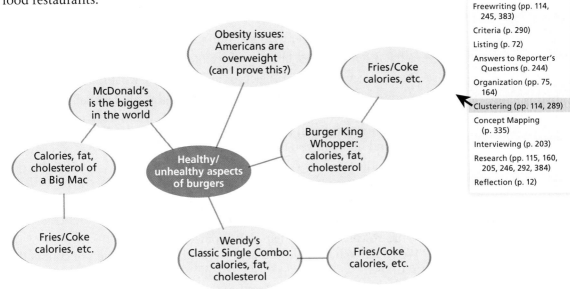

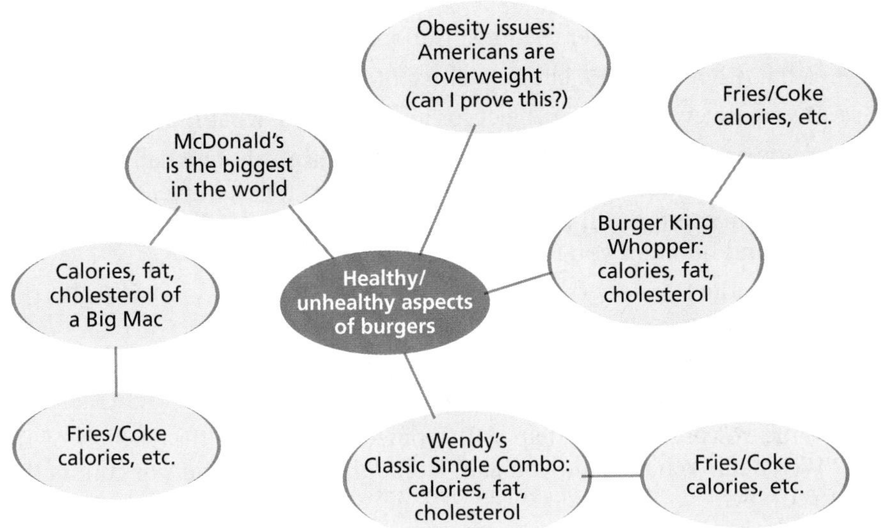

EXAMPLES OF INVENTION

Constructing and Supporting Evaluative Criteria

To evaluate any subject, you need to begin by considering the basis on which you will make your evaluation, as well as how you might support your criteria. Consider the various aspects of the subject on which you might base your evaluation. Here are just a few possibilities:

- Physical aspects such as size, weight, shape, taste, smell, and sound
- Quality, including warranty period, type of warranty offered, component quality (steel vs. plastic, for example), and power aspects (size)
- Aesthetic aspects (how the item feels to use, drive, listen to, sit in, wear, and so on), color, and proportion
- Entertainment-value aspects (what will you use this product for?)
- Comparative aspects, such as the following:
  - Which career would give me the greatest satisfaction? Why?
  - What is the best place to study? Why?
  - Which political candidate should get my vote? Why?

In most evaluations, you will need to show how your subject can be measured against similar subjects and explain the basis of your comparison. If you

For more on making comparisons, see Chapter 13.

are comparing two automobiles, for example, you could compare them in terms of price, gas mileage, and maintenance, among other criteria.

Once you have a basis for comparison, the first step in deciding the criteria for your evaluation is to look over your invention work and consider what you have learned so far about your subject. Try to answer these questions:

- What do you consider the most important aspect of your subject?
- What other qualities, either positive or negative, does this subject have?
- If you are evaluating a subject for its usefulness, what must it do?
- If you are evaluating a product or service, think about what you will use it for. If you are evaluating a child's car seat, for example, the most important criterion will probably be safety. What do you mean by the term *safe*, and how can you tell if a particular car seat is safe?
- If a product or service needs to be reliable, what do you mean by that term, and how can you determine reliability?
- What criteria are absolutely necessary for the subject to possess? What criteria are important, but perhaps not as necessary?
- What research might help with your evaluation? Will a search of the Web help? What would you gain from talking with others or conducting a survey?

Writing Activity

Constructing and Supporting Criteria

Construct a list of possible criteria for your evaluation. For each of your criteria, explain, in no more than one sentence, why it is important in evaluating your subject. Also, in no more than one sentence, outline what kind of evidence you might use to support each criterion.

EXAMPLES OF INVENTION

Brainstorming (pp. 158, 332)
Freewriting (pp. 114, 245, 383)
Criteria (p. 290)
Listing (p. 72)
Answers to Reporter's Questions (p. 244)
Organization (pp. 75, 164)
Clustering (pp. 114, 289)
Concept Mapping (p. 335)
Interviewing (p. 203)
Research (pp. 115, 160, 205, 246, 292, 384)
Reflection (p. 12)

Annlee Lawrence's Criteria

After Annlee Lawrence completed some brainstorming and freewriting about her subject, she made a list of the criteria for evaluating fast-food restaurants and did some additional freewriting to discover what they meant and what she thought about each one. Here is an excerpt:

- Why should anyone care about eating a burger?
- What does "obesity" mean? Who says it's important?
- Why is "fat" bad and are there different kinds of fat?
- How does cholesterol hurt people? And I read somewhere that there is both good and bad cholesterol—I wonder if any of each is in a burger?

- And everyone knows that we want to consume fewer calories, right?
- Does any of this affect taste?
- What about the other stuff we usually eat with a burger? Fries? A Coke?

I guess I know it's important to not be overweight and all, but I wonder if eating a burger now and then really matters. Aren't there some people who eat them all the time, though? I mean, with fries and all? How bad could that be? I need to learn more about fat and calories and things, so I can point to what is bad (and if anything is good) about America's burgers.

Once I learn some stuff—now, where can I learn the fat content, etc. of burgers? Does McDonald's and Wendy's and Burger King post them somewhere? Online? It'd be kind of funny if I had to go and buy a burger at each place, just to find out how unhealthy it might be!

And once I have some information, how can I present it so readers can understand and make a wise choice, based on my evaluation?

Exploring Your Ideas with Research

Although personal opinions are sometimes sufficient evidence for an evaluation, in more formal settings, you will need to support your claims with outside research. One advantage of conducting research is that the information you find will help you form your judgment about your subject. It's important not to make that judgment too soon; often you won't know what you really think until you have done a lot of invention work, conducted much of your research, and have even written a draft or two.

Research, of course, can give you solid evidence—verifiable information, such as figures, statistics, data, or expert testimony—to help support your final evaluation. The kind and amount of research you will need to do will vary according to the rhetorical situation: who your audience is and what you are trying to accomplish. Use the reporter's questions of *who, what, when, where, why,* and *how* to get started on your research. After you have determined the information you need, decide what kind of research you should conduct to gather that information, in the library and on the Internet. You may also need to do field research.

For help with locating sources of information and with field research, see Chapter 19; for help with taking notes and documenting your sources, see Chapter 20.

As you review your notes, look for information that will help you show to what degree your subject does, or does not, meet a given criterion. Look as well for any conclusions that others have drawn about the subject of your evaluation—and consider if and how your evaluation differs from theirs. While you can use others' opinions in support of your conclusion, hearing and reading what others have said will often provide new ideas and suggest additional avenues for research.

As you conduct your research, you may find that other writers have reached judgments that differ from yours. You will want to address—and counter—their opinions in your comments, in order to strengthen your evaluation.

Writing Activity

Conducting Research

Using the list of qualities of effective evaluative writing on pages 274–276, review your invention writing and your list of criteria, and note what you already know about your issue. Next, determine whether you need to do research to come up with additional criteria or evidence, learn more about similar subjects, or muster stronger counterarguments.

In no more than two pages, outline a research plan. In your plan, indicate the following:

- What you already know about your subject
- What questions you still have
- Who or what sources might answer your questions
- Who might provide other perspectives on your subject
- Where you might look for further information
- When you plan to conduct your research

Gather, read, and take notes on your subject from these outside sources. Use an electronic journal to record images, URLs, and other information that you find as you conduct your research.

Annlee Lawrence's Research Strategy

EXAMPLES OF INVENTION

Brainstorming (pp. 158, 332)
Freewriting (pp. 114, 245, 383)
Criteria (p. 290)
Listing (p. 72)
Answers to Reporter's Questions (p. 244)
Organization (pp. 75, 164)
Clustering (pp. 114, 289)
Concept Mapping (p. 335)
Interviewing (p. 203)
Research (pp. 115, 160, 205, 246, 292, 384)
Reflection (p. 12)

Annlee Lawrence needed to research the nutritional content of typical meals available from the three restaurants she was evaluating. She developed the following research plan:

- I'll check both online and at the stores themselves, to see if the information is provided.
- I need to try to compare apples-to-apples as much as I can—that is, I want to compare similar-size hamburgers, and similar-size fries and drinks (otherwise it would be an unfair evaluation and my readers would not benefit and probably wouldn't believe me).
- I should check in the library for information on why these things (calories, fat, cholesterol) are bad for people.
- I may also find in the library some useful information about the companies I'm focusing on (McDonald's, Wendy's, Burger King). I know there are others (Sonic, A&W), but I want to concentrate on the big three, as they're everywhere.

A WRITER'S *Responsibility* | Constructing Ethical Evaluations

As humans, we all make judgments, yet we rarely analyze the process that we use to make those judgments. However, whenever you make an evaluation, your judgments will have an impact, and because of that impact, you have certain responsibilities. When you make an evaluation in a civic writing situation, you have a responsibility to all who will be affected by the decision that will eventually be made. Remember, too, that the audience for a civic evaluation will include some who will disagree, and that potential for disagreement makes your honesty and sense of responsibility even more important. If you misrepresent some aspect of your evaluation, someone can use that distortion to discredit your entire evaluation. Writing an ethical evaluation means you must present statistics and other data accurately, without skewing them in your favor. If you have asked only a few of your classmates about the effectiveness of your campus recycling program, for example, you cannot say, "The majority of students who attend my college think that campus recycling is effective."

Reviewing Your Invention and Research

After you have conducted your research, review your invention work and notes and think about the information you collected from outside sources and how that information matches the criteria you have for your evaluation. You may be ready to decide on a working thesis statement—a statement that summarizes the main point of your evaluation—at this point. Even though you might already have a general idea of the conclusion your evaluation is leading you to, your thesis should come *from* your complete evaluation. It is best to decide on your thesis when you have done a lot of invention work (listing, brainstorming, clustering, and other strategies) and research. You might even wait until after you construct your first draft.

Writing Activity

Considering Your Research and Focusing Your Ideas

Examine the notes you have taken from your research. Then, using your criteria as a starting point, see how your information matches the criteria you have established.

Organizing Your Evaluation

Once you have some sense of the criteria you will use and how your subject matches those criteria, consider how you might organize your evaluation. The questions that you need to ask yourself when deciding on your organization are all rhetorical:

- Who is the audience for your evaluation?
- Why might they be interested in your evaluation, or how you can make them interested in it?

For more on design and visuals, including examples of different kinds of graphics, see Chapter 18.

Digital Literacy Using Computer Software to Create Hierarchies

If there's one thing computers are good at, it's establishing hierarchies (systems of ranking, prioritizing, and organizing things). When you're writing an essay that evaluates something, the computer screen can serve as a workshop space, where you can move around ideas and concepts.

You can use different programs—and sometimes different windows within the same software application—to design charts, outlines, tables, Venn diagrams, timelines, and other visual space-holders for your information. Use color, line, shape, and space to move information around on the plane of the computer screen, looking for categories and interesting interrelations among your ideas and segments of information.

- What is your purpose for writing—that is, what will your readers learn about your subject by reading your evaluation? How will that knowledge help them with their evaluation?

For more on the inductive and deductive methods, see Chapter 8.

The answers to these questions can help you decide what you need to emphasize, which in turn will help you choose an organizational approach.

Here is a brief outline of three possible organizational approaches for writing an evaluation:

Options FOR Organization

Options for Organizing Evaluations

First Inductive Approach	Second inductive Approach	Deductive Approach
Outline why you are making the evaluation. Discuss/explain the criteria. Explain how well your subject or subjects match (or fail to match) the various criteria. Discuss which subjects are "best," according to the evaluative criteria you have established. Explain your thesis statement in your conclusion.	Begin with a discussion of the subject or subjects that you are evaluating. Explain its or their strengths and weaknesses. Outline how the positive and negative points match each of your criteria. Explain how the subject or subjects you are evaluating fulfill those criteria (this, then, is your thesis statement).	Begin with the conclusion that you have reached about the subject or subjects (your thesis statement). Explain why and how you reached that conclusion using a compare-and-contrast format; compare and contrast each aspect of what you are evaluating in relation to the criteria.

Constructing a Complete Draft

Once you have generated some initial thoughts and ideas, selected the criteria for judging your subject, and reviewed your notes from your reading and research, your next step is to write a first draft, which is often called a working draft. Your first draft is your opportunity to expand, explain, and develop your ideas.

connect
mhconnectcomposition.com
Drafting and Revising QL9005

Before beginning your draft, review the writing you have done so far. What are the relative advantages of evaluating several items or of concentrating on just one? Why? Review the criteria that you have developed and decide which you want to emphasize. If your instructor and/or peers have given you suggestions, consider how you will incorporate their advice into your evaluation. As you prepare to write, ask yourself the following questions:

- What is the most effective way to explain my criteria?
- In what ways does the subject of my evaluation match up with (or fail to match up with) the criteria I have selected?
- What is my final evaluation?
- How can I express my main point effectively as a thesis statement?

As you draft your evaluation, stop occasionally to read your work, imagining that you are reading it for the first time. Because your draft is an exploratory text, ask yourself the following questions:

For more on comparison, definition, and description, see Chapter 13.

- How have I compared my subject with similar items?
- How effectively have I added details demonstrating how well the subject matches my criteria?
- What visual information might I use to explain my evaluation?
- How clear is my final judgment?

Synthesizing and Integrating Sources into Your Draft: Creating Charts or Graphs to Show Your Data

INTEGRATING SOURCES

When writing an evaluation, the ability to synthesize a variety of ideas becomes especially important. In many ways, simply doing an evaluation is a kind of synthesis—the act of taking differing pieces of information and putting them together to form a new piece of information. As you look at the specific details of the subject that you are evaluating, you will be able to make the determining judgments needed for your evaluation. Using details from your research will then help your readers follow your line of thought so that they can understand the reasoning behind your judgments.

When researching and writing an evaluation, you may find that some of your evaluation will be based on numerical data, and one useful way to show those data is in the form of a chart or graph. We can see how student writer Annlee Lawrence incorporates cumulative data into her evaluative narrative both to explain to and to show her readers the total caloric intake of some popular fast-food meals:

When I researched the nutritional content of these three meals, I found that all three have high calorie content (see fig. 1). The Whopper Combo from Burger King has been a favorite of Americans for generations. But is it as good for your body as it is to your taste buds? When I researched the nutritional information, I discovered that this meal has a grand total of 1230 calories. In contrast, Wendy's Classic Single Combo has 1060 calories, and McDonald's Quarter Pounder Combo has 1000.

While Lawrence listed the meals in descending order of caloric intake, some readers simply get overwhelmed with reading numbers. One way to make a clearer argument is to do what Lawrence did: incorporate numbers into your narrative but also use graphs to visually depict the data. We can see how Lawrence breaks down the fast-food meals into three components (burger, fries, and Coke), and shows the comparative calories of each.

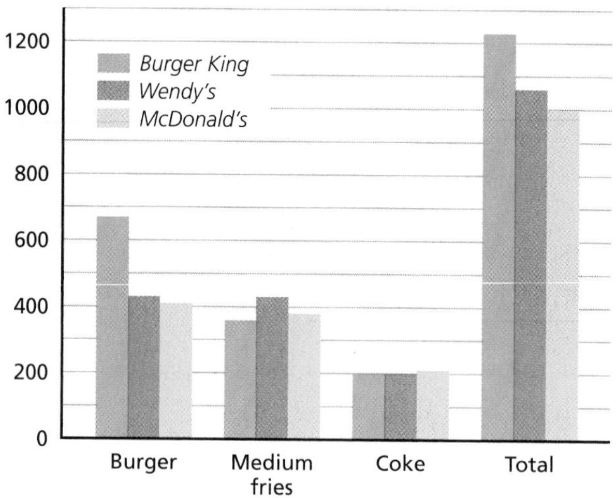

Because student writer Lawrence had many pieces of data, she converted them into the form of a simple column chart. Consider how such a chart makes it easy for readers to see what Lawrence has to say about the calorie content of various fast-food products.

Parts of a Complete Draft

connect
mhconnectcomposition.com
Introductory paragraph overview QL9006

Introduction: One of the qualities of a successful evaluation is that it grabs and holds readers' attention. Strategies that will help you hook your readers include the following:

- **Begin by explaining why you are making the evaluation—your rhetorical purpose—followed by a discussion of your criteria.** It is also often helpful to include an explanation of why you selected these criteria. This is usually the approach taken by articles in consumer magazines such as *Consumer Reports*.

- **Indicate your conclusion at the beginning.** You will then explain in the body of your text why and how you reached that conclusion.
- **Set the scene for your evaluation.** Depending on your topic, you might open your evaluation with a description of your subject.

Body: If you are using the inductive approach, indicate what you want to evaluate and on what basis at the beginning, and then work through the process (and through the body of your evaluation) as you go. If you are using the deductive method, begin by stating your judgment, and then use the body of your paper to support it, often by comparing and contrasting your subject with other subjects of the same type.

Conclusion: Regardless of the organizational method you employ, make sure that your judgment of your subject—your evaluation—is clearly stated. Remember that in an evaluation, your ultimate conclusion is usually your thesis statement, or main point, but your conclusion can serve other purposes as well. A conclusion in evaluative writing often does the following:

connect™
mhconnectcomposition.com
Concluding paragraph overview QL9007

- **Summarizes how each supporting piece of evidence helps support your main point.** In a lengthy, detailed evaluation, a summary of your findings can help readers recall the main points that you are making.
- **Reaches out to your audience.** An appeal to the audience is an especially effective way to end an evaluation, as often you want them to not only agree with your evaluation but also to do something with what they have learned.

Title: As you compose your evaluative writing, a title should emerge at some point—perhaps late in the process. The title should reflect your judgment of your subject, and it should catch your readers' attention and make them want to read your essay.

Digital Literacy — Storing Image Files

It is always a good idea to store the photographs you find in your research in a separate computer file, so you will have easy access to them when you start constructing your evaluation. Name your images and folders so that you can easily find the pictures you wish to use. For example: "Rodeo_rider.jpg," or "calfroper1.gif" will help you more easily find images you've saved than "pic1" or "image_3".

Be aware that image files come in different formats: .jpg, .gif, .bmp, and .tif are some common image file extensions. If a picture will not open on your computer, it may be because you don't have a program on your computer that is capable of handling that image's format.

For more on using visuals, see Chapter 18.

VISUALIZING *Variations* | Using Visuals to Support Your Evaluation

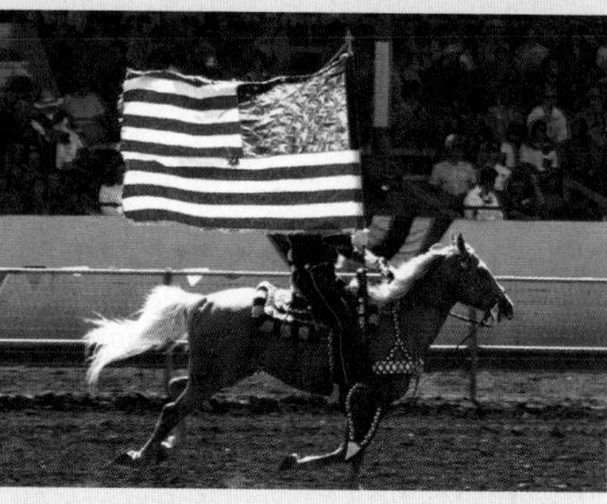

If you decided to respond to Scenario 2 (page 273), which asks that you to write a review, you might include photographs to illustrate what you are evaluating.

For instance, if you were evaluating the local rodeo or a Fourth of July parade, you could use a photograph to illustrate the event. What if your criteria for reviewing, or evaluating, this cultural event included *plenty of activities, tradition*, and *audience involvement?*

Think about what this photograph shows and what it might suggest to a reader:

- Part of American history; part of a long-standing tradition
- The involvement of animals; this horse is decorated with fancy hardware
- Lots of people watching in the audience

What do you think this picture would add to our evaluation of a local rodeo?

For any photograph you are considering, then, ask yourself the following questions:

- What might this photograph show about my subject?
- How can I select a photograph that will support a point I want to make and help me justify my overall judgment about my subject?

Writing Activity

Constructing a Full Draft

After reviewing your notes, invention activities, and research, and carefully considering all of the information that you generated and the comments you received, construct a complete first draft of your evaluation, using the organizational approach that you have decided on. Remember that your evaluation will evolve as you write, so your ideas will most likely change as you compose this first draft. Remember also that you will be learning as you write. While you may have some sense of whether your subject fits your criteria, expect to modify your position as you develop your evaluation essay.

Annlee Lawrence's First Draft

After deciding on an organizational approach and a tentative thesis, Annlee Lawrence was ready to begin her first, or working, draft. She did not worry about errors and instead concentrated on getting her main ideas on paper. Note that she started her paper by outlining what she was going to do, without revealing her conclusions. This inductive approach is one of the possible organizational methods described on page 294. As she wrote, Lawrence did not worry about grammar, punctuation, and mechanics; instead, she concentrated on getting her main ideas into her draft. (The numbers in circles refer to peer comments—see page 302.)

Who Has the Better Burger?

Annlee Lawrence

Did you know that McDonald's operates more than thirty thousand restaurants in more than one hundred countries on six continents? In the United States, McDonald's represents 43% of the total fast-food market. McDonald's feeds more than forty-six million people a day—more than the entire population of Spain! Surgeon General David Satcher comments, "Fast food is a major contributor to the obesity epidemic." It's no wonder that sixty percent of America is overweight or obese. Obesity, if left unabated, will surpass smoking as the leading cause of preventable death in America. So why is it that we can't seem to stay away from our beloved Big Macs or Whoppers? Probably because our lives demand it at times. We don't have time to prepare a full-blown meal, so we have created fast food to fit with our fast-paced lives. So unfortunately, obesity can't be helped in today's society, but can be avoided through moderation of consumption. Generally speaking, most fast food is unhealthy. But if you had to pick one that was the healthiest, which would it be? I felt that for this evaluation, the most important criteria for determining a "healthy" burger should be calories, total fat, and cholesterol. I chose some of the favorite meals to evaluate: the Whopper Combo from Burger King, Wendy's Classic Single Combo, and McDonald's Quarter Pounder Combo.❶

The Whopper Combo from Burger King has been a favorite of Americans for generations. But is it as good to your body as it is to your taste buds? When I researched the nutritional information, I discovered that the sandwich itself has 670 calories, 95 milligrams of cholesterol, and 39 grams of total fat. A medium fry has 360 calories and 18 grams of fat. Not to mention the medium Coke that contains 200 calories. All this adds up to be a grand total of 1230 calories, 57 grams of fat, and 95 milligrams of cholesterol.❷

Because I used the Burger King Whopper, I picked a similar sandwich from Wendy's, the Classic Single Combo. The burger has 430 calories, 20 grams of total fat, and 75 milligrams of cholesterol. A medium fry has 430 calories, 20 grams of fat, and a medium coke has 200 calories. This all adds up to 1060 calories, 40 grams of total fat, and 75 milligrams of cholesterol.

Last but not least, there is the McDonald's Quarter Pounder Combo. Despite popular opinion, this burger is the best for you. It has 411 calories, 16 grams of fat, and 65 milligrams of cholesterol. A medium fry has 380 calories, 19 grams of fat, and a medium Coke has 210 calories. The total calories would be 1000, total fat 35, and total cholesterol is 75 milligrams.

So if you do get caught up in a hurry and feel like grabbing a burger, then get the McDonald's Quarter Pounder. The McDonald's Quarter Pounder has 7 fewer grams of fat than the Wendy's Classic Single and 24 fewer grams of fat than the Burger King Whopper. Even their fries have 5 fewer grams of fat than Wendy's and 2 fewer than Burger King. This doesn't mean that you should go and buy out McDonald's. Obviously, as the movie *Super-Size Me* proved, even the "healthy" fast food isn't good for you. But if eaten in moderation, fast food is one of the best things to happen to America.[3]

Works Cited[4]

Wendy's Nutrition Facts & Topics. Web. 14 November 2008. <http://www.wendys.com/food/NutritionLanding.jsp

Burger King Nutritional Information. Web. 14 November 2008. <http://www.bk.com/Nutrition/PDFs/brochure.pdf>.

Get the Nutrition Facts for a McDonald's Menu Item. Web. 14 November 2008. <http://nutrition.mcdonalds.com/bagamcmeal/chooseCustomize.do

Revising

Once you have a full draft of your evaluation, you still have much to do. First, however, you should set the draft aside so that you can gain some critical distance. You can then read it with fresh eyes.

As you revise your early drafts, hold off on doing a great deal of heavy editing. When you revise, you will probably change the content and structure of your paper, so time spent working to fix problems with grammar, punctuation, or mechanics at this stage is often wasted.

When you reread the first draft of your evaluation, here are some questions to ask yourself:

- How effectively have I explained or indicated my criteria?
- What else might my audience want or need to know about my subject?

WRITER'S *Workshop* | Responding to Full Drafts

Working with one or two other classmates, read each evaluation and offer comments and questions that will help each of you see your papers' strengths and weaknesses. Consider the following questions as you do:

- What is your first impression of this draft? How effective is the title at drawing you in? Why? What are your overall suggestions for improvement? What part(s) of the text are especially strong?
- How clear and understandable is the point of the evaluation?
- How has the writer explained the subject of the evaluation? How might he or she develop the explanation further to make it more effective?
- How clearly and thoroughly has the writer explained and justified the criteria? What details need to be added or clarified?
- How effectively has the writer applied his or her criteria?
- How adequately are all assertions supported with evidence?
- If the writer makes comparisons, how clear are they? Where might additional comparisons be called for?
- How could the writer more clearly match the criteria to the subject? Are there any criteria that the writer discusses but never applies to the subject?
- What terms need to be defined?
- How effective is the organization of this evaluation? Why?
- How might visuals help the writer support his or her criteria more effectively?
- How clearly does the writer present and discuss any opposing points of view on this subject?
- How adequately is the writer's overall evaluation supported by the evidence he or she has presented?

- How else might I interest my audience in my evaluation of this subject?
- What did I find out about my subject that I did not include in my evaluation?
- How clearly have I defined any terms my readers might not know?
- Could some aspects of my evaluation be more effectively presented as a graph or chart?

Technology can help you revise and edit your writing more easily. Use your word processor's track-changes tool to try out revisions and editing changes. After you have had time to think about the possible changes, you can "accept" or "reject" them. Also, you can use your word processor's comment tool to write reminders to yourself when you get stuck with a revision or some editing task.

Because it is so difficult even for experienced writers to see their emerging writing with a fresh eye, it is almost always useful to ask classmates, friends, or family members to read drafts of your persuasive writing.

Student Comments on Annlee Lawrence's First Draft

Using the questions on page 301, Annlee Lawrence's classmates made some suggestions on her first draft. Below are comments she received, keyed to the first draft on pages 299–300.

1. "These seem like good criteria, but why did you choose them? Do you need a stronger reason for your criteria here?"
2. "These are a lot of statistics to digest at once (sorry!). I got lost. Can you give all this in a table or chart?"
3. "Seems like the ending contradicts the rest of your essay. Why is fast food good for America? The ending seems wrong here."
4. "Don't you have a quote in the first paragraph from the Surgeon General? There's no citation for it here."

Responding to Readers' Comments

Once they have received feedback on their writing from peers, instructors, friends, and others, all writers have to decide what to do with that feedback. Since your writing is your responsibility, you must determine how to deal with reader responses to your work.

The first thing to do with any feedback is to consider carefully what your readers have to say about your text. For example, Annlee Lawrence's readers had the following reactions:

- One reader wondered why she chose the criteria she did. Lawrence needs to think about whether she needs to justify her criteria for her readers.
- Another reader felt overwhelmed by all of the statistical information in the paper and suggested a chart. Lawrence needs to think about what one or more charts might add to her paper, and what type of chart or graph she might use.
- A reader felt dissatisfied with her ending. How might Lawrence improve her conclusion?
- A reader pointed out problems with Lawrence's documentation, which affected the credibility of her evaluation.

As with any feedback, it is important to listen carefully to it and consider what your reader has to say. Then it is up to you, as the author, to decide how to come to terms with these suggestions. You may decide to reject some comments, of course; other comments, though, may deserve your attention. You may find that comments from more than one reader contradict each other. In that case, use your own judgment to decide which reader's comments are on the right track.

In the final version of her paper on pages 304–307, you can see how Annlee Lawrence responded to her reader's comments, as well as read her review of her first draft.

Knowledge of Conventions

mhconnectcomposition.com

Correcting problems with subject-verb agreement QL9010

Correcting problems with pronoun case QL9011

When effective writers edit their work, they attend to genre conventions, documentation, format, usage, grammar, and mechanics. By attending to these conventions in your writing, you make reading a more pleasant experience for readers.

Editing

connect

mhconnectcomposition.com

Revising and Editing overview (also Drafting) QL9008

After you revise, you have one more important step—editing and polishing. When you edit and polish, you make changes to your sentence structure and word choice to improve your style and to make your writing clearer and more concise. You also check your work to make sure it adheres to conventions of grammar, usage, punctuation, mechanics, and spelling. If you have used sources in your paper, you should make sure you are following the documentation style your instructor requires.

Because it is sometimes difficult to identify small problems in a familiar text, it often helps to distance yourself so that you can approach your draft with fresh eyes. Some people read from the last sentence to the first so that the content, and their familiarity with it, doesn't cause them to overlook an error. We strongly recommend that you ask classmates, friends, and tutors to read your work to help you find editing problems that you may not see.

See Chapter 20 for more on documenting sources using MLA or APA style.

To assist you with editing, we offer here a round-robin editing activity focused on careful word choice, which is a common concern in writing to evaluate.

WRITER'S *Workshop* | Round-Robin Editing with a Focus on Careful Word Choice

Evaluative writing often requires careful word choice (diction). It is critical to select words that clearly represent what you intend to say. For example, notice how the revision to this word choice problem improves the clarity of this sentence:

> We don't have time to prepare a full-blown meal, so we ~~have created~~ *rely on* fast food to fit with our fast-paced lives.

People in general have not "created" fast food, but they have come to rely on the convenience that it provides.

Working with several peers, consult a good college dictionary and the portion of a handbook that covers word choice. If you are uncertain about a specific word choice, ask your instructor for help.

ROUND-ROBIN EDITING WITH A FOCUS ON

Genres, Documentation, and Format

For advice on writing in different genres, see the Online Appendix. For guidelines for formatting and documenting papers in MLA or APA style, see Chapter 20.

If you are writing an academic paper in response to Scenario 1, you will need to follow the conventions for the discipline in which you are writing and the requirements of your instructor. If you are working on Scenario 2, a review, you can be somewhat more informal than you would be in an academic paper.

If you have used material from outside sources, including visuals, you will need to give credit to those sources, using the documentation style required by the discipline you are working in and by your instructor.

A Writer Shares Her Evaluation: Annlee Lawrence's Final Draft

Here is Annlee Lawrence's final draft. Note that she has addressed the questions and concerns that her classmates had.

ANNLEE LAWRENCE

EVALUATIVE ESSAY

Who Has the Healthier Burger?

Did you know that McDonald's Corporation operates more than thirty thousand restaurants in more than one hundred countries on six continents? In the United States, McDonald's represents 43% of the total fast-food market (*Super Size Me*). Restaurants that are part of the McDonald's organization feed more than forty-six million people a day—more than the entire population of Spain. While the global reach of McDonald's and other fast-food chains is impressive, it is also dangerous. As Surgeon General David Satcher comments, "Fast food is a major contributor to the obesity epidemic" (*Super Size Me*). 1

It's no wonder that 60% of Americans are overweight or obese. Obesity, if left unchecked, will soon surpass smoking as the leading cause of preventable death in America. So why can't we seem to stay away from our beloved Big Macs or Whoppers? Probably because our lives demand it at times. Busy Americans often don't have time to prepare a home-cooked meal, so they rely on fast food to fit in with their fast-paced lives. Unfortunately, then, fast food is a part of today's society, but obesity can be avoided through moderation of consumption. Generally speaking, most fast food contains high—and therefore unhealthy—levels of calories, fat, and cholesterol, three dangerous aspects of an unhealthy lifestyle (Dietary Guidelines). But some fast-food meals are not as bad for you as others. For this evaluation, I 2

Notice how Lawrence offers support for her criteria: information from the Surgeon General's guidelines.

chose three popular meals: the Whopper Combo from Burger King, Wendy's Classic Single Combo, and McDonald's Quarter Pounder Combo.

When I researched the nutritional content of these three meals, I found that all three have high calorie content (see fig. 1). The Whopper Combo from Burger King has been a favorite of Americans for generations. But is it as good for your body as it is to your taste buds? When I researched the nutritional information, I discovered that this meal has a grand total of 1230 calories. In contrast, Wendy's Classic Single Combo has 1060 calories, and McDonald's Quarter Pounder Combo has 1000. 3

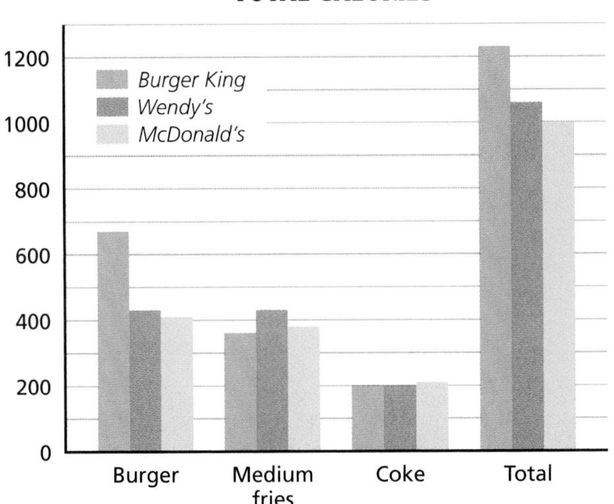

Fig. 1 Total calories in three fast-food meals.

The Burger King Whopper meal not only has the highest calorie count, it also has the highest fat content at 57 grams of total fat (see fig. 2). The next lowest is Wendy's Combo meal at 40 grams of total fat. The lowest of the three is McDonald's Quarter Pounder Combo at 35 grams of fat. 4

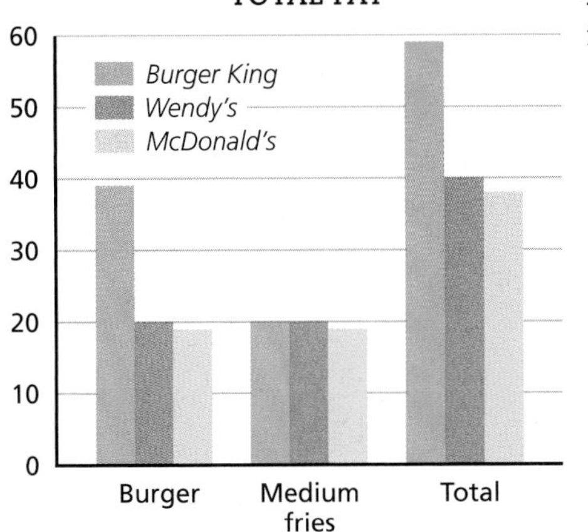

Fig. 2 Total fat in three fast-food meals.

In the following section, Lawrence has incorporated information from external sources to support her thesis.

One of Lawrence's classmates commented on her criteria:

These seem like good criteria, but why did you choose them? Do you need a stronger reason for your criteria here?

One peer reviewer had this comment:

These are a lot of statistics . . . Can you maybe give all this in a table or chart?

Note how Lawrence put that data into three charts.

5 Last but not least is the cholesterol content (see fig. 3). A high level of cholesterol in the blood can increase the risk of heart disease. Once again, the Burger King Whopper meal has the highest level at 95 milligrams. Wendy's meal has the next highest level at 75 milligrams, and this time McDonald's Quarter Pounder Combo has the lowest level of cholesterol at 65 milligrams.

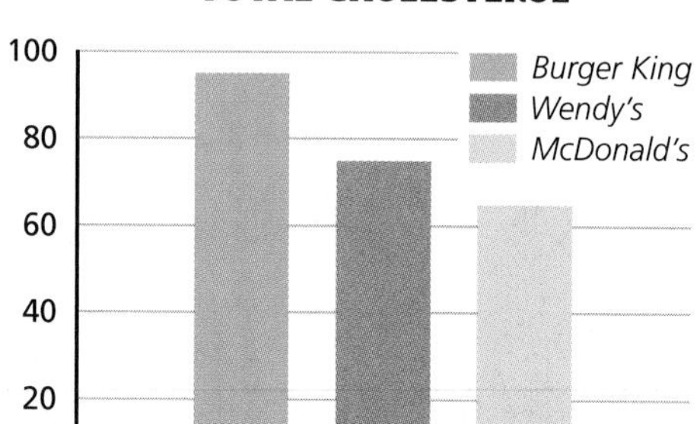

Fig. 3 Total cholesterol in three fast-food meals.

6 So if you are in a hurry and feel like grabbing a burger, you are probably better off getting the McDonald's Quarter Pounder meal, which has fewer calories and lower fat content than the other two meals. This doesn't mean, however, that you should make a habit of eating at McDonald's or any other fast-food restaurant chain, especially if you have a genetic predisposition to high cholesterol levels. Obviously, as the movie *Super Size Me* proved, even the "healthy" fast food isn't good for you when consumed on a regular basis. But if eaten in moderation, fast food is one of the best things to happen to busy Americans.

Works Cited

AOA Fact Sheets. American Obesity Association. Web. 2 May 2005. 14 October 2005. <http://www.obesity.org/subs/fastfacts/obesity_US.shtml>.

Burger King Nutritional Information. Web. 14 November 2008. <http://www.bk.com/Nutrition/PDFs/brochure.pdf>.

Get the Nutrition Facts for a McDonald's Menu Item. Web. 14 November 2008. <http://nutrition.mcdonalds.com/bagamcmeal/chooseCustomize.do>.

McDonald's Investor Fact Sheet 2006. Web. 14 October 2005. <http://mcd.mobular.net/mcd/90/8/26/>.

Super Size Me. Dir. Morgan Spurlock. Hart Sharp Video. 2004. Film.

Lawrence's classmate felt the ending of her first draft had problems:

Seems like the ending contradicts the rest of your essay. Why is fast food good for America? The ending seems wrong here.

She has made a slight change here to address this comment.

This paper follows MLA guidelines for in-text citations and works cited.

One of Lawrence's classmates pointed out that she had problems with her documentation:

Don't you have a quote in the first paragraph from the Surgeon General? There's no citation for it here.

Her revised list includes a citation for the Surgeon General's *Dietary Guidelines*.

United States Office of the Surgeon General. *Dietary Guidelines for Americans 2005*. 12 January 2005. Web. 10 April 2005. <http://www.healthierus.gov/dietaryguidelines/index.html>.

Wendy's Nutrition Facts & Topics. Web. 14 November 2008. <http://www.wendys.com/food/NutritionLanding.jsp>.

QUESTIONS FOR WRITING AND DISCUSSION

Rhetorical Knowledge: The Writer's Situation and Rhetoric

1. **Audience:** Who do you see as Lawrence's audience?
2. **Purpose:** Lawrence seems to have another purpose for her evaluation, in addition to writing this paper for a class assignment: to help her classmates. How well does she fulfill that larger purpose?
3. **Voice and tone:** What voice/tone strategies does Lawrence use to establish her *ethos*?
4. **Responsibility:** How effectively does Lawrence represent the facts about calories and other nutritional data in her evaluation?
5. **Context, format, and genre:** Lawrence is writing as a college student who eats fast food. How does that affect her credibility in this evaluation? Can you tell what genre Lawrence's evaluation might be? Is it a report? While Lawrence makes effective use of graphs—usually a sign of a report—she does not use heads or subheads.

Critical Thinking: The Writer's Ideas and Your Personal Response

6. What is your initial response to Lawrence's essay?
7. Lawrence focuses on only three criteria for her evaluation. How sufficient is that, do you think, for her to construct an effective evaluation? Why?

Composing Processes and Knowledge of Conventions: The Writer's Strategies

8. How effective is the evidence that Lawrence provides? What other evidence might she have used?
9. How effectively does Lawrence use the quotation and information from the Surgeon General?

Inquiry and Research: Ideas for Further Exploration

10. Interview several of your classmates, explaining Lawrence's conclusions. What is their reaction to her evaluation? Might it influence their dining decisions in the future?

 Self-Assessment: Reflecting on Your Goals

Now that you have constructed a piece of evaluative writing, go back and reconsider your goals. To help reflect on the goals that you have achieved, respond in writing to the following questions:

Rhetorical Knowledge

- *Audience:* What have you learned about addressing an audience in evaluative writing?
- *Purpose:* What have you learned about the purposes for constructing an evaluation?
- *Rhetorical situation:* How did the writing context affect your evaluative text? How did your choice of subject affect the research you conducted and the way you presented your evaluation?
- *Voice and tone:* How would you describe your voice in this essay? Your tone? How do they contribute to the effectiveness of your evaluation?
- *Context, medium, and genre:* How did your context determine the medium and genre you chose, and how did those decisions affect your writing?

Critical Thinking, Reading, and Writing

- *Learning/inquiry:* What process did you go through to focus on a main idea, or thesis? How did you judge what was most and least important in your evaluation?
- *Responsibility:* How did you fulfill your responsibility to your readers?
- *Reading and research:* What did you learn about evaluative writing from the reading selections in this chapter? What research did you conduct? How sufficient was the research you did?
- *Skills:* As a result of writing this evaluation, how have you become a more critical thinker, reader, and writer? What skills do you hope to develop further in your next writing project?

Writing Processes

- *Invention:* What invention strategies were most useful to you?
- *Organizing your ideas and details:* What organization did you use? How successful was it?
- *Revising:* What are the strongest and the weakest parts of your essay? Why? If you could go back and make an additional revision, what would it be?
- *Working with peers:* How did your instructor or peer readers help you by making comments and suggestions about your writing? List some examples of useful comments that you received. How could you have made better use of the comments and suggestions you received?

- *Visuals:* Did you use photographs or other visuals to help explain your evaluation to readers? If so, what did you learn about incorporating these elements?
- *Writing habits:* What "writerly habits" have you developed, modified, or improved on as you constructed the writing assignment for this chapter? How will you change your future writing activities, based on what you have learned about yourself?

Knowledge of Conventions

- *Editing:* What sentence problem did you find most frequently in your writing? How will you avoid that problem in future assignments?
- *Genre:* What conventions of the genre you were using, if any, gave you problems?
- *Documentation:* Did you use sources for your paper? If so, what documentation style did you use? What problems, if any, did you have with it?

If you are preparing a course portfolio, file your written reflections so that you can return to them when you next work on your portfolio. Refer to Chapter 1 (pages 11–12) for a sample reflection by a student.

mhconnectcomposition.com

Annlee Lawrence Reflects on Her Writing QL9009

Chapter 10

Writing to Explain Causes and Effects

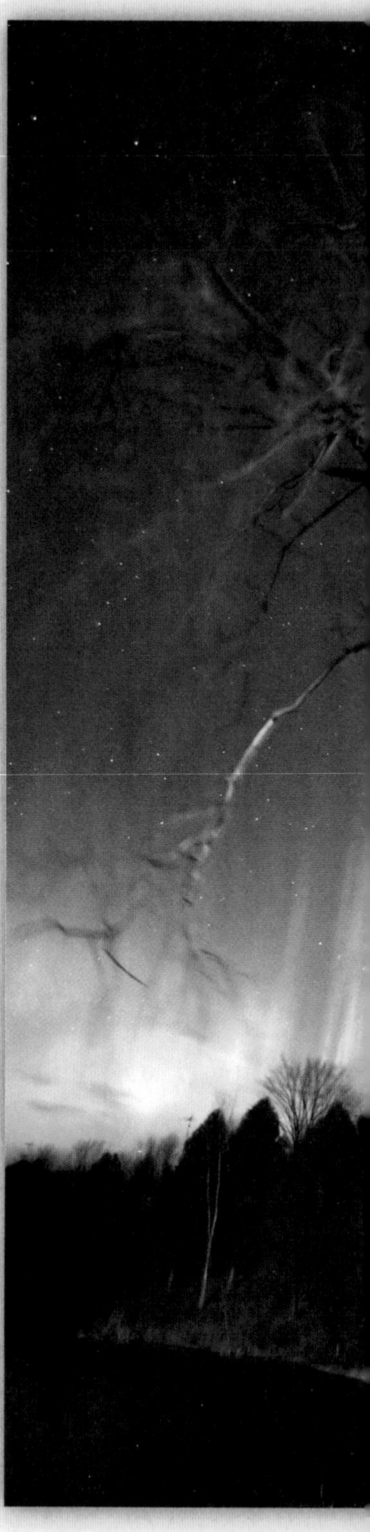

Here is the space weather report from NASA for one day in October 2003:

> Giant sunspots 484 and 486 remain visible on the sun, posing a continued threat for X-class solar explosions. Indeed, on Sunday, Oct. 26, 2003, there were two such blasts—one from each sunspot. The explosions hurled coronal mass ejections (CMEs) into space and somewhat toward Earth.
>
> Because of these events, sky watchers should be alert for auroras during the nights ahead. . . . Forecasters estimate a 25 percent chance of severe geomagnetic storming when the incoming CMEs sweep past Earth and deliver (probably glancing) blows to our planet's magnetic field. (Sun & Space Weather News 2003, http://cse.ssl.berkeley.edu/secnews/s-a-news03.html)

We are often curious about how and why things happen. We wonder what causes natural phenomena such as the north-

ern lights (aurora borealis), we want to know what caused the extinction of certain species, and we have a vested interest in knowing the causes of diseases such as cancer, Alzheimer's, or schizophrenia.

Consider the events that take place in your life: You are surrounded by *changes* that occur, *trends* you can observe (and wonder why they happen), *behavior* that is unusual or surprising. All have *causes*, reasons why they happened. In fact, *why* is probably the best question you can ask as you explore any cause-and-effect relationship.

In some cases, discovering the cause is an end in itself. For instance, we may one day know precisely why the dinosaurs became extinct about 60 million years ago, but we may not be able to use that information to change life as it is currently lived on Earth. In other cases, though, we can use information gained from causal analysis to eliminate or avoid the causes of certain effects. For instance, in recent years, scientists have come to understand—and share with the public—the strong cause-and-effect relationship between tobacco use and certain kinds of cancer. Although identifying and understanding relationships between causes and effects can be challenging, the act of writing will help you to become more aware of them. Because life includes many causes and effects, writing about them can help you to make sense of sequences of related events.

Setting Your Goals:

Rhetorical Knowledge

- **Audience:** Your success will partially depend on how well you have analyzed your audience. How can you make your audience interested in this cause-and-effect relationship?
- **Purpose:** Your main purpose is to convince readers that a cause-and-effect relationship exists. Your purpose may be to identify a cause and determine its effect(s). Or your purpose may be to determine a series of causes and effects—often called a *causal chain*.
- **Rhetorical situation:** Think about the factors that affect where you stand in relation to your subject.
- **Voice and tone:** Present yourself as a logical writer who provides reliable information.
- **Context, medium, and genre:** Decide on the most effective medium and genre to use to present your causal analysis. Visuals such as flowcharts are often an effective way of helping audiences understand causal relationships.

Critical Thinking, Reading, and Writing

- **Learning/inquiry:** Think critically about whether an actual cause-and-effect relationship exists. It may be coincidental that one event happens right after another or that two phenomena often occur together.
- **Responsibility:** Recognize that causes and effects may be more complex than you first realize. Any given phenomenon or event is likely to have many causes and to produce many effects.
- **Reading and research:** As you conduct research about a causal relationship, make sure you understand the nature of the relationship well enough to be able to document the causality.

Writing to Explain Causes and Effects

10 Chapter

Writing Processes

- **Invention:** Begin by recording possible answers to the question you are considering using an invention strategy such as brainstorming or listing.
- **Organizing your ideas and details:** Once you have recorded some ideas, think about how to organize your main points and what supporting evidence you need to provide.
- **Revising:** Read your work with a critical eye, to make certain that it displays the qualities of a good causal analysis.
- **Working with peers:** Peer review is a crucial part of the process of writing a causal analysis because it enables you to get a sense of how an audience will respond to your claim that a cause-and-effect relationship exists.

Knowledge of Conventions

- **Editing:** When you edit a causal analysis, make sure that the subordinate clauses are attached to independent clauses and are therefore part of complete sentences.
- **Genres for cause-and-effect writing:** In your college classes, you will be required to follow the conventions for an academic essay. Other, nonacademic writing situations may call for a variety of genres.
- **Documentation:** You will probably need to rely on sources outside of your experience, and if you are writing an academic essay, you will be required to cite them using the appropriate documentation style.

mhconnectcomposition.com

Writing to Explain Causes and Effects Tutorial QL10001

Rhetorical Knowledge

When you write about causes and effects, you need to have a specific purpose in mind, some sense of your audience, and an idea of an effective way to substantiate the cause-and-effect relationships you are considering. How can you prove your claim that a cause-and-effect relationship exists?

Writing about Causes and Effects in Your College Classes

Many of the assignments for your college classes will ask you to determine the causes of an event, a trend, or a phenomenon. Here are some examples:

- Your dance instructor may ask you to explain why and how dance steps and movement have evolved over time.
- Your biology instructor may ask you to explain what causes leaves to turn color and drop from trees in certain parts of the world in the fall.
- In a sociology course, you might investigate the possible effects of antipoverty programs on the crime rate in low-income neighborhoods.

The "Ways of Writing" feature presents different genres that can be used when writing about causes and effects in your college classes.

Writing about Causes and Effects for Life

Much of the writing constructed in professional settings is designed to solve problems. The first step in solving any problem is determining why the problem exists:

- *Why* is quality control so much better at one plant than the others?
- *Why* can't we increase sales to the level we need to become profitable?

Many professionals in the work world spend a good deal of their time determining causes and effects:

- A team of medical researchers writes a paper reporting on a study that reveals a cause-and-effect relationship between vitamin C deficiency and osteoporosis.
- A teacher wonders why some students have difficulty reading and studies them to find out the causes of their problems.
- A police officer writes evidence in an accident report to show that excessive speed caused a driver to lose control of his car.

When writers focus on community issues, they often need to find and explain answers to *why* questions:

- A citizens' group submits a written report to the county health board arguing that more restaurant inspections lead to fewer incidences of *E. coli* food poisoning.
- A homeowner writes a letter to the editor of a county newspaper arguing that a nearby golf course is the source of the chemical residue recently discovered in local well water.

You will also encounter many occasions for thinking and writing about causes and effects in personal settings. It is critical to understand why things happen, and journals are an excellent place to explore such cause-and-effect relationships. For example, a young couple might keep a daily journal on the activities of their infant daughter. After a few weeks, when they reread their entries, they might notice a pattern suggesting that when they feed their daughter one kind of formula, she sleeps fewer hours at night.

The "Ways of Writing" feature presents different genres that can be used when writing about causes and effects in life.

Scenarios for Writing | Assignment Options

connect
mhconnectcomposition.com
Writer's Workshop: Applying Learning Goals to Cause-and-Effect Writing QL10002

Your instructor may ask you to complete one or both of the following assignments that call for writing about causes and effects. Each of these assignments is in the form of a *scenario*, which gives you a sense of who your audience is and what you need to accomplish with your causal analysis.

Starting on page 332, you will find guidelines for completing whatever scenarios you decide—or are asked to—complete. Additional scenarios for college and life may be found online.

Writing for College

SCENARIO 1 **Academic Paper: Causes and Effects in One of Your Other College Courses**

Consider the topics that you are studying this semester that involve causes and effects. Choose a topic that interests you, and then come up with a question about that topic that will lead you to investigate causes and/or effects. Here are some possibilities:

- **Geology:** What causes an earthquake?
- **Music:** How did hip-hop change popular music?
- **Art:** How did the invention of the camera affect the kinds of painting that artists did in the nineteenth century?
- **Physics:** What causes the lift that makes it possible for airplanes to fly?

Alternatively, you might consider some general cause-and-effect relationships that you have noticed. Here are a few examples:

Ways of Writing to Explain Cause and Effect

Genres for Your College Classes	Sample Situation	Advantages of the Genre	Limitations of the Genre
Academic essay	Your health and wellness professor asks you to explain the possible causes of eating disorders in college-age female students.	In an academic essay you can examine an important issue in detail to determine cause.	Effective academic essays require substantial supporting evidence.
PowerPoint presentation	Your writing professor asks you to present how professional athletes influence the actions of teenage males.	A *PowerPoint* presentation allows you to provide visuals that accompany your talk.	You have to be careful not to offer too many or too few details.
Brochure	To promote an expanded campus recycling program, your brochure needs to explain the cause(s) for the expanded program and its benefits.	A brochure is an effective medium for concisely presenting material in words and visuals.	A brochure allows only limited space for presenting material.
Formal laboratory report	Your botany professor asks you to construct a formal lab report showing the relationship of a warmer climate to recent issues with bark beetles infesting your community's elm trees.	A formal lab report is a common venue for showing such a cause-and-effect relationship.	Lab reports typically do not appeal to a wide audience.
Genres for Life	**Sample Situation**	**Advantages of the Genre**	**Limitations of the Genre**
Brochure	You decide to construct a brochure that explains why a certain stretch of highway is dangerous and so causes more accidents.	A brochure gives readers a quick overview of your topic.	A brochure provides limited space to explain causes and effects.
Formal business plan	To get a loan for a new product line, you construct a business plan showing how these new products will increase profits.	Lending institutions often require a formal business plan before they decide whether to offer a loan.	Some intangibles—such as the work ethic of employees—cannot easily be documented in a business plan.
Poster	To help children understand that they need to wash their hands before eating, you construct a poster showing how germs can cause them to become sick.	A poster is a useful visual teaching tool for young readers.	Posters offer limited space for presenting material.
Web site	You want to create a Web site that explains how high school dropouts hurt the community because they often cannot find jobs that pay well.	A Web site can have a large school-age readership.	Constructing effective Web sites is time-consuming and Web sites might not reach the entire target group.
Editorial	Through an editorial, you want to explain to residents of your town how a slight increase in sales tax will benefit the community.	An editorial lets you outline details about the cause-and-effect relationship between the small tax increase and the benefits for your community.	Because editorials tend to be short, it can difficult to present enough evidence to support your position.

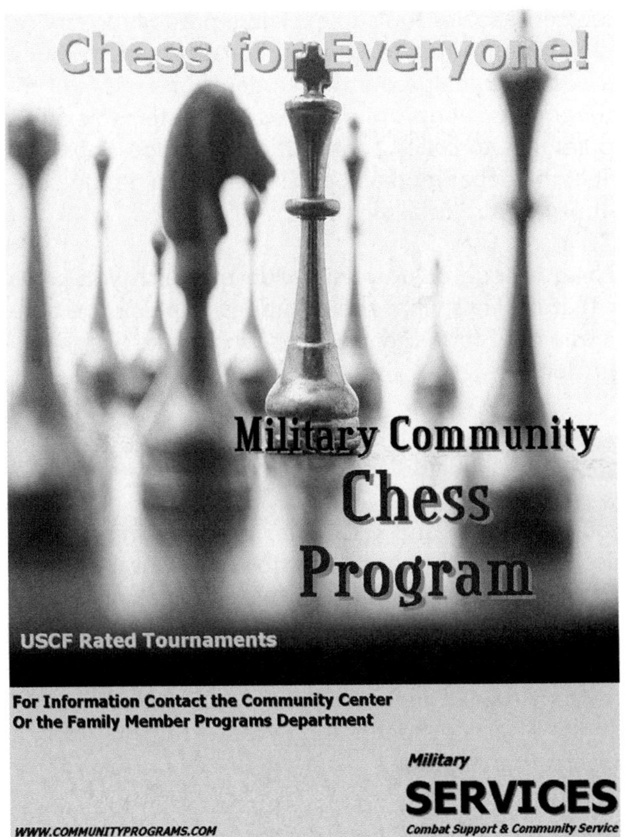

FIGURE 10.1 Poster for a Chess Club

- **College:** Why does the cost of attending college always seem to increase?
- **Community:** Why do some neighbors around the college resent having students rent homes nearby?
- **Classroom:** Why do some students take so long to finish college?

Writing Assignment: For this assignment, you can choose among several options. One possibility is to select an effect and then write about its causes. Another possibility is to select a cause and then write about its effects. Your goal is to convince an audience of instructors and students in the discipline that your causal analysis is credible.

Writing for Life

SCENARIO 2 Personal Writing: A Poster to Describe a Campus Club

A poster is an effective medium for telling a brief message. Posters often include photographs or other visual elements, and they sometimes are printed in full color and on glossy paper. Figure 10.1 shows a poster for a chess club.

Small businesses use posters as sales tools to explain a product or service. Health agencies use posters to inform clients about health-related issues. Graduate schools provide posters to help potential students understand program and graduation requirements. Nonprofit agencies use posters to explain the work they do and sometimes to solicit contributions. College clubs (the rugby team, the botany club, the debating team, and so on) often design posters to serve as recruiting tools for potential members.

Writing Assignment: For a college or university club of which you are a member, design a poster that outlines what the club does, explains the benefits of joining, and includes a brief form that students who would like to join can fill in and send to your club.

connect
mhconnectcomposition.com
Additional Scenarios QL10003

Rhetorical Considerations in Cause-and-Effect Writing

- **Audience:** While your instructor and classmates are your initial audience, you should also consider other audiences for your causal analysis. What evidence will convince your readers that you are making a valid claim about a cause-and-effect relationship?
- **Purpose:** Your general purpose is to convince readers that a cause-and-effect relationship exists. How can you establish the causes of something (an effect), establish the effects of something (a cause), or show how a series of causes and effects are related?
- **Voice, tone, and point of view:** Why are you interested in the cause-and-effect relationship that you have chosen to write about? What preconceptions about it do you have? What are your attitudes toward the topic and the audience? How will you convey those attitudes?
- **Context, medium, and genre:** Keeping the context of the assignment in mind, decide on a medium and a genre for your writing. How will your writing be used? If you are writing for an audience beyond the classroom, consider what will be the most effective way to present your information to this audience.

For more on choosing a medium and genre, see Chapter 17 and the Online Appendix.

Critical Thinking, Reading, and Writing

Before you begin to write your causal analysis, read examples of writing about causes and effects to get a feel for this kind of writing. You might consider how visuals could enhance your causal analysis, as well as the kinds of sources you will need to consult.

The qualities of writing about causes and/or effects include a focused presentation of the effect(s) or cause(s), a clearly stated claim that a cause-and-effect relationship exists, and sufficient evidence to support the claim. The writer also has the responsibility to research carefully, to avoid logical fallacies, and to consider other points of view. These qualities and responsibilities are discussed in the section that follows.

Learning the Qualities of Effective Writing about Causes and Effects

When you consider what causes what, or what the effects of something are, you need to convince others that the relationship you see in fact exists. Here are the qualities of writing that analyzes causes and/or effects successfully:

- **Presentation of focused cause(s) or effect(s).** At the beginning of your essay, introduce the event, activity, or phenomenon for which you wish to establish cause(s), or effect(s), or both. To focus the causes or effects, you should limit the time period that you are considering. This does not mean you cannot write about long periods of time (for a geology paper, you almost have to do so). Rather, always keep the time period in mind as you determine exactly what to focus on so you can reasonably cover your topic given the limits of your assignment.
- **A clearly stated claim that a cause-and-effect relationship exists.** After you have done enough research to be certain that a cause-and-effect relationship exists, you will be prepared to state the nature of that relationship. State the claim so that readers understand it, especially since they may know little or nothing about your topic.
- **Sufficient evidence to support your claim.** To support your claim, present evidence that readers will consider persuasive. Such evidence may consist of the following:
    - The results of empirical studies or historical research found in scholarly and popular books, in journals, and on Web sites
    - Your own observations, experience, or reading
    - Testimony from interested or affected parties ("Interviews with other students indicate that . . .") or experts ("Professor X, a noted authority, asserts that . . .")
    - The use of examples that demonstrate that your suggested cause or causes actually do cause the effect
- **Clear, logical thinking.** People often jump to conclusions when they see two events happening at the same time and assume there is a cause-and-effect relationship (see the discussion of *post hoc, ergo propter hoc* in the box on page 336). So consider these issues as you search for cause-and-effect relationships:
    - **Does the effect have a single cause, or multiple causes?** Things are rarely as simple as they first appear to be. More often than not, an effect will have multiple causes. Carefully analyze and research all the causes that may contribute to a particular effect.

  - **What are the contributing causes, and do they lead to a precipitating cause?** Often, a number of causes together contribute to what might be called a *precipitating cause,* the final cause that sets the effect in motion. Several contributing causes might set up a single precipitating cause. For example, although the football fan might blame the kicker who missed a last-second field goal for the team's loss of the important game, there surely were many other reasons that contributed to the loss (dropped passes, poor execution of running plays, missed tackles, and so on).
  - **Is a particular cause remote or immediate?** It is sometimes useful to examine a chain of causes so that you understand what came first, what happened next, and so on. Writing down the sequence of causes and effects will help you see the events in the **causal chain** as they happened over time.
  - **Is a particular cause necessary or sufficient?** A **necessary cause** is one that must be present for the effect to occur. A **sufficient cause** is one that, if present, always triggers a particular effect. For example, for a teenager to be able to borrow the family car, his or her family must have a car—that cause is *necessary* to the effect of the teenager being able to borrow it. The teenager's forgetting to put gas into the family car before bringing it back, however, is a *sufficient* cause for the parents to refuse to lend it again; other causes would be sufficient as well (bringing the car home dirty or running into a utility pole and denting the fender are also possible causes for the parents' decision), so forgetfulness is not a necessary cause.

For more on writing effective arguments, including claims, evidence, types of appeals, and counterarguments, see Chapter 14.

- **Anticipation of possible objections or alternative explanations.** While your causal analysis may be highly plausible, there are almost always other possible causes for the same effect or other possible effects of the cause that you are considering. Be prepared to acknowledge those other potential causes or effects and to show why your causes or effects are more likely.

Reading, Inquiry, and Research: Learning from Texts That Explain Cause-and-Effect Relationships

The readings that follow are examples of writing about causes and effects. As you read them, consider the following questions:

- To what extent has the writer focused on causes, on effects, or on both causes and effects?
- What parts of the selection seem the strongest? Why do you think so?
- How can you use the techniques of cause-and-effect writing exemplified here in your writing?

JUAN WILLIAMS

The Ruling That Changed America

CAUSE-AND-EFFECT ESSAY

1 Fifty years later, the *Brown* decision looks different. At a distance from the volcanic heat of May 17, 1954, the real impact of the legal, political, and cultural eruption that changed America is not exactly what it first appeared to be.

2 On that Monday in May, the high court's ruling outlawing school segregation in the United States generated urgent news flashes on the radio and frenzied black headlines in special editions of afternoon newspapers. One swift and unanimous decision by the top judges in the land was going to end segregation in public schools. Southern politicians reacted with such fury and fear that they immediately called the day "Black Monday."

3 South Carolina Gov. James Byrnes, who rose to political power with passionate advocacy of segregation, said the decision was "the end of civilization in the South as we have known it." Georgia Gov. Herman Talmadge struck an angry tone. He said Georgia had no intention of allowing "mixed race" schools as long as he was governor. And he touched on Confederate pride from the days when the South went to war with the federal government over slavery by telling supporters that the Supreme Court's ruling was not law in his state; he said it was "the first step toward national suicide." The *Brown* decision should be regarded, he said, as nothing but a "mere scrap of paper."

4 Meanwhile, newspapers for black readers reacted with exultation. "The Supreme Court decision is the greatest victory for the Negro people since the Emancipation Proclamation," said Harlem's *Amsterdam News*. A writer in the *Chicago Defender* explained, "neither the atomic bomb nor the hydrogen bomb will ever be as meaningful to our democracy." And Thurgood Marshall, the NAACP lawyer who directed the legal fight that led to *Brown*, predicted the end of segregation in all American public schools by the fall of 1955.

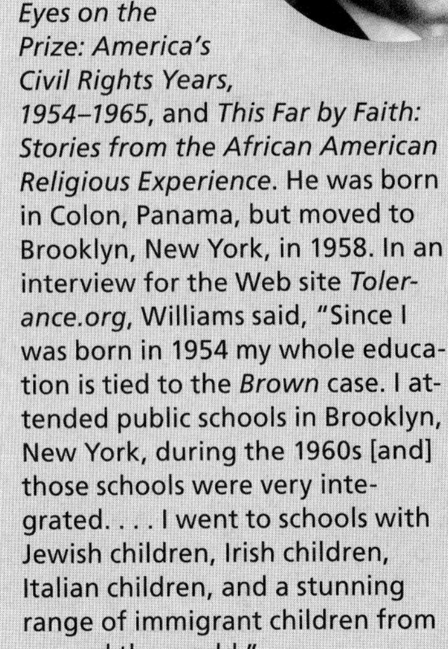

Juan Williams is the author of *Thurgood Marshall: American Revolutionary*, the nonfiction bestseller *Eyes on the Prize: America's Civil Rights Years, 1954–1965*, and *This Far by Faith: Stories from the African American Religious Experience*. He was born in Colon, Panama, but moved to Brooklyn, New York, in 1958. In an interview for the Web site *Tolerance.org*, Williams said, "Since I was born in 1954 my whole education is tied to the *Brown* case. I attended public schools in Brooklyn, New York, during the 1960s [and] those schools were very integrated. . . . I went to schools with Jewish children, Irish children, Italian children, and a stunning range of immigrant children from around the world."

Williams attended Haverford College and graduated with a degree in philosophy in 1976. For more than twenty years, Williams was an editorial writer, op-ed contributor, and White House reporter for the *Washington Post*. His work has appeared in *Newsweek, Fortune, Atlantic Monthly, Ebony, Gentlemen's Quarterly*, and the *New Republic*. Williams is currently a senior correspondent for National Public Radio.

This essay originally appeared in the April 2004 issue of the *American School Board Journal*.

Slow Progress, Backward Steps

Ten years later, however, very little school integration had taken place. 5
True to the defiant words of segregationist governors, the Southern states had hunkered down in a massive resistance campaign against school integration. Some Southern counties closed their schools instead of allowing blacks and whites into the same classrooms. In other towns, segregationist academies opened, and most if not all of the white children left the public schools for the racially exclusive alternatives. And in most places, the governors, mayors, and school boards found it easy enough to just ask for more time before integrating schools.

That slow-as-molasses approach worked. In 1957, President Eisen- 6
hower had to send troops from the 101st Airborne into Little Rock just to get nine black children safely into Central High School. Only in the late '60s, under the threat of losing federal funding, did large-scale school integration begin in Southern public schools. And in many places, in both the North and the South, black and white students did not go to school together until a federal court ordered schoolchildren to ride buses across town to bring the races together.

Today, 50 years later, a study by the Civil Rights Project at Harvard 7
University finds that the percentage of white students attending public schools with Hispanic or black students has steadily declined since 1988. In fact, the report concludes that school integration in the United States is "lower in 2000 than in 1970, before busing for racial balance began." In the South, home to the majority of America's black population, there is now less school integration than there was in 1970. The Harvard report concluded, "At the beginning of the 21st century, American schools are now 12 years into the process of continuous resegregation."

Today, America's schools are so heavily segregated that more than 8
two-thirds of black and Hispanic students are in schools where a majority of the students are not white. And today, most of the nation's white children attend a school that is almost 80 percent white. Hispanics are now the most segregated group of students in the nation because they live in highly concentrated clusters.

At the start of the new century, 50 years after *Brown* shook the nation, 9
segregated housing patterns and an increase in the number of black and brown immigrants have concentrated minorities in impoverished big cities and created a new reality of public schools segregated by race and class.

The Real Impact of *Brown*

So, if *Brown* didn't break apart school segregation, was it really the earth- 10
quake that it first appeared to be?

Yes. Today, it is hard to even remember America before *Brown* because the ruling completely changed the nation. It still stands as the laser beam that first signaled that the federal government no longer gave its support to racial segregation among Americans. 11

Before *Brown*, the federal government lent its power to enforcing the laws of segregation under an 1896 Supreme Court ruling that permitted "separate but equal" treatment of blacks and whites. Blacks and whites who tried to integrate factories, unions, public buses and trains, parks, the military, restaurants, department stores, and more found that the power of the federal government was with the segregationists. 12

Before *Brown*, the federal government had struggled even to pass a law banning lynching. 13

But after the Supreme Court ruled that segregation in public schools was a violation of the Constitution, the federal attitude toward enforcing second-class citizenship for blacks shifted on the scale of a change in the ocean's tide or a movement in the plates of the continents. Once the highest court in the land said equal treatment for all did not allow for segregation, then the lower courts, the Justice Department, and federal prosecutors, as well as the FBI, all switched sides. They didn't always act to promote integration, but they no longer used their power to stop it. 14

An irreversible shift had begun, and it was the direct result of the *Brown* decision. 15

The change in the attitude of federal officials created a wave of anticipation among black people, who became alert to the possibility of achieving the long-desired goal of racial equality. There is no way to offer a hard measure of a change in attitude. But the year after *Brown*, Rosa Parks refused to give up her seat to a white man on a racially segregated bus in Montgomery, Ala. That led to a yearlong bus boycott and the emergence of massive, nonviolent protests for equal rights. That same year, Martin Luther King Jr. emerged as the nation's prophet of civil rights for all Americans. 16

Even when a black 14-year-old, Emmit Till, was killed in Mississippi for supposedly whistling at a white woman, there was a new reaction to old racial brutality. One of Till's elderly relatives broke with small-town Southern tradition and dared to take the witness stand and testify against the white men he saw abduct the boy. Until *Brown*, the simple act of a black man standing up to speak against a white man in Mississippi was viewed as futile and likely to result in more white-on-black violence. 17

The sense among black people—and many whites as well—that a new era had opened created a new boldness. Most black parents in Little Rock did not want to risk harm to their children by allowing them to join in efforts to integrate Central High. But working with local NAACP officials, the parents of nine children decided it was a new day and time to make 18 history. That same spirit of new horizons was at work in 1962 when James Meredith became the first black student to enroll at the University of Mississippi. And in another lurch away from the traditional support of segregation, the federal government sent troops as well as Justice Department officials to the university to protect Meredith's rights.

The next year, when Alabama Gov. George Wallace felt the political necessity of making a public stand against integration at the University of Alabama, he stood only briefly in the door to block black students and then stepped aside in the face of federal authority. That was another shift toward a world of high hopes for racial equality; again, from the perspective of the 21st century, it looks like another aftershock of the *Brown* decision. 19

The same psychology of hope infected young people, black and white, nationwide in the early '60s. The Freedom Rides, lunch-counter sit-ins, and protest marches for voting rights all find their roots in *Brown*. So, too, did the racially integrated 1963 March on Washington at which Martin Luther King Jr. famously said he had a vision of a promised land where the sons of slaves and the sons of slave owners could finally join together in peace. The desire for change became a demand for change in the impatient voice of Malcolm X, the militant Black Muslim who called for immediate change by violent means if necessary. 20

In 1964, a decade after *Brown*, the Civil Rights Act was passed by a Congress beginning to respond to the changing politics brought about by the landmark decision. The next year, 1965, the wave of change had swelled to the point that Congress passed the Voting Rights Act. 21

Closer to the Mountaintop

This sea change in black and white attitudes toward race also had an impact on culture. Churches began to grapple with the Christian and Jewish principles of loving thy neighbor, even if thy neighbor had a different color skin. Major league baseball teams no longer feared a fan revolt if they allowed more than one black player on a team. Black writers, actors, athletes, and musicians—ranging from James Baldwin to the Supremes and Muhammad Ali—began to cross over into the mainstream of American culture. 22

The other side of the change in racial attitudes was white support for equal rights. College-educated young white people in the '60s often defined themselves by their willingness to embrace racial equality. Bob Dylan sang about the changing times as answers "blowing in the wind." Movies like *Guess Who's Coming to Dinner* found major audiences among all races. And previously all-white private colleges and universities began opening their doors to black students. The resulting arguments over affirmative action in college admissions led to the Supreme Court's 1978 decision in the 23

Bakke case, which outlawed the use of quotas, and its recent ruling that the University of Michigan can take race into account as one factor in admitting students to its law school. The court has also had to deal with affirmative action in the business world, in both hiring and contracts—again as a result of questions of equality under the Constitution raised by *Brown*.

But the most important legacy of the *Brown* decision, by far, is the growth of an educated black middle class. The number of black people graduating from high school and college has soared since *Brown*, and the incomes of blacks have climbed steadily as a result. Home ownership and investment in the stock market among black Americans have rocketed since the 1980s. The political and economic clout of that black middle class continues to bring America closer to the mountaintop vision of racial equality that Dr. King might have dreamed of 50 years ago. 24

The Supreme Court's May 17, 1954, ruling in *Brown* remains a landmark legal decision. But it is much more than that. It is the "Big Bang" of all American history in the 20th century. 25

QUESTIONS FOR WRITING AND DISCUSSION

Rhetorical Knowledge: The Writer's Situation and Rhetoric

1. **Audience:** Williams is writing for an audience that, more likely than not, takes the decision in *Brown vs. Board of Education* for granted. How does he show his audience the real importance of the decision?
2. **Purpose:** Williams wants readers to understand that even if U.S. public schools are still largely segregated, *Brown vs. Board of Education* was perhaps the most important Supreme Court decision of the twentieth century. How successful is he in convincing you?
3. **Voice and tone:** Williams begins his article with measured language, much as you'd expect from a newspaper reporter. He then intersperses his reporting with several short, one-sentence paragraphs of commentary (for example, see paragraphs 13 and 15). How does this tone affect your response to what you read?
4. **Responsibility:** Williams needs to make sure his readers understand the social situation in the United States in 1954. How effectively does he do that?
5. **Context, format, and genre:** This essay is written as a retrospective, looking back over U.S. history in the fifty years since the Supreme Court decision. How sufficiently does Williams provide the historical background for you as readers today? How well does he establish the appropriate context? How does he use the conventions of an academic essay?

Critical Thinking: The Writer's Ideas and Your Personal Response

6. Before reading Williams's article, how aware were you of the impact of *Brown vs. Board of Education*? Can you think of another Supreme Court ruling that has had as significant an impact?
7. At the end, Williams asserts that *Brown vs. Board of Education* was instrumental in helping to establish the emerging black middle class. Given this observation, and given that school enrollment patterns are determined by housing patterns that depend on economic status, why are schools more segregated today?

Composing Processes and Knowledge of Conventions: The Writer's Strategies

8. Because for many people, fifty years after the fact, *Brown vs. Board of Education* is simply an entry in history books, how does Williams make the decision real for his current readers?
9. Williams structures his argument to show that *Brown vs. Board of Education* did not accomplish what it intended, but that it eventually did more. How effective is his argument? Why?

Inquiry and Research: Ideas for Further Exploration

10. Investigate other Supreme Court decisions. Which seem to have had greater impact than expected at the time they were made?

ROBERT REICH

The Real Reason Why Highway Deaths Are Down

BLOG

Robert Reich is a professor of public policy at the University of California, Berkeley. From 1993 to 2001, he served as secretary of labor. He has written numerous books, including *The Work of Nations, The Future of Success, Locked in the Cabinet,* and *Supercapitalism.* His many articles have appeared in periodicals such as the *New Yorker, Atlantic Monthly, New York Times, Washington Post,* and *Wall Street Journal.* He has written a blog, Robert Reich's Blog (http://www.robertreich.blogspot.com/), since April 2006. It is labeled as "his personal journal." The following blog entry appeared August 20, 2008, just as the U.S. economy was beginning to decline. Reich points to the economy as a major factor in reducing highway deaths. Recent studies indicate that text messaging while driving is more dangerous than drinking alcohol and driving. Which cause is of greatest concern to you? Why?

The U.S. saw a 3.9 percent drop in traffic fatalities since 2006. That's according to the latest report from the National Highway Traffic Safety Administration. So what are we doing right? 1

Transportation Secretary Mary Peters credits the decline to safer vehicles. I doubt it. The cars on our roads last year weren't all that much safer than they were the year before. Basically they were the same cars, because sales of new cars plummeted. 2

Some hypothesize that our roads themselves have become safer, but our roads didn't suddenly improve. In fact, too many of America's highways are literally falling apart for lack of adequate maintenance. One major bridge even caved in. 3

Some think the drop in highway fatalities is due to drivers being more careful—buckling their seat belts, obeying traffic laws. Secretary Peters also credits "more aggressive law enforcement." But here, too, the evidence is weak. Seat belt laws have been in effect in most states for years. And law enforcement efforts on our roads have not noticeably changed. 4

If anything, many of us behind the wheel are less careful these days. We're paying less attention to driving and more to chattering on cell phones, fiddling with iPods and Blackberries, and adjusting global positioning devices. 5

And more of us are driving motorcycles, accounting for a growing number of highway deaths. 6

So what's the real explanation? It's the economy, stupid. When the economy tanks, as it began to do last year, fewer people are on the road. It's not just the high gas prices. The same pattern can be seen in other major downturns. 7

When unemployment rises, fewer people commute to work. When incomes fall, fewer people drive to the malls or to movies and restaurants, because they have less money to spend. And fewer people on the roads mean fewer highway accidents and deaths. 8

The last time we saw this big a drop in highway deaths was 1991, which was also the last time we experienced this big a plunge in our economy. 9

Highway fatalities rose again in the mid-90's as the economy revived. Given how the economy is now going, 2008 will probably turn out to be among the safest years on record.

QUESTIONS FOR WRITING AND DISCUSSION: LEARNING OUTCOMES

Rhetorical Knowledge: The Writer's Situation and Rhetoric

1. **Audience:** Who is Reich's primary audience? What makes you think that?
2. **Purpose:** What is Reich trying to accomplish in this blog entry?
3. **Voice and tone:** What is Reich's attitude toward the topic and the audience?
4. **Responsibility:** How does Reich demonstrate that he takes seriously his responsibilities as a writer?
5. **Context, format, and genre:** If Reich were to revise this blog entry into an academic essay, what revisions would he need to make? Some blog entries are informal essays, like this one. What features of the entry mark it as informal?

Critical Thinking: The Writer's Ideas and Your Personal Response

6. Reich's second sentence in paragraph 7 reads, "It's the economy, stupid." How do you respond to this sentence?
7. The last sentence in the first paragraph reads, "So what are we doing right?" What was your initial reaction to that sentence? When you finished reading the blog entry, what was your reaction to that sentence?

Composing Processes and Knowledge of Conventions: The Writer's Strategies

8. How credible does Reich seem in this blog entry? Why do you think that?
9. Why does Reich mention the National Highway Safety Administration in the first paragraph?

Inquiry and Research: Ideas for Further Exploration

10. Read some of Reich's other blog entries (http://www.robertreich.blogspot.com/). How would you describe his tone in these entries? Listen to some of his podcasts, which can be found on National Public Radio (www.npr.org). How does his tone sound?

GENRES *Up Close* Writing an Educational Poster

Because people are busy juggling the demands of the professional, civic, and personal arenas of their lives, they sometimes do not have time to read longer texts such as full academic essays. At other times, writers want to grab and use readers' attention when readers are on the go—walking on sidewalks or down hallways, riding on buses or trains, or standing in line at places of business. To reach busy readers on the go, writers sometimes use educational posters, which provide information in a condensed form, with a mixture of visual and verbal elements. Effective educational posters have the following features:

- They focus on a single narrow topic.
- They include a balance of words, images, and white space (space where no words or images appear).
- They are uncluttered. They include plenty of blank space.
- They have relatively few words—just enough to make a point.
- They can be read from a distance—at least ten feet away—when displayed on a wall.

The type size should be at least 24-point.

As you read the following poster, consider how these features are implemented.

PIKE COUNTY GENERAL HEALTH DISTRICT

EDUCATIONAL POSTER

Cover Food

The Pike County General Health District is a government agency in Waverly, Ohio. The PCGHD is charged with protecting the health of the county's residents. The following poster describes what happens when a fly lands on food. How effective is this poster in convincing you to cover your food from flies?

The poster focuses on a single, narrow topic—why you should cover your food.

The balance of words, images, and white space is a bit off—the text dominates the poster.

The poster has more text than is typical.

The type size is large enough to be read at a distance.

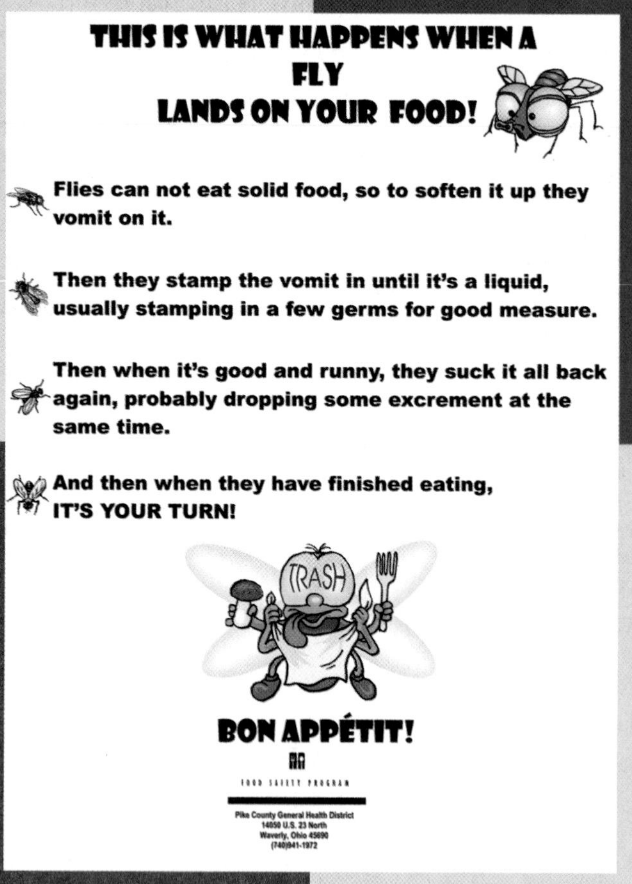

THIS IS WHAT HAPPENS WHEN A
FLY
LANDS ON YOUR FOOD!
Flies can not eat solid food, so to soften it up they vomit on it.
Then they stamp the vomit in until it's a liquid, usually stamping in a few germs for good measure.
Then when it's good and runny, they suck it all back again, probably dropping some excrement at the same time.
And then when they have finished eating,
IT'S YOUR TURN!
TRASH
BON APPÉTIT!
FOOD SAFETY PROGRAM
Pike County General Health District
14050 U.S. 23 North
Waverly, Ohio 45690
(740)941-1972

QUESTIONS FOR WRITING AND DISCUSSION: LEARNING OUTCOMES

Rhetorical Knowledge: The Writer's Situation and Rhetoric

1. **Audience:** Who is the audience for this poster about flies on food?
2. **Purpose:** What is the purpose of describing what happens when flies land on food?
3. **Voice and tone:** What attitude does the Pike County General Health District seem to display in this educational poster?
4. **Responsibility:** How does this poster demonstrate that the Pike County General Health District takes its responsibilities seriously?
5. **Context, format and genre:** Why does the image appear after most of the words in this poster? Why is an educational poster an appropriate genre for this topic?

Critical Thinking: The Writer's Ideas and Your Personal Response

6. What did you learn from this educational poster?
7. After reading this educational poster, how likely are you to follow the advice at the bottom of the poster?

Composing Processes and Knowledge of Conventions: The Writer's Strategies

8. How might this educational poster be improved by changing (location, size, and so on) the words, images, and white space?

Inquiry and Research: Ideas for Further Exploration

9. Conduct a Web search to learn more about the effects of flies' landing on your food.

Writing Processes

As you work on your assignment, revisit the qualities of an effective cause-and-effect paper (see pages 319–320), and remember that the writing process is recursive—that is, writers move back and forth among all of the activities. After you engage in invention strategies and conduct some research, you may start writing, or you may decide to do some more research.

For a tip on organizing your computer files, see page 70.

Invention: Getting Started

connect
mhconnectcomposition.com
Drafting and Revising QL10005

As you work, try to answer these questions:

- What do I already know about this event, phenomenon, or trend?
- What do I know about its cause(s) or effect(s)?
- Where can I learn more about the causal relationships involved? What relevant personal experiences or observations can I contribute?
- What might my audience already know about the cause-and-effect relationship I am exploring?
- What might my audience's point of view be?
- What questions do I have? What do I want and need to find out?

As with any kind of writing, invention activities improve with peer feedback and suggestions. Consider sharing the invention work you have done so far with several classmates or friends in order to understand your rhetorical situation more clearly and to generate more useful information.

EXAMPLES OF INVENTION

Writing Activity

Brainstorming

Brainstorming is an invention technique that can help you focus your causal analysis and come up with possible causes and/or effects. Working with the questions above, spend a few minutes writing everything you can think of about the causal relationship you plan to discuss. Don't worry about putting this information into sentences or paragraphs; simply record it using any words that come to mind.

Deborah Schlegel's Brainstorming

Deborah Schlegel became interested in the topic of global warming in her environmental studies class. She decided to write a cause-and-effect essay about global warming in response to Scenario 1 (see page 315). Schlegel began by brainstorming to focus her topic and to choose whether to look at the causes of global warming, its effects, or both:

- Could global warming be caused by too much heat on the planet, whether that comes from the sun or from humans or animals?
- There was something a few years ago about the stuff they used for air conditioning in homes and cars and buildings—Freon?—that ruined the ozone layer, the part of our atmosphere that keeps some of the warming things away from Earth.
- NASA had some reports showing how the ozone layer was changing, shrinking. There's also something like higher greenhouse gas production.
- I wonder what governments might do about global warming?
- What can the average person do?
- How does global warming affect people, ecosystems, etc.?
- Are there any positive effects from global warming, or are all of its effects negative?
- It seems to me that someone thinks that global warming is a good idea, but only if your community isn't on the ocean, where it will be flooded!

Exploring Your Ideas with Research

Usually, when you are writing about cause-and-effect relationships, you will need to provide evidence to support your claims. Although you may be able to draw on your own experience to provide evidence, you will also need to offer verifiable information such as facts, statistics, expert testimony, experimental results, and examples. For instance, if you were writing about cause-and-effect relationships in the areas of health or safety, two good sources of information are the Centers for Disease Control and the U.S. Department of Transportation, both of which have Web sites filled with reliable information.

To find evidence from outside of your own experience, you will need to do research to answer questions such as the following:

- What facts or other verifiable information will provide solid evidence that a cause-and-effect relationship actually exists? Where can I find this information? What sources will be most reliable?
- What expert testimony can I provide to support my thesis about causes or effects, or both? What authorities might I interview?
- What statistical data support my contention that a cause-and-effect relationship exists?
- How can I best explain the data to my readers so that (1) they can easily understand them and (2) my evidence supports my conclusions?

The subject you focus on, and the kind of essay you are constructing, helps to determine the kind of research you conduct. For example, you could conduct several kinds of research:

- For Scenario 1, in which you focus on a topic in one of your courses, interviewing classmates, professors, and/or administrators is a useful way to learn about different perspectives.
- For Scenario 2, in which you create a poster, look at posters on and off campus. Which are particularly effective?

As we have seen, Deborah Schlegel already had an interest in global warming when she began her cause-and-effect assignment. She wanted to explore this topic in more depth and detail. At her college library, she searched the library's newspaper index for sources using the keywords "global warming" and "ice age," and found some newspaper articles that might be helpful. Sources she located included the following newspaper article:

"Atlantic Surf Seekers Get Big Chill." *Arizona Republic*. 4 November 2003. B10.

She also conducted a Web search using the search engine Google and found more information. Her sources included news organizations like the Cable News Network (CNN):

"Study Hints at Extreme Climate Change." CNN. 28 October 1999. 1 November 2003 <http://www.cnn.com/NATURE/9910/28/climate.change.enn/>.

After researching, Schlegel had information that she could use to formulate a thesis, or main idea, about what causes global warming and what its effects might be.

Writing Activity

Conducting Research

What sources could help you answer the questions you have about your topic and formulate a working thesis? The following questions will help you focus your research:

- What do you already know about the subject from your invention work?
- What cause-and-effect connections can you make?
- For what cause-and-effect connections do you need to provide some evidence?
- Whom might you quote as an expert?
- Where can you find statistics that will support your claim?
- Where might you look for more information and evidence?

Reviewing Your Invention and Research

After you have conducted your research, review your invention work and the information you collected from outside sources. Once you have a general idea of the cause(s) and/or effect(s) your research is leading you to, try to develop what is called a *working thesis statement:* If you had to explain the cause-and-effect relationship now, based on what you have learned, what would it be? Through the process of writing itself, you will learn more about your topic and possible cause-and-effect relationships, so you will modify and develop the working thesis statement as you draft and revise your text.

Writing Activity

Concept Mapping

Concept mapping takes clustering a step further and is especially useful for cause-and-effect papers because it helps you see the relationships between causes and their possible effects. Concept mapping asks you to show connections or relationships, so constructing such a map is an especially a useful invention activity for a cause-and-effect paper.

EXAMPLES OF INVENTION

Brainstorming (pp. 158, 332)
Freewriting (pp. 114, 245, 383)
Criteria (p. 290)
Listing (p. 72)
Answers to Reporter's Questions (p. 244)
Organization (pp. 75, 164)
Clustering (pp. 114, 289)
Concept Mapping (p. 335)
Interviewing (p. 203)
Research (pp. 115, 160, 205, 246, 292, 384)
Reflection (p. 12)

Deborah Schlegel's Concept Mapping

To clarify for herself—and perhaps for readers—the causal chain leading from global warming to an ice age, Deborah Schlegel looked over the research she had conducted and constructed the following concept map.

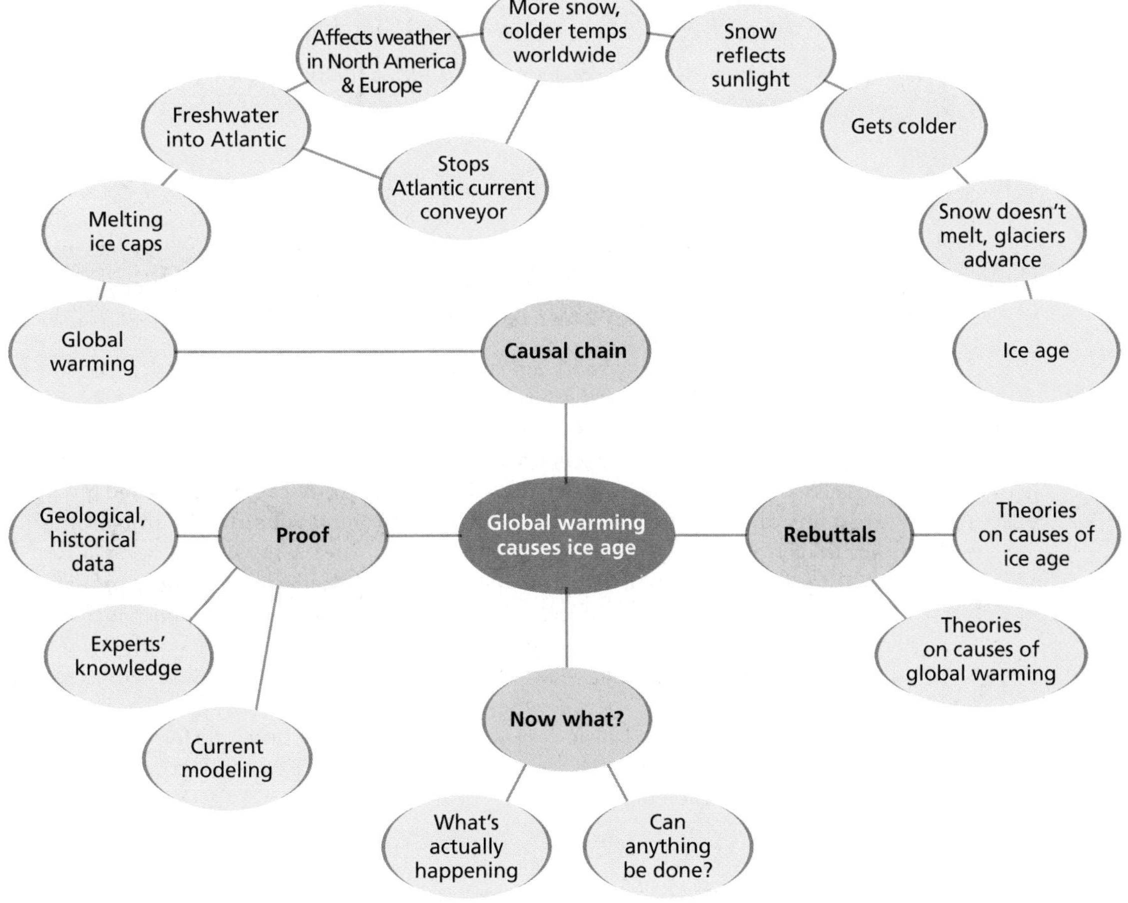

Writing Activity

Considering Your Research and Focusing Your Ideas

Examine the notes you have made based on your research. Then, using the *who, what, where, when, why,* and *how* questions as a starting point, see what information you have. For example, if you were working on a brochure for a campus club you are involved with, here are the kinds of questions you might ask to get started on your brochure:

- **Who:** Who are the members (or perhaps the officers) of your club, and why are they involved? Who is a reader of your brochure, and why should that reader be involved with your club?
- **What:** What activities is your club involved with? What happens at your meetings? What benefits are there to being a member of your group?
- **Where:** Where do you meet? (A photo might be useful here.)
- **When:** When do you meet? How often and for how long?
- **Why:** What is the purpose of your club??
- **How:** How does your group do what it does? Are there dues, and what do they pay for?

A WRITER'S *Responsibility* | Determining True Causes and Effects

Events that happen at the same time may or may not be related causally—be sure you are not asserting a relationship that does not in fact exist, or mistaking a cause for an effect, or vice versa. An ethical writer works diligently to avoid the logical fallacy of *post hoc, ergo propter hoc,* a Latin phrase meaning "after this, therefore because of this." If you argue that X caused Y simply because X preceded Y, you are guilty of this logical fallacy. What are some examples of *post hoc, ergo propter hoc* thinking that you have recently witnessed?

Often, in cases where two events happen at the same time and are probably causally related, it still may not be obvious which is the cause and which is the effect. For instance, educational experts have observed that students with low self-esteem often underperform in school. But do people who have low self-esteem perform poorly in school because they have low self-esteem, as has been assumed in the past? Or do they have low self-esteem because they perform poorly in school, as some psychologists now believe? A responsible writer needs to consider both of these possibilities.

Organizing Your Cause-and-Effect Paper

Once you have a working thesis and supporting evidence for your cause-and-effect paper, you need to consider how you might organize your text. The questions to ask yourself are all rhetorical:

- Who is the audience for your paper?
- Why might they be interested in your reasoning about causes and/or effects, or how can you make them interested in it?
- What is your purpose for writing—that is, why do your readers need to understand this cause-and-effect relationship? What will your readers learn about your subject by reading your paper?

Once you have determined your purpose, you can choose the organizational approach that is best suited to it. Here are three possible organizational approaches that you might choose for your paper.

Options FOR Organization

Organizing a Cause-and-Effect Essay

Identify an Effect and Then Determine Its Cause(s)	Identify a Cause and Then Determine Its Effect(s)	Determine a Series of Causes and Effects
Introduce the effect.	Introduce the cause.	Introduce one of the causes or one of the effects.
Explain the importance of the effect.	Explain the importance of the cause.	Explain the importance of the cause or the effect that you have identified.
List possible causes.	List possible effects.	List possible causes and effects.
Assert probable cause-and-effect relationship(s).	Assert probable cause-and-effect relationship(s).	Assert probable chain of causes and effects.
Note that there may be several causes.	Note that there may be several effects.	Provide evidence to support your claim about series of causes and effects.
Provide evidence to support your claim about cause-and-effect relationship(s).	Provide evidence to support your claim about cause-and-effect relationship(s).	Address skeptics' doubts.
Address skeptics' doubts—others say these causes do not cause the effect, so address those objections.	If others might see different effects from your cause, address their objections.	Conclude by summarizing the cause-and-effect relationships you discussed in your paper.
Conclude by summarizing the cause-and-effect relationships you discussed in your paper.	Conclude by summarizing the cause-and-effect relationships you discussed in your paper.	

Constructing a Complete Draft

Once you have chosen the most effective organizational approach for your audience and purpose, you are ready to construct the rest of your draft. As you work, keep the following in mind:

- Draw on your invention work and your research. If necessary, do more invention work and/or more research.
- As you try out tentative ideas about possible causes and/or possible effects, ask peers about what they consider necessary to support your ideas.
- Ask yourself and peers whether visuals might help make your case.

For more on constructing visuals, see Chapter 18.

INTEGRATING SOURCES

Synthesizing and Integrating Sources into Your Draft: Summarizing Information from Sources

When considering cause-and-effect relationships, effective writers integrate a variety of sources into their texts to support their claims. Although writers can quote or paraphrase source material, they often find it helpful to summarize source information about cause-and-effect relationships because such explanations can be too long to integrate effectively as quotations or paraphrases. As noted on pages 565–566 in Chapter 20, summaries need to encapsulate others' ideas accurately and concisely.

On pages 348–355 in this chapter, writer Deborah Schlegel quotes, paraphrases, and summarizes source material in her essay on global warming. When she summarizes source material, she clearly strives to be accurate and concise, as illustrated in the following passage (paragraph 4) from her essay:

> When temperatures heat up, increased amounts of freshwater enter the northern Atlantic Ocean. This effect happens for two reasons. First, the warmer temperatures cause the Arctic ice cap and the sea ice that surrounds it to melt. Second, runoff into the ocean increases, caused by increased rain and snow in the northern latitudes of North America. NASA's Earth Observing System (EOS) science report ("The Earth Observing System Science Plan") points to the models on global climate change, all showing that these are the two ways global warming will cause the amount of freshwater entering the Atlantic Ocean to increase. Clearly, increased global temperatures cause an increase in freshwater entering the Atlantic Ocean.

Notice how the summary includes a source citation, enclosed in parentheses to set it off from Schlegel's words. The citation indicates to readers that this paragraph is a summary of someone else's words and ideas, rather than Schlegel's original ideas. Further, in the paragraph's last sentence, Schlegel emphasizes the point of the summary, explaining how it supports her claim.

In short, when you summarize and integrate others' ideas into your texts, aim to do the following:

- Concisely condense the source material.
- Accurately encapsulate the information in the source material.
- Cite the source of the information.
- Indicate how the summary supports your claim(s).

Parts of a Complete Draft

Introduction: To write an introduction that captures readers' attention, you might want to try one of the following strategies:

connect
mhconnectcomposition.com
Introductory paragraph overview QL10006

- **Give your audience a reason for being interested by vividly portraying how this topic makes a difference in their lives.**
- **Make a statement that suggests the unexpected.** Juan Williams uses this strategy in "The Ruling That Changed America" (page 321):

  Fifty years later, the *Brown* decision looks different. At a distance from the volcanic heat of May 17, 1954, the real impact of the legal, political, and cultural eruption that changed America is not exactly what it first appeared to be.
- **Examine a surprising causal relationship (that you can substantiate) to hold an audience's interest.**

Body: There are many strategies you can use to show cause and effect. In the body of your causal analysis, you may list and discuss possible causes and effects. You will likely also refute skeptics' claims. For example, in a causal analysis on the dangers of smoking, you might note that while many smokers may feel their habit endangers only themselves, research data indicates the harmful effects of second-hand smoke. You could then present the data as evidence.

Digital Literacy — Using Graphics and Video to Explain Cause-and-Effect Relationships

Graphics, and even video, can help you explain complex cause-and-effect relationships. If your instructor allows, see if you can find a short video clip (one to three minutes long) that shows the causal relationship you are explaining. Many Web search engines include video searches. Or you might explore a large video site such as YouTube (http://youtube.com). If you have access to a digital video camera or own a video-capable cell phone or smart phone, you can create a short video clip yourself. For example, if you are writing about the effects of proper grip, motion, and follow-through on curveball execution in baseball, you could ask a campus baseball player to demonstrate while you record video of various techniques. Consider recording a voice-over that explains the movements involved.

connect
mhconnectcomposition.com
Concluding paragraph overview QL10007

Conclusion: In your conclusion, you need to reinforce the connections between the causes and effects that you have established. Do not assume your reader will make the same connections you have. Ask yourself the following questions:

- How effectively have you shown that the effect was a result of the cause?
- How well have you tied together all of the different ideas you have been working with?
- How clearly have you articulated your perspective so your audience has no doubt about what you have been trying to prove?
- Have you given your reader a sense of closure?

Title: As you construct your cause-and-effect paper, a title should emerge at some point—often late in the process. The title should reflect the cause-and-effect claim that you are considering.

VISUALIZING *Variations* | Choosing Visuals That Illustrate Cause-and-Effect Relationships

If preparing a causal analysis for a civic or professional writing situation, you will often need to present the results of your analysis to a group. If preparing an oral presentation using either *PowerPoint* slides or transparencies, what content would you need to include, and how would you format it? Consider:

- Slides allow you to "show" as well as "tell." What information will you "show" and what will you "tell"?
- How can you use graphics most effectively?
- Your writing is very visible on slides. Have you edited carefully?
- Programs for creating presentation slides often provide options for background templates. How can you pick a background that will complement your slides?

For more on oral presentations, including the use of PowerPoint, see Chapter 16.

For example, for a presentation to a civic association, consider how to format an overhead transparency showing an increase in the number of bicycle/pedestrian accidents during the past year. You might start with plain black type:

In the past year, bicycle/pedestrian accidents have increased 70%

You could add shading to highlight the most important part of the sentence:

In the past year, bicycle/pedestrian accidents have increased 70%

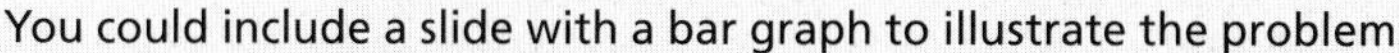

You could include a slide with a bar graph to illustrate the problem:

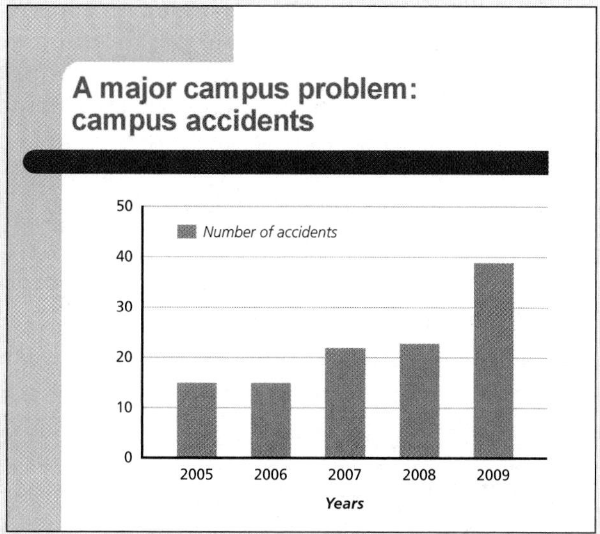

For any visual that you are considering, ask yourself the following questions:

- What does this visual show about the cause-and-effect relationship?
- How do I select a chart or graph that will support a point I want to make?
- What other visuals might show that a cause-and-effect relationship exists?

Writing Activity

Constructing a Full Draft

After reviewing your notes and research and invention activities, and carefully considering all of the information that you have generated, you are ready to construct a first complete draft, using the organizational approach that you have decided on. Remember that your thinking about the nature of the cause-and-effect relationship may evolve as you draft your paper, so your ideas will most likely change as you compose the first draft of your essay.

As you draft, keep in mind that you are proving that something occurred as a direct result of something else. Make sure you have support for your claims about cause-and-effect relationships.

There is no one right way to start composing. However, if you have an organizational plan that you are comfortable with, you might begin by filling in parts of the sections that you feel best about or those where you feel you have the best information. You can always put everything together later.

An Excerpt from Deborah Schlegel's First Draft

In this excerpt from her first draft, note how Deborah Schlegel incorporates evidence from a variety of sources to prove her claim. As she wrote, Schlegel did not worry about grammar, punctuation, and mechanics; instead, she concentrated on getting her main ideas onto paper. (The numbers in circles refer to peer comments—see pages 345–346.)

Global Warming
Deborah Schlegel

The arguments are endless over what is causing our global temperatures to rise. Is it higher amounts of green house gases such as CO_2 and aerosols in the atmosphere caused by man? Or is it something totally unavoidable such as where we are in the sunspot cycle or the increased solar output of our Sun? How does this affect all of us?①

The Earth's oceans are ringed by several ocean currents linked together forming what is called the Global Ocean Conveyor. Like the conveyor belt this brings to mind, these currents move water around the globe cooling the atmosphere above them when they're carrying cold water on the surface and warming the atmosphere when they carry warm surface water. This giant conveyor belt is driven by very cold, very salty water that sinks to the bottom of the ocean and creeps along slowly—moving also the water above it. . . .

Stopping the Global Ocean Conveyer means there will no longer be warm surface water arriving from the equatorial regions and the Caribbean. The jet stream will no longer be able to pick up warm air to distribute over Europe, causing that area to become colder. The jet stream will be delivering colder air to each point east of Europe—Northern Asia and the Northern Pacific. Onshore winds will no longer be warming the East Coast of North America—that area will become colder. In a snowballing effect, because the jet stream will be passing over colder water and colder landmasses, the weather everywhere will be affected. Any place that currently depends on warming from ocean currents, directly or indirectly, will become colder.②

Those who've lived in northern climates where it snows all winter know once it snows, the temperatures go down further and stay down. With no warm winds coming, the same thing will happen in our story. To make matters worse, the snow that stays on the ground will reflect sunlight back up making the temperatures even colder. This surface reflection of incoming solar radiation is called albedo. NASA's Earth Observing System satellites have measured the albedo value of non-melting snow-covered surfaces at 80% to 90% (Goddard Space Center 264). This means that 80% to 90% of the sunlight falling on these snow-covered areas will reflect back into space, leaving only 10% to 20% of the heat. And remember that we now have many more regions of the Earth covered with snow than we used to. The reflection of sunlight causes temperatures to fall even further—it's called a vicious cycle.

Now we get to the ice age part. When snow keeps falling, it packs down, becoming ice. The more snow, the more the ice thickens. As the ice thickens, more stress is put on the deep ice. When enough stress is placed on it, the ice will begin to move or flow—it will advance. In fact, this is the definition of a glacier—an ice sheet that advances. An ice age is declared when widespread glaciers advance. In our story, we are now in an ice age. . . .

The first group of disbelievers falls into the "it isn't what we've traditionally thought causes ice ages, so this new theory can't be trusted" category. Every new theory in science since Galileo announced the sun didn't travel around the Earth has had to deal with this group.③ Past theories of ice age causes include events that put a lot of dust and particles into the atmosphere thus blocking out the sun (massive volcanic eruptions or increased space dust from meteors and/or comets), less energy from the sun reaching the earth (from variations in the Earth's orbit, lessened solar output, or changes in the Earth's tilt), or events that block ocean and air currents such as the shifting of the continental plates or massive mountain ranges like the Himalayas lifting up.

The other group of critics questions whether the specific models used in predicting the events in our story will in fact lead to an ice age or questions whether any model could predict such a complex event that is in the future. It is true that computer models are only as good as the data being used in them. So there are several points we want to make sure are present in any model we consider the validity of. Was the research done by a scientifically reputable institution? Was it published in a scientifically reputable journal? Were the results of the model replicated by other reputable institutions? . . .

Dr. Richard Alley, a professor of geosciences at Pennsylvania State University says that Global Ocean Conveyer disruptions and sudden climate changes are ". . . nothing new—only the realization that they have occurred" (Wood). He states that while we used to think climate changes, like aging, happened gradually, recent studies of ice cores dating back 100,000 years ago show sudden shifts. "Large, abrupt and widespread climate changes occurred repeatedly in the past across most of the Earth, and followed closely after freshening of the North Atlantic" (Wood).

It is true we can't predict the future with absolute certainty, but we can look at past trends and see where we might be going. Where are we now? And we continue to see increases in those factors that may cause the currents to stop. The Geophysical Fluid Dynamics Lab found CO_2 levels are continuing to rise 0.4% per year and have risen 28% since preindustrial times indicating continued global warming ("Climate Impact"). A Danish study from the University of Bremen found a decrease in the amount of Arctic sea ice each year since 1978, with 2002 seeing the smallest amount of ice observed for at least 100 years (Kaleschke). The melting of this sea ice is a continuing source of fresh water for the North Atlantic.

All of this means that we—all human beings, everywhere on earth—may be in for some serious climate changes, and that those changes will be more negative than positive.❹

Revising

Once you have a draft, put it aside for a day or so. This break will give you the chance to come back to your text as a new reader might. Read through and revise your work, looking especially for ideas that are not explained completely, terms that are not defined, and other problem areas. As you revise your early drafts, hold off on doing a great deal of heavy editing.

When you reread the first draft of your paper, here are some questions to ask yourself:

- How effectively have I explained my thesis so the reader knows what I intend to prove?
- What else might my audience want or need to know about my subject?
- How else might I interest my audience in my causal analysis?
- What did I find out about my subject that I did not include in my causal analysis?
- Have I clearly explained and defined any terms my readers might not know?
- Would any aspects of my causal analysis be more effective if presented visually?

Technology can help you revise and edit your writing more easily. Use your word processor's track-changes tool to try out revisions and editing changes. After you've had time to think about the possible changes, you can "accept" or "reject" them. Also, you can use your word processor's comment tool to write reminders to yourself when you get stuck with a revision or some editing task.

WRITER'S *Workshop* | Responding to Full Drafts

Working with one or two classmates, read each paper and offer comments and questions that will help each of you see your paper's strengths and weaknesses. Consider the following questions as you do:

- What is your first impression of this draft? How effectively does the title draw you into the paper? Why? What part(s) of the text are especially effective for showing a cause-and-effect relationship?
- How well does the writer stay on track? If he or she loses focus, where does it happen?
- How logical is the paper? What strengths and weaknesses do you see in the writer's logic?
- How effective is the introduction? What suggestions can you make to improve the introduction?
- What do you think is the author's thesis or main point? How could it be expressed or supported more effectively?
- In the main part of the paper, are there parts that need more explanation? Where would you like more details or examples?
- How credible is the writer's case that a relationship exists? How credible are his or her sources?
- Might visuals such as charts, tables, graphs, or photographs help the writer to explain or support his or her claims about causes and/or effects more simply and clearly?
- How clearly and effectively does the writer present any opposing points of view on this subject? How effectively does he or she answer opposing viewpoints?
- What could be added or changed to make the conclusion more effective? To what extent does it make you want to learn more about this topic?
- What are the main weaknesses of this paper?—How might the writer improve the text?

Student Comments on Deborah Schlegel's First Draft

Using the questions above, Deborah Schlegel's classmates made some suggestions on her first draft. Below are comments she received, keyed to the first draft on pages 342–344:

1. "I suggest that you provide more information after your first paragraph, to give us more background on how the climate works and how do we know that?"
2. "This is pretty informal, especially the use of 'we.' I realize that you're trying to 'draw your readers in' to make them interested in your paper—how else might you do so?"

3. "It was Copernicus, not Galileo, who first suggested the earth moves around the sun. Make sure your facts are right!"
4. "Interesting and thoughtful first draft, with good quotations to support your claims. I'd like to read even more on the human causes of global warming and climate change. Are there any illustrations that you found in your research that might help readers *see* what you mean?"

Responding to Readers' Comments

Once they have received feedback on their writing from peers, teachers, friends, and others, writers have to figure out what to do with that feedback. Because your writing is your responsibility, you must determine how to deal with reader responses to your work. For example, how might you deal with this reader's comment that Deborah Schlegel received on her paper?

> "Interesting and thoughtful first draft, with good quotations to support your claims. I'd like to read even more on the human causes of global warming and climate change. Are there any illustrations that you found in your research that might help readers *see* what you mean?"

One way Schlegel could have responded was to do just what the reader suggested: to find and add some pictures, charts, or tables to *show* what she has in mind.

The first thing to do with any feedback, then, is to consider seriously what your reader has to say. The classmates who read Schlegel's paper:

- Asked for more information and background after the initial paragraph
- Told the writer to get her facts right
- Noted that the tone is fairly informal and wondered how else she might interest readers in the subject of the paper

Schlegel needed to address all of these questions or concerns. As with any feedback, it is important to listen to it carefully and consider what your reader has to say. Then it is up to you, as the author, to decide *how* to come to terms with these suggestions. You may decide to reject some comments, of course; other comments, though, may deserve your attention. You may find that comments from several readers contradict each other. In that case, use your own judgment to decide which reader's comments are on the right track.

In the final version of Schlegel's paper on pages 348–355, you can see how she responded to her reader's comments, as well as to her own review of her first draft.

Knowledge of Conventions

In your college classes, writing about a cause-and-effect relationship is usually academic writing, so you will be required to follow the conventions for an academic essay. Other situations may call for a variety of genres, including memos, essays, blog postings, letters to the editor, and even formal position papers. Such documents often include tables, charts, graphs, or photos. Be aware of the conventions for any genre you use.

Editing

After you revise, you have one more important task—editing and polishing. At the editing stage, make changes to your sentence structures and word choices to improve your style and to make your writing clearer and more concise. Also check your work to make sure it adheres to conventions of grammar, usage, punctuation, mechanics, and spelling. Use the spell-check function of your word-processing program, but be sure to double-check your spelling personally (your computer cannot tell the difference between, say, *compliment* and *complement*). If you have used sources in your paper, make sure you are following the documentation style your instructor requires.

As with overall revision of your work, this final editing and polishing is most effective if you can put your text aside for a few days and come back to it with fresh eyes. We strongly recommend that you ask classmates, friends, and tutors to read your work to find editing problems that you may not see. To assist you with editing, we offer here a round-robin editing activity focused on making sure that subordinate clauses are attached to independent clauses.

connect
mhconnectcomposition.com
Revising and Editing overview (also Drafting) QL10008
Correcting confusing shifts QL10010
Correcting faulty parallelsim QL10011

See Chapter 20 for more on documenting sources using MLA or APA style.

WRITER'S *Workshop* | Round-Robin Editing with a Focus on Subordinate Clauses

Writing about causes and effects benefits from the careful use of **subordinate clauses.** A subordinate clause has a subject and a verb, but it cannot stand on its own because it begins with a subordinating conjunction (such as *although, because, while, if,* or *since*) and is a sentence fragment:

FRAGMENT *Because my car did not start this morning.*

Because subordinate clauses cannot stand on their own, they need to be attached to an independent clause:

SENTENCE *Because my car did not start this morning,* I was late for class.

or

SENTENCE I was late for class *because my car did not start this morning.*

Working with several classmates, look for the subordinate clauses in your papers, and make sure they are attached to independent clauses. If you are uncertain about a specific convention for using subordinate clauses, consult a handbook or ask your instructor.

ROUND-ROBIN EDITING WITH A FOCUS ON

Genres, Documentation, and Format

For advice on writing in different genres, see the Online Appendix. For guidelines for formatting and documenting papers in MLA or APA style, see Chapter 20.

If you are writing an academic paper in response to Scenario 1, follow the conventions appropriate for the discipline in which you are writing and the requirements of your instructor. However, if you are responding to Scenario 2, follow the guidelines for educational posters so that it meets the needs and requirements of your intended audience.

If you have used material from outside sources, including visuals, give credit to those sources, using the documentation style required by the discipline you are working in and by your instructor.

A Writer Shares Her Causal Analysis: Deborah Schlegel's Final Draft

Below is Deborah Schlegel's finished cause-and-effect paper. Note that she has addressed the questions and concerns that her classmates had, adding information and examples based on their suggestions.

DEBORAH SCHLEGEL

CADEMIC RESEARCH REPORT

Weather Forecast: Bikinis or Parkas?

One classmate wrote to Schlegel the following comment:

I suggest that you provide more information after your first paragraph, to give us more background on how the climate works and how do we know that?

In her final draft, Schlegel provides significant background.

Climate researchers have recently come up with good and bad news about the global warming crisis. The good news first—maybe it wasn't such a bad idea to move to hot Phoenix after all, and we may not have to worry about global warming. The bad news? Teenagers may have spent too much money on summer clothes. A growing number of scientists are warning that global warming may cause really big-time global cooling—an ice age. 1

To understand how this seeming contradiction could happen, we'll follow a path that leads from the Arctic ice cap to the Atlantic Ocean and around the world on the same ocean current the turtles rode in *Finding Nemo*. But first we start with the current crisis, global warming. I also want to note that while some politicians do *not* believe that global warming is a real and serious problem, the majority of scientists—the great majority—are positive that the earth is warming up, and that humans are a primary cause of global warming. 2

The arguments are endless over what is causing our global temperatures to rise. Is it the higher amounts of greenhouse gases such as CO_2 and 3 aerosols in the atmosphere caused by humans? Is it the higher amounts of greenhouse gases like methane being pumped into the atmosphere by the large numbers of cows living on this planet? Or is it something totally unavoidable, such as where we are in the sunspot cycle or the increased solar output of our sun? Whatever the causes are, temperatures are rising, and it is this increase that is the beginning of the story.

When temperatures heat up, increased amounts of freshwater enter the northern Atlantic Ocean. This effect happens for two reasons. First, the warmer temperatures cause the Arctic ice cap and the sea ice that surrounds it to melt. Second, runoff into the ocean increases, caused by increased rain and snow in the northern latitudes of North America. NASA's Earth Observing System (EOS) science report ("The Earth Observing System Science Plan") points to the models on global climate change, all showing that these are the two ways global warming will cause the amount of freshwater entering the Atlantic Ocean to increase. Clearly, increased global temperatures cause an increase in freshwater entering the Atlantic Ocean. 4

Earth's oceans are ringed by several ocean currents linked together, forming what is called the Global Ocean Conveyor. Like a conveyor belt, these currents move water around the globe, cooling the atmosphere above them when they're carrying cold water on the surface and warming the atmosphere when they carry warm surface water. This giant conveyor belt is driven by very cold, very salty water that sinks to the bottom of the ocean and creeps along slowly—also moving the water above it. The turtles in the film *Finding Nemo* rode a portion of the Global Ocean Conveyor that slides around Australia and down its east coast (not as quickly as shown in the movie, but then, that was fiction). The portion of this conveyor in the Atlantic, the Gulf Stream, is an important force in driving the whole system. 5

How fast the Gulf Stream moves is determined by thermohaline circulation—what the temperature of the water is (thermo-) and how salty it is (-haline). Ideally, the Gulf Stream brings warm, salty water from the equatorial and Caribbean regions up to the North Atlantic. There the winds of the jet stream, moving from west to east, take out a fair amount of the heat and move it to the North Atlantic regions and Europe. The journal *Natural Science* likens the amount of heat sent on via the jet stream ". . . to the total energy output of a million nuclear power plants" ("A New European Ice Age?"). That's why Europe has such balmy temperatures for its latitude. London is as far north as Moscow, the Aleutian Islands and Edmonton, Canada. Rome shares its latitude, but not its Mediterranean weather, with Upper Mongolia and northern Montana. The East Coast of the United States also benefits from warmer temperatures through this heat transfer. 6

One of Schlegel's peers wondered about using other strategies besides the word "we."

This is pretty informal, especially the use of "we." I realize that you're trying to "draw your readers in" to make them interested in your paper—how else might you do so?

While Schlegel still sometimes uses the word *we*, she also engages her readers by asking questions.

As the surface water of the Gulf Stream cools, it becomes denser, sinks to a depth of about two kilometers, and begins its slow progress around 7 the world. As the dense water leaves an area, it pulls in new water from the equatorial and Caribbean regions, and the cycle continues. That is, the cycle continues as long as the water traveling north becomes denser and sinks. However, an increase in cold, freshwater entering the North Atlantic cools the surface temperatures and, because it's freshwater, makes the ocean currents less salty. Cooler surface temperatures and less salty currents, in turn, cause a slowdown in the Gulf Stream. If there is a lot of cold, freshwater, the surface temperatures no longer have enough heat to transfer to the jet stream as it passes over, nor are the waters salty enough to sink and continue driving the Global Ocean Conveyer. The Global Ocean Conveyer could stop. No more nice winters for London, Rome, and the rest of Europe. But that's not all.

The end of the Global Ocean Conveyer would mean an end to warm 8
surface water arriving from the equatorial regions and the Caribbean. The jet stream would no longer be able to pick up warm air to distribute over Europe, causing that area to become colder. The jet stream would be delivering colder air to each point east of Europe—Northern Asia and the Northern Pacific. Onshore winds would no longer be warming the East Coast of North America—that area would become colder. Because the jet stream would be passing over colder water and colder landmasses, the weather everywhere would be affected. Any place that currently depends on warming from ocean currents, directly or indirectly, would become colder.

The results of these colder temperatures when winter comes would 9
be devastating. The North Atlantic regions, the British Isles, Europe, Japan, and the Pacific Northwest normally receive heavy rains in the winter. If their winter temperatures were colder, this precipitation would fall instead as snow. Snow would fall in many places that had never or rarely seen it previously. Snow stays on the ground during the entire winter in the northern latitudes, waiting for the warm winds of spring (called chinooks in the northern United States and Canada) to melt it. But without a Global Ocean Conveyor, the system that transfers warm temperatures from the tropics to the northern climates via the ocean currents would no longer exist. So this snow would stay on the ground.

Those who've lived in northern climates, where it snows all winter, 10
know that once it snows, the temperatures go down further and stay down. With no warm winds coming, the same effect would happen in the scenario just described. To make matters worse, the snow on the ground would reflect sunlight back up, making the temperatures even colder. This surface reflection of incoming solar radiation is called *albedo*. NASA's Earth Observing System satellites have measured the albedo value of non-melt-

ing snow-covered surfaces at 80% to 90% ("The Earth Observing System Science Plan"). This means that 80% to 90% of the sunlight falling on these snow-covered areas will reflect back into space, leaving only 10% to 20% of the heat. With many more regions of the Earth covered with snow, the reflection of sunlight would cause temperatures to fall even further in a vicious cycle. Snow and ice would also act as an insulating blanket to keep ground temperatures cold. It takes a large amount of energy to warm up this insulated blanket, but that energy would no longer be available.

When snow keeps falling, it packs down, becoming ice. The more snow, the thicker the ice. As the ice thickens, more stress is put on the deep ice. When enough stress is placed on it, the ice begins to move or flow—it advances. In fact, this is the definition of a glacier—an ice sheet that advances. An ice age occurs when widespread glaciers advance. In our scenario, we would now be in an ice age. 11

You shouldn't sell off your tank tops and shorts yet, though. Not everyone in the scientific community agrees with this scenario. In fact, scientists have never agreed on a cause for the ice ages that have occurred in the past. Because no one was recording and preserving data then, we have no record of the events leading up to the ice ages or the events that caused them to end. What scientists do have is physical evidence—clues they can put together and run through computer models to see how they relate to what's happening in our climate today. 12

One group of disbelievers argues that this new theory isn't what we've traditionally thought causes ice ages, so it can't be trusted. Every new theory in science since Copernicus announced that the sun doesn't travel around the Earth has confronted similar resistence. Past theories of the causes of ice ages include the occurrence of massive volcanic eruptions or increased amounts of space dust from meteors or comets, events that put large amounts of dust and particles into the atmosphere and block out the sun; decreases in the amount of the sun's energy reaching the earth caused by variations in Earth's orbit, lessened solar output, or changes in the Earth's tilt; or events that block ocean and air currents such as the shifting of the continental plates or the lifting up of massive mountain ranges like the Himalayas. These theories all have problems. An ice age has not followed every time one of these events has occurred, and some ice ages have occurred without any of these events happening first. If any of these theories are valid, they must be only a part of the picture, not the main contributing factor. 13

A student reader caught an error of fact:

It was Copernicus, not Galileo, who first suggested the earth moves around the sun. Make sure your facts are right!

Like any good researcher, Schlegel makes sure all her facts are correct in her final draft.

Another group of critics questions whether the specific models used to predict the events in our scenario indicate that our current situation will in fact lead to an ice age. These critics question whether any model could predict such a complex future event. Computer models are only as good as the data being used in them, so before accepting the results of 14 these models we must consider the validity of the research. Was it done by a scientifically reputable institution? Was it published in a reputable, peer-reviewed journal? Were the results of the model replicated by other reputable institutions?

15 In considering possible causes of ice ages, we have good sources of computer modeling. Several studies looking at the effects of global warming have come up with models that support a global cooling. The government-funded Geophysical Fluid Dynamics Lab working with Princeton University has used a computer model to look at the effects on our climate of CO_2 increases. The global warming that resulted led to a shutdown of the Global Ocean Conveyor. The model indicated that this shutdown would occur within a decade and that the conveyor would take several centuries to recover (Raphael). Scientists at the Physics Institute of the University of Bern in Switzerland duplicated these results using a different model (Stocker and Schmitter).

16 Researchers at Woods Hole Oceanographic Institute on Cape Cod looked at evidence gathered over the past ten or fifteen years and concluded that we may be heading for the colder climate predicated by our scenario. As the President and Director of the Institute, Dr. Robert B. Gagosian, puts it, ". . . we've seen ominous signs that we may be headed toward a potentially dangerous threshold. If we cross it, Earth's climate could switch gears and jump very rapidly—not gradually—into a completely different mode of operation."

17 Scientists at the Woods Hole Oceanographic Institute found that in the past decade, the North Atlantic waters have become dramatically fresher—they are losing their saltiness (Gagosian). If this trend continues, we may get to see firsthand whether or not the predictions of these models are accurate.

18 While computer climate models have not existed long enough for us to see if their long-term predictions will hold, we can look at evidence we have from past eras and see what happened before previous ice ages occurred. While studying fossilized remains of plankton algae drilled from the bottom of the mid-Atlantic, Scott Lehman and Julian Sachs, former University of Colorado–Boulder researchers now at Columbia University's Barnard College, found that the temperature of the Atlantic dropped prior to the beginning of ice ages and rose prior to their ending. These temperature changes were abrupt and "seem to be almost entirely ocean driven" (qtd. in "Study Hints at Extreme Climate Change"). These temperature changes seem to indicate changes in how the Gulf Stream was distributing warmer water. Lehman and Sachs also note that the "temperatures in the Sargasso Sea during the last ice age fluctuated up to 9 degrees Fahrenheit" (fig. 1).

One classmate had this comment:

I'd like to read even more on the human causes of global warming and climate change. Are there any illustrations that you found in your research that might help readers see what you mean?

One of the ways that Schlegel responded was to include the illustration on the following page.

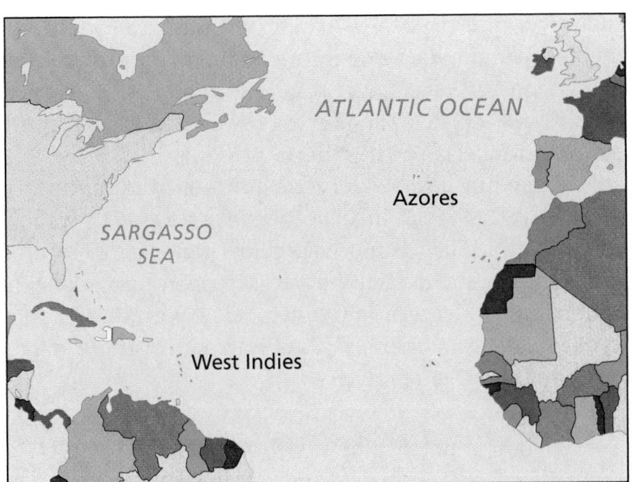

Fig. 1 Temperatures in the Sargasso Sea during the Last Ice Age. "Study Hints at Extreme Climate Change." CNN. 28 Oct. 1999. 1 Nov. 2003. <http://www.cnn.com/NATURE/9910/28/climate.change.enn/>.

19 Dr. Richard Alley, a professor of geosciences at Pennsylvania State University, says that Global Ocean Conveyer disruptions and sudden climate changes are "nothing new—only the realization that they have occurred [is]" (qtd. in Wood). He states that while we used to think climate changes, like aging, happened gradually, recent studies of ice cores dating back 100,000 years show sudden shifts. Alley notes that "large, abrupt and widespread climate changes occurred repeatedly in the past across most of the Earth, and followed closely after freshening of the North Atlantic" (qtd. in Wood).

20 While we can't predict the future with absolute certainty, we can look at past trends and see where we might be going. Where are we now? The Gulf Stream and Global Ocean Conveyor are still running, although one climate scientist, Dr. Andrew Weaver at the University of Victoria in British Columbia, suspects they might be slowing down. His work shows that the Scandinavian Glacier is growing and suggests this may be the result of less warm air reaching that far corner of the North Atlantic (Wood). Records of past climates suggest that when the Gulf Stream stops, it does so within a few decades of the first sign that it is slowing down (Raphael).

21 And we continue to see increases in those factors that may cause the currents to stop. The Geophysical Fluid Dynamics Lab found CO_2 levels are continuing to rise 0.4% per year and have risen 28% since preindustrial

times, indicating continued global warming. A Danish study from the University of Bremen found a decrease in the amount of Arctic sea ice each year since 1978, with 2002 seeing the smallest amount of ice observed for at least 100 years (Kaleschke). The melting of this sea ice is a continuing source of freshwater for the North Atlantic.

So what is happening now? Water temperatures off Atlantic City, New 22
Jersey, were colder in 2003 than in any other year since 1911, when record keeping began ("Atlantic Surf" B10). These colder water temperatures were seen as far south as Florida. In fact, the water temperatures along the East Coast were almost three degrees Fahrenheit below normal. Next time you see a sale on parkas, take another look. And you might want to start selling those tank tops and shorts after all!

This paper follows MLA guidelines for in-text citations and works cited. Note that URLs are optional.

Works Cited

"A New European Ice Age?" *Natural Science*. 1 Nov. 1997. Web. 24 Oct. 2003 <http://naturalscience.com/us/cover/ cover5.html>.

"Atlantic Surf Seekers Get Big Chill." *Arizona Republic*. 4 Nov. 2003. B10. Print.

Gagosian, Robert B. "Triggering Abrupt Climate Change." *Argentinean Foundation for a Scientific Ecology Web Site*. Web. 24 Oct. 2003 <http://mitosyfraudes.8k.com/Calen/ TriggerIceAge.html>.

Kaleschke, Lars. "New Trend of Arctic Sea Ice Decrease?" Sept. 2002. University of Bremen, Denmark. Web. 1 Nov. 2003 <http://iup.physik.uni-bremen.de:8084/decade.html>.

Raphael, Catherine. "Climate Impact of Quadrupling Atmospheric CO_2—An Overview of GFDL Climate Model Results." Geophysical Fluid Dynamics Lab. Web. 24 Oct. 2003 <http://www.gfdl.gov/~tk/climate_dynamics/index.html>.

Stocker, T. F., and A. Schmittner. "Influence of CO_2 Emission Rates on the Stability of the Thermohaline Circulation." 1997 University of Bern, Switzerland. Web. 24 Oct. 2003 <http://www.climate.unibe.ch/~stocker/abstracts/stocker97nat.html>.

"Study Hints at Extreme Climate Change." CNN. Web. 28 Oct. 1999. 1 Nov. 2003 <http://www.cnn.com/NATURE/9910/28/climate.change.enn/>.

"The Earth Observing System Science Plan." Goddard Space Flight Center. 1999. Web. 1 Nov. 2003 <http://eospso.gsfc.nasa.gov/science_plan/>.

"The Great Ice Age." US Department of the Interior/US Geological Survey. Web. 1 Nov. 2003 <http://pubs.usgs.gov/gip/ice_age/ice_age.pdf>.

Weart, Spencer. "Past Cycles: Ice Age Speculations." *The Discovery of Global Warming*. 2003. American Institute of Physics. Web. 24 Oct. 2003 <www.aip.org/history/climate/cycles.htm>.

Wood, Anthony R. "After Mild Winters, a Possible Sea Change." *Philadelphia Inquirer.* 8 Dec. 2002. Web. 1 Nov. 2003 <http://www.philly.com/mld/inquirer/4689103.hrm?template+contentMdules/printstory.jsp>.

QUESTIONS FOR WRITING AND DISCUSSION

Rhetorical Knowledge: The Writer's Situation and Rhetoric

1. **Audience:** Who is the intended audience for this essay?
2. **Purpose:** What is Schlegel's purpose in writing this essay?
3. **Voice and tone:** What tone does Schlegel take in this essay?
4. **Responsibility:** How responsibly has Schlegel written? How effectively does she present and counter opposing viewpoints?
5. **Context, format, and genre:** Schlegel is writing as a student in a first-year writing course. How does this context affect her writing? If Schlegel were writing in a different context, how might her essay change? Schlegel has written an academic research report, which should carefully define a topic and then prove a thesis based on their research. Has she done so?

Critical Thinking: The Writer's Ideas and Your Personal Response

6. What is your initial response to Schlegel's essay?
7. Does Schlegel focus mainly on causes? Effects? A series of causes and effects?

Composing Processes and Knowledge of Conventions: The Writer's Strategies

8. How well do you think Schlegel has researched her topic? How can you tell? What additional research might she have done?
9. What part(s) of Schlegel's essay are the most convincing? Why? The least convincing? Why?

Inquiry and Research: Ideas for Further Exploration

10. Interview several friends about the causes and/or effects of global warming, and record their comments. Write about the similarities and differences that you discover in the comments you have received.

Self-Assessment: Reflecting on Your Goals

Now that you have constructed a piece of writing that explains causes and effects, review your learning goals, which you and your classmates may have considered at the beginning of this chapter (see pages 312–313). To help reflect on the learning goals that you have achieved, respond in writing to the following questions:

Rhetorical Knowledge

- *Audience:* What have you learned about addressing an audience in this kind of writing?
- *Purpose:* What have you learned about the purposes for writing about causes and effects?
- *Rhetorical situation:* How did the writing context affect your writing about cause(s) and/or effect(s)? How did your choice of subject affect the research you conducted?
- *Voice and tone:* How would you describe your voice in this essay? Your tone? How do they contribute to the effectiveness of your writing?
- *Context, medium, and genre:* How did your context determine the medium and genre you chose, and how did those decisions affect your writing?

Critical Thinking, Reading, and Writing

- *Learning/inquiry:* While working on your paper, what did you learn that you might be able to generalize about in the causal relationship you focused on?
- *Responsibility:* How did you show that the effect or effects you wrote about were really the result of the cause or causes you identified?
- *Reading and research:* What did you learn from the reading selections in this chapter? What research did you conduct? What additional research might you have done?
- *Skills:* What skills have you learned while being engaged in this project? How do you hope to develop them further in your next writing project?

Writing Processes

- *Invention:* What invention skills have you learned in writing about causes and effects? Which skills were most useful to you?
- *Organizing your ideas and details:* Describe the process you used to identify the causes and then the effects you wrote about. How did you decide to organize your paper, and how successful was your organization?
- *Revising:* What one revision did you make that you are most satisfied with? If you could go back and make an additional revision, what would it be?

- *Working with peers:* How have you developed your skills in working with peers? How did you make use of feedback you received from both your instructor and your peers? How could your peer readers help you more with your next assignment? How might you help them more, in the future, with the comments and suggestions you make on their texts?
- *Visuals:* Did you use visuals to explain your cause(s) or effect(s) to readers? If so, what did you learn about incorporating these elements?
- *Writing habits:* What "writerly habits" have you developed, modified, or improved on as you constructed the writing assignment for this chapter? How will you change your future writing activities, based on what you have learned about yourself?

Knowledge of Conventions

- *Editing:* What sentence problem did you find most frequently in your writing? How will you avoid that problem in future assignments?
- *Genre:* What conventions of the genre you were using, if any, gave you problems?
- *Documentation:* Did you use sources for your paper? If so, what documentation style did you use? What problems, if any, did you have with it?

mhconnectcomposition.com

Deborah Schlegal Reflects on Her Writing QL10009

If you are constructing a course portfolio, file your written reflections so that you can return to them when you next work on your portfolio. Refer to Chapter 1 (pages 11–12) for a sample reflection by a student.

Writing to Solve Problems

You see, hear, and read about problems and possible solutions to those problems all the time. In developing countries, governments and nongovernmental organizations struggle with problems such as poverty or disease. Closer to home, your community might experience a high dropout rate in your local high school or a shortage of affordable housing. When you write to propose solutions, you first identify an existing problem and then suggest one or more possible ways to solve it. For example, the Web site for ACCION International has identified world poverty as a problem and has proposed a possible solution. ACCION started its lending program more than forty years ago, providing loans to what it calls "Microentrepreneurs," so those business owners can grow their own small companies. In turn, the interest they pay provides funding for even more small-business loans.

When you are faced with a smaller-scale problem than world poverty, perhaps one in your own life or your friends' lives, you will

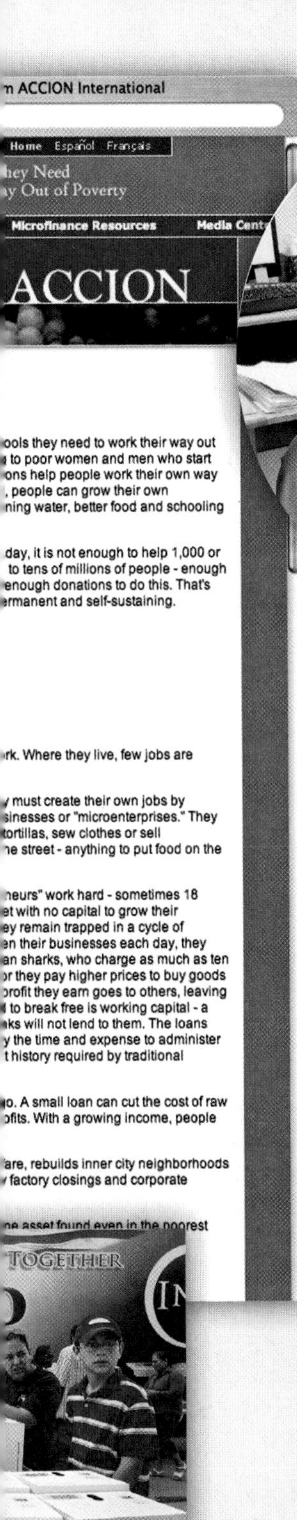

often propose your own solution to it. When you suggest counseling to an unhappy friend, you are proposing a solution—a known treatment—to an emotional problem: depression. When you recommend a heating and air conditioning repair company to a friend with a broken furnace, you are proposing a solution—the repair company—to a more practical problem: the faulty furnace.

When you propose any solution, however, others may already have suggested different solutions to the same problem. Therefore, you must support your own proposal with convincing evidence—not just opinions—and demonstrate that the proposal has a reasonable chance of success.

Setting Your Goals:

Rhetorical Knowledge

- **Audience:** To convince your audience to accept your solution, pay careful attention to your readers' views on and attitudes toward the problem. Who will be interested in your solution? What are their needs, values, and resources? What arguments are most likely to convince this audience?
- **Purpose:** One purpose of any proposal is to convince readers of the existence of a problem and the need for a solution. Another purpose is to convince readers that the solution(s) you propose is (are) the best one(s) possible.
- **Rhetorical situation:** Think about the factors that affect where you stand in relation to your subject. What is compelling you to write your proposal essay?
- **Voice and tone:** When you write to solve problems, you will need to be persuasive. As a result, make sure your tone engages your readers and does not in any way threaten or offend them.
- **Context, medium, and genre:** Decide on the most effective medium and genre to use to present your proposal to the audience you want to reach. Visuals such as charts, graphs, and photographs may help you make your case.

Critical Thinking, Reading, and Writing

- **Learning/inquiry:** When you propose a solution, you first need to think critically to determine whether the problem exists and needs to be solved and whether your proposed solution is viable. Also think critically about the kind of evidence that will convince your readers. Further, evaluate a range of possible solutions to find one or more that are not only viable but effective.
- **Responsibility:** As you read solutions proposed by others, you have the responsibility to consider their solutions fairly as well as critically. You cannot ignore other good ideas simply because you do not agree with them.
- **Reading and research:** Readers will find your solution more acceptable if you have carefully and critically examined the problem and the issues surrounding your solution, supporting it with strong evidence, not unproven assumptions and assertions.

Writing to Solve Problems

Chapter 11

Writing Processes

- **Invention:** Start by recording the ideas that you have about your problem, using an invention strategy such as brainstorming or listing. After recording your initial ideas and findings, you will also need to conduct research.
- **Organizing your ideas and details:** Once you have some ideas down, think about how you might organize your main points, what evidence you might need to provide to support them, and how you might deal with competing solutions to the problem.
- **Revising:** As you write, you may change your opinion about your problem and solution. Once you have a draft, read your work with a critical eye to make certain that it displays the qualities of an effective proposal.
- **Working with peers:** "Test" your solution on your classmates.

Knowledge of Conventions

- **Editing:** One of the hallmarks of effective proposals to solve problems is the use of inclusive language—language that makes diverse readers feel like part of the team that is solving the problem.
- **Genres for writing to solve problems:** In your college classes, proposing a solution usually involves academic writing, so you will probably be required to follow the conventions for an academic essay. Nonacademic writing situations may call for a variety of genres.
- **Documentation:** When writing to solve problems, you will probably need to rely on sources outside of your own experience. Make sure you document them using the appropriate style.

mhconnectcomposition.com

Writing to Solve Problems Tutorial QL11001

Rhetorical Knowledge

Readers of any proposal will ask themselves, "Why should I believe *you*?" All successful proposals have one important aspect in common: the establishment of a credible *ethos*. The nature of your subject and your audience will help determine the balance between logical arguments and emotional appeals that you will need to maintain.

Writing to Solve Problems in Your College Classes

In many of your college classes, your instructor will present you with a problem and ask you to propose a solution. For your classes, you want to examine any problem academically and in depth, with a level of detail ensuring that your readers see and understand the problem. After all, if readers cannot understand the problem, and perhaps see how it affects them, then why should they pay any attention to your proposed solution(s)? Here are some examples of problems you could write about in your college classes:

- In your political science class, you may be asked to propose a solution to the problems associated with the electoral college.
- In a course in environmental studies, you might be asked to propose ways to reduce U.S. dependence on fossil fuels.
- In your geology course, you might be asked to write a research proposal to study the problem of erosion in a nearby canyon.
- In your botany course, you might be assigned a problem/solution paper to examine the effects of global warming on the oak trees that surround your downtown county courthouse and plaza.

The "Ways of Writing" feature presents different genres that can be used when writing to solve problems in your college classes.

Writing to Solve Problems for Life

Writing to solve problems is prevalent in all areas of your life. Many people feel that all they ever do in their professional lives is propose solutions to problems. Consider the following examples:

- An employee writes to her company's personnel director to propose a solution to the high turnover rate in her division.
- A new member of a company's product development division writes to his supervisor to suggest ways to reduce the time and costs required to develop and test new products.

People who are active in their communities often propose solutions as part of their civic life. Because problems continually emerge, every community constantly needs ideas to help solve its problems. You might, for example, write a letter to a local newspaper in which you propose a plan for raising funds for a nonprofit organization.

In your personal life, you will also encounter problems that need to be solved. Some will no doubt be large and potentially life altering. Suppose your mother, who lives alone, is suffering from Alzheimer's disease. You might send an e-mail to your siblings, proposing several possible solutions that you will discuss in a conference call. Or suppose your child is having a problem at school. You might send a letter to your child's teacher.

The "Ways of Writing" feature presents different genres that can be used when writing to solve problems in life.

Scenarios for Writing | Assignment Options

connect
mhconnectcomposition.com
Writer's Workshop: Applying Learning Goals to Writing about Solving Problems QL11002

Your instructor may ask you to complete one or both of the following assignments that call for a solution to a problem. Each of these assignments is in the form of a *scenario*. The list of rhetorical considerations on page 366 encourages you to think about your audience; purpose; voice, tone, and point of view; and context, medium, and genre.

Starting on page 382, you will find guidelines for completing whatever scenario you decide—or are asked—to complete. Additional scenarios for college and life may be found online.

Writing for College

SCENARIO 1 **Solving a Social Problem from One of Your Courses**

Think about a problem that you have learned about in another class you are taking this term. To complete this assignment, assume that the instructor has asked you to choose a problem and propose a solution for it, which you will present to your classmates. You must first decide which problem you wish to address and then look at various options for solving the problem. Here are some possible social problems to consider:

- **Education:** In some states, the dropout rate is relatively high.
- **Criminal justice:** In some cities, motorists run red lights more frequently than they do in other communities.
- **Business administration:** In many sectors of the U.S. economy, relatively few women have high-level management positions.
- **Health:** The incidence of diabetes is relatively high among some segments of the population in the United States.

Writing Assignment: Propose a solution to the problem that you have selected. Be sure to focus on solving one aspect of the problem, thus narrowing it down to a manageable size.

Ways of Writing to Solve Problems

Genres for Your College Classes	Sample Situation	Advantages of the Genre	Limitations of the Genre
Academic essay	In your sociology class, your professor asks you to examine some social problem (the effect of television violence or advertising on young people; unhealthy fast food in our diets; and so on) and suggest possible solutions.	Your research on both the problem and potential solutions will be useful to young people who may engage in potentially unhealthy behaviors.	Some societal problems are too large to cover in one paper.
Proposal	Your college success class professor asks you to write a paper detailing why some students leave school and to propose some ways to keep them enrolled.	An proposal is good for defining a problem and then presenting research on potential solutions.	To get information from your fellow students, you will need to interview them—perhaps many of them—which is time-consuming.
Oral presentation	Create an oral presentation for your world history class outlining a problem in another country and suggesting some solutions to that problem.	This oral presentation will force you to define the problem succinctly and then present possible solutions to it.	Illustrations will be crucial and some problems are difficult to define orally and to show visually.
Letter to your campus newspaper	Your writing professor asks you to draft a letter to the editor of your campus newspaper about a problem on campus (litter, speeding cars, and so on).	Your school newspaper is a useful arena to publicize the problem and to ask fellow students to help with the solution.	A letter allows only limited space, and some problems and solutions are hard to describe briefly. It might not be published.
Business report	Your business instructor asks you to outline an unusual business problem and to suggest solutions.	Finding a unique problem in the business world may help you and your readers understand how to solve unusual issues.	If your problem and solution are too esoteric, no one will care, as they may think they will never have to deal with such an issue.
Genres for Life	**Sample Situation**	**Advantages of the Genre**	**Limitations of the Genre**
Brochure	With several neighbors, you want to construct a brochure in which you outline a local problem and suggest possible solutions.	A brochure provides a quick and easy way to share information about the problem, as well as your proposed solution.	A brochure provides limited space to present both the problem and the solution.
Memo	You have been asked to write a memo to the president of your firm, telling her about a serious problem and suggesting possible solutions.	A memo forces you to write concisely and specifically.	A memo is restrictive in terms of space (no one wants to read a ten-page memo).
Wiki	You want to construct a wiki that allows neighbors to share information on a problem that affects them (graffiti, dangerous intersections, and so on) and to suggest and comment on possible solutions.	A wiki is an easy and uncomplicated way for people to share what they know about problems and potential solutions.	Someone will need to monitor the wiki for improper comments; readers need a reason to return to read and post on the wiki.
Web page	Every five years your extended family has a large-scale reunion, but there are always problems (travel time and cost, location for the reunion, and so on). Construct a Web page outlining these problems and and suggesting possible solutions.	A Web page gives everyone the same information at the same time; you can constantly update it, and you can provide links so you do not need to type all details into the page.	A static Web page does not allow for interaction (as a wiki does).
Performance improvement plan	A person you supervise at work has low sales for the quarter. You need to explain the problem and to suggest solutions to it.	Your plan has to outline both the problem and suggested solutions in sufficient detail so your employee has a real opportunity to improve his behavior.	If you are not complete in your "plan for improvement," your employee might not do what he needs to do to solve the problem.

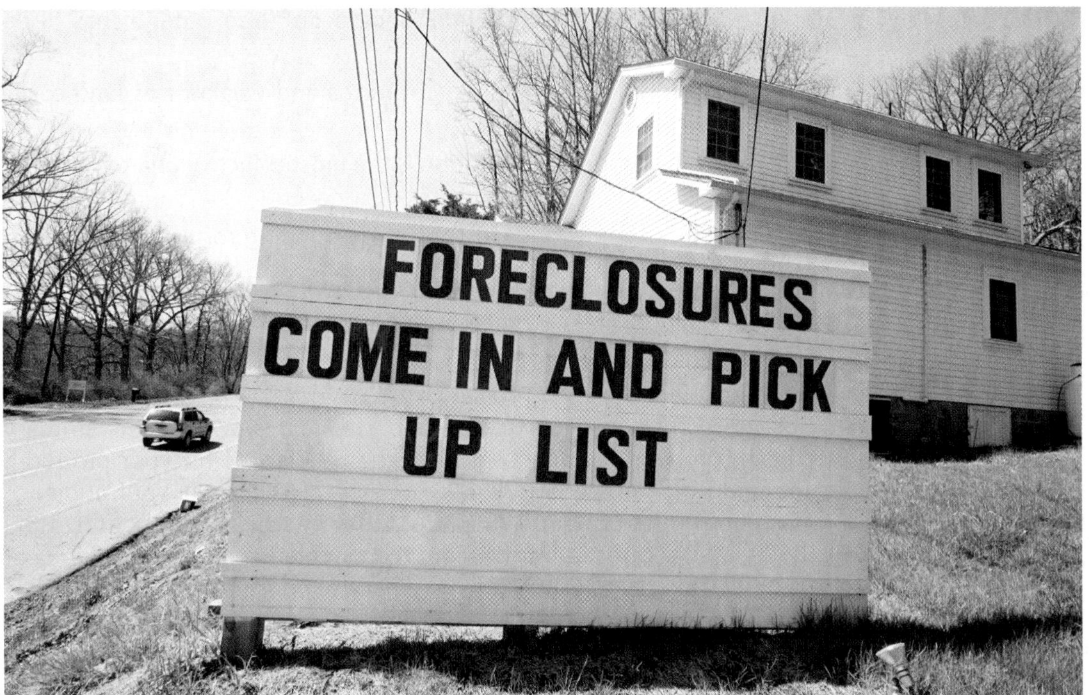

An increase in the number of mortgage foreclosures during an economic downturn can be problematic in communities with high unemployment.

Writing for Life

SCENARIO 2 Civic Writing: Proposal to Solve a Community Problem

Think about some problem in your community, such as litter that does not get picked up, a shortage of shelters or food banks for the homeless, gang violence, job losses, high housing prices, a lack of parks, or big-box stores moving in or closing down. As you consider a local problem, keep in mind that you will need to define that problem and prove that it exists to your readers. Unless they can understand the problem, your solution will not make any sense.

Writing Assignment: Write a formal proposal, which you plan to present to the city council, outlining and explaining the problem, as well as your suggested solution. For more on the format of a formal proposal, see pages 367–368. In your proposal, be sure to do the following:

- State the problem, in enough detail that readers will understand it and its importance to your community.
- If your research turns up any background information (what the causes of the problem are, how long it has been a problem, what others have

done to try to solve the problem, and so on), also outline that background information.

- List possible solutions, with their strengths and weaknesses (and costs, if applicable).
- Explain why your suggested solution is the most effective one to solve the problem.
- Ask for action of some kind (further study, funding for the solution, and so on).

connect
mhconnectcomposition.com
Additional Scenarios QL11003

Rhetorical Considerations

- **Audience:** While your instructor and classmates will be the primary audience, you should also consider other audiences for your proposal, depending on the scenario you have chosen. What will your audience know about this problem? Why should they be concerned about it? How can you make your solution(s) seem reasonable to them? What kinds of responses would you expect them to have to your proposal?
- **Purpose:** Your purpose is to identify a particular problem and propose a viable solution. How will you convince your audience the problem needs attention?
- **Voice, tone, and point of view:** You may choose to write about a problem that you have strong feelings about. How much has your view of the problem—or even your view that it *is* a problem—been determined by your value system? How will you deal with your preconceptions about the problem, and how might these preconceptions affect your tone? What attitudes, if any, do you hold toward members of your audience, and how might that affect how you present your information?
- **Context, medium, and genre:** Keeping the context of the assignment in mind, decide on a medium and a genre for your writing. How will your writing be used? If you are writing for an audience beyond the classroom, consider what will be the most effective way to present your proposal to this audience.

For more on choosing a medium and genre, see Chapter 17 and the Online Appendix.

Critical Thinking, Reading, and Writing

Before you begin to write your proposal, consider the qualities of a successful proposal. It also helps to read one or more proposals to get a feel for this kind of writing. Finally, you might consider how visuals could enhance your proposal, as well as the kinds of sources you will need to consult.

Effective writing that solves problems contains a clearly defined problem and a well-articulated solution that is targeted for a specific audience. In addition, this kind of writing will include convincing evidence for the proposed solution's effectiveness, as well as a well-documented review of alternative solutions. Finally, an effective proposal will include a call to action.

Learning the Qualities of Effective Proposals

A proposed solution to a problem should include the following qualities:

- **A clearly defined problem.** An effective proposal first establishes the existence of a problem that is both understandable and manageable within the scope of the assignment.

For more information on cause and effect, see Chapter 10.

- **An awareness of the audience.** Your readers need to believe that the problem you are writing about actually exists and that your proposed solution will work. Therefore, use what your audience already knows and believes to shape your proposal. For instance, if your audience readily accepts that there is a problem, you need not spend time and effort on establishing that; you can focus almost exclusively on the proposed solution. If, however, your readers may be unaware of the problem, or may not believe it *is* a problem, you will need to spend time making them aware of it and convincing them to be concerned about it.
- **A well-explained solution.** Your readers need both to understand your solution and to find it reasonable. One way to help any audience understand your proposal is to use language that the audience understands and to provide definitions of unfamiliar terms.
- **Convincing evidence for the effectiveness of the solution.** You will need to prove that your solution is viable and that it is the best answer to the probem by supporting your assertions with evidence such as expert testimony, case studies, experimental studies, and examples of similar solutions to similar problems. A solution needs to be feasible, affordable, and effective.

  You will also need to anticipate readers' objections to your proposed solutions so that you can address them. The cost of any solution almost always comes up as an objection, so you need to be prepared to deal with that ("While this solution is expensive in the near future, I will demonstrate how the costs will actually save us money in the long run").
- **A well-documented review of alternative solutions.** While your proposed solution should be able to stand on its own merits, for your proposal to convince the most skeptical readers, you must also acknowledge alternative ways to solve the problem and then carefully show why the alternatives will not work, or work as well, thus demonstrating that your solution is the best option.
- **A call to action.** There is little point to proposing a solution to a problem unless someone actually implements that solution. At the end of your proposal, you should urge those who can take action to solve the problem to do so.

Reading, Inquiry, and Research: Learning from Texts That Propose Solutions

As you read the selections, consider the following questions:

- How effective is the writer at convincing you that there is a problem that needs to be addressed?
- To what extent has the writer offered a workable solution?
- How convincing is the evidence? Why?
- How effectively does the writer anticipate opposing views and look at alternative solutions?
- How can you use the techniques of proposal writing exemplified here in your writing?

MICHELLE MISE POLLARD

The Nursing Crisis: The Solution Lies Within

PROPOSAL ESSAY

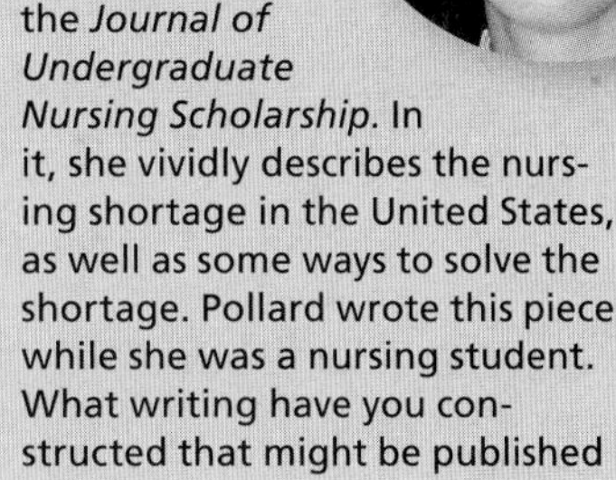

As a nursing student at the University of North Carolina, Charlotte, Michelle Pollard wrote this paper for the *Journal of Undergraduate Nursing Scholarship.* In it, she vividly describes the nursing shortage in the United States, as well as some ways to solve the shortage. Pollard wrote this piece while she was a nursing student. What writing have you constructed that might be published one day?

Abstract

The nursing crisis, in our country, has reached such epidemic proportions that congressional testimony indicates a need for immediate action. Exploring the causes, finding clues to the attrition, and understanding the implications of this worsening shortage can help us to search for solutions. This paper attempts to express how solutions may lie within the nursing profession itself to stop the outflow of nurses from the profession and to increase the inflow of new individuals to the profession. 1

Introduction

On September 25th 2001, a congressional hearing took place to address the problem of the current nursing shortage, which has reached critical proportions. Members of the House of Representatives met and heard nurses tell stories of poor working conditions that include inadequate staffing, heavy workloads, use of mandatory overtime, lack of sufficient support staff, and inadequate wages. One such nurse from a Washington area hospital said eliminating mandatory overtime, setting better nurse to patient ratios and giving staff nurses a voice in hospital policy were more important than higher pay. "Until you fix the working environment, the salary issue is kind of moot" (Romig, 2001, p. 733). The current nursing shortage, unlike those of the past, appears to be headed toward a path of rapid decline. 2

This unstable environment in the healthcare setting has been blamed on many issues that stem from changes in healthcare to societal attitudes about the nursing profession. Steps can be taken and words spoken that can lessen the declivity[1] of nursing professionals. This has become an issue that affects all Americans and immediate steps need to be taken to stop the worsening progression of this threat to healthcare as we know it. 3

[1] declining number

Exploring the Causes

An aging population of patients that are often in need of more intense and specialized care from qualified medical professionals, of which nurses comprise the largest percentage, is adding fuel to the fire of this worsening crisis (Heinrich, 2001). The increase in the number of higher acuity patients with the added burden of a shrinking nursing population results in a bleak picture for the future of the profession. 4

According to congressional testimony by the House Education and Workforce Committee, the nursing workforce is aging and there are not enough new nurses entering the profession to replace those retiring or leaving (Heinrich, 2001). According to Senator Jim Jeffords (2001), I-Vt, the average age of a nurse is presently between 42–45 and by 2010 nearly 40% of the nursing workforce will be over the age of 50 and nearing retirement. "Our nation has suffered from nursing shortages in the past. However, this shortage is particularly severe because we are losing nurses from both ends of the pipeline," Jeffords said. 5

Clues to Attrition

Not only are the majority of nursing professionals aging, but many young people are choosing other careers. A recent study reported that women graduating from high school in the 1990s are 35% less likely to become nurses than women who graduated in the 1970s (Heinrich, 2001). Women today have more job options, many of which offer better pay, more job satisfaction, and perceived better working conditions ("Nursing Shortage," 2001). 6

Experienced nurses are opting out of nursing after many years, as well, looking for less stressful and more lucrative careers. A survey done by the Federation of Nurses and Health Professionals found that half of the currently employed RNs had considered leaving the patient care field for reasons other than retirement over the past two years (Heinrich, 2001). 7

Understanding the Implications

The shortage of qualified nursing personnel is an issue that affects anyone who is a provider or consumer of healthcare in this country. Consumers are affected directly by quality of care from nurses who feel they are overworked and overstressed due to the increasing demands on their time. Physicians are affected, as well, in their everyday practice and dealings with nurses and patients. According to one physician, "we are increasingly feeling the strain of a hospital nursing staff who are stretched too thin" (Stapleton, 2001, p. 30). The situation inevitably leads to a question of quality of care in settings such as hospitals. 8

As employers of the largest segment of healthcare professionals, administrators of hospitals and other facilities are also directly affected by 9 the nursing shortage. A poll by the American Hospital Association (AHA) reports from a survey of 700 hospitals that there are approximately 126,000 nationwide RN positions currently vacant ("Publication," 2001). Maryland, for example, reported a statewide vacancy rate for hospitals of 14.7%, up from 3.3% in 1997. California reported a vacancy rate of 20% among its hospitals (Heinrich, 2001).

Proposing Solutions

There is no tried and true solution to a problem that has been seen before by 10
this profession, but how do we stop the downward spiral as we lose current and future nurses to other, more attractive career choices? Efforts made to improve the workplace environment may both reduce the likelihood of nurses leaving the field and encourage more young people to enter the nursing profession. Governmental agencies can help bring new nurses into the profession by offering money for tuition assistance as well as all related expenses. Hospitals and other healthcare agencies can offer more attractive employment packages and listen firsthand to the issues surrounding the dissatisfaction of their nursing staff. Nurse managers that work closely with top administrators and have voices that leaders listen to can take a stand for nursing as a whole. The reports show that nurses would have increased job satisfaction if they had better working relationships with supervisors who have real power and autonomy (Welch, 2001, p. 24). But the majority of the burden for improving the job satisfaction lies within each of us as nurses.

Improving the workplace environment has to start from within the 11
profession itself. As Mueller (2001) notes in an article in *Creative Nursing,* "we know we are proceeding into a serious global nursing shortage. . . . And we are discovering that some of the solutions lie within each one of us" (p. 3). As nurses we have voices that can be heard through all the administrative and governmental offices, but we must find ways to speak collectively and constructively. Oftentimes nurses are not assertive in telling the story of what it is that causes them to be dissatisfied, and many degrade the profession by complaining and not acting to improve it. Do we not hurt ourselves as well as the profession by discouraging qualified individuals from choosing nursing as a career? To express ourselves completely and honestly, we must first look to develop personally and professionally. We, as nurses, need to implement a plan of action to further enhance our professionalism and solicit new members. My suggestions for such a plan include:

- First, "Do no harm"; do not degrade the profession by words, actions, or deeds.
- Become a teacher, mentor, role model to young professionals.
- Develop a strategy for community awareness and respect for the profession.

- Strive to continue to elevate our own personal standards and the standards of our profession (i.e., educational requirements should be MSN[2] for managers and teachers).
- Find ways to enhance the collective voice of nursing in your workplace, state, country.
- Finally, have pride and enjoy the wonderful and rewarding career that you have chosen.

These ideas can help our profession gain a sense of why it is we are important to society and why we are irreplaceable to the healthcare system. By continuing to discuss only the negative nursing experiences, we discourage many prospective nurses from entering the profession altogether. Nurses need to share stories of how wonderful and rewarding a career in nursing can be. "I have never been bored or disinterested in nursing because I've been able to have so many roles in many settings . . . nursing is intellectually stimulating as I read articles in nursing, attend conferences and meetings and use that knowledge in my practice . . . I could share that I have had the pleasure of participating in the professional growth and development and that almost everyday new opportunities present themselves to me because I am a nurse . . . and that I haven't regretted a day or a moment for having chosen nursing as a career" states Christine Mueller, RN, PhD (2001, p. 5). 12

It is stories like these that will bring those future nurses into a career that can be more rewarding than most. How many other careers allow you to be a part of the milestones of life like birth and death, recovery from illness and trauma, and make a difference in the lives of those who cross your path? Nurses are the backbone of the patient care setting, offering holistic care unlike any offered by other members of the healthcare team. And as nurses we have an obligation to save our profession from further deterioration and overall worsening of the nursing shortage. 13

Whether you are a bedside nurse or a top nursing executive, it is the responsibility of us all to make our voices heard throughout the halls of our hospitals, state legislatures, and this country. We must show why it is important to improve conditions and what a wonderful and rewarding career nursing is and can be to many individuals who have much to offer this outstanding and admirable profession. If we, ourselves, have immense pride and respect for what it is we do, we have to influence others to share this frame of mind in order to make a difference in the careers we have chosen. Be proud and speak loudly, letting everyone know what a noble and caring profession it is that we share. 14

---

[2] Master of Science in Nursing degree

References

Boehner, J. (2001, September 25). *Nursing shortage.* FDCH Congressional testimony.

Bozell, J., Holcomb, S., & Kornman, C. (2002). Cut to the chase [Electronic version]. *Nursing Management, 33*(1), 39–40.

Heinrich, J. (2001, July 10). *Emerging nurse shortages due to multiple factors.* FDCH government account reports. Retrieved from http://ehostvgw20.epnet.com

Jeffords, J. (2001, November 1). *Jeffords' legislation to strengthen nursing profession passes health committee.* FDCH press releases. Retrieved from http://ehostvgw20.epnet.com

Mueller, C. (2001). The breadth and depth of nursing. [Electronic version]. *Creative nursing, 7*(4), 3–5.

Nursing shortage: It's likely to get worse before it gets better [Electronic version]. (2001, August). *Occupational Health Management, 11*(8), 85.

Parker, C. (2001). Nursing shortage, working conditions intertwined at congressional hearing [Electronic version]. *AHA News, 37*(39), 1.

Publication paints a bleak picture [Electronic version]. (2001, August). *Occupational Health Management, 11*(8), 89.

Romig, C. (2001). The nursing shortage demands action now—state and federal legislation passed [Electronic version]. *AORN Journal, 74*(5), 733.

Stapleton, S. (2001). Where's the nurse? [Electronic version]. *American Medical News, 44*(23), 30.

Thompson, T. (2001, September 28). Tommy Thompson holds news conference on the nursing shortage. *FDCH Political Transcripts.* Retrieved from http://ehostvgw20.epnet.com.

Welch, M. (2001–2002). The nursing shortage may be permanent [Electronic version]. *Connecticut Nursing News, 74*(4), 24.

Workforce: The people part of getting ready [Electronic version]. (2001, October). AHA News, 37(40), 6.

QUESTIONS FOR WRITING AND DISCUSSION: LEARNING OUTCOMES

Rhetorical Knowledge: The Writer's Situation and Rhetoric

1. **Audience:** The author of this article is writing for nurses. How effectively has she addressed this audience? What can you point to that tells you who her readers might be? To what other audience might you suggest this argument be made?
2. **Purpose:** In addition to suggesting how the nursing crisis might be solved, do you see any other purpose for Pollard's essay?
3. **Voice and tone:** How believable is Pollard? What can you point to in the essay that gives its author *ethos*?
4. **Responsibility:** What can you point to in the essay to show how Pollard is accurately using statistical information?
5. **Context, format, and genre:** How effective is the format of this essay? Why?

Critical Thinking: The Writer's Ideas and Your Personal Response

6. To what extent do threatened or actual shortages affect your own career area? Or to what extent does your chosen field have the opposite problem: too many people attempting to enter it?
7. What is Pollard's solution? How concrete is it?

Composing Processes and Knowledge of Conventions: The Writer's Strategies

8. Pollard lists ways the nursing profession can help itself in six bullet points. All of these steps seem easy to do from the outside. To what extent will these solutions have an impact on the problem?
9. What in the essay do you disagree with? That is, what aspects of Pollard's proposed solution do you think are unworkable?

Inquiry and Research: Ideas for Further Exploration

10. If your school has a nursing program, find out what enrollments are like. Are there more or fewer students now than there were ten years ago? What enrollment trends do you see?

GIBOR BASRI

An Open Letter to the Campus Community

LETTER

Gibor Basri is the founding Vice Chancellor for Equity and Inclusion at the University of California, Berkeley, where he is also professor of astronomy. He has published widely on star formation and other topics in astronomy. After a series of events on and near the UC Berkeley campus, he sent this e-mail message to students, faculty, and staff. The e-mail was signed by Basri, as well as Chancellor Robert Birgeneau, Associated Students of the University of California President Roxanne Winston, and Vice Chancellor for Student Affairs Harry Le Grande. These days, there is much in the news about how political discussions, even on a college campus, are less civil: people want to shout at one another, rather than to discuss issues calmly. What is the "discussion climate" on your campus or in your community?

Subject: An Open Letter to the Campus Community
From: "Gibor Basri, Vice Chancellor—Equity & Inclusion (Campus-wide)" <CALmessages@berkeley.edu>
Date: Mon., November 17, 2008, 6:55 pm
To: "Students" <CALmessages@berkeley.edu>

1 Recent events both on and off campus have prompted us to send this open letter to the campus community. In order for all of us to thrive and succeed, our campus must be safe and welcoming, and disagreements need to be managed in a respectful and civil manner. At Berkeley, we are passionate about the matters that shape our world; debate, free speech, and political activism are proudly defining characteristics of our campus. But we must also ensure that debates and advocacy take place in a reasoned and civil way that increases understanding and does not promote intolerance and hate.

2 Unfortunately, there have been a number of troubling incidents that make us acutely aware of the need for continued vigilance, constructive dialogue and concerted action to protect these values. In addition, we believe that it is essential for every member of the campus community to be aware of the venues and vehicles that are available for dialogue, conflict resolution and the reporting of incidents, including acts of retaliation, that appear to violate our principles, values, and standards of conduct.

3 Most recently a dispute between students with differing views of the Israeli-Palestinian conflict led to a physical altercation and citations issued by the police. Physical assault and violence are never acceptable. We as a campus will not tolerate such incidents and reiterate our condemnation of them. Other disturbing and unacceptable incidents this semester have included hate graffiti, racially derogatory remarks directed at specific students, and potentially criminal acts of retribution. The cumulative impact of these incidents has left many on campus feeling uncertain about how,

exactly, the campus is responding and disappointed in the behavior of a few students who have been provocative or tried to take matters in their own hands. It is expected that students themselves will take leadership and responsibility for upholding campus values.

We are taking vigorous steps to address the current situation. University administration and student leaders are working to make sure that all voices are being heard and tensions are lessened. The UC Police Department is continuing to investigate the recent altercation, graffiti, and other matters. Campus groups are holding activities such as forums, town halls, and other forms of civil dialogue between people with differences including this week's Peace Not Prejudice events (www.calpnp.com). 4

The values of civility and tolerance require constant attention, thought, and action. To help promote them, in 2005 the University adopted Principles of Community (berkeley.edu/about/principles.shtml) which include the expectations we hold for respectful behavior from all members of the campus community. In addition, the campus has a number of resources which provide proper channels to deal with provocations which violate our values. You can turn to any of these offices: ASUC Student Advocate, the Office of Campus Climate and Compliance, Office of the Dean of Students, the Gender Equity Resource Center, the Center for Student Conduct and Community Standards, staff in the Office of Multicultural Student Development, the UC Police Department, and the staff and student ombuds offices. 5

Developing a long-term strategy for improving campus climate is part of the charge of the new division of Equity & Inclusion, under the leadership of Vice Chancellor Gibor Basri. The division is developing further policies and practices which will help promote an inclusive and welcoming climate. One of these will be a Campus Climate Team that will help monitor and rapidly respond to future incidents. We will be updating and expanding the campus website for reporting bias related incidents (stophate.berkeley.edu) and using technology to build an on-line community of those who want to make Berkeley safer and more inclusive. We are actively soliciting suggestions from students, student groups, staff, and faculty on ways to make UC Berkeley more civil and respectful of differences. We will be reporting regularly on the progress of these activities. 6

Students, faculty, and staff can also help by practicing civility with all members of our community and working to promote understanding and acceptance. We encourage everyone to participate in the debates and discussions that have made Berkeley famous throughout the world and to do so in the spirit of intellectual engagement, rational argumentation, respectful discourse, and regard for the common good. The vibrancy of Berkeley's intellectual environment is made possible by our rich diversity. 7

Let us use this opportunity to help lead the way away from bigotry and hate towards a flourishing multicultural society.

(signed: Chancellor Robert Birgeneau, ASUC President Roxanne Winston, Vice Chancellor Gibor Basri, Vice Chancellor Harry Le Grande)

QUESTIONS FOR WRITING AND DISCUSSION: LEARNING OUTCOMES

Rhetorical Knowledge: The Writers' Situation and Rhetoric

1. **Audience:** How is the e-mail message tailored to the audience—faculty, staff, and students at the University of California, Berkeley?
2. **Purpose:** What solutions are the authors of the letter proposing?
3. **Voice and tone:** How does the open letter model the kinds of respect that the authors are requesting?
4. **Responsibility:** Why do the authors include off-campus incidents in the letter?
5. **Context, format, and genre:** Why did the authors choose to send this message via e-mail? What other media might also be effective? Although the authors label the e-mail message an open letter, e-mails have some of the features of memos. What are some of those features?

Critical Thinking: The Writer's Ideas and Your Personal Response

6. If you were a student at Berkeley, how would you respond to this message?
7. If you found yourself in one of the situations described in the message, how would you respond at that moment?

Composing Processes and Knowledge of Conventions: The Writer's Strategies

8. Why did these four individuals sign the letter? Why did Basri not send it with just his signature?
9. How do the signatories establish their collective *ethos* in the letter?

Inquiry and Research: Ideas for Further Exploration

10. Conduct a Web search to find out how other colleges and universities have dealt with the kinds of problems described in this message.

GENRES *Up Close* Writing a Proposal

Proposals often offer solutions to problems, but they also can suggest actions to take in situations where there is no real problem. For example, you can propose that you and your friends take in a particular movie, dine at a certain restaurant, or watch a particular sporting event. If you and your friends have similar tastes in movies, food, or sports, you may not have to support your proposal with reasons—for example, "I read online reviews that raved about this movie" or "That restaurant has the best pasta dishes in town" or "This is being billed as the most competitive game of the season."

Other kinds of proposals can outline future research projects, suggest ways to improve a company's already strong productivity, put forward ideas for enhancing an organization's marketing procedures, or seek funding for a research project. Such proposals are not designed to solve problems per se, but they do point the way to seizing opportunities.

Whether you are writing a proposal to solve a problem or to seize an opportunity, the genre features are similar. In particular, proposals do the following:

connect
mhconnectcomposition.com
Memo breakdown QL11004

- Define a problem to be solved or an opportunity to be seized.
- Delineate a plan of action for solving the problem or seizing the opportunity.
- Make the case that the proposed solution is the most practical, feasible, and effective.
- anticipate questions, objections, and alternative solutions/methods of seizing opportunities.
- Conclude with what the writer would like to happen next.

How does the following proposal memo fit these conventions?

AMY BASKIN AND HEATHER FAWCETT

Request for a Work Schedule Change

MEMO

Amy Baskin is a freelance writer who has published in magazines such as *Canadian Parent, Canadian Living, Today's Parent, Canadian Family,* and *Education Today.* She has also taught children and adults for more than two decades.

Heather Fawcett is a writer and an advocate for children with special needs. Early in her career, she was a technical writer in the computer industry. Her textbook *Techniques for Technical Communicators* has been used on college and university campuses in Canada and the United States.

This proposal memo is excerpted from Baskin and Fawcett's book *More Than a Mom—Living a Full and Balanced Life When Your Child Has Special Needs. www.morethanamom.net.*

Do you or someone you know have flexible work hours? What benefits and problems can you see with such an arrangement?

Background

Karen works weekdays 9:00 to 5:30 as a technical writer for an aerospace plant. Karen's husband, Murray, doesn't start work until 9:30, but often must work late into the evening. They have two school-age children. Their youngest, Helen, has cerebral palsy.

Karen would like to work flextime, so that she can be home with her daughters after school. That would allow her to schedule more therapy appointments for Helen, as well as help the girls with their homework. It would also save the family significant babysitting costs.

She will request a 6:00 a.m. to 2:30 p.m. workday.

Proposal Memo

To: John Doe
From: Karen MacDonald
Re: Request for Flextime
Date: May 17, 2006

1 As a team member of HI-Tech's Technical Writing Division for six years, I'd like to propose changing my work hours to 6:00 a.m. to 2:30 p.m., instead of 9:00 to 5:30.

2 I believe that, with this earlier schedule, I would be able to improve my written output by at least a third. As I'm sure you know, writing and editing requires a great deal of solitary concentration. Although I enjoy the camaraderie of our open-concept office, I am frequently disrupted by nearby phone calls and discussions. With the earlier schedule, I would have several hours to work without distraction before most of my coworkers arrive each day.

3 An earlier schedule would also allow me to schedule my daughter's medical appointments after work, meaning I'd be able to take significantly less time off, yet still see to her needs.

Overview of the memo—defines the problem/opportunity.

Delineates a plan of action to solve the problem/seize the opportunity.

Anticipates questions and objections.

I feel that my work record as a reliable, self-directed, and self-disciplined employee makes me an ideal candidate for flextime work. 4

Since I rarely interact directly with customers, customer service should not be compromised. Should an urgent matter arise after I'd left work for the day, I would still be accessible by cell phone. 5

My meetings with engineers can be easily rescheduled to take place before 2:30. I could still arrange to work a later schedule on days when my presence would be critical in the late afternoon—for example, if a client requested a 3:00 meeting. 6

To ensure success, I propose we meet weekly in the first month to review the arrangement. I would continue to report on my progress in weekly department meetings. 7

Concludes with what the writer would like to happen next.

We can use the timelines currently in our product schedule to track my projects and measure productivity. 8

I would like to discuss this proposal with you further to address any potential concerns you might have. I understand that you are responsible for the success of this department and must determine whether this plan works for our team as a whole. I suggest a trial period of one month, after which the arrangement could be assessed and revised, if necessary. I understand that if the plan is not working, I might be required to return to my original schedule. 9

QUESTIONS FOR WRITING AND DISCUSSION: LEARNING OUTCOMES

Rhetorical Knowledge: The Writer's Situation and Rhetoric

1. **Audience:** The audience for Karen MacDonald's proposal memo is her supervisor. How has MacDonald shaped the memo to address the supervisor's needs?
2. **Purpose:** MacDonald's goal is stated in the "Re" line—she is requesting flextime. Besides announcing her goal with the phrase "Request for Flextime," what other phrases might be effective in the "Re" line?
3. **Voice and tone:** How does MacDonald's tone affect the persuasiveness of her memo proposal?
4. **Responsibility:** How does MacDonald demonstrate that she is a responsible parent and employee?
5. **Context, format, and genre:** If MacDonald had decided to make this request in a face-to-face meeting rather than in a memo, what would be different? If there is a follow-up meeting with her supervisor to discuss the proposal, what more might MacDonald say to strengthen her case? If MacDonald had written a letter rather than a memo to make her proposal, how would the letter differ from the memo?

Critical Thinking: The Writer's Ideas and Your Personal Response

6. If you were MacDonald's supervisor, how would you respond to her proposal? Why?
7. What is the most compelling section of MacDonald's proposal?

Composing Processes and Knowledge of Conventions: The Writer's Strategies

8. How does MacDonald address potential objections to her proposal? How effectively does she do that?
9. How MacDonald establish her *ethos* in the proposal? How effectively does she do that?

Inquiry and Research: Ideas for Further Exploration

10. Conduct a Web search to see how some companies use flextime. Who seems to benefit from flextime?

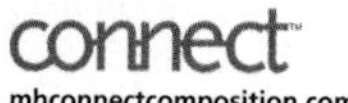

mhconnectcomposition.com

Writing to Solve Problems Animated Walkthrough QL11005

Writing Processes

As you work on your assignment, remember the qualities of an effective paper that proposes a solution to a problem (see page 367). Also recall the recursive nature of the writing process—that is, after you engage in invention and conduct some research, you may start writing, or you may decide to do some more research. In fact, the more writing experience you get, the more you will realize that no piece of writing is ever finished until your final draft.

Invention: Getting Started

As with any writing that you do, the more invention activities that you can draw on, the more effective your paper will be. Try to answer these questions while you do your invention work:

- What do I already know about the problem?
- What possible solutions do I already have in mind to propose?
- Where might I learn more about this problem? What personal experience might I have that is relevant?
- What might my audience already know about this problem?
- What might their point of view be?
- What questions do I have about the problem or about possible solutions?

Writing Activity

Freewriting

Keeping the questions above in mind, freewrite to jot down everything you know about the problem. Be sure to also list any questions you still have. That should give you a good sense of what research you still need to conduct. Once you jot down what you know about the problem, you not only can focus on what else you need to understand about it (for more research) but also can start thinking about possible solutions. Do not worry about putting what you know, what questions you have, and so on into complete sentences; the idea is to get down on paper everything you know about the problem and potential solutions. That gives you a useful starting point.

For more on freewriting and other strategies for discovery and learning, see Chapter 3.

Esther Ellsworth's Freewriting

Student writer Esther Ellsworth, who is planning to major in biology, decided to look at the problems of current land-use policy in Arizona—as well as solutions to these problems. She began with the following short piece of freewriting:

> Arizona is such a beautiful state—lots of wide-open spaces with panoramic views of mountains. The state still has lots of undeveloped land, but what will happen to it as the population continues to explode? Arizona is one of the fast-growing states in the U.S., and there's no end in sight. What can be done to preserve as much natural beauty as possible. We owe it to future generations. Is there a way to bring government agencies, citizens' groups, and developers together so that everyone is on the same page?

EXAMPLES OF INVENTION

Brainstorming (pp. 158, 332)
Freewriting (pp. 114, 245, 383)
Criteria (p. 290)
Listing (p. 72)
Answers to Reporter's Questions (p. 244)
Organization (pp. 75, 164)
Clustering (pp. 114, 289)
Concept Mapping (p. 335)
Interviewing (p. 203)
Research (pp. 115, 160, 205, 246, 292, 384)
Reflection (p. 12)

Exploring Your Ideas with Research

Once you have used invention techniques to decide on a problem and explore what you know about it, you need to conduct research to investigate the problem further and develop possible solutions to it.

Although your own experience may provide some evidence for the effectiveness of your proposed solution, personal experience usually needs to be supplemented by other forms of evidence: quotations from experts, examples, statistics, and estimates of time and financial resources drawn from reliable sources. One way to organize your research is to use the qualities of effective proposals to guide your research activities. Here are some possibilities:

- **A clearly defined problem:** As you do research on your problem, look at how others have defined it and narrowed it to make it more manageable.
- **An awareness of the audience:** Your research should give you a sense of how other writers have defined and addressed their audiences. Also, you should note how other writers have treated people's perceptions of the problem that you are trying to solve. What do they assume that people know about the problem? What do they assume that people do not know about the problem? How much do they assume that people care about the problem?
- **A well-articulated solution:** For most kinds of problems in the world, you will not be the first person to propose solutions. Look at how other writers have articulated their solutions.

Digital Literacy

Conducting Primary Research Online

Your writing about problems and solutions can be improved if you investigate the kinds of solutions that would satisfy the larger community. To do so, you can use online resources to conduct primary research. To collect data or feedback from members of the community that will be affected by your solution, you can create a survey to collect their opinions, observations, and ideas, either developing a simple e-mail distribution list and sending a small number of questions to targeted respondents or taking advantage of free spaces for collecting peoples' opinions and reactions on popular sites such as Facebook, MySpace, and SurveyMonkey.

- **Convincing evidence for the solution's effectiveness:** You will need to find evidence that your proposed solution is viable. Look for expert testimony, the results of experimental research, and case studies.

For advice on conducting primary research, see Chapter 19.

- **A well-documented review of alternative solutions:** You cannot be certain that your proposed solution is the most effective one unless you have carefully reviewed a range of possible solutions. As you consider them, keep an open mind—you might find a solution that is more effective than the one that you first offered.
- **A call to action:** As you do your research, look at the language that other writers have used to inspire their readers to action.

Writing Activity

Conducting Research

Using the list of qualities for effective writing to solve problems, begin by listing what you already know about the problem and potential solutions. Then note what research you still need to conduct and possible sources to consult.

Esther Ellsworth's Notes on Her Research

Reminder to self: Don't forget to include all the citations for the sources that I'm planning to use. Do this for everything or I'll be sorry later.

A clearly defined problem: I have a general sense of the problem from driving around the state—especially the metropolitan areas—and from the news coverage of land use issues, but I need to look at some scholarly sources. This might be the kind of problem that the Morrison Institute for Public Policy (a respected "think tank") has considered.

An awareness of the audience: I think that I have a pretty good handle on the audience for this; it's fairly diverse. However, I should look at how others have addressed audiences. I wonder if the Sierra Club has a magazine or a local chapter? I'll bet there have been editorials and letters, too, in the local paper—I'll have to look there.

A well-articulated solution: I need to read a little more here, and I need to think about this. I have sort of a sense of what might be done, but I need to think about how to write this. One thing I want to read through is the local paper, the *Arizona Republic*, as it has stories all the time about land and space issues.

Convincing evidence for the solution's effectiveness: Here I need to read what the skeptics are writing. If I do that, I'll know what evidence to provide. Some of the land-use think tanks (e.g., Lincoln Institute of Land Policy) may have information from both the advocates and skeptics. I also need to check the Government Documents section of the campus library.

EXAMPLES OF INVENTION

Brainstorming (pp. 158, 332)
Freewriting (pp. 114, 245, 383)
Criteria (p. 290)
Listing (p. 72)
Answers to Reporter's Questions (p. 244)
Organization (pp. 75, 164)
Clustering (pp. 114, 289)
Concept Mapping (p. 335)
Interviewing (p. 203)
Research (pp. 115, 160, 205, 246, 292, 384)
Reflection (p. 12)

A well-documented review of alternative solutions: If I don't look at a range of solutions, I might reinvent the wheel or miss a really good solution. I need to keep an open mind. Also, if I don't look at other possibilities, sceptics will think that I'm hiding something.

A call to action: I'll rely a lot on others here. I'll see how others have called for action—and how folks have responded to those calls. I know that the think-tank reports will include calls to action.

Reviewing Your Invention and Research

After finding sources and reading them critically, to reconsider your thinking about your problem and your proposed solution in light of the qualities of an effective solution. Also begin thinking about a tentative thesis—your statement of your proposed solution. Keep an open mind, though. As you draft and revise your proposal, you may continue to refine your thesis. In some cases, you might even change it drastically. People who develop the best solutions usually leave open the possibility that a better solution could occur to them at any time.

For more on developing a thesis, see Chapter 13.

Esther Ellsworth Considers Her Research and Focuses Her Ideas

After reading through various sources and taking notes, Ellsworth wrote the following in her research journal:

> My reading has given me a better handle on the problem and its possible solutions. I think I'm ready to state that lawmakers need to pass laws that mandate a comprehensive—not simple—plan for land use. I think that I know what needs to be in a comprehensive plan, and I'll mention those components in my proposal.

A WRITER'S *Responsibility* | Constructing Writing to Solve Problems

When you propose a solution to a problem, you have multiple responsibilities. You have a responsibility to be honest about the scope and magnitude of the problem: Who is affected, and how much are they affected? In addition, if there are costs associated with your proposal, it is your responsibility to provide an accurate estimate of those costs.

You also have a responsibility to consider a range of viable solutions and to evaluate carefully the effectiveness, affordability, and limitations of each. In doing so, you establish your credibility with your readers by demonstrating that you have looked at a number of solutions, that you have thoroughly investigated each one, and that you have made a carefully considered recommendation. By presenting each option fairly and by showing how *your* solution is the best, you also make your own position more credible and believable.

Organizing Your Information

Once you know the problem you will be writing about and the solution you will be proposing, you need to consider how you might organize this material. The questions that you need to ask yourself are all rhetorical:

- Who is your audience?
- Why might they be concerned about the problem you are discussing, and why might they be willing to accept your solution? Is it in your audience's best interest to find a solution for your problem?
- What is your purpose for writing—that is, why do your readers need this solution?
- What is the most important aspect of the problem you are proposing to solve?

One method for organizing a solution to a problem is the **whole-problem pattern.** If you are following this pattern, you first grab the readers' attention and introduce the problem and then use the paragraphs that follow to explain and illustrate it. If you think that readers are already familiar with the problem, this part of the paper could be fairly short, consisting of only a paragraph or two. If you think that readers are not familiar with the problem, however, then you might need to devote several pages to explaining and illustrating it. Then offer your proposed solution or set of solutions, respond to objections that you think readers might have, and conclude with a call to action.

A second organizational approach is to **segment the problem.** This approach is useful if the problem is relatively complex and has several components. First, you explain and illustrate the problem, but in a general way. Next, you focus on each part of the problem that needs special attention, offering a solution and responding to objections that you anticipate specific to each part. Finally, you offer suggestions for implementation and conclude with a call to action.

A third organizational approach, which involves a **sequence of steps,** is appropriate if the solution has multiple steps. After introducing the problem, you offer an overview of a series of steps that will solve the problem. You then explain each step in detail, provide evidence that it will work, and address any objections to it.

Here is a summary of these three organizational structures.

Options FOR Organization

Organizing a Proposal Essay

Whole-Problem Pattern	Segmenting the Problem	Sequence of Steps
Introduce the problem and its background.	Introduce the problem and its background.	Introduce the problem and its background.
Explain the problem.	Explain the problem.	Explain the problem.
Offer a solution or set of solutions.	Explain one part of the problem, offer a solution, and respond to objections.	Offer a multistep solution with an overview of the steps.
Respond to anticipated objections to the solution.	Explain another part, offer a solution, and respond to objections.	Offer a detailed explanation of the first step.
Offer suggestions for implementing the solution.	Deal similarly with remaining parts.	Offer a detailed explanation of the second step.
Conclude with a call to action.	Offer suggestions for implementing the solution.	Deal with any additional steps that might be necessary.
	Conclude with a call to action.	Conclude with a call to action.

Constructing a Complete Draft

Once you have chosen the organizational approach that works best given your audience and purpose, you are ready to construct the rest of your draft. Remember that your thinking about the problem and its solution(s) will evolve as you write, so as you work on the draft, keep the following in mind:

- Draw on your invention work and your research. As you draft, you may discover that you need to do more invention work and/or more research.
- As you try out tentative solutions to the problem, ask peers about the kinds of evidence you need to demonstrate that the solution is viable.
- Ask yourself and peers whether visuals might help make your case.

connect
mhconnectcomposition.com
Drafting and Revising QL11006

INTEGRATING SOURCES

Including Others' Perspectives in Narratives (p. 76)
Quoting Sources (p. 118)
Paraphrasing Sources (p. 164)
Incorporating Numerical Data (p. 208)
Incorporating Partial Quotes (p. 250)
Creating Charts or Graphs to Show Your Data (p. 295)
Summarizing Information from Sources (p. 338)
Including Research Information (p. 387)

Synthesizing and Integrating Sources into Your Draft: Including Research Information

If you are working on a large research assignment, you will end up with a wealth of information, so using that information in your text can be a challenge: How can you condense it to help the reader understand it? This problem is especially acute when some of your research comes from texts that provide you with a large amount of information. One way to condense such research is to summarize what you learn and then to use those summaries in your text (for more on summarizing, see pages 565–566).

Often student writers, when faced with a mountain of information, try to use it all—and so the information overwhelms the text. The student has turned over control of the text to all of the research she or he found, and the text is no longer the writer's. You can avoid giving up control of your text by using summaries of the research in your writing to support the claims.

Student writer Esther Ellsworth selected a *big* subject to write about: land-use planning in the state of Arizona. In working with such a large subject, Ellsworth collected a lot of information, some of which came from a text rich with ideas: "Overview of Growth in Arizona: Critical Statistics." Ellsworth faced the challenge of selecting the most important ideas and presenting that information to her readers, in an understandable manner.

Simply listing what she found would have given Ellsworth's readers a lot of information, but some of it would not have related to her point. So, she summarized what she learned and used those summaries in her writing. Here is an example:

> Arizona lawmakers need to work with national officials to adjust the federal regulations that make it impossible to designate State Trust Lands as permanent preservation zones. The easiest way to do this would be to create, with the federal government's approval, a "Conservation Area" classification within the State Land Department. The new designation would give an undeveloped area permanent status as a non-development zone; its land would remain free of structures, and only the state government, with public approval, could build roads or utilities on it. The property could still generate revenue for the state by being leased to ranchers and farmers ("Overview" 29), but cities would never be allowed to encroach on the territory, companies would never be allowed to mine the land, and power plants would never pollute the area's air. The space would be free of concrete and steel; it would be open to animals, plants, and people. (paragraph 14)

Note that a lot of possible approaches to the problem are listed here, but in a format—a summary—that makes them clear and understandable to the reader. Note, too, how Ellsworth ends her paragraph with the positive aspects of using the ideas she summarized, as then the area "would be free of concrete and steel; it would be open to animals, plants, and people." She thus relates her summarized information back to her main point.

To use summaries in your writing, do the following:

- Introduce the summarized information (never just put it into your text without some of your words as an introduction).
- Connect the summary back to your main point, so your readers can easily see how the summarized information supports your argument.
- Accurately report and document where the information came from.

Parts of a Complete Draft

Introduction: Regardless of your organizational approach, begin with a strong introduction to capture your readers' attention and introduce the problem that you are proposing to solve. To accomplish these two goals, you might do one or more of the following:

connect
mhconnectcomposition.com
Introductory paragraph overview QL11007

- **Provide a brief history of the problem.**
- **Quote an authority who knows the problem well.** In "The Nursing Crisis," Michelle Mise Pollard begins her report with an account of a nurse's testimony to Congress.
- **Cite salient statistics that demonstrate the nature of the problem.**
- **Provide information about the problem that will surprise—and possibly concern—readers.** Pollard should get the attention of anyone reading her text when she notes that the nursing crisis affects "anyone who is a provider or consumer of health care in this country."

Body: When you propose a solution to a problem, you should determine the most effective organizational approach for the purpose you are trying to achieve and the audience you are addressing. The reading selections in this chapter, for example, use the organizational approaches outlined on pages 386–387 to good effect. Whether you present a whole problem, segment the problem, or give a step-by-step solution, be sure to show why other solutions will not work or have already failed. Sometimes a problem has not been solved because previous solutions addressed only its symptoms, not its root cause. If this is the case, you need to show that your solution will take care of the root problem.

- **Present a whole problem and then give solutions.** Although she has no one solution to the whole problem of the nursing shortage, Pollard does propose that any real solution will succeed only if all of the people who have a stake in solving this problem work together to find a solution and not just try to fix small pieces of it.
- **Give a step-by-step solution to the problem.** Pollard suggests specific actions to take, in the bulleted list she provides on page 371.

Conclusion: In your conclusion, review your proposed solution, reach out to your audience, and, usually, call for readers to take action to implement the proposal. Your conclusion could include the following:

connect
mhconnectcomposition.com
Concluding paragraph overview QL11008

- An outline of the problem you are working to solve
- A summary of your main points, with an explanation of why your solution would work
- A call to action—what you would like your reader to *do* now that he or she knows about the problem and your suggested solution

VISUALIZING *Variations* | Alternative Forms for Solving Problems

Assume that rather than writing an essay to propose a solution, you design a brochure. Consider the example of an abandoned mall and a proposed multiuse complex called SkySong. What pictures or drawings might be useful to a potential customer, keeping in mind that the project is reaching out not only to businesses but also to people who might want to live in SkySong?

For the residential part of the project, this visual and exerpt from the descriptive text that accompanies it is designed to catch a potential renter's eye:

Source: Courtesy SkySong, rendering by Pei Cobb Freed & Partners

- 325 one-, two-, and three-bedroom floor plans ranging in size from ±551 to ±1,583 square feet
- 1,000-space parking garage for residents and tenants
- Private balconies
- Community pool, spa, and exercise facility
- State-of-the-art high-speed Internet and communications facilities

Title: As you compose your proposal, a title should emerge at some point—often very late in the process. The title should, of course, reflect the problem that you are addressing and might or might not hint at the solution. If you hint at a controversial solution in the title, however, you risk alienating readers whom you might otherwise win over with the strength of your argument.

The following details are directed at possible business clients:

- Two 4-story buildings, each approximately 150,000 square feet, frame the eastern half of the east-west boulevard intersecting the center. Built with flexibility in mind, the buildings are designed to accommodate any tenant's space needs, whether small start-up companies, expanding businesses, or regional operations.

Consider these questions:

- This drawing, has the look and feel of a photograph. Why might the artist who rendered this drawing want it to *seem real*, as if the buildings and people really exist?
- What does this drawing contribute to the proposal for SkySong? What could similar drawings contribute to a proposal in the form of a brochure?

Writing Activity

Constructing a Complete Draft

Using the writing you did when selecting an organizational approach for your problem/solution paper, write a complete first draft of your paper. Be sure to explain your problem in detail and to outline your solution and explain why it is the best way to solve the problem your paper focuses on.

An Excerpt from Esther Ellsworth's First Draft

In this excerpt from her first draft, note how Esther Ellsworth presents the problem to her audience. As she wrote, Ellsworth did not worry about grammar, usage, punctuation, and mechanics; instead, she concentrated on getting her main ideas onto paper. (The numbers in circles refer to peer comments—see page 394.)

Land Use Planning in Arizona

Esther Ellsworth

Population growth, and the urban expansion that accompanies it, is beginning to destroy Arizona's outdoor flavor. Because we have no statewide plan for land use, development goes unchecked and undirected; cities sprawl, and growth also hits both rural communities and historically unsettled areas. As people watch, the open land for which Arizona is famous begins to disappear; office buildings, housing developments, and utility plants swallow it up. Residents see this occurring, and they become worried about state land preservation and planning.①

❷Land conservation is necessary for several reasons, first of which is the fact that open spaces can be used by virtually every member of the public, allowing all people to enjoy the outdoors. Guarding environments from exploitation by developers and businesses keeps public land available for all citizens' benefit. Protected environments offer space to everyone, space where people can go hiking or camping, where they can go boating or bird watching, where they can hunt or fish. With protected environments, people are free to enjoy the land in its most natural, undisturbed state. . . .

In order to have viable land use programs, we must have projects that are supported by all community sectors. . . . Just like education, immigration, and criminal justice concerns, land use will have to become part of Arizona's core political dialogue.❸

Arizona land preservation efforts must consider the state's present territory divisions and usage plans. . . . We can decide to save many of Arizona's wild areas from urbanization, and we can officially pledge to protect our environment's biodiversity.❹

The passage of Preserve Arizona also presents the challenge of linking small conservation areas to one another. . . . But neither boundary-specification nor Preserve Arizona is comprehensive enough to protect this state's land resources.❺

In almost any discussion of land use, developers and environmentalists put themselves at odds, polarizing the conversation and refusing any compromise. Therefore, if they are ever to recognize their roles as stewards of the land, both groups will have to take a step back from the argument. They must leave behind their extreme beliefs—advocating either no growth planning or total growth restriction—because both these approaches are harmful to the state. (If Arizona's open space is exploited, it will not be able to yield profit *for anyone* in the future, and if all development is stopped, we will endanger our present economic health.) The best approach to the question of land use, instead, is compromise. Our cities will continue to grow, but we can slow their rapid expansion by preserving areas in and around them. We can also preserve large tracts of land in the state's rural regions, thereby preventing most urbanization of these areas.❻❼❽

Revising

Once you have a draft, put it aside for a day or so. This break will give you the chance to come back to your text as a new reader might. Reread and revise your work, looking especially for ideas that are not explained completely, terms that are not defined, and other problem areas. As you work to revise your early drafts, postpone doing a great deal of heavy editing. When you revise, you will probably change the content and structure of your paper, so time spent working to fix problems with sentence style or grammar, punctuation, or mechanics at this stage is often wasted.

As you revise, here are some questions to ask yourself:

- How effectively have I explained and outlined the problem(s), so my readers can understand those issues?
- What else might my audience want or need to know about my subject?
- How might I explain my solution(s) in sufficient detail and with enough examples so my readers can see how my ideas are logical solutions to the problem?
- How clearly have I explained and defined any terms my readers might not know?
- What other visual aids might help explain the problem and/or my solution?

WRITER'S *Workshop* | Responding to Full Drafts

Working with one or two other classmates, read each paper and offer comments and questions that will help each of you see your papers' strengths and weaknesses. Consider the following questions as you do:

- What is your first impression of this draft? How effectively does the title draw you into the paper? What part(s) of the text are especially effective at explaining the problem or the writer's proposed solution?
- How successfully does the introduction grab readers' attention? What other attention grabbers might the writer try?
- How well has the writer explained the problem to someone who is unfamiliar with it? How might the writer explain it more effectively?
- How effective is the organizational approach?
- How carefully did the writer document sources in this draft?
- How well has the writer explained the proposed solution?
- How well has the writer addressed objections that skeptics might raise?
- How has the writer suggested ways to implement the proposed solution?
- Might visuals help the writer to present the problem or its solution more effectively?
- How effectively does the conclusion call people to action?
- What do you see as the main weaknesses of this paper? How the writer might improve the text?

Student Comments on Esther Ellsworth's First Draft

Using the questions above, Esther Ellsworth's classmates made some suggestions on her first draft. Below are comments she received, keyed to the excerpt from the first draft on pages 391–92.

1. "You probably need to do more of an introduction that grabs our attention more than this does."
2. "Here you might do something to build a link between these paragraphs—perhaps some language about the proposal."
3. "Can you add something here about how to conduct these dialogues in ways that will help to solve the problem rather than make it worse?"
4. "What have people tried to do in the past? What will be the benefits of your proposed solution?"
5. "Is there anything else that needs to be done to solve the problem?"
6. "What about people who think that your proposal will restrict freedom and harm commerce?"
7. "You need some sort of conclusion."
8. "Of course, in your revised version, you'll need to include all of your citations."

Responding to Readers' Comments

Once you have received feedback from your classmates, your instructor, and others about how to improve your text, you have to determine what to *do* with their suggestions and ideas. The first thing to do with any feedback is to really listen to it and consider carefully what your readers have to say. For example, how might Esther Ellsworth have responded to these reader suggestions?

- One reader was not taken by Ellsworth's introduction. When a peer reviewer indicates that an introduction does not excite him or her, that means that *some* readers might just stop reading at that point.
- Another reader asked for a smoother transition between two sections.
- A reader requested more historical background and information.

All of these questions or concerns were issues that Ellsworth needed to address. As with any feedback, it is important to listen to it carefully and consider what your reader has to say. Then it is up to you, as the author, to decide *how* to come to terms with these suggestions. You may decide to reject some comments, of course; other comments, though, may deserve your attention. You may find that comments from more than one reader contradict each other. In that case, you need to use your own judgment to decide which reader's comments are on the right track.

In the final version of her paper on pages 396–402, you can see how Esther Ellsworth responded to her readers' comments, as well as to her own review of her first draft.

Knowledge of Conventions

By paying attention to conventions when they edit their work, effective writers help to meet their readers' expectations. Experienced readers expect proposals to follow accepted conventions.

Editing

When you edit and polish your writing, you make changes to improve your style and to make your writing clearer and more concise. You also check your work to make sure it adheres to conventions of grammar, usage, punctuation, mechanics, and spelling. If you have used sources in your paper, make sure you are following the documentation style your instructor requires.

connect
mhconnectcomposition.com
Revising and Editing overview (also Drafting) QL11009

Because it can be difficult to identify small problems in a familiar text, it often helps to distance yourself from it so that you can approach the draft with fresh eyes. Some people like to put the text aside for a day or so; others try reading aloud; and some even read from the last sentence to the first so that the content, and their familiarity with it, doesn't cause them to overlook an error. We strongly recommend that you ask classmates, friends, and tutors to read your work to help find editing problems.

See Chapter 20 for more on documenting sources using MLA or APA style.

To assist you with editing, we offer here a round-robin editing activity on inclusive language.

ROUND-ROBIN EDITING WITH A FOCUS ON

WRITER'S *Workshop* | Round-Robin Editing with a Focus on Inclusive Language

When you propose solutions to problems, be especially careful to use inclusive language—language that does not exclude people based on gender, ethnicity, marital status, or disability. Using inclusive language makes readers feel that they are included in the group that is solving the problem.

Look for instances in your work where you may have inadvertently used language that excludes a group based on gender, ethnicity, marital status, or disability. If you are uncertain about whether a particular word or phrase is a problem, consult a grammar handbook or ask your instructor.

connect
mhconnectcomposition.com
Correcting gender bias and pronoun-antecedent agreement QL11011

For advice on writing in different genres, see the Online Appendix. For guidelines for formatting and documenting papers in MLA or APA style, see Chapter 20.

Genres, Documentation, and Format

If you are writing an academic paper in response to Scenario 1, you will need to follow the conventions appropriate for the discipline in which you are writing. For Scenario 2, you may need to follow the conventions of a formal proposal.

A Writer Proposes a Solution: Esther Ellsworth's Final Draft

Below is the final draft of Esther Ellsworth's proposal. As you read her essay, consider whether you think her solutions will work.

ESTHER ELLSWORTH

PROPOSAL ESSAY

Comprehensive Land Use Planning in Arizona

One of Ellsworth's classmates made the following comment on her initial draft:

You probably need to do more of an introduction that grabs our attention more than this does.

Ellsworth responded with a new opening paragraph that attempts to catch the reader's attention by alluding to various American myths.

The *American West*. What visions of grandeur that phrase brings to mind! Repeating it aloud, I think of tumultuous rivers, steep mountains, deep canyons, wide expanses of desert, large stands of trees. I think of pioneers migrating to this area, of people coming in search of something more than they ever had before—money, adventure, freedom from religious persecution, rebirth—something to be found in the wide open spaces of the land. I think of the native peoples who have inhabited this territory for centuries, not claiming ownership but instead simply living on the land for generations. I think of this place that I and so many others have called home. 1

Land—open land—is central to the identity of a western state. It is the very fact that our cities are two or three hours apart, that we have open areas without any significant development, that gives the West its character. Yet, more and more, we are losing this characteristic. Developers keep speculating, turning once-rural areas into huge planned communities. Cities keep sprouting up and spreading out, encroaching on the wilderness around them. And people keep moving to Arizona, attracted by the state's open land and renowned natural beauty, by the good weather and good recreation. 2

This population growth, and the urban expansion that accompanies it, is beginning to destroy Arizona's outdoor flavor. Because we have no statewide plan for land use, development goes unchecked and undirected; cities sprawl, and growth also hits both rural communities and historically unsettled areas. As people watch, the open land for which Arizona is 3 famous begins to disappear; office buildings, housing developments, and utility plants swallow it up. Residents see this occurring, and they become worried about state land preservation and planning. People recognize that Arizona's lack of conservation measures is a problem, but they do not know what to do about it. They do not understand that a series of legislative actions can create the plan for comprehensive land use that Arizona needs.

Land conservation is necessary for several reasons. First of all, open spaces can be used by virtually every member of the public, allowing all people to enjoy the outdoors. Guarding environments from exploitation by developers and businesses keeps public land available for all citizens' benefit. Protected environments provide space for everyone, space where people can go hiking or camping, where they can go boating or bird watching, where they can hunt or fish. With protected environments, people are free to enjoy the land in its most natural, undisturbed state. 4

Open space is also important ecologically. By preserving the native species and genetic variation of an area, open space preserves biodiversity. Animals and plants thrive in unrestricted territories, because the land gives them access to migratory routes, new habitats, and new mating populations (Nabhan 37–39). Thus, land conservation allows Arizona's unique creatures and ecosystems to prosper: Our state is home to many protected species, and it is the site of several reintroduction efforts for California condor and Mexican wolf populations, both of which are endangered. Arizona is also one of the only places in the world to have Sonoran Desert flora and fauna, and regions like southern Arizona's "sky island" mountain ranges (the Tucson Mountains, Santa Ritas, and Catalinas) or northern Arizona's Colorado Plateau provide research opportunities for numerous scientists ("Colorado" 1; Ellsworth). The importance of preserving this state's biodiversity, for both species protection and academic study, is clear. 5

Some people claim that preservation of biodiversity should not receive as much attention as it does, that it stands in the way of states' economic health. Today, however, the opposite of that statement is true: Preserving biodiversity in Arizona is financially important and beneficial for everyone involved. Ecotourism, or "visitation to natural areas that involves no consumptive use of those areas," is an extremely profitable and reliable economic foundation for many communities (Leones 56). Ecotourism also happens to be one of Arizona's primary methods of attracting visitors to the state; each year, about five million people come to see the Grand Canyon alone, and the money they spend supports local economies ("Grand" 1). If the Canyon were only a hole in the ground without an incredibly diverse ecosystem, if it did not host an amazing variety of animals and plants, people would not be nearly so anxious to see it. But the canyon is *not* just a "hole in the ground," and like many areas in our state, its unadulterated natural beauty makes it attractive to visitors. This sort of beauty—found 6

Ellsworth received this comment from a classmate:

Here you might do something to build a link between these paragraphs—perhaps some language about the proposal.

Her response was to add language that helps to serve as a bridge between the two paragraphs.

also in places like the Chiricahua Mountains and the West Fork of Oak Creek—brings visitors, and ultimately better financial health, to the state.

For all of these reasons, open space is worthy of conservation. We realize, as Arizona citizens, that land use and planning are issues we need to address; they affect so many aspects of our lives that we cannot ignore them any longer. In Arizona, there is a growing need to develop a statewide vision for land appropriations, and the public has to decide how to set aside land for conservation. 7

In response to a very short paragraph that briefly alluded to community involvement and political dialogue, one student made the following comment:

Can you add something here about how to conduct these dialogues in ways that will help to solve the problem rather than make it worse?

Ellsworth's response was to expand paragraph 8 in order to "show" community involvement and political dialogue rather than merely "tell" about it.

In order to have viable land use programs, we must have projects that are supported by all members of the community. The Sierra Club might advocate one approach while the governor's office and utility companies prefer another, and if no one is willing to construct a third, compromise plan, conservation efforts will fail. Many people want to approach land use planning as a problem to be solved quickly, as something they can look at once and then leave behind (Martori), but such thinking is also sure to fail. Because Arizona's land use patterns and needs will always change, it is impossible to establish policy that will not require periodic review. To be successful in conservation efforts, Arizona leaders and citizens must consider land use to be an ongoing concern, something that will be part of every future campaign and administration. "Governing growth will always require a perspective and process capable of balancing strong and independent values," ASU Public Affairs Professor John Stuart Hall says, and he is certainly correct (14). Just like education, immigration, and criminal justice concerns, land use will have to become part of Arizona's core political dialogue. 8

As we discuss land protection and development, we must also be careful not to turn our conversations into tense political debates. This inclination toward divisiveness inhibits the communication and consensus that are necessary for the successful establishment of a statewide land use plan. If people argue continuously, they have difficulty understanding one another's worries, and they do not work well together. Until Arizona's citizens decide to establish common ground in conservation discussions, until they recognize a shared desire to take care of the state's land, they will not make much progress with planning. "We must struggle together," Phoenix writer Larry Landry states in one opinion piece, "to replace animosity with civility in our dialogue on the future of our community, to recognize the need to bring balance into the growth versus no-growth debate . . ." (80). Until this happens, conservation efforts will have little success. 9

Advocates of land preservation in Arizona must consider the state's present territory divisions and usage plans. Right now, about 80% of the state is undeveloped. Most of these areas are managed by American Indian tribes, local and state governments, the Bureau of Land Management, and the U.S. Forest Service ("Overview" 29). A person could rightly ask, then, why more preservation efforts are necessary if so much land is *already* held 10 in the public's interest. The most direct response to this query, the reason we need further conservation measures, is that many people have tried to develop commercial and residential sites in these so-far-undisturbed areas—areas meant for the general public's use—and under present laws, such action is permissible. Under Arizona law, individuals and companies are allowed to purchase territory from the State Land Department, even though the areas are designated State Trust Lands (properties to be leased or sold only for the benefit of education and criminal justice programs). Because of the present structure, the Land Department manages to sell areas without much oversight from courts or the public. Citizens therefore have no way to preserve State Trust Lands for conservation, and they lose much of "the open landscape [that is] so vital to [Arizona's] functioning ecosystem" (Walsh 143). If, as some argue, we do not need to reconsider State Trust Land rules, how, then, can we ever hope to preserve our open areas from development? If, on the other hand, we reserve the right to decide the future of the Trust Lands, we can create conservation codes for the state, designating certain areas for preservation and leaving others open to the possibility of development. By taking this step, we can decide to save many of Arizona's wild areas from urbanization, and we can officially pledge to protect our environment's biodiversity.

People have tried to solve Arizona's land conservation dilemma several times in the past, but they have not developed an all-encompassing preservation program. In 1998, when Arizona voters passed Proposition 303 (the Preserve Arizona Initiative), they did not effect the kind of change that can really save the state's open lands from development. Under Preserve Arizona, $20 million of state funding will be available every year to help local governments purchase land for conservation. But with this measure, citizens still have little assurance that Arizona's significant tracts of open space will be protected. The Preserve Arizona plan will help to guard small parcels from development by setting aside land in projects like the Scottsdale McDowell Mountain Preserve, but in the end, it will only create a fragmented string of conservation parks. 11

Here, one of Ellsworth's classmates asked for some historical perspective:

What have people tried to do in the past? What will be the benefits of your proposed solution?

Her response was to describe some past Arizona efforts at land management.

The passage of Preserve Arizona also presents the challenge of linking small conservation areas to one another. If animals and plants living in Preserve Arizona territories are to thrive, each of the small protected parcels must be connected to other wild spaces. According to some people, such a requirement makes it necessary for cities to implement "greenbelt" or growth boundary policies. (A greenbelt is a permanent conservation area around a city; a growth boundary is a temporary development limit that is adjusted every few years.) But while these actions are helpful biologically, allowing animals to migrate, they are unlikely to solve the problem of open space preservation. Growth boundaries are simply too unpopular among politicians and developers to be viable conservation methods. 12

Many officials maintain that boundaries make housing costs skyrocket, and politicians therefore hate the idea of implementing boundaries here in Arizona (DeGrove 88). It is wise to be skeptical of complaints against boundaries, however. In Portland, Oregon, which has had a growth boundary since 1973, residents have not noted significant cost-of-living increases (DeGrove 88), and Arizona cities could choose to adopt some version of the urban boundary idea, making it work in conjunction with Preserve Arizona. But neither boundary-specification nor Preserve Arizona is comprehensive enough to protect this state's land resources.

One classmate wanted to know if there were other options:

Is there anything else that needs to be done to solve the problem?

Ellsworth responded by mentioning alternative options.

In addition to Preserve Arizona and urban boundary plans, the state needs to develop two major policies: It must adjust State Trust Land rulings to designate some of these territories as permanent conservation spaces, and it must give individuals a way to designate their own properties as conservation lands. 13

Arizona lawmakers need to work with national officials to adjust the federal regulations that make it impossible to designate State Trust Lands as permanent preservation zones. The easiest way to do this would be to create, with the federal government's approval, a "Conservation Area" classification within the State Land Department. The new designation would give an undeveloped area permanent status as a non-development zone; its land would remain free of structures, and only the state government, with public approval, could build roads or utilities on it. The property could still generate revenue for the state by being leased to ranchers and farmers ("Overview" 29), but cities would never be allowed to encroach on the territory, companies would never be allowed to mine the land, and power plants would never pollute the area's air. The space would be free of concrete and steel; it would be open to animals, plants, and people. 14

One of Ellsworth's classmates asked:

What about people who think that your proposal will restrict freedom and harm commerce?

She responded by trying to anticipate the position of potential critics and give arguments to show that her proposal would not restrict freedom.

Some Arizona residents would definitely object to setting aside these lands as Conservation Areas; the idea of non-development zoning is anathema for them because it seems like a restriction of freedom. But land conservation actually *guarantees* citizens' freedoms. It may prohibit certain individuals from disturbing the land, but it allows all citizens the freedom to use the area, and it is thus the most fair use for all involved. Through leasing to ranchers and farmers, Conservation Areas provide money for state education and criminal justice programs, and they ensure the preservation of places that are important and beneficial to all of Arizona. Also, not all State Trust Lands would become Conservation Areas; about 10 percent would still remain available for the Land Department to sell, lease, or preserve as it deems appropriate. 15

Once the Conservation Area system is in place, private individuals would have a means of designating their own properties for preservation. Currently, tax systems make it very difficult for large landowners to keep their areas free of development. If individuals who own large pieces of land 16 do not use the territory for commercial purposes, like farming or ranching, they pay exorbitant property taxes. Upon reaching retirement age, many of these people find that they cannot afford to keep their land because the taxes are simply too high. Individuals who want to preserve their family's heritage and land have no way to do so, and consequently much of Arizona's agricultural and ranching lands have been sold to developers in the past few decades. If we were to allow landowners to make their properties Conservation Areas, however, and give them a tax break for doing so, we would make possible another way to preserve open spaces. It is true that each of the territory additions would be rather small (Arizona's remaining tracts of private land are not very extensive), but nonetheless, they would increase the amount of preserved open space in Arizona.

In almost any discussion of land use, developers and environmentalists put themselves at odds, polarizing the conversation and refusing any compromise. Therefore, if they are ever to recognize their roles as stewards of the land, both groups will have to take a step back from the argument. They must leave behind their extreme beliefs—advocating either no growth planning or total growth restriction—because both of these approaches are harmful to the state. If Arizona's open space is exploited, it will not be able to yield profit for *anyone* in the future, and if all development is stopped, we will endanger our present economic health. The best approach to the question of land use, instead, is compromise. Our cities will continue to grow, but we can slow their rapid expansion by preserving areas in and around them. We can also preserve large tracts of land in the state's rural regions, thereby preventing the urbanization of these areas. 17

Restricting growth and planning for conservation does not limit individual freedom; instead, these actions free us all from future problems with land use. They free us to enjoy the open spaces of Arizona. They free us to use the land for recreation and sustainable commerce (ranching and agriculture). By controlling cities' growth and general land use, we ensure every individual's ability to enjoy state lands in the years to come. We ensure the survival of our unique environment, and we ensure the beauty of this territory. Developing a comprehensive land use plan for Arizona will not be easy, but the legislation is possible, and developing it is a challenge we ought to accept. 18

One classmate pointed out that Ellsworth didn't really have a conclusion in her initial draft. She responded with a concluding paragraph.

Works Cited

"Colorado Plateau Information Network." Web. 22 Nov. 1998 <http://ecosys.usgs.nau.edu/>.

DeGrove, John M. "State Responses to Urban Growth: Lessons for Arizona." *Growth in Arizona: The Machine in the Garden.* Tempe: Morrison Institute for Public Policy/ASU, 1998. Print.

This paper follows MLA guidelines for in-text citations and works cited.

Since the draft originally submitted to classmates didn't contain any formal documentation, one classmate reminded Ellsworth to add it:

Of course, in your revised version, you'll need to include all of your citations.

Ellsworth included a formal list of works cited in her final draft.

Ellsworth, Clare. Personal interview. 25 Oct. 1998.

"Grand Canyon National Park." Web. 22 Nov. 1998 <http://www.nps.gov/grca/>.

Hall, John Stuart. "Arizona's Growth Continuum and Policy Choices." *Growth in Arizona: The Machine in the Garden.* Tempe: Morrison Institute for Public Policy/ASU, 1998. Print.

Landry, Larry. "Restore the Focus on Planning." *Growth in Arizona: The Machine in the Garden.* Tempe: Morrison Institute for Public Policy/ASU, 1998. Print.

Leones, Julie, and Bonnie Colby. "Tracking Expenditures of the Elusive Nature Tourists of Southeastern Arizona." *Journal of Travel Research* 36.3 (1998): 56.

Martori, Peter. "Land Use and Urban Growth in Arizona." Flinn Foundation Public Policy Seminar Series, Session 1.17, Oct. 1998. Lecture.

"Overview of Growth in Arizona: Critical Statistics." *Growth in Arizona: The Machine in the Garden.* Tempe: Morrison Institute for Public Policy/ASU, 1998. Print.

Nabhan, Gary Paul, and Andrew R. Holdsworth. "State of the Desert Biome." *Growth in Arizona: The Machine in the Garden.* Tempe: Morrison Institute for Public Policy/ASU, 1998. Print.

Walsh, James P. "Losing Ground: Land Fragmentation in Rural Arizona." *Growth in Arizona: The Machine in the Garden.* Tempe: Morrison Institute for Public Policy/ASU, 1998. Print.

QUESTIONS FOR WRITING AND DISCUSSION: LEARNING OUTCOMES

Rhetorical Knowledge: The Writer's Situation and Rhetoric

1. **Audience:** Who is the intended audience for Ellsworth's proposal? What makes you think that?
2. **Purpose:** What does Ellsworth hope will happen when people read her proposal?
3. **Voice and tone:** How has Ellsworth used language to help establish her *ethos* as someone who is knowledgeable about the problem of land use?
4. **Responsibility:** Comment on Ellsworth's use of sources to support her proposal. How responsibly has she used her sources? Why?
5. **Context, format, and genre:** Ellsworth wrote this paper for a first-year writing course. If she were to change this piece of writing to an editorial for her local newspaper, what revisions would she need to make? Effective problem/solution papers feature a well-defined problem and then present a viable solution. Does Ellsworth do both in her paper? If so, how? If not, what could she do?

Critical Thinking: The Writer's Ideas and Your Personal Response

6. What is your initial response to Ellsworth's paper?
7. How is Ellsworth's paper similar to other proposed solutions that you have read?

Composing Processes and Knowledge of Conventions: The Writer's Strategies

8. How effectively does Ellsworth organize her proposal? What other organization would have worked?
9. How does Ellsworth provide evidence that her solution is viable? What other evidence might she have provided?

Inquiry and Research: Ideas for Further Exploration

10. Interview family members and neighbors about their feelings on what is happening to your community and the surrounding areas.

Self-Assessment: Reflecting on Your Goals

Having finished your proposal assignment, take some time to reflect on the thinking and writing you have done. It is often useful to go back and reconsider your learning goals. In order to better reflect on these learning goals, respond in writing to the following questions:

Rhetorical Knowledge

- *Purpose:* What have you learned about the purposes for writing a proposal?
- *Audience:* What have you learned about addressing an audience for a proposal?
- *Rhetorical situation:* How did the writing context affect your writing about the problem you chose and the solution you proposed? How did your choice of problem and solution affect the research you conducted and how you made your case to your readers?
- *Voice and tone:* What have you learned about the writer's voice in writing a proposal?

Critical Thinking, Reading, and Writing

- *Learning/inquiry:* As a result of writing a proposal, how have you become a more critical thinker, reader, and writer?
- *Responsibility:* What have you learned about a writer's responsibility to propose a good and workable solution?
- *Reading and research:* What research did you conduct for your proposal? Why? What additional research might you have done?
- *Skills:* What critical thinking, reading, and writing skills do you hope to develop further in your next writing project? How will you work on them?

Writing Processes

- *Invention:* What process did you go through to identify the problem and the solution you wrote about? How helpful was this process? What research skills have you developed while writing your proposal?
- *Organizing your ideas and details:* How successful was your organization? What drafting skills have you improved? How will you continue to improve them?
- *Revising:* What revising skills have you improved? If you could go back and make an additional revision, what would it be?
- *Working with peers:* How did you make use of the feedback you received? How have you developed your skills in working with peers? How could your peer readers help you more on your next assignment? How might you help them more?

- *Visuals:* Did you use visuals to help explain your problem and solution? If so, what did you learn about incorporating these elements?
- *Writing habits:* What "writerly habits" have you developed, modified, or improved on as you constructed the writing assignment for this chapter? How will you change your future writing activities, based on what you have learned about yourself?

Knowledge of Conventions

- *Editing:* What sentence problem did you find most frequently in your writing? How will you avoid that problem in future assignments?
- *Genre:* What conventions of the genre you were using, if any, gave you problems?
- *Documentation:* Did you use sources for your paper? If so, what documentation style did you use? What problems, if any, did you have with it?

If you are constructing a course portfolio, file your written reflections so that you can return to them when you next work on your portfolio. Refer to Chapter 1 (pages 11–12) for a sample reflection by a student.

Esther Ellsworth Reflects on Her Writing QL11010

chapter 12

Writing about Creative Works

Geometry

I prove a theorem and the
house expands:
the windows jerk free to
hover near the ceiling,
the ceiling floats away with
a sigh.

As the walls clear
themselves of
everything
but transpar-
ency, the
scent of
carnations
leaves with
them. I am out
in the open

and above the windows
have hinged into
butterflies,
sunlight glinting where
they've intersected.
They are going to some
point true and unproven.

—*Rita Dove*

When you think of "literature," do you think of a poem like "Geometry" by Rita Dove? Or do you associate "literature" with some other literary genre? Literature isn't necessarily restricted to novels, short stories, plays, and poetry. It can be defined more broadly to include film and television shows, graphic novels, hypertext, song lyrics—basically, any story told in any kind of medium. You may associate writing about literature exclusively with academic courses, but people think and write about literature and other creative works in many places both inside and outside the classroom. In presentations in civic and professional situations, speakers often allude to a scene or a character from a well-known novel, play, television series, or film to make a point. In your personal life, you may have already posted brief reviews of books on the Web sites of book vendors such as Amazon.com. Throughout your life, as you engage in spoken and written conversations about a novel you have read, a film you have seen, or the lyrics of your favorite song, you'll be thinking, talking, and writing about literature.

Writing about Creative Works

This chapter offers strategies for writing about creative works. Much of what you will read and write about in your college classes will be creative works, such as literature, art drama, poetry, sculpture, film, and photography. After you graduate, you might write to others about plays you see, films you watch, museum exhibits you attend, and so on. And you might evaluate or comment on those same kinds of creative works in your professional life.

Your writing will take the form of any number of genres:

- For an art class, you might construct an academic paper that evaluates a period in the life of an artist.
- For a literature class, you might construct a fictional dialogue between two characters from a novel your class read.
- You might send an e-mail to your extended-family members about an art exhibit you just saw and want to recommend.
- You might draft a letter to the editor of your local paper complaining about its lack of coverage for a new exhibit at your local museum.

As always, the genre you select is determined by the subject, your audience, your thoughts about the creative work, and so on. The "Ways of Writing" feature outlines genres that are suitable for writing about creative works for your college classes and for your life outside the classroom.

Ways of Writing about Creative Works

Genres for Your College Classes	Sample Situation	Advantages of the Genre	Limitations of the Genre
Literary Analysis	For your creative nonfiction class, you are asked to construct an essay comparing and contrasting the writing styles of two authors.	"Comparing and contrasting" the styles of these authors will give you and your readers will gain insight into how they construct their texts.	There are many other aspects of the writing of these authors that you could also examine, so you are a little restricted here.
Rhetorical Analysis	Your writing professor asks you to examine the rhetorical aspects of the text: how the author uses the rhetorical appeals of *ethos, logos*, and *pathos*; how the components of the text work together; and so on.	An academic rhetorical analysis gives you and your classmates insight into how the text functions.	A rhetorical analysis examines a text through a specific lens; there are many other ways to consider how a text works.
Oral presentation	For your art class, you are asked to construct a 15-minute PowerPoint presentation, that illustrates how an artist's work was received and changed over her lifetime.	This presentation will help you and your classmates understand how the work of an artist changes and grows over a period of years.	You will have only a limited time to make your presentation; illustrations will be crucial to your presentation.

Genres for Your College Classes	Sample Situation	Advantages of the Genre	Limitations of the Genre
Book Review	For your literature class, you are asked to review the latest novel by one of your favorite writer sand to let others know something about this writer's work.	This review will allow you to read the book, analyze what the writer has done, and then evaluate the book—placing it in the context of other novels by the same author.	You are only basing your review on your own knowledge and are not researching what others have said.
Music trace	For your intro to blues class, you are asked to selected a blues artist and write about his or her influence on contemporary music.	A trace will help you understand the way music evolves over time and how some artists have a strong impact over time.	Focusing on one artist for the trace might create a narrow view of musical influence.
Genres for Life	**Sample Situation**	**Advantages of the Genre**	**Limitations of the Genre**
Poster	You are involved in a local drama production, and you want to construct a poster to advertise the play.	Your poster can be duplicated and displayed around town to advertise your production.	A poster provides only a limited amount of space; illustrations are needed to catch the eye of passing viewers; some information (location, cost, times, and so on) also needs to be prominently displayed, which further limits available space.
E-mail	You just attended an art exhibit that you want your family to know about, so you decide to construct an e-mail to family members explaining why they should attend the exhibit.	E-mail forces you to write concisely but with sufficient detail to convince family members to attend the exhibit; you also can attach photographs or other illustrations that might help persuade them to attend.	An e-mail generally should not be longer than about a page, so you have limited space to present your argument.
Wiki	You want to share information about local art exhibits and performances on a wiki.	A wiki is an easy and uncomplicated way for people interested in local arts to share and to modify the entries to correct dates, times, venues, actors, etc. as those aspects of the performance change.	Someone may need to monitor the wiki for inappropriate entries and to ensure incorrect information is not listed.
Web page	You want to construct a Web page to showcase the creative work of a family member (photographs; counted cross-stitch; watercolors, and so on).	Your Web page provides both text and photographs, and can have links to related areas.	A Web page does not allow for interaction (as a blog or a wiki does).
Letter to the editor	You recently attended the opening of a new exhibit at your local museum, and you want to tell readers of the local paper how interesting and engaging it was.	Your letter lets you share your personal comments and evaluation of the exhibit.	A letter to the editor gives you limited space; not all readers of the paper read the letters to the editor. It might not be published.

Writing Effectively about a Creative Work

Although you may be asked simply to explore a work of literature or art or music, in most cases, you will be expected to make a point about the work and provide evidence to support that point. You do not necessarily have to convince your readers to accept your point of view, but you do want readers to understand and appreciate your perspective. You may be asked to do the following:

For more on writing an evaluation, see Chapter 9.

- Evaluate the work.
- Analyze the entire work or some aspect of it (character, plot, theme, setting, sounds, colors, symbolism, imagery, or another element).
- Compare a character or characters to characters in other works.
- Explain the historical significance of the work.
- Explain how the work causes a reaction in the reader/viewer, and explore why that reaction occurs.

Effective writing about creative works includes these elements:

- **A clear thesis about the work.** Your main point or thesis statement should clearly state your main idea about the work. In the rest of your essay, you should support, explain, and expand on this main point.
- **Textual support for your assertions.** When making claims about a work, point to specific evidence in the work that supports your claims. Using evidence from a short story or other literary work usually involves paraphrasing or directly quoting from the text or poem. To provide evidence from a film, you would describe specific scenes.

For more information about supporting assertions, see pages 230–231.

- **Attention to the elements of the work.** If you are reading a work of literature, read it more closely than you would read other kinds of texts, such as a newspaper or even a college textbook.

  When you read a literary work, such as a short story, you are reading not just to understand—what happens in the story—but also for character development, theme, figurative language, and other elements that are commonly found in literary works. In other words, you are reading for the literary qualities of the text:

  - **Characters.** The people in the story—who is the story about? Who does what? How? Why?
  - **Setting.** The time and location of the story.
  - **Point of view.** The perspective of the narrator—the person telling the story. The narrator may or may not be a character in the story. The story may be told from a first-person (*I*) perspective or from a third-person (*he, she, they*) perspective, and the narrator may or may not know what other characters are thinking.
  - **Plot.** The sequence of events in a story—what happens. In a work of fiction such as a short story or film, the plot usually reaches a crisis point or climax and then a resolution.

- **Theme.** The meaning of the story; the general statement that the story makes about life. Common themes in fiction deal with life's big questions, such as why seemingly good people suffer or what "love" is.
- **Style.** Sentence structure and variation, word choices, the use of irony, and overall tone. Writing style is one way literary authors define themselves and their texts. Here is an example of Ernest Hemingway's style from the opening of his short book *The Old Man and the Sea.*

  He was an old man who fished alone in a skiff in the Gulf Stream and he had gone eighty-four days now without taking a fish. In the first forty days a boy had been with him. But after forty days without fish the boy's parents had told him the old man was now definitely and finally *salao,* which is the worst form of unlucky, and the boy had gone at their orders in another boat which caught three good fish the first week. It made the boy sad to see the old man come in each day with his skiff empty and he always went down to help him carry either the coiled lines or the gaff and harpoon and the sail that was furled around the mast. The sail was patched with flour sacks and, furled, it looked like the flag of permanent defeat.

- **Figures of speech/imagery.** Literary works often contain **figurative language,** which evokes images in the reader's mind, and symbols. Writers use **symbols** within a work to represent or indicate other things. They also use **metaphors** to represent one thing as if it were another ("her hair is velvet"), **similes** to say that one thing is similar to another using the word *like* ("her smile is like the sun"), and **imagery** to generate a group of closely related details that, taken together, evoke an idea.

For more on the elements of creative works, see pages 424–425.

- **Sufficient context.** The evidence you provide your audience depends on whom you see as that audience and what they need to know about the work if they are to accept your claim. Your audience's familiarity with the work helps you determine how much you will need to summarize or how much detail to include, what characters you will need to describe, and what else from the story you need to explain so that readers will understand your point.

One effective strategy for approaching this assignment is to read or view the creative work you're interested in several times. The first time, you might simply read or view the work to comprehend or understand it. The second time, you might read or view the work with an eye for the literary features described in the list above. During this second reading, make notes in the margins or in a journal. After that second reading, review your marginal comments to see what in the work seems to have grabbed your attention the most. For instance, your comments may focus on characterization more than anything else. If so, consider that focus to be a cue to pay extra attention to characterization as you read or view the work a third time.

For more on reading critically and writing to learn, see Chapters 2 and 3.

Writing Responsibly about a Creative Work

When you write about creative works, you need to balance several kinds of responsibilities:

- Present your own thinking about the work you are writing about instead of simply repeating the thoughts of others.
- Support your assertions about the work that you are analyzing. The best way to support your ideas is to excerpt or paraphrase relevant passages from the text carefully, making sure to present them accurately, document them correctly, and avoid claiming others' ideas or words as your own. Also consider passages that could be used to refute your assertions.
- Use excerpts from the work fairly, in context.

For more on documenting sources properly, see Chapter 20.

Writing to Learn about Literary Works

Literature can take you places you may never get to, show you lives very different from—or similar to—your own, and help you understand your life, feelings, and relationships. When you *write* about literature, you open up a new world of learning. By putting your thoughts into some order and onto paper, you can learn more about what you think and believe about ideas implicit in the work. As you read the following short story, look for the literary qualities discussed on pages 410–411.

JOHN EDGAR WIDEMAN

Ascent by Balloon from the Yard of Walnut Street Jail

SHORT STORY

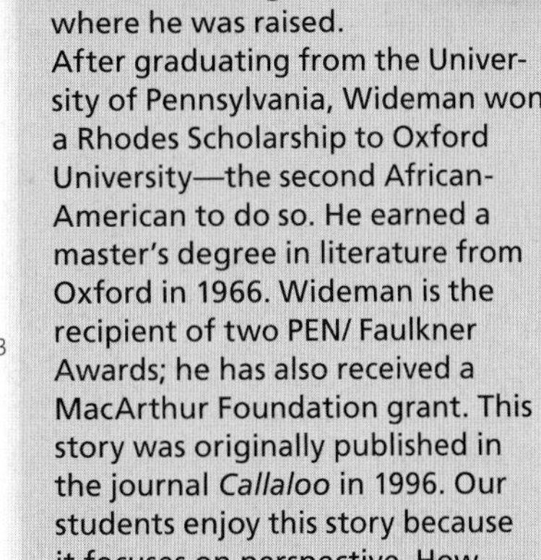

John Edgar Wideman is the author of *The Homewood Trilogy* (1981–83), written about life in the black middle-class section of Pittsburgh, where he was raised. After graduating from the University of Pennsylvania, Wideman won a Rhodes Scholarship to Oxford University—the second African-American to do so. He earned a master's degree in literature from Oxford in 1966. Wideman is the recipient of two PEN/ Faulkner Awards; he has also received a MacArthur Foundation grant. This story was originally published in the journal *Callaloo* in 1996. Our students enjoy this story because it focuses on perspective. How do you respond to the narrator's perspective?

1 I am the first of my African race in space. For this achievement, I received accolades and commendations galore. Numerous offers for the story of my life. I'm told several unauthorized broadsides, purporting to be the true facts of my case from my very own lips, are being peddled about town already. A petition circulates entreating me to run for public office.

2 Clearly my tale is irresistible, the arc of my life emblematic of our fledgling nation's destiny, its promise for the poor and oppressed from all corners of the globe. Born of a despised race, wallowing in sin as a youth, then a prisoner in a cage, yet I rose, I rose. To unimaginable heights. Despite my humble origins, my unworthiness, my sordid past, I rose. A Lazarus in this Brave New World.

3 Even in a day of crude technology and maddeningly slow pace, I was an overnight sensation. A mob of forty thousand, including the President himself, hero of Trenton and Valley Forge, the father of our country as some have construed him in the press, attended the event that launched me into the public eye.

4 The event—no doubt you've heard of it, unless you are, as I once was, one of those unfortunates who must wear a black hood and speak not, nor be spoken to—the event that transformed me from convict to celebrity received the following notice in the Pennsylvania Gazette:

"On January 19, 1793, Jean-Pierre Blanchard, French aeronaut, ascended in his hydrogen balloon from the yard of Walnut Street Jail in Philadelphia to make the first aerial voyage in the United States. In the air forty-six minutes, the balloon landed near Woodbury, New Jersey and returned the same evening to the city in time for Citizen Blanchard to pay his respects to President Washington, who had witnessed the ascension in the morning." 5

Though I am not mentioned by name in the above, and its bland, affectless prose misses altogether the excitement of the moment, the notice does manage to convey something of the magnitude of the event. Imagine men flying like birds. The populace aghast, agawk, necks craned upward, every muscle tensed as if anticipating the tightening of the hangman's knot, its sudden yank, the irresistible gravity of the flesh as a trap door 6 drops open beneath their feet. Men free as eagles. Aloft and soaring over the countryside. And crow though I was, my shabby black wings lifting me high as the Frenchman.

I was on board the balloon because little was understood about the effect of great height upon the human heart. Would that vital organ pump faster as the air grew thinner? Would the heart become engorged approaching the throne of its maker, or would it pale and shrink, the lusty blood fleeing, as once our naked parents, in shame from the Lord's awful gaze? Dr. Benjamin Rush, a man of science as well as a philanthropic soul, well known for championing the cause of a separate Negro church, had requested that a pulse glass be carried on the balloon, and thus, again, became a benefactor of the race, since who better than one of us, with our excitable blood and tropically lush hearts, to serve as guinea pig. 7

The honor fell on me. I was the Frenchman's crew. Aboard to keep the gondola neat and sanitary, a passenger so my body could register danger as we rose into those uncharted regions nearer my God to thee. 8

Jean-Pierre Blanchard was not my first Frenchman. Messrs. De Beauchamp and De Tocqueville[1] had visited my cell in the Walnut Street Jail on a humanitarian, fact-finding mission among the New World barbarians to determine whether this Quaker invention, "the penitentiary," reformed criminals and deterred crime. The Frenchmen were quite taken with me. Surprised to discover I was literate. Enchanted when I read to them from the dim squalor of my cage the parable of the Good Shepherd, the words doubly touching, they assured me, coming from one who was born of a degraded and outcast race, one who, they assumed, had experienced only indifference and harshness. 9

No. Beg pardon. I'm confusing one time with another. Events lose their shape, slide one into another when the time one is supposed to own becomes another's property. An excusable mistake, perhaps inevitable when one resides in a place whose function is to steal time, rob time of its possibilities, deaden time to one dull unending present, a present that is absolutely not a gift, but something taken away. Time drawn, quartered and eviscerated, a sharp pain hovering over the ghost of an amputated limb. Too much time, no time, time tormenting as memories of food and blankets when you lie awake all night, hungry shivering in an icy cell. No clocks. Only unvarying, iron bars of routine solitary confinement mark your passage, your extinction outside time. 10

I would meet De Tocqueville and De Beauchamp years after the flight with Jean-Pierre Blanchard. By then I'd been transferred from Walnut 11

---

[1] French author of *Democracy in America,* an account of his travels in the early years of the republic.

Street Jail to the new prison at Cherry Hill. There, too, I would have the distinction of being the first of my race. Prisoner Number One; Charles Williams: *farmer; light black; black eyes; curly black hair; 5′7 1/2″; foot 11″; flat nose, scar on bridge of nose, broad mouth, scar from dirk on thigh; can read.*

First prisoner of any race admitted to Cherry Hill. Warden Samuel Wood greeted me with no acknowledgment nor ceremony for this particular historic achievement. Later that day, when I complained of dampness in my cell, he reminded me that the prison being new, on its shakedown cruise so to speak, one could expect certain unanticipated inconveniences. The good Warden Wood allowed me a berth in the infirmary until my cell dried out (it never did), but unfortunately the infirmary was also dank and chilly, due to lack of sunlight and ventilation, the cold miasma from marshy soil sweating up through the prison's foundation stones. So I began my residence with a hacking cough, the subterranean air at Cherry Hill as thick and pestilential as the air had been wholesome and bracing in the balloon. 12

I'm complaining too much. All lives are a combination of good times and bad, aren't they. We all suffer a death sentence. Today I wish to celebrate the good, that special time rising above the earth. So up, up, and away then. 13

A cloudless morning. In minutes we drift to a height that turns Philadelphia into a map spread upon a table. The proud steeple of Christ Church a pen protruding from an ink well. After the lazy, curved snake of river, the grid of streets laid straight as plumb lines. I pick out the State House, Independence Hall, the Court House, Carpenters Hall, the market on High Street. And there, the yard of the Walnut Street Jail, there at 1, 2, 3, . . . count them . . . 4, 5, Sixth Street, the Jail and its adjacent yard from which we'd risen. 14

People are ants. Carriages inch along like slugs. Huge silence beats about my ears. A wind, clear and safe as those rare dreams that enfold me, slip me under their skirts and whisk me far from my cell. 15

But I must not lose myself in the splendor of the day until I execute the task that's earned me a ride. Once done, I can, we can, return to contemplating a world never seen by human eyes till just this unraveling, modern instant.

I place the glass on my flesh, count the pulse beats 1, 2, 3, . . . as I practiced counting rungs on the ladder of streets rising, no, *sliced* one after another, beginning at Water Street along the Delaware's edge. 16

Near the end of that momentous year, 1793, a plague of yellow fever will break out in the warren of hovels, shanties and caves along the river and nearly destroy Philadelphia. My Negro brethren, who inhabit that Quarter in large numbers, will perform admirably with enormous courage, skill and compassion during the emergency. Nursing the afflicted, burying 17 the dead. One measure of the city's desperation in that calamitous year, a petition that circulates (unsuccessfully) suggesting we, the immates of the jail, be allowed to serve and, thereby risking our lives, purchase freedom. This is the year that famous prisoner, the French King, is executed and my brethren will build their separate church, the African Episcopal Church of St. Thomas at Fifth and Walnut, a location empty at the moment, though cleared and ready. See it, a mere thumb print opposite the Jail from this elevation.

The Quakers, with their concern for the state of my soul, their insistence I have boundless opportunity to contemplate my sins, to repent and do penance, arrange matters in the Jail so I have ample time to consider things consequential and not. I've often pondered late at night when I cannot sleep, the symmetry between two events of that busy year, 1793: the separation of black from white in God's House, the plague that took so many citizens' lives. One act, *man's,* an assertion there is not enough room in the house of worship; the second act, *God's*, making more room. 18

During the terrible months when the city teetered on the brink of extinction, when President Washington together with all Federal and City officials decamped to more salubrious locations, various treatments, all futile, were prescribed for the deadly fever. Among the treatments, phlebotomy, the opening of a vein to draw blood from a victim, was quite popular until its opponents proved it killed more often than it cured. 19

My brethren, trained and guided by the ubiquitous Dr. Rush, applied his controversial cure: an explosive purge of mercury and calomel, followed by frequent, copious bleedings. Negro nurses became experts, dispensing pharmaceutical powders and slitting veins with equal dexterity. Out with the bad air. In with the good. I couldn't resist a smile when I pictured my brethren moving through white peoples' houses during broad daylight as freely as I once glided through the same dwellings after dark. Emptying purses, wallets, pockets, desk drawers, I, too, relieved my patients of excess. 20

In the prison also, we must drive out bad blood. Though all of us are infected by the fever of lawlessness, some prisoners are incurably afflicted. One such wretch, Matthew Maccumsey, Number 102. His crime: speech. Too much talk and at the wrong times and often in an obstreperous, disruptive, disrespectful manner, threatening the peace and economy of the entire system of absolute silence. 21

Ice water ducking, bagging with black hood, flogging, the normal and natural deterrents all applied and found wanting in lasting effect, the iron gag was prescribed. Number 102 remanded for examination and treatment to Dr. Bache, the nephew, I've heard, of the famous Dr. Franklin, the kite-flyer. 22

A committee, convened a decade later to investigate continuing complaints of questionable practices at the prison, described the gag in these words: a rough iron instrument resembling the bit of a blind bridle, having an iron palet in the center about an inch square and chains at each end to pass around the neck and fasten behind. This instrument was placed in the prisoner's mouth, the iron palet over the tongue, the bit forced back as far as possible, the chains brought round the jaws to the back of the neck; the end of one chain was passed through the ring in the end of the other chain drawn tight to the "fourth link" and fastened with a lock. 23

Rousted out of sleep before first light, groggy, frightened, I knew by the hour, the hulking stillness of the figures gathered into the narrow corridor outside my cell, I was being summoned for a punishment party. Seeing the faces of other prisoners of color in the glaring torchlight, I rejoiced inwardly. This night at least I was to be a punisher, not the punished. The guards always enlisted blacks to punish whites and whites to punish blacks, by this unsubtle stratagem, perpetuating enmity and division. 24

We forced No. 102's hands into leather gloves provided with rings, crossed his arms behind his back and after attaching the rings to the ends of the gag chain drew his arms upwards so their suspended weight pulled the gag chains taut, causing the chains to exert pressure on jaws and jugular, trapping blood in the averted head, producing excruciating pain, the degree of which I could gauge only by observing the prisoner's eyes, since the gag at last had effectively silenced him. 25

Niggified, ain't he, a guard exclaimed, half in jest, half in disgust as 102's lifeless, once pale face, blackened by congealed blood, was freed of the gag. 26

Again, I'm muddling time. The pacifying of 102 came later at Cherry Hill. My job on the balloon was to record the reaction of my own African pulse to heavenly ascent. Higher and higher it rose. The striped French balloon. The stiff, boat-shaped basket beneath it, garlanded with fresh flowers, red, white and blue bunting. Inside the gondola the flags of two great republican nations. We intended to plant them wherever we landed, claim for our countrymen joint interest in the rich, undiscovered lands far flung across the globe. 27

Watching the toy town shrink smaller and smaller beneath me, all its buildings and inhabitants now fittable on the end of a pin, for some unfathomable reason as I rose irresistibly to a heretofore undreamed-of height for any person of my race, as I realized the momentousness of the occasion, all the planning, sacrifice and dumb luck that had conspired to place me here, so high, at just that fantastic, unprecedented, joyous moment, as I began to perceive how far I'd risen and how much further, the sky literally the limit, still to rise, a single tear welled out from God-knows-where. 28

From my swaying perch high above everyone I watch our shadow eclipse a corner of the yard, then scuttle spider-like up the far wall of the Walnut Street Jail. 29

Observed from the height of the balloon I'd be just another ant. Not even my black hood pierced with crude eyeholes would distinguish me as I emerged from the night of my cell, blinking back the sudden onslaught of crisp January sunlight. 30

My eyes adjusted to the glare and there it was, finally, the balloon hovering motionless, waiting for someone it seemed, a giant, untethered fist thrust triumphantly at the sky. 31

From the moment it appears, I am sure no mere coincidence has caused the balloon to rise exactly during the minute and a half outdoors I'm allotted daily to cross the prison yard, grab tools, supplies and return to my cell. If Citizen Blanchard's historic flight had commenced a few seconds sooner or later that morning, I would have missed it. Imagine, I could have lived a different life. Instead of being outdoors glancing up at the heavens, I could have been in my cell pounding on the intractable leather they apportion me for cobbling my ten pairs of shoes a week. In that solitary darkness tap-tap tapping, I wouldn't have seen the striped, floating sphere come to fetch me and carry me home. 32

How carefully I set the pulse glass above a vein. Register the measured ebb and flow, each flicker the heart's smile and amen. 33

QUESTIONS FOR WRITING AND DISCUSSION

1. **Your Personal Response:** What strikes you most about the way the story comments on race?
2. **Character:** How do you react to the narrator calling himself a "guinea pig" in paragraph 7?
3. **Setting:** What is the significance of Philadelphia as the setting for Wideman's story?
4. **Point of View:** If the point of view were third person instead of first person, how would that change the story?
5. **Plot:** How are events in this story related to one another? Which events in the story cause other events? Which events seem unrelated?
6. **Theme:** What is Wideman's narrator saying about life?
7. **Style:** Find examples of figurative language in the story. What effect does Wideman's figurative language have on you as a reader?
8. **For Further Exploration:** Read other stories by Wideman, and compare them to "Ascent by Balloon from the Yard of Walnut Street Jail."

Writing Activity

Analyzing a Feature of a Creative Work

In response to a literary work selected by you or by your instructor, choose one of the following features and jot down everything that comes to mind about it. Your notes will serve as a starting point for your writing about that work.

- Character
- Setting
- Point of view
- Plot
- Theme

GENRES *Up Close* Writing a Book Review (of Fiction)

Book reviews serve several purposes. First, they help readers decide whether to make a trip to the local library or bookstore to borrow or buy the reviewed books. Second, they offer readers alternative perspectives on books so that they can compare their own responses with those of reviewers. A book review typically includes some description of the book, an analysis of its features, and some evaluation of the book. When a book review focuses on a work of fiction, it also includes some information about and analysis of common features of fiction—characters, plot, setting, narration, theme, genre, and style.

The genre features of a review of a book of fiction include the following:

- **Information about the author.** For example, what other works has the author written? How successful have the author's other works been?
- **A brief summary of the work.** Reviewers need to help readers understand what the book is about, but they should not provide so many details that the reading experience is ruined for the reader. For example, a good review does not give away the ending of the story.
- **Analysis of components of the work.** These include characters, plot, setting, narration, theme, genre, and style.
- **A description of the work comparing it to other works.** How does this work of fiction relate to other works by the same writer and/or by other writers?
- **Rating of enjoyment.** How much did the reviewer enjoy reading the work?
- **A recommendation.** Reviewers often imply or state explicitly whether the work is worth reading.

GENRES UP CLOSE

EVIEW OF AN ILLUSTRATED BOOK

JOANNA RUDGE LONG

Haiku for Cats

Wabi Sabi, by Mark Reibstein, illustrated by Ed Young

Joanna Rudge Long, a graduate of Swarthmore College, writes and lectures about children's literature. Her writing has appeared in the *New York Times, Kirkus Reviews,* and the *Horn Book Magazine.* She has served as a judge for the prestigious May Hill Arbuthnot Honor, awarded to an author who has made major contributions to the field of children's literature. In the following review, she writes about the appeal of *Wabi Sabi* to readers of all ages. Can you qualify this assertion?

When writers craft reviews of illustrated books, they often devote substantial portions of the reviews to discussing the visual elements in the books. Long begins her review by talking about the illustrator and his previous work before she comments about the book itself. In fact, she says something about the images in almost every one of her paragraphs.

In a long, distinguished career, Ed Young has often conveyed the depth of apparently simple stories through his illustrations. "Lon Po Po: A Red-Riding Hood Story from China" (1989) won him a Caldecott Medal with its dramatic pictures (including a particularly fearsome wolf), creatively enhanced by the thematic use of light and shadow—which also resonates in his dedication: "To all the wolves of the world for lending their good name as a tangible symbol for our darkness." He added a dimension to the Indian fable of the blind men and the elephant with "Seven Blind Mice": Six mice, in rainbow colors, misconstrue the bits of the elephant they touch, but the seventh—white, like refracted light—explores the whole and grasps the truth. 1

Like these stories, Mark Reibstein's "Wabi Sabi"—choosen this fall as a New York Times Best Illustrated Children's Book—has a familiar scenario: a cat named Wabi Sabi seeks her name's meaning, elicits various responses and comes home wiser. From P. D. Eastman's "Are You My Mother?" to J. R. R. Tolkien's hobbits, it's a reliable formula, famously summarized in T. S. Eliot's "Four Quartets": "We shall not cease from exploration / And the end of all our exploring / Will be to arrive where we started / And know the place for the first time." 2

But while the plot of "Wabi Sabi" is simple, its purpose is demanding: to present an elusive concept of origins "in ancient Chinese ways of understanding and living, known as Taoism and Zen Buddhism." As Reibstein puts it: "Wabi sabi is a way of seeing the world that is at the heart of Japanese culture. It finds beauty and harmony in what is simple, imperfect, natural, modest and mysterious. . . . It may best be understood as a feeling, rather than as an idea." Remarkably, Reibstein and Young capture the essence of all of this with clarity, elegance and a kind of indirection that seems intrinsic to the subject. 3

The book's structure is intricate. Young responds to three different strands of text. The first—the prose narrative—is direct and informal. ("It had never occurred to her before that wabi sabi was anything more than her name"). Then each episode concludes with a haiku—an oblique glimpse of what the animal characters call "hard to explain." ("The pale moon resting / on foggy water. Hear that / splash? A frog's jumped in." On each spread there's another haiku, a decorative grace note in delicate Japanese characters (translations appear at the end, along with transliterations of these classics by Basho and Shiki). 4

Wabi Sabi's quest and the splendid pictures will please younger children (though probably not as young as the publisher's recommended range of 3 to 6). The rest of us will be better prepared to appreciate the subtle interconnections among dialogue, poetry and collages fashioned from "time-worn human-made as well as natural materials." Even this medium is a metaphor for the gentle philosophy explored here. The art is rich in leaf greens and glowing reds; in the textures of hair straw, crazed paint or rough paper. Young captures moments of transcendent beauty—a frog visible 5 through moon-struck water (crumpled, iridescent paper)—and his art incorporates traditional haiku references (a pale moon, symbol of autumn).

Life-size, the cat invites us in, peering intently from the large, square jacket. Opening it, we find that she's among pine trees, which (since the book is hinged at the top) are now above her. That top hinge is brilliant. It recalls Japanese wall hangings, and it reinforces the theme by compelling us to see this familiar object from a new angle. Also, like many a cat intent on her own agenda, this book's no lap sitter. It's a challenge to hold and angle it comfortably, to turn pages with hands accustomed to accessible right-hand corners. 6

Long comments about how the illustrations at the end of the book reflect the main character's growth. What would be lost if she had chosen not to spend so much time on the interrelationship of the text and the illustrations?

Wabi Sabi completes her quest after several small, satisfying epiphanies. Meanwhile, the lovely illustrations grow less detailed until, home at last, the cat is simply silhouetted on white, the single, freely brushed character above her declaring, "Free of possessions." If wabi sabi is "a feeling, rather than an idea," this outcome feels just right. 7

QUESTIONS FOR WRITING AND DISCUSSION

1. **Audience:** In paragraph 5, why does Long mention adult readers of this children's book?
2. **Purpose:** Early in the review Long focuses on the book's illustrator more than the writer, and she continues to focus heavily on the illustrations throughout the review. Why do you think that she does this?
3. **Voice and Tone:** What is Long's attitude toward the book?
4. **Responsibility:** What features of this review suggest that Long is a responsible writer?
5. **Context, Format, and Genre:** In the online version of this review, Long includes some hyperlinks (e.g., "J.R.R. Tolkien" and "T.S. Eliot" in paragraph 2). Why is that useful in an online review?
6. **Context, Format, and Genre:** What genre features of a book review are apparent in this reading?

Writing Activity

Preparing to Write a Book Review

A book review usually includes some description of the book, an analysis of its literary qualities (such as characters, plot, setting, and narration) if it is fictional, an evaluation of the book, and information about the author. Select a favorite childhood book or a work by an author whose writing you are familiar with. Using the genre of e-mail, craft a brief review recommending it to a friend. In your review, highlight one or two features that you think will particularly appeal to your audience.

Writing about a Creative Work

As you read, view, or listen to the creative work you are writing about, consider using some of the reading strategies presented in Chapter 2 and the strategies for discovery and learning presented in Chapter 3 to engage more fully and more critically in the work. Also look for the literary qualities discussed on page 410.

For a tip on organizing your computer files, see page 70.

Selecting a Creative Work to Write About

You can use a variety of invention activities to select and then explore your creative work. If your instructor has not assigned a particular creative work, spend some time exploring short stories or other works. Try to answer these questions:

- Which works have you recently read or seen that interest you the most? Why?
- Which works have evoked the strongest emotional responses in you? What are those emotions?
- Which works have made you think the most?

For more on invention strategies, see Chapter 3.

Recording Your Initial Responses

After selecting a creative work, record your responses to it. If you do not do this important step, you may be tempted to adopt someone else's views in place of your own. Record your responses to the following questions:

- What kinds of emotions does this work evoke in you?
- How does this work make you think about life?

- In one sentence, what is the theme of this work?
- What language in the work do you find most interesting or effective?

Finding a Feature to Analyze

The following questions will help you think analytically about the various features of a creative work. Keep in mind that to consider each aspect of the work thoroughly, you will need to read it and take notes carefully and thoughtfully—never just skim. Your notes will help you decide what you will focus on and gather evidence from the work itself to support the claim you will make in your essay.

Character: There are many ways to analyze characters. To find an approach that works and that interests you, consider using a concept that you have learned in another course, such as the psychological stages people go through when facing death or social stratification to interpret the motivations of a character or group.

You can also analyze characters by thinking about them in the same way you think about people in general. You might ask the following questions:

- What motivates the actions of this character?
- What do you admire or dislike about this character? Why?
- How effectively does this character communicate with other characters?
- What role does this character play in the story?
- Why do other characters treat this character as they do?

Setting: The physical setting is where a story takes place.

As you read or view the creative work to analyze the setting, consider the following kinds of questions:

- What information can you glean from the details provided about the setting?
- How does the setting affect the atmosphere in which the story occurs or the events that take place in the story?
- If the story is set in some specific time in history, how historically accurate are the details?

Point of view: *Point of view* is a term describing what the narrator knows (and does not know). In some stories, the narrator is *omniscient;* he or she knows what all of the characters are thinking. In other stories, the narrator is a character in the story, and his or her knowledge is limited to what he or she sees, hears, or thinks.

As you contemplate point of view, consider the following questions:

- Is the narrator a character (first-person narration)? Is the narrator someone outside the story (third-person narration)? If the narration is third person, is the narrator omniscient? Or is the narrator limited to describing what characters do and say rather than what they think?

- Why do you think that the author used this particular point of view to tell the story?
- How would the story be different if the author had used another point of view?

Plot: A *plot* is what happens in the story. Most plots involve a *conflict*, either between characters, within a character, or between a character and nature or circumstance. In many stories, the conflict leads to a crisis, which is then resolved.

To write about the plot of a particular story, consider these questions:

- How are the events in the story related to one another?
- When do events begin and end?
- How do specific events in the story affect individual characters?
- How is the crisis resolved?

Theme: To explore the theme of a work, you might consider the following questions:

- How does the story make you think about life or people?
- What, if anything, is the moral of this story?

Style: Although many stylistic devices are used in literature and film, you are probably familiar with some of the more common ones.

- A **simile** is an indirect comparison that includes the word *like* or *as*. ("His coat was like a faded carpet.")
- A **metaphor** is a direct comparison in which one thing is described as something else. ("The hummingbird was a tiny blue helicopter.")
- **Personification** involves attributing human qualities to animals, objects, or even ideas. ("Sensing my frustration, the computer screen went blank.")
- **Hyperbole** is exaggeration so extreme that it is clearly not meant to be taken literally ("His car was the size of a canal barge"), while **understatement** is a statement surprising in its lack of force ("'We're experiencing some difficulties,' the pilot said as we noticed the distinct smell of smoke").
- **Irony** is a tone in which the writer's meaning contrasts sharply with what is stated. ("'I'm thrilled to be here,' she said from her hospital bed.")

Consider the following questions about style:

- What uses of language are especially interesting? Why?
- Can you find examples of simile, metaphor, personification, hyperbole, and understatement in the work?
- Does the writer use irony? How is it used, and why?

Integrating Visuals When Writing about Creative Works

If you are writing about a visual medium such as film, you might want to include visuals as part of your discussion. Visuals that might be available for writing about films include publicity stills and frame enlargements. (If you post your writing on the Web, however, you will probably need permission to include these images.) For example, Figure 12.1 shows an image from one of the *X-Men* films based on a series of graphic novels, a genre in which illustrations tell most of the story. In writing about one of these films, you might combine a still image, such as Figure 12.1, with a cover image, such as Figure 12.2, from one of the graphic novels to illustrate a point about the costumes in the film.

As you look at possible visuals to include, consider these questions about the effective use of visuals in writing about a creative work:

- In what ways does the illustration illuminate the film?
- What does the illustration show a reader that it would be hard to show with text alone?
- What other types of visuals might be useful in writing about the film?

FIGURE 12.1 Wolverine, played by Hugh Jackman in the *X-Men* films.

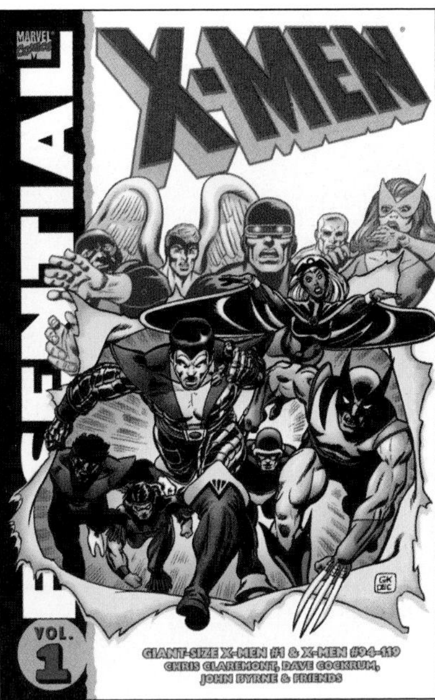

FIGURE 12.2 Cover for one of the graphic novels in the *X-Men* series. What other kinds of illustrations might help you to analyze an aspect of the *X-Men* films or novels?

Digital Literacy

Performing Quantitative Analyses

You can find many classic works of literature online in literature archives. Usually, these are editions and translations that are in the public domain. You can download these works from a reputable Web site such as Project Gutenberg (http://www.gutenberg.org/catalog/), then copy and paste them into a word processor. If a work is stored on your computer, you can perform simple types of *quantitative analysis*, which is useful for investigating and writing about the way the author uses words and phrases to develop themes and stylistic patterns. For example, you can use your word processor's "Find" feature to do the following:

- Count the number of times the author uses a certain word or words. The repetition of a word or idea creates a cumulative effect on readers.
- Focus on the consistency with which the author uses the word or words and what that might mean.
- Argue that the word is used primarily by a specific character or group of characters.
- Examine the actual grammar and syntax of passages in which the word appears, to show how the author explores its implications.

Chapter 13

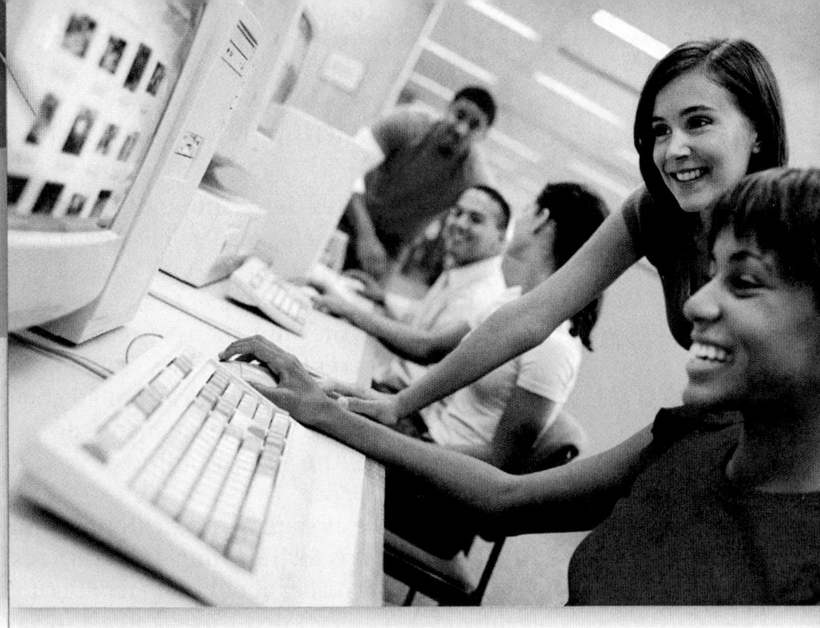

Using Strategies That Guide Readers

Whatever your purpose, you can use a range of rhetorical strategies to help readers understand your writing. At the levels of the individual sentence, the individual paragraph, and the full piece of writing, you will need strategies to help readers make connections. This chapter starts by focusing on the basic building blocks of any piece of writing—writing a thesis statement and paragraphs. Next, we look at how to link sentences and paragraphs together using cohesive devices. Then we explore strategies to narrate, describe, define, classify, compare, and contrast. Finally, we look at different ways you can outline and map your writing to ensure that the writing strategies you use are effective. All of these strategies can be used for the writing projects in Chapters 4–11.

Announcing a Thesis or Controlling Idea

mhconnectcomposition.com
Thesis statement overview QL13001

A **thesis** announces the main point, major claim, or controlling idea in an essay. A clear thesis helps readers because it prepares them for what they will be reading.

Although a thesis statement can focus your attention as you write, it is usually helpful to write your thesis statement after you have done invention work and research. Invention activities can help you clarify your thinking about a topic. Research can help you learn more about it. Once you have done invention and research, a thesis statement can help you construct a well-focused draft. Of course, the exact wording of your thesis statement might change as you draft your paper.

The best thesis statements are limited and focused and offer some sense of the support that is forthcoming. If your thesis statement merely states a fact, it just informs the reader about that fact; it is not arguable. If you offer a personal feeling as a thesis ("I don't like coffee"), people could certainly argue with it, but your evidence would be purely subjective ("I don't care for the flavor") and therefore not persuasive. If your thesis statement is general and vague ("Movies are more expensive now than they were last year"), there might not be much to write in support of your thesis. Providing two figures—the average price of movies last year and the average price this year—proves your assertion.

Here are two examples of weak thesis statements, which then were revised into stronger thesis statements:

WEAK I can't stand war movies.

REVISED *Letters from Iwo Jima* is an effective war movie because it forces Americans to view, and even sympathize with, combatants traditionally seen as enemies.

REASON There is no way to support your personal feeling—that you do not like war movies—with evidence. But you could provide evidence for the ways *Letters from Iwo Jima* helps viewers see enemy combatants in a new light.

WEAK The National Hockey League is in trouble.

REVISED The National Hockey League has lost fan support because of the 2004–2005 lockout.

REASON The weak version is too general and vague. The revised version gives a specific reason for the trouble.

It is important to *qualify* your thesis statement by using terms such as *probably* or *likely* to make it more acceptable to an audience.

Writing Activity

Looking for Weak Thesis Statements

Examine a copy of your campus or local newspaper, looking at the various articles for examples of weak thesis statements. Bring some examples to share with your classmates, and be prepared to indicate how you would improve the weak statements you located.

Writing Paragraphs

A **paragraph** is a collection of connected sentences that focus on a single idea. With few exceptions, your writing projects will consist of paragraphs, each developing an idea related to your topic. In your writing, you need to think about both the effectiveness of individual paragraphs and the way they are organized and connected to support your purpose. Consider the following example, which might appear in a paper about Abraham Lincoln's career:

> During his years as president, 1861–1865, Abraham Lincoln experienced great stress from a combination of causes. **First,** the Civil War, which broke out weeks after his March 1861 inauguration, wore on him daily until its end in April 1865. **Second,** typhoid took the life of Willie, his beloved eleven-year-old son, in February 1862. **Third,** his wife, Mary Todd Lincoln, suffered from depression and other forms of mental illness, problems that became more acute during the years in the White House.

Although the specifics may vary, effective paragraphs generally have the following features:

- **Focus on a single main idea.** The more tightly you focus a paragraph on a main idea, the more you will help readers navigate the paragraph. Note that in the example paragraph every sentence is focused on the causes of Lincoln's stress. If you want to alert your readers to other information that will come later in your paper, use a *forecasting sentence*. In the example about Lincoln, the sentence that mentions Mary Lincoln's depression could forecast that the paper will have more to say about that topic.
- **Have a topic sentence.** A topic sentence guides readers by expressing a paragraph's main idea, the idea that the other sentences in the paragraph support or develop. In the example about Lincoln, the first sentence, which is underlined, serves as the topic sentence.
- **Use different levels of specificity.** All paragraphs have at least two levels of specificity. In the paragraph about Lincoln, the topic sentence clearly introduces the idea of stress and its various causes, and the second, third, and fourth sentences are more specific.

- **Use connective words and phrases.** Used within a paragraph, connective words and phrases, discussed in more detail on pages 435–437, can show precisely how the sentences in the paragraph support the topic sentence and relate to one another. In the example paragraph, the words *First, Second,* and *Third* (in bold type) tell readers that each of the sentences they begin offers a separate cause of Lincoln's stress.
- **Include a logical connection to the next paragraph.** When readers finish a paragraph, they expect that the next paragraph will be connected to it in some readily apparent way. After reading the paragraph that focuses on the sources of stress that Lincoln experienced, readers expect that the next paragraph will also be related to Lincoln's stress.

Placement of Topic Sentences

In the paragraph about Lincoln, the topic sentence is the first sentence, a placement that lets readers know right away what the paragraph will be about. Sometimes, however, you will want to place a topic sentence at the end of a paragraph to develop suspense or to summarize information. This strategy can be especially effective in persuasive writing because it allows the writer to present evidence before making an assertion. Here is an example:

> Less than a quarter of our agricultural land is used to feed people directly. The rest is devoted to grazing and growing food for animals. Ecosystems of forest, wetland and grassland have been decimated to fuel the demand for land. Using so much land heightens topsoil loss, the use of harsh fertilizers and pesticides, and the need for irrigation water from dammed rivers. <u>If people can shift away from meat, much of this land could be converted back to wilderness</u>.
>
> Joseph Pace, "Let's Go Veggie!"

Sometimes a paragraph has no topic sentence. Instead, the topic sentence is implied. In cases where the point is fairly clear to readers, a writer may decide to leave it unstated. In the following paragraph, the implied (unstated) topic sentence could be something like, "Lynn had endured an abusive marriage":

> When I first met Lynn, she seemed withdrawn and disoriented. She had just taken the biggest step of her 25 years; she had left an abusive husband and she was scared: Scared about whether she could survive on her own and scared of her estranged husband. He owned a small restaurant; she was a high school dropout who had been a waitress when she met him. During their three years of marriage he had beaten her repeatedly. Only after he threw her down a flight of stairs had she realized that her life was in danger and moved out. I don't think I fully grasped the terror she had lived until one summer day when he chased Lynn to the door of my house with a drawn gun.
>
> Barbara Ehrenreich, "A Step Back to the Workhouse"

Moving to a New Paragraph

Paragraph breaks signal that a writer is moving from one idea to another. Consider again the example paragraph on Lincoln in which every sentence is related to causes of stress. We could develop that paragraph further by adding sentences that maintain that focus. Look at what happens, though, when we add a sentence that does not fit the focus on causes of stress:

> . . . Third, his wife, Mary Todd Lincoln, suffered from depression and other forms of mental illness, problems that became more acute during the years in the White House. To alleviate the stress, Lincoln often read the plays of Shakespeare.

The last sentence in this paragraph does fit the general topic of Lincoln's experience with stress, but it does not fit the tight focus on causes in this paragraph. Instead, it introduces a related but new idea. The solution is to make the last sentence the topic sentence of the next paragraph:

> . . . Third, his wife, Mary Todd Lincoln, suffered from depression and other forms of mental illness, problems that became more acute during the years in the White House.
>
> To alleviate the stress, Lincoln often read the plays of Shakespeare. Among those that he read most frequently were *King Lear, Richard III, Henry VIII, Hamlet*, and *Macbeth*. About his favorite play, *Macbeth*, he wrote the following in a letter to the actor James H. Hackett on August 17, 1863: "I think nothing equals *Macbeth*. It is wonderful."

Notice that this new paragraph provides details about Lincoln and stress that are even more specific than the ones in the preceding paragraph.

Opening Paragraphs

The opening paragraphs of an essay announce the topic and the writer's approach to that topic. In an opening paragraph the writer needs to establish a relationship with readers and help them connect the topic to what they already know and care about. Some common strategies for opening paragraphs include the following:

- Tell an interesting anecdote.
- Raise a thought-provoking question.
- Provide salient background information.
- Offer a view that the writer and readers hold in common.
- Forecast the rest of the essay.

Writing Activity

Introductions

For each of the following excerpts from opening paragraphs, describe the strategy that the writer is using. Does it make you want to read more? Why or why not?

> The official poverty rate in 2003 was 12.5 percent, up from 12.1 percent in 2002. In 2003, 35.9 million people were in poverty, up 1.3 million from 2002. For children under 18 years old, both the poverty rate and the number in poverty rose between 2002 and 2003, from 16.7 percent to 17.6 percent, and from 12.1 million to 12.9 million, respectively.
>
> U.S. Census Bureau, "Poverty: 2003 Highlights"

> The most vulnerable victims of poverty are the world's children. Nearly 28,000 children die *every day*—more than 10 million per year—most from preventable diseases and malnutrition. Yet, the handful of preventable diseases that kill the majority of these children can be treated and prevented at very little cost. Measles can be prevented with a vaccine costing just 26 cents. Diarrheal disease, which results from poor sanitation and unsafe drinking water, can be treated with pennies' worth of oral rehydration salts. Malaria kills nearly one million children each year, despite the fact that treatment for acute malaria costs just pennies.
>
> results.org

> Tina Taylor was a model of what welfare reform was supposed to do. Taylor, 44, a single mother, had spent six years on public assistance. After 1996, when changes were made in welfare law to push people into work, she got a job that paid $400 a week and allowed her family to live independently. For the first time in a long time, she could afford to clothe and feed her two children, and even rent a duplex on the beach in Norfolk.
>
> Griff Witte, "Poverty Up as Welfare Enrollment Declines; Nation's Social Safety Net in Tatters as More People Lose Their Jobs"

Concluding Paragraphs

Readers remember best what they read last. Although it is not that helpful to simply restate what your essay is about in your conclusion, you can use it to do the following:

- Restate your thesis and remind readers of your key points.
- Emphasize the significance of your perspective on your topic.
- Bring your writing to closure.

Writing Activity

Conclusions

For each of the following concluding paragraphs, explain what the writer has done and decide how effective you think each conclusion is.

> Each day of my life there are times when I reflect back to working on the farm. And every day people notice that I am different from the rest of my peers. At school, teachers and organization leaders are impressed by my time management skills and the amount of responsibility I take on. At work, my boss continues to ask me where he can find some more hard working people. I simply tell him, "Try hiring some farm girls. I hear they turn out pretty good."
>
> Jessica Hemauer, "Farm Girl"

> The Supreme Court's May 17, 1954, ruling in *Brown* remains a landmark legal decision. But it is much more than that. It is the "Big Bang" of all American history in the 20th century.
>
> Juan Williams, "The Ruling That Changed America"

Using Cohesive Devices

Within paragraphs, effective writers use a variety of cohesive devices to show readers how sentences are connected to one another. The major devices include connective words and phrases, word repetition, and pronoun reference. To help readers understand how paragraphs are related to one another, writers use transitional sentences as well as headings.

Using Connective Words and Phrases

You can guide readers with logically connected sentences and paragraphs, making these connections explicit through the use of **connective words and phrases.** These connections fall into three main categories: temporal, spatial, and logical.

TEMPORAL CONNECTIONS

Time: now, then, during, meanwhile, at this moment

> I worked all weekend. Meanwhile, my colleagues watched football all day Saturday and Sunday.

Frequency: often, occasionally, frequently, sometimes

> Sally likes unplanned trips. Sometimes, she'll even show up at the airport and then decide where to fly for the weekend.

Temporal order: first, second . . . ; next; before (that); after (that); last; finally

> Let's eat dinner. After that, let's see a movie.

SPATIAL CONNECTIONS

Location: nearby, outside, inside

> I stood by the window. Outside, a moose ran down the street.

Spatial order: first, second . . . ; last, next

> Jane sat in the corner. Next to her sat Jill.

LOGICAL CONNECTIONS

Addition: further, furthermore, moreover, additionally, in addition, and, also

> Martha Flynn is a powerful council member in our city. Further, she may be headed for other powerful positions in the future.

Opposition/contrast: on the other hand, however, in contrast, on the contrary, but, conversely, nevertheless, yet, instead, rather

> I don't eat meat for ethical reasons. On the other hand, I do wear leather shoes.

Comparison: likewise, similarly, analogously

> George H. W. Bush led the United States to war in the 1990s. Likewise, George W. Bush led the United States to war in 2001.

Causation: because, as a result, as a consequence, therefore, thus, accordingly, consequently, so, then, on account of

> He didn't pay his phone bill. As a result, the phone company discontinued his service.

Clarification: in other words, that is,

> He rarely does his homework. In other words, he's not a very good student.

Qualification: under the [these] circumstances, under other circumstances, under these conditions, in this context

> John McCain spent years as a prisoner of war in North Vietnam. Under these circumstances, it's remarkable that he is so well adjusted.

Conclusion: finally, in summary, to sum up, in conclusion, therefore

> The new Toyota Camry has been rated one of the safest cars on the road. Therefore, we should consider buying one.

Illustration: for example, for instance, in particular, specifically

> Luz wears colorful clothes. For example, yesterday she wore a bright red sweater to her math class.

Using Word Repetition

Repeating a word or phrase from one sentence to the next helps readers make a connection between those two sentences:

> In a new study on the occurrence of dating **violence** among teenagers, University of Arkansas researchers found that 50 percent of high schoolers have experienced some form of physically **violent** behavior in their relationships. More surprising, the research revealed that male and female students perpetrate **violence** at an equal rate and that, of the two, females may be inflicting more serious forms of abuse on their partners.
>
> Megan Mooney and Patricia Petretic-Jackson, "Half of High School Students Experience Dating Violence, UA Study Shows"

Using Pronoun Reference

Pronouns substitute for nouns. When writers use pronouns to replace nouns, those pronouns point backward or forward to the nouns that they replace:

> During **his** years as president, 1861–1865, Abraham Lincoln experienced great stress from a combination of causes. First, the Civil War, which broke out weeks after **his** March 1861 inauguration, wore on **him** daily until its end in April 1865. Second, typhoid took the life of Willie, **his** beloved eleven-year-old son, in February 1862. Third, **his** wife, Mary Todd Lincoln, suffered from depression and other forms of mental illness, problems that became more acute during the years in the White House.

Writing Activity

Focusing on Cohesive Words

Working alone or with one or two classmates, identify the cohesive devices (and lack of cohesive devices) in the following paragraph. Also, edit the paragraph by adding cohesive devices that you think might strengthen connections between sentences.

> The want to consume is nothing new. It is has been around for millennia. People need to consume resources to survive. However, consumption has evolved as people have ingeniously found ways to help make their lives simpler and/or to use their resources more efficiently. Of course, with this has come the want to control such means. Hence, the consumption patterns have evolved over time based on the influence of those who can control it. As a result, there is tremendous waste within this system, to maintain such control and such disparities.
>
> Anup Shaw, "Creating the Consumer"

Using Transitional Sentences and Paragraphs

Writers use **transitions** to help readers move from one section of an essay to another. These sentences or paragraphs often summarize what has come before and forecast what will come next. Here are two examples:

> Those are the advantages of an interest-only home loan. Now let me explain their major disadvantages.
>
> Although after that presentation I admired her intellect even more, her next decision caused me seriously to question her judgment.

Using Headings

In short pieces of writing, you may not need to use headings. For longer pieces of writing and in certain genres, though, headings and even subheadings can help readers more quickly understand the focus of the paragraphs that come after them. They tell readers that the paragraphs they precede are a related group and are all on the same topic, specified in the heading.

Keep the following guidelines in mind when you write headings:

- Generally, use only one level of heading for a five-page paper.
- Be sure all content under a heading relates to that heading.
- Make your headings specific.

VAGUE	Properties of Glass
SPECIFIC	Chemical Properties of Glass

- At each level, make headings parallel in grammatical structure, font, and level of specificity.

NOT PARALLEL	The Chemistry of Glass, Physical Properties
PARALLEL	Chemical Properties, Physical Properties

- Design headings so that they stand out from the text.

DOESN'T STAND OUT	Common Uses of Glass
DOES STAND OUT	**Common Uses of Glass**

If you are writing an academic paper, you should follow the requirements of the documentation style you are using for the style of your headings.

For more on headings in MLA and APA style, see Chapter 20.

Writing Activity

Focusing on Headings and Subheadings

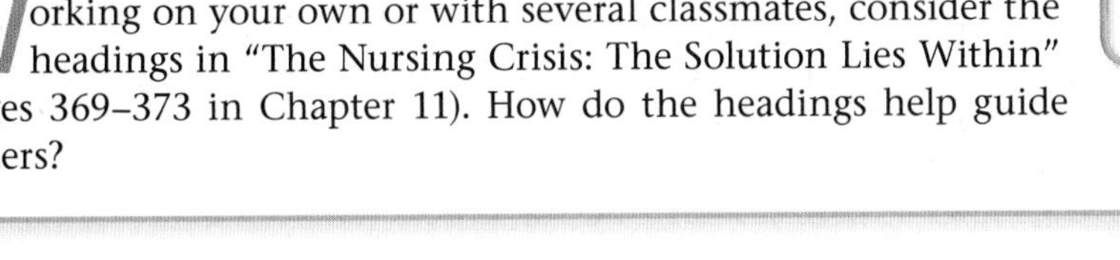

Working on your own or with several classmates, consider the headings in "The Nursing Crisis: The Solution Lies Within" (pages 369–373 in Chapter 11). How do the headings help guide readers?

Writing Narratives

Both in everyday speech and in many kinds of writing, **narration** is a common strategy. When you narrate, you relate an event or a series of events or, in the case of a process, you give a series of steps. Most narratives are organized by time, or **chronologically**, from the beginning to the end of an event, a series of events, or a process. Obviously, narration is relevant to much of our discourse in all areas of our lives because our lives are filled with events and processes:

- At dinner, you tell your family or friends about an event at school or work that day.
- In a science course, you record what happened when you conducted a laboratory experiment.
- As a witness to a traffic accident, you tell the investigating police officers what happened.

In this section we consider two kinds of narratives: narratives that relate an event or a series of events and narratives that relate a process.

Narrating Single Events or a Series of Events

Often in everyday conversation, you narrate single events. Narrating a single event is also a common way of organizing part or all of a piece of writing. You might write an essay about an event that affected your life, an article on the

For more on narrating an event or a series of events, see Chapter 4.

opening of a store in your neighborhood, or a research report on the Montgomery bus boycott in 1955. You can also narrate a series of events in a piece of writing. You might write an account of your life, of the growth of the McDonald's restaurant chain, or of the American civil rights movement in the 1950s and 1960s.

When you narrate an event or a series of events, you will most often order your details chronologically—what happened first, what happened next, and so on. As an alternative, however, you might discuss the importance of the event or events first, and then proceed to the details so that your readers will understand why they, too, ought to be interested in what happened.

Chronological Structure: Because life's events occur chronologically, it is usually easiest to narrate them that way. It is also usually easier for readers to mentally process narratives that unfold chronologically. Even a short narrative paragraph such as the following one can suggest a chronological ordering of events:

> Once my aunt found a freckle on her chin, at a spot that the almanac said predestined her for unhappiness. She dug it out with a hot needle and washed the wound with peroxide.
>
> Maxine Hong Kingston, "No Name Woman"

Point of View: The narrator of a story can have any of several points of view, so when you construct a narrative, select a point of view to write from.

In the *first-person* point of view, the narrator tells the story from the perspective of a participant or character in the story:

> When I went to kindergarten and had to speak English for the first time, I became silent.
>
> Maxine Hong Kingston, "Tongue Tied"

In a narrative told from a *third-person* point of view, the narrator is not a participant or character in the story. The narrator consistently uses third-person pronouns or proper nouns to talk about the actions of characters:

> On December 1, 1963, shortly after President Kennedy's assassination, Malcolm X addressed a public rally in New York City. He was speaking as a replacement for Elijah Muhammad as he had done many times before. After the speech, during a question and answer period, Malcolm X made the remark that led to his suspension as a Muslim minister. In answer to a question, "What do you think about President Kennedy's assassination?" Malcolm X answered that he saw the case as "The chickens coming home to roost." Soon after the remark, Malcolm X was suspended by Elijah Muhammad and directed to stop speaking for ninety days.
>
> John Henrik Clarke, from the Introduction to *Malcolm X: The Man and His Times*

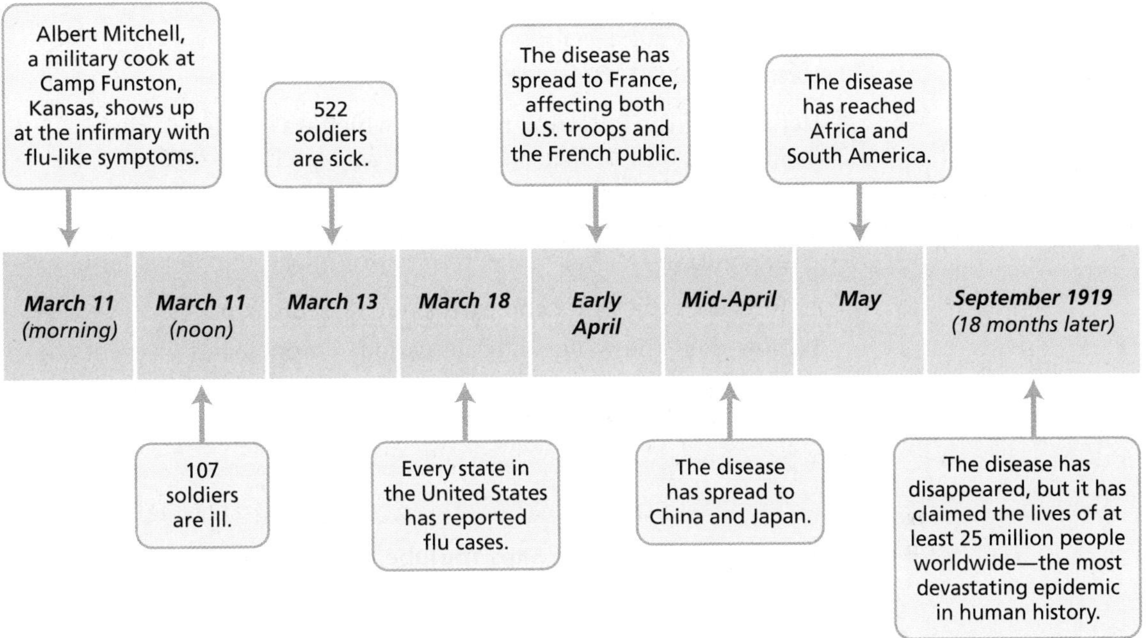
Albert Mitchell, a military cook at Camp Funston, Kansas, shows up at the infirmary with flu-like symptoms.
522 soldiers are sick.
The disease has spread to France, affecting both U.S. troops and the French public.
The disease has reached Africa and South America.
March 11 (morning)
March 11 (noon)
March 13
March 18
Early April
Mid-April
May
September 1919 (18 months later)
107 soldiers are ill.
Every state in the United States has reported flu cases.
The disease has spread to China and Japan.
The disease has disappeared, but it has claimed the lives of at least 25 million people worldwide—the most devastating epidemic in human history.

FIGURE 13.1 Timeline for the 1918 Flu Epidemic

Developing Tension: Narrative tension is the feeling readers have when they are concerned about what will happen to a character. The more readers care about a character, the more they want to know how the character will get through a conflict. Narratives with tension are more interesting to readers. To establish tension in narratives, writers show conflicts between characters who hold differing values or perspectives. For example, the following sentences develop tension:

> My mother's parents didn't want her to marry my father, so the young couple eloped on a blustery day in November.
>
> Tom and I were best friends, but then one day I saw him stuff a DVD into his shirt in a department store.

Resolving the Tension or Conflict: Just as readers are intrigued by narrative tension, they are interested in seeing how tensions are resolved. Most readers look forward to a sense of closure by the end of the story.

Incorporating Visuals in Narratives: When you narrate a series of events, you have the opportunity to cover a significant period of time, as well as the complications involved in a more extended narration. If the chronology becomes complex, you might find it useful to guide readers with a summarizing visual such as a timeline. Figure 13.1, for instance, is a brief timeline for the flu epidemic of 1918.

For more on a type of writing that uses narration extensively, see Chapter 4, "Writing to Share Experiences."

Writing Activity

Analyzing Narrative Strategies

After reading the following narrative, which was posted in the business section of DenverPost.com, on March 13, 2007, respond in writing to the following questions:

1. What does the image of SpongeBob SquarePants add to the article? Why?
2. Why does the writer end with a report on stock prices?
3. How does the writer indicate various chronologies of events in the narrative?
4. How do verb tenses function in the narrative?

Viacom Sues YouTube for $1 Billion
Seth Sutel AP Business Writer

NEW YORK—MTV owner Viacom Inc. sued the popular video-sharing site YouTube and its corporate parent, Google Inc., on Tuesday, seeking more than $1 billion in damages on claims of widespread copyright infringement.

Viacom claims that YouTube has displayed more than 160,000 unauthorized video clips from its cable networks, which also include Comedy Central, VH1 and Nickelodeon.

The lawsuit, filed in U.S. District Court in New York, marks a sharp escalation of long-simmering tensions between Viacom and YouTube and represents the biggest confrontation to date between a major media company and the hugely popular video-sharing site, which Google bought in November for $1.76 billion.

YouTube's soaring popularity has been a cause of fascination but also fear among the owners of traditional media outlets, who worry that YouTube's displaying of clips from their programs—without compensation—will lure away viewers and ad dollars from cable and broadcast TV.

Viacom is especially at risk because much of its programming is aimed at younger audiences who also are heavy Internet users.

Last month Viacom demanded that YouTube remove more than 100,000 unauthorized clips after several months of talks between the companies broke down.

YouTube said at the time that it would comply with the request and said it cooperates with all copyright holders to remove programming as soon as they're notified.

In a statement, Viacom lashed out at YouTube's business practices, saying

Fans of SpongeBob SquarePants and his friends, shown here in a scene from *The SpongeBob SquarePants Movie,* will not be able to view scenes from the popular Nickelodeon cartoon show on the YouTube Web site. Viacom Inc., which owns Nickelodeon, has insisted that all of its content be removed from YouTube and is suing the popular video sharing site for more than $1 billion, claiming copyright infringement.

it has "built a lucrative business out of exploiting the devotion of fans to others' creative works in order to enrich itself and its corporate parent Google."

Viacom said YouTube's business model, "which is based on building traffic and selling advertising off of unlicensed content, is clearly illegal and is in obvious conflict with copyright laws."

Viacom said YouTube has avoided taking the initiative to curtail copyright infringement on its site, instead shifting the burden and costs of monitoring the video-sharing site for unauthorized clips onto the "victims of its infringement."

A representative for Google didn't immediately respond to a request for comment.

Other media companies have also clashed with YouTube over copyrights, but some, including CBS Corp. and General Electric Co.'s NBC Universal, have reached deals with the video-sharing site to license their material. CBS Corp. used to be part of Viacom but has since split off into a separate company.

Universal Music Group, a unit of France's Vivendi SA, had threatened to sue YouTube, saying it was a hub for pirated music videos, but later reached a licensing deal with the company.

In addition to damages, Viacom is also seeking an injunction prohibiting Google and YouTube from using its clips.

Google shares dropped $4.82, or 1.1 percent, to $449.93 in Tuesday morning trading on the Nasdaq Stock Market, while Viacom's Class B shares rose 43 cents, or 1.1 percent, to $40 on the New York Stock Exchange.

Narrating Processes

When you narrate a process, you tell how something is done (informative/explanatory process narrative), or you tell others how to do something (instructional/directive process narrative).

Informative/Explanatory Process Narratives: Informative or explanatory process narratives tell readers how something is done so that they can understand a process, not so that they can replicate the process. For example, you might write an informative process analysis about the following:

- How a legislative bill becomes a law
- How a seed germinates
- How a company's supply chain works

Instructional/Directive Process Narratives: While the purpose of informative or explanatory process narratives is to enhance the reader's understanding of a process, the purpose of an instructional or a directive process narrative is to help readers learn how to do something. For instance, you might explain the following processes so that readers can replicate them:

- How to make a great pizza at home
- How to use the online library catalog at your school
- How to fill out a ballot petition

Digital Literacy: Constructing a Timeline

To construct a timeline like the one in Figure 13.1, you can use a timeline template in your word processor (you can download it to your computer from online resources; Microsoft products will usually do this for you; the "help" feature should walk you through this process with one or two mouse clicks). It works best to construct your timeline in a separate document. Once you have prepared the timeline, you can copy and paste it into your project document. Alternatively, you can copy and paste the timeline into a PowerPoint slide and then insert the slide into your document file. As a PowerPoint slide, it's more easily moved as a graphic unit within your document.

Writing Descriptions

When you describe, you sketch people, places, and things verbally. Usually, you will aim to establish an overall feeling about what you are describing, such as the feeling evoked in the following passage:

> A dark mist lay over the Black Hills, and the land was like iron. At the top of the ridge I caught sight of Devil's Tower upthrust against the gray sky as if in the birth time the core of the earth had broken through its crust and the motion of the world was begun. There are many things in nature that engender an awful quiet in the heart of man; Devil's Tower is one of them.
>
> N. Scott Momaday, "The Way to Rainy Mountain"

Because it is so common, **description** will be part of many of your writing projects in all four areas of life. However, the approach you take to description will depend on what you are describing. Here we focus on three approaches that can be especially effective—naming, sensory, and spatial.

Naming in Description

When you describe someone or something, you need to name that person or thing, as well as its features. For example, if you were to describe the room where you sleep, you might name objects such as the bed, dresser, chair, artwork, walls, ceiling, and floor. Consider the effect of naming in the following excerpt from Robert Sullivan's book *Rats:*

> A rat is a rodent, the most common mammal in the world. *Rattus norvegicus* is one of the approximately four hundred different kinds of rodents, and it is known by many names, each of which describes a trait or a perceived trait or sometimes a habitat: the earth rat, the roving rat, the barn rat, the field rat, the migratory rat, the house rat, the sewer rat, the water rat, the wharf rat, the alley rat, the gray rat, the brown rat, and the common rat. The average brown rat is large and stocky; it grows to be approximately sixteen inches long from its nose to its tail—the size of a large adult human male's foot—and weighs about a pound, though brown rats have been measured by scientists and exterminators at twenty inches and up to two pounds. The brown rat is sometimes confused with the black rat, or *Rattus rattus*, which is smaller and once inhabited New York City and all of the cities of America but, since *Rattus norvegicus* pushed it out, is now relegated to a minor role.

A Sensory Approach to Description

A thorough sensory description includes details from all five senses—sight, sound, taste, smell, and touch. In a vivid sensory description, the reader experiences vicariously what the writer has described. To generate such a description, you might use the questions in the following table. With minor modifications, you can use these questions to develop descriptions of a wide range of items.

Sense	Questions to Consider	Responses
Sight	What does it look like?	
	What do I see when I look at it?	
Hearing	What sounds does it make?	
	What sounds are associated with it?	
Taste	How does it taste?	
	What tastes are similar to it?	
	What tastes are associated with it?	
Smell	What does it smell like?	
	What smells are similar to it?	
	What smells are associated with it?	
Touch	What does it feel like to the touch?	
	What tactile associations do I have with it?	

Of course, for some subjects, you will rely on details from only one or two senses. The sense you will use most often when writing description is sight. Remember that other senses can also have an impact on readers, however. The sense of smell, for example, tends to evoke memory in humans more powerfully than any other sense.

In the following description of "good bread," notice how the writer appeals to several of the senses:

> Good bread. Its pleasure is deeply soul satisfying. It's not a superficial pleasure. It's down deeper than that. It may come from a perfect crust, with texture, definition, a caramelized crusty crunch with just the right give and not too thick. And it may come from a light, airy crumb, and you know it's been crafted by gentle, knowing hands that have shaped thousands of loaves just like this. And it may come from that lingering, wheaty fullness that makes you think of a soft sun-tinted breeze flowing its tide through a field of just-ripe, golden, amber-at-sunset wheat, ready for harvest.
>
> Ken's Artisan Bakery and Café (Portland, Oregon), "What Is Good Bread?"

A Spatial Approach to Description

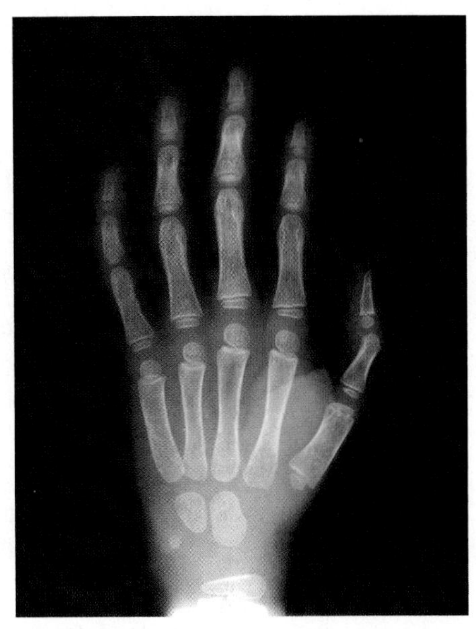

FIGURE 13.2 An X-ray of a child's hand

When you describe something *spatially*, you describe it in terms of both its own physical dimensions and its relationship to the objects around it. An approach that is primarily spatial can include sensory details or a visual, which may even be the predominant part of the description. For example, Figure 13.2 is an x-ray of a child's hand. Below is a brief spatial description of the x-ray.

> The hand is composed of many small *bones* called carpals, metacarpals and phalanges. The two bones of the lower arm—the radius and the ulna—meet at the hand to form the wrist.
>
> The *carpal bones* are a set of eight short bones forming the wrist; they are disposed on two rows of four bones each. These bones, the size of a marble, provide the wrist's litheness and mobility.
>
> The palm of the hand is composed of five *metacarpal bones* laid out from the wrist, as a fan. The articulation of the first metacarpal bone with the carpal bones, permits the movement of touching, with the thumb, the tips of all fingers.
>
> It is from this movement that the human hand can acquire the efficiency necessary to grab and manipulate objects.
>
> Every hand is composed of 14 long bones named the *phalanges*. These bones compose the fingers and the thumb. Each finger has three phalanges and the thumb only two.
>
> McGill University, School of Architecture

Writing Activity

Writing an Effective Description

Working on your own or with several classmates, choose a topic to describe. First, generate a list of questions that an interested reader might have about the topic. Second, answer each of the questions to generate descriptive details. Third, use those details to write a short descriptive paragraph, using the approaches described above.

For more on two types of writing that use description extensively, see Chapter 4, "Writing to Share Experiences," and Chapter 7, "Writing to Analyze."

Writing Definitions

Definitions help your readers understand the terms that you are using. Clear definitions are especially important if you are writing about a topic that you know more about than your readers do, about an issue over which there are differences of opinion—including over the meanings of terms—or about a topic for which precision is crucial. You will find occasions to use definitions in all four areas of life:

- In a letter to one of your U.S. senators, you define "the working poor" as you argue for legislation to assist low-income families.
- When you take a friend to a baseball game, you define "earned run average" when "ERA" appears after a pitcher's name on the big screen in left field.
- In an economics course, you define "gross domestic product" in a paper about economic growth in India and China.

Kinds of Definitions

You can use any of several kinds of definitions depending on how much information your readers need. Sometimes you can define a term by simply giving your readers a **synonym**, a more familiar word or phrase that could be used in place of the term you are defining. However, defining a word with a synonym has limitations. Consider some synonyms for the word *war: warfare, combat, conflict, fighting, confrontation, hostilities*, and *battle*. Depending on the context, these words cannot necessarily be used interchangeably.

More useful than a synonym in many cases is an essential definition. **Essential definitions** are sentence definitions that include three parts: (1) the name of what is being defined, (2) the general category for the item being defined, and (3) the form or function that distinguishes the item being defined from similar items in the same general category. Here are some examples:

Name	Category	Form or Function
A toaster	is a small kitchen appliance	that browns bread.
A mixer	is a small kitchen appliance	that combines ingredients.

If a synonym or an essential definition is sufficient, you can incorporate it in an extended definition. An **extended definition**, which can take up one or more paragraphs, may include both of these briefer types of definition, as well as additional information and examples. It is especially helpful when you need to define a concept that is abstract or complex. For instance, here is an extended definition of a *mugwump:*

This archetypal American word derives from the Algonquian dialect of a group of Native Americans in Massachusetts. In their language, it meant "war leader." The Puritan missionary John Eliot used it in his translation of the Bible into their language in 1661–63 to convey the English words "*officer*" and "*captain*."

Mugwump was brought into English in the early nineteenth century as a humorous term for a boss, bigwig, grand panjandrum, or other person in authority, often one of a minor and inconsequential sort. This example comes from a story in an 1867 issue of *Atlantic Monthly*: "I've got one of your gang in irons—the Great Mugwump himself, I reckon—strongly guarded by men armed to the teeth; so you just ride up here and surrender."

It hit the big time in 1884, during the presidential election that set Grover Cleveland against the Republican James G. Blaine. Some Republicans refused to support Blaine, changed sides, and the *New York Sun* labelled them *little mugwumps*. Almost overnight, the sense of the word changed to *turncoat*. Later, it came to mean a politician who either could not or would not make up his mind on some important issue, or who refused to take a stand when expected to do so. Hence the old joke that a mugwump is a person sitting on the fence, with his mug on one side and his wump on the other.

Michael Quinion, *World Wide Words*

Notice that the definition indicates what a mugwump is, explains the origin of the word and its history, and provides concrete examples.

Writing Activity

Identifying Features of a Definition

Consider the following definition of a Luddite:

A Luddite is a person who fears or loathes technology, especially new forms of technology that threaten existing jobs. During the Industrial Revolution, textile workers in England who claimed to be following the example of a man named Ned Ludd destroyed factory equipment to protest changes in the workplace brought about by labor-saving technology. The term *Luddite* is derived from Ludd's surname. Today, the term Luddite is reserved for a person who regards technology as causing more harm than good in society, and who behaves accordingly.

Tech Target Network

1. What are the features of this definition?
2. How might you clarify the definition?

For more on a type of writing that uses definitions extensively, see Chapter 8, "Writing to Convince."

Writing Classifications

When you classify, you group—or divide—items into categories based on one of three principles— completeness, exclusiveness, or consistency:

- **Completeness** means that all items need to be included in a classification. If you were classifying automobiles, you would need to make certain that SUVs were included in your scheme.
- **Exclusiveness** means that none of your categories should overlap with any other category. For example, the categories *movies about monsters* and *scary movies* don't work because some movies about monsters are scary (*The Thing*) and would fit in both categories.
- **Consistency** means that the same criteria need to be used to determine the contents of each category. If you are classifying animals and two of your categories are *mammals* and *birds*, your third category should not be *extinct animals* because that introduces different criteria into your system.

For more on a type of writing that uses classification extensively, see Chapter 7, "Writing to Analyze."

Many topics can be classified, which means that you will find classification a useful organizing strategy for many kinds of writing:

- Before purchasing a laptop computer for business travel, you might classify some possible laptops you are considering by weight—ultra-light (under three pounds), light (three to five pounds), moderate (six to eight pounds), and heavy (more than eight pounds).
- In deciding which candidates to support in an election, you might classify them according to their stated positions on issues that are important to you.
- As you write a menu for your next week's meals, you could use the categories in the food pyramid shown in Figure 13.3.

Writing about Comparisons and Contrasts

The related strategies of **comparison**—looking at how subjects are similar—and **contrast**—looking at how they are different—are common not just in writing but in thinking. People find that they are crucial tools in thinking about and differentiating many aspects of the world around them.

In all areas of life, you will use comparison and contrast:

- In an art history class, you might compare and contrast the features of two schools of art such as impressionism and surrealism.
- In an e-mail to a friend, you might compare and contrast two romantic comedies that you recently saw at movie theaters.
- You might compare and contrast the features of two network servers that your company is considering for purchase.

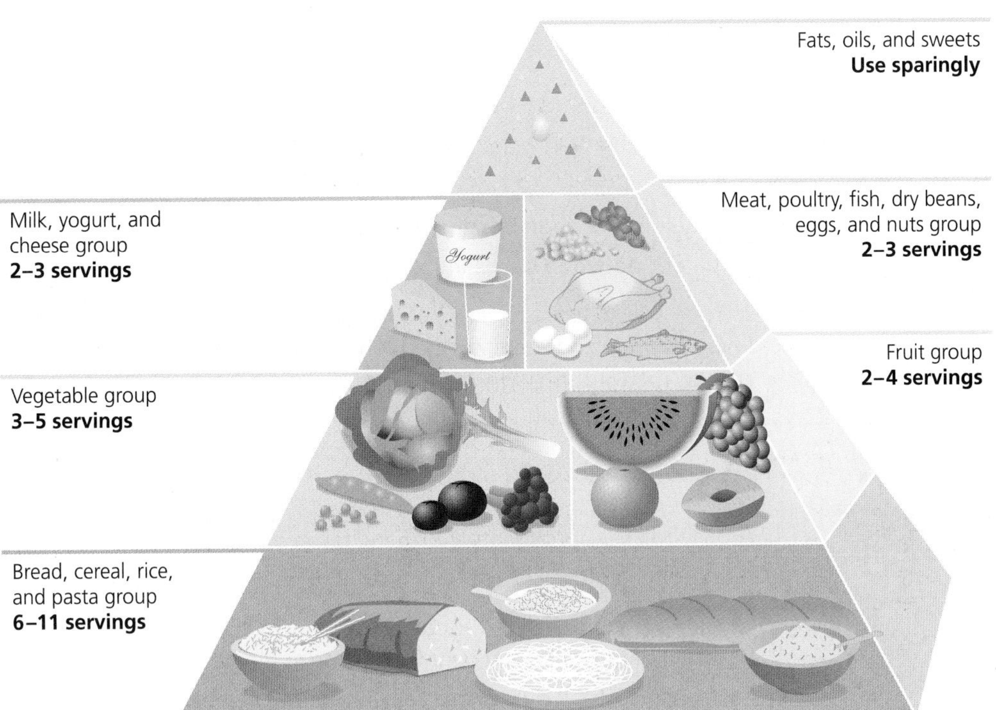

FIGURE 13.3 The Food Pyramid

Approaches to Comparison and Contrast

The two major approaches to comparing and contrasting two items are point-by-point and block. In the **point-by-point approach**, you discuss the two items together for each point of comparison/contrast. In the **block approach**, you discuss all of your points of comparison/contrast about one item first and then all points about the other item second. Here are two abbreviated outlines for a paper comparing the sports of baseball and fast-pitch softball, each using one of the two organizational approaches.

Point-by-Point Approach

I. Pitching
  A. Method
    1. Overhand or sidearm in baseball
    2. Underhand in fast-pitch softball
  B. Speed
    1. Up to 100 miles per hour in baseball
    2. Up to 70 miles per hour in fast-pitch softball

II. Field dimensions
   A. Mound
      1. Elevated to about 12 inches in baseball
      2. Level with the field in fast-pitch softball
   B. Infield
      1. Ninety feet between bases in baseball
      2. Sixty feet between bases in fast-pitch softball
   C. Outfield
      1. Over 400 feet to the centerfield fence in baseball
      2. Usually no more than 300 feet to the centerfield fence in fast-pitch softball

III. Equipment
   A. Balls
      1. A baseball is approximately 2.75 inches in diameter
      2. A fast-pitch softball is approximately 3.5 inches in diameter
   B. Bats
      1. Baseball bats are usually over 2.5 inches in diameter
      2. Fast-pitch softball bats are usually under 2.3 inches in diameter

Block Approach

I. Baseball
   A. Pitching
      1. Overhand or sidearm
      2. Up to 100 miles per hour
   B. Field dimensions
      1. Pitcher's mound approximately 12 inches high
      2. Ninety feet between bases
      3. Over 400 feet to centerfield fence
   C. Equipment
      1. Baseball approximately 2.75 inches in diameter
      2. Bats usually over 2.5 inches in diameter

II. Fast-Pitch Softball
   A. Pitching
      1. Underhand
      2. Up to 70 miles per hour
   B. Field dimensions
      1. Pitcher's circle level with the field

2. Sixty feet between bases
3. Usually no more than 300 feet to centerfield fence

C. Equipment
1. Softball approximately 3.5 inches in diameter
2. Bats usually under 2.3 inches in diameter

If you compare two items with many features, you should usually use the point-by-point approach. Regardless of the approach that you use, however, you can help guide your readers by doing the following:

- Focusing on the major similarities and differences
- Including the same points of comparison/contrast for both items
- Covering the points in the same order for both subjects
- Using transition words to move from point to point

Writing Activity

Comparing/Contrasting

Read "Facing Poverty with a Rich Girl's Habits" on pages 62–64 in Chapter 4, "Writing to Share Experiences." Construct an outline of the major points of comparison/contrast that Suki Kim offers when she describes her life in South Korea and her life in the United States. Does she use a point-by-point approach or a block approach?

Using Outlines and Maps to Organize Your Writing

Regardless of the organizing strategies that you use, outlines and visual maps can be helpful tools. Commonly used outlines and maps include scratch outlines, formal outlines, and tree diagrams.

connect
mhconnectcomposition.com
Outline Tutorial QL13002

SCRATCH OUTLINES

Scratch outlines work well early in the process of composing. As rough sketches of your thoughts, they can help you get ideas on paper without much concern for the final organization of the project. A scratch outline might be little more than a list of ideas in the order in which they might appear in the final project. Here is an example:

connect
mhconnectcomposition.com
Scratch and formal outline QL13003

Solving the Problem of Childhood Obesity

- Open with a story about obesity to grab readers' attention.
- Provide some background/history.

- Describe the problem with statistics.
- Explain the causes of the problem: poor nutrition (food pyramid), large serving sizes, lack of exercise.
- Describe the consequences of childhood obesity: diabetes, adult cardiovascular problems.
- For each cause, offer a possible solution: teaching parents how to read nutritional labels; educating children and parents about serving sizes; persuading schools to require physical education; and persuading parents to engage their children in more exercise.
- Conclude.

FORMAL OUTLINES

Formal outlines can be useful once you have done some invention work and research. In a formal outline, you arrange your ideas in a series of levels. The first level is marked with roman numerals (I, II, III), the second level with capital letters (A, B, C), the third level with numbers (1, 2, 3), and the fourth level with lowercase letters (a, b, c). Each level must have at least two entries. The entries in a formal outline can be in sentences (a sentence outline) or in words or phrases (a topic outline) as in the following example:

Solving the Problem of Childhood Obesity

I. Opening story about obesity
II. Background/history of obesity
III. Description and explanation of the problem
    A. Statistical overview of the problem
    B. Causes of the problem
        1. Poor nutrition (food pyramid)
        2. Large serving sizes
        3. Lack of exercise
    C. Consequences of problem
        1. Diabetes
        2. Cardiovascular problems in adulthood
IV. Possible solutions
    A. Instruction for parents on how to read nutritional labels
    B. Education for children and parents about serving sizes
    C. Recommendation that schools require physical education and that parents engage their children in more exercise
V. Conclusion

If you wanted a more detailed plan, with sentences that you could actually use in your paper, you could prepare a sentence outline like the following:

Solving the Problem of Childhood Obesity

I. Many children, such as Heather H., begin the cycle of dieting and gaining weight as early as age 10.

II. Obesity has been increasing in the United States, especially among children and adolescents.

III. Here are some recent, and quite startling, statistics about childhood obesity.

IV. There are several reasons for this problem, including poor nutrition, ever-increasing portion sizes, and children's reluctance to exercise.

   A. The first reason is that today's children, who live in one of the wealthiest countries in the world, suffer from poor nutrition.

   B. Another reason is that we all seem to expect large serving sizes in every restaurant these days.

   C. Finally, many children don't exercise, preferring to stay indoors for video games and online chats with their friends.

V. The consequences of childhood obesity can be dire.

   A. Diabetes can be one major and severe consequence.

   B. Childhood obesity also leads to cardiovascular problems when children grow up.

VI. Fortunately, some doctors and other experts are turning their time and attention to this problem, and have come up with some unique ideas.

   A. Parents need to learn how to read food labels, so here are some instructions for doing so.

   B. Both children and parents need to understand what a reasonable "serving size" looks like.

   C. Several exercise programs are available that schools can provide to young students—exercise that will be fun and helpful to them.

VII. Childhood is too important a time to spend obsessing about weight, but children should be encouraged to eat a healthful diet and exercise regularly to avoid the dieting treadmill that Heather H. and others like her are on.

TREE DIAGRAMS

Like outlines, tree diagrams show hierarchical relationships among ideas; Figure 13.4 gives an example.

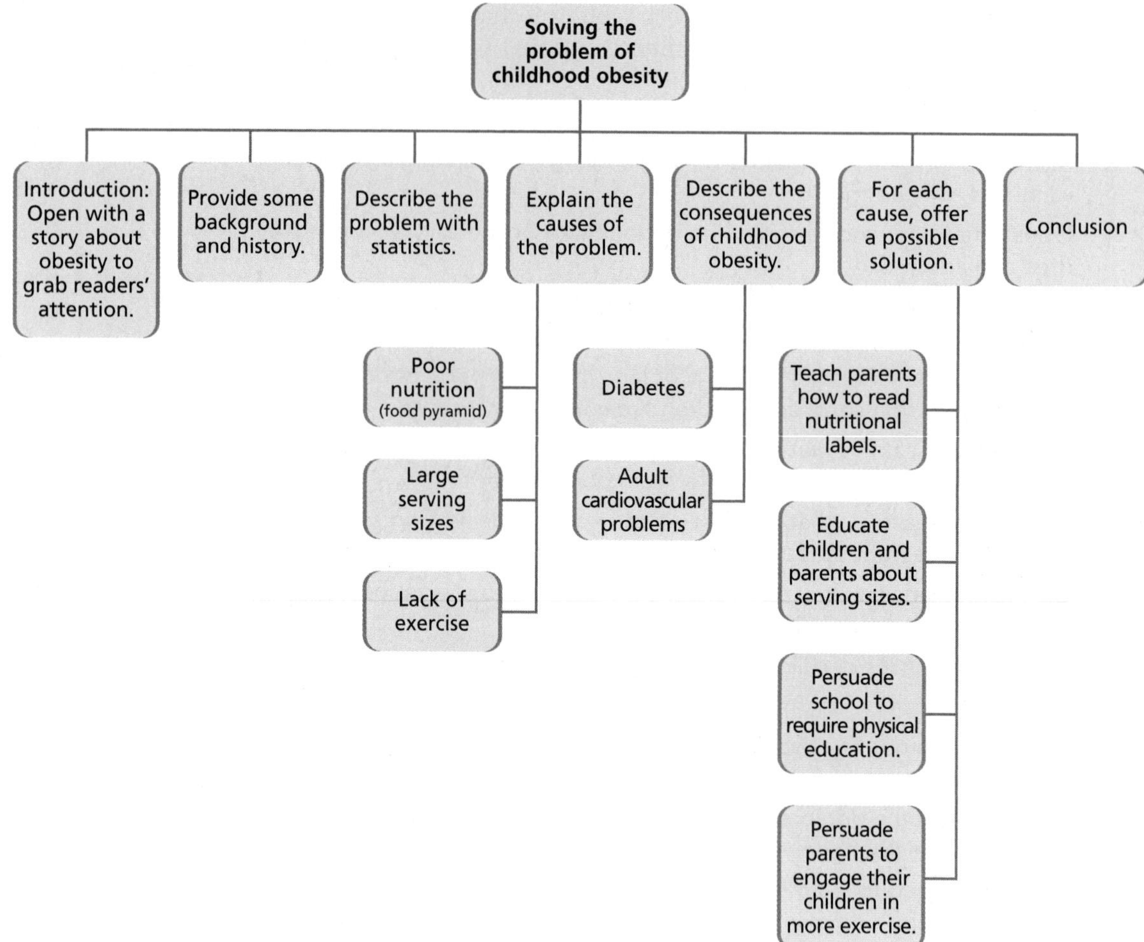

FIGURE 13.4 Tree Diagram for a Paper on Childhood Obesity

Chapter 14

Using Strategies for Argument

Often in our culture, the word *argument* has a negative connotation, as if to *argue* really means to *fight* about something. But the term *argument* in many academic, professional, and civic settings and in most writing situations means to debate with someone about an issue or to attempt to convince someone to accept your point of view. That does not mean your debating partners, listeners, or readers will end up agreeing with you (or you with them), but rather that, at the end of your argument, your audience will say, "I understand what you mean and can appreciate your position. I don't necessarily agree with everything you've said, but I can see where you're coming from." This kind of argument must have as its thesis an assertion that is debatable, not a certainty, and must generate responses somewhere on the following continuum:

Strongly Disagree ⟷ **Strongly Agree**

Assertions that are capable of evoking such responses are appropriate **thesis statements** or **claims** for arguments. The fundamental aim of an argument is to move the audience along this continuum of responses toward agreement.

Effective arguers get to know their audiences well enough to understand where on this continuum their responses are likely to lie, and they choose argument strategies based on that knowledge. Of course, some members of the audience will be willing to move farther along the continuum than others.

If "winning" an argument means that the other side sees, understands, and appreciates your position, then your goal is to present your thesis and supporting evidence in a logical manner, so that your reader can at least understand—and perhaps agree with—your position.

Argument and Persuasion

When you present an argument, you want readers at a minimum to understand what you mean and to see your perspective. The concept of **argument**, then, is somewhat different from and broader than that of **persuasion.** When you have persuaded someone, you have convinced that person to believe something (this legislative bill is better than that one) or to do something (provide the funding needed for longer library hours).

In a sense, an argument is the means of persuasion: You cannot persuade someone about anything without an effective argument. So, while you certainly hope that you will be able to persuade the president of your school to increase library hours, your overall goal is to construct and present a sound, effective argument. Put another way, after members of your audience read your argument, they may or may not agree with you in part or in full, but if your argument is effective, they will at least think, "I understand this writer's position, and he or she has made a strong case."

Each of the chapters in Part 3 of this book asks you to construct a certain kind of argument, with the goal of attempting to persuade your readers in a variety of ways. For example, Chapter 8 ("Writing to Convince") asks you to argue for a position on a controversial issue, while Chapter 9 ("Writing to Evaluate") asks for your judgment on the quality of a product, event, place, or other subject. In both cases, you may not necessarily cause your readers to change their minds—by switching sides on the issue or rushing out to see the film you recommended. Rather, they will understand your position and the reasons and evidence that support that position. Likewise, for Chapter 10 ("Writing to Explain Causes and Effects"), and Chapter 11 ("Writing to Solve Problems"), you are asked to argue a debatable claim, whether it be a cause-and-effect relationship, or a solution to a problem. Readers may not completely agree with your claim, but if it is soundly argued, they should at least be willing to consider it.

Rhetorical Appeals

The philosopher Aristotle was one of the first to notice that effective speakers use three kinds of appeals to help make their arguments convincing. An **appeal** in this sense is a means of convincing your audience to agree with your argument, and perhaps of convincing them to do something. We introduced the three kinds of appeals—*logos, ethos,* and *pathos*—in Chapter 2 (pages 20–23) in the context of rhetorical analysis. Here we focus on using them to construct an effective written argument. You already use these various appeals when you want to convince your friends to do something with you, for example, or to talk your parents or children into going somewhere.

Logical Appeals

Logical appeals, or, using the Greek word, *logos,* are appeals made through your use of solid reasoning and appropriate evidence, including statistical and other types of data, expert testimony, and illustrative examples.

Always consider what kind(s) of evidence will best convince your audience. For example, if you are writing to evaluate something (perhaps a film, a restaurant, or an art museum), quoting known and accepted authorities on the subject is often persuasive. If you are writing to solve a problem, historical information also can be useful, showing, for instance, how other communities have dealt with similar issues or problems.

No matter what kind of evidence you use to support your argument, that evidence must come from reliable sources. *For more information on evaluating sources, see Chapter 19.*

Ethical Appeals

Ethical appeals, or appeals to *ethos,* focus on your character. When you establish your *ethos,* you communicate to readers that you are credible, intelligent, knowledgeable, fair, and perhaps even altruistic, concerned about the welfare of others. You can establish your ethos by doing the following:

- Present yourself as knowledgeable about your subject matter.
- Acknowledge points of view that differ from yours, and deal fairly with them. For example, you might write, "Other people might say that ______ ______________ is less costly than what I'm proposing, and they would be right—my plan does cost more. But the benefits far outweigh the cost, and here is why. . . ."
- Provide appropriate information, including facts and statistics. Some audiences will be receptive to statistical information; others will be more receptive to quotations from experts in the field. Still others might look for both types of evidence.

Emotional Appeals

Appeals to readers' emotions, or *pathos,* can help readers connect with and accept your argument. However, effective arguers use emotional appeals judiciously, avoiding appeals that astute readers might consider exploitive.

There are many ways to appeal to readers' emotions. Here are some possibilities:

- Identify who is or will be affected positively or negatively by a situation or course of action that you are arguing for and ask the audience to identify with them.
- Show how the situation or course of action has emotionally affected people elsewhere.
- Arouse indignation over a current situation by showing how it is inconsistent with a community's value or concerns.

You use all three appeals frequently in everyday life. To convince a friend to go to see a film with you, for example, you might mention that the film, although new and relatively unknown, received an award from the Sundance Film Festival, an appeal in which you draw on the *ethos* of the famous film festival; you might point out that the early showings cost only half as much as the nighttime shows (*logos*); or you might plead that you have no one else to go with and hate going to movies alone (*pathos*).

The Rhetorical Triangle: Considering the Appeals Together

Most effective arguments combine rhetorical appeals because audiences respond to a variety of appeals. The three kinds of appeal complement one another, as is suggested by the rhetorical triangle shown in Figure 14.1. Each aspect of an act of communication—the writer, the reader, the message—is connected to the other two aspects.

FIGURE 14.1
The Rhetorical Triangle

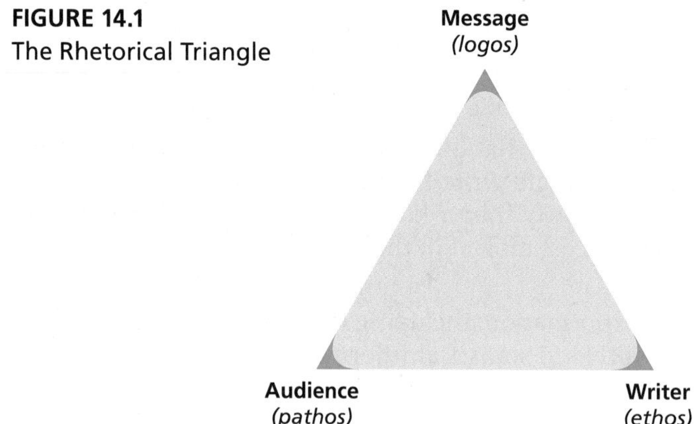

Writing Activity

Considering Your Audience

Construct two brief letters, no longer than a page. For each letter, assume that you want twenty-four-hour, seven-day-a-week access to your college's library.

- For your first letter, your audience is your classmates. How would you argue for your position in a letter to them? What needs would you list, to show those you have in common?
- For your second letter, your audience is the president of your college or university. How would you argue for your position to him or her?

With several classmates, discuss the differences between your letters.

Three Approaches to Argument

In this chapter, we cover three ways to conceptualize argument: classical, Toulmin, and Rogerian. All three approaches are widely used as ways to think about and to design effective arguments. Understanding how they function will help you not only to understand the arguments you read or hear but also to construct your own written arguments.*

- The *classical* approach is a way of organizing an argument to make sure you, as a writer, have covered all important aspects of your argument.
- The *Toulmin* way of considering an argument is to examine how the argument functions: how one aspect provides reasons and evidence for another, what definitely needs to be explicitly stated and what does not, and so on.
- The *Rogerian* approach to argument helps those involved in any argument understand and (perhaps appreciate) other points of view and how those might relate to their own positions.

Classical Strategies for Arguing

About 2,400 years ago, the Greek philosopher Aristotle formalized what we now call the **classical scheme** of argument by listening to effective public speakers and then figuring out what made their arguments effective. Amazingly, Aristotle's ideas remain relevant today. If you are using the classical scheme, this is the sequence you follow:

Aristotle

- Introduction
- Main claim
- Evidence supporting claim
- Discussion of other perspectives
- Conclusion

This approach is called the **deductive** way to reason because you state your claim and then help the reader understand (or deduce) how the evidence supports your claim. Here is a simplified example of how the deductive approach might work in asking for a raise:

- Introduction and main claim — I'd like to talk with you about getting a raise. I've been with the company for two years now, and for several reasons I feel that I deserve a raise at this point in my career here.

*Thanks to our good friend and colleague Doug Downs for reminding us of the differences among these three concepts.

- Evidence supporting claim
  - First, I am very effective now at doing work in the office as well as working with customers outside the office.
  - Second, I've taken classes to learn several new software programs, and I'm now fully proficient at using them.
  - Third, I've shown that I can take on lots of responsibility because I've handled several important projects in the past two years.
  - Fourth, my end-of-year rankings have consistently improved.
- Discussion of other perspectives (acknowledging, conceding, and/or refuting them) — Now, I know there was that one dissatisfied customer, but if you'll recall, I managed to satisfy her (at last!) by providing extra service.
- Conclusion — Therefore, I deserve a raise.

The advantage of the deductive method is that you state your position and make your case before your reader starts thinking about other perspectives. Because readers understand what your point is *early* in your text, they find it easier to follow your argument.

If you are using another method, commonly known as the **inductive** approach, you first present and explain all of your reasons and evidence, then draw your conclusion—your main claim. In other words, you provide the evidence first and then the conclusion at the end. The advantage is that your reader may come to the same conclusion before you explicitly state your position and will therefore be more inclined to agree with your view.

For more on deductive and inductive reasoning, see Chapter 8.

An inductive approach to asking for a raise could use the same evidence to support the claim, discussion of other perspectives, and conclusion, but begin without a main claim:

- Introduction — I'd like to speak with you about my job performance here at our company now that I've been here for two years.

Parts of a Classical Argument

Thinking about the parts of an argument makes the task of arguing more manageable. When you put the parts together, the results can lead to an effective whole.

The classical argument as presented here has five parts occurring in a certain order. However, as you write your own arguments, you may find that not every part is essential in every case and you may also find it useful to rearrange or combine the parts. The five parts are as follows:

1. **Introduction** (*exordium*): In the introduction, you gain the attention of the audience and begin to establish your credibility. To accomplish this, you need to have analyzed your audience. Your overall goal in the introduction is to prepare your audience to be receptive to your case.

   Here are some strategies that can work well in introductions for arguments:

   - Show how the issue affects the audience.
   - Show how the issue affects the community in general.
   - Outline what a reader might do about the issue.
   - Ask a question to grab the reader's attention.
   - Explain what will happen if the reader does not get involved and take action.
   - Begin with a compelling quotation.

Digital Literacy **Using Music in Arguments**

If you have ever listened closely to the words of popular songs, whether they are examples of rock, blues, jazz, musical theater, hip-hop, or rhythm and blues, you've probably noticed that many song lyrics follow the patterns of argument. Mining popular culture for examples that can help you build an argument can be quite effective.

If you are asked to write an essay that persuades, consider searching your music collection for interesting and powerful metaphors, statements, and stories you can use as quotations. Whether you collect CDs, download tunes, call up videos on YouTube, listen to podcasts, or even write and produce your own music, it is possible to consider your collection of music as a collection of *arguments*. Be careful, though, to provide context and reasons for choosing the particular quotations that seem to support your view.

Often, you can insert a sound file into a PowerPoint presentation, which can add an interesting dimension to a persuasive oral presentation. Be cautious about posting any music online, however. All music—no matter how brief the excerpt—is protected by copyright and is not considered fair use unless it is in the public domain.

2. **Narration** (*narratio*): Here you briefly explain the issue and provide some background or context for the argument you will make, as well as explain why it is important. If your readers understand why the issue is important to *them,* they are more likely to be interested and involved in your argument. You can use a narrative to do the following:

   - State the crucial facts that are generally agreed on.
   - List the main issues or aspects that you will consider in your argument.
   - Introduce the main reasons that support your argument.

3. **Confirmation** (*confirmatio*): This is the main body of your argument. Here you offer evidence to support your thesis or claim. Evidence can consist of facts, statistics, expert opinion, and other information. For example,

if you are arguing that students should get involved in the upcoming campus elections, data relating to issues that are part of the election campaign can help them understand how the issues affect them personally.

4. **Refutation** (*refutatio*): If you can argue about a statement, that means ideas or values are in dispute—that is, an issue is undecided and there is another side to your argument. Dealing with that other side, or **counterargument**, is a crucial step: If you fail to deal with the opposition's counterarguments, your readers may think that you are unaware of them or that you are trying to conceal their existence.

   To refute counterarguments, you first need to discover what they are through research or audience analysis. For example, as you share ideas and drafts with your classmates, ask them what arguments the other side might make to address this issue or problem.

   As you consider opposing viewpoints, you need to decide how to handle them. Refutation is only one of several options. Some counterarguments may not be significant enough to merit further consideration; it may be enough simply to acknowledge them. If you are trying to convince students to vote in a campus election, you might simply acknowledge the objection that one vote does not make a difference: "I understand what you mean, because I used to think that way. And it's true that one vote rarely makes 'the difference' in any election." Or you might decide to refute the objection, noting that "what one person can do is to talk to other people, and convince them that they need to vote, and talk to them about the issues, and then all of a sudden that one person has gotten a lot of other people involved."

   Other ways to deal with objections to your argument include the following:

   - Agree that *part* of the opposing view is valid, and then demonstrate how the rest of the argument is unsound.
   - Accept that the opposing view is valid, but note that what the opposition suggests costs too much / is impractical / will not work because _______________ has been tried and been unsuccessful in other places or has some other problem.
   - Discredit any authorities they cite in their favor ("Since Jones wrote that, three studies have been published showing that his conclusions were incorrect . . .").

5. **Conclusion** (*peroration*): Here you conclude your argument and, possibly, call for action. In the conclusion, you can do one or more of the following:

   - Summarize your case.
   - Stir readers' emotions.
   - Suggest an action or actions that the audience might take.
   - Refer back to the start of your essay, tying everything together.
   - List your main points, touching on your evidence for each.

Example: The Classical Scheme in Action

DAVID WOLMAN

Time to Cash Out: Why Paper Money Hurts the Economy

David Wolman is a contributing editor at *Wired,* where this essay first appeared. He is the author of *Righting the Mother Tongue* and *A Left-Hand Turn Around the World,* and he has written for magazines such as *Newsweek, Discover, Outside* and *Forbes.* Wolman's work has also been anthologized in the *Best American Science Writing* series.

Two years ago, Hasbro came out with an **electronic version** of Monopoly. Want to buy a house? Just put your debit card into the mag-stripe reader. Bing! No more pastel-colored cash tucked under the board. Turns out it wasn't Lehman Brothers but Parker Brothers that could smell the future. At least, that's what participants at this year's **Digital Money Forum** believe. In March, after a long day of talks with titles like "Currency 2.0" and "Going Live With Voice Payments," forum attendees at London's plush Charing Cross Hotel gathered for drinks—and, yes, a few rounds of Monopoly Electronic Banking Edition. 1

Introduction: Here Wolman sets the stage, so to speak, as he introduces his argument.

Unfortunately, the world's governments remain stuck in the past. To maintain our stock of hard currency, the US Treasury creates hundreds of billions of dollars worth of new bills and coins each year. And that ain't money for nothing: The cost to taxpayers in 2008 alone was $848 million, more than two-thirds of which was spent minting coins that many people regard as a nuisance. (The process also used up more than 14,823 tons of zinc, 23,879 tons of copper, and 2,514 tons of nickel.) In an era when books, movies, music, and newsprint are transmuting from atoms to bits, money remains irritatingly analog. Physical currency is a bulky, germ-smeared, carbon-intensive, expensive medium of exchange. Let's dump it. 2

Narration: Wolman states his point about the outmoded nature of physical currency. Wolman tries to get readers thinking: Does physical currency cost more than it's worth? Is it bad for the environment? What examples from your own experience suggest that physical currency no longer makes sense?

Markets are already moving that way. Between 2003 and 2006, non-cash payments in the US increased 4.6 percent annually, while the percentage of payments made using checks dropped 13.2 percent. Two years ago, card-based payments exceeded paper-based ones—cash, checks, food stamps—for the first time. **Nearly 15 percent** of all US online commerce goes through PayPal. Smartcard technologies like **EagleCash** and **FreedomPay** allow military personnel and college students to ignore paper money, and the institutions that run dining halls and PXs save a bundle 3

Confirmation: Wolman provides multiple examples of how governments, businesses, and individuals are moving to electronic currency.

by not having to manage bills and coins or pay transaction fees for credit cards. Small communities from British Columbia to the British Isles are experimenting with alternative currencies that allow residents to swap work hours, food, or other assets of value.

Objection and Refutation: Wolman himself offers an objection to his argument and then refutes the objection by giving a specific example of a new technology that is now available.

4 But walled-garden economies are a long way from a fully cashless society. As *Wired* **first noted 15 years ago**, to rely exclusively on an emoney system, we need a ubiquitous and secure network of places where people can transact electronically, and that system has to be as convenient as—and more efficient than—cash. The infrastructure didn't exist back then. But today that network is in place. In fact, it's already in your pocket. "The cell phone is the best point-of-sale terminal ever," says **Mark Pickens**, a microfinance analyst with the **Consultative Group to Assist the Poor**. Mobile phone penetration is 50 percent worldwide, and mobile money programs already enable millions of people to receive money from or "flash" it to other people, banks, and merchants. An added convenience is that cell phones can easily calculate exchange rates among the myriad currencies at play in our world. Imagine someday paying for a beer with frequent flier miles.

Objection and Refutation: Wolman gives a second objection. He then answers with a potential solution. What other solutions would you suggest?

5 Opponents used to argue that killing cash would hurt low-income workers—for instance, by eliminating cash tips. But a modest increase in the **minimum wage** would offset that loss; government savings from not printing money could go toward lower taxes for employers. And let's not forget the transaction costs of paper currency, especially for the poor. If you're less well off, check-cashing fees and 10-mile bus rides to make payments or purchases are not trivial. Yes, panhandlers will be out of luck, but to use that as a reason for preserving a costly, outdated technology would be a sad admission, as if tossing spare change is the best we can do for the homeless.

Conclusion: Asks the readers to think about how we can use existing technologies to make life better. Notice the "value charged" language he uses.

6 Killing currency wouldn't be a trauma; it'd be euthanasia. We have the technology to move to a more efficient, convenient, freely flowing medium of exchange. Emoney is no longer just a matter of geeks playing games.

Writing Activity

Identifying a Classical Argument

With several of your classmates, find an essay in a newsmagazine (such as *Time* or *Newsweek*) that is written in the form of a classical argument. Identify each part of the argument:

- Introduction
- Narration
- Confirmation
- Refutation
- Conclusion

Toulmin Strategies for Arguing

Another important model of argument was developed by philosopher Stephen Toulmin in his 1958 book *The Uses of Argument*. As with Aristotle's classical scheme, you already use the main aspects of Toulmin's approach: Every day you make assertions ("All students need to be involved in the upcoming election") and then use "*because* statements" to provide support for those assertions ("because if they are not, they won't have their needs and positions represented to those in power"). Toulmin called your assertion a **claim** and the *because* statement **data**. For example, if you are trying to convince your classmates to become involved in campus politics, you might claim that their involvement is vital to their own interests. But unless your classmates believe that getting involved will affect them (in amount of tuition they pay, for example), they will not be able to understand why they ought to take the time and make the effort to become involved. So you, as the person making the argument, must consider whether your audience will know why it is important for them to participate, and if you determine that they may not, it is up to you to provide those specific reasons.

Stephen Toulmin

What Toulmin adds to this fairly intuitive way of constructing any text is the notion of a **warrant:** *why* the data support the claim. Sometimes you need to say why explicitly; other times you can assume that your reader understands this connection.

In **Toulmin's model of argumentation**, then, three components are considered essential to any argument:

- **Claim:** the conclusion or point that you will argue and hope to convince readers to agree with. For example, your claim might be "A major objective of this country's space program should be to land a crew of astronauts on Mars."

- **Data:** the reasons you give to support your claim. Your data may take the form of *because* statements. You might support your claim about Mars by saying "because knowing about Mars will help us understand our own planet and the life it supports because Mars may have had water—and life—at one time."
- **Warrant:** the connection between the claim and the data, explaining why the data support the claim. Often this connection is obvious and can go unstated. For example, the data and claim above are connected by the idea that it is important that we understand our planet.

Three other components of an argument are considered optional: the backing, the rebuttal, and the qualifier:

- **Backing:** If you are not sure that your readers will see the connection between data and claim, you need to state the warrant and support it as well. The support for the warrant is the backing. If you felt you could not assume the warrant about understanding our planet, you might need to state it explicitly: "Understanding our own planet and the life it supports is crucial to our survival as a species, and knowing about Mars will help us do that."
- **Rebuttal:** When you rebut the opposition's position, you prove that your position is more effective—for example, that it is acceptable to more people. You might acknowledge the potential objection that space missions with astronauts are costly but argue that the potential benefits outweigh the costs: "While space flight with astronauts is expensive, in terms of our total economy those costs are small and the possible knowledge that we would gain by putting a human being instead of a machine in charge of data collection is priceless."
- **Qualifier:** In response to opposing positions and points, you may need to in some way limit or modify, or qualify, your claim. You can do this by indicating precisely the conditions under which your claim does and does not apply. Qualifiers often include words such as *sometimes, possibly, may,* and *perhaps*.

Example: The Toulmin Model in Action

STANLEY FISH

But I Didn't Do It!

Both a professor and an attorney, Stanley Fish has held teaching and administrative positions in several large American universities. A world-renowned scholar of the seventeenth-century poet John Milton, Fish is the author of more than a hundred articles and books, many of which have been translated into other languages. Fish has won many awards and honors, including the Hanford Book Award, the PEN/Spielvogel-Diamonstein Award, and the Milton Society Award. He also received a nomination for the National Book Award. The following opinion piece was first published in the *New York Times* in 2006. Although we don't always agree with Stanley Fish, we always learn from his thinking.

Emboldened by the State of Virginia's apology for slavery—the measure passed both houses unanimously—some Georgia lawmakers are in the process of introducing a similar resolution in their legislature. The reasoning behind the apology movement is straightforward: a great wrong was done for centuries to men and women who contributed in many ways to the prosperity of their country and were willing to die for it in battle; it's long past time to say we're sorry. 1

Unstated warrant: Slavery was and is a horrible part of American history. Fish probably assumes that he does not need a *because* statement as readers will agree that slavery was terrible.

Resistance to the apology movement is also straightforward. There is the fear that because an apology is an admission of responsibility for a prior bad act, apologizing might establish a legal or quasi-legal basis for reparations. And there is also the objection that after so many years an apology would be merely ceremonial and would therefore be nothing more than a "feel good" gesture. 2

This is the issue Fish is dealing with. He is rebutting the assertion that an apology for slavery is a bad idea because no one who is currently alive, including the individual members of the Georgia legislature, kept slaves.

But the objection most often voiced is that the wrong people would be apologizing to the wrong people. That was the point made by Tommie Williams, the Georgia Senate majority leader, when he said: "I personally believe apologies need to come from feelings that I've done wrong," and "I just don't feel like I did something wrong." 3

Williams's counterpart in the house, Speaker Glenn Richardson, made the same claim of innocence on behalf of his colleagues. "I'm not sure what we ought to be apologizing for," given that "nobody here was in office." 4

Claim: The Georgia lawmaker's resistance to an apology is based on faulty reasoning.

Mr. Richardson's statement at least has the merit of recognizing that an apology would not be made by an individual—the idea isn't to go to some slave cemetery and speak to a gravestone—but by an institution. He 5

Data: The members of the Supreme Court, by relying on precedent, carry on the work of the members who preceded them and are responsible for earlier members' actions because they are all part of that institution.
Unstated warrant: The Supreme Court's authority derives from its reliance on, and respect for, precedent.
Warrant: Justices should overrule previous decisions in which the court ruled incorrectly.
Warrant: Legislatures are analogous to courts.
Data: Case where the U.S. Congress passed legislation providing reparations to Japanese-Americans unjustly treated during World War II.
Data: President George H. W. Bush formally apologized to Japanese-Americans.
Qualifier: Fish admits he doesn't intend to answer the greater question of whether an apology should be issued; rather, he limits his argument to addressing one reason offered by members of the Georgia legislature for not apologizing.
Conclusion: The fact that the Georgia legislators did not personally keep slaves is not a valid reason to resist apologizing.

just thinks that because no present member of the institution was around at the time of the injury, an apology would make no sense.

6 But this is very bad reasoning, and you can see why if you read just a few recent Supreme Court cases on any subject. Invariably, the justice delivering the court's opinion will cite a precedent from a case decided 50 or 100 years ago, and say something like, "In Smith v. Jones, we ruled that . . . " But of course he or she didn't actually—that is, personally—rule on anything in 1940 or 1840, so what's with the "we"?

7 The answer is that by using "we" to refer to an action taken before any present member of the court had reached the age of reason or was even alive, the justices acknowledge that they are part of an ongoing enterprise, and as such are responsible for its history; not as individuals, but as persons charged with the duty of carrying on a project that precedes them and will survive them.

8 At times "carrying on" includes revising and even repudiating earlier stages in that project. By overruling a precedent—a rare occurrence, to be sure—the justices say, collectively and on behalf of everyone who has ever donned the robe, "Oops, we got that one wrong; sorry, here's another try."

9 Legislatures do not overrule; they repeal, but the principle is the same. Legislators meeting on the first day of a new term don't say, "O.K., let's start all over again and figure out what laws we would like to have on the books." Instead, they regard themselves as picking up a baton passed to them by their predecessors whose actions they now "own," even in those instances when no legislator now sitting performed them. The vast majority of those actions will continue in force, but a few will be revisited, and of those, a smaller number will be modified or even reversed.

10 Sometimes a mistake now acknowledged can be remedied by changing the law. Sometimes that remedy would come too late, and another form of response is called for, as when the United States passed the Civil Liberties Act of 1988, deploring the internment of Japanese-Americans during World War II and authorizing payments of $20,000 to each surviving internee.

11 Ronald Reagan signed that act into law, and two years later President George H. W. Bush formally apologized for "the wrongs of the past."

12 Does that mean that Georgia should apologize, too? Not necessarily. The question is a political as well as a moral one, and it is not my intention here to answer it. All I am saying is that while there may be good reasons to resist apologizing, the "we didn't personally do it and those it was done to are dead" reason isn't one of them.

Writing Activity

Using a Toulmin Argument

Consider an issue you think is important to your classmates. Construct a brief Toulmin argument in which you identify your claim and the warrants your classmates need to believe in order to accept your argument. This issue could be something of local interest, such as campus parking, or a matter of national significance, such as health care.

Rogerian Strategies for Arguing

Rogerian argument, which is based on the work of psychologist and mediator Carl Rogers, allows for the fact that at times we will take perspectives on issues that conflict with the views of people with whom we have important relationships. Suppose you and a close friend disagree about how to solve the problem of alcohol-related traffic fatalities. Although you could use classical argumentative strategies to win this argument, in the long term, your relationship might be better served by a conversation in which you try to see the other point of view.

Carl Rogers

Differences of opinion occur in all four areas of life—the academic, the professional, the civic, and the personal. And in all four areas, we have relationships that we want to maintain. We might therefore do better to resolve our differences without trying to "win." Although the strategies of classical argument may work well in settings where the participants are clearly opponents trying to convince a third party (two lawyers making their case to a jury, for instance), they do not work so well when the participants need to maintain a collegial, friendly, or even loving relationship. And although such strategies may work well when your topic is relatively uncontroversial or your audience is disposed to agree with your claim, they may be more likely to alienate than to persuade your audience when your topic is controversial and your audience is hostile to your claim. You might think of Rogerian argument as a "kinder, gentler" way to argue—and one that might often serve you well.

The ultimate goal of Rogerian argument is to negotiate differences and cooperate to reach a resolution that benefits or is in some way acceptable to both parties. Thus, in Rogerian argument, it is useful to begin by thinking about commonalities—that is, by thinking about and understanding opposing views and asking yourself, "Even though we may have some differences, what do we have in common?" or "Even though we may not think alike, how can we work together effectively to solve this problem?" Rogerian argument asks you to "feed back" opposing arguments. This requires you to understand the other person's position, and to think enough about that position to articulate it. This does not mean that you agree with the other position, of course, but that saying (or writing) it shows you understand and that you recognize the other of the argument. In a way, Rogerian arguments sound something like, "I understand your position on this point," which is much softer than saying, "I think your position is dead wrong!"

Rogerian arguments have several components:

- **Introduction:** The introduction includes a description of the issue you hope to come to a consensus on. As you state a goal, keep your tone positive and invite others to participate in solving the problem or reaching agreement.
- **Summary of opposing views:** Be as accurate and as neutral as you can in stating the views of those who may disagree with you. Show that you have the skills, character, and fairness to see and appreciate the merits of opposing views.
- **Statement of understanding:** After you have stated the opposing views, demonstrate that you understand why others might hold such views. If possible, indicate the conditions under which you too could share those views.
- **Statement of writer's position:** The previous three parts have prepared your readers to listen to your views, and here is the place to state them. Invite your audience to consider your views in the same way that you have considered theirs.
- **Statement of contexts:** Building on the statement of your position, be specific about the kinds of conditions under which you hope others will find merit in your position.
- **Statement of benefit:** Explain how your position or solution will benefit those who might oppose you. End on a positive and hopeful note.

Example: Rogerian Strategies in Action

RICK REILLY

Nothing but Nets

Rick Reilly has been voted National Sportswriter of the Year eight times. He wrote the weekly "Life of Reilly" column for *Sports Illustrated* for many years, and he frequently contributes to *Time* magazine. Reilly's nonfiction books include *Who's Your Caddy?* and *The Life of Reilly: The Best of* Sports Illustrated's *Rick Reilly.* Reilly also has published the novel *Missing Links* and is the winner of many awards, including the New York Newspaper Guild's Page One Award for Best Magazine Story. The following article was first published in *Sports Illustrated* in 2006. Our students find this essay humorous and enlightening.

I've never asked for anything before, right? Well, sorry, I'm asking now. 1

We need nets. Not hoop nets, soccer nets or lacrosse nets. Not New Jersey Nets or dot-nets or clarinets. *Mosquito* nets. 2

Problem: Reilly is a sportswriter who is not writing about game nets, but the need for mosquito nets.

See, nearly 3,000 kids die every day in Africa from malaria. And according to the World Health Organization, transmission of the disease would be reduced by 60% with the use of mosquito nets and prompt treatment for the infected. 3

Introduction: Reilly outlines the severity of the problem.

Three thousand kids! That's a 9/11 every day! 4

Put it this way: Let's say your little Justin's Kickin' Kangaroos have a big youth soccer tournament on Saturday. There are 15 kids on the team, 10 teams in the tourney. And there are 20 of these tournaments going on all over town. Suddenly, every one of these kids gets chills and fever, then starts throwing up and then gets short of breath. And in seven to 10 days, they're all dead of malaria. 5

Reilly works hard to put the problem into a language that everyone can understand.

We *gotta* get these nets. They're coated with an insecticide and cost between $4 and $6. You need about $10, all told, to get them shipped and installed. Some nets can cover a family of four. And they last four years. If we can cut the spread of disease, 10 bucks means a kid might get to live. Make it $20 and more kids are saved. 6

Reilly points out how inexpensive the nets are.

Benefit: For $10 you can save a child's life.

So, here's the ask: If you have ever gotten a thrill by throwing, kicking, knocking, dunking, slamming, putting up, cutting down or jumping over a net, please go to a special site we've set up through the United Nations Foundation. The address is: *UNFoundation.org/malaria*. Then just look for the big *SI's Nothing But Net* logo (or call 202–887–9040) and donate $20. *Bang*. You might have just saved a kid's life. 7

Note how Reilly writes about a shared, common ground with any reader who ever played a sport (which would include almost everyone).

Writer's position: Reilly works to defuse the money objection to his proposal, and he does so in a humorous way. Sure, he says, he wants to raise a million dollars . . . but then he shows how that large amount can come from many small donations.

Benefit: no overhead costs— all donations pay for nets.

Benefit: Look at how many lives could be saved.

Or would you rather have the new Beastie Boys CD? 8

You're a coach, parent, player, gym teacher or even just a fan who likes watching balls fly into nets, send $20. You saved a life. Take the rest of the day off. 9

You have *ever* had a net in the driveway, front lawn or on your head at McDonald's, send $20. You ever imagined Angelina Jolie in fishnets, $20. So you stay home and eat on the dinette. You'll live. 10

Hey, Dick's Sporting Goods. You have 255 stores. How about you kick in a dime every time you sell a net? Hey, NBA players, hockey stars and tennis pros, how about you donate $20 every time one of your shots hits the net? Maria Sharapova, you don't think this applies to you just because you're Russian? Nyet! 11

I tried to think how many times I have said or written the word "net" in 28 years of sports writing, and I came up with, conservatively, 20,000. So I've already started us off with a $20,000 donation. That's a whole lot of lives. Together, we could come up with $1 million, net. How many lives would that save? More than 50 times the population of Nett Lake, Minn. 12

I know what you're thinking: *Yeah, but bottom line, how much of our $1 million goes to nets?* All of it. Thanks to Ted Turner, who donated $1 billion to create the U.N. Foundation, which covers *all* the overhead. "Every cent will go to nets," says Andrea Gay, the U.N. Foundation's Director of Children's Health. 13

Nets work! Bill and Melinda Gates have just about finished single-handedly covering every bed in Zambia. Maybe we can't cover an entire Zambia, but I bet we could put a serious dent in Malawi. 14

It's not like we're betting on some scientist somewhere coming up with a cure. And it's not like warlords are going to hijack a truckload of nets. "Theoretically, if every person in Africa slept at night under a net," says Gay, "nobody need ever die of malaria again." You talk about a net profit. 15

My God, think of all the nets that are taken for granted in sports! Ping-Pong nets. Batting cage nets. Terrell Owens's bassinet. If you sit behind the plate at a baseball game, you watch the action *through* a net. You download the highlights on Netscape and forward it on the net to your friend Ben-net while eating Raisinets. Sports is nothing *but* net. So next time you think of a net, go to that website and click yourself happy. Way more fun than your fantasy bowling league, dude. 16

One last vignette: A few years back, we took the family to Tanzania, which is ravaged by malaria now. We visited a school and played soccer with the kids. Must've been 50 on each team, running and laughing. A taped-up wad of newspapers was the ball and two rocks were the goal. Most fun I ever had getting whupped. When we got home, we sent some balls and nets. 17

I kick myself now for that. How many of those kids are dead because we sent the wrong nets? 18

Writing Activity

Constructing a Rogerian Argument

With several of your classmates, construct a Rogerian argument, focusing on some campus or national issue or problem.

Some Common Flaws in Arguments

Any argument, no matter how effective, can be marred by **logical fallacies,** or flaws in reasoning. Although sometimes introduced deliberately into an argument with the aim of misleading readers, such flaws are often inadvertent, and avoiding them requires the kinds of critical thinking discussed in Chapter 2. The following list includes the most common and easily avoided fallacies.

- **Appealing to irrational fears:** All humans have fears, and it is often easy to exploit those fears. Someone making the argument that cattle ranchers should test each cow every month, even though there have been only a few isolated cases of mad cow disease in the United States, would be exploiting an irrational fear.
- **Appealing to pity:** Although appeals to pity and other emotions can be justified at times, this kind of appeal can mask an otherwise weak case. If a student who is failing a course because she has missed many classes and performed poorly on exams appeals to her instructor by pleading, "If I fail this course, I won't graduate on time," she is obviously masking a weak case.
- **Appealing to prejudice:** Also known as *ad populum,* this fallacy occurs when the writer appeals to a preexisting prejudice. A common example is the practice of putting an image of the American flag on a bumper sticker that advocates a particular product or stance, with an appeal to patriotism thus substituting for an argument for the product or stance. For example, Figure 14.2 is an advertisement for the American Civil Liberties Union (ACLU) that uses the American flag to indicate that their cause is patriotic. How does this image influence your initial reaction to the ad?

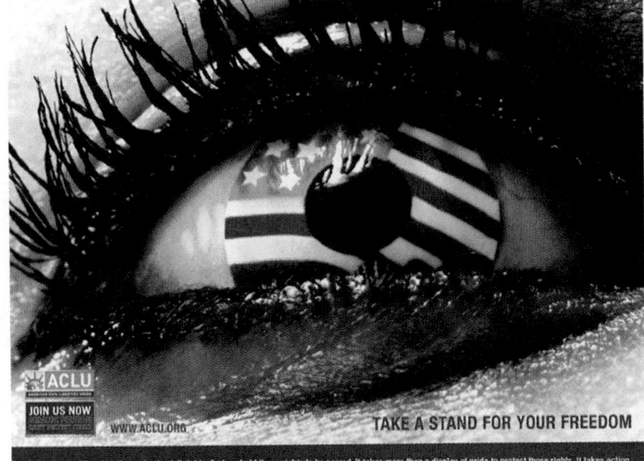

FIGURE 14.2 An advertisement for the ACLU, using the familiar stars and stripes as part of its appeal

- **Appealing to tradition:** The most common form of this appeal is the statement "We've always done it this way in the past."
- **Arguing from a lack of knowledge or evidence:** We can illustrate both forms of this flaw with the following example: You have looked for a needle in a haystack, and your search has been unsuccessful. From this lack of evidence, one person might argue that there must be a needle in that haystack if you would only search more carefully. From the same lack of evidence, a second person might argue that there is no needle in the haystack. In reality, of course, neither conclusion can be supported.
- **Attacking the opponent's character:** Often called an *ad hominem* attack, this fallacy is sometimes used in an attempt to direct attention away from the logic of a case—usually a strong case—by evoking a negative emotional response to the person making the case. In an effort to make an opponent seem like a hypocrite, a person might say, "My opponent argues that vegetarianism is a moral choice, but I notice that he wears leather shoes—so it is acceptable to *wear* part of an animal, but not to eat part of one? That is hypocritical!" The opposite fallacy (*pro hominem*), which is also common, involves directing attention away from a case—usually a weak case—by evoking a positive emotional response to the person making it. A legislator might appeal to the public to support an unworthy bill by praising the record of the colleague who introduced it: "Because Representative Smithers has produced good ideas in the past, we should vote for her plan to drill for oil in Central Park."
- **Attributing false causes:** Usually called *post hoc, ergo propter hoc* ("after this, therefore because of this"), this fallacy occurs when someone assumes that event A caused event B because event A occurred before event B. A common example is superstitious thinking: "I've been having so much bad luck recently because I broke a mirror/walked under a ladder/crossed the path of a black cat." This fallacy is common in civic life. In political campaigns, for example, an incumbent will often claim that his or her policies have caused the economy to improve, whereas a challenger will charge that the incumbent's policies have caused crime rates to increase. All sorts of events occur before other events in the world, but that does not mean that they cause those other events.
- **Bandwagon appeal:** Here the arguer is essentially saying "Many people are doing it, especially people whom you admire, so it must be a good thing to do. You should do it too." Television beer commercials frequently use this appeal when they show a group of young, attractive people having a great time at a party: If those people are having such a good time drinking that brand of beer, anyone who drinks it will also have a good time.
- **Begging the question (circular reasoning):** This fallacy treats a questionable assertion as if it has already been answered or fully explained, as in the following example: "My friend would never cheat because he's an honest person." To assert that someone is honest is not to provide evi-

dence that he did not or would not cheat; this assertion merely restates the idea that the person would not cheat but has nothing to do with whether he actually did cheat.

- **Complex question:** In this ploy, an arguer asks a question that actually has two parts and demands a one-part response. For instance, the question "When did you stop beating your dog?" has embedded in it the assumption that you used to beat your dog. The person to whom it is addressed would be right to reply, "Hold on. Let's first establish whether I have ever beaten my dog in the first place."
- **Either-or reasoning:** Also known as "false dichotomy," this fallacy occurs when writers give readers two opposing choices (either A or B) when other possibilities also exist. For instance, a person might state, "You can major in business administration, or you can plan on getting a crummy job."
- **Faulty analogy:** In this fallacy, the writer makes a comparison that is in some way misleading or incomplete—or that does not even relate to the topic being discussed. A reporter who writes, "The president hit a home run with his labor bill" is using a faulty baseball analogy. The president is not a baseball player and is supposed to be working with Congress, not against them.
- **Guilt by association:** This fallacy occurs when a writer seeks to discredit an opponent by associating the opponent with some unpopular person, group, or idea, as when politicians attempt to brand their opponents with labels such as "free-spending liberal" or "hard-right conservative." Such labels imply that *all* liberals are "free spending" or that all conservatives are "hard-right"—and both labels have negative connotations.
- **Overgeneralization:** This fallacy occurs when someone reaches a conclusion based on insufficient evidence, especially atypical examples. For instance, your friend engages in overgeneralization when, after an automobile accident in which she was not wearing a seat belt but sustained only minor injuries, she says, "See. Seat belts aren't necessary."
- **Oversimplification:** People sometimes search for simple answers to complex problems. For instance, some might say that the solution to gang violence in high schools would be simply to require students to wear uniforms in school. Of course, the problem of gang violence is complex, and its solution will not be that easy.
- **Red herring (or non sequitur):** This fallacy occurs when the writer introduces irrelevant material to divert attention from the issue being considered. The fallacy gets its name from the practice of dragging a red herring—a fish—along the ground to distract hunting dogs from the scent that they are following. A student who says to his teacher, "I know that I was late for class today, but I've been on time every other day" is using a red herring to throw the teacher off the scent of the real issue: The student is late.

- **Slippery slope:** This fallacy claims that once something starts, it must continue, just like a person sliding down a slippery slope. An example is the student who says, "We've got to fight that proposed fee for using the computer center. If that fee is enacted, pretty soon they'll be charging fees for using the restrooms on campus."
- **Stacking the deck:** Here the writer presents evidence for only one side of the case. A student who says, "I should get an A because I handed in all my homework," while neglecting to mention that she got a C on the midterm and final exams, is stacking the deck.
- **Straw person:** This fallacy occurs when an arguer distorts the opponent's argument and then attacks that distorted argument. For instance, a few decades ago, when equal rights for women was a hotly contested issue, some people made statements such as "Equal rights for women means that women will have the right to use men's restrooms. What is this country coming to?" Unisex restrooms were not part of what women's rights advocates were arguing for—so they served as a straw person.
- **Universal statements:** Such statements often include words such as *always, never, all, everyone, everybody, none,* or *no one*. Of course, some statements that include those words are true—for instance, "All humans are mammals." However, when writers use those words to describe human behavior or beliefs, those statements are usually problematic. For example, the statement "Men never share their feelings, but women always do" could be easily contradicted with just one or two cases.

Writing Activity

Searching for Logical Fallacies

To help you learn to identify logical fallacies, in your local or campus newspaper, find several instances of logical fallacies (Hint: Often, letters to the editor provide rich material!). Bring copies to class, share them, and explain the logical fallacies to your classmates.

Chapter

15

Using Strategies for Collaboration

Although writing can be a solitary activity, it is often a collaborative endeavor. For instance, researchers in the sciences, education, and engineering often co-author research proposals and reports. In business, teams often write project proposals and reports. In local, state, or national legislatures, many people collaborate to write bills to present to their colleagues. When groups of neighbors or parents are concerned about some local problem, they will often collaborate on a letter to the editor of their local newspaper or to the school board. In your writing classroom, you will probably have the opportunity to get feedback from your classmates, and in other courses, you are likely to encounter assignments that require you to work as part of a team.

Working with Peers on Your Single-Authored Projects

As you work on your own writing projects, working with peers can yield many benefits. Early in the process of crafting a project, peers can help you generate ideas by challenging you to consider other perspectives. Later in the process, peers can point out ways to revise your writing so that readers will find it more understandable, informative, or persuasive. Peers can also help edit your prose.

In the chapters in Parts 2 and 3 of this book, "Writer's Workshop" activities help you solicit feedback from peers. It is your responsibility to encourage peers to offer candid assessments of your work. Peers should not be nasty, of course, but they *should* give you a clear sense of how well your writing is fulfilling its purpose.

Strategies for Working with Peers on Your Projects

Feedback from peers can help you at any point in a project. Although it is important to seek and use the perspectives that peers can offer, it is equally important to remember that *you* are ultimately responsible for the project. Given this principle, the following guidelines can be useful:

- Peers can indicate what is working well—and not so well. When peers ask for more information, you should consider adding that information to your next draft.
- Peers' questions are usually more helpful than their suggestions.

Using Digital Tools for Peer Review

It may be difficult to find time to meet face-to-face with peers outside of class. Digital tools for peer review can help. Even if it is easy to meet face-to-face, though, writers still need to use digital tools. Here are some common tools that you can use:

- The track-changes feature of your word-processing software makes it easy to see the changes that different reviewers are suggesting in a document. You can then accept or reject any or all suggested changes.
- The "comment" feature of most word-processing software makes it easy to offer a suggestion or pose a question to the writer.
- Many instructors use a course-management system to offer courses either completely or partially online.
- Wikis offer writers the opportunity for peer review. Changes to documents in wikis are automatically tracked. Changes can easily be made by anyone with access to the document.

Working with Peers on Multiple-Authored Projects

Working with your classmates on multiple-authored projects can have many benefits. One long-term benefit is that it will prepare you for co-authoring documents with your colleagues in the workplace. Another benefit is that working with a group can infuse a project with a rich array of perspectives.

Group work also presents challenges, however. Some members of the writing team may be inclined to contribute too much to the project while others sometimes seem to contribute too little. Another challenge is that some co-authors may insist on doing things their way without listening to potentially effective ideas from others.

Strategies for Working with Peers Effectively

Working with peers can be challenging because they may question your thinking in new and sometimes uncomfortable ways. In college, this kind of interaction is especially likely because your classmates may have personalities and/or cultural backgrounds that differ substantially from yours. Although encountering a variety of backgrounds and perspectives can move you out of your comfort zone, it can also be a catalyst for learning.

Collaboration can take place in several ways. You might find yourself working on an entire project with the same team. Or you might find yourself using one classmate or a small group of your classmates as peer reviewers for drafts of one another's works. The "Writer's Workshop" sections in Parts 2 and 3 go over many different strategies for peer review of single-authored works.

To make the most of your work with peers, try some of the following strategies:

- **Listen empathically to your group members' comments and questions.** Empathic listeners strive to understand why someone is making a particular comment or raising a particular question.
- **Assign roles to members of the group.** One member of the group can be the *recorder,* whose duty is to keep track of who says what. Another member of the group can be the *question-asker,* posing questions to encourage everyone to think more critically or deeply. Yet another group member can be the *facilitator,* whose role is to keep the discussion focused and moving forward. It is important that every group member have some *specific responsibility* to perform.
- **Provide positive and constructive feedback.** Every piece of feedback can be stated more or less negatively or more or less positively. Further, every negative or less positive statement can be recast into a more positive form:

Digital Literacy **Using a Wiki to Collaborate**

Working in groups can be a challenge, especially when your group members are trying to schedule out-of-class work time together. You might want to consider using a free online groupware site, or even a wiki. A wiki is an interactive Web site that allows members to create, add, delete, and change content. Each group member can edit existing content and develop separate materials on linked pages. Wikis and groupware document sites eliminate the confusion of keeping track of multiple e-mails in your inbox. Some popular sites to try out free of charge include *Google Groups* (http://groups.google.com), *Google Docs* (http://docs.google.com), *pbwiki* (http://pbwiki.com), *wetpaint* (http://www.wetpaint.com), and *Wikispaces* (http://www.wikispaces.com).

Less Positive	More Positive
There's an error in his sentence.	You could edit the sentence this way:
This paragraph is underdeveloped.	You could develop this paragraph by adding this:
You don't have a conclusion.	What are you planning to say in the conclusion?

- **Pay attention to interpersonal dynamics.** Before the group begins discussing the assigned topic, ask each member of the group to respond to the following kinds of questions:
  - What can the group do to function most effectively?
  - What seems to impede our group from functioning effectively?
  - What encourages you to contribute effectively to the group?
- **Do round-robin sharing.** To ensure that every member of the group contributes equally, go around the table clockwise, with each person contributing one after the other. Do this as many times as necessary to solicit everyone's contributions.
- **If possible, keep the group relatively small—three or four members.** Larger groups become hard to manage, and it becomes difficult to coordinate calendars or to reach consensus.
- **Consider your class and your peer group to be intertwined communities.** Make a commitment to improve the work of each community and each member of the community. If every member makes such a commitment, everyone will benefit.
- **Celebrate your accomplishment.** When the project is completed, treat yourselves, perhaps by enjoying coffee or lunch together.

One way to ensure the success of any group endeavor is to plan. The tasks that follow will help you to plan various aspects of your work with your group.

DEFINE SUCCESS FOR THE GROUP

What will count as success, and how can the group achieve it? You might use the following chart, for example, to define success and to identify the means for achieving it.

Defining Group Success

Sign of Success	Method(s) for Achieving
Everyone shows up for our meetings at the agreed-on time.	Add meetings to daily planners and/or PDAs.
Everyone participates equally.	Use a round-robin approach for sharing ideas during discussions.

DEVELOP A PLAN FOR DEALING WITH GROUP PROBLEMS

Potential problems include a group member who dominates a discussion, doesn't carry a fair share of the load, or misses a deadline. If a problem does surface, deal with it immediately. Dealing with small problems immediately can keep them from becoming bigger problems. If a problem arises, do *not* focus on who is to blame; instead, focus on finding a solution.

SET SHORT-TERM AND LONG-TERM GOALS

Before the group begins a particular work session, decide what you want to accomplish in the session—your short-term goal. As you work, stay focused on that goal until you achieve it. If the group will work together over multiple sessions, decide on a long-term goal to achieve by the last session. Then establish short-term goals for each session along the way.

Project Goals

Long-Term Goals	Short-Term Goals
Complete the project by November 16.	Complete library research by October 3.
	Complete interviews by October 10.

DEVELOP A PLAN FOR COMPLETING THE PROJECT

Identify the subtasks that need to be completed along the way, as well as a timeline for completing each subtask. Write down who is responsible for each task, and make certain that each member of the group has a list of everyone's responsibilities. As each deadline for a subtask approaches, ask the responsible member or members to report on progress.

MAKE A CALENDAR OF GROUP MEETINGS

Group meetings can be held face-to-face, by telephone, or in online chat rooms. For each meeting, establish an agenda and identify what each person needs to do before the meeting. Also, decide who will serve as the discussion leader for each meeting, and assign a different discussion leader for each meeting.

Calendar for Meetings

Meeting Date	Agenda Item(s)	Individuals' Preparation	Discussion Leader
October 11	Examine interviews	Hanna: Bring three copies of transcripts of interviews with rental-property owners.	Hanna
		Molly: Bring three copies of transcripts of interviews with renters.	Molly
		Meghan: Bring three copies of transcript of interview with city attorney.	Meghan

Using Digital Tools to Facilitate Multiple-Authored Projects

Whether or not collaborative meetings are held in person, digital tools can support the process. Here are some tried-and-true suggestions for using digital tools:

- Agree on a sequence for working on each digital file to avoid duplication of effort.
- For revising, use the track-changes and comment features of your word-processing software. That way other members of the group can see the changes that you are making.
- When you send a file to another member of the group for revising or editing, copy the other members of the group so that they can be certain who is working on the document and can see the progress on the project.
- When you name files, include the current date in the file name, such as "rental_paper_10–18–08." Don't delete older versions of files because you may need them to recover a deleted paragraph or to recover a file that has become corrupted.

Chapter 16

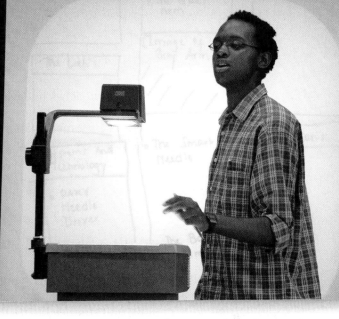

Making Effective Oral Presentations

Along with invention, arrangement, memory, and style, *delivery*—the way you present a message—is one of the five canons of rhetoric. In most of this book, we have dealt with written or visual forms of delivery. In this chapter, however, we will consider oral presentations, a form of delivery that is becoming increasingly important in all areas of life.

- In your academic life, you will be asked to make presentations in some of your classes.
- In your professional life, you will often be asked to present your ideas to your colleagues and to clients.
- In your civic life, you may speak before the local school board, or to the city council, or in front of any number of civic or political organizations.
- In your personal life, you may be called on to give a speech at an occasion such as a wedding, a funeral, or a school reunion, or you may speak at a less formal gathering of your family or friends.

As with written communication, oral presentations are *rhetorical acts*. To prepare an effective oral presentation, you need to ask yourself the same questions that you would ask for any writing situation:

- What do I want to accomplish? In other words, what is the purpose of this presentation?
- Who is my audience? What do they already know about my topic?
- What is the context surrounding this presentation?
- How much do I already know about my topic, and what else do I need to learn about it?

Once you have decided what you want to accomplish with a particular audience on a specific occasion, you will have a better understanding of how you need to prepare: what kind of research you need to conduct, what types of information you need to collect, and what kinds of visuals you should prepare.

Developing Your Presentation

You can use several approaches to develop an oral presentation. For more formal presentations on complex topics, you might decide to write the full text of your presentation. In some situations, you might decide to read your full text, especially if you have to use specific words at specific moments during your presentation. In other situations, you might write the full text and then prepare an outline of it. You might then speak from that outline on a sheet of paper and/or on a set of PowerPoint slides.

Establishing a Clear Structure

As with any piece of discourse that you construct, an oral presentation needs to have a clear organization that helps you to achieve your purpose. For most oral presentations, you will need to do the following:

- Construct an effective, thought-provoking, and attention-grabbing *introduction*. Remember that during your presentation, your listeners may be tempted to let their attention wander. Therefore, part of your job is to draw them in, to tell them something that will interest them, and to indicate quickly how your topic affects them.
- Let your audience know the *main point(s)* that you plan to make. Often called **forecasting**, this technique is especially important in oral presentations. If you have five main points that you want to cover, name them. Each time you move to the next point, make note of that, too ("The third point I want to make is . . ."). It often helps to provide the audience with a written outline of your points.
- Include sufficient evidence to *support* each one of your claims. You will be much more credible as a speaker if you support your claims with facts, examples, statistics, and testimony from experts.
- Be sure to *point back* to your main point so that it will be easy for your listeners to understand exactly how each point that you make or piece of information that you provide relates to your thesis.
- Use *visual aids* to outline the structure of your talk, if the situation calls for them. Your PowerPoint or overhead slides should outline the points you want to make, which you will then elaborate on. The message of each visual needs to be readily apparent.
- Use your *conclusion* to summarize and emphasize your main point, and to outline briefly how everything in your presentation supports it.

For more on supporting claims with evidence, see Chapters 8 and 14.

For more on using transitions, see Chapter 13.

VISUALIZING *Variations* | *PowerPoint* Presentations

Consider the most *ineffective* ways to use overhead slides or a PowerPoint presentation:

- The speaker uses very small type, so any text would be hard for the audience to read.
- The speaker spends part of the designated speaking time setting up or becoming familiar with the projection equipment.
- The speaker simply reads the visuals to the audience.
- The speaker uses every PowerPoint special effect on every slide.
- The speaker faces *away from* the audience while reading the text on the screen.
- The speaker walks to the screen and uses a finger to point to words on the screen.

Now contrast that to a presentation with *effective* qualities:

- Each visual aid uses appropriate type sizes, colors, and graphics to illustrate the speaker's main points.
- Before the presentation, the speaker learns how to use the equipment and sets it up.
- The speaker talks directly to the audience, using the text on each visual only as starting points, which he or she then elaborates and explains.
- The speaker uses PowerPoint special effects sparingly.
- The speaker talks directly to the audience, making eye contact and looking for signs that the audience is "getting" what the presentation is about.
- If necessary, the speaker uses an inexpensive laser pointer to point to specific words on the screen.

Suppose you were assigned to write an academic paper focusing on whether students litter on your campus, and you needed to prepare an oral presentation as part of that assignment. The slide in Figure 16.1 is one possible way for you to start a PowerPoint presentation on that topic.

The photograph can help you get your audience's attention and focus them on your topic. Each subsequent PowerPoint slide can contain the same heading, but provide the points you want to discuss in your presentation. Your second slide (Figure 16.2) might offer examples that suggest that students really are *not* slobs.

You will elaborate on these **talking points** as you make your presentation, discussing each one in detail and providing more information to support each point as you make it. For example, for the first point you could add the following information:

For more on visuals for presentations, see Chapter 18.

- Student organizations collect all recycled products in classrooms and office buildings.
- Student groups make money through this recycling effort.

(continued)

(continued)

Are students really slobs?

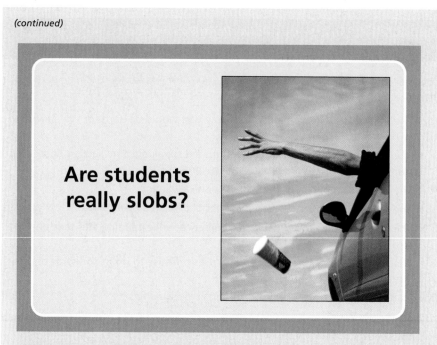

FIGURE 16.1 An Opening Slide for a Presentation

Are students really slobs?

Not necessarily. At our college, students

- help with the campus recycling program.
- are responsible for cleaning their dorm rooms.
- are subject to weekly inspections.
- are fined if their bathrooms are not clean.
- serve on a task force to keep our campus beautiful.

FIGURE 16.2 A Second Slide

- Students work together in the dorms to collect recycled products.
- Several student leaders serve on the Campus Recycling Board (CRB).

As you speak, then, you will flesh out each point with specific examples that are not on the slide but that provide information and details for your audience.

Considering Your Audience

Your *audience* is your primary concern as you plan, develop, and deliver your presentation. Every decision you make depends on your awareness of that audience, from considering what they already know about your subject, to what they need to know to believe what you tell them, to how you should present yourself to that audience. So consider: How do you want to come across to your audience? As informed and logical? As thoughtful? Probably. Or as someone shouting at them? Or droning at them? Probably not.

Digital Literacy: Enhancing Oral Presentations with Visuals and Audio

Using graphic, audio, and video files to enhance your oral presentations is not just a good idea—in this day and age, it's often expected. Audiences are not usually critical of video that is less than perfect as long as it illustrates an important point. Before incorporating media into your oral presentation, however, use the following checklist to make sure your presentation goes smoothly:

- Examine the room, lecture hall, or space where you will be presenting. Note the size and shape of the room, the seating arrangements, and the available equipment.
- If you are using video or sound media, make sure you have allowed enough time for the video or audio clip to play.
- Keep it brief. Do not give the audience time to get uncomfortable or restless while the video or sound is playing.
- *Always* plan a fallback handout, visual chart, or anecdote in the event that the technologies available in the room suddenly fail.
- Choose music, video clips, and images that are relevant to your presentation and that strengthen your claims and positions.
- Practice your presentation, including the time it takes to start and stop each video or sound element.
- Ask a friend, co-worker, or classmate to be your test audience, and be open to this person's feedback. Video and sound elements should illustrate, add meaning to, and clarify main points, not distract or confuse your audience. If your test audience tells you that it's not clear why you have incorporated media, ask for comments and suggestions.
- Give the audience time to react. If they *do* enjoy the media you've incorporated, give them a moment to laugh or applaud before you continue with your presentation.

One way to move your audience in the direction you would like them to go is through what magician and author Steve Cohen calls "command [of] the room." He recommends that you do the following:

- Look listeners in the eye. This might seem hard to do, especially if you are speaking before a large crowd, but you can always find someone to look at and speak to directly. Find these folks in several parts of your audience, and soon it will look like you are speaking personally to *everyone* in that audience.
- Hold that eye contact longer than you might expect to.
- Speak in a conversational tone and manner.
- Remember the 45-degree rule: If you are concerned that you might wobble as you speak, make sure to put one foot in front of the other, at about a 45-degree angle. It's impossible to wobble when you stand that way.

Finally, always make certain that your listeners can hear you, projecting your voice to the farthest member of your audience. To make certain that the audience can hear you, begin your presentation by asking, "Can folks in the back of the room hear me if I speak at this volume?" It's also a good idea to ask people to raise their hands and cup their ears if they can't hear you.

Writing Activity

Analyzing and Evaluating a Speech

Author Dale Dauten suggests listening to the "top 100 speeches" and other speeches available at http://www.americanrhetoric.com/. Visit that Web site and listen to a famous speech. In no more than two pages, write a brief analysis by responding to the following questions:

- What do you think made this speech famous?
- How effective do you think it was? Why?
- How effective do you think its original audience found it? Why?
- How was it organized?
- What were the main points of the speech?

Eliminating the Fear of Speaking in Public

The fear of speaking in public is always at or close to the top of lists of common fears. However, a bit of nervousness before a presentation can be a positive thing. If you are not nervous, you can be overconfident and not do a very effective job. Here are some techniques that can help you overcome stage fright:

- Be overprepared. Know what you want to say. Know your subject. If you plan to use visual aids, be prepared for the unexpected—for example, a broken projector.
- Practice *out loud* several times before your presentation. The more you practice, the better your presentation will be, period. *Thinking* what you want to say and actually *saying it aloud* are really two different things. When you just think about a presentation, your mind tends to fill in the words you leave out. But when you force yourself to practice out loud, you will end up with a much more polished presentation.
- Time your presentation, so you know that it fits whatever time parameters you have been given. There's nothing worse than having your host hold up a sign that says "TWO MINUTES LEFT" when you still have eight minutes of material left in your presentation.
- Another way to eliminate the fear of speaking, or at least to avoid showing that fear, is to use a clipboard to hold your notes. A piece of paper held in your hand might shake, but a clipboard will not.
- *Visualize* making a successful presentation before you make it. *See yourself* in front of your audience. *Listen* to them applaud. *See* them nod in agreement. *See yourself speaking with them* afterward. Picture what you want to happen, and it will.
- As you speak, do not let minor distractions bother you. If you hear noise from an adjoining room or from the street outside, ignore it. Do not assume that the person in the back row who appears to be laughing is laughing at you. Any number of things will distract you. You need to ignore them and concentrate on what you want to say.

Other Tips for Making Effective Oral Presentations

- Show enthusiasm.
- Use hand gestures purposefully.
- Become aware of any tics (such as, saying "um," playing with your hair, or rubbing your nose) and eliminate them. One strategy is to video record your speech and then watch it with a friend or classmate. Another strategy is to watch for these distracting behaviors while practicing in front of a mirror.
- Before a presentation and immediately following it, invite members of the audience to ask questions at the end of the presentation.
- Do not rely solely on visuals, especially a PowerPoint presentation. Because digital technology can fail, be prepared to give a presentation even if the computer or the projector fails to function properly.

- After practicing your presentation with a script or notes, also practice giving it with a bulleted list of your main points. Put that list on a 3″ × 5″ card.
- Always say "thank you" at the end of your presentation. You will find it to be surprisingly effective (and thoughtful).

Activity

Making an Oral Presentation

Using one of the papers that you wrote for Part 2 or 3 of this textbook, prepare and deliver an oral presentation. Revise and adapt your paper to suit your new medium and purpose, by establishing a clear structure, using effective visual aids, and considering your audience, according to the strategies described in this chapter.

If you have a video camera and can record your presentation so you can play it back and critique yourself, so much the better. But in any case, when you practice, think of your work as *rehearsal:* Go through your presentation from start to finish, without stopping. If you get tongue-tied or drop your notes or the projector does not work, just continue as if you were actually giving your speech.

Chapter 17

Choosing a Medium, Genre, and Technology for Your Communication

As long as humans have recorded their experiences, they have used technologies that act as tools to record their ideas.

A portion of a prehistoric cave painting from caves in Lascaux, France, the image that opens this chapter is approximately 17,000 years old. Although we know little about the person or people who made this image, we can surmise that painting was a useful technology for communicating with the intended audience. We do know that this medium (painting on a cave wall) allowed ancient humans to record images that might be decorative, might be symbolic, might tell a story, or might have performed a combination of these functions. Although the form of communication—or **genre**—this cave painting was created in has been lost, its medium is certainly durable, having survived for thousands of years.

Communication technologies are as varied as paint on a cave wall or a canvas, a piece of chalk, a ballpoint pen, or a word-processing program. Whatever a writer's purpose, the availability of a particular tool often helps to determine what **medium**—method of delivery—that writer uses to communicate.

When writers use a specific communication technology, they need to understand the impact that the technology will have on that communication. You do not always have a choice of which technology or medium you can use. But when you do, you need to understand the potential and limitations of each, and you need to make your choice in a rhetorically sound way. This chapter will provide an overview of communication technologies, suggestions on evaluating publishing options, and guidelines for choosing the most effective genre and medium for your work. It will also discuss design considerations and computer-mediated technologies.

Communication Technologies

Communication technology is not necessarily an electronic device. Because writing is itself a technology, every tool that we use to write is a kind of communication technology. Some communication technologies, such as word-processing software, encourage revision while others, such as pen and paper, act to discourage it. On the other hand, a handwritten letter, while difficult to revise, may make a more personal connection with your reader than a word-processed document. And pens and note paper are easier to carry than laptop computers and do not require an electrical outlet, a battery, or an Internet connection to function.

For an overview of technologies for computer-mediated communication, see pages 497–504.

Writing is inextricably linked to the technology that produces it. Understanding your own process and what communication technologies will work most effectively and efficiently for you in a given writing situation is important to your success as a writer.

Publishing Your Work

When you write letters or even when you write for an academic purpose, you are usually writing to one person or to a small number of people. As a result, your communication is generally private. When you *publish* your written work, however, you make it public. You can publish your writing in a variety of ways, from printing a newsletter and distributing copies to a limited group of people to constructing a page on the Web that is accessible to anyone. Although publishing your work can be exciting, it also involves both responsibilities and risks.

As recently as the 1970s, the only way to publish a piece of writing was in some kind of print medium. Publishing meant typesetting a manuscript and reproducing it on a printing press, a process that was both time-consuming and expensive. With the advent of the Internet, however, and specifically the hypertext environment of the Web, today's students have technology and publishing options and opportunities that were unheard of in the past. Now anyone who constructs a Web page on a server connected to the Internet publishes a document that is available to the entire world. If you are like our students, for example, you probably spend some time with MySpace and Facebook. While these are not academic "publishing" by any means, they are a way for you—a student—to publish and share information with students everywhere.

If you publish to a broad audience, and especially if you publish on the Web, you need to remember that those who view your work will be forming an opinion of you and your ideas that is based solely on what they see and read. Comments made in haste, without thought and reflection, can sometimes come back to haunt their authors. Members of your audience will also respond in some way to the design of your document or Web page—to the colors, the typeface, the size of type, the arrangement of items on the page or screen, and so on. If you make assertions, they will expect you to provide proof. As with any other form of written communication, they will also expect you to follow the conventions of spelling, grammar, punctuation, and mechanics. If you do not, you will weaken your credibility.

Whether you publish in print or in an electronic medium, you will enhance your credibility if you choose an appropriate genre.

Selecting a Genre and a Medium

At the beginning of any writing task that has an audience beyond their immediate circle, writers need to decide which established form of writing, or genre, to write in and the best medium in which to publish their work.

The chapters in Parts 2 and 3 include further details about genres.

In choosing a genre and medium, you need to consider carefully the audience, the context, and the purpose for your writing. For example, if you are writing a set of instructions for the operation of a propane camp stove, you can expect that the people who will read those instructions will usually be outdoors and often in isolated locations. The instructions will be more useful and effective, then, if they are published in print and in a size that is easy to pack and carry. On the other hand, if you are providing information about the academic support resources available on your campus and most of the students on the campus have high-speed Internet access, the best way to reach this audience may be to publish the information on a Web site.

Deciding on a Genre for Your Work

The genre you use for your writing is usually determined by your rhetorical purpose: Who is your audience, and what are you trying to accomplish with that audience? Sometimes, of course, whoever asks you to write will dictate the genre:

- Your employer asks you to construct a formal proposal.
- Your art teacher asks you to construct and present an oral report that uses visuals in the form of handouts, overhead projector slides, or a PowerPoint presentation (for more on presentation software, see page 503).
- Your Aunt Hanna asks you to send her a letter outlining your recent move to a new city, and she especially likes photographs printed in the letter.
- Your college president requests e-mail responses to a proposed new student fee.

Much of the time, though, you will select the appropriate genre based on your audience and rhetorical purpose:

- If you want to suggest to the president of your college that your campus library needs longer operating hours, a formal letter or proposal is probably the best approach (Chapter 8 focuses on persuasive writing).
- If you want to provide information to your community about an upcoming campus art exhibit, a brochure or poster might be the best genre (Chapter 6 focuses on informative writing).

For more on some common genres, see the Online Appendix.

- If you want to analyze an upcoming school bond tax proposal, a wiki or blog might be useful genres with which to present your analysis—and ones that allow others to also chime in (Chapter 7 focuses on analytical writing; for more on blogs and wikis see page 499.

Once you have decided on the genre, you will have to decide which medium will be the most effective in presenting the information (or your argument, evaluation, request, and so on). And your writing might take several forms. For example, if you are writing to share an experience (see Chapter 4), you might outline your shared experience in one of these forms:

- In print form, as an essay for your writing class
- On the Web, including several pictures, to share with family and friends
- As a PDF file on the Web that readers can download and print
- In an audio or video clip that you can e-mail readers and/or make available as a Web link

Deciding Whether to Use Print, Electronic, or Oral Media

Few academic papers are handwritten these days. Usually, you need to turn in an assignment printed in type on paper or in some kind of electronic medium. Often you have no choice; your instructor will specify a medium and format. However, in other situations your instructor might not specify the medium and format, and instead expect you to make the proper rhetorical choice.

Because the same information can usually be provided in both print and electronic forms, the medium you choose often depends on how that information is going to be used. Consider how each one also helps you accomplish different tasks better than the other.

Features of Paper and Electronic Documents

Criteria	Medium: Print on paper	Medium: Electronic
Portability	Easily portable	Can be sent almost instantly over the Internet; needs devices for portability such as a laptop, PDA, or Smartphone
Control of design	Relatively easy to control	Less easy to control—issues can be screen size and resolution
Ability to search	More difficult to search—needs a good index	Easy to search—can use hot-linked keywords
Revision	Once printed, difficult to revise—have to go back to the electronic version	Easy to revise

Paper documents work best when you are providing information in a narrative or sequential organization. Much academic writing, which is often argumentative, works well in print form because argument, which involves stating and supporting a thesis, is best presented as a linear sequence of points. On the other hand, if you are providing information that does not need to be read sequentially or chronologically, then hypertextual electronic formats, in which readers can use links to move easily from one section to another, offer an advantage over paper documents.

Writing Activity

Selecting a Medium

With several of your classmates, consider the following writing tasks. For each one, decide what medium might be appropriate to get your message across to the audience indicated.

- A group consisting of you and your neighbors wants to collect comments and information on a problem with an illegal dump near a school and present them to the town council.
- To increase public awareness of the different organizations on campus, your group has been asked to send information to various civic clubs such as the Rotary, Kiwanis, and Elks. With the material will be a request for donations to your school organizations.

Considering Design

In addition to choosing a genre and medium for your work, you will need to decide on a design for it. We know that many people absorb information more readily when it is presented in a diagram or a chart. And we know that how a document looks will affect our response to it. Chapter 18 covers the principles of good design and provides guidelines for incorporating visual material in your writing.

No matter what design functions you use, your goal in using them should be to make your message more effective.

Technologies for Computer-Mediated Communication

Your choice of a medium for your work may depend not only on the writing situation and the genre you have chosen but also on the availability of computers and the Internet to you and your audience, and on your—and their—comfort level with using them.

When you think about the way you use computers during your writing process, you probably think about using word-processing software to compose, revise, and edit your various drafts. Although these uses are important, they are not the only way that computers can help you during your writing process. You might use a computer to find information on the Internet or to access library databases. In addition, you can use word-processing software at other times besides composing, such as when you are taking notes or brainstorming, listing, and doing other invention work. You can even use other technologies, such as e-mail, for exploring topics and sharing ideas and drafts with peers.

The following technologies give you additional tools and options for writing and publishing your work in different media.

E-mail

Many of us use e-mail frequently. Familiar though it may be, e-mail is a powerful technology. To make the best use of it, you need to be aware of some basic rhetorical issues.

connect
mhconnectcomposition.com
Email QL17001

- **Tone:** E-mail messages range from very informal to formal, depending on your audience. If you are writing to a close friend, a family member, or even a classmate, you may feel comfortable using nonstandard words such as "gonna" or "dunno" or acronyms such as BTW (by the way) or ASAP (as soon as possible). However, using nonstandard language in your e-mail correspondence with supervisors, instructors, or people you don't know may harm your credibility with your audience.
- **Audience:** While you may send an e-mail to a specific person, *that* person might forward your e-mail or include it in another e-mail to someone you don't even know, so be aware of and cautious about what you say.
- **Ethos:** Your e-mail address will be seen by everyone you send e-mail to. If you send e-mail from work or school, your address is often assigned to you—and usually consists of a form of your name. However, when you set up a personal e-mail account, you can choose your own address, which will therefore say something about you. Like a vanity license plate on a car, addresses that are overly cute are inappropriate in a professional environment. Consider using different addresses for different purposes.

For more on e-mail as a genre, see the Online Appendix.

Threaded Discussions

connect
mhconnectcomposition.com
Netiquette QL17002

A **threaded discussion** is simply e-mail that, instead of being sent to individual addresses, is posted on the virtual equivalent of a bulletin board. Participants add their comments in the appropriate place—either as an extension of a previous message or as a new topic or "thread." The advantage is that everyone can see what the other participants are saying.

Threaded discussions can help instructors and students perform a variety of writing tasks. If the class is being offered entirely online, threaded discussions are a substitute for in-class discussions. If the class meets face-to-face, threaded discussions are one way to work collaboratively on a class assignment or participate in a discussion outside of class.

Synchronous Chat

At its most basic level, **synchronous chat** is simply a way to communicate with someone else in real time using text. Two types of synchronous chat are the virtual text-based worlds in MUDs (Multi User Domains) and MOOs (MUDs Object Oriented). These days most people who use synchronous chat are likely to be using some kind of instant messaging (IM).

Although instant messaging and other forms of synchronous chat are a great way to communicate with distant friends or relatives, you can also use the same technology for a variety of group or team activities. Synchronous chat provides an incredibly powerful environment for brainstorming. Because most chat software has a logging function, you can keep a written record of your conversation or brainstorming session and use it later in your writing.

For a definition of brainstorming, see Chapter 3, page 35.

Blogs

Blogs are a type of online journal. Like pen-and-paper journals, blogs often feature personal, reflective writing, but blogs are posted on the Web and are therefore public documents. Because blogs are consciously written as public documents, they are often about subjects that might interest large numbers of people, such as politics or sports or entertainers. However, they tend to retain their personal flavor because there is seldom, if ever, any accountability for what gets written in a blog. Some blogs are the work of a single author, others are interactive. They allow, and even encourage, multiple writers to take part in the conversation. An Internet site like Globe of Blogs (www.globeofblogs.com) lists thousands of blogs on a wide variety of topics.

Wikis

A **wiki** is "a page or collection of Web pages designed to enable anyone who accesses it to contribute or modify content" (http://en.wikipedia.org/wiki/Wiki). A wiki allows readers not only to read what is posted (as in a blog) but also to add or modify the content. In a real sense, then, a wiki is a living document that changes according to the thoughts about and written responses to information and ideas already posted. Perhaps the most famous wiki is the online encyclopedia Wikipedia, there are many other uses for a wiki:

- Businesses use wikis to share information and to let employees add and correct information.
- Families, especially extended families, can use a wiki to post information on family members, family reunions, and so on.
- College students can use a wiki to share information, to work on collaborative writing assignments, and so on.
- Teachers use wikis to share curricular material, lesson plans, assignment prompts and so on.

Word-Processing Software

Word processors such as Microsoft *Word, OpenOffice,* and *WordPerfect* have always performed four basic functions: inserting text, deleting text, copying and moving text, and formatting text. One important advantage that word processors offer is that they are a very forgiving technology. Changes are easy to make. This ability to revise texts easily opens up all kinds of possibilities for writers. Major revisions become easier because moving chunks of text from one place to another takes only a few simple manipulations of the mouse. Editing your text becomes easier because you can make minor changes with just a few keystrokes, instead of having to retype the entire paper. In addition, other functions allow a writer or writers to edit a text and peer reviewers to make comments on it.

For more on effective document design and the use of visuals, see Chapter 18.

Further, the options for designing a word-processed document are increasing all the time. While all documents need to be well written, readers now expect word-processed documents to look professional as well. Formatting options include, but are not limited to, type fonts and sizes, tables, boxes, and visual effects such as numbered and bulleted lists. If a writer needs to include graphics, they can be inserted directly into the word-processed document.

Digital Literacy **Learning New Software Programs**

Use the "barter system" to discover how you and your classmates can help one another become more proficient with various software applications. Make a list of all the computer programs (software applications) you have used, and compare the list with those made by your friends. Are there programs you would like to learn to use? Are there programs you can show someone else how to use better? Take advantage of any free time you have in the computer classroom or computer lab to help someone else—or ask for someone's help—in using unfamiliar programs that will aid them in their classes or on the job.

Writing Activity

Using Editing Features

Using whatever word-processing software you have available, investigate some of its editing features. Is there a "track-changes" feature? If so, try it. Is there a "comment" feature?

Working in teams of two, each student should write a paragraph or two on what you think is the most interesting or challenging feature of your word-processing program. Save your writing as an electronic file, and then share it with your teammate. Edit your teammate's file, using the track-changes and comment features.

Peer-Review Applications

As increasing numbers of writers use computer software to collaborate, the software keeps improving. The programs that writers use for this purpose fall into two distinct categories: collaborative tools built into standard word-processing programs, as discussed on page 500, and Web-based editing programs.

One type of Web-based editing program is a wiki—software that allows open editing of Web documents. A wiki is useful when writing teams work over distance and do not necessarily share the same computer operating systems or Web-browsing software. This flexibility makes wikis useful for student projects.

One Web-based program that allows peers to comment on your work is available to you as part of the Online Learning Center for this text. This software permits you and the other members of your assigned peer group to make comments about one another's writing and to view and respond to those comments.

Graphics Software

Today, it is possible to enhance your documents using a variety of visual information: tables, charts, graphs, photos, drawings, and other visual images. Although you can design some tables using a word-processing program and graphs and charts using a spreadsheet, other images need to be digitized (that is, put into a form that can be read by a computer). The easiest way to render many visuals in a digital format is to use a graphics program such as *PaintShop-Pro, Illustrator,* or *FreeHand.* If you are taking photographs yourself, you can use a digital camera. If you have a printed image, however, you can easily digitize it by using a scanner.

Once the image is digitized, you can manipulate it by using graphic editing software such as *PhotoShop.* Image-editing software allows you to change the size or resolution of the digital image, crop out unneeded elements, or change the contrast. However, image-editing software also makes it possible to change images inappropriately. Just because it is easy to change a photo does not mean that you *should* change it. The ease with which we can alter images raises serious ethical questions.

Digital Literacy: Protecting Your Computer

Letting someone use your computer can result in downloads and icons you don't want or need popping up on your screen or freezing your computer when you least expect it. Especially when your school computer is used for "recreational" purposes, files and programs can clog up your machine, causing resource issues that can mean an expensive trip to the tech support service. It's better to limit the number of people who use your computer and to resist the urge to use someone else's computer. Most colleges provide computer labs on campus, and the staff at the computer lab can usually help you with any problems that arise.

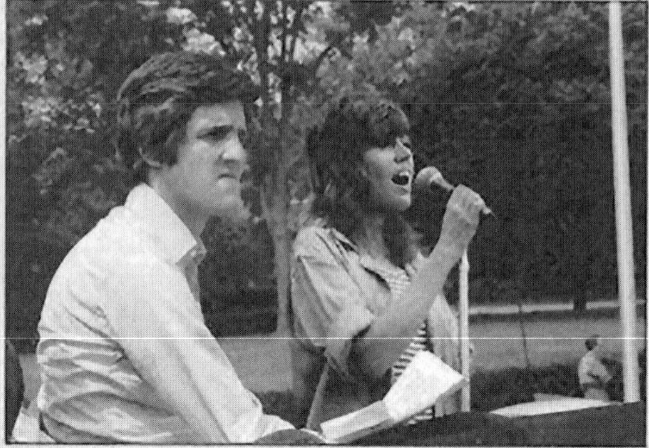

Fonda Speaks To Vietnam Veterans At Anti-War Rally

Actress And Anti-War Activist Jane Fonda Speaks to a crowd of Vietnam Veterans as Activist and former Vietnam Vet John Kerry (LEFT) listens and prepares to speak next concerning the war in Vietnam (AP Photo)

FIGURE 17.1 This photograph of John Kerry and Jane Fonda, supposedly appearing together at an anti-war rally, is fake. It was fabricated by combining the two photographs shown below it.

We have all seen examples of famous photographs that have been altered to include a person who was not in the original image. Although some doctored photos might be considered funny, others are fabricated with the intention of misleading readers. For example, a fake photo of a young John Kerry attending an anti-war rally with Jane Fonda surfaced during the 2004 presidential campaign season. Figure 17.1 shows the fake photo, along with the two photos that were combined to construct the fake.

The fake photo enraged many people because John Kerry, who was using his status as a Vietnam War veteran as part of his presidential campaign, is shown standing next to Jane Fonda, well known for her controversial visit to

North Vietnam during that war. Perhaps not surprisingly, this fake photo was cited as evidence that Kerry was unpatriotic.

A WRITER'S *Responsibility* | Using Image-Editing Software Ethically

If you are thinking of altering a photo, the first question you need to ask yourself has both ethical and legal implications: Do I have the right to change someone else's image without that person's permission? Unless you already own the image or have the owner's permission to use it and alter it, making changes may very well violate the creator's copyright. Because you will need the owner's permission to use the image, make sure you also get permission to change the image if you would like to do so. You may think that cropping out what you consider to be unnecessary parts of a photo might not be an issue, but the copyright owner might see the issue differently. Second, you need to be sure that by making changes you are not misrepresenting your subject or misleading your readers.

Desktop Publishing Software

Desktop publishing software such as *Quark* and *InDesign* allows writers to produce documents on their personal computers that are ready to be professionally printed. Although people who are comfortable with computers and have some training in layout and design can readily do some simple desktop publishing tasks, most people need training or practice in its use. Most desktop publishing programs are designed to construct short documents, and people often use them to prepare flyers, brochures, and newsletters. Such software gives you control over your document, including more precision in placing and manipulating images and more control over *leading* (the spacing between the lines) and *kerning* (the spacing between letters).

Presentation Software

At some point in their careers, almost all professionals make oral presentations. Sometimes professionals need to make a presentation to an audience of peers or higher-level employees. At other times they may need to do a sales presentation or present a report on a project in a more informal setting. Most professional presenters include some kind of visual component to help keep their audience's attention focused on the presentation. In the past, presenters often used large charts or posters, slides, or overhead transparencies. Now, most professionals use presentation software such as *PowerPoint.* Presentation software allows you to format slides for a presentation easily and professionally. If you do not have access to *PowerPoint,* you can use *Impress,* a compatible, open-source (free) program that is part of the *OpenOffice* desktop software suite. *Google Docs,*

Chapter 16 covers strategies for effective oral presentations another free Web-based presentation program, allows you to import *PowerPoint* files and easily share and collaborate on presentations online.

For more on oral presentations and presentation software, see Chapter 16.

When using presentation software, you need to remember that your slides should complement your presentation, not be its focus. When you give a presentation, you want your listeners to pay the most attention to what you say. If you use a graphic, the graphic should add to, not detract from, the content of the slide. Think of your bullet points as "talking points" or even as hyperlinks. What you actually say is the equivalent of clicking on a link in a Web page for more information.

Technologies for Constructing Web Pages

Web pages are computer files that can be viewed using software called a **browser.** Examples of browsers are *Internet Explorer, Safari,* and *Firefox*. Web pages are coded using hypertext markup language (html). The html coding places information in the document that allows the browser to display the page properly. There are many ways to construct a Web page:

- Use the "save as a Web page" option in your word-processing software. This option has the advantage of being easy and is appropriate for very simple, straightforward Web pages.
- "Hand code" the hypertext markup language (html) (this means writing the actual mark-up tags in a text editor like *Notepad* or *TextEdit*). This option gives you more control over the design of your site, but it is time-consuming.
- Use an html editor like *Dreamweaver.* Because html has become increasingly complex, most professionals now use html editors.
- Use a Web-based page construction tool like *Google Page Creator.* Web-based tools usually have both visual (word processor–like) and html editor modes. They have the added advantage of instantly providing you with an opportunity to view your page exactly as it will appear online before you publish it.

For more on writing Web pages, see the Online Appendix.

Although you need to be sensitive to the look and feel of your Web pages, ultimately what will matter most is their content. The most important question will be, "How effectively am I getting my message across to the audience that I am targeting?"

Communicating with Design and Visuals

The two documents on this page combine written and visual elements. The poster at the top of the page was created with specialized graphics software, commonly available in university or college computing labs. The flyer below uses one of several widely available word-processing software programs.

Whether you are designing an elaborate poster or a simpler one, use the same standard design principles that are the focus of this chapter.

When you apply the principles of design you need to consider your writing situation and make rhetorical choices. Here are some questions to consider:

- What are you trying to accomplish with your text, and how might design images help you achieve your goals?
- What kind(s) of design elements and images might appeal to your audience?
- How can the available technology affect the design and image choices you make?

for the Eradication of Poverty,
1997-2006
"Eradicationg poverty is an ethical, social, political and economical imperative of humankind."
Millennium development goal:
"...To halve, by the year 2015, the proportion of the world's people whose

Q. If I'm a high school student struggling in one of my classes, how can I get extra help?
A. FREE tutoring at ABCD Parker Hill/Fenway!
Subjects Available:
- Algebra - Trigonometry
- Calculus - Grammar
- Essays - Biology
- Physics - American History/Literature
Plus More!
Neighborhood Service Center
ABCD Parker Hill/Fenway
For more information contact:
Tejwattie Balgobin
Special Projects Coordinator
Think you need tutoring?
Do you want:
- To improve your grade in algebra?
- To get a better understanding about the peri
tables in chemistry?
- To get help writing an essay?
- To get assitance with tonight's homework?
If you answered yes to any of the above question
may qualify for our FREE tutoring program! Call
day for more information!

Principles of Document Design

Whatever their rhetorical choices might be, writers can use the design principles of proximity, contrast, alignment, and repetition to craft more effective texts.

Proximity

Whenever you vary the amount of space between and around text elements so that related items are close to one another and unrelated items are separated from one another, you are employing the principle of **proximity.** For instance, consider the following three versions of a shopping list:

Version A	Version B	Version C
wireless network router	wireless network router	wireless network router
watercolors	wireless mouse	wireless mouse
English dictionary	blank CDs	blank CDs
blank CDs	English dictionary	
pastels	thesaurus	English dictionary
thesaurus	book of quotations	thesaurus
wireless mouse	oil paints	book of quotations
oil paints	watercolors	
book of quotations	pastels	oil paints
		watercolors
		pastels

Which list would make it easier for you to find these nine items in the shortest amount of time? Most people would probably find the third list easiest to use because the information is organized into three categories. We might label those categories "Computer Equipment," "Reference Books," and "Art Supplies." The spaces between the three categories help separate one group from another.

For some documents, such as brochures and newsletters, writers can also use borders and color to group common items and separate them from dissimilar items. (Color type may not be appropriate for many academic papers.)

As illustrated by the flyer advertising tutoring services at the beginning of this chapter, borders can also make sections of your written text stand out.

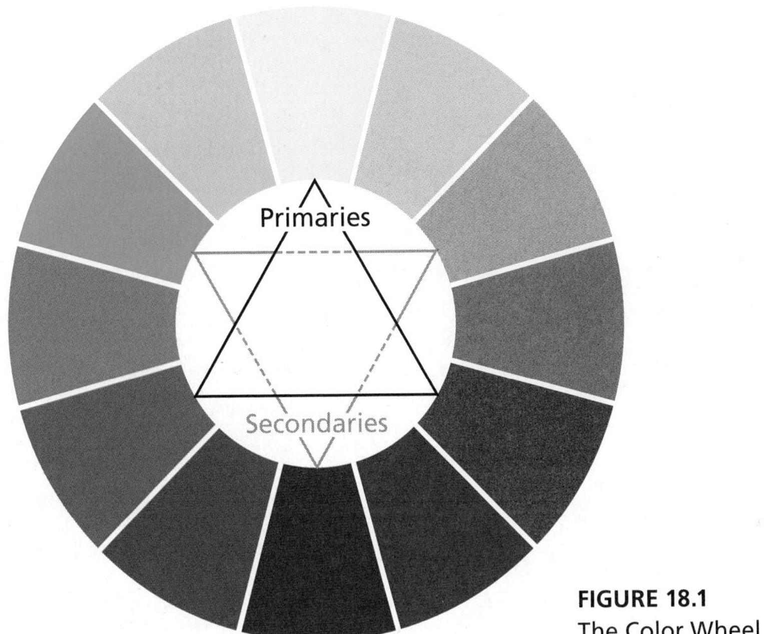

FIGURE 18.1
The Color Wheel

Contrast

Contrast is the design feature that sets some aspects of a page apart from others. You can use contrast by employing design features such as bold or italic type, underlining, indentation, and color to indicate the hierarchy of importance among text elements and to create certain effects. For instance, you can use contrast to make headings at different levels of importance visually distinct.

Color can also add visual interest and contrast to your texts. If you use more than one color in a document, however, consult the color wheel shown in Figure 18.1 to determine which colors work best together.

As the color wheel indicates, the **primary colors** are red, yellow, and blue. The **secondary colors,** located at points halfway between the three primary colors on the wheel, are formed by combining primary colors: Red and yellow combine to make orange; blue and yellow combine to make green; and red and blue combine to make violet. Other colors are formed by combining primary colors with secondary colors.

Complementary colors are directly across from each other on the wheel—for instance, yellow and violet, red and green, and blue and orange. Placing complementary colors next to each other has the effect of *jarring* the reader. Placing adjacent colors together, on the other hand, has a *pleasing* effect. Pairing colors separated by two or three positions on the color wheel can have a *vivid* or *bold* effect.

Colors are sometimes considered to be warm and cool. *Warm* colors—red, orange, and yellow—are energetic and bold. *Cool* colors—green, blue, and

FIGURE 18.2 A Poster Using Warm Colors

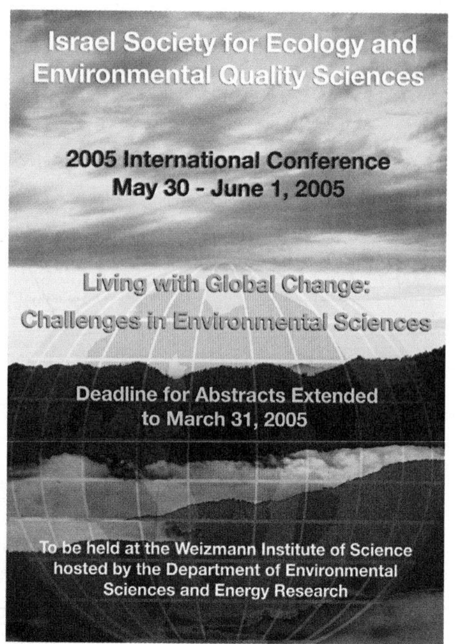

FIGURE 18.3 A Poster Using Cool Colors

violet—sometimes have a soothing, calming effect. Consider the poster shown in Figure 18.2 above. Two warm colors, yellow and red, appear together in this poster. Because red and yellow are also both primary colors, the red text on the yellow background is especially eye-catching.

Now consider the poster shown in Figure 18.3, announcing a conference on ecology and environment. The background for this poster includes green and blue, both cool colors that have a calming effect.

Alignment

Alignment is the design feature that provides a consistency in the placement of text and graphical elements on a page. Writers also use alignment to indicate relationships among text elements. As readers of English, we are accustomed to text that is aligned on the left side of the page. Other alignments are possible, however, and you can vary alignments to achieve different effects.

Unless your text is very brief, your best choice for most academic writing is usually to align your text at the left margin to make it easier for your readers to process. For other contexts—for example, a professional report—you might align your text at both margins, or *justify* it, for a professional look; most books and periodicals make extensive use of this type of alignment. If your text is short and you want to achieve an eye-catching effect on a poster or a brochure, you might consider using right or center alignment.

Repetition (or Consistency)

When you use **repetition** or **consistency,** you apply the same design features to text elements with similar rhetorical functions, doing so consistently throughout the text. Note how the consistent use of bullets in front of the items in our grocery list sets them off even more for readers.

Shopping List

Computer Store	Bookstore	Art Supply Store
• Wireless network router	• English dictionary	• Oil paints
• Wireless mouse	• Thesaurus	• Watercolors
• Blank CDs	• Book of quotations	• Pastels

There are many ways to follow the principle of repetition or consistency in a document: following a documentation style accurately, designing to make things easier to read, using typefaces and fonts consistently, using a carefully developed heading structure, and using bullets, numbers, letters, graphics, and white space consistently.

USING A SINGLE DOCUMENTATION FORMAT

Chapter 20 provides guidelines for citing sources and formatting academic papers. Following a single, consistent format throughout your paper makes it easier for readers to determine the type of source you are citing, find it in your works-cited or references list, and consult it themselves if they choose to do so.

DESIGNING TO MAKE DOCUMENTS EASIER TO READ

The principles of proximity, contrast, alignment, and repetition aren't the only means that document designers use to help make texts more readable. The appropriate typeface (serif for print, sans serif for electronic), and the use of headings, bullets, and white space all act to shape a document that makes things easier for readers. While good design principles help readers read more quickly, they also enable readers to more easily find pieces of information in long documents.

USING TYPEFACES AND TYPE SIZES CONSISTENTLY

A **typeface** is a design for the letters of the alphabet, numbers, and other symbols. A **type font** consists of all the available styles and sizes of a typeface. For most academic documents, you probably need to use only one or possibly two typefaces. Typefaces belong to one of two general categories: serif and sans serif. A **serif** typeface has small strokes or extenders at the top and the bottom of the letter, and letters may vary in thickness. **Sans serif** (without serif) type has no small strokes or extenders, and the letters have a uniform thickness. Usually, serif type is considered easier to read, especially in longer texts. For that reason, most newspapers, magazines, and books, including this one, use serif type for body text and sans serif type in headings and other kinds of displayed type, for contrast. Here are some examples of serif and sans serif type:

Serif Typefaces	Sample Sentence
Times New Roman	Carefully select the typeface that you use in your texts because the type can affect how easily readers can process your text.
Courier New	Carefully select the typeface that you use in your texts because the type can affect how easily readers can process your text.
Sans Serif Type	**Sample Sentence**
Arial	Carefully select the typeface that you use in your texts because the type can affect how easily readers can process your text.
Century Gothic	Carefully select the typeface that you use in your texts because the type can affect how easily readers can process your text.

All of the samples above are in 12-point type, which is a standard size for academic papers (1 point is equivalent to 1/72 of an inch). Notice that different typefaces take up different amounts of space. In some writing situations, space costs money; if so, you should consider a smaller face such as Times New Roman or Arial over a larger one such as Courier or Century Gothic. In other situations, such as a slide presentation, you may need a larger face.

Most computers offer a wide range of typefaces to choose from, including unusual and ornate varieties. You should use these typefaces sparingly, however, because they can be difficult to read, especially for longer texts.

USING HEADINGS CONSISTENTLY

Headings signal the content of your paper and help readers understand its organization. When headings are worded and styled consistently, readers know which sections are at a higher or lower level of generality than others. You can use different sizes of type; different typefaces; and underlining, bold, and italic to signal different levels of generality. Treat headings at the same level the same way—the same font size and style, the same location on the page, and the same capitalization.

You should also use parallel structure for all headings at a given level, as in the following example:

Parts of the City
  Shopping in the Business District
  Discovering the Residential Areas
  Enjoying the Waterfront
  Relaxing in the Parks

Digital Literacy **Integrating Visual and Graphical Elements**

Projects written for digital media should integrate visual and graphical elements in ways that make logical and rhetorical sense. Here are some suggestions:

- Choose appropriate color schemes.
- Use *labels* and *captions* that clarify visual information.
- Use elements that *explain* and *create context* for images, video, and sound that you use. Use media that *support* your main ideas and arguments, rather than simply accompanying them.
- Be prepared to prove ownership and/or rights to the media you have incorporated.

USING BULLETS, NUMBERS, ROMAN NUMERALS, AND LETTERS CONSISTENTLY

You can use bullets, numbers, Roman numerals, or letters—or some combination of these elements—for several purposes. Most frequently, they are used to indicate items in a list or an outline. Any of these markers can be effective for a short list of items, as shown on page 512.

If you are presenting steps in a process or items in a certain order, numbers are usually a more effective choice, and a combination of Roman numerals, letters, and numbers is standard in outlines. Bullets can be used to set off the items in a list effectively, although they can be problematic in longer lists because readers may have to count down the list of items if they need to discuss a particular point in the list. Of course, you should use bullets, numbers, Roman numerals, and/or letters consistently throughout a text.

For more on how to construct an outline, see Chapter 13.

Bullet	Numbers (with Bullets)	Roman Numerals (with Letters)	Letters (with Numbers)
Car Models	Car Models	Car Models	Car Models
• Ford	1. Ford	I. Ford	A. Ford
• Taurus	• Taurus	A. Taurus	1. Taurus
• Focus	• Focus	B. Focus	2. Focus
• Mustang	• Mustang	C. Mustang	3. Mustang
• Chevrolet	2. Chevrolet	II. Chevrolet	B. Chevrolet
• Impala	• Impala	A. Impala	1. Impala
• Malibu	• Malibu	B. Malibu	2. Malibu
• Corvette	• Corvette	C. Corvette	3. Corvette

USING WHITE SPACE CONSISTENTLY

White space is any part of a document that is not covered by type or graphics. The margins at the edges of a document are white space, as are the spaces between lines and above and below titles, headings, and other elements. Use white space consistently throughout a document. You should always leave the same amount of space above headings at the same level. (If you are using MLA or APA style, you will need to follow the guidelines provided by the style you are following for margins and spacing—see Chapter 20.)

USING GRAPHICS EFFECTIVELY

Graphics can appear in academic papers as well as a number of other types of documents that you might prepare. The different kinds of graphics are discussed on pages 514–527. Generally, you should use the same kind of graphic to illustrate similar points or concepts. To achieve consistency, you need to consider the following:

- What you want to accomplish with each graphic
- What the overall look of each image is
- How the graphics are marked in the text with labels and captions
- How you should introduce the graphics within your text

Select the kind of graphic that best accomplishes your purpose. To most effectively indicate the composition of a pizza, for example, you might choose a pie chart like that shown in Figure 18.4, which shows the ingredients used to make a sausage and mushroom pizza weighing 1.6 kg. The sum of the numbers shown equals 1.6 kg, the weight of the pizza. The size of each slice shows us the fraction of the pizza made up from that ingredient. Figure 18.5 shows the same

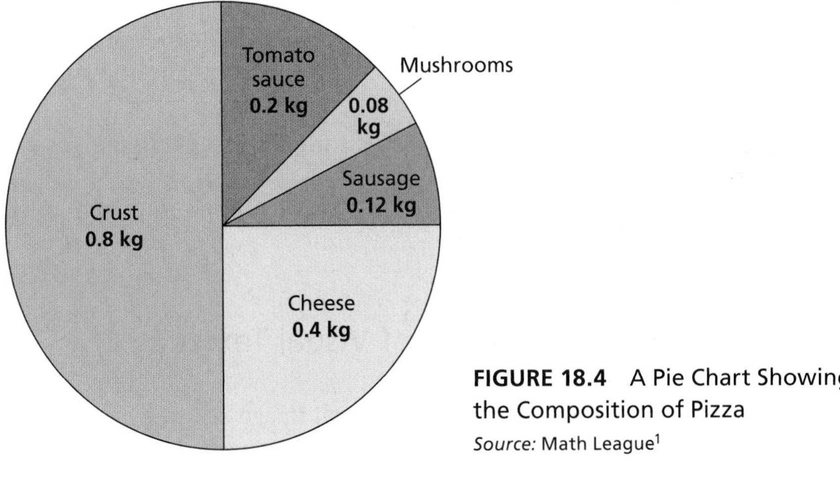

FIGURE 18.4 A Pie Chart Showing the Composition of Pizza
Source: Math League[1]

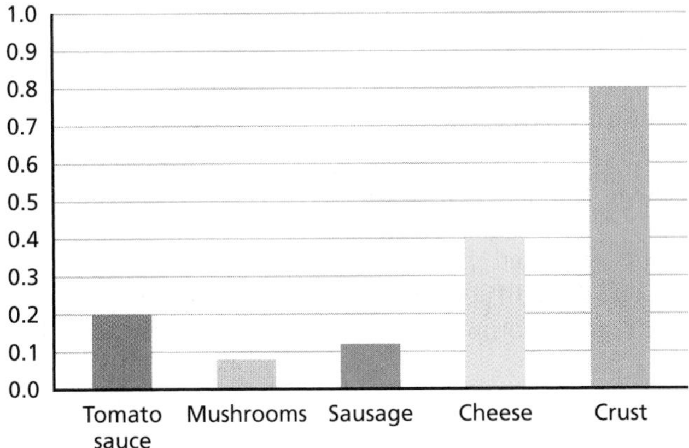

FIGURE 18.5 A Bar Graph Presenting the Same Data as the Pie Chart

data but given as a bar graph—as you can tell, the bar graph does not explain or present the information as effectively as the pie chart does.

To present graphics effectively, follow these guidelines:

- **Give the graphics in your document a consistent look.** For example, use one-color or multicolor drawings rather than mixing one-color and multicolor drawings. If you use multiple colors, use the same ones in each graphic (for more on the use of color, see pages 507–508).
- **Introduce and explain each graphic.** If you do not do so, then it is possible that your readers will not understand why the image is there or what it is intended to convey. For the bar graph in Figure 18.5, for example,

[1] Complete source information for the figures in this section can be found in the Credits on pages 000–00.

you should introduce it before putting it into your text ("This next graph shows how mushrooms make up the least amount, in weight, of the ingredients in a typical pizza") and follow the image with an explanation of how the bar graph connects to your topic.

- **Place graphics in a document strategically.** Place each visual as close as possible to the text discussion that refers to it. If you are following APA style, however, you have the option of placing visuals at the end of your paper.

Common Kinds of Visual Texts

When you consider adding a visual image or images to a document, you should do so to help accomplish your overall purpose. Do not add a visual just to have a picture or chart or table in your text; rather, use it as a way to support your thesis and achieve your goal for that piece of writing. Visuals such as tables, bar and line graphs, drawings, diagrams, maps, and cartoons can be effective tools.

Tables

Tables organize information in columns and rows for readers, helping them make comparisons between or among pieces of information or sets of numerical data. Consider, for instance, Table 18.1, which compares how information has been stored using different media. By looking at the table, we can see that information is being stored more in all media but film. The same data given in a paragraph would be difficult to compare. By reviewing the table, however, readers can easily make comparisons up and down rows, across columns, and

Table 18.1 Worldwide Production of Original Information, If Stored Digitally, in Terabytes, circa 2002

Storage Medium	2002 Upper Estimate	2002 Lower Estimate	1999–2000 Upper Estimate	1999–2000 Lower Estimate	% Change Upper Estimates
Paper	1,634	327	1,200	240	36%
Film	420,254	76,69	431,690	58,209	–3%
Magnetic	5,187,130	3,416,230	2,779,760	2,073,760	87%
Optical	103	51	81	29	28%
Total	**5,609,121**	**3,416,281**	**3,212,731**	**2,132,238**	**74.5%**

Notes: Upper estimates assume information is digitally scanned; lower estimates assume digital content has been compressed.
Source: How Much Information 2003. http://www2.sims.berkeley.edu/research/projects/how-much-info-2003/execsum.htm#stored. Accessed February 12, 2009.

across rows and columns. Notice that between 1999–2000 and 2002, the upper estimates of information stored on paper increased at a greater percentage than information stored on optical media.

USING TABLES EFFECTIVELY IN YOUR TEXTS

Word-processing programs will usually allow you to format information into tables automatically—consult the Help screen for the program you are using. Spreadsheet programs also allow you to construct tables.

To decide if a table will be appropriate for your purpose and audience, answer the following questions:

- Do I have data or information that could appear in tabular form?
- How would a table help me organize this data or information for readers?
- How do I want or need to organize the data or information in the table so that readers can find the information they need or I want them to see?

Bar and Line Graphs

Bar and line graphs provide another way to present numerical information to your readers. Both types of graphs plot data along a horizontal line (the *x*-axis) and a vertical line (the *y*-axis). Like a table, a **bar graph** allows readers to make comparisons. For example, the graph in Figure 18.6 allows readers to compare actual or projected energy use in three different parts of the world over a period of fifty years.

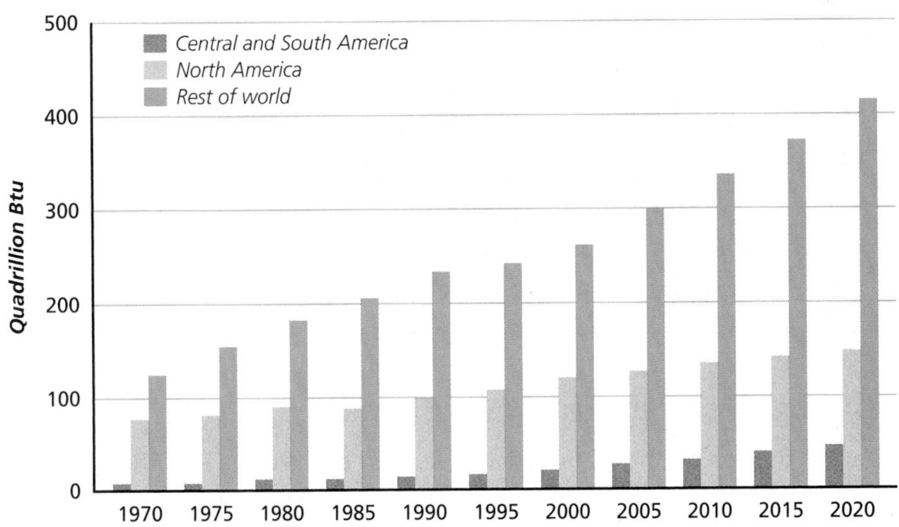

FIGURE 18.6 Bar Graph Showing Energy Consumption in the World from 1970 to 2020 *Source:* U.S. Government Energy Information Administration

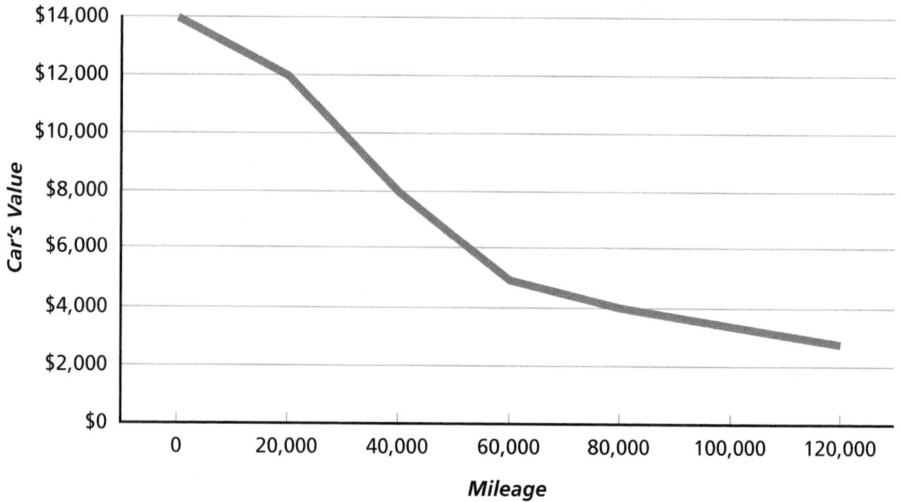

FIGURE 18.7 A Line Graph Illustrating the Relationship between Mileage and Value *Source:* Math League

A **line graph** shows readers a change or changes over a period of time. Figure 18.7 is a line graph illustrating the relationship between a car's mileage and its value.

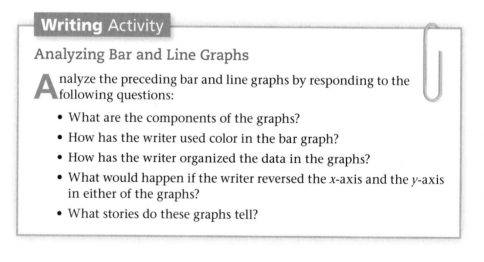

Writing Activity

Analyzing Bar and Line Graphs

Analyze the preceding bar and line graphs by responding to the following questions:

- What are the components of the graphs?
- How has the writer used color in the bar graph?
- How has the writer organized the data in the graphs?
- What would happen if the writer reversed the *x*-axis and the *y*-axis in either of the graphs?
- What stories do these graphs tell?

USING GRAPHS EFFECTIVELY IN YOUR TEXTS

You can use bar or line graphs that have been constructed by others in your paper as long as you give proper credit to the source. You can also use a spreadsheet program or *PowerPoint* to construct graphs from data you have discovered or generated on your own, or you can use an online graphing site, such as "Create a Graph" (http://nces.ed.gov/nceskids/Graphing/), hosted by the

National Center for Educational Statistics. If you do not have access to a computer, however, you can construct the graph yourself, using graph paper. If you use data from a source to construct your graph, you need to give credit to that source.

See Chapter 20 for help with citing sources for your data.

To use bar and line graphs effectively in your texts, consider the following questions:

- Do I have sets of numerical data that I would like readers to compare?
- Do I have data that indicate a change over a period of time?
- What could a bar or line graph add to my text?
- If I am using a bar graph, how should I organize it?
- How should I explain the graph in my text?
- Do I have access to the technology (a color printer, for example) that will enable me to construct the graph and/or present it effectively?

Charts

A **chart** is a visual text that allows you to show the relationships among different items or among the parts of a whole. Consider Figure 18.8, which shows what various stain colors look like on oak. Notice how the chart holds one variable constant—the kind of wood—so that readers can make consistent comparisons among stain colors.

Two kinds of charts that are very common in academic writing, as well as in writing for other areas, are pie charts and flowcharts. A **pie chart** shows

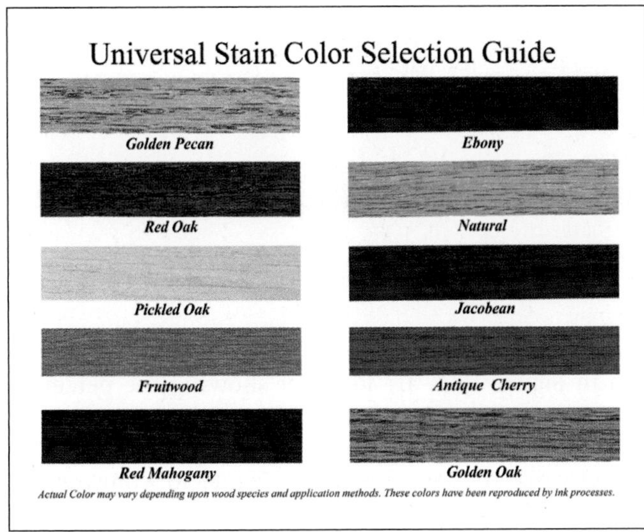

FIGURE 18.8 Chart Showing Wood Stains

FIGURE 18.9
Flowchart That Is Also a Decision Tree
Source: Gary Ensmenger

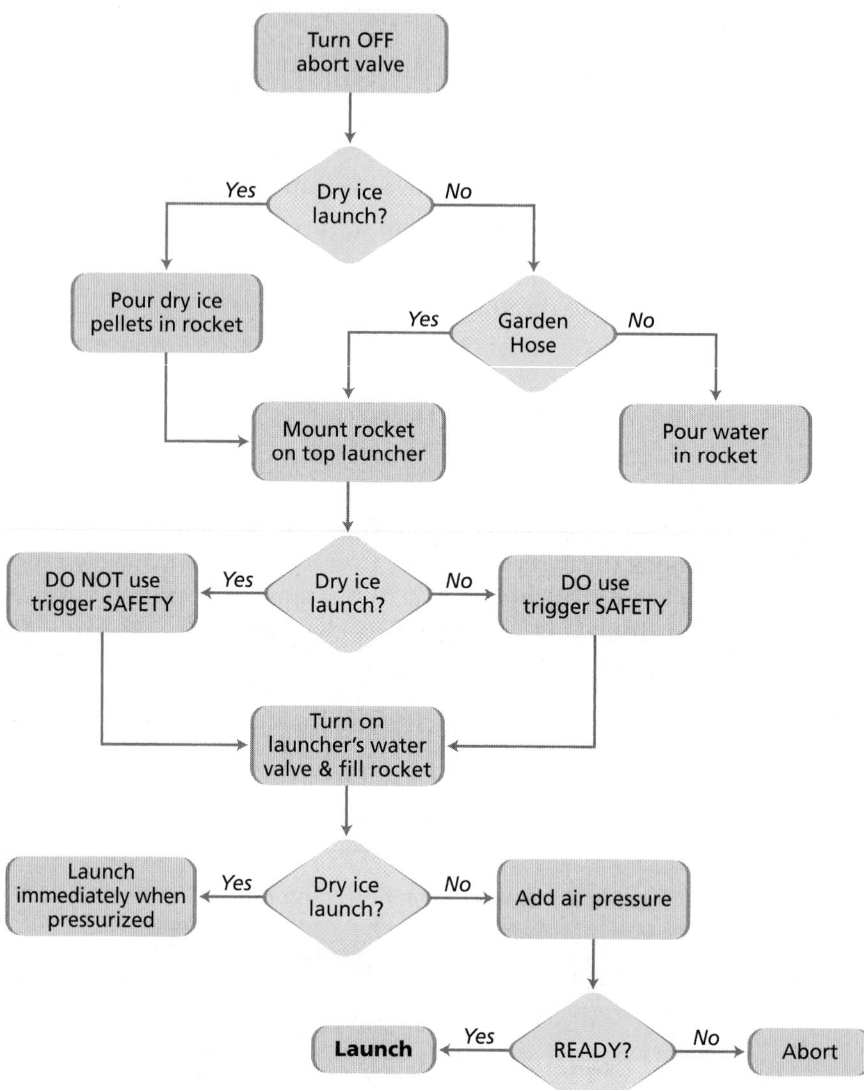

readers the components that make up the whole of something. Pie charts, like the one shown in Figure 18.4, are ideal for showing the percentages of each part of an item.

A **flowchart** shows how a process works. Many readers find it easier to understand processes when they see flowcharts. Figure 18.9 illustrates the complex process of launching a water rocket. Notice that the chart is also a kind of *decision tree,* with yes or no responses that direct readers' progress through the chart.

USING CHARTS EFFECTIVELY IN YOUR TEXTS

As with graphs, you can use charts that have been produced by others in your paper as long as you give proper credit to the source. You can construct your own charts the old-fashioned way—drawing them by hand—or you can use a drawing program. Spreadsheet programs and *PowerPoint* also enable you to produce charts and import them into your paper.

To use charts effectively in your texts, consider the following questions:

- Is there a process, a key relationship, or the components of something within my text that I could illustrate with a chart?
- How will the chart help my audience better understand a particular point in my paper?
- How can I organize the chart so that readers can see patterns in the information?
- Do I have access to the technology (a color printer, for example) that will enable me to construct the chart and/or present it effectively?

Photographs

Photographs are common in our lives. We see them daily in magazines and newspapers, as well as on Web sites, billboards, and posters. Because photographs are filled with details, a single photograph can replace hundreds or even thousands of words. Imagine how difficult it would be to describe your best friend's physical appearance to a stranger using words alone. On the other hand, a photograph could not give your reader a detailed view of your friend's personality.

Consider two well-known photographs of Abraham Lincoln. The first (Figure 18.10) portrays Lincoln with his son Tad. The second (Figure 18.11) portrays Lincoln with Allan Pinkerton, who headed the Union spying operations, and Major General John A. McClernand. A writer could use either photograph to illustrate what Lincoln's life was like during the Civil War years, which corresponded with his years in the White House. The photograph that shows Lincoln with his son gives readers a sense of his personal life. It does not tell the whole story, however, including his love for Tad and his other two children—Willie and Robert—and his heartbreak when his favorite child, Willie, died from typhoid fever

FIGURE 18.10 Abraham Lincoln with His Son Tad

FIGURE 18.11 Lincoln with Allan Pinkerton (left) and Major General John A. McClernand

in 1862, at age eleven. These are details that a writer would include in the text. Similarly, the photograph of Lincoln with Pinkerton and McClernand does not give a complete picture of his working relationship with them; for that, words are needed.

Writing Activity

Considering Photos

With your classmates, prepare a list of six well-known places, people, or objects. Bring one photograph of each place, person, or object to class. Compare and contrast your photos with those that other students have brought by responding to the following questions:

- What does each photograph reveal about its subject? What does each photograph leave out?
- What does each photograph reveal about the person who took it?
- How could you use each photograph in a piece of writing?
- What purposes could each photograph have in a given type of writing?

USING PHOTOGRAPHS EFFECTIVELY IN YOUR WRITING PROJECTS

With the advent of inexpensive digital photography, it is easy to store, retrieve, manipulate, and send photographs. Although it is easy to integrate digital photographs into your documents, note that low-resolution photos are grainy when printed on paper. *Resolution* refers to the number of pixels (or dots) in the image. High-resolution photos have more pixels per inch than low-resolution photos. The following table gives the recommended resolutions (300 dots per inch) for several photograph sizes:

Size of Photo	Recommended Resolution for Printed Photograph
2″ × 2″	600 × 600 pixels
2″ × 3″	600 × 900 pixels
4″ × 6″	1200 × 1800 pixels
5″ × 7″	1500 × 2100 pixels

In your written texts, you may use photographs that have been produced by others if you give proper credit to the source of the photograph. If you are publishing the photograph on a Web site or in some other print or electronic medium, you will need to obtain permission to use it from the copyright holder unless it is in the public domain. If a photograph is in the **public domain**, no one owns the copyright for the image, and you may use it without obtaining permission.

To decide when and how to use photographs in your writing, consider the following questions:

- What kind of photograph will most effectively support my purpose?
- What impact will a photograph have on my text?
- How will my audience respond to each of the photographs that I am considering?
- Where might I place the photograph in my text? Why?
- Do I need permission to use a particular photograph?
- How might I ethically manipulate the photograph to use in my text? For example, can I crop, or cut out, part of the photograph that includes extraneous material?
- If the photograph is an electronic document, is the resolution high enough for use in a print document?
- Will the technology that is available to me accurately reproduce the photograph?

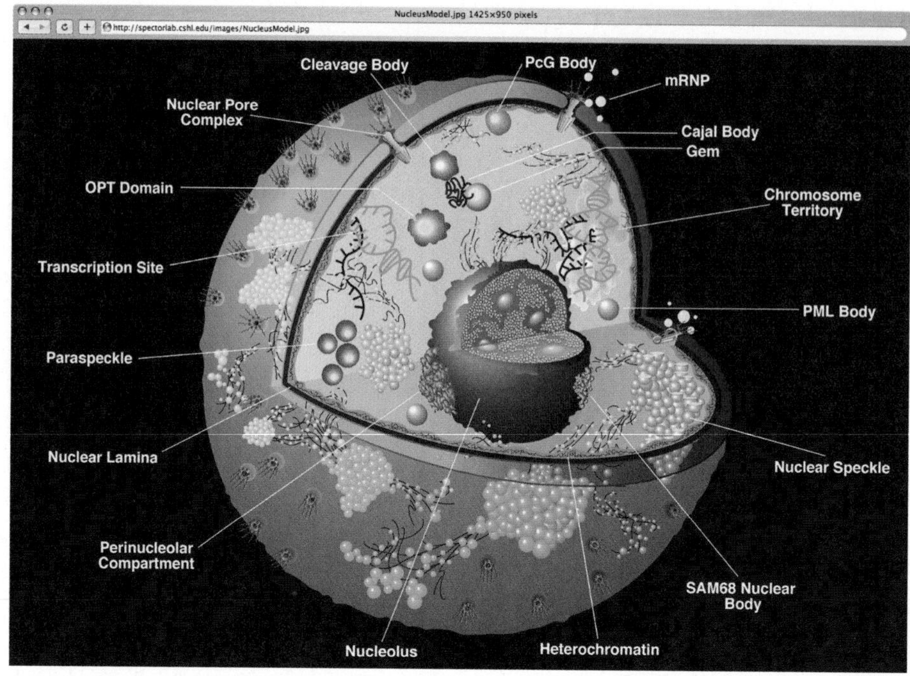

FIGURE 18.12
Drawing of a Cell Nucleus
Source: Spector Lab

Drawings

Like photographs, **drawings** enable readers to visualize a subject. Drawings are common in technical and scientific writing because writers in those fields frequently need to give readers detailed descriptions of objects, many of which are so small or so far away that it is difficult to see and photograph them. Consider the drawing of a cell nucleus in Figure 18.12. Notice how this drawing includes **labels**—words that name its parts. What is missing from this drawing, however, is an explanation of the functions of the nucleus and its many parts. Only words can provide that information. In other words, the visual and verbal elements in a text need information, and only writers can provide those words to complement and supplement each other.

Writing Activity

Considering Drawings

Find an example of a drawing in one of your textbooks, in a newspaper or magazine, or on a Web site. Discuss how successfully the text and drawing you have found work together to achieve the writer's purpose.

USING DRAWINGS EFFECTIVELY IN YOUR TEXTS

You can produce a drawing by hand. If you have access to a scanner, you can then scan your finished drawing, generating a computer file. Or, you can use a drawing program that allows you to generate a digital file directly on your computer. If you pick up a drawing from a source for use in your paper, you will need to give proper credit to that source. If you are publishing the drawing, you will need to obtain permission to use it.

To use drawings effectively in your texts, consider the following questions:

- What in my text could I illustrate with a drawing?
- How could a drawing meet the needs of my audience?
- Can I use an existing drawing, or do I need to construct one?
- Do I need permission to use an existing drawing?
- Do I have access to software that I can use to construct the drawing?

Diagrams

Diagrams are drawings that illustrate and explain the arrangement of and relationships among parts of a system. Venn diagrams, for example, consist of circles representing relationships among sets. Consider the Venn diagram in Figure 18.13, which illustrates how sustainable development depends on relationships among the environment, the economy, and equity. Of course, this diagram by itself does not explain the exact nature of these relationships. To do that, a writer needs to define each of the terms in the diagram—*environment, economy, equity*—and then explain how they interact to form sustainable development.

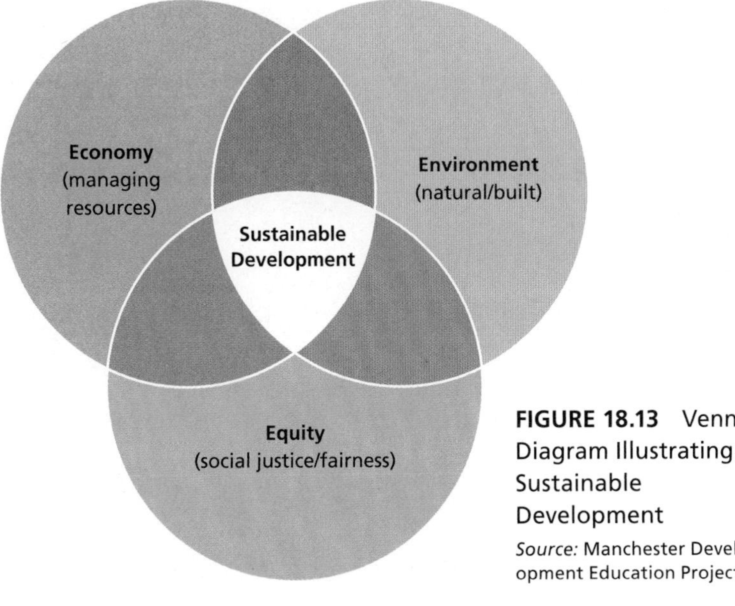

FIGURE 18.13 Venn Diagram Illustrating Sustainable Development

Source: Manchester Development Education Project

USING DIAGRAMS EFFECTIVELY IN YOUR WRITING

As with drawings, you can either construct a diagram by hand and scan it or use a drawing program. If you use a diagram from a source, you will need to give proper credit to that source. If you are publishing the diagram, you will need to obtain permission to use it.

To use diagrams effectively in your writing, consider the following questions:

- What in my text could I illustrate with a diagram?
- What effect will the diagram have on my readers?
- Can I use an existing diagram, or do I need to construct one?
- Do I need permission to use an existing diagram?
- Do I have access to software that I can use to construct the diagram?

Maps

Cartographers use **maps** to record and show where countries, cities, streets, buildings, colleges, lakes, rivers, and mountains are located in the world or in a particular part of it. Of course, consumers of maps use them to find these places. We use printed or downloaded maps to drive from one location to another. On the evening news, we see maps showing where events take place and what kind of weather is occurring in neighboring states and countries. We even use maps to help us visualize fictional places such as the territories described in the *Lord of the Rings* trilogy (Figure 18.14).

FIGURE 18.14 Map from the *Lord of the Rings* Trilogy

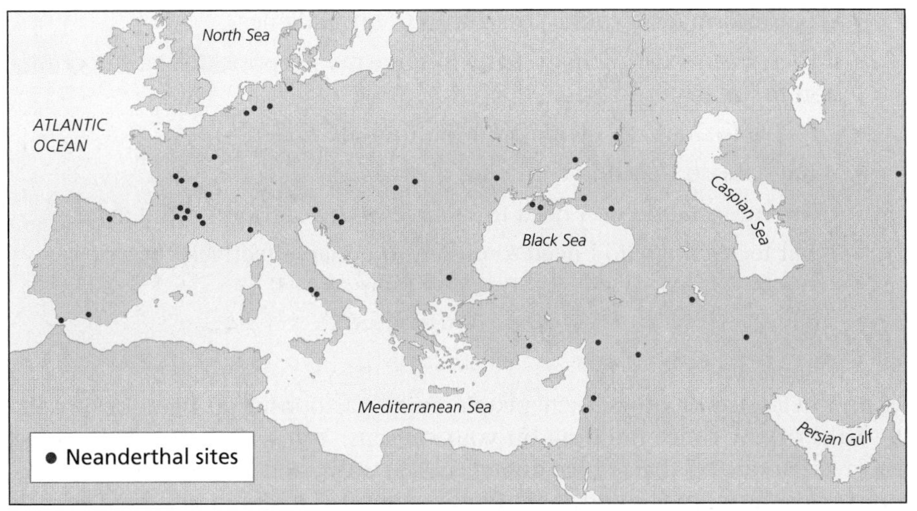

FIGURE 18.15 Neanderthal Range Map *Source:* National Geographic Society

Many different academic disciplines use maps. Anthropologists use maps to illustrate where species have lived, as in Figure 18.15, which shows the range of the Neanderthals—an extinct species of humans—in Europe.

Writing Activity

Analyzing Maps

Choose one of the two maps in Figures 18.14 and 18.15 and respond to the following questions:

- What is the purpose of this map?
- What additional information would make the map more useful?
- What would a writer need to explain to readers so that readers could use the map effectively?
- How does the map adhere to the principles of proximity and contrast (see pages 506–507)?
- How might the captions for the maps be revised to be more informative?

USING MAPS EFFECTIVELY IN YOUR TEXTS

In most cases, you will need to use maps from other sources, giving credit and obtaining permission to use them if necessary. To use maps effectively in your texts, consider the following questions:

- What information could a map offer to my audience?
- If there is an existing map that will serve my purpose, do I need permission to use it?
- If I have to draw my own map, what tools do I need?
- What data do I need to construct the map?
- What information do I need to include in the caption for the map?
- What technology do I need to present the map effectively?

Cartoons

To find evidence of how much people enjoy cartoons, you need only walk the halls of any office building on your campus. You will notice that people display cartoons on their office doors, cubicle walls, and bulletin boards. **Cartoons** make humorous—and sometimes poignant—observations about people and events. Consider the cartoon in Figure 18.16. One feature of most cartoons is that their visual and verbal elements complement each other. The visual part of the cartoon gives the topic a human or humanlike face, and the verbal part offers a specific comment.

USING CARTOONS EFFECTIVELY IN YOUR TEXTS

In most cases, when you use cartoons in your text, they probably will have been produced by other people. Make sure that you are able to give the source information for any cartoon that you include. If you are publishing your paper on the Web or in another medium, you will need to obtain permission to use

GLASBERGEN
"My presentation lacks power and it has no point.
I assumed the software would take care of that!"

FIGURE 18.16 Cartoon Reprinted by permission of Randy Glasbergen

the cartoon from the copyright holder. If you draw your own cartoon, you will need to do so by hand and then scan it to produce a computer file that you can incorporate into your text.

To use cartoons effectively in your texts, consider the following questions:

- How will a cartoon support my purpose?
- Given that readers usually associate cartoons with humor and/or satire, how might humor or satire affect my readers?
- Do I need permission to use a published cartoon, or is it in the public domain?

Designing New Media

Most of the principles of good design for print texts still hold for new media with minor exceptions. For example, serif fonts appear to be more readable in print while sans serif fonts are more readable online. Whether you are crafting Web pages, *PowerPoint* presentations (meant to be presented as static presentations or as videos), or any other forms of new digital media, you should keep basic principles of effective design in mind.

There is a school of thought championed by Web usability expert Jakob Neilsen, recommending that Web pages should err on the side of simplicity and avoid "bells and whistles." There are valid arguments for this. However, remember that design is a rhetorical decision. How you design anything, whether it is a static Web page or a video, should be driven by your understanding of how to get your message across to your intended audience most effectively. Strike a balance between being engaging and eye-catching while not being overpowering.

The best way to achieve this visual balance is to think rhetorically. Is your target audience likely to respond most positively to a background of bright or muted colors? Will they most likely prefer to read long passages of text, or might they respond better to salient points in a bulleted list accompanied by a carefully scripted audio track?

Using Visuals Rhetorically

As you consider using visuals, think about using them rhetorically to achieve some specific purpose with a specific audience.

Considering Your Audience

Readers are more likely to expect visuals in some genres than in others. Lab reports, for example, commonly include tables and graphs. This principle applies to any visuals that you plan to use in your writing. As you consider using a particular visual, ask yourself the following questions:

- Does my audience need this visual, or is it showing something that my readers already know very well? What information might a visual add?
- How will this audience respond to this visual?
- What other visual might they respond to more favorably?
- Will this audience understand the subtleties of this visual?
- How do I need to explain this visual for this particular audience?

Considering Your Purpose

As we saw in Parts 2 and 3 of this book, you will have a general purpose for any writing project—to record and share experiences, to explore, to inform, to analyze, to convince or persuade, to evaluate, to explain causes and effects, to solve problems, or to analyze creative works. To the extent possible, every part of your paper should contribute to that purpose. Any phrase, clause, sentence, paragraph, or section of your paper that does not support your purpose needs to be revised or deleted. The same principle applies to any visual that you are considering. Diagrams, for example, most often have an informative purpose. A cartoon, in contrast, is almost always humorous but often makes a statement. Photographs are often used to make the rhetorical appeal of *pathos,* as they can evoke an emotional response in the reader. Figure 18.17, for example, is a photograph from the Web page for Feed the Children, a charitable organization.

FIGURE 18.17 A Photograph from the Web Page for Feed the Children, a Charitable Organization

Before using any visual, ask yourself these questions:

- How will this visual support my purpose?
- How might this visual detract from my purpose?
- Why is this visual necessary?
- What other visual or visuals might support my purpose more effectively?

Using Visuals Responsibly

Just as you need to consider the purpose of using any visual, you also need to consider how using visuals responsibly will enhance your credibility as a writer.

Permissions

Whenever you plan to use a visual, you need to make certain that you have permission to use that visual. If you have constructed a table, graph, or chart from data that you have gathered, then permission is not needed. If you use a visual prepared by someone else, or use data from a source to produce a visual, you should always give credit to your source, even if the visual or data are from a government source and/or are in the public domain (that is, outside of copyright and available to anyone who wants to use it). For most academic papers, it is usually not necessary to request permission to use a visual. If your writing will be made available to an audience beyond your classroom, however, you will need to ask for permission to use any visual from a source that you include. Some visuals that you find on the Web are in the public domain, but if you are in doubt about a particular visual, contact the Web manager of the site where you found it to ask what permissions are required.

The subjects of photographs have certain rights as well. If you take a photograph of a friend, you need to ask your friend for permission to use it if your project will have an audience beyond the two of you. If your friend does not want the photo used in a course paper or on a Web site, you are ethically and legally obligated to honor those wishes. To be certain that there is no misunderstanding, ask your friend to sign an agreement granting you permission to use the photo for clearly specified purposes. If you later want to use the photo for other purposes, ask your friend to sign another agreement. But you should never put undue pressure on someone to sign such an agreement.

Distortions

Just as you should not distort quoted or paraphrased material (see Chapter 20), you should also be careful not to distort the content and the physical properties of any visuals you include in your paper. In Chapter 17, for instance, we

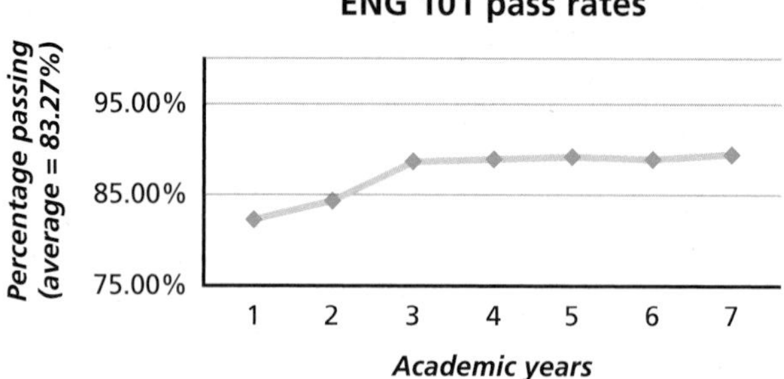

FIGURE 18.18 Chart That Distorts Information

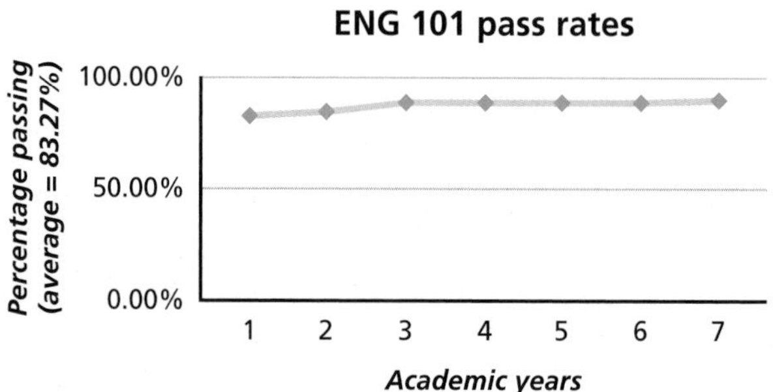

FIGURE 18.19 Chart That Presents the Same Information Honestly

show a fabricated photo of Jane Fonda and John Kerry on stage together (page 502). Sometimes the data in charts and graphs is misrepresented—consider, for example, Figure 18.18, which shows the pass rates for students in English 101. Clearly, the pass rate improved by year 3 and has remained fairly stable since then. *If* this chart maker wants to show a dramatic improvement in the pass rate, then it makes sense to use a scale that runs from 75% to 95%. On the other hand, a full scale (from 0 to 100%) makes the improvement in pass rates much less obvious and dramatic, as shown in Figure 18.19.

There may be times, however, when some forms of distortion can be helpful and ethical. For instance, consider the two maps shown in Figure 18.20. The first one shows the forty-eight contiguous states as they typically appear on a map. Such maps show the relative sizes—measured in square miles—of the states. The second map is designed to show the distribution of wire-service news stories about certain cities and states. Notice that New York and Washington, DC, get lots of attention in wire-service news stories. This deliberately distorted image helps to make a serious point about the news.

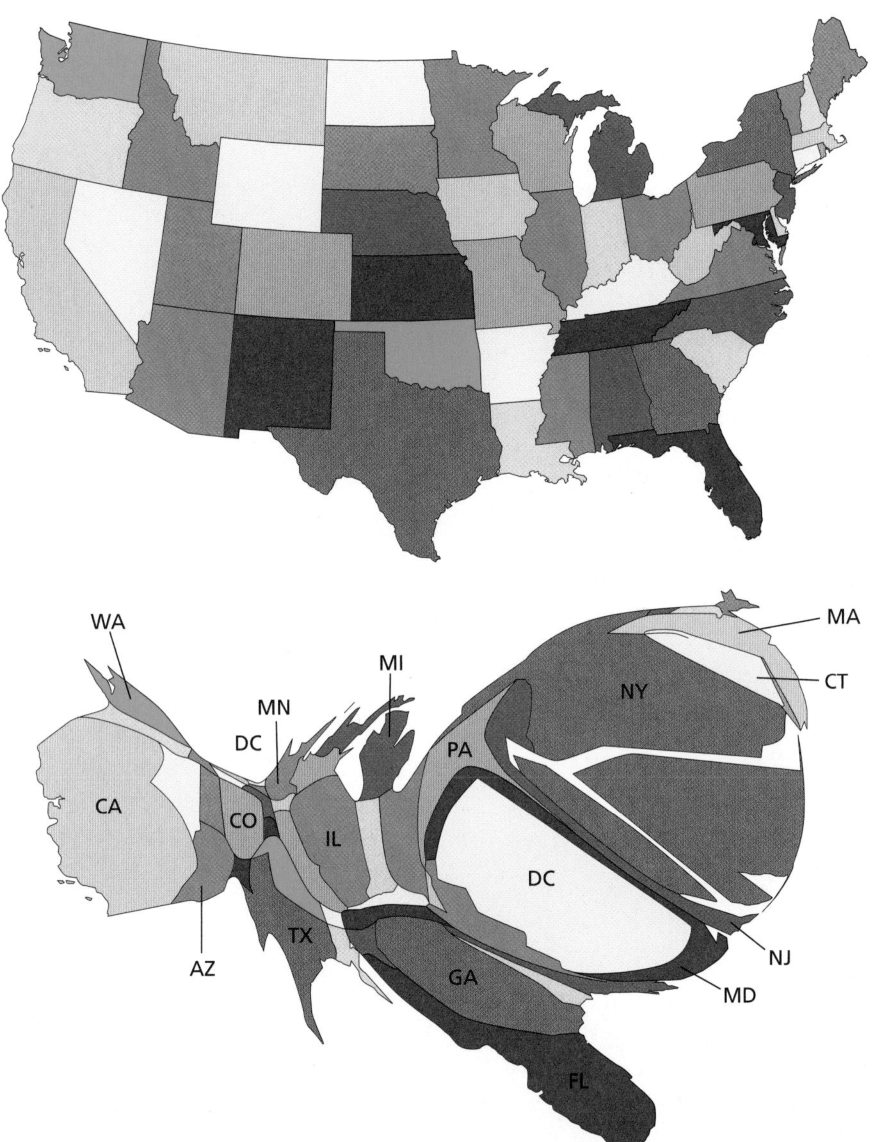

FIGURE 18.20 Regular Map of the United States and Distorted Map That Illustrates a Point about News *Source:* Maps by M. E. J. Newman and M. T. Gastner

Chapter 19

Finding and Evaluating Information

In the past, **research** meant searching through actual library stacks. Because of the almost instant access to a wealth of sources that technology makes possible, finding information today may appear to be much easier than it was in the past, but the reality is that it is simply different. Although you can still find books and print journals on library shelves, and they are still useful resources, today researchers often start a project with a search of the library's online catalog or database or a search of the World Wide Web.

Before the advent of electronic sources, researchers usually assumed that they could generally rely on the accuracy of the printed texts found in college or university libraries. Although those sources still exist, anyone can now publish anything on the Web or more easily self-publish content as a book. So much information is available on the Internet that it is vital to focus your search as carefully as possible so that you turn up only the most relevant sources. It is also more critical than ever for you to evaluate the quality of what you do find.

Also, researchers still go out into the field to conduct other kinds of research. In this kind of hands-on investigation, you gather information through observation and experimentation as well as, when working with humans, interviews and surveys.

Conducting Effective Library and Web-Based Research: An Example

For more on field research, see pages 553–554.

You already have plenty of experience in conducting research. Have you ever used a classmate's opinion of an author or a band to influence a friend to read that author's book or to see that band? If so, you were using the results of a type of field research called **interviewing** as evidence.

The research that you do for any writing task is a rhetorical act. That is, you conduct research for a specific purpose, with a particular audience in mind, in a specific writing situation. Consider how you might approach the following assignment for a psychology class:

> Respond to this question: Why do adolescent males (and sometimes females) change their behavior when they join a gang? Based on your research, write a 3- to 4-page paper that provides compelling reasons for this behavior, providing specific evidence to support your position.

This assignment is fairly straightforward: Your purpose is to fulfill this assignment, and your audience is your psychology professor. The assignment even provides you with a **research question.** Your answer to this question will form the thesis of your research paper. But where will you find the evidence that will help you decide on your answer to this question—your thesis—and support that thesis? How will you locate it? How will you be able to tell if the evidence is credible and reliable?

Often it will be your responsibility to formulate research question. When you find yourself in that situation, keep these principles in mind:

- Keep the question focused. For example, "What caused the Civil War?" is a huge question. However, "Why did Confederate forces fire on Fort Sumter on April 12, 1861?" is much more manageable.
- Make sure you will be able to get good information on your question. You may be interested in the role Venezuelan oil plays in the U.S. economy, especially from the Venezuelan perspective. However, if you discover that most of the information for this topic is in Spanish and you can't read that language, you will probably not be able to go forward with this question.
- Consider whether you can find an adequate number of resources to answer your question. For example, are the people you hope to interview available and willing to speak with you? Can you really arrange to do field research at some far-off location?

Library Research

Often the first place to look when conducting research to answer a question is the reference section of your college library. There you will find sources such as general and specialized encyclopedias and dictionaries. For example, you might start your research for the psychology paper about gangs and adolescents by defining "adolescent," perhaps by looking it up in a medical dictionary:

> A young person who has undergone puberty but who has not reached full maturity; a teenager.
>
> —American Heritage Medical Dictionary®

Based on this definition, you determine that your research will focus on males and females between the ages of thirteen and nineteen. You decide to conduct a search in your online college library catalog. (Librarians are also available online in many libraries. Almost every library has a reference librarian, and he or she is a truly useful resource. It is always helpful to discuss your research question with the reference librarian. He or she will probably be able to point you to some reference sources that might be useful.

All college libraries have a book **catalog** of some kind. In addition to the book catalog, your library probably subscribes to various electronic **databases** such as *Academic Search Premier.* Databases are indexes of articles that are available in periodicals; many also provide complete texts of the articles themselves. To look for articles in popular or trade magazines, for instance, you would search one database, while you would use another database to find articles in academic journals, and still another database for articles in newspapers.

Digital Literacy

Using Academic Databases

The following are popular academic databases that can help you with research in different disciplines. Keep in mind that the names of academic databases do change; your reference librarian can help you find a database that will be useful for your particular project.

- *Academic Search Premier*
- *ERIC*
- *General Science Index*
- *Google Scholar*
- *Humanities Index*
- *JSTOR*
- *LexisNexis Academic*
- *ProQuest*
- *Social Science Index*

SEARCHING A LIBRARY CATALOG

For any electronic search, you need to come up with an appropriate word or phrase, or **keyword,** that will be found in the kind of source you are seeking. To find useful keywords for a search of your library's catalog, it is often a good idea to start by consulting the *Library of Congress Subject Headings (LCSH),* a book that lists subject headings in use in most library systems. It will tell you how subject areas are categorized in the library and will therefore help you come up with search terms that will turn up books on your subject.

Note that the search term "gang behavior" is just one of a range of possibilities. It is often useful to use a number of search terms. You can also pull up more information on each entry and examine other relevant references there that might be useful to your research.

Here is a research hint: Whenever you find a book on your research subject in your college library, spend a few minutes examining the *other* texts that surround the one you just located. Books about the same topic are shelved together, so once you find one book on the topic you are researching, many others will be nearby.

SEARCHING AN ONLINE DATABASE

Now that you have several books that you might want to examine for information on gang behavior, you should also search one or more of the databases your college's library subscribes to. A search of a typical database—in this case, *Academic Search Premier*—using the keywords "male" and "gang" might turn up abstracts (summaries) of articles like this one:

> *GANG* WORLD. By: Papachristos, Andrew V.. Foreign Policy, Mar/Apr2005 Issue 147, p48–55, 8p, 3c, 1bw; Abstract: The article discusses the rise of street ***gangs*** around the world. The image of a young, minority, "inner-city," ***male gang*** member is transmitted, exploited, and glamorized across the world. The increasing mobility of information via cyberspace, films, and music makes it easy for ***gangs, gang*** members, and others to get information, adapt personalities, and distort ***gang*** behaviors. Two images of street ***gangs*** dominate the popular consciousness—***gangs*** as posses of drug-dealing thugs and, more recently, ***gangs*** as terrorist organizations. Although the media like to link ***gangs*** and drugs, only a small portion of all ***gangs*** actually deal in them. Similarly, the name Jose Padilla is inevitably followed by two epithets—al Qaeda terror suspect and street ***gang*** member. The link between the two is extremely misleading. One of the most urgent challenges for policymakers is distinguishing between the average street ***gang*** and groups that operate as criminal networks. Globalization and street ***gangs*** exist in a paradox: ***Gangs*** are a global phenomenon not because the groups themselves have become transnational organizations, but because of the recent hypermobility of ***gang*** members and their culture. Individual ***gangs*** flaunt their Internet savvy by posting complex Web sites, including some with password protection. As the global economy creates a growing number of disenfranchised groups, some will inevitably meet their needs in a ***gang***. INSETS: Want to Know More?; When ***Gangs*** Go Bad.; (*AN 16195307*) **HTML Full Text** **PDF Full Text** (1.7 MB)

Note that the abstract indicates that this article deals with "gang culture," so this one seems especially promising (and because the full text of the article is available online, you can print the essay with a click of your mouse). Note also that *Academic Search Premier*, the search database we used for this search, may not be available in all libraries. We use it here to illustrate a possible search database; your college or university will provide a similar search database.

Another online database that many colleges offer their students is *LexisNexis*, which indexes a range of newspapers, other periodicals, and a wide range of other kinds of documents. Figure 19.1 shows the first part of a search using the keyword "adolescent gangs."

Several of the articles listed by *LexisNexis* appear to be potentially useful. Since they are available as full-text articles, you can click on the title and immediately check them for relevance.

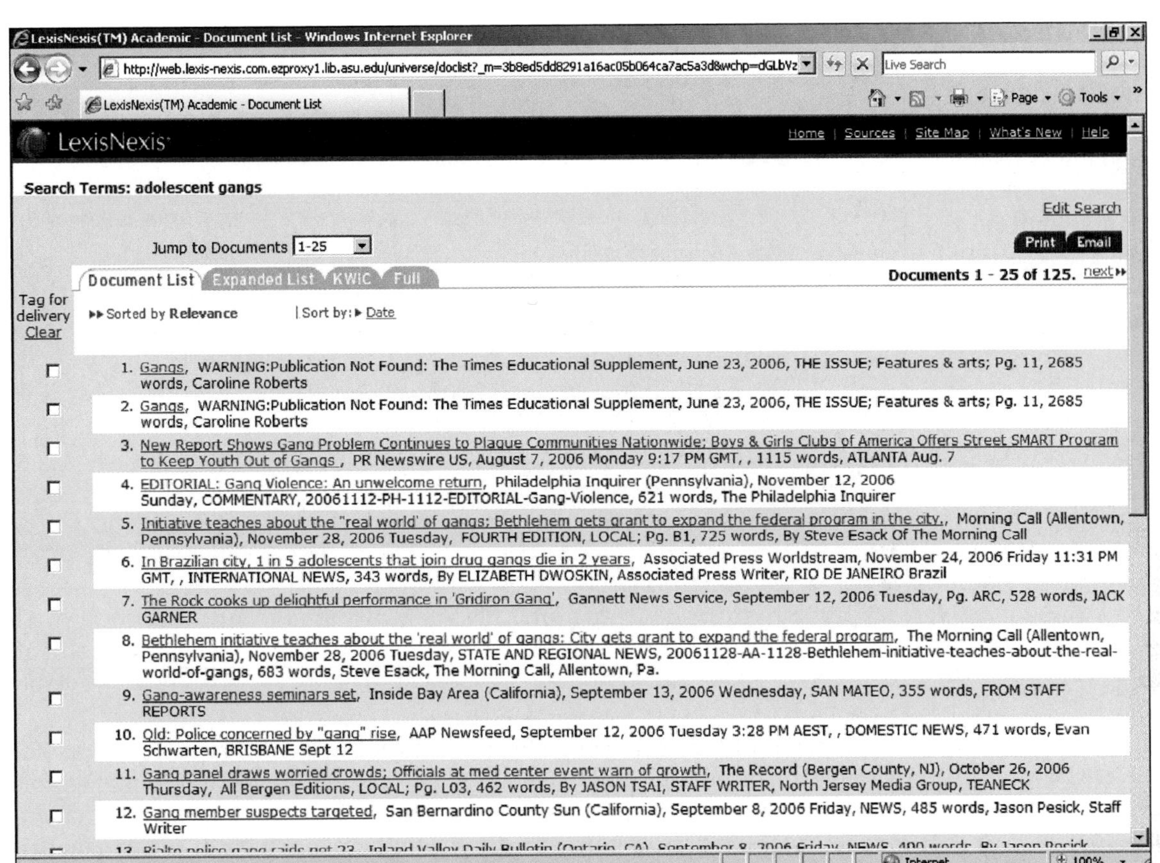

FIGURE 19.1 Search of the LexisNexis Database Using the Search Term "Adolescent Gangs" *LexisNexis* and *Knowledge Burst* logo are registered trademarks of Reed Elsevier Properties Inc. Used with permission of *LexisNexis.*

Research on the Web

You continue your search on the Web, which is the largest part of the global network of computers known as the Internet. The Web is hyperlinked, which means that one useful site will often provide links to many more.

If you have conducted Web searches, you probably quickly learned that different **search engines**, software programs that find sites on the Web, locate different information—that the search engine Google (www.google.com), for example, will give you different results from what Yahoo! (www.yahoo.com) or Bing (www.bing.com) does. You may also have used a "meta-search" engine such as Dogpile (www.dogpile.com), which searches *other* search engines, so the results you retrieve are from a range of searches. Usually, it is a good idea to use several different search engines.

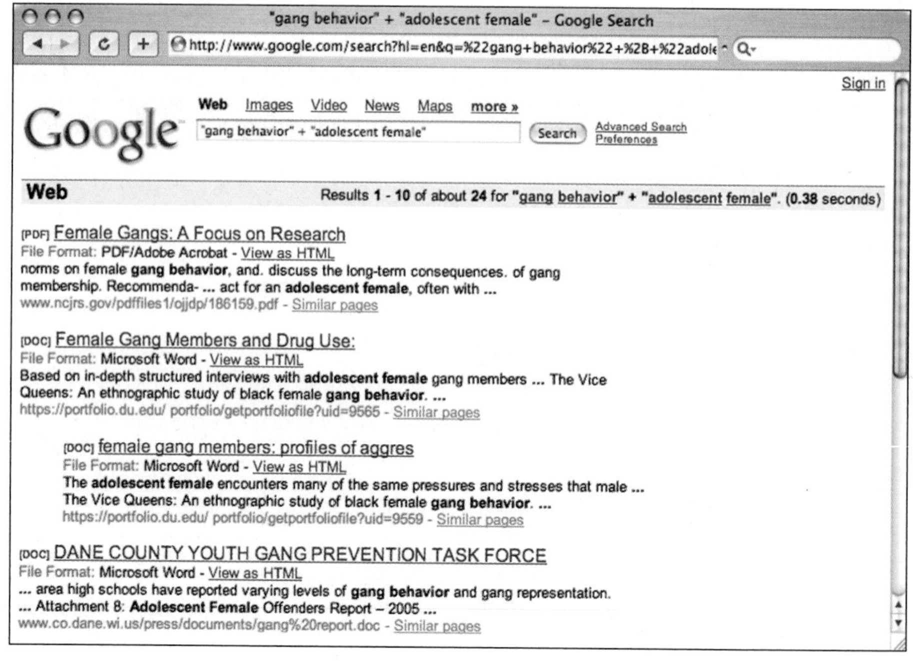

FIGURE 19.2 Result of a Search Using the Google Search Engine and the Keywords "Gang Behavior" + "Adolescent Female" Reprinted by permission of Google Brand Features

A search of the Web using Google and the keywords "gang behavior," for example, turns up over 1.47 *million* hits. This result provides an unmanageable number of choices. The best way to limit the number of hits that a search engine returns is to narrow what the search engine is looking for. You can do this easily on Google by enclosing multiple keywords within quotation marks so that the search engine looks for them when they appear together as a phrase. Simply by enclosing the search term "gang behavior" in quotation marks, you can limit the result to 46,700 hits, for example. This helps, but 46,700 options are still far too many. As a next step, you might qualify the search even more. If you are looking for information about female gangs, for example, you might try searching with the keywords "gang behavior" + "female." Doing so gives you a list of 13,000 hits. Although that's better, it's still not really good enough. You can then modify the search even further by trying this combination of keywords: "gang behavior" + "adolescent female." This time the response, shown in Figure 19.2, is only 24 hits, a manageable number. By closely defining your search terms and using them in combination, you can narrow your search and come up with the best possible online sources.

One other option you might consider if you are working on an academic paper is Google Scholar, which searches only scholarly Web sites. Searching Google Scholar using the keywords "gang behavior" + "adolescent female" gives you the result shown in Figure 19.3. You can also search for images on the Web. Using an image search on Google, for example, you may find a photo of gang activity which you can use to illustrate your paper.

FIGURE 19.3
Result of a Search Using the Google Scholar Search Engine and the Keywords "Gang Behavior" + "Adolescent Female"

Writing Activity

Developing a List of Questions and a Research Plan

For one of your current writing projects, develop a list of intriguing research questions. These are questions that require complex answers, not just facts. After each question, indicate where you would go to find answers and what you would do there.

Selecting Sources

Whenever you do research, you will encounter a wide range of sources. You have to determine what sources will be useful to you for your particular writing situation. We will outline a number of sources here and then discuss how you might *evaluate* the various kinds of information you locate.

The kind(s) of sources that you select depend on what you are trying to learn. You would not, for example, expect to find in books information on events that took place less than a year ago. For that kind of information, you would need to look for publications that publish more current information.

Each type of source has advantages and disadvantages, so it is usually best to use a variety of sources.

Books

Book from Cambridge University Press

Books such as the one shown here have historically been a researcher's first choice for much academic research because what you learn from them has almost always been well researched and the statistical information validated. However, even books have to be subjected to more intensive questioning these days, as it is now relatively easy for just about anyone to publish a book. Books in an academic library, however, have been carefully evaluated by librarians and are usually reputable. One disadvantage of the research you will find in a printed book is that it often takes several years to write, review, and publish a book—so the information often is not as current as that in other sources.

Academic Journals

American Journal of Psychiatry

Academic essays appear in **journals** such as the *American Journal of Psychiatry*. Journals are most often sponsored by universities. Essays in most academic journals are written by scholars in the field and are "peer reviewed," which means that other scholars have read the article, commented on it, and made a judgment about its validity and usefulness. Journal articles are usually well-researched. Also, academic essays usually come with a "works cited" or "references" page, which lists all of the sources the writer used. Often, these lists point to useful sources about the topic you are working on.

For example, your library search focusing on adolescent males and females and gangs might turn up this essay, published in the *American Journal of Psychiatry:* "What Happens to 'Bad' Girls? A Review of the Adult Outcomes of Antisocial Adolescent Girls" by Kathleen A. Pajer, M.D., M.P.H. In addition to the essay, you find a "works cited" section with eighty-three entries, references to other journal articles and books that Dr. Pajer used in her text. These will lead you to more information about teenage gangs.

Newspapers

Newspapers, especially those with a national focus such as the *New York Times*, are considered reliable sources. Often, local papers will get their information from national sources.

A *LexisNexis* search for newspaper articles on a topic will provide you with recent information. You need to remember, however, that while newspapers are very current sources, because they are following stories in progress, sometimes the information they provide may change as more complete information on a story becomes available.

Popular Magazines

Magazines, especially newsmagazines such as *Time* and *Newsweek*, have a broad perspective on national issues and often provide useful background and historical information. Many make the contents of the print magazine available online. Often the magazine will offer additional content online, as well as forums for readers to respond to articles and to one another.

A search at Time.com, for example, turns up possible sources for your paper on gangs, as shown in Figure 19.4.

Newsweek Magazine

TIME Magazine - Search Results

http://www.time.com/time/searchresults?N=0&Ntk=NoBody&Nty=1&Nr=OR%28p_record

TIME

Tuesday, September 4, 2007

Home

Gangs

Search

Refine Your Search

Refine By Dates
- Past 7 Days (2)
- Past 30 Days (17)
- Past Year (146)

From
Ma 17 1923

To
Sep 10 2007

Refine

Years limited by available results

Refine by Section
- Politics (5)

Refine by Author
- Corliss, Richard (162)
- Lacayo, Richard (24)
- McGirk, Tim (36)
- Morrow, Lance (33)
- Schickel, Richard (50)
- More...

Refine by Publication
- Time Domestic (5267)
- Time Asia (166)
- Time Europe (106)

Refine by Type
- Articles (5608)
- Blog (13)

Refine by Article Length
- Long (1948)
- Medium (2140)
- Short (1533)
- Cover Story (250)

Search Results:

Your search for **"Gangs"** found **5,621** results

Page: **1** | 2 | 3 | 4 | 5 | 6 | 7 | 8 | 9 | 10 | Next >>

Sponsored Links

Gangs
www.ask.com Better pictures & more relevant results on Ask.com. Use Ask.com.

See Sponsored Links For: Gangs

Sorted by **newest** | oldest | relevance

Making a Difference at Home
Sep. 10, 2007 | By Caroline Kennedy
Inspired by their work abroad, Peace Corps volunteers return to the U.S. as teachers, bringing the lessons they learned to the kids who need them most
844 words | view cover

Postcard: Philadelphia
Sep. 3, 2007 | By Brendan Lowe
...was seen as closely linked to more violent crimes, whether explicitly as **gang** markings or simply as a sign of neighborhoods in disrepair. But in...
605 words | view cover

Making a Difference at Home
Aug. 29, 2007 | By Caroline Kennedy
Inspired by their work abroad, Peace Corps volunteers return to the U.S. as teachers, bringing the lessons they learned to the kids who need them most
846 words

Healing Katrina's Racial Wounds
Aug. 27, 2007 | By Russell McCulley/New Orleans
Amid all the problems that New Orleans has faced, relieving black-white distrust has proven to be one of the toughest
965 words

Covers

Apr. 24, 1972

TIME
GANG WAR

- Table of Contents
- Large Cover

Featured Cover Stories

THE YOUTH CRIME PLAGUE
Jul. 11, 1977 | view cover

A Boy and His Gun
Aug. 2, 1993 | view cover

Life In Hell: A Baghdad Diary
Aug. 14, 2006 | view cover

More Cover Stories (250)

Photo Essays

FIGURE 19.4

Search of the Time.com Web Site Using the Keyword "Gangs"

Business Traveler Magazine

Trade or Commercial Magazines

Trade or commercial/professional magazines, such as *Business Traveler*, have a specific audience, which consists of the members of a group with a common interest or profession. If the magazine is published for a professional organization, a portion of the members' dues usually pays for the magazine. Other magazines are for-profit publications that serve the industry as a whole. These publications often are written specifically for their target audience. They also can provide lots of information from an insider's perspective, so you may need to be very familiar with the field.

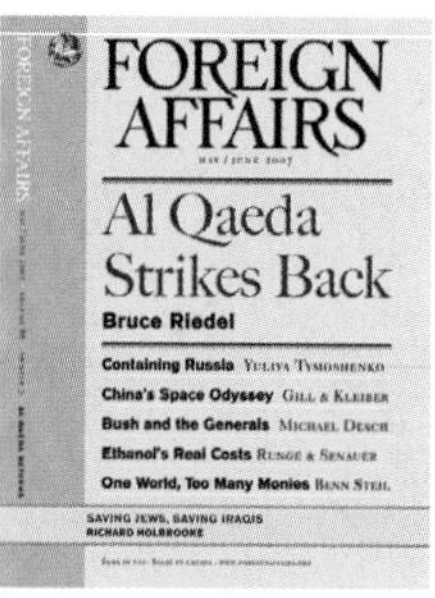

Foreign Affairs Magazine

Public Affairs Magazines

Magazines that focus on public affairs, such as *Foreign Affairs*, generally publish articles on national issues, so they are useful sources for papers about these issues. Their essays are usually thoughtfully researched and documented.

Specialty Magazines

Magazines about travel, different regions of the country, cooking, and other specialized topics are often useful if you are searching for the kinds of information they provide. Examples include *Arizona Highways*. Others, such as *BusinessWeek*, cater to a specific field and often have useful statistics and other types of information related to that field.

Arizona Highways Magazine

The Internet

The Internet, especially the Web, offers a huge range of information, all available very quickly. As you will see on pages 546–552, it sometimes takes a bit of work to figure out exactly who controls a Web site and the information it presents, so information you obtain from the Web must be used with caution.

It is extremely difficult to generalize about the Internet because it remains a dynamic, ever-evolving source of information and, often, misinformation. Any attempt to categorize Internet sources is, at best, a rough estimate, but we can point to at least five different kinds of online resources.

- **Web sites that serve as what used to be called the "home page" of an organization.** Most of these are now much more complex and sophisticated than they were in the early years of the Web, but they may very well be the first place you choose to look for information about any organization or group. Although the quality of the information you find on these Web sites may be good, you need to remember that because they are maintained by the organization itself, they tend to give a very positive view of the organization.

FIGURE 19.5 Home Page for the Internal Revenue Service

- **Web sites that provide information to the general public.** Many of these Web sites are maintained by governmental agencies. Their subject matter and complexity vary depending on whether they are constructed and maintained by local municipalities, state agencies, or the federal government. In most instances, the information found on these sites is very reliable. Figure 19.5, for example, is the home page for the site maintained by the Internal Revenue Service.
- **Online periodicals and newspapers.** As noted earlier, almost every print publication now has an online version. Some local newspapers, such as the *Daily Hampshire Gazette* (www.gazettenet.com) of Northampton, Massachusetts, have a free news section and a section only for paid subscribers. Much of the content from each day's edition of the *New York Times* (www.nytimes.com) is available free online, but only to those who register. Many magazines allow online viewers to read most of their articles, while others publish snippets online and allow full access only to subscribers.

  Some academic journals, such as *Kairos* (http://english.ttu.edu/Kairos/), are published only online. Like most academic journals, they are peer-reviewed, and the information in them is as reliable as that found in print academic journals.

FIGURE 19.6 Page from *Diet Blog* Reprinted by permission of Jim Foster, Editor, www.diet-blog.com

connect
mhconnectcomposition.com
Using blogs in research QL19001

- **Blogs.** A blog is usually maintained by one person who shares his or her thoughts on a given topic or set of topics and may post links to other sites on the Web as well as comments from other writers. While some blogs are maintained by experts in a particular field, others are written by people who want to spread their own point of view on anything from politics to what kind of software is better. Use them with caution. Figure 19.6 is an example of a blog on dieting.

For more information on evaluating sources see pages 546–552.

- ***Wikipedia.*** *Wikipedia* is a collaborative online encyclopedia. The articles on *Wikipedia* are written by volunteers, and it is possible for anyone to edit already existing articles. Although there are some safeguards to protect certain pages, some information found on *Wikipedia* may be suspect. You may think of it as a good starting place, in much the same way

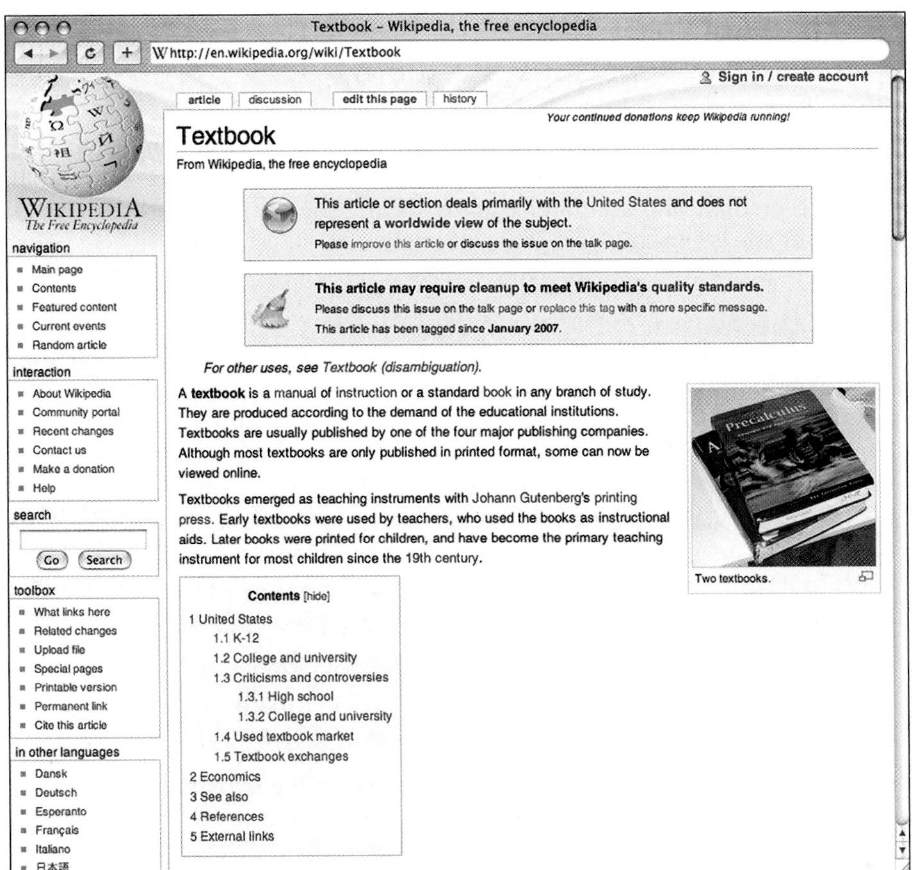

Textbook - Wikipedia, the free encyclopedia

http://en.wikipedia.org/wiki/Textbook

Sign in / create account

article | discussion | edit this page | history

Your continued donations keep Wikipedia running!

WIKIPEDIA
The Free Encyclopedia

navigation
- Main page
- Contents
- Featured content
- Current events
- Random article

interaction
- About Wikipedia
- Community portal
- Recent changes
- Contact us
- Make a donation
- Help

search

Go Search

toolbox
- What links here
- Related changes
- Upload file
- Special pages
- Printable version
- Permanent link
- Cite this article

in other languages
- Dansk
- Deutsch
- Esperanto
- Français
- Italiano
- 日本語

Textbook

From Wikipedia, the free encyclopedia

This article or section deals primarily with the United States and does not represent a worldwide view of the subject.
Please improve this article or discuss the issue on the talk page.

This article may require cleanup to meet Wikipedia's quality standards.
Please discuss this issue on the talk page or replace this tag with a more specific message.
This article has been tagged since **January 2007**.

For other uses, see Textbook (disambiguation).

A **textbook** is a manual of instruction or a standard book in any branch of study. They are produced according to the demand of the educational institutions. Textbooks are usually published by one of the four major publishing companies. Although most textbooks are only published in printed format, some can now be viewed online.

Textbooks emerged as teaching instruments with Johann Gutenberg's printing press. Early textbooks were used by teachers, who used the books as instructional aids. Later books were printed for children, and have become the primary teaching instrument for most children since the 19th century.

Two textbooks.

Contents [hide]

1 United States
1.1 K-12
1.2 College and university
1.3 Criticisms and controversies
1.3.1 High school
1.3.2 College and university
1.4 Used textbook market
1.5 Textbook exchanges
2 Economics
3 See also
4 References
5 External links

FIGURE 19.7 *Wikipedia* Entry for "Textbook"

that a traditional encyclopedia is a place to start for background, but you should not rely on it for all of your information on a topic. It is always wise to look for additional sources of information beyond *Wikipedia*. You should also be cautious about citing it as a source in your academic papers. Figure 19.7 shows the *Wikipedia* entry for "textbook."

For more about Wikipedia, see "Growing Wikipedia Revises Its 'Anyone Can Edit' Policy" by Katie Hafner, in Chapter 6.

Writing Activity

Planning Your Research

For a college class in which you have been asked to conduct research on a particular topic, select a potential topic, and then list the sources you might look at and what you might expect to find in them. Also plan when and where you will conduct your research.

Evaluating Your Sources: Asking the Reporter's Questions

Finding sources is only the beginning of your task in conducting research; you also need to evaluate the information you locate. How do you determine that a source is credible and accurate? Usually, asking the questions a reporter asks when he or she is working on a story will help you.

Who Is the Author?

Scholarly Book on the Subject of Gangs

Who is the author of the research? What can you learn about that author? If the work is an essay or an entire book, you may be able to find biographical information about the author or authors. For example, let's say you are conducting research on gangs and find this book in your college library: *Teen Gangs: A Global View*, edited by Maureen P. Duffy and Scott Edward Gillig, and published by Greenwood Press. Here is what the publisher says about the two editors in its online catalog:

> **MAUREEN P. DUFFY** is Associate Professor and Chair of the Counseling Department at Barry University, Miami Shores, Florida.
>
> **SCOTT EDWARD GILLIG** is Professor and Coordinator of the mental health counseling specialization at Barry University.

Both editors are university professors, which means the book most likely contains thoroughly researched and well-documented articles by respected authors. If you examine Greenwood's catalog or Web site, you will see that it specializes in nonfiction books primarily for schools and that it also publishes library reference titles. So you know the editors are both professors and the book is not self-published. Although you cannot tell much about the reputation of Greenwood Press from its Web site alone, all of the information you have found indicates that the articles in this text were probably written by people who are credible authorities in their field.

What Is the Text About? What Is the Quality of the Information?

To determine the answer to this question, you will need to ask the following additional questions:

- What is the focus of the printed or online text you are considering?
- How thoughtful and research-based is it?
- Does the text take a balanced, thoughtful approach?

You'll also want to make sure the text is relevant to your topic.

For instance, in your research on why adolescent males or females change their behavior when they join gangs, suppose you visit the Web site at www

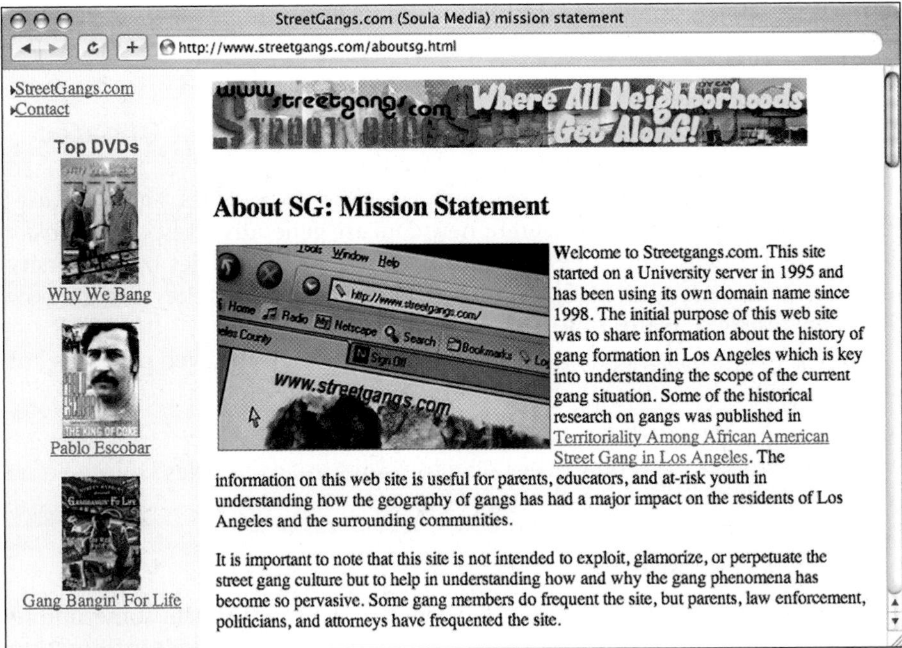

FIGURE 19.8 Mission Statement for the Web Site Streetgangs.com

.streetgangs.com. The mission statement shown in Figure 19.8 indicates that the site appears to be controlled by an individual and has been since 1995. This does not mean that the information on the site is not credible, only that you will need to consider the source if you decide to use anything from this Web site.

The final paragraph of the section about the history of the Web site adds this information:

> We receive dozens of email every day so forgive us if we cannot personally respond to your message, but we will do our best to answer ALL serious questions. We receive over 6 million page visits monthly so please do not email us to help you with your high school paper or to ask silly questions. Please see the *bibliography* for tips on good books to read and for articles to download, or visit the *topics* to read recent news articles. If you have a serious question about gangs visit the *billboard* where your question may have already been asked. If you would like to write an article for *Street Gangs Magazine* please follow the *submission guidelines* and forward your essay. Media requests should be made from the *contact page.*

With so much interest in street gangs, it is certainly possible that this Web site gets "over 6 million page visits monthly." How does the tone of these comments affect your view of this site?

Even at sites or blogs maintained by individuals, you can sometimes learn valuable information and find useful links. For example, Streetgangs.com offers a "100 page bibliography" for sale, but the site includes sample pages to give you a sense of the information the site makes available.

When Was the Text Published or the Web Site Last Updated?

Generally, the more current the information a source provides, the more useful it is to you. In academic research, new data are generally a response to *older* data. In fact, one of the benefits of reading books and articles by university scholars is that they almost always refer to earlier research as they outline how their new research relates to it.

At www.streetgangs.com, there is no notice of when the Web page was last updated, but in the copyright section you will find this notice:

> Copyright © Notice, Terms & Conditions
> Copyright © 1995–2006, Street Gangs, Gangs in Los Angeles
> P.O. Box 18238, Los Angeles CA, 90018, USA
> 800.249.1324
> All Rights Reserved

This notice tells you that someone has worked on this Web site sometime in 2006. The page also includes a link to the biography and contact information for A. Alonso, who is evidently responsible for the site, another bit of evidence that the site is controlled by an individual.

Why Was This Information Published?

What can you determine about why the information was published? What is the text's purpose? Who appears to be the target audience? If you can determine to whom the text appeals, you might gain a sense of its purpose.

You cannot know for sure why an essay was published, or a book printed, or a Web site constructed, but you can make some good guesses:

- Essays in academic journals are often published to share new knowledge. This is especially true of articles in scientific journals, which publish the results of scientific research, but even in journals that focus on the humanities or on professional fields, professors publish what they have learned from their reading and thinking.

  Because articles in academic journals are peer-reviewed, other scholars in the field will get the chance to comment on and make suggestions (and criticisms) about any essay before it is published. So generally you can expect the information in journal articles to be reliable. Journals are also major venues that scholars and practitioners use to communicate and share information within professional and scientific fields.
- Academic books provide professors with a way to distribute large amounts of information and insight to their peers, and while some make money for their author and publisher, many do not, so the profit motive is not a strong factor in publishing an academic text. Academic texts are

also peer-reviewed, so other scholars in the field will have examined the information, data, and conclusions in a text prior to publication. During the publishing process, those peer reviewers will have the opportunity to contribute their ideas, criticisms, and suggestions. Academic texts are generally published by university presses.

- **Articles in newsmagazines and newspapers** present items in the local, national, or worldwide news. Most often, editors work diligently to present the news in an unbiased manner, but most newspapers and even some magazines have editorial pages or sections.

  As with anyone else, newspaper and magazine editors and writers have their own particular viewpoints and ways of looking at what they report on—in other words, there is always *some* bias in anything that is said or written. At any particular time and place, you might be able to label newspapers and magazines according to their general tendencies. But these ways of seeing and writing about the news vary over time, as editors and writers come and go.

  How can you, as a reader, get some sense of the biases of the newsmagazines and newspapers you read for your research? One way is to compare how the same information is presented in the different magazines or newspapers. Read two or more editorials on the same topic. Look for facts related to a story that appears in one publication but not in the other: What might that tell you about each? Consider how the same story is presented in two different publications. How big is the headline? How much space is devoted to the article? Is it on the front page or on an interior page?

- **Web sites** give all kinds of information. However, not all Web sites give completely accurate and reliable information. You have to evaluate a Web site just as you would any other source. For information on evaluating Web sites, see "A Writer's Responsibilities" (page 552).

Writing Activity

Analyzing Newspapers

Most newspapers have a particular political slant, which is often clear in their editorials but is also evident in the way various news stories are presented. If you examine the newspapers from several large cities, such differences will be readily apparent. Select a major story that is currently in the news, and compare how three newspapers cover it. What kind of photographs accompany the story? What do their editorials say about it? How much "newsprint" space is devoted to the story? Where do the stories appear?

Compare what you have learned with the information that several of your classmates have gathered about coverage of the same story or a similar story.

Writing Activity

Examining a Web Site to Determine Its Audience

Select one of the following Web sites and, in no more than two pages, outline who you think is the intended audience for the site, what you think its purpose is, and why you make that assertion. Indicate who maintains the site (if you can tell) and when it was last updated.

http://www.gangwar.com/dynamics.htm
http://www.csun.edu/~hcchs006/gang.html
http://ojjdp.ncjrs.org/pubs/reform/ch2_e.html
http://www.gangstyle.com/

Where Was the Item Published?

It is becoming increasingly difficult to differentiate between library research and online research because so many traditional library resources are now located online. In addition, many libraries provide portals to online databases and other online sites. As a result, whether information resides in a physical building or is stored on a server, you will need your critical thinking skills more than ever to determine its value.

As with any research activity, your decision about where to search for information depends on what you are trying to learn. If the answer to your research question requires demographic data, you might find that all the reliable and most current census information is on different Web sites maintained by various agencies of the U.S. government. Web-based research is rarely sufficient for a project of any depth, however. For example, you probably can learn more about local census trends and data from your local newspaper.

Articles and other source materials published on the Web can appear professional and unbiased, but it is often difficult to find information that allows you to evaluate fully the credibility of a Web page. To do so, you need to determine what person, company, or organization constructed the site and stands behind it. If you learn that you are examining a personal Web site instead of one sponsored by a government agency or a university, you need to take that fact into account. Although organizations will often have their own agenda, they usually can devote more resources to the construction and maintenance of a Web site than an individual can. Web suffixes generally indicate the source of a Web site:

- **.edu** indicates an educational institution. Information you find at such a location has generally been approved by the school. However, many colleges and universities also provide Web space for students and faculty members, and those individuals may post information that has *not* necessarily been approved by the school.

- .com indicates a for-profit company. The suffix *.com* is a shortened form of *commercial* and usually designates a business-oriented site.
- .org indicates an organization. The *.org* Web suffix is generally used for nonprofit organizations.
- .gov indicates some level of government (state, national, or local).
- .net indicates Web sites generally used by Internet service providers (ISPs) and companies that provide Web hosting, like www.concentric.net. Some commercial businesses also use the *.net* extension, but usually not as their main Web site. Some Internet service providers allow their customers to use their "net" extension for sharing things like photographs, such as www.photo.net.
- .biz is most often used for small-business Web sites.
- .info is, like *.com*, an unrestricted domain: Anyone can use it. According to Network Associates, the company that assigns and allocates Web addresses, *.info* is the most popular extension beyond *.com, .net,* and *.org.*

For more information on Web suffixes and addresses, see http://www.networksolutions.com/. Network Solutions offers a "WhoIs" search function for nearly all sites on the Web except personal ones. Conducting a "WhoIs" search will give you information about the sponsor of any particular Web page. This search not only tells you who "owns" the domain name, but also provides e-mail contact information. If the Web page you're looking for is not listed, then it is probably a personal page.[1]

How Accurate Is the Information in This Source?

Anyone who checks out in a supermarket and sees tabloid headlines about aliens and Elvis sightings understands that not all news stories that appear in print are necessarily accurate. How do you know what information to believe and what information to view with skepticism?

- One of the best ways of determining accuracy in any publication is finding out who published it. As we have noted, books published by university presses and articles published in academic journals are peer-reviewed. You can usually expect that large newspapers such as the *New York Times* will print the most accurate information available at the time. Over time, some information published in reliable periodicals or newspapers may change or be corrected. The publication is then likely to publish the updated information.
- Another way of determining accuracy is to investigate the author's track record. Of course, it's important to make sure that the author's area of expertise is in the subject you are researching. A famous actor who writes a

[1] Thanks to William Sherman, University of Northern Colorado, for this information.

diet book may or may not be a credible source of information on proper nutrition.

To determine the accuracy of information on a Web site, you might consider the Web sites it provides links to. Often, following some of the links will give you information about the site's credibility. For example, the Web site Streetgangs.com showed these links in December 2006:

- Gang member receives 50 years, Dec 8, 2006
- Stopping gang activity is a noble goal, but the end doesn't always justify the means, Nov 30, 2006
- Delgadillo names U.S. prosecutor as 'gang czar', Nov 28, 2006
- Police, FBI target San Fernando Valley gang crimes, Nov 22, 2006

Links that connect to reputable newspapers or television stations would indicate that whoever is maintaining the Web site is providing readers with connections to legitimate news articles, thus adding to the credibility of the Web site. However, the links listed above lead to stories that have bylines but give little indication of what organization the writer works for. Some simply say "Times Staff." What impact do links such as these have on the way you view the information available on this site?

A WRITER'S *Responsibility* | Evaluating Web Sites

Ask yourself the following questions when evaluating the credibility of a Web site.

- Who is the author or sponsor of the site? What can you find out about the author or sponsor? Why might they sponsor the site? What benefit might the sponsor receive from the Web site?
- What does the site's address tell you about it? What does the suffix that appears at the end of the address tell you about it: *.edu* for educational, for example, or *.com* for commercial? Is there a tilde (~) in the address, which indicates a personal site?
- What is the purpose of the site? Is the purpose to provide information? To sell a product or service? To persuade readers to accept a particular point of view?
- How professional is the tone, and how well designed is the site? How carefully has it been edited and proofread? How many grammatical and spelling errors are there?
- Consider the quality of the author's arguments. Does the content contain logical fallacies? How fairly does the author deal with opposing views?
- Can you find a date when the site was published or most recently updated?
- What kinds of links does the site provide? How legitimate or credible are the sites the links lead to?

Field Research

As we have seen, much of the time you will gather information for your research projects from books, periodicals, the Web, and other preexisting sources. At other times, you may need to gather first-hand information. Sometimes you can get the information you need by simply observing people, wildlife, or natural phenomena. At other times, the best method of gathering information from human subjects may be to ask questions of individual people or groups of people, either directly or in writing. However you do it, the act of gathering information on your own is called **field research** because you need to go out "into the field." The most common kinds of field research you might find yourself doing are observation, personal interviews, and surveys.

Working with Human Participants

Much field research has to do with human behavior. Any time you are doing research that involves human participants, you are expected to behave ethically and to do or say nothing that might in any way harm your participants. To ensure that researchers follow ethical practices, all academic institutions (and many private organizations) have Institutional Review Boards (IRBs). All research projects that use human participants must be approved by your organization's IRB or its designated representative. All IRBs have their own rules. Check with your instructor about your school's human participants policy.

Informed Consent

Whether you are required to submit a formal proposal to your school's IRB or simply need to work closely with your instructor, if you are going to be working with human participants, you need to get their permission by having all of the participants in your field research sign an Informed Consent Form. Most institutions have templates for these forms readily available.

Observations

Watching and recording what you see might be the most effective way to help you answer your research question. If viewing people, animals, or other phenomena over a short time will provide you with useful information, you may choose observation as your research method.

OBSERVING HUMANS

If you are writing an informative or analytical paper, you may need to observe human behavior as part of your research. To make your observations, you might station yourself at a particular place in a shopping mall, at an athletic event, or at a busy intersection and record, in detail, certain behaviors. For example, you might record how many vehicles passing through an intersection near your college actually come to a complete stop at the stop sign. You would need to keep track of the total number of vehicles passing by as well as the specific number of vehicles that demonstrate the particular behavior you are watching for. It is, of course, possible to make even more detailed observations, such as what car models drivers who run stop signs are driving. To make detailed observations such as these, it helps to prepare by setting up categories. Once you are in the field observing and recording, you probably won't have time to develop new ones.

OBSERVING OTHER PHENOMENA

For writing projects that lend themselves to observation, see Chapters 5, 6, and 7.

You can also observe other natural and human-influenced phenomena. Some researchers observe animal behavior; others watch tornadoes and other weather patterns. The specific nature of what you are observing will determine the tools you will need and the methods you will use.

Writing Activity

Conduct an Observation

People often comment on how students are tied to technology. How valid is this assertion? One way to test this assumption might be to sit for an hour in your student union or some other place where students from your campus gather. Watch the behavior of the students. Are they talking with one another in person, or are they using technology to communicate, listen to music, or watch videos? Take notes of what you see. You might want to establish some categories. Are students talking on cell phones? Are they using laptops? Are they listening to iPods? Write a short report on your findings.

Interviews

Because most of us are comfortable talking with other people, we often think that interviewing someone will be easy. However, interviews are rarely an easy way to do meaningful research. Effective interviews that yield useful information happen only when the interviewer prepares ahead of time. As you prepare, it's important to remember that some of the interviews you may see on television or hear on the radio are not necessarily good examples of interviewing.

You can employ several strategies to prepare and conduct a successful interview:

- Call ahead to make an appointment instead of just showing up in your subject's office. You might obtain more information than you might otherwise have been able to get.

- Do your homework ahead of time so that you have good questions ready to ask, have anticipated the nature of the responses, and have good follow-up questions at hand. Being able to anticipate the nature of the interview will enable you to steer the interview in the direction in which you need it to go.
- Be prepared to take notes. Before you interview someone for an assignment, practice (using your interview questions) with a classmate or a friend.
- Consider bringing along some kind of recording device. If you plan to record the interview, make sure you have your subject's permission before the interview begins. Some people are willing to talk but do not wish to be recorded.
- Be polite and friendly during the interview. It is usually a good idea to follow up an interview with a thank-you note.

Although your specific interview questions will depend on your topic and the person you are interviewing, you will usually want to prepare two kinds of questions: open-ended and directed. **Open-ended questions** let the person being interviewed develop his or her answers at length. **Directed questions** seek more specific kinds of information. As part of her research for a paper on violence in the movies, for example, Magda was interested in learning about how people react when they are watching violent movies. To find out, she decided to interview the local manager of a theater chain that sometimes shows violent, R-rated movies. To prepare for the interview, Magda developed the following list of questions:

1. What would you consider a violent movie?
2. What specific content in a movie makes it violent?
3. Are all movies that contain scenes with (the content from the previous questions) necessarily violent? If not, why not? What's the determining factor?
4. Do you show many movies like that? If so, how many per month?
5. Why do you think people watch violent movies?
6. What age groups seem to watch violent movies?
7. Do audiences at violent movies behave differently from audiences at other types of movies, such as comedies?
8. Are audiences at violent movies more or less likely to buy more at the concession stand?
9. Do audiences at violent movies leave behind more or less trash in the theater?
10. Are audiences at violent movies more or less likely to leave through an unauthorized exit?
11. Are audiences at violent movies generally noisier or quieter?

Some of the questions in Magda's list, such as 1–3, were open-ended. Others, such as questions 7–11, were more directed, perhaps indicating the direction of her thinking as she developed her thesis.

Avoid what can be called "forced-choice questions," questions that presuppose only a few specific choices and force your subject to answer one of them. Asking "Do you think the football team is bad or just plain awful this year?" assumes the team really is bad and that your subject will agree. A better question would be "What's your opinion of the football team this year?"

Writing Activity

Conducting an Interview

Assume that you are a reporter for your school's newspaper. Your editor has assigned you to interview the president of your campus on a topic of your choice. Develop a list of ten questions, some open-ended, some directed, that you want to ask the president.

Also stay away from leading questions that have built-in *assumptions* the person you are interviewing might not agree with. A question like "Don't you think that conducting surveys provides a richness that other research methods can't match?" assumes (1) that the interviewee will interpret "richness" in the same way you do, and (2) that both of your definitions of "can't match" will also agree. It would be more effective to ask the question in a more neutral way: "Are there any advantages, in your view, to surveys over other kinds of field research? If so, what might they be?"

Surveys

Although interviews are useful sources of information and have the advantage of enabling a direct exchange between the subject and the interviewer, the number of people that one person can interview is limited. Some research projects require you to collect information from a larger number of people than you could possibly interview. To get information from a large number of people quickly and efficiently, you can use a **survey.** Although on the surface a survey may look like just a set of questions, an effective survey is carefully designed, and its questions are very specifically framed. A good survey will either target a particular group of people or solicit information about the participants to provide you with a context for their answers.

CONSTRUCTING A SURVEY

Several strategies will enable you to put together an effective survey:

- Keep the survey a reasonable length. Ask only those questions that are necessary. Many people think that all surveys need to start with questions that ask for certain basic demographic information, but you need gather only information that is important for your research.
- Make sure the questions you ask call for an appropriate response. If a reasonable answer to the question is "yes," or "no," make sure there are only two possible responses. If a wider range of responses is appropriate, a scale such as "strongly agree, agree, no opinion, disagree, strongly disagree" may be more useful.
- Consider whether you want to ask only *closed-ended* or *directed* questions that call for specific answers, such as "List your age," or if you also want to ask *open-ended* questions, such as "Describe your experience at the Math Testing Center." Closed-ended questions are easier to tabulate, but open-ended questions will provide you with more examples and narrative detail.
- If you ask open-ended questions that call for written responses, give your respondents enough room on the form to answer fully.
- The question itself should not influence the response. Asking a question like "Do you think there are not enough parking spaces on campus?" leads the respondent to say "yes." A more effective way to get the same information would be to ask, "What is your opinion of the campus parking situation?"
- Have a strategy for tabulating the open-ended responses. Are you going to try to categorize them? Are you planning to use them as anecdotal examples?
- Consider using an electronic survey, such as those provided by SurveyMonkey.com. These companies often allow you to conduct free surveys but limit the number of responses you can receive to 100 or so. An electronic survey lets you reach a wider audience: You can simply e-mail the survey link. Also, you may find that those you want to complete your survey are more likely to fill out an electronic form than a paper one—and the electronic survey will help you collect and collate your data.

Digital Literacy **Creating Electronic Note Cards**

To avoid scrolling within one document looking for chunks of information to paste into your draft, consider dividing your research into a number of documents, grouping chunks of source text in clearly named, easy-to-identify files. These files will function more or less like electronic note cards in your project's main folder on your computer. Don't forget to type or paste bibliographic information for each source within its document file.

ADMINISTERING YOUR SURVEY

Test your survey before you administer it. That way, if a question or two proves to be faulty, you can make changes. Have several people respond to your survey, asking them to indicate any confusing questions. Also consider whom you would like to respond to your survey, targeting your audience as specifically as possible. A general rule of thumb is that the more people you can ask to take your survey—the larger the data set—the more useful the results will be. It is also important to make sure that you are surveying the right population. If you are looking for information on what kind of coffee drinks are most popular on your campus, for example, you should survey only coffee drinkers.

Writing Activity

Develop a Survey

Often people who are thinking of opening a small business conduct a survey of their potential clientele to test their business plan's chances for success. Think of a possible product or service that seems to be lacking in your community. Then identify the customers your business will serve. Develop a set of survey questions that will give you a good sense of whether others share your perceived need for this business.

Chapter

20

Synthesizing and Documenting Sources

Effective academic writing does not just emerge out of a writer's mind. Academic writers are expected to know what others have said on their topic, using the work of other writers to help establish a foundation for an argument, substantiate an argument, or set up a point that they will then challenge or support. This process of building your own arguments using support and arguments from other writers is called **synthesis.** As they synthesize ideas, academic writers need to use sources, acknowledging the thinking that already exists on an issue and giving credit to those who developed it. When developing an argument in an academic essay, for instance, you will be expected to review the relevant work of previous researchers and summarize their results. You will then be able to build your own arguments, working from theirs. And you will need to give these researchers credit. To help you synthesize other people's writing and documenting sources, this chapter covers plagiarism, quotations, paraphrasing, and summaries, as well as MLA and APA documentation styles.

For more on synthesis, see Chapter 2.

An Overview of Documentation

When you document sources appropriately, you accomplish several important purposes:

- Documentation indicates what you as the writer did not produce—in effect, it indicates where you have used summary and paraphrase: "This isn't my idea and here is where it came from." Or it indicates a quotation: "These aren't my words, and here is the name of the person who wrote them."
- Documentation that follows a system such as the one recommended by the Modern Language Association (MLA) or the American Psychological Association (APA) provides readers with a list of sources—called the list of Works Cited in MLA style or References in APA style—so they can consult the works listed.
- Proper documentation, within the text and in the list of sources, makes it easy for the reader to locate and read a particular source the writer has cited or even a specific quotation in that source.
- Proper documentation of appropriate sources lends *ethos* and credibility to you as a writer and enhances your argument.

Different academic disciplines have different style guides that offer a range of conventions for writers to follow, including conventions for documentation. Here we will present the conventions for documentation given in the style guides of the MLA and the APA. MLA style is used for papers in humanities disciplines, including English; APA style is used for papers in social science disciplines. The current editions of both manuals are as follows:

Gibaldi, Joseph. *MLA Handbook for Writers of Research Papers*. 7th ed. New York: MLA, 2009.

American Psychological Association. (2010). *Publication manual of the American Psychological Association* (6th ed.). Washington, DC: Author.[1]

Other disciplines recommend a variety of styles. Here are some of those other options:

- *Scientific Style and Format: The CSE Manual for Authors, Editors and Publishers* (7th ed.). If your academic work is in the sciences, you may be required to use the style suggested by the Council of Scientific Editors (CSE), formerly the Council of Biology Editors (CBE).
- *Information for Authors*. This volume, published by the Institute of Electrical and Electronics Engineers (IEEE), is used by engineers.
- *The Chicago Manual of Style* (15th ed.). *CMS* is another widely used style. In fact, if you are expected to do on-the-job writing that requires documentation, more likely than not you will use *CMS*.

When you use information from sources to support your thesis, you must be careful to give appropriate credit to the author of each source. Failing to do so is plagiarism. You can choose from among several options for presenting information that you have taken from other writers' work: quotations, paraphrases, or summaries.

Plagiarism

We've all heard lots of discussion about plagiarism. Yet, too often, both teachers and students are reacting without ever really understanding what plagiarism is. It's crucial that students and teachers understand what constitutes plagiarism. The best definition of **plagiarism** is from the Council of Writing Program Administrators in their "Defining and Avoiding Plagiarism: The WPA Statement on Best Practices": "In an instructional setting, plagiarism occurs when a writer deliberately uses someone else's language, ideas, or other original (not common-knowledge) material without acknowledging its source" (http://www.wpacouncil.org/positions/WPAplagiarism.pdf). If you read that statement carefully, you'll see that the key concept in plagiarism is the *intent to deceive.* In fact, the act of knowingly submitting someone else's work as your own is the basic ingredient of what constitutes plagiarism. There are two somewhat related problems that students, especially those who are new to using research in their writing, often have problems with: inadequate or incorrect citations, and "patchwriting."

connect
mhconnectcomposition.com
Intentional and unintentional plagiarism QL20001

Inadequate or Incorrect Citations

One of the most common problems students have when integrating material from sources into their writing is inadequate or incorrect citations. Accurate use of citation can be confusing to new researchers, and instructors often see students make mistakes in citing sources. The best thing for you to remember is that you must be sure to cite material you get from other sources. If you are integrating material from sources, whether you use it in a direct quotation, a paraphrase, or a summary, you must cite it appropriately. You'll also need to have the appropriate citation in your Works Cited list at the end.

Patchwriting

Rhetoric and composition scholar Rebecca Moore Howard uses the term "patchwriting" to describe when students unintentionally put passages from sources into their own writing without proper attribution. This commonly happens when students use inappropriate paraphrase or summary or just aren't quite sure how to incorporate the ideas of others into their work. To avoid patchwriting, make sure your paraphrases and summaries are really in your words and that you are using proper citation when you incorporate the ideas of others into your work.

Anti-plagiarism Software

Search technologies that enable all of us to find information more quickly and thoroughly than ever before also can be used by instructors to check whether the work students are turning in is original or taken from somewhere else. Anyone who finds a suspicious passage in a piece of writing can simply Google the passage, making sure the whole passage is enclosed in quotation marks, and see if it appears elsewhere. Using similar search technologies, some companies have marketed what has come to be called *anti-plagiarism software.* Some schools buy licenses to such software. The most commonly used is *Turnitin* or *SafeAssign,* which is part of *Blackboard.* Instructors who use this kind of software let their students know that assignments are going to be submitted. In fact, many instructors encourage their students to submit drafts of assignments so that the software can point out potentially problematic passages and inadequate citation. Using anti-plagiarism software in this way gives students the opportunity to have their drafts checked for both patchwriting and inadequate citation, so they can revise their papers before submitting the final draft.

Quotations

mhconnectcomposition.com
Direct quotation QL20002

When the most effective way to make a point is to use another author's exact words, you are using a **quotation.** Use a direct quotation in the following situations:

- When the exact wording is particularly striking
- When the author is considered to be especially authoritative
- When you take issue with the author's statement

If you are using MLA style and your quotation is shorter than five lines, you should enclose it in quotation marks and incorporate it into your text. Because the quotation is incorporated into the sentence, a comma is used after the introductory phrase. At first it might feel a bit awkward or clumsy when you integrate quoted material into your writing; however, you will get better with practice. Using verbs such as *notes, comments, observes,* and *explains,* will help you introduce quotations smoothly and meaningfully.

For information on how to cite quotations, paraphrases, and summaries within text, see pages 568–571 for MLA style and pages 594–596 for APA style.

> Writing about the power of computers, Sherry Turkle says, "When I want to write and don't have a computer, I tend to wait until I do" (29).

When the quotation is longer than four lines and you are using MLA style, start the quotation on a new line and indent all lines of the quotation one inch. The quotation should be double spaced and does not need to be enclosed in quotation marks. If the quotation is introduced with an independent clause, that clause is followed by a colon.

An early researcher in virtual environments writes of their compelling nature:

> Why is it so hard for me to turn away from the screen? The windows on my computer desktop offer me layers of material to which I have simultaneous access: field notes; previous drafts of this book; a list of ideas not yet elaborated but which I want to include; transcripts of interviews with computer users; and verbatim logs of sessions on computer networks, on bulletin boards, and in virtual communities. (Turkle 29)

If you are using APA style, quotations of fewer than forty words should be enclosed in quotation marks and incorporated into the text, as follows:

Writing about the power of computers, Sherry Turkle (1995) says, "When I want to write and don't have a computer, I tend to wait until I do" (p. 29).

Block quotations are used in APA style when the quotation is at least forty words long. They are indented only five spaces and double spaced, and are not enclosed in quotation marks.

An early researcher in virtual environments writes eloquently of their compelling nature:

> Why is it so hard for me to turn away from the screen? The windows on my computer desktop offer me layers of material to which I have simultaneous access: field notes; previous drafts of this book; a list of ideas not yet elaborated but which I want to include; transcripts of interviews with computer users; and verbatim logs of sessions on computer networks, on bulletin boards, and in virtual communities. (Turkle, 1995, p. 29)

Paraphrases

Use **paraphrases** when you put someone else's ideas into your own words. Because you are using someone else's ideas, you need to make appropriate citations. However, you will use your own words and sentence structure. If you choose to borrow unique phrases from the original, those phrases should be placed in quotation marks. Here, for example, is a block quotation in APA style:

In his book *The World Is Flat, New York Times* columnist Thomas L. Friedman (2005) notes that when Netscape went public in 1995, it had significant ramifications for the emerging global economy:

> Looking back, what enabled Netscape to take off was the existence, from the earlier phase, of millions of PC's, many already equipped with modems. Those are the shoulders Netscape stood on. What Netscape did was bring a new killer app—the browser—to this installed base of PC's making the computer and its connectivity inherently more useful for millions of people. (p. 57)

If you don't want to use a direct quotation, you can paraphrase Friedman's information by changing it into your own words. However, in paraphrasing, you need to be careful that you do not commit **plagiarism** by using language and/or sentence structures that are too close to the original. The following paraphrase uses language that too closely mimics the original.

Faulty Paraphrase

> In *The World Is Flat* (2005), Thomas L. Friedman looks back to 1995 and notes that what enabled Netscape to take off when it went public was that it could stand on the shoulders of the millions of already existing PC's, many already equipped with modems. Its new killer app—the browser—helped millions of people make connecting more useful. (57)

In contrast, the following paraphrase is entirely in the writer's own words and sentence structures:

Acceptable Paraphrase

> In *The World Is Flat* (2005), Thomas L. Friedman looks back to 1995 and notes that Netscape could make a significant impact on the emerging global economy when it went public because of its browser. When Netscape brought this new software application—the browser—to the users of modem-enhanced PC's, it made those connected computers much more useful. (57)

Suppose you were writing about the film *Harry Potter and the Sorcerer's Stone* and wanted to cite ideas from Roger Ebert's review of it. Here is a paragraph from Ebert's review:

> *Harry Potter and the Sorcerer's Stone* is a red-blooded adventure movie, dripping with atmosphere, filled with the gruesome and the sublime, and surprisingly faithful to the novel. A lot of things could have gone wrong, and

> none of them have: Chris Columbus' movie is an enchanting classic that does full justice to a story that was a daunting challenge. The novel by J. K. Rowling was muscular and vivid, and the danger was that the movie would make things too cute and cuddly. It doesn't. Like an Indiana Jones for younger viewers, it tells a rip-roaring tale of supernatural adventure, where colorful and eccentric characters alternate with scary stuff like a three-headed dog, a pit of tendrils known as the Devil's Snare and a two-faced immortal who drinks unicorn blood. Scary, yes, but not too scary—just scary enough.

Faulty Paraphrase

A faulty paraphrase would mimic Ebert's sentence structure in the original text. Here is an excerpt from Ebert's paragraph:

> The novel by J. K. Rowling was muscular and vivid, and the danger was that the movie would make things too cute and cuddly. It doesn't.

A poor paraphrase would look similar:

> According to Ebert, the novel by J. K. Rowling was brawny and brilliant, and the danger was that the movie would make things too delightful and cuddly. It does not.

The following acceptable version conveys Ebert's idea but with a different sentence structure.

Acceptable Paraphrase

> According to Ebert, the film avoids the trap of making Harry's story too cutesy while remaining true to the novel's power.

Summaries

When you include a **summary** of your source's ideas, you condense the material presented by another author into a briefer form. While similar to paraphrasing, summaries condense information into a substantially smaller number of words. You might summarize a paragraph or even a page of material in only a sentence or two. To summarize a chapter, you might need several paragraphs. A summary of a larger work might be several pages in length. Once again, however, the summary must be entirely in your own words and sentence structures to avoid plagiarizing the original. Here are unacceptable and acceptable summaries of the Ebert passage.

Unacceptable Summary

> Roger Ebert notes that the film is an adventure movie with lots of atmosphere and that it does full justice to Rowling's challenging novel. Colorful and eccentric characters alternate with scenes that are scary but not too scary.

Acceptable Summary

> In Roger Ebert's opinion, the film is a faithful rendition of the first Harry Potter novel, a rousing adventure story in the tradition of the *Indiana Jones* films. It offers a not overly frightening experience along with Rowling's "colorful and eccentric characters."

For more on writing a summary, see Chapter 2, pages 28–30.

Note that if you use phrases from the original in your summary, you should enclose them in quotation marks.

Syntheses

As noted on pages 30–32 in Chapter 2, **synthesis** is the act of blending information from multiple sources and melding it with the writer's own ideas. A synthesis could involve quoting, paraphrasing, and/or summarizing source material. To avoid plagiarism when synthesizing source material, you need to clarify which ideas are taken from which sources and which ideas are your own. For example, in the opening paragraph of his essay on gangs and adolescent behavior, writer Aaron Zook is reviewing some of the literature on the topic:

> Since the early 1920s, researchers have closely studied the relationship between street gangs and violent crime from a variety of perspectives: crimino-logical, sociological, and psychological (Thabit, 2005). Whatever the underlying causes for gang membership, the results seem clear; members of street gangs admit to a far greater rate of serious crime, and to far more severe acts of violence (Penly Hall, Thornberry, & Lizotte, 2006) than non-gang members of the same age, race, and socioeconomic background (Battin-Pearson, Thornberry, Hawkins, & Krohn, 1998). According to the Web site Safeyouth.org (n.d.), gang violence is certainly cause for concern:
>
> > Gang members are responsible for much of the serious violence in the United States. . . . Teens that are gang members are much more likely than other teens to commit serious and violent crimes. For example, a

> survey in Denver found that while only 14% of teens were gang members, they were responsible for committing 89% of the serious violent crimes.
>
> Many researchers have therefore come to the conclusion that gangs necessarily cause violence and deviant behavior.

Notice how Zook uses parenthetical citations to identify the sources for information that he has taken from multiple sources. Notice too in the last sentence how Zook uses his own words to draw a conclusion from the material that he summarized and quoted earlier in the paragraph. However, if his sentence had read, "Many researchers have therefore come to the conclusion that gang members are responsible for much of the serious violence in the United States," he would have been plagiarizing because the sentence includes exact words and phrases from the original block quotation.

UNACCEPTABLE SYNTHESIS

> Many researchers have therefore come to the conclusion that gang members are responsible for much of the serious violence in the United States.

ACCEPTABLE SYNTHESIS

> Many researchers have therefore come to the conclusion that gangs necessarily cause violence and deviant behavior.

or

> Many researchers have therefore come to the conclusion that "gang members are responsible for much of the serious violence in the United States."

Ellipses

If you decide that a quotation is too long and want to condense it, you can do so by placing an ellipsis (three periods with a space between each) in place of the omitted words. If the ellipsis occurs at the end of the sentence, you will need to place the sentence's period preceding the first ellipsis with a space between the first ellipsis point and the period of the sentence. Make sure when you use an ellipsis that you do not change the meaning of the original quotation. For example, compare the original quotation from Marshall McLuhan and the condensed version:

ORIGINAL QUOTATION

> As the alphabet neutralized the divergencies of primitive cultures by translation of their complexities into simple visual terms, so representative money reduced the moral values in the nineteenth century.

CONDENSED VERSION

> In *Understanding Media*, Marshall McLuhan compares the visual technology inherent in the alphabet with money, saying, "As the alphabet neutralized the divergencies of primitive cultures . . . so representative money reduced moral values in the nineteenth century" (141).

Brackets

If you find that something within a quotation is not clear and you need to add information so that your readers will understand it better, you can do so by using square brackets [ ]:

> In their book *Freakonomics*, Steven D. Leavitt and Stephen J. Dubner confirm that often commonly held stereotypes seem to apply to reality:
>
> > For instance, men [on online dating sites] who say they want a long-term relationship do much better than men looking for an occasional lover. But women [on the same sites] looking for an occasional lover do great. (82)

MLA Documentation Style

There are two components to MLA style: parenthetical in-text citations and a works-cited list that appears at the end of the paper. Every source cited within the body of the paper appears in the works-cited list.

MLA Style: In-Text Citation

mhconnectcomposition.com
When to cite QL20003

In MLA style, parenthetical in-text citations are used in conjunction with the list of works cited to give readers the information they would need to locate the sources that you have quoted, paraphrased, or summarized. The intent in MLA style is to give only as much information in the text as the reader needs to find the detailed bibliographical information in the list of works cited—generally, the author and the page number of the material cited. The following are examples of how to cite different types of sources within your text using MLA style, starting with the most basic citation: a work with one author.

A WORK WITH ONE AUTHOR

Suppose that you quote from page 282 of Deborah Tannen's *You Just Don't Understand: Women and Men in Conversation*, published in 1990. In MLA style, your in-text citation would be "(Tannen 282)." MLA in-text citations do not include punctuation, and the page number is given simply as a number.

The parenthetical citation is placed directly after the cited material. Here is an example using a block quotation in MLA style:

connect
mhconnectcomposition.com
Parenthetical citation QL20004

> In talking about gender differences, this phenomenon is noted:
>
> > Complementary schismogenesis commonly sets in when women and men have divergent sensitivities and hypersensitivities. For example, a man who fears losing freedom pulls away at the first sign he interprets as an attempt to "control" him, but pulling away is just the signal that sets off alarms for the woman who fears losing intimacy. (Tannen 282)

In this example, the author's name is not mentioned in the text that precedes the quotation. When the author's name is mentioned in the preceding sentence, however, the parenthetical citation includes only the page number, as in the following example:

> Deborah Tannen, a researcher who has written extensively about the language differences of men and women, notes, "Understanding each other's styles, and the motives behind them, is a first move in breaking this destructive cycle" (282).

If a parenthetical citation follows a quotation that ends a sentence, place the period after the parenthetical citation. However, if the quotation appears as a block (see above), place the period before the citation.

A WORK WITH MORE THAN ONE AUTHOR

Use all the authors' last names. If there are more than three authors, you can use the first author's last name with *et al.* following it.

> Glassick, Huber, and Maeroff state that "teaching, too, must in the end be judged not merely by process but by results, however eloquent a teacher's performance" (29).

> Ultimately, it is the results of teaching, not the method or the quality of the teacher's performance, that we must evaluate (Glassick, Huber, and Maeroff 29).

TWO OR MORE WORKS BY THE SAME AUTHOR

If you are citing ideas from two or more works by the same author, use the title of the work to distinguish which source you are citing.

It is important to establish good relations with the people you work with by engaging in non-work related conversation. Both men and women do so, but the subjects of their conversations differ (Tannen, *Talking from 9 to 5* 64).

AN UNKNOWN AUTHOR

Use a shortened version of the title.

Employees of Google believe their corporate culture to be antithetical to that of Microsoft ("Google" 15).

A GOVERNMENT AGENCY OR A CORPORATE AUTHOR

Use the name of the organization.

Policy makers and citizens are warned that "Arizona is not positioned well to attract and keep the knowledge workers it needs" (Morrison Institute 6).

AN ANTHOLOGIZED WORK

Cite the author of the anthologized piece, not the editor of the collection. However, give the page numbers used in the collection.

John Perry Barlow asks the important question: "The enigma is this: If our property can be infinitely reproduced and instantaneously distributed all over the planet without cost, without our knowledge, without its even leaving our possession, how can we protect it?" (319).

A SECONDARY SOURCE

Whenever possible, cite the original source. However, if you do need to use a quotation from a secondary source, use *qtd. in*.

Jonathan Shaw muses, "I don't think mankind is ready, spiritually or mentally, for the transformations it's undergoing in the technological era: tattooing is a mute plea for a return to human values" (qtd. in Dery 284).

AN ONLINE SOURCE

Unless your source has some kind of numbering system or is a pdf file, you will not usually be able to provide page numbers for your quotation or paraphrase. Give the author or, if the author's name is not available, the title of the online work you are citing.

According to Christopher Beam, there are a number of methods that Internet service providers can use to block Web sites if a government orders them to do so.

MLA Style: Constructing a List of Works Cited

Because the list of works cited at the end of your paper is intended to work together with your in-text citations, it includes only the sources you cite within your text, not the works that you read but did not cite. The list should be double-spaced, and its entries are listed alphabetically by the last name of the first author. The first line of each entry is even with the left margin; any subsequent lines are indented by one-half inch.

connect
mhconnectcomposition.com
MLA and APA parenthetical citation overview QL20005

All entries in the list are formatted following the same rules. In the following pages, you will find, for each common type of entry, a sample entry for a work in MLA style and, on pages 599–608, for many of the same works in APA style. First, though, to see some important differences between the two styles, consider these pairs of entries:

MLA Paivio, Allan. *Mental Representations.* New York: Oxford UP, 1986. Print.

APA Paivio, A. (1986). *Mental representations.* New York: Oxford University Press.

MLA Miller, George A. "The Magical Number Seven, Plus or Minus Two: Some Limits on Our Capacity for Processing Information." *Psychological Review* 63 (1956): 81–97. Print.

APA Miller, G. A. (1956). The magical number seven, plus or minus two: Some limits on our capacity for processing information. *Psychological Review, 63,* 81–97.

Notice in particular the following:

- In both styles, entries consist of three essential pieces of information, separated by periods: author, source, and publication information for the source (place of publication and publisher for the book; journal title and volume number for the article). Note the difference in the placement of information: In APA style, the year of publication follows the author's name rather than coming later in the entry as it does in MLA style.
- In MLA style, authors' first and middle names are given in full if that is how they are given in the source; in APA style, only initials are given.
- In MLA style, all major words in titles are capitalized; in APA style, only the first word, words following a colon, and names are capitalized in the

FIGURE 20.1 MLA Style: A Flowchart for Determining the Model Works-Cited Entry You Need

Is My Source a Complete Print Book or Part of a Print Book?

No ↓	Yes, go to the next question below.	Go to this entry.
	Is it a book with only one author?	1
	Are you citing more than one book by this author?	2
	Is it a book with multiple authors?	3
	Is the book by an organization of some kind?	4
	Is the author unknown or unnamed?	5
	Does the book also have a translator?	11
	Is it a later publication or edition of the book?	6, 7
	Is it a multivolume work or part of a multivolume work?	13
	Is it part of a series?	14
	Does the book have an editor or a translator?	8, 11
	Is the book an edited collection or anthology?	8
	Is it a work in a collection or anthology?	9
	Is it an introduction, a preface, a foreword, or an afterword?	12
	Is it an entry in a dictionary or reference work?	22
	Is it a published interview?	10

Is My Source from a Print Periodical Such as a Journal, a Magazine, or a Newspaper?

No ↓	Yes, go to the next question below.	Go to this entry.
	Is it from a scholarly journal?	
	Do the journal's page numbers continue from one issue to the next?	15
	Does each issue start with page 1?	16
	Is it from a magazine?	17
	Is it a review?	20
	Is it from a newspaper?	18
	Is it an editorial?	19
	Is it a letter to the editor?	21

connect
mhconnectcomposition.com
MLA Style: Determining the model works-cited entry you need QL20006

titles of books and articles. All major words are capitalized in the titles of periodicals, however.

- In both styles, titles of books and periodicals are given in italics. In MLA style, titles of articles are enclosed in quotation marks; in APA style, they are not.
- In MLA style, the medium of the source is identified—for example, Print, DVD, or Web Performance.

The section that follows includes model entries for different types of print and nonprint sources in MLA style. Figure 20.1 provides you with a flowchart that will help you find the model entry that is closest to the source that you need to cite.

Is My Source a Print Source but Not from a Journal, a Magazine, or a Newspaper?

No	Yes, go to the next question below.	Go to this entry.
↓	Is it an entry in a dictionary or reference work?	22
	Is it a government document?	23
	Is it a pamphlet?	24
	Is it the proceedings from a conference?	25
	Is it an unpublished doctoral dissertation?	26
	Is it a published or an unpublished letter?	27
	Is it a map or chart?	28
	Is it a cartoon?	29
	Is it an advertisement?	30

Is My Source a Nonprint Source from an Online Subscription Database or the World Wide Web?

No	Yes, go to the next question below.	Go to this entry.
↓	Is it a professional or personal Web site?	31
	Is it an article?	
	Is it a scholarly article retrieved from a database?	32
	Is it an article from an online journal?	34
	Is it an article from an online magazine?	35
	Is it an article from an online newspaper?	36
	Is it an online book?	33
	Is it a blog entry?	37
	Is it an entry on a wiki?	38
	Is it a posting to an electronic forum?	39
	Is it an e-mail message?	40

Is My Source a Nonprint Source That Is Not Published Online?

No	Yes, go to the next question below.	Go to this entry.
↓	Is it a television or radio program?	41
	Is it an audio recording?	42
	Is it a film, video recording, or DVD?	43
	Is it a nonperiodical publication on CD-ROM?	44
	Is it a personal, e-mail, or telephone interview?	45
	Is it an oral presentation?	46
	Is it a performance?	47
	Is it a work of art?	48

Consult with Your Instructor about How to Cite Your Source.

mhconnectcomposition.com

MLA Style: The parts of a works-cited entry QL20007

PRINT DOCUMENTS

Books

The basic items in an entry for a book are the author's name or authors' names, the title, and the publication information, consisting of the place of publication, publisher, date of publication, and medium. See Figure 20.2 for guidelines on where to find the elements of a works-cited entry for a book in MLA style.

1. Book with one author: The most basic form includes the author's name, the title of the book, in italics, and the publication information.

publication information
author — title — city — publisher — date

Gould, Stephen Jay. *The Mismeasure of Man.* New York: Norton, 1981. Print.

2. Two books by the same author: In MLA style, the author's name appears only in the first entry. For all subsequent entries, three hyphens are used instead of the name. The entries are listed in alphabetical order according to title.

Tannen, Deborah. *Talking from 9 to 5.* New York: Morrow, 1994. Print.

- - -. *You Just Don't Understand: Women and Men in Conversation.* New York: Ballantine, 1990. Print.

3. Book with multiple authors: In MLA style, only the first author's name is inverted; the other authors' names are given first name first. MLA style uses *and* before the last author's name. In MLA style, if a book has more than three authors, you may give all the names or give the name of the first author followed by *et al.* (For an example of the use of *et al.*, see no. 8.)

Covey, Stephen R., A. Roger Merrill, and Rebecca R. Merrill. *First Things First.* New York: Simon, 1994. Print.

4. Book by a corporate entity or organization:

Adobe Systems Inc. *Adobe Acrobat 5.0: Getting Started.* San Jose: Adobe, 2001. Print.

5. Book by an unknown author:

The Chicago Manual of Style: The Essential Guide for Writers, Editors, and Publishers. 15th ed. Chicago: Chicago UP, 2003. Print.

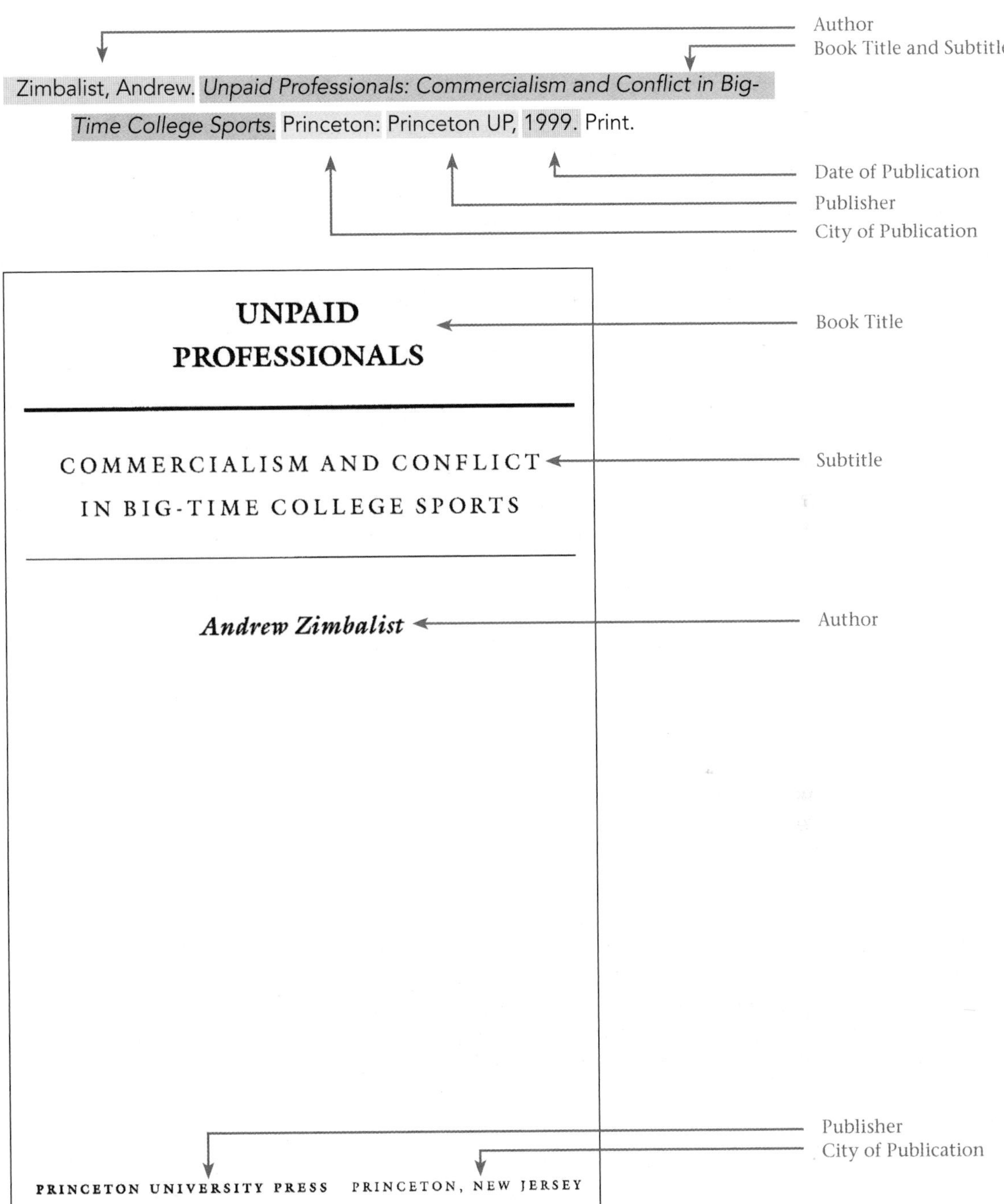

FIGURE 20.2 The Parts of a Works-Cited Entry for a Book in MLA Style
(continued page 576)

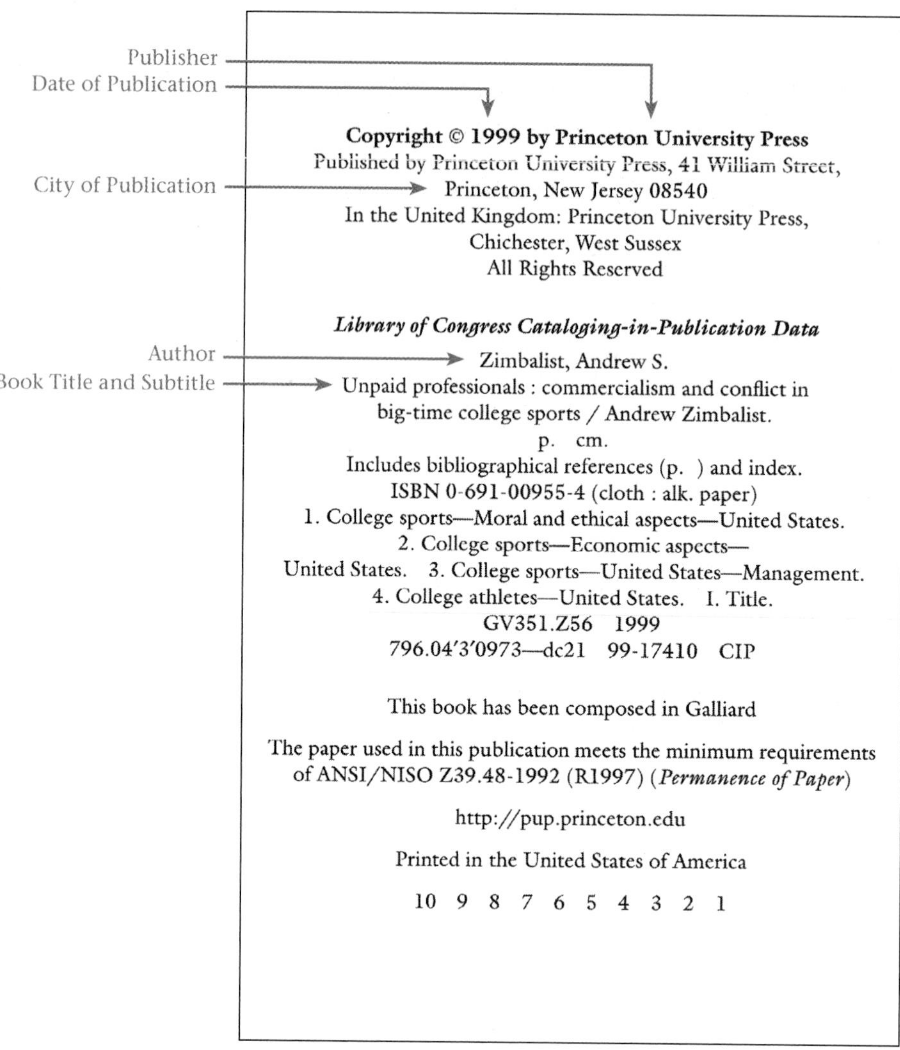

Copyright © 1999 by Princeton University Press
Published by Princeton University Press, 41 William Street,
Princeton, New Jersey 08540
In the United Kingdom: Princeton University Press,
Chichester, West Sussex
All Rights Reserved

Library of Congress Cataloging-in-Publication Data
Zimbalist, Andrew S.
Unpaid professionals : commercialism and conflict in
big-time college sports / Andrew Zimbalist.
p. cm.
Includes bibliographical references (p.) and index.
ISBN 0-691-00955-4 (cloth : alk. paper)
1. College sports—Moral and ethical aspects—United States.
2. College sports—Economic aspects—
United States. 3. College sports—United States—Management.
4. College athletes—United States. I. Title.
GV351.Z56 1999
796.04'3'0973—dc21 99-17410 CIP

This book has been composed in Galliard

The paper used in this publication meets the minimum requirements of ANSI/NISO Z39.48-1992 (R1997) (*Permanence of Paper*)

http://pup.princeton.edu

Printed in the United States of America

10 9 8 7 6 5 4 3 2 1

FIGURE 20.2 Continued

6. Republished book: Including the original date of publication is optional in MLA style. If you do include this date, place it immediately following the title.

Dickens, Charles. *Hard Times*. 1854. Ed. David Craig. Baltimore: Penguin, 1969. Print.

7. Book in a later edition:

Corbett, Edward P. J. *Classical Rhetoric for the Modern Student*. 3rd ed. New York: Oxford UP, 1990. Print.

8. Edited collection:

Inman, James A., and Donna N. Sewell, eds. *Taking Flight with Owls: Examining Electronic Writing Center Work*. Mahwah: Erlbaum, 2000. Print.

Harrington, Susanmarie, et al., eds. *The Outcomes Book: Debate and Consensus after the WPA Outcomes Statement*. Logan: Utah State UP, 2005. Print.

9. Work in a collection or an anthology: Include the full range of pages for the work you are citing, not just the pages you used or quoted from.

Anson, Chris M., and Richard Jewell. "Shadows of the Mountain." *Moving a Mountain: Transforming the Role of Contingent Faculty in Composition Studies and Higher Education*. Ed. Eileen E. Schell and Patricia Lambert Stock. Urbana: NCTE, 2001. 47–75. Print.

10. Published interview:

Hawisher, Gail. "Making the Map: An Interview with Gail Hawisher." *Feminist Cyberscapes: Mapping Gendered Academic Spaces*. Interview with Kristine Blair and Pamela Takayoshi. Ed. Kristine Blair and Pamela Takayoshi. Stamford: Ablex, 1999. 177–91. Print.

11. Translation:

Eliade, Mircea. *The Sacred and the Profane: The Nature of Religion*. Trans. Willard R. Trask. New York: Harcourt, 1959. Print.

12. Introduction, preface, foreword, or afterword:

Burns, Hugh. Foreword. *Technology and Literacy in the Twenty-First Century: The Importance of Paying Attention*. By Cynthia L. Selfe. Carbondale: Southern Illinois UP, 1999. ix–xvii. Print.

13. Multivolume work: If you have used more than one volume of a multivolume work, note the total number of volumes in the work after the title or editor information. (Refer to the actual volume and page numbers used in your in-text citation).

Campbell, Joseph. *The Masks of God*. 4 vols. New York: Viking, 1972. Print.

If you have used only one volume of a multivolume work, cite only the volume you have used.

Elias, Norbert. *The History of Manners.* Vol. 1. New York: Pantheon, 1982. Print.

14. Book in a series: If you are using a book that is part of a series, include the title of the series with no italics or quotation marks after the publication information and medium. Include the number of the series if it is present.

Shortand, Michael, ed. *Science and Nature: Essays in the History of the Environmental Sciences.* Oxford: British Society for the History of Science, 1993. Print. BSHS Monograph Ser. 8.

Periodical Articles

The basic items in an entry for a periodical article are the author's name or authors' names, the title of the article, and information about the publication in which the article appeared, including its title, volume number (if applicable), date, page range, and publication medium. See Figure 20.3 for guidelines on where to find the elements of a works-cited entry for a periodical article in MLA style.

15. Article in a scholarly journal with continuous pagination: The volume number follows the title.

authors — title of article

Thayer, Alexander, and Beth E. Kolko. "Localization of Digital Games: The Process of Blending for the Global Games Market."

title of periodical — volume no. and date — page range — medium

Technical Communication 51 (2004): 477–88. Print.

16. Article in a scholarly journal that is paginated by issue: When an article is from a journal that restarts its page numbers with each issue, the issue number follows the volume number and a period.

Howard, Rebecca Moore. "Power Revisited: Or, How We Became a Department." *Journal of the Council of Writing Program Administrators* 16.3 (1993): 37–49. Print.

17. Magazine article: Magazines may or may not include volume and issue numbers. In any case, in MLA style, volume numbers are not given. Instead, dates are provided. If magazines are published weekly or biweekly, the day is included along with the month, which is abbreviated. If the entire article does not appear on consecutive pages, give the first page number and a plus sign (+).

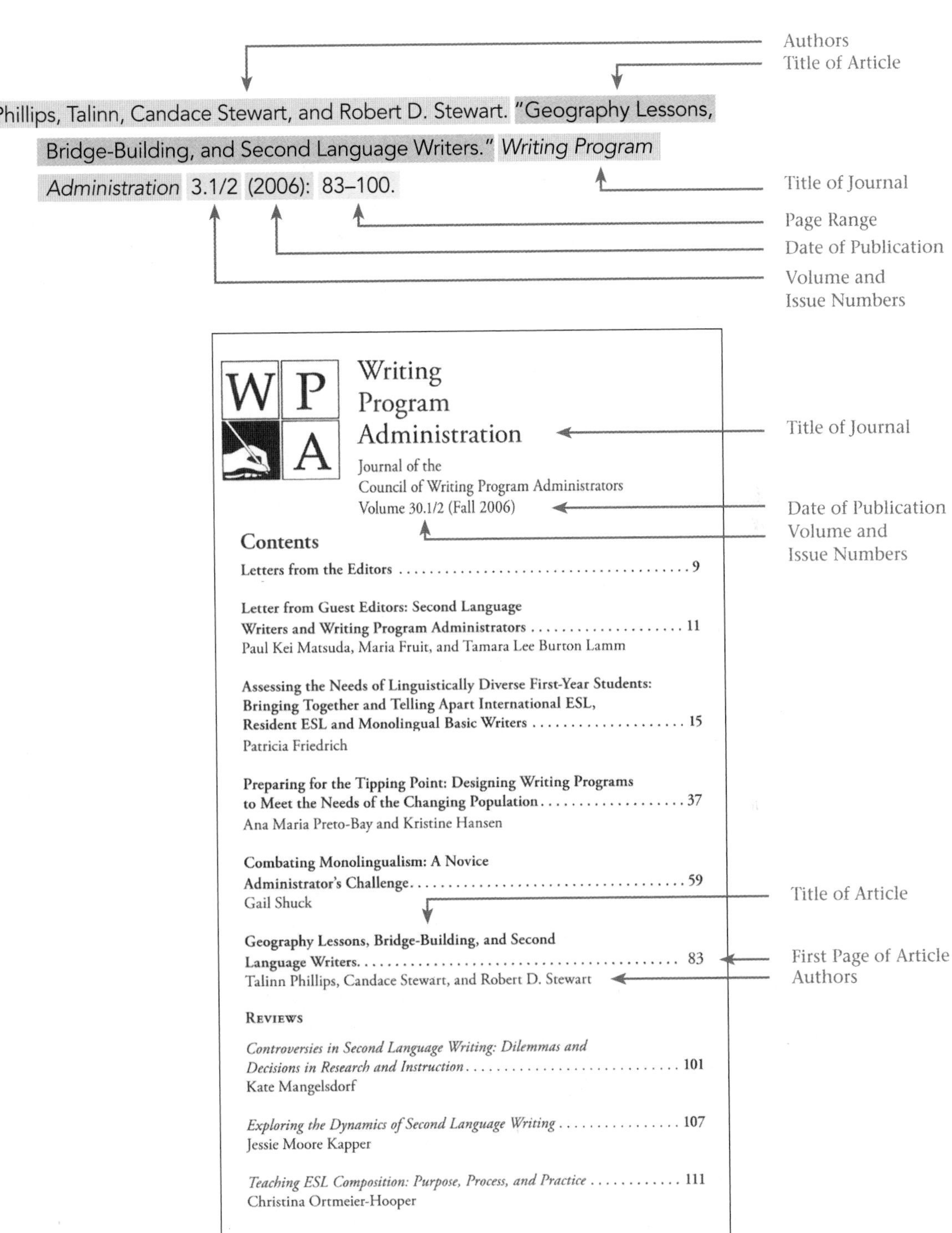

FIGURE 20.3 The Parts of a Works-Cited Entry for a Journal Article in MLA Style

Foust, Dean, Michael Eidem, and Brian Bremner. "AFLAC: Its Ducks Are Not in a Row." *BusinessWeek* 2 Feb. 2004: 52–53. Print.

Wilson, Chauncey E. "Usability and User Experience Design: The Next Decade." *Intercom* 1 Jan. 2005: 6–9. Print.

18. Newspaper article: Entries for newspaper articles include the edition, when it is given (because different editions print different items), along with the date of publication and the section and page numbers. You should include the city of origin of a local newspaper within square brackets if it is not part of the title of the newspaper (for example, *Capital Times* [Madison]). You should also eliminate *The* at the beginning of the names of newspapers. When articles appear on discontinuous pages, give the first page number and a plus sign (+).

Fatsis, Stefan. "A More Modern Masters." *Wall Street Journal* 9 Apr. 2002: B1+. Print.

19. Editorial: If an editorial is unsigned, use the form below. For signed editorials, begin the cite with the author's name.

"Moral Scoreboard." Editorial. *Arizona Republic* [Phoenix] 18 Feb. 2004: B10. Print.

20. Review: If there is no author for the review, alphabetize it by the title of the review. If the review also has no title, alphabetize by the title of what is being reviewed, even though your entry will begin with *Rev. of.* When citing a review, use the format appropriate for its place of publication.

Jablonski, Jeffrey. Rev. of *The New Careers: Individual Action and Economic Change*, by Michael B. Arthur, Kerr Inkson, and Judith K. Pringle. *Technical Communication Quarterly* 12 (2003): 230–34. Print.

21. Letter to the editor:

Rosati, Colette. Letter. *Arizona Republic* [Phoenix] 18 Feb. 2004: B10. Print.

Other Print Sources

22. Entry in a dictionary or reference work: In MLA style, entries in reference works are treated like entries in collections. If the author is known, begin with the author. Otherwise, start with the title of the entry. If the reference work is commonly known and regularly updated, you can simply give the edition and the date of publication.

"Express Mail." *Merriam-Webster's Collegiate Dictionary.* 11th ed. 2003. Print.

Pfeiffer, Robert H. "Sumerian Poetry." *Princeton Encyclopedia of Poetry and Poetics*. Ed. Alex Preminger. Enlarged ed. Princeton: Princeton UP, 1974. Print.

23. Government document: When the author of the document is not known, the agency is given as the author. Most publications from the U.S. federal government are published by the Government Printing Office (GPO). Give GPO as the publisher unless the title page indicates otherwise, as in the citation below.

United States. Dept. of Health and Human Services. National Institutes of Health. *Toxicology and Carcinogenesis Studies of Resorcinal (CAS No. 108-46-3) in F344/N Rats and B6C3F$_1$ Mice (Gavage Studies)*. Research Triangle Park: National Institutes of Health, 1992. Print.

24. Pamphlet or brochure: Pamphlets and brochures are short documents and are usually held together by staples rather than a more formal binding. They are treated as books.

A Guide to Visiting the Lands of Many Nations & to the Lewis & Clark Bicentennial. St. Louis: National Council of the Lewis & Clark Bicentennial, 2004. Print.

25. Published conference proceedings: The entire collection is treated as a book. Individual articles are treated as though they were in a collection by different authors.

Buchanan, Elizabeth, and Nancy Morris. "Designing a Web-Based Program in Clinical Bioethics: Strategies and Procedures." *Proceedings of the 15th Annual Conference on Distance Teaching & Learning*. Madison: U of Wisconsin, 1999. 65–70. Print.

26. Unpublished doctoral dissertation:

Edminster, Judith R. "The Diffusion of New Media Scholarship: Power, Innovation, and Resistance in Academe." Diss. U of South Florida, 2002. Print.

27. Letter: If the letter you are citing has been published, treat it as you would a work in an anthology, but also include the date.

Hemingway, Ernest. "To Maxwell Perkins." 7 February 1936. *Ernest Hemingway: Selected Letters, 1917–1961*. Ed. Carlos Baker. New York: Scribner, 1981. 437–38. Print.

If the letter you are citing is a personal letter, start with the writer's name followed by "Letter to the author" and the date.

Morris, Patricia M. Letter to the author. 28 Dec. 2005. MS.

28. Map or chart:

San Francisco Bay. Map. San Francisco: California State Automobile Association, 2004. Print.

29. Cartoon:

Benson, Steve. Cartoon. *Arizona Republic* [Phoenix] 28 Dec. 2006: 17. Print.

30. Advertisement: Identify the product or company being advertised. Give the appropriate publication information for the medium where the ad appeared.

Bristol-Myers Squibb. Advertisement. *Time*. 25 Dec. 2006: 81. Print.

ONLINE SOURCES

Because online sources change constantly, citing them is more complicated than citing print sources. In addition to the author's name (if known) and the title of the document and overall Web site, provide publication information (if known, such as the sponsoring organization and the date the site was last updated), the publication medium, and the date the document was accessed. Because URLs change often, they should be included at the end of citations only when readers might have trouble locating the document using author and title searches. When the document you are citing has a print as well as an electronic version, you may choose to provide publication information for both versions. See Figure 20.4 for guidelines on where to find the elements of a works-cited entry for an article accessed from an online database.

Digital Literacy

Inserting URLs in Citations

MLA style calls for placing URLs inside angle brackets. However, when you type a period after the closing angle bracket, your word processor's "auto-correct" function will probably eliminate both angle brackets, so you will have to go back and retype them. To avoid having to do this step each time, modify your word processor's auto-correct settings so that they do not include angle brackets. Try to avoid breaking URLs across lines; if you must break them, break them only after a slash (/).

31. Basic professional or personal Web site:

American Medical Association. Home page. AMA. 2008. Web. 17 Feb. 2008.

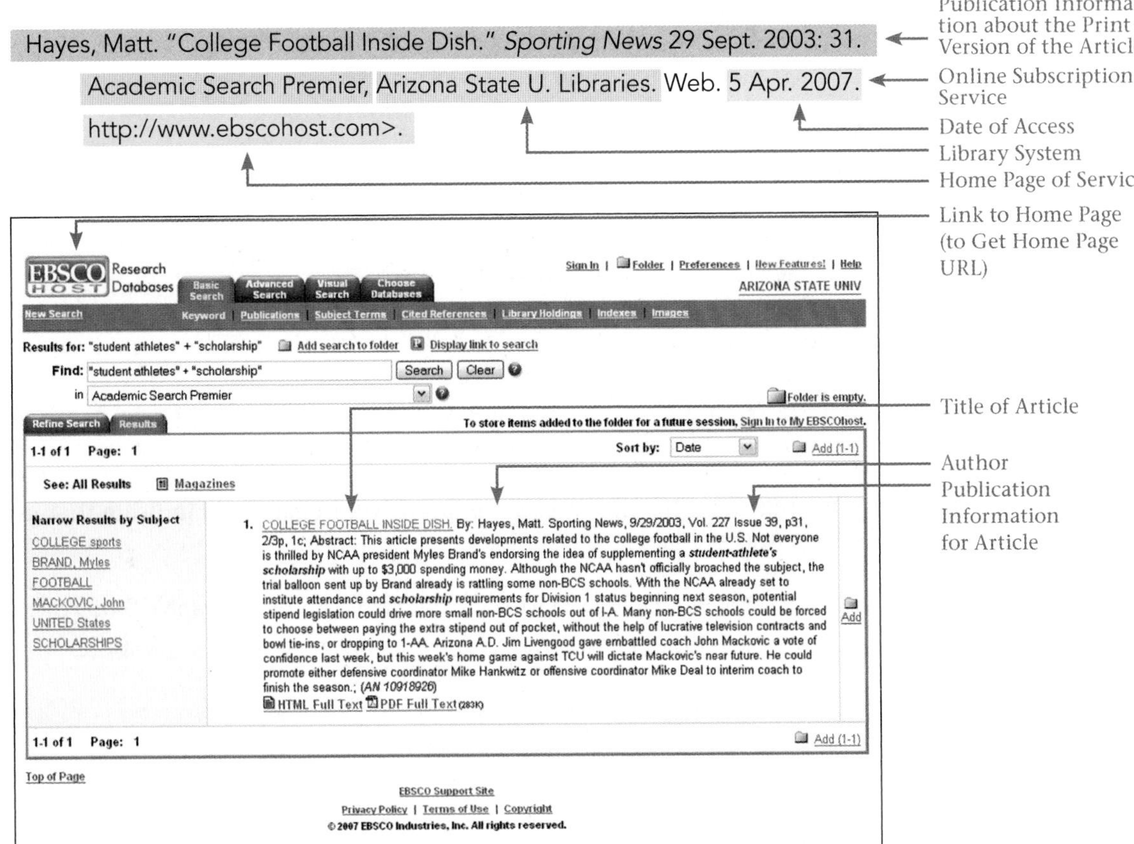

FIGURE 20.4 The Parts of a Works-Cited Entry for a Periodical Article Accessed from an Online Subscription Database

32. Scholarly article retrieved from a database:

author — title of article

Selber, Stuart A. "Beyond Skill Building: Challenges Facing Technical Communication Teachers in the Computer Age." *Technical*

title of journal — volume no., date, page range — database

Communication Quarterly 3 (1994): 365–91. *EBSCOHost.*

medium — date of access

Web. 18 Feb. 2004.

Bennet-Kastor, Tina. "Spelling Abilities of University Students in Developmental Writing Classes." *Journal of College Reading and Learning*, 35.1 (2004): 67–82. ERIC. 30 March 2007.

33. Online book:

author title of the online book title of the web site

Howells, William Dean. *Familiar Spanish Travels. Project Gutenberg.*

sponsoring agency date site was updated medium

Project Gutenberg Literacy Archive Foundation. 2008. Web.

date accessed

18 Feb. 2008. <http://www.gutenberg.nt>

URL included because "gutenberg.com" an obvious guess and similar site would not lead reader to correct site

34. Article from an online journal: When the online article is a digitized version of a print document, include the page numbers that you would find in print. However, if the document appears only in electronic form, page numbers may not exist. In that case, use *n. pg.* in your citation to indicate that no pagination was available.

Salvo, Michael J. "Deafened to Their Demands: An Ethnographic Study of Accommodation." *Kairos* 7.1 (2002): n. pg. 17 Web. Feb. 2004.

35. Article from an online magazine:

Cooper, Matthew, and Karen Tumulty. "Bring on the Cash!" *Time.* 16 Feb. 2004. Web. 17 Feb. 2004.

36. Article from an online newspaper:

Novovitch, Barbara. "It's Home Stupid Home, but the 'Clods' Can Read." *New York Times.* 17 Feb. 2004. Web. 23 Feb. 2005.

37. Blog entry: Use the MLA format for general Web sites. Include the name of the author (bloggers often use pseudonyms); the name of the entry, enclosed in quotation marks; the name of the blog; the date of the entry (if available); the publication medium; and the date of access.

Rice, J. "Network Academics." *Yellow Dog.* 30 Mar. 2007. Web. 31 Mar. 2007.

38. Wiki entry: Include the title of the entry, in quotation marks, the title of the wiki (italicized), the name of the sponsoring agency, the date the page was last updated, the publication medium, and the date you accessed the entry.

"Rhetoric." *Wikipedia*, Wikimedia Foundation. 14 Nov. 2008. Web. 30 Nov. 2008.

39. Posting to an electronic forum such as a mailing list (listserv): This basic format is used for all online forums including Web-based postings.

Peckham, Irvin. "Re: Update on AP and Dual Enrollment." Online posting. *WPA-L*. 21 Sept. 2003. Web. 17 Feb. 2004.

40. E-mail message:

Bernhardt, Stephen B. "RE: Congrats!" E-mail to the author. 17 Feb. 2004.

OTHER NONPRINT SOURCES

41. Television and radio programs: The basic elements for entries that cite radio and television programs include the title of the episode, the title of the program, or series, the name of the network, the call letters and the city of the local station, the broadcast date, and the medium of reception.

"Dogs and More Dogs." *Nova*. Narr. John Lithgow. PBS. KAET, Phoenix. 3 Feb. 2004. Television.

"Scientists Succeed in Cloning Human Embryo." *All Things Considered*. Narr. Joe Palca. NPR. WGBH, Boston, 12 Feb. 2004. Radio.

42. Audio recording: A citation emphasizing a particular song would follow the format below. The cite ends with the medium accessed, such as *CD, LP,* or *Audiocassette.*

Jackson, Alan. "Drive." *Drive*. Arista, 2002. CD.

43. Film, video recording, or DVD: In MLA style, the citation usually starts with the title and the director. The distributor, year of release, and medium are necessary. Other items, such as performers, are optional.

The Lord of the Rings: The Two Towers. Dir. Peter Jackson. Perf. Elijah Wood and Ian McKellan. 2002. New Line Home Entertainment, 2003. DVD.

44. Nonperiodical publication on a CD-ROM:

The OWL Construction and Maintenance Guide. Ed. James A. Inman and Clinton Gardner. Emmitsburg: IWCA, 2002. CD-ROM.

45. Personal, e-mail, or telephone interview: Indicate whether the interview was conducted in person, by e-mail, or by telephone following the name of the person you interviewed.

Schwalm, D. Personal interview. 21 Feb. 2004.

46. Oral presentation:

Russell, David R. "Teacher's Perception of Genre across the Curriculum: Making Classroom/Culture Connections Visible." Conf. on College Composition and Communication Convention. Atlanta Hilton, Atlanta. 26 Mar. 1999. Address.

47. Performance: If you are citing a play, an opera, a concert, or a ballet performance, start with the title, followed by the authors (*By*), and any other pertinent information (such as the director, identified as *Dir.*), the site where performed, the city, and the performance date; also note that it was a *Performance.*

The Norse Family. By Jerry Jones. Dir. Walter Onger. Mesa Performing Arts Center, Mesa. 28 Dec. 2007. Performance.

48. Work of art:

di Chirico, Giorgio. *The Philosopher's Conquest.* 1914. Oil on canvas. Joseph Winterbotham Collection. Art Institute of Chicago.

MLA Style: Sample Student Paper

Follow these guidelines if you are required to use MLA style:

- Note that a separate title page is not required. Instead, on the first page, put your name, your professor's name, the course number, and the date in the upper-left-hand corner, one inch from the top of the page, and follow with the title of your paper. The title should be centered, with major words capitalized (not articles and prepositions), and it should not be underlined or in a special typeface.
- Double-space the entire paper, including the information mentioned above, block quotations, and your list of works cited.
- Leave one-inch margins on all sides.
- Put page numbers in the upper-right-hand corner, one-half inch from the top. Just before each page number, put your last name.
- Indent paragraphs one-half inch from the left-hand margin.
- Begin your list of works cited on a new, consecutively numbered page. Include the title *Works Cited* one inch from the top. Center the title; do not use a special typeface for it.

The student paper that follows, "Money for Nothing," by Jessie Katz, is an example of a paper that uses MLA style.

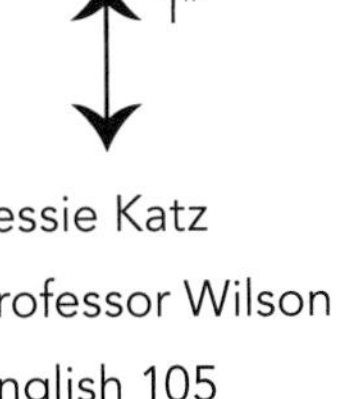

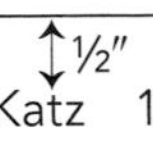

Katz 1

Jessie Katz

Professor Wilson

English 105

February 15, 2006

1″

Student's name.

Professor's name.

Course title.

Date.

Money for Nothing

Title centered; major words capitalized.

For followers of college sports, February is a particularly exciting time of year. With the recent culmination of the football season in the bowl games and the anticipation of upcoming March Madness, all eyes seem glued to ESPN and the sports section of the newspaper as the drama of the season's games, rivalries, and players unfolds. In this charged atmosphere, the public turns its attention toward student-athletes and has ample occasion to contemplate the extraordinary lives that these young people lead. Indeed, some student-athletes apparently have it all: Aside from their national recognition and virtual stardom on and off of their campuses, these athletes also often receive special on-campus housing, state-of-the-art training facilities, and, perhaps most notably, substantial scholarships from their schools.

1″

According to the National Collegiate Athletic Association (NCAA), colleges and universities award $1 billion in athletic scholarships annually to over 126,000 student-athletes (*Online*). NCAA defines athletic aid as "a grant, scholarship, tuition waiver, or other assistance from a college or university that is awarded on the basis of a student's athletic ability"; and a student-athlete is a member of the student body who receives athletic aid from his or her school sometime during his or her freshman year. Regardless of financial need or academic promise, athletic scholarships may cover tuition, fees, room and board, and books. Although nearly all Division I and Division II schools grant athletic scholarships, awarding this type of aid does little to benefit the academic prestige, community, or economic condition of colleges or universities. Giving scholarships based solely on athletic merit may in fact undermine the purpose of institutions of higher education, so colleges and universities need to reexamine the extraordinary amounts of money they currently spend on athletic aid to their students.

Shortened version of title of source enclosed in parentheses.

Thesis statement.

Like any social institution, colleges and universities exist to promote a certain set of goals. Even though mission statements differ from school to school, these

Quotation longer than four lines indented 1 inch and double-spaced. Sentence that introduces it usually ends with colon. Page number given at end.

organizations usually share three major objectives: academic scholarship through instruction and research, service to the university's community, and economic development of the university and its surroundings. For instance, Arizona State University, one of the nation's premier research institutions and member of the PAC-10, has a mission statement typical of a state university. Its *2005–2006 General Catalog* reads as follows:

> Arizona State University's goal is to become a world-class university in a multicampus setting. Its mission is to provide outstanding programs in instruction, research, and creative activity, to promote and support economic development, and to provide service appropriate for the nation, the state of Arizona, and the state's major metropolitan area. To fulfill its mission, ASU places special emphasis on the core disciplines and offers a full range of degree programs—baccalaureate through doctorate, recognizing that it must offer quality programs at all degree levels in a broad range of fundamental fields of inquiry. ASU will continue to dedicate itself to superior instruction; to excellent student performance; to original research, creative endeavor, and scholarly achievement; and to outstanding public service and economic development activities. (23)

Universities, including ASU, promote their goals through their facilities, through their academic and community programs, and especially through their people, the large majority of whom are students. Students represent both a college's main source of income and its main product; and when a school awards a scholarship, it makes an investment in an individual who it feels will make a special contribution to its goals. However, granting athletes aid does not directly contribute to the three primary goals that most colleges and universities share.

Although they are part of institutions that society entrusts with the passage and creation of knowledge through scholarship and research, people often suspect that athletic departments disregard the academic success of student-athletes. Certainly not all student-athletes fit the "dumb jock" stereotype, but an alarming amount of data shows that these individuals fall behind their peers in the classroom. Academic underachievement in student-athletes starts at the recruitment level. To become a member of the NCAA and gain the privilege of practicing and playing sports and obtaining a sports scholarship at a Division I or Division II college, incoming freshmen must graduate from high school, complete at least fourteen core courses (including English, math, and physical and social sciences), have a minimum grade point average of 2.0, and achieve a minimum score of 820 on the SAT (*Online*). While these requirements appear reasonable, NCAA receives too many applicants and has a staff that is too small to carefully examine each potential student's high school record. Thus, academic advisors "cheat the system," as is evidenced in a 1997 scandal in which exceptional high school athletes attended and paid certain high schools that adjusted their deficient standardized test scores (Zimbalist 35). In the most extreme cases of academic under-preparedness, student-athletes enter institutes of "higher" education without basic literacy and math skills. Since NCAA evaluates high school courses rather than college courses, after student-athletes are accepted into college, the regulation of student-athlete academic education becomes less centralized, falling to the universities' athletic departments, which may be motivated to keep student-athletes in the game and not on the academic chopping block. Instances abound in which advisors recommend lenient professors and classes with titles like Leisure and the Quality of Life, Sports Officiating, and Popular Music (Arizona State University). Surely, if and when academic education becomes subordinate to athletics, colleges and universities are counterproductive in funding their student-athletes' "scholarship."

Source cited in parentheses, with page number.

Organization as author.

One of the most disturbing facts concerning athletics in colleges and universities is that a substantial number of athletes are leaving these schools without a degree. In an effort to remedy the academic deficiencies prevalent in college sports, NCAA instituted the Academic Progress Rate (APR) program in 2004 (Bartter 1). Using a complex formula to assign each team an APR, NCAA supports teams with an APR of 925, the minimum value that predicts that the team will graduate at least half of its athletes, and higher. According to a recent study by the University of Central Florida, of the fifty-six Division I football teams selected to play in the 2006 Bowl games, twenty-three teams (including the previous national champion, University of Southern California) received an APR below 925, and twenty-seven teams had a graduation rate under 50%. For all Division I

Katz 4

student-athletes, the U.S. Department of Education reports a 62% graduation rate, although the graduation rates for "the elite sports" (men's basketball and football) are considerably lower, with a basketball graduation rate of 44% and a football graduation rate of 54% (Wolverton). Admittedly, the total student-athlete graduation rate exceeds the graduation rate (60%) of non-athletes, but the success of many of these student-athletes may be bolstered by the financial support they receive. Consequently, a vast sum of the money that colleges give to their athletic students does not support the achievement of a degree, the most important tangible reward that a college or university can give a student. Indeed, unlike academic or music scholarships, which directly contribute to a college degree, athletic scholarships fund a pursuit unrelated, and at times even counterproductive, to what ASU's mission statement calls "fundamental fields of inquiry." Considering the tough odds of playing professional sports (1 in 1,233), student-athletes who do not graduate miss out on the invaluable and marketable skills and knowledge that a degree signifies (Zimbalist 31). Thus, granting athletic scholarships does not necessarily lead to academic returns for the university or the student-athlete.

Katz cites studies to support her thesis about athletic aid.

Despite the academic arguments against granting athletic scholarships, some institutions defend their awarding of financial aid based solely upon athletic performance with the argument that athletics contribute to the community service facet of a college's or university's stated mission. Certainly, a strong athletic program may benefit the community in a variety of healthy ways; a winning team engenders school spirit in its students and faculty, entices the citizens who live near the college to take an active interest in at least one aspect of the school, and earns state and national recognition and exposure, which may attract students and lead to increased enrollment. However, college athletics can be seen as having as many detrimental as positive effects on its community. In some instances, the same school spirit that fills the students with a sense of pride and place leads to very disreputable, unsportsmanlike conduct in the student body. In 2001, about 2,000 University of Arizona basketball fans flooded streets, destroyed cars, and set fires after the NCAA tournament in Minneapolis (Rotstein); and in 2003, University of West Virginia students set over 100 fires and rioted in the streets after their football team defeated Virginia Tech (French 89). The athletes themselves also sometimes engage in activities that harm the communities; underage drinking and drug use occur in the athlete population as they do the general college population, and more serious events (such as allegations of rape against members of the University of Colorado football team in 2001 and the 2005 Baylor University incident in which one basketball player murdered his teammate) become highly publicized scandals. These events weaken considerably the positive impacts college athletics may have on schools' communities and undermine other community services, such as volunteer work, that students without any sort of scholarship perform. While athletics may benefit the community in many ways, they also have too many harmful effects on the community for colleges to justify the current levels of spending that many of them devote to athletic scholarships.

Katz responds to counter-argument about possible benefits of student athletics.

Perhaps the most common justification for granting student-athletes athletic scholarships is that college athletics is a major source of revenue for institutes of higher learning: through scholarships, athletes are allowed a portion of the money that they bring to their schools. This justification operates on the assumption that athletics do indeed attract capital to colleges and universities; yet an increasing amount of evidence shows that athletics departments actually cause a substantial deficit to the institutions that house them. The financial information from college athletics departments can be very misleading: in 1994, NCAA reported that Division I-A athletics programs earned an average of about $13,632,000 and spent about $12,972,000, yielding an apparent profit of $660,000 (French 80). These numbers, though, did not account for the fact that some universities subsidized their athletic departments. If the direct transfers to athletics programs from their universities that year were subtracted from the average earnings, the result would reveal that these programs actually had a $174,000 deficit. In fact, some athletics departments had so little money that they could not even afford to fund their athletes' scholarships; instead, there is evidence of some universities dipping into the scholarship funds reserved for students with demonstrated financial need or academic merit (French 82).

Another misconception about athletic funding is that winning teams attract more monetary gifts from donors and alumni. A study by Cornell University

Katz 6

Information from authoritative source introduced by signal phrase within text.

Katz responds to two additional counterarguments; responds to second counterargument by citing study and quoting expert.

Secondary source introduced in text, with *qtd. in* used in parenthetical citation.

management and economics professor Robert Frank, discussed in a 2004 *Sports Illustrated* article, demonstrates that "the presumed indirect benefits of sports, such as the spike in alumni giving and an enlarged applicant pool, are by all indications minimal." In fact, Frank discovered that "the revenues needed to compete have escalated to the point where the average big-time athletic program runs in the red. And when success brings a spike in donations, the money is routinely earmarked for the athletic program—not the general university fund" (qtd. in Fish). Therefore, even if a profit from student athletics is earned, universities usually cannot and do not use the money to advance their missions. Southern Methodist University President Gerald Turner confirms these conclusions: "I've been a university president now for about 20 years and I have never found any relationship between alumni giving to academic programs and the success of the athletic program" (qtd. in Fish). When colleges and universities award athletic scholarships, it may be less of a sound financial investment than boosters hope.

Without a doubt, athletics have an important entertainment role in a university setting. Yet, behind the Rose Bowl and March Madness, athletics programs are not as beneficial to their scholarly institutions as they may seem. It's time for colleges and universities to concentrate on their central missions—to promote academic scholarship, service to the university's community, and economic development of the university and its surroundings—instead of justifying the exorbitant expenditures of funds on programs that are more popular than they are useful to the school, the student, and the community at large.

Katz 7

Works Cited

Arizona State University. Office of the Executive Vice President and Provost of the University. *Arizona State University: 2005–2006 General Catalog.* Tempe: Academic and Administrative Documents, 2005. Print.

Bartter, Jessica. "Institute Study by Lapchick Looks at APR Rates and Graduation Rates for 2005–06 Bowl-Bound Teams." 5 Dec. 2005. Devos Sport Business Management Program, College of Business Administration, University of Central Florida. Web. 8 Feb. 2006.

Fish, Mike. "Separate Worlds: Studies Show Big-Time Athletics Don't Impact Academic Donations." *Sports Illustrated.* 14 Sept. 2004. Web. 9 Feb. 2006.

French, Peter A. *Ethics and College Sports: Ethics, Sports, and the University.* Lanham: Rowman, 2004. Print.

The Online Resource for the National Collegiate Athletic Association. 2005. NCAA. Web. 7 Feb. 2006.

Rotstein, Arthur H. "Arizona Fans Turn Rowdy." *USA Today.* 3 Apr. 2001. Web. 12 Feb. 2006.

Wolverton, Brad. "Under New Formula, Graduation Rates Rise." *Chronicle of Higher Education* 52.21 (2006): A41. Web. 10 Feb. 2006.

Zimbalist, Andrew. *Unpaid Professionals: Commercialism and Conflict in Big-Time College Sports*. Princeton: Princeton UP, 1999. Print.

New page, title centered; double space between title and first line of works-cited list.

Entries double-spaced, in alphabetical order.

First line of each entry at left margin; all other lines indented 1/2 inch.

Note that URLs are optional for Web sources.

APA Documentation Style

APA Style: In-Text Citation

In APA style, parenthetical in-text citations are used in conjunction with the list of references at the end of a paper to give readers the information they would need to locate the sources that you have quoted, paraphrased, or summarized. In-text citations include year of publication along with the author and page number. Suppose, for example, that you are quoting from page 282 of Deborah Tannen's *You Just Don't Understand: Woman and Men in Conversation*, published in 1990. In APA style, a parenthetical in-text citation would be "(Tannen, 1990, p. 282)". If you give the author's name within your sentence, however, the date appears in parentheses following the name. APA parenthetical citations have commas between the elements and "p." before the page number. Page numbers are needed only when you are citing a quotation or specific information.

The following are examples of how to cite different types of sources within your text using APA style.

A WORK WITH ONE AUTHOR

> Deborah Tannen (1990), in talking about gender differences, observes, "Complementary schismogenesis commonly sets in when women and men have divergent sensitivities and hypersensitivities" (p. 282).

A WORK WITH MORE THAN ONE AUTHOR

For a source with up to five authors, use all the authors' last names in the first citation. If you give their names in parentheses, put an ampersand (&) between the last two names. After the first citation, use the first author's name followed by *et al.* for a work by three or more authors.

> Glassick, Huber, and Maeroff (1999) state that "teaching, too, must in the end be judged not merely by process but by results, however eloquent a teacher's performance" (p. 29).

> Ultimately, it is the results of teaching, not the method or the quality of the teacher's performance, that we must evaluate (Glassick, Huber, & Maeroff, 1999, p. 29).

For a source with six or more authors, use *et al.* with every citation, including the first.

AN UNKNOWN AUTHOR

Use a shortened version of the title.

> Employees of Google believe their corporate culture to be antithetical to that of Microsoft ("Google," 2006).

A GOVERNMENT AGENCY OR A CORPORATE AUTHOR

Give the complete name of most organizations every time you use them. After the first use, however, you can use an abbreviation for organizations with unwieldy names and well-known or easily understood abbreviations.

> The Federal Emergency Management Agency (FEMA, 2007) offers officials many suggestions in a new brochure. You can obtain a copy of FEMA's brochure at our main office.

A SECONDARY SOURCE

If you need to use a quotation from a secondary source, use *as cited in* to let your readers know that you are doing so.

> Jonathan Shaw muses, "I don't think mankind is ready, spiritually or mentally, for the transformations it's undergoing in the technological era: tattooing is a mute plea for a return to human values" (as cited in Dery, 1996, p. 284).

AN ONLINE SOURCE

Cite in the same way that you would cite a print source. For a source with paragraph numbers, use *para.* or ¶. If you cannot find a date for the source, use the abbreviation *n.d.* (for "no date").

> According to Christopher Beam (2006), there are a number of methods that Internet service providers can use to block Web sites if a government orders them to.

A BLOCK QUOTATION

In APA style, block quotations are used for quotations of more than forty words and are indented one-half inch or five spaces, as in the following example:

> Tannen (1990), in talking about gender differences, notes this phenomenon:
>
> > Complementary schismogenesis commonly sets in when women and men have divergent sensitivities and hypersensitivities. For example, a man who fears losing freedom pulls away at the first sign he interprets

FIGURE 20.5 APA Style: A Flowchart for Determining the Model References Entry You Need

connect
mhconnectcomposition.com
APA Style: Determining the model references entry you need QL20008

Is My Source a Complete Print Book or Part of a Print Book?

No	Yes, go to the next question below.	Go to this entry.
↓	Is it a book with only one author?	1
	Are you citing more than one book by this author?	2
	Is it a book with multiple authors?	3
	Is the author unknown or unnamed?	5
	Is the book by an organization of some kind?	4
	Does the book also have a translator?	10
	Is it a later publication or edition of the book?	6, 7
	Is it a multivolume work?	12
	Does the book have an editor or a translator?	8,10
	Is the book an edited collection or anthology?	8, 9
	Is it a work in a collection or an anthology?	9
	Is it an introduction, a preface, a foreword, or an afterword?	11
	Is it a published interview?	13
	Is it an entry in a dictionary or reference work?	22

Is My Source from a Print Periodical Such as a Journal, a Magazine, or a Newspaper?

No	Yes, go to the next question below.	Go to this entry.
↓	Is it from a scholarly journal?	
	Do the journal's page numbers continue from one issue to the next?	14
	Does each issue start with page 1?	15
	Is it from a magazine?	16
	Is it a review?	19
	Is it from a newspaper?	17
	Is it an editorial?	18
	Is it a letter to the editor?	20
	Is it an article in a newsletter?	21

> as an attempt to "control" him, but pulling away is just the signal that sets off alarms for the woman who fears losing intimacy. (p. 282)

Note that the year of publication is given in parentheses immediately following the author's name and not with the page number.

APA Style: Constructing a References List

For a comparison of the MLA and APA styles for citing books and periodical articles, see page 571.

The section that follows includes model entries for different types of print and nonprint sources in APA style. Figure 20.5 provides you with a flowchart that will help you find the model entry that is closest to the source that you need to cite.

Is My Source a Print Source but Not from a Journal, a Magazine, or a Newspaper?

No	Yes, go to the next question below.	Go to this entry.
↓	Is it an entry in a dictionary or reference work?	22
	Is it a government document?	23
	Is it an unpublished doctoral dissertation?	24
	Is it an academic report	25

Is My Source a Nonprint Source from an Online Subscription Database or the World Wide Web?

No	Yes, go to the next question below.	Go to this entry.
↓	Is it a professional or personal Web site?	26
	Is it an article?	
	Is it a scholarly article retrieved from a database?	27
	Is it from an online journal?	29
	Is it from an online magazine?	30
	Is it from an online newspaper?	31
	Is it an online book?	28
	Is it a posting to an electronic forum?	32
	Is it an e-mail message?	33
	Is it a blog entry?	34
	Is it an entry in a wiki?	35
	Is it computer software?	36

Is My Source a Nonprint Source That Is Not Published Online?

No	Yes, go to the next question below.	Go to this entry.
↓	Is it a television or radio program?	37
	Is it an audio recording?	38
	Is it a film, video recording, or DVD?	39
	Is it an oral presentation?	40

Consult with Your Instructor about How to Cite Your Source.

PRINT DOCUMENTS

Books

The basic elements in an entry for a book are the author's name or authors' names, the date of publication, the title, and the publication information, consisting of the place of publication and the publisher. See Figure 20.6 for guidelines on where to find the elements of an entry in a list of references for an edited collection in APA style.

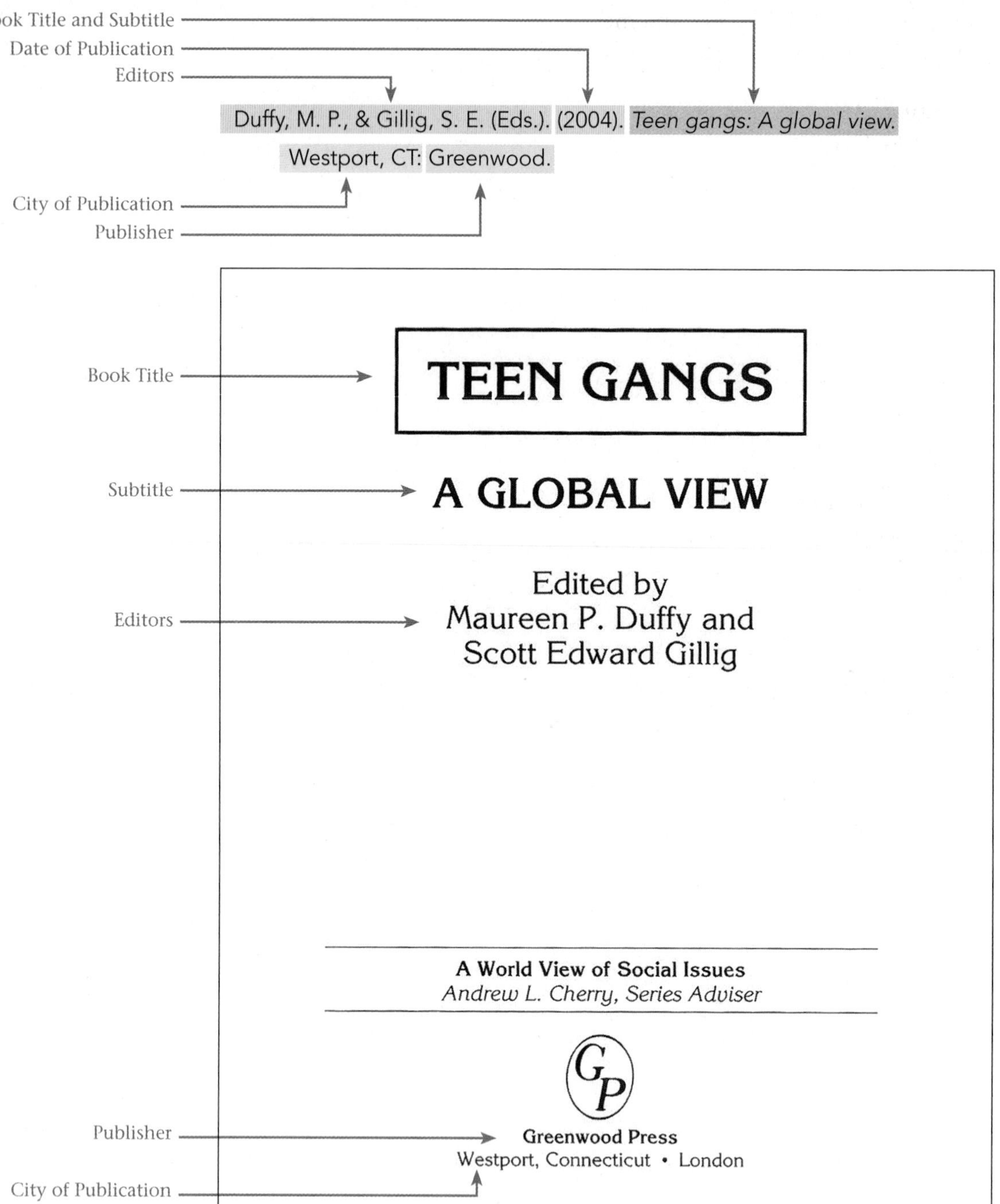

Book Title and Subtitle
Date of Publication
Editors
Duffy, M. P., & Gillig, S. E. (Eds.). (2004). *Teen gangs: A global view.*
Westport, CT: Greenwood.
City of Publication
Publisher
Book Title
TEEN GANGS
Subtitle
A GLOBAL VIEW
Edited by
Editors
Maureen P. Duffy and
Scott Edward Gillig
A World View of Social Issues
Andrew L. Cherry, Series Adviser
GP
Publisher
Greenwood Press
Westport, Connecticut • London
City of Publication

FIGURE 20.6 The Parts of a Reference Entry for an Edited Collection

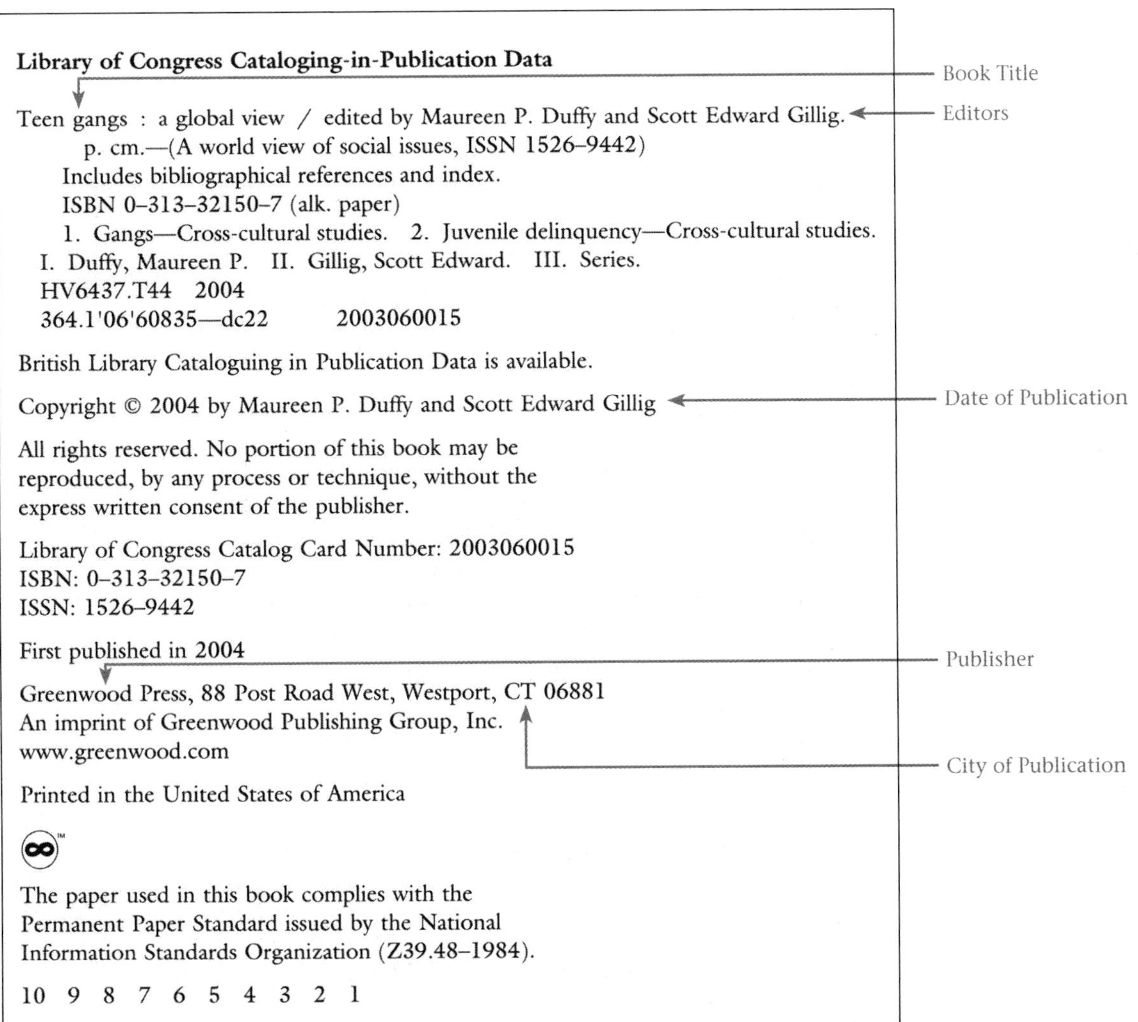
Library of Congress Cataloging-in-Publication Data

Teen gangs : a global view / edited by Maureen P. Duffy and Scott Edward Gillig.
p. cm.—(A world view of social issues, ISSN 1526-9442)
Includes bibliographical references and index.
ISBN 0-313-32150-7 (alk. paper)
1. Gangs—Cross-cultural studies. 2. Juvenile delinquency—Cross-cultural studies.
I. Duffy, Maureen P. II. Gillig, Scott Edward. III. Series.
HV6437.T44 2004
364.1'06'60835—dc22 2003060015

British Library Cataloguing in Publication Data is available.

Copyright © 2004 by Maureen P. Duffy and Scott Edward Gillig

All rights reserved. No portion of this book may be reproduced, by any process or technique, without the express written consent of the publisher.

Library of Congress Catalog Card Number: 2003060015
ISBN: 0-313-32150-7
ISSN: 1526-9442

First published in 2004

Greenwood Press, 88 Post Road West, Westport, CT 06881
An imprint of Greenwood Publishing Group, Inc.
www.greenwood.com

Printed in the United States of America

The paper used in this book complies with the Permanent Paper Standard issued by the National Information Standards Organization (Z39.48-1984).

10 9 8 7 6 5 4 3 2 1

1. Book with one author: In APA style, the date of publication follows the author's name. The author's first and middle name are given as initials, and the title of the book is italicized. Only the first word of the title is capitalized, as well as any proper nouns and the first word following a colon.

connect
mhconnectcomposition.com
APA Style: The parts of a references entry QL20009

author date of publication title city state publisher

Gould, S. J. (1981). *The mismeasure of man.* New York, NY: Norton.

2. Two entries by the same author: The entries are listed in chronological order, with the earliest publication first. If more than one work was published in the same year, the works are ordered alphabetically based on the first letter of the title. Each work is given a lowercase letter after the date: for example, "(2004a)" for the first entry published in 2004 and "(2004b)" for the second entry. These letters would appear with the dates in the in-text citations.

Tannen, D. (1990). *You just don't understand: Women and men in conversation.* New York, NY: Ballantine Books.

Tannen, D. (1994). *Talking from 9 to 5.* New York, NY: Morrow.

3. Book with multiple authors: All authors' names are inverted. Use an ampersand to separate the last two entries. Give the names of all authors up to six; if there are more authors, follow the sixth name with *et al.*

Covey, S. R., Merrill, A. R., & Merrill, R. R. (1994). *First things first.* New York, NY: Simon & Schuster.

4. Book by a corporate entity or organization: When the publisher is the same as the author, use the word *Author* where the publisher's name is usually given.

Adobe Systems Inc. (2001). *Adobe acrobat 5.0: Getting started.* San Jose, CA: Author.

5. Book by an unknown author:

The Chicago manual of style: The essential guide for writers, editors, and publishers (15th ed.). (2003). Chicago, IL: University of Chicago Press.

6. Republished book: The original date of publication must be included.

Dickens, C. (1969). *Hard times.* (D. Craig, Ed.). Baltimore, MD: Penguin Books. (Original work published 1854)

7. Book in a later edition:

Corbett, E. P. J. (1990). *Classical rhetoric for the modern student* (3rd ed.). New York, NY: Oxford University Press.

8. Edited collection:

Inman, J. A., & Sewell, D. N. (Eds.). (2000). *Taking flight with owls: Examining electronic writing center work.* Mahwah, NJ: Erlbaum.

See also Figure 20.6 on pages 598–599.

9. Work in a collection or an anthology: In APA style, the page numbers come after the title and before the publication information.

Anson, C. M., & Jewell, R. (2001). Shadows of the mountain. In E. E. Schell & P. L. Stock (Eds.), *Moving a mountain: Transforming the role of contingent faculty in composition studies and higher education* (pp. 47–75). Urbana, IL: NCTE.

10. Translation:

Eliade, M. (1959). *The sacred and the profane: The nature of religion* (W. R. Trask, Trans.). New York, NY: Harcourt. (Original work published 1957)

11. Introduction, preface, foreword, or afterword:

Burns, H. (1999). Foreword. In C. L. Selfe, *Technology and literacy in the twenty-first century: The importance of paying attention* (pp. ix–xvii). Carbondale, IL: Southern Illinois University Press.

12. A multivolume work published over more than one year:

Campbell, J. (1959–1968). *The masks of god* (Vols. 1–4). New York, NY: Viking.

13. Published interview:

Blair, K., & Takayoshi, P. (1999). Making the map: An interview with Gail Hawisher. [Interview with G. Hawisher] In K. Blair & P. Takayoshi (Eds.), *Feminist cyberspaces: Mapping gendered academic spaces* (pp. 177–191). Stamford, CT: Ablex.

You should cite an interview published in a periodical as you would a periodical article (see nos. 14, 15, and 16). APA categorizes personal interviews as personal communications: Because such an interview cannot be recovered, there is no need to include an entry for it in a reference list, but the interview should be cited in the body of the text (see nos. 33 and 40).

Periodical Articles

The basic items in an entry for a periodical article are the author's name or authors' names, the date of publication in parentheses, the title of the article, and information about the publication in which the article appeared, including its title, volume and issue number (if applicable), and the page range for the article. See Figure 20.7 for guidelines.

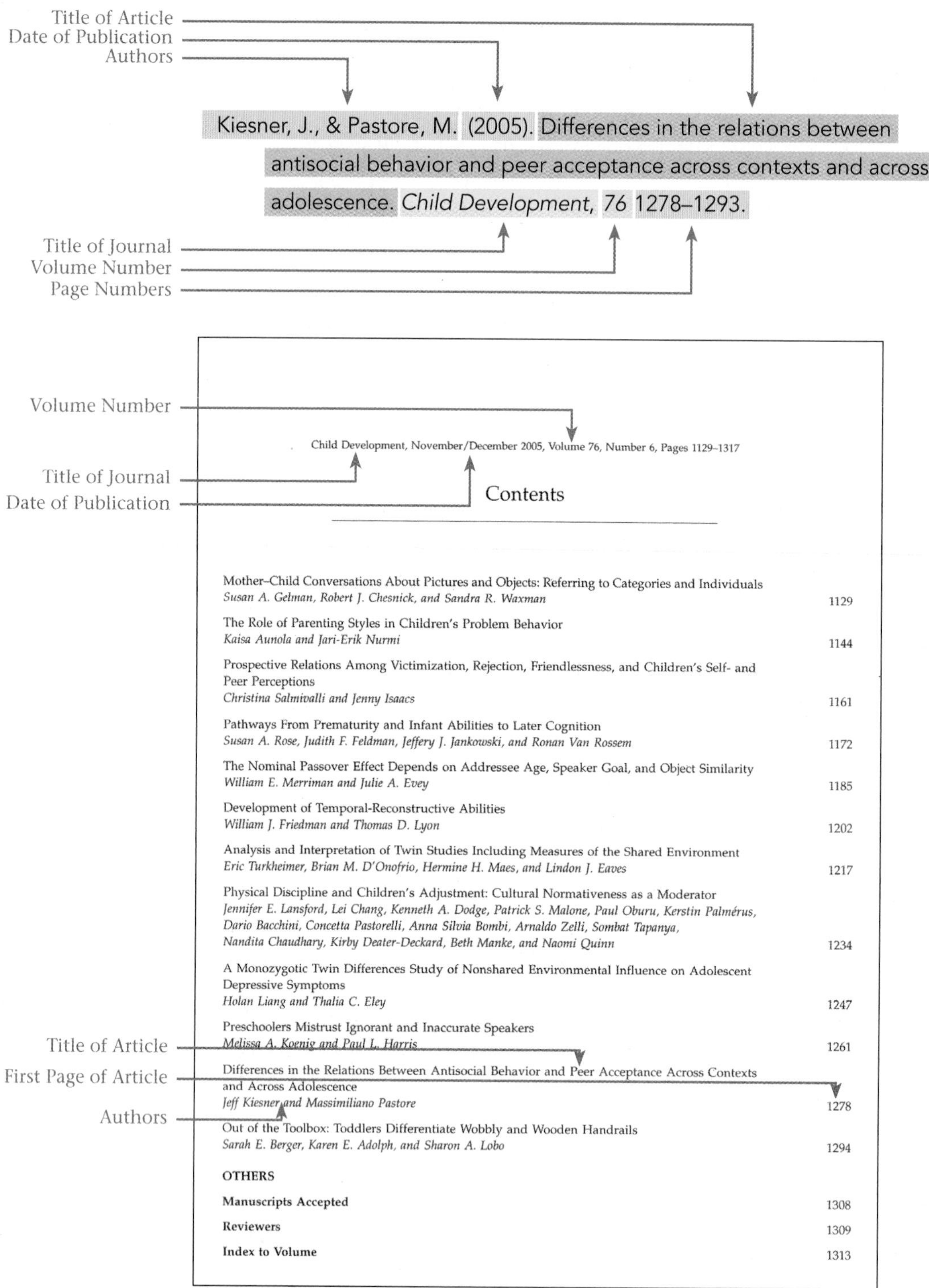

Child Development, November/December 2005, Volume 76, Number 6, Pages 1129–1317

Contents

FIGURE 20.7 The Parts of a Reference Entry for a Journal Article

14. Article in a scholarly journal with continuous pagination: In APA style, the volume number is italicized. APA style also uses full page numbers.

authors date of publication title

Thayer, A., & Kolko, B. E. (2004). Localization of digital games: The

title of periodical

process of blending for the global games market. *Technical*

volume no. and page range

Communication, 51, 477–488.

15. Article in a scholarly journal that is paginated by issue: When an article is from a journal that restarts the page numbers with each issue, the issue number follows the volume number in parentheses in APA style.

Howard, R. M. (1993). Power revisited: Or, how we became a department. *Writing Program Administration: Journal of the Council of Writing Program Administrators, 16*(3), 37–49.

16. Magazine article: Magazines may or may not include volume and issue numbers. In an entry in APA style, the volume number should be included, placed within commas between the name of the magazine and the page numbers of the article: "(*Scientific American, 290,* 54–61)." In the first example below, *BusinessWeek* is a magazine that does not use volume numbers.

Foust, D., Eidem, M., & Bremner, B. (2004, February 2). AFLAC: Its ducks are not in a row. *BusinessWeek*, 52–53.

Wilson, C. E. (2005, January). Usability and user experience design: The next decade. *Intercom, 52,* 6–9.

17. Newspaper article: When articles appear on discontinuous pages, as they often do, APA style requires you to list all the page numbers.

Fatsis, S. (2002, April 9). A more modern masters. *Wall Street Journal*, pp. B1, B4.

18. Editorial: If there is a title, it should precede "[Editorial]."

Moral scoreboard. [Editorial]. (2004, February 18). *The Arizona Republic*, p. B10.

19. Review: If the review is titled, give the title in the usual position, preceding the bracketed information.

Jablonski, J. (2003). [Review of the book *The new careers: Individual action and economic change,* by M. Arthur, K. Inkson, & J. K. Pringle]. *Technical Communication Quarterly, 12,* 230–234.

20. Letter to the editor:

Rosati, C. (2004, February 18). Let's throw the book at Valley street racers [Letter to the editor]. *The Arizona Republic,* p. B10.

21. Newsletter article, no author: Unsigned articles should be alphabetized in the list of references by the first word of the title. If there is a volume number, place it between the name of the publication and the page numbers, separated by commas. The following example from the newsletter of the Heard Museum of Native Cultures and Art has no volume number.

Shared images: The jewelry of Yazzie Johnson and Gail Bird. (2007, January/February). *Earthsong,* 8.

Other Print Sources

22. Entry in a dictionary or reference work: APA style uses page numbers even when the entries are alphabetical.

Express Mail. (1993). In *Merriam-Webster's new collegiate dictionary* (p. 411). Springfield, MA: Merriam-Webster.

Pfeiffer, R. H. (1974). Sumerian Poetry. In *Princeton Encyclopedia of Poetry and Poetics* (pp. 820–821). Princeton, NJ: Princeton University Press.

23. Government document: Like MLA style, APA style lists the agency as the author of the report when the author is not known. If you list a subdepartment or agency, make certain that you also list the higher department if the subdepartment is not well known. If the publisher is not the Government Printing Office (GPO), list the highest known agency or department as the author. If the document has a specific publication number, list it after the title.

National Institutes of Health. (1992). *Toxicology and carcinogenesis studies of Resorcinol (CAS No. 108-46-3) in F344/N rats and B6C3F$_1$ mice (Gavage Studies)* (NIH Publication No. 92-2858). Research Triangle Park, NC: Author.

24. Unpublished doctoral dissertation:

Edminster, J. R. (2002). *The diffusion of new media scholarship: Power, innovation, and resistance in academe* (Unpublished doctoral dissertation). University of South Florida.

25. Academic report:

Melnick, R., Welch, N., & Hart, B. (2005). *How Arizona compares: Real numbers and hot topics.* Tempe: Arizona State University, Morrison Institute for Public Policy.

ONLINE SOURCES

Unlike MLA, APA prefers that the exact URL be given in the reference entry, along with the Digital Object Identifier (DOI). It is not necessary to include publication information (location: publisher) for sources for which there is a URL or DOI. The URL or DOI will allow a reader to locate information about the publisher, if desired. If the content is likely to change, give a retrieval date. For content that is fixed, such as a journal article, no date is necessary. See Figure 20.8 for guidelines.

The DOI is a unique number that is registered with a specific agency that follows the standards of the International DOI Foundation (IDF). It works similarly to the system that registers domain names on the Internet and helps people locate a specific reference, such as a journal article or an online book. If you were searching for an article on the topic of adolescent female gang behavior, you might find this article. You can see the DOI in the fourth line on the left. When a DOI is provided, it is not necessary to include a URL, as example 29 on p. 607 illustrates.

Journal of Human Behavior in the Social Environment, 19:231–241, 2009

ISSN: 1091-1359 print/1540-3556 online
DOI: 10.1080/10911350802694584

Spirituality as a Protective Factor Against Female Gang Membership

ELIZABETH S. MARSAL
Department of Criminal Justice, East Carolina University, Greenville, North Carolina

26. Basic professional or personal Web site:

American Medical Association. (2004). Home page. Retrieved February 17, 2004, from http://www.ama-assn.org/

Publication Information about the Print Version of the Article

Sullivan, M. L. (2005). Maybe we shouldn't study "gangs": Does reification obscure youth violence? *Journal of Contemporary Criminal Justice 21*(2), 176. Retrieved from CSA Illumina database.

Online Subscription Service

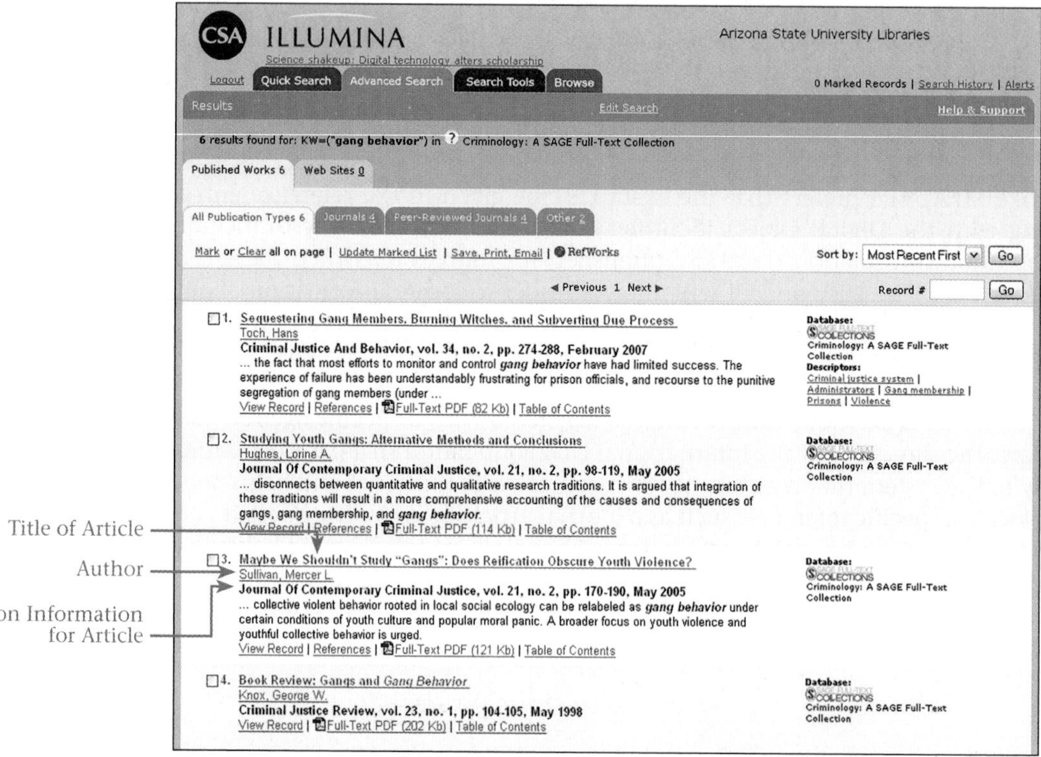

FIGURE 20.8 The Parts of a Reference Entry for a Journal Article Accessed from an Online Subscription Database

27. Scholarly article retrieved from a database: Include the issue number as well as the volume number.

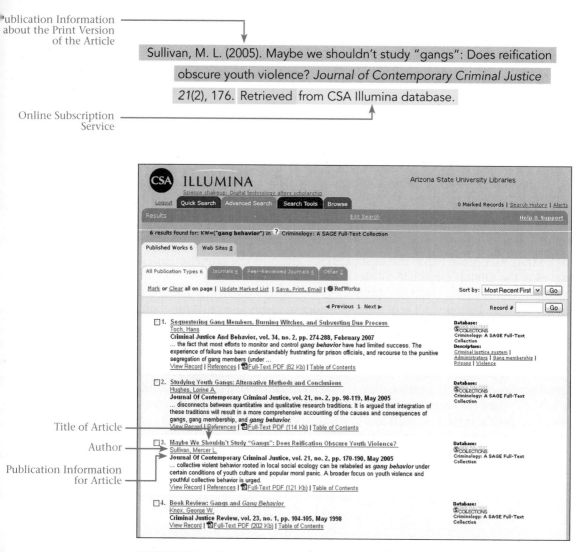

author date of publication title of article

Selber, S. A. (1994). Beyond skill building: Challenges facing technical communication teachers in the computer age.

title of journal volume no. and page range

Technical Communication Quarterly, 3(4), 365–391.

name of database

Retrieved from EBSCOHost database.

28. Online book:

Howells, W. D. (1913). *Familiar Spanish travels.* Retrieved from http://www .gutenberg.net/etext05/sptrv10.txt

29. Article from an online journal with a DOI: In APA style, the volume number is italicized.

Marsal, E. S. (2009). Spirituality as a protective factor against female gang membership. *Journal of Human Behavior in the Social Environment, 19:* 231–241. doi: 10.1080/10911350802694584

Note: For journal articles that are published online and are unchanged from their print version, you can use the format for a journal article (no. 14 or 15), but add [*Electronic version*] following the title of the article. A retrieval statement is not necessary.

30. Article from an online magazine:

Cooper, M., & Tumulty, K. (2004, February 16). Bring on the cash! *Time.* Retrieved from http://www.time.com/time/election2004/article/ 0,18471,591298,00.html

31. Article from an online newspaper:

Novovitch, B. (2004, February 17). It's home stupid home, but the "clods" can read. *New York Times.* Retrieved from http://www.nytimes .com/2004/02/17/education/17PROF.html

32. Posting to an electronic forum such as a mailing list (listserv): In APA style, list only electronic references that have been archived and are retrievable.

Peckham, I. (2004, February 17). Update on AP and dual enrollment. [Electronic mailing list message.] Retrieved from http://lists.asu.edu/cgi-bin/ wa?A2=ind0309&L=wpal&D=1&O=D&F=&S=&P=52156

33. E-mail message: In APA style, e-mail is cited only in the text as "personal communication," followed by the date of the e-mail.

34. Blog entry: Provide the name of the author (bloggers often use pseudonyms), date, title of entry, the words "Message posted to," name of blog, and the URL.

Rice, J. (2007, March 30). Re: Network academics [Web log message]. Retrieved from http://ydog.net/?page_id=345

35. Wiki entry:

Rhetoric. (n.d.). Retrieved March 30, 2007, from http://en.wikipedia.org/wiki/Rhetoric

36. Computer software: If you download software, include "Available from" and the URL.

AllWrite! 2.0 with Online Handbook. [Computer software]. (2003). New York, NY: McGraw-Hill.

OTHER NONPRINT SOURCES

37. Television and radio programs: In APA style the names of the writers, directors, and producers are given as appropriate. Indicate whether the source is a television or radio broadcast in square brackets.

Buckner, N., & Whittlesey, R. (Writers, Directors, Producers). (2004, February 3). Dogs and more dogs. *Nova* [Television broadcast]. Boston, MA, and Washington, DC: Public Broadcasting Service.

Turpin, C. (Executive Producer). (2004, February 12). Scientists succeed in cloning human embryo. *All things considered* [Radio broadcast]. Washington, DC: National Public Radio.

38. Audio recording:

Jackson, A. (2002). Drive. On *Drive* [CD]. New York, NY: Arista.

39. Film, video recording, or DVD:

Jackson, P. (Director). (2002). *The lord of the rings: The two towers* [DVD]. United States: New Line Home Entertainment.

40. Oral presentation: Because live lectures are not recoverable data, in APA style, they are cited parenthetically in the text but are not included in the list of references. However, when professional presentations are made from texts that can be recovered, they are cited.

Russell, D. R. (1999, March). Teacher's perception of genre across the curriculum: Making classroom/culture connections visible. Paper presented at the Conference on College Composition and Communication Convention, Atlanta, GA.

APA Style: Sample Student Paper

The student paper that follows, "How Do Gangs Affect Adolescent Behavior?" by Aaron Zook, is an example of a paper that uses APA style.

If you write a paper using APA style, follow these guidelines:

- Include a separate title page. Center the title one-third of the way down the page, using capital and lowercase letters; do not use a special typeface for it. Give your name, the course name and number, and the date, all also centered and double spaced, on separate lines below the title. In the upper-right-hand corner, give the page number, preceded by a short version of the title, which you will include on each page of your paper.
- On the second page of your paper, provide an abstract of the paper if your instructor requires one. An abstract is a brief (approximately 100–120 words) summary of your paper's contents. If you include an abstract, the paper itself begins on the third page. Repeat the title on the first page of your paper, centering it one inch from the top. Double-space to the first line of your text.
- Double-space the entire paper, including any block quotations and the items in your list of references.
- Insert 2 spaces after punctuation at the end of a sentence.
- Leave one-inch margins on all sides.
- Place page numbers in the upper-right-hand corner after the running head, five spaces after the shortened version of the title.
- Indent paragraphs and block quotations one-half inch from the left margin.
- Note that some papers use headings to label sections of the text. If you use headings, center them and double-space above and below them.
- Put your list of references on a new page, with the title "References" centered at the top.

Title is centered, one-third of the way down the page.

Name, title of course, name of professor, and date are centered and double-spaced on separate lines below the title.

How Do Gangs Affect Adolescent Behavior?

Aaron Zook

Psychology 101

Professor Jones

March 23, 2010

1" ½"

HOW GANGS AFFECT BEHAVIOR 2

How Do Gangs Affect Adolescent Behavior?

1" Since the early 1920s, researchers have closely studied the relationship between street gangs and violent crime from a variety of perspectives: criminological, sociological, and psychological (O'Connor, 2006). Whatever the underlying causes for gang membership, the results seem clear; members of street gangs admit to a far greater rate of serious crime, and to far more severe acts of violence (Hall, Thornberry, & Lizotte, 2006) than non-gang members of the same age, race, and socioeconomic background (Battin-Pearson, Thornberry, Hawkins, & Krohn, 1998). According to the Web site Safeyouth.org (n.d.), gang violence is certainly cause for concern:

> Gang members are responsible for much of the serious violence in the United States. . . . Teens that are gang members are much more likely than other teens to commit serious and violent crimes. For example, a survey in Denver found that while only 14% of teens were gang members, they were responsible for committing 89% of the serious violent crimes.

1"

Many researchers have therefore come to the conclusion that gangs necessarily cause violence and deviant behavior. As a matter of policy, then, it seems clear that the solution to a number of social ills is to break up, disrupt, or prevent the formation of gangs. Other programs seek to prevent young people from joining gangs through interventions of various types and levels of effectiveness. Most of these efforts take it as a given that gangs seriously distort behavior, even among individuals who already belong to "high-risk" demographic groups. Adolescents living in poverty or other disadvantaged circumstances; those attending violent and/or failing schools; members of criminalized peer groups; and children from violent and/or extremely dysfunctional households or demonstrating a predisposition toward antisocial behavior all seem to be at greater risk for future gang membership (Battin-Pearson et al., 1998), but a number of studies have shown that their own behaviors are considerably more violent while they belong to a gang than they were before or after membership (Gordon et al., 2004). After years of study, researchers still do not clearly understand how and why gangs exert such a powerful influence on behavior. A crucial answer might be found in the typical composition of a gang. Overwhelmingly, gangs are made up of

1"

Title repeated on first page of paper, centered.

Double-space from title to first line of paper.

Information from sources cited with parenthetical references.

Quotation longer than forty words indented 1/2 inch or 5 spaces and double-spaced. Introductory sentence ends with a colon. Because no date is given in source, abbreviation *n.d.* is included.

Et al. used after the first citation for multiple authors. *Et al.* used for first citation of work with six authors.

HOW GANGS AFFECT BEHAVIOR 3

Zook presents synthesis of his findings.

Opening paragraph sets up the issue.

First point: Difficulty of defining gangs.

Government agency as author.

adolescents and young adults. The median age of violent gang members has been estimated to be eighteen; members tend to join in their late teens, and contrary to popular fallacies and urban legends, youths generally leave a gang with few or no consequences within a year of joining (Thomas, 2005). Clearly, then, the gang problem can and should be understood in large part as a youth problem; researchers might come to a deeper understanding of the nature and impact of gangs by shifting some emphasis in their research from violence to adolescent adjustment behaviors.

The research community has by no means reached a consensus as to the precise definition of street gangs, however. The telltale sign that a group is a gang—one that most researchers, police organizations, the popular media, and gang members themselves agree on—is a tendency to commit violent acts (Katz & Jackson-Jacobs, 2004), but violence is not an adequate condition in itself. Why, for example, are Crips and Bloods considered gangs, but not Skin-heads? Likewise, organized crime is now rarely considered "gang behavior," though early studies included these types of organizations. Yet all of these form distinct social groups and are involved in criminal behaviors (Thomas, 2005). One common distinction researchers draw is based on the motivation behind the group's violent activities. Does the group sell drugs or stolen merchandise? Do they operate according to an ideology or shared set of racial or cultural prejudices? Or are they primarily concerned with "turf," status, or violence for its own sake (U.S. Department of Education, n.d.)? Contemporary studies tend to maintain that only the latter group of motives typify "gangs" and have been particularly concerned with the seemingly random nature of the various criminal behaviors that many such gangs exhibit. The criminal acts seem to have largely symbolic value, consistent with the way many street gangs are associated with the use of emblems, dress, and a shared name easily identified by all of their members (Katz & Jackson-Jacobs, 2004).

Experts in gang behavior have advanced numerous explanations for the most troubling examples of violent gang behavior: random drive-by shootings, seemingly unmotivated killings and aggravated assaults, car-jackings, and so on. Ritual initiations, turf wars, cycles of retribution between competing gangs, and intra-gang status have all been identified as motivators (Fagan & Wilkinson, 1998). Other hypotheses focus on the greater availability of guns and drugs, and still others on the model of shared or diffuse moral culpability (Thornberry, Krohn, Lizotte, & Chard-Wierschem, 1993), a phenomenon that has also been observed in riots and cases where soldiers have committed wartime atrocities. Yet another explanation has involved the culpability of the media and the police in promoting gang imagery: The very definition of gangs as violent entities increases members' levels of violence. In other words, certain youths seek the rewards they think gang membership will afford them—status; protection; group identity; and entertainment, drugs, and sex (U.S. Department of Education, n.d.)—and are willing to engage in violent acts because "that's what a gang is." The image is reinforced by the news and popular media and by the folklore of the gang itself. It has also been argued that both gang members' own accounts of their activities and police statistics may be misleading. Because of the status violence confers on a perpetrator, a subject could conceivably exaggerate his or her criminal behavior in surveys and interviews as a means of bragging. Further, crime statistics reflect arrest and incarceration rates which, considering the general conspicuousness of gang members and police efforts to target these groups, could conceivably skew higher for gang offenders than for criminals who do not belong to gangs. A number of studies, less sensational in their findings and therefore less visible in the mainstream media, have found that most gang members spend the majority of their time simply "hanging out," albeit often within the context of drug or alcohol use (Katz & Jackson-Jacobs, 2004). In a sense, then, lacking any overarching objective such as profit or ideology, some gangs may see continued violence as a means of justifying their own existence and retaining members who would otherwise grow restless and leave.

Second point: Various explanations of gang behavior, leading to most satisfactory one.

If retention is indeed the motivation for violent gang behavior, then it seems unlikely that some special feature of gangs in their day-to-day operation enables violent extremes of behavior; rather, it is the symbolic value of the gang "family" that makes them sufficiently attractive to justify violence, the risk of death or imprisonment, and the common perception (however false) that one can never leave the gang. It seems likely that certain characteristics typical

Citation of source with no author indicated.

Concludes with assertion that his arguments have led to: cultural factors contribute to gang violence.

of adolescents—the desire to create a self-identity, establish a sense of belonging, and both derive status from and earn status within groups (Ausubel, 2002)—make them vulnerable to the allure of such symbolism. It also seems likely that, in addition to environmental and psychological factors such as peer pressure and/or facilitation (Gifford-Smith, Dodge, Dishion, & McCord, 2005) or poor self-esteem ("At last," 1995), cultural factors also aggravate the problem of gang violence. That is to say, while many studies have rightly focused on how crumbling inner cities, poverty, and lack or loss of opportunity and hope affect a teen's predisposition toward gang affiliation, it might be worthwhile to examine how society itself provides gangs with false or mythical status that might add to their attraction.

HOW GANGS AFFECT BEHAVIOR 6

References

At last—a rejection detector! (1995, November). *Psychology Today, 28*(6). Retrieved from http://www.psychologytoday.com/

Ausubel, D. P. (2002). *Theory and problems of adolescent development* (2nd ed.). Lincoln, NE: iUniverse.

Battin-Pearson, S. R., Thornberry, T. P., Hawkins, J. D., & Krohn, M. D. (1998, October). *Gang membership, delinquent peers, and delinquent behavior* (Juvenile Justice Bulletin NCJ 17119). Retrieved from Office of Juvenile Justice and Delinquency Prevention: http://ojjdp.ncjrs.gov/jjbulletin/9810_2/contents.html

Fagan, J., & Wilkinson, D. L. (1998). Social contexts and functions of adolescent violence. In D. S. Elliott, B. Hamburg, & K. R. Williams (Eds.), *Violence in American schools: A new perspective* (pp. 55–93). New York, NY: Cambridge University Press.

Gifford-Smith, M., Dodge, K. A., Dishion, T. J., & McCord, J. (2005). Peer influence in children and adolescents: Crossing the bridge from developmental to intervention science. *Journal of Abnormal Child Psychology, 33,* 255–265. doi: 10.1007/s10802-005-3563-7

Gordon, R. A., Lahey, B. B., Kawai, E., Loeber, R., Stouthamer-Loeber, M., & Farrington, D. P. (2004). Antisocial behavior and youth gang membership: Selection and socialization [Abstract]. *Criminology, 42,* 55–88. doi: 10.1111/j.1745-9125.2004.tb00513.x

Hall, G. P., Thornberry, T. P., & Lizotte, A. J. (2006). The gang facilitation effect and neighborhood risk: Do gangs have a stronger influence on delinquency in disadvantaged areas? In J. F. Short, Jr., & L. Hughes (Eds.), *Studying youth gangs.* Lanham, MD: Altamira Press.

Katz, J., & Jackson-Jacobs, C. (2004). The criminologists' gang. In C. Sumner (Ed.), *The Blackwell companion to criminology* (pp. 91–124). doi:http://dx.doi.org/10.1002/9780470998960.ch5

National Youth Violence Prevention Center. (n.d). *Youth gangs.* Retrieved from http://www.safeyouth.org/scripts/teens/gangs.asp

New page, title centered; double-space between title and first line of reference list.

Entries double-spaced, in alphabetical order.

First line of each entry at left margin; all other lines indented 1/2 inch or 5 spaces.

This paper was written prior to the publication of the 6th edition of the *APA Publication Manual* and follows the style of the 5th edition.

O'Connor, T. (2006, Nov. 30). *Social disorganization theories of crime* [Lecture notes]. Retrieved from http://www.apsu.edu/oconnort/crim/crimtheory10.htm

Thomas, C. R. (2005, April). Serious delinquency and gang membership. *Psychiatric Times 22*(4). Retrieved from http://www.psychiatrictimes.com/home

Thornberry, T. P., Krohn, M. D., Lizotte, A. J., & Chard-Wierschem, D. (1993). The role of juvenile gangs in facilitating delinquent behavior. *Journal of Research in Crime and Delinquency, 30*(1), 55–87. Abstract retrieved from http://jrc.sagepub.com/

U.S. Department of Education. (n.d.). *Youth gangs: Going beyond the myths to address a critical problem.* Retrieved from http://www2.ed.gov/admins/lead/safety/training/gangs/problem_pg3.html

Walker-Barnes, C. J., & Mason, C. A. (2001). Ethnic differences in the effect of parenting on gang involvement and gang delinquency: A longitudinal, hierarchical linear modeling perspective. *Child Development, 72,* 1814–1831. Abstract retrieved from http://www3.interscience.wiley.com/cgi-bin/home

Appendix A
Constructing a Writing Portfolio

Constructing a writing portfolio gives you the opportunity to select, display, and reflect on the work you have done in this course. Although there are many ways to construct a portfolio, this chapter offers you some common suggestions and guidelines that others have found useful. An important purpose for constructing the portfolio is to provide you with support for the claims that you will make about your writing in the course. In short, a portfolio helps you support this statement: "Here is what I have learned this semester, and here is the evidence that I have learned these writing strategies and conventions."

Your instructor will guide you on how much evidence to include in the portfolio to support your claims about what you have learned. In some cases, a single example of your work will be sufficient evidence. In other cases, you may need to provide several examples. For instance, to demonstrate that you know how to adapt a message for a particular audience, you might need to show how you have done so for two or three different audiences.

What Is a Portfolio and Why Should I Construct One?

In the past, graphic artists and photographers were the only professionals who tended to keep portfolios of their work. These artists used portfolios to show potential clients their previous work and to give them a sense of what to expect in the future. More recently, many other professionals, such as technical or professional writers, have found that keeping a portfolio is helpful when they look for work.

Although no one will deny that the quality of the final product is important, from an educational perspective, how you arrived at that final product may be just as important as, or even more important than, the result you achieved. By looking at your process (the path you took to get to your endpoint) in a portfolio, your instructor can better assess your strengths and weaknesses as a writer.

When instructors or other readers look at a single piece of your writing, they may come away with a narrow view of your writing capabilities. They may see only a particular kind of writing, with its strengths and weaknesses. However, when readers look at a portfolio of your work, they gain a fuller picture of the writing you have accomplished.

Because the portfolio represents what you have learned throughout the course, the ideal time to read this appendix and to begin constructing your portfolio is during the first week of the course. That will give you many opportunities to select and reflect on your work while that work is still fresh in your mind. Students who construct the most effective portfolios usually work on them a little each week.

Selecting Materials for Your Portfolio

As you decide what to include in your portfolio, ask yourself these questions:

- What have I learned about writing in each of the four areas of life—academic, professional, civic, and personal?
- What have I learned about writing for various purposes?
- What rhetorical skills and knowledge have I developed?
- What critical reading skills have I developed?
- What critical thinking skills have I developed?
- What have I learned about composing processes—invention, drafting, revising, and editing?
- What have I learned about working effectively with peers?
- What knowledge of conventions have I developed?
- What have I learned about writing responsibly?
- What have I learned about using technology?

As you respond to each of the questions listed above, consider a follow-up question: *What evidence will demonstrate that I have developed this set of skills or knowledge?* Think about all the work that you have done in the course. Among the print or electronic evidence—tangible evidence—available to you are the following:

- Invention work (listing, brainstorming, clustering, and freewriting)
- Research notes (from your library and online research, field research, and interviews)
- Reading notes (comments you made on the reading you did for the class)
- Drafts of papers
- Peers' written comments on your work
- Online discussions about your work
- Polished versions of your papers
- Reflections on your papers (that you write when you submit your papers)

Among the evidence that may not appear on paper or disk are the following:

- Discussions with peers about your writing
- Discussions with your instructor about your writing

You will, of course, need to transcribe evidence that exists only in your memory so that you can make it available to those who read your portfolio.

Reflecting on What You Have Written

As noted earlier, it is useful to reflect on your work regularly throughout the semester while that work is fresh in your mind. A week or a month later, you may not remember why you followed up on a peer's comments or how you might approach the topic differently if you were to write about it again. Remember that *reflective writing* asks you to do just what its name suggests: to think back on, to consider, to reflect on the work you did for the course. Consider answering the questions at the end of each chapter in Parts 2 and 3 of this book as a way to start that reflective process.

There are several ways to keep track of your reflective writing. You may choose to keep a handwritten or electronic journal, or you may want to keep your own course blog where you regularly reflect on your course writing.

For more on journals, see pages 27–28.

As you reflect on the work that you use as evidence in your portfolio, you might consider another question: *Why does this piece of evidence effectively demonstrate that I have developed a certain set of skills or knowledge?* Your response to that question should also appear in your portfolio because it illustrates that you are confident about what you have learned during the course.

As you reflect on your polished essays, you might wish to include a paragraph for each that begins, "If I had the opportunity to revise this paper further, I would . . ." This kind of statement acknowledges the situation that exists in most courses: There is rarely enough time to revise as thoughtfully as you could even if the course were two semesters long.

Organizing Your Portfolio

There are many ways to organize your portfolio, and your instructor will let you know how he or she would like your portfolio to be arranged and organized. Some colleges and universities have specific portfolio requirements; if yours does, you will receive guidance on what you need to do.

Sometimes, your teacher will ask you to organize your portfolio in a *chronological* manner, starting with the first piece of writing you did for the class and ending with your final piece of writing. Other organizational schemes you may find especially useful include the following:

- **By learning goals:** This is an efficient and effective way to organize your portfolio. For example, the Writing Program Administrators Outcomes Statement (see page xl), which is prominent in this book, includes four categories of learning goals: (1) rhetorical knowledge; (2) critical thinking, reading, and writing; (3) processes; (4) knowledge of conventions; and (5) composing in electronic environments. If you use this scheme, you may wish to follow the order given here, or you may wish to reorganize the categories to reflect what you consider to be most important. Once you have decided on the order of the learning goals, those goals can become headings in your portfolio. Under each heading, then, you could respond to the three questions noted earlier:

- What have I learned? How have I grown as a writer?
- What evidence demonstrates that I have learned this—that I have grown?
- Why is this evidence the most convincing evidence that I can choose?

For an example from a writing portfolio organized by learning goals, see pages 622–624.

- **By purpose:** If you use this organizational scheme, you could list the chapter titles from Parts 2 and 3 of this book as your headings—for example, "Writing to Explore," "Writing to Convince," "Writing to Propose Solutions," and so on. This pattern may allow you to focus on each purpose more fully, but it also may cause you to repeat statements about learning goals. That is, for each purpose, you might have to say, "Here's how I learned to adapt my message to an audience." If you do use this organizational pattern, you still can use the same questions:
  - What have I learned? How have I grown as a writer?
  - What evidence demonstrates that I have learned this—that I have grown?
  - Why is this evidence the most convincing evidence that I can choose?

Portfolio Formats

You may decide to submit—or your instructor may request that you submit—your portfolio in one of the following formats:

- **As a print document** in a three-ring binder.
- **As an electronic file,** either on a flash drive or CD. If you use this format, consider constructing a hypertext document so that readers can click on links to see other parts of your portfolio.
- **As a Web site.** This format enables you to provide links to other parts of your portfolio, as well as links to other Web sites or pages that you have found useful during the semester.

In the example shown in Figure A.1, note how student Eileen Holland has organized her electronic portfolio. As background for her work in her first-year writing course, she provided examples of her writing from elementary and secondary school. Because she was an avid reader who believed that reading helped her as a writer, she provided information about several of her favorite writers. Then she included materials to demonstrate that she learned skills and knowledge from the four areas of the Writing Program Administrators Outcomes Statement. Finally, she looked to the future by projecting what she hoped to learn in upcoming semesters.

<table>
<tr><th colspan="2">Electronic Portfolio
Introduction and Table of Contents
by Eileen Holland</th></tr>
<tr><td>My Writing in Elementary School

My Writing in High School

My Favorite Writers
Garrison Keillor
Jared Diamond
Sarah Vowell

Categories of Learning
Rhetorical Knowledge
Critical Thinking, Reading, and Writing
Processes
Knowledge of Conventions

My Future Goals for Learning to Write</td><td>Welcome to my writing portfolio for first-year composition. As my contents indicate, I've been interested in writing since elementary school because my teachers gave me fun writing projects and lots of encouragement. In high school, I was fortunate enough to work with teachers who offered me lots of constructive feedback; some of my friends did the same. I've also been inspired by writers such as Garrison Keillor, Jared Diamond, and Sarah Vowell.

In this portfolio I demonstrate how I have developed skills and knowledge in this course. In particular, I demonstrate how I have learned in four areas: (1) Rhetorical Knowledge; (2) Critical Thinking, Reading, and Writing; (3) Processes; and (4) Knowledge of Conventions. In addition to describing what I have learned, I also offer evidence from my work this semester to prove that I have learned the kinds of knowledge and skills that we have studied.

When I finished high school, I thought that I knew all that I needed to know about writing. In this course, though, I have come to appreciate that learning to write is a never-ending journey. My teacher, who has been writing for more than five decades and teaching writing for almost three decades, told us that she's still learning to write. In class we talked about all sorts of people who keep learning to perform well in their fields until they retire—teachers, professional athletes, entertainers, engineers, painters, architects. Humans keep on learning.</td></tr>
</table>

FIGURE A.1 Sample Portfolio Entry

A Portion of a Sample Portfolio

The following portfolio excerpt comes from Chelsea Rundle, who constructed it in a second-semester writing course. Note how she used the Writing Program Administrators Outcomes Statement to organize her portfolio. Also note how she used evidence from her work to demonstrate what she had learned.

PORTFOLIO

Chelsea Rundle

I cannot believe the semester is coming to a close already. Even though it has seemed quite short, I have learned a lot over the course of this semester. In English 102, I learned that a good paper topic is one that I am passionate about and is feasible. Picking topics that were particular to my major—applied biology—helped me explore different issues/trends in the field of biology and medical science through writing my English papers.

In my first paper, I explored the concept of personalized medicine by researching what others thought about it and then stepping back and forming my opinion on the topic. For the second paper, writing to convince, I addressed a topic I am very passionate about—CT scans causing radiation cancer. I was able to look at how these two topics affect one another because CT scans are an integral process in personalized medicine.

The topic for my evaluation was the biology program at ASU Tempe versus the biology program at another ASU campus. I picked this topic because I am planning on attending one campus for one more year, but I do not know what campus to attend after that. Even though in my evaluation I came to the conclusion that the other campus's biology program would be better for me—I am still not sure. You made the comment on one of my drafts that I should try taking a biology course at ASU Tempe. I may take your advice and try taking a course over there before making a final decision regarding which university to attend. Also, I am not certain what future career I want to enter into. It may be best for me to figure that out before picking which campus I want to attend.

For my proposing a solution paper, I chose a topic that I am passionate about but is not particular to my major. Instead, I chose a topic personal to me and those living in my neighborhood—a new parking regulation passed by the Home Owner's Association (HOA) that does not allow any vehicles to be parked on the street. I chose this topic because my sister will be getting her driver's license soon and I just bought a new truck, so my family will have too many vehicles to fit in our garage and driveway. You suggested that I go to the city council with my final paper, and I just might. The parking regulation has been a problem for a number of families in my neighborhood. If I get enough people to side with me and show the HOA why the regulation is a problem and what some possible solutions to the problem are, I have faith we can get the HOA to change their minds. We'll see.

While writing these four papers and revising them, I have expanded my writing knowledge and have learned how to strengthen my writing skills. I will demonstrate what I have learned in this portfolio. In the portfolio for writing goals and objectives, I used only examples from English 102 because it is the only class I took this semester in which I learned about writing.

RHETORICAL KNOWLEDGE

- Focus on a Purpose

In writing the first argument, I stayed focused on a purpose: persuading the audience to see the dangers of CT scans. To do this, I used a claim, support for my claim, and the refutation of counterarguments. In refuting counterarguments I addressed multiple viewpoints on the issue while showing the reader why my claim is correct. The following is a refutation of a counterargument I used to strengthen the paper:

> Some argue that radiation cancer is not caused by CT scans, but can be caused by other factors. This is absolutely true, for radiation, or the release of energy, can be given off by a number of sources including household electrical appliances, heaters, the sun, and x-ray machines. For example, I recall my parents telling me that they were always warned as children not to stand too close to the microwave, or they would get cancer. This is hardly the case, for the type of radiation given off by electrical appliances and heaters isn't harmful enough to cause cancer. However, radiation cancer is caused by high exposure to the sun and x-ray machines. Therefore, as

> exposure to CT scans—a form of x-ray technology—increases, so does the risk of radiation cancer.

- Respond to the Needs of Different Audiences

When writing a paper particular to my major, I had to think about the needs of my audience. It is important to explain a topic and give background information at the beginning of the paper to avoid confusion. It is hard for readers to form an opinion from reading your paper if they don't understand the topic you are writing about. It is also important to not offend your audience, so the writer must determine how to use the three appeals—logos (logic), ethos (ethics), and pathos (emotions)—appropriately. Balancing logos, ethos, and pathos is a major challenge in writing an effective paper. Peer reviews helped me determine where more background information was needed.

To provide background information to the reader in a draft of my argument on the topic of CT scans, I wrote:

> The word <u>tomography</u> originates from the Greek word <u>tomos</u>, meaning "slice," and <u>graphia</u>, or "describing." CT scans, a form of tomography, have been used for years as the predominate method for medical imaging. The scans produce a three-dimensional image of an object's internal structure based on several x-ray images. Original uses of CT scans are to diagnose different cancers, guide biopsies and similar procedures, and to plan surgery or radiation treatment ("Computed").

Also regarding how to respond to the needs of audiences—I learned that it is crucial to maintain a negotiable stance while writing an argument. Arguments are rarely two-sided, so it is important to be open to all sides. If you form an opinion without getting all the facts and hearing other viewpoints, you can't honestly say your claim is correct. It is difficult to persuade your audience to see things from your perspective if you don't know all the perspectives yourself. . . .

Appendix B

Writing Effective Essay Examinations

In many of your college classes, you will be asked to take essay examinations—to sit and write (sometimes on a computer, most often by hand), for a specified period of time, about the material you have learned. Writing essay exams differs in several ways from writing academic papers that you might work on for several weeks. When you write an essay exam, you will find that the following is true:

- You usually have to rely on your memory.
- You don't have much time to figure out what you would like to say.
- You can't get feedback from your instructor and classmates.
- You usually do not have much time for revision.

It is no wonder, then, that some students worry about in-class essay examinations. Our purpose here is to help you overcome any possible fears about essay examinations by giving you some specific strategies to use before and during such tests.

Keep in mind that essay examination situations may come along throughout your life. In your career or in a civic organization, for example, you may be asked to write quickly and without the luxury of invention work or peer feedback:

- As a small-business owner, you might have to draft and complete a cost estimate and quotation in a customer's home.
- As a member of a city council or town board, you may need to comment on a political issue at a town meeting or in response to a question from the media.
- If you write advertising copy or are a journalist, you will frequently have tight deadlines to contend with.

Think of college essay examinations as a way of preparing for life after college, when you often will have to write from memory in a short period of time.

To write an effective response to a question on an essay examination, you will need to do the following:

- Know and understand the information that the examination will cover.
- Be able to relate that information to other topics and ideas you have read about and discussed in class.
- Analyze and understand the question(s) that you are asked to address.

- Construct a thoughtful answer to the question(s), and get your ideas onto paper in the available time.
- Deal with any pre-exam stress issues that you might have. Much of what causes stress for any kind of examination occurs when students are not prepared for the exam, so just being ready can make a big difference in your anxiety level.
- Deal with the examination *scene*—whether you are writing by hand or on a computer, what distractions there might be (other students, noise), and so on.

Getting Ready: Information Gathering, Storage, and Retrieval

When you read and take notes for your college classes, remember that one day you probably will be tested on this information.

Chapter 2 provides useful strategies for reading effectively, and Chapter 3 offers strategies for writing about course material, so we suggest that you revisit those chapters with an eye to using them to help prepare you for essay examinations. Teachers don't expect students to remember everything covered in classes, but you will be expected to recall and understand the main concepts and to relate them to other ideas. As you read and listen in class, make note of the major concepts, and be sure you can explain them.

One reading strategy, for instance, requires you to annotate what you read, not only listing the main points but also jotting down any comments and questions you have about the text. This "talking back" to the text helps you remember what you've read and develop your own ideas and positions on the issues you read about—positions you may be asked to argue in an in-class essay examination.

For more on annotating, see Chapter 2, pages 18–20.

Considering Questions

As you read and listen to class lectures and participate in class discussions, consider the kinds of questions an instructor might ask you to write about. What are the big issues or ideas that have been covered in class or that you have encountered in your reading? As you think of possible questions, record them in your journal. Then set aside some time to write responses to those questions.

For example, in a humanities class where you are considering various periods in the world of art, it is quite possible that, for an in-class essay examination, your teacher will ask you to situate a group of specific artists in the historical context in which they lived and worked. In a political science class, you may be asked to write about how the specific political issues of the day influenced a particular political party or movement. In your history class, you may be asked to explain how the historical events that took place over a period of time led to the start of a war. It is important to recognize that you probably can make a good guess at what questions a teacher will ask on an essay examination, so it is worthwhile for you to consider what those questions might be—before the exam—and how you might answer them.

Analyzing Questions

In addition to thinking about and predicting what questions you might be asked, it is important to understand what the questions are asking you to do.

Because instructors know that students have only a limited time to respond to an essay examination, they generally will ask questions that have a narrow focus. For example, in a history class, a question for a major writing assignment might be worded like this:

Discuss the events that led up to the second Iraq war.

For an in-class examination, where students have only a brief time to respond, however, a question might be worded like this:

In no more than two pages, explain what was defined as Iraq's "no fly zone."

The following question is a writing prompt designed to elicit a brief response and is similar to prompts used on placement examinations—those tests that determine which writing class is appropriate for a student. How might you answer it?

Ernest Hemingway once commented, "As you get older, it is harder to have heroes, but it is sort of necessary." To what extent do you agree or disagree with his observation? Why? Support your opinion with specific examples.

What is this essay question asking you to *do?* If you have not studied Hemingway, this question might worry you, but consider this: The question is not about Hemingway; rather, it asks for your response to what he said about having heroes. Do you think that, in order to construct an effective essay, you might want to define what a hero is to you? That you might want to provide some examples of your own heroes? That when you answer the real question—whether you agree with Hemingway's comment—you will need to provide some specific examples to show what you mean?

When you see the test question(s) for your essay examination, ask yourself what the question(s) asks you to *do:*

- Does it ask you to *analyze* something—to explain how the parts make up the whole? Consider how you might answer this question:

Analyze the use of the magic of flying in relation to the other illusions in the* Harry Potter *films.

For more on analysis, see Chapter 7.

- Does the question ask you to *evaluate* an idea or text or work of art? Consider how you might answer this question:

For more on evaluation, see Chapter 9.

***Of the short stories you read in English class this semester, explain which makes the most effective use of* imagery.**

- Does the exam question ask you to *show connections* between historical trends, or causal chains—to demonstrate that one event led to or caused other events? Here, of course, your answer will need to show clearly the connections that you see. How might you answer this question?

For more on cause and effect, see Chapter 10.

How did the Gulf of Tonkin incident influence the start of the Vietnam War?

- Does the test ask you to *compare* one or more ideas or texts with others? Or does it ask you to *contrast* concepts or ideas or texts? If you are asked to compare things, then you will look for similarities between them; if you are asked to contrast, then you will look for (and provide examples of) differences. How might you answer the following question, from a political science class?

For more on comparison and contrast, see Chapter 13.

Briefly compare Canada's and Australia's reactions to the second Iraq war.

- Does the question ask you to *define* something? When you define something, you most often explain what you think it *is*, and then also set it against what it is *not*. Usually, questions that deal with definitions ask for more than just a dictionary definition.
- Does the question ask that you *discuss* an idea or concept or text? In examination terms, "discuss" means to present the most important features of an idea or concept and then analyze them. You will need to provide examples or other kinds of evidence to support your analysis. "Discuss" in an examination question also leaves your options fairly open—that is, you can discuss briefly or discuss in detail. In an essay *exam*, you can only discuss *briefly*, so consider only the main points you want to make and how you can support those specific points.

For more on definition, see Chapter 13.

- Does the question ask you to *illustrate* something—that is, to provide specific examples to explain the characteristics of the idea or concept?
- Does the examination ask you to *explain* an idea or concept? Think about how you might answer this question:

Explain the significance of* rills *on the lunar surface.

- Does the exam ask you to *critique* something (a work of art, a short story, a poem, an idea), outlining and explaining the something's strengths and weaknesses? Consider how you might answer this question:

Critique William Faulkner's use of* time *in "A Rose for Emily."

For more on rhetorical analysis, see pages 20–23.

- Does the exam question ask that you *review* or *summarize* a particular philosophy or train of thought?
- Does the exam ask you to *analyze* a topic (a text, a local agency, a business plan), to explain how the various aspects of that topic function and work together? Does it ask you to construct a *rhetorical analysis?*

If you are faced with a multiple-part question that seems difficult to answer, draw some lines between each section—in effect, break down the question into its component parts. For example, here is a multipart question:

Noting the recent changes in campus safety problems, argue that your campus needs more or less police protection, but without causing a siege or locked-in mentality for the student body.

Go through and mark each part of the question:

1. Noting the recent changes in campus safety problems
2. argue that your campus needs more or less police protection
3. but without causing a siege
4. or locked-in mentality for the student body

Part 1 asks that you outline what changes in campus safety issues have recently taken place.

Part 2 asks that you take a position on the amount of police protection your campus needs (if you argue for more protection, what does that mean: more police on campus? More police on foot patrol? Bicycle police? Should they be more heavily armed? Should there be police dogs?).

Part 3 asks that you define what a "siege mentality" would be for the students. Part 4 of asks much the same: for a definition and explanation of what a "locked-in mentality" is.

Breaking down a complex question in this manner allows you to see and thus consider each part of the question, an analysis that helps ensure that you will answer all of its parts.

Constructing Thoughtful Answers

Once you understand exactly what the question is asking you, it is helpful to jot down your main ideas. Then think about what organizational method you might use.

Also think about whether it is a *short-* or *long-answer* essay exam. If you have an hour for the essay exam, for example, and there are ten questions, that gives you an average of six minutes to answer each question, a fairly good tip-off that you are working with a short-answer examination. For your answers to be effective, you will need to get right to the point and then state any supporting evidence as concisely as possible.

On the other hand, if you have ninety minutes to respond to one question on an exam, then you have time to brainstorm the ideas you might want to present, to construct a brief cluster diagram of how the parts of your answer relate to each other, and to do other invention work. And as you are writing the exam, you will have time to explain each aspect of your answer in greater detail than on a short-answer exam.

Often, the test question itself will give you a strong clue as to what kind of organization might be effective. For example, consider this sample question from a history class:

An understanding of the past is necessary for understanding the current situation.

Explain what you think the above statement means. Discuss the similarities between the 1964 presidential election, in which Lyndon Johnson soundly defeated Barry Goldwater, and the 2008 presidential election, in which Barack Obama soundly defeated John McCain. How does an understanding of past events help us to understand what happens in the present?

This is a three-part question, which means that a three-part answer might be the most efficient and effective strategy. If you break down the question into its parts, you have the following:

- *Explain* what the statement means. The first part of your answer should do just what the question asks, in your own words and from your own perspective: What do you think the statement means?
- *Discuss* the similarities, as the question asks you to do. What historical trends and events brought about Lyndon Johnson's election? What similar trends and events contributed to Barack Obama's election?
- *Discuss* how past events (in this case, the 1964 presidential election) help us understand a similar event that took place forty-four years later. Do these two events mean a similar election might again happen in 2052?

One type of organization that works well for essay examinations is what is commonly called the "classical scheme." This method of organizing ideas dates back at least to Aristotle, who noticed that effective speakers most often do the following:

1. State their position and what is important (what is "at stake" in the argument).
    a. State their first piece of evidence, always connecting it back to the main point
    b. State their second piece of evidence, connecting it back to the main point
    c. State the third piece of evidence . . .
    d. And so on
2. Briefly outline any objections to the main point; then explain why those objections are incorrect, or at least show how their position can accommodate the objection.
3. Summarize their position, restating their main points.

For more on the classical scheme, see Chapter 14.

If you follow the classical scheme, you will do the following:

- Construct a solid thesis statement, clearly indicating the main point that you want to make in your answer.

- Provide an effective and logical organizational pattern to follow.
- State your main point right at the start, forcing yourself to use supporting details that always relate back to that main idea. (If an idea or piece of supporting evidence does *not* help you accomplish what the test question asks you to do, then why is it there?)
- Acknowledge the other side of an issue or situation or idea, which tells your instructor that you are aware that there are other perspectives or approaches.
- Tie everything together at the end (which is what a conclusion should do).

Dealing with the Examination Scene

You probably have your favorite place to write, where it is quiet (or there is music playing), and where everything you need is at hand (pencil, pen, computer, paper, erasers, coffee), and so on. But you *rarely* will have such an ideal setting for an in-class examination—unless you construct it.

Because you usually know when an exam will take place, it's a good idea to prepare your test-taking environment as best you can, so the writing situation the examination presents is as normal and comfortable as possible. If you usually use a pencil to write, then make sure you have several sharpened pencils with you—or better yet, a good-quality mechanical pencil. If you are allowed to use notes as you write the exam, make sure your notes are clearly written and legible. Here are some other ways to prepare to construct an effective essay examination:

- Know the material that you will be tested on, by using effective studying techniques (tape-recording and then listening to your notes; rewriting your in-class notes on your computer, to help impress them in your memory and also to make them available in readable form; working with others in study groups; and so on).

See Chapter 3, "Writing to Discover and to Learn," for more on study strategies.

- Consider what questions you might be asked by constructing your own test questions. This activity forces you to look at the material from a different viewpoint (teacher rather than student), by asking, What would I like my students to know and understand about this material? What way might be the best way for them to demonstrate that knowledge?
- *Before* taking the exam, think about how you will spend the time you are allotted. Surprisingly, few students really think about how they will spend the hour or ninety minutes or whatever time they will be given for the exam. If you have a plan going into the exam, then you will use your time more wisely. So think about how to use the time you will be allowed effectively, and then consider how much time you might spend on each of these tasks:
  - Understanding the question
  - Getting some ideas onto paper

- Organizing those ideas
- Actually writing the exam
- Revising your response, once you have it on paper
- Editing your work
- Proofreading your work

Note whether some questions are worth more points than others; if so, then it makes sense to spend *more time* on the questions that are worth more. If you encounter a question that you cannot immediately answer, skip it and go on to other questions. That gives you some time to think about it as you work on other answers.

Terry Dolan Writes an Essay Examination

College student Terry Dolan received this prompt for a sixty-minute essay examination:

PROMPT

In his 2005 book *The World Is Flat,* Thomas Friedman talks of "ten forces that flattened the world." Name three of Friedman's ten forces, and explain how they helped to flatten the world.

TERRY DOLAN'S RESPONSE

In his book *The World Is Flat,* Thomas Friedman talks of ten forces that flattened the world. I will discuss how three of these forces—the fall of the Berlin Wall, Netscape going public, and open-sourcing—helped to flatten the twenty-first-century world.

On November 9, 1989, the Berlin Wall fell. While this was a major victory for the forces of democracy in East Berlin and East Germany, it also stood as a symbol for the eventual fall of communism in all of Europe. By opening up Eastern Europe, and eventually the old Soviet Union, to free market capitalism, the end of the Berlin Wall was Friedman's first "flattener." Friedman also talks about the IBM PC computer and how its introduction helped to facilitate the flattening process begun by the fall of the Berlin Wall. The computer with a modem helped to connect people in the old communist bloc with new computer and economic networks.

Friedman's second flattening force happened when the browser Netscape went public. Netscape was a major force because it really opened up the World Wide Web and the Internet for the general population. Before Netscape, the only way people had access to the Internet was in text-only environments. Although that type of access may have been interesting, it mainly attracted scientists and educators. Netscape let people use graphics, and eventually sound and video, online as well. One of the important advantages Netscape offered is that it could be used on any type of computer—PCs, Macs, or Unix boxes.

One important off-shoot of Netscape that helped flatten the world was the fact that when people began to send pictures, audio, and video files over the Internet, they needed more bandwidth. To accommodate this need, companies started laying more fiber optic cable. As a result, phone prices started dropping as well, enabling people to communicate more and faster.

Another flattener, according to Friedman, is the open-source movement. Unlike most software, you can download open-source software for free. Friedman explains that it works on the same model as scientific peer review. People participate in developing the software for the good of the group and the notoriety it gives them. The main open-source software that Friedman discusses is the Apache Web server. Friedman talks about how many of the main Internet Web sites run on Apache servers. Because there is no cost involved in buying the software, just about anyone who knows how can run a Web server.

An even more important example of open-source software is probably the Linux operating system. Linux is a kind of Unix, a powerful computer operating system. The advantage to Linux is that it's cheap (you can download it for free) and flexible (lots of computer people are constantly working to make it even better). The disadvantage to Linux is that most software is written to run on PCs. But more and more open-source software is being written to run on Linux boxes. You can now get Open Office and similar open-source programs that will let you do just about anything you could do with Microsoft software. All the open-source programs are free. You can also get Firefox, a web browser that runs on Linux. In other parts of the world, lots of computers run on Linux and use open-source software.

Finally, what I think is the most interesting point about all of Friedman's flatteners is that they're all about technology, mainly computer technology, and how that helps all of us connect to one another faster and better. Technology is what's making the world flat.

Credits

TEXT CREDITS

PAGE xl, xli: "WPA Outcome Statement for First-Year Composition," adopted by the Council of Writing Program Administrators (WPA), April 2000. This work is licensed under a Creative Commons license: http://creativecommons.org/by/nd/3.0/us/.

CHAPTER 2

p. 19: Eric Bangeman, "The Ethics of "Stealing" a WiFi Connection." Copyright © 2008 Condé Nast Publications. All rights reserved. Originally published in *Ars Technica*. Reprinted by permission. **p. 29:** Carlton Vogt, "Downloading Music: Harmful to the Artist, the Record Company, or Neither?," Ethics Matters column in *InfoWorld* and on www.infoworld.com.

CHAPTER 4

p. 47: "A Priceless Lesson in Humility," Copyright © 2008 by Felipe Morales, part of the This I Believe Essay Collection found at www.thisibelieve.org, Copyright © 2005–2009, This I Believe, Inc. Used with permission of This I Believe, Inc. **p. 47:** www.thisibelieve.org, Copyright © 2005–2009, This I Believe, Inc. Used with permission of This I Believe, Inc. Explorer screen shot reprinted with permission from Microsoft Corporation. **p. 57:** Tanya Barrientos's "Se Habla Espanol" Copyright © 2004 by Tanya Barrientos. From *Border-Line Personalities* edited by Michelle Herrera Mulligan and Robyn Moreno. Compilation Copyright © 2004 by Michele Herrera-Mulligan and Robyn Moreno. Reprinted by permission of HarperCollins Publishers and the author. **p. 66:** Excerpt from *Growing Up* by Russell Baker. Reprinted by permission of Don Congdon Associates, Inc. Copyright © 1982 by Russell Baker.

CHAPTER 5

p. 107: John Lurz, "DeMystify Thyself: Working Closely with Brilliance and Getting the Hang of It," *Princeton Alumni Weekly (PAW)*, October 23, 2002. Used with permission.

CHAPTER 6

p. 139: Copyright © 2005 by National Youth Leadership Council, www.nylc.org. All rights reserved. **p. 143:** "Clocking Cultures," Carol Ezzell, *Scientific American*, September 2002. Reprinted with permission. Copyright 2002 by Scientific American, Inc. All rights reserved. **p. 154:** *Journal of Leadership and Organizational Studies* by Pamela Brandes, Stephanie L. Castro, Matrecia S.L.

James, Arthur D. Martinez, Timothy A. Matherly, Gerald R. Ferris, Wayne A. Hochwarter. Copyright © 2008 by Sage Publications Inc. Journals. Reproduced with permission of Sage Publications Inc. Journals in the format Textbook and Other book via Copyright Clearance Center. **p. 162:** "Did You Know" note from the University of Nebraska at Lincoln is reprinted by permission of the University of Nebraska-Lincoln Landscape Services. **p. 167:** "Easy Voter Guide: California Edition" is reprinted by permission of the League of Women Voters of California, www.easyvoter.org. **p. 160:** Rates of Biodegradability is reprinted by permission of Worldwise, Inc.

CHAPTER 7

p. 180: "Fear Factor: Psychologists help people conquer anxieties and phobias," Robin Gerrow, is reprinted by permission of the author. **p. 191:** "Putting in the Hours," James M. Lang, The Chronicle of Higher Education, May 16, 2003. Copyright © 2003, The Chronicle of Higher Education. Reprinted with permission. **p. 195:** From *Strapped: Why America's 20- and 30- Somethings Can't Get Ahead* by Tamara Draut. Copyright © 2005 by Tamara Draut. Used by permission of Doubleday, a division of Random House, Inc., and by permission of Tamara Draut. For on-line information about other Random house, Inc. books and authors, see the Internet web site at http://www.randomhouse.com. **p. 199:** Jesse Hassenger, "Irony as a Disguise." Reprinted with permission from the author. **p. 210:** Bar graph showing Penn State Tuition Increases for the Past Five Years based on data from "Through the Roof," Bill Schackner, Pittsford Post-Gazette, 7/15/2006.

CHAPTER 8

p. 235: "Letter Responding to Dowd," Brian J.G. Pereira, *The New York Times*, September, 2004. Reprinted by permission of Dr. Brian J.G. Pereira. **p. 240:** Liz Emrich, "Slut-O-Ween," Open Salon, October 19, 2008. http://open.salon.com/content.php?cid=31400. Used with permission. **p. 247:** Definition of "objectification." Copyright © 2006 by Houghton Mifflin Harcourt Publishing Company. Reproduced by permission from *The American Heritage Dictionary of the English Language, Fourth Edition*. **p. 253:** Chart and data on temperature differences is reprinted by permission of Dr. Charles Ophardt, Professor of Chemistry, Elmhurst College, Elmhurst, IL.

CHAPTER 9

p. 266: American Film Institute's List of 100 Greatest American Movies is reprinted by permission of the American Film Institute. **p. 277:** R. Albert Mohler, "Ranking the Presidents: A New Look at the Best and the Worst," Wednesday, June 09, 2004. http://www.albertmohler.com/commentary_read.php?cdate=2004-06-09. Reprinted with permission of the author. **p. 282:** Movie review of Star Trek, "A Fresh Frontier: In the best prequel ever, 'Star Trek' reboots the franchise and reminds us why we love it" by Ty Burr, *Boston Globe*, May 5, 2009. © 2009 Globe Newspaper Company. Reprinted with permission. **p. 285:** Movie review of *Star Trek*, "Take it to the bridge: A reboot full of pure energy and cracking comic timing, the new first generation of an old favourite is a delight" by Peter Bradshaw, *The Guardian*, May 8, 2009. Copyright Guardian News & Media Ltd 2009. Used with permission.

CHAPTER 10

p. 310: "Sunspots Cause Trouble" from Space and Weather News website, October 27, 2003. Reprinted with permission of Dr. Tony Phillips. **p. 321:** "The Ruling That Changed America," Juan Williams is reprinted from *American School Board Journal*, April 2004. Copyright © 2004 National School Boards Association. All rights reserved. **p. 327:** Robert Reich, The Real Reason Why Highway Deaths Are Down, August 20, 2008, http://robertreich.blogspot.com/2008_08_01_archive.html. Used with permission. **p. 353:** Map showing temperatures in the Sargasso Sea during the last ice age from "Study hints at extreme climate change," *Environmental News Network*, October 28, 1999. Reprinted by permission of ENN.com.

CHAPTER 11

TA 11.1: "Why Microlending," Accion, is reprinted by permission. **p. 492:** "The Nursing Crisis: The Solution Lies Within," Michele Mise was originally published in the *Journal of Undergraduate Nursing Scholarship*, Fall 2002. Reprinted by permission of the author, Michele Mise. **p. 502:** Gibor Basri, "An Open Letter to the Campus Community." Used with permission. **p. 507-508:** Amy Baskin and Heather Fawcett, "Request a Work Schedule Change with a Flexibility Proposal Memo," from the book *More Than a Mom: Living a Full and Balanced Life When Your Child Has Special Needs*, Appendix 3; copyright © 2006 Amy Baskin and Heather Fawcett. Woodbine House, 2006. Used with permission of the authors. **p. 390:** Courtesy of SkySong, rendering by Pei Cobb Freed & Partners.

CHAPTER 12

p. 407: "Geometry" from *The Yellow House on the Corner*, Carnegie-Mellon University Press, © 1980 by Rita Dove. Reprinted by permission of the author. **p. 411:** Hemingway, Ernest. *The Old Man and the Sea*. New York: Charles Scribner's Sons, 1952. **p. 413:** Wideman, John Edgar. Ascent by Balloon from the Yard of Walnut Street Jail. *Callaloo* 19:1 (1996), 1-5. © 1996 Charles H. Rowell. Reprinted with permission of The John Hopkins University Press.

CHAPTER 13

p. 432: Excerpt from Barbara Ehrenreich, "A Step Back to the Workhouse." First published in *Ms.* magazine, November 1987. Reprinted by permission of Ms. magazine, © 1987. **p. 442:** "Viacom Sues YouTube for $1 Billion," by Seth Sutel, APAA Business Writer. Used with permission of The Associated Press Copyright© 2009. All rights reserved. **p. 445:** Excerpt from *Rats: Observations on the History and Habitat of the City's Most Unwanted Inhabitants* by Robert Sullivan. Bloomsbury USA, Granta Books. **p. 446:** "What is Good Bread?" is reprinted by permission of Ken Forkish, Ken's Artisan Bakery and Café. **p. 449:** Definition of "Mugwump" is reprinted by permission of Michael Quinion, World Wide Words. **p. 449:** Definition of "Luddite" from TechTargetNetwork is reprinted by permission of WhatIs.com

CHAPTER 14

p. 465: "Time to Cash Out: Why Paper Money Hurts the Economy" by David Wolman, from Wired.com, 05.22.09, http://www.wired.com/culture/culturereviews/magazine/17-06/st_essay. Used with permission. **p. 473:** Reprinted courtesy of *Sports Illustrated*: "Nothing but Nets" by Rick Reilly, May 1, 2006. Copyright 2006, Time Inc. All rights reserved.

CHAPTER 18

p. 505: ESOL Flyer from Fenway Neighborhood Service Center is reprinted by permission of Action for Boston Community Development, Inc. **Fig. 18.1, p. 507:** Colorwheel is reprinted by permission of Stanford Brands, Newell Rubbermaid, Inc. **Fig. 18.3, p. 508:** Poster for Israel Society for Ecology and Environmental Quality Sciences is reprinted by permission of Weizmann Institute of Science. **Fig. 18.4, p. 513:** Pie chart showing composition of a slice of pizza are reprinted by permission of Mathematics Leagues, Inc. **Table 18.1, p. 514:** Table 1.2 from How Much Information 2003, http://www2.sims.berkeley.edu/research/projects/how-much-info-2003/execsum.htm#stored, accessed February 12, 2009. Used with permission. **Fig. 18.5, p. 513:** Bar graph showing composition of a slice of pizza are reprinted by permission of Mathematics Leagues, Inc. **Fig. 18.7, p. 516:** Relationship between a Car's Mileage and Its Value is reprinted by permission of Mathematics Leagues, Inc. **Fig. 18.8, p. 517:** Universal Stain Color Selection Guide is reprinted by permission of Come To Buy, Inc., www.ComeToBuy.com. **Fig. 18.9, p. 518:** Bigfoot Water Rocket Launcher Flowchart is reprinted by permission of Gary Ensmenger, President, Bigfoot Stilt Company. **Fig. 18.12, p. 522:** Drawing of a cell nucleus is reprinted by permission of David L. Spector, Cold Spring Harbor Laboratory, New York. **Fig. 18.13, p. 523:** Venn diagram on sustainable development is reprinted by permission of Manchester Development Education Project. **Fig. 18.15, p. 525:** Neanderthal Range Map is reprinted by permission of Richard G. Klein. **Fig. 18.18, p. 526:** Reprinted by permission of Randy Glasbergen. **Fig. 18.20, p. 531:** Two maps of the U.S., one plain and one distorted, from "Diffusion-based methods for producing density-equalizing maps," Michael Gastner and Mark Newman, PNAS, May 18, 2004. Copyright © 2004 National Academy of Sciences, USA. Reprinted with permission.

CHAPTER 19

p. 535: Definition of "adolescent," adapted. Copyright © 2007 by Houghton Mifflin Harcourt Publishing Company. Reproduced by permission from *The American Heritage Medical Dictionary, Revised Edition*. **p. 536:** Search result for keywords, "male" and "gang" are reprinted by permission of EBSCO Publishing. **Fig. 19.1, p. 537:** Lexis/Nexis and the Knowledge Burst Logo are registered trademarks of Reed Elsevier Properties, Inc. used with the permission of Lexis/Nexis. **Figs. 19.2, 19.3, pp. 538, 539:** Reprinted by permission of Google Brand Features. **Fig. 19.4, p. 541** Screen image from TIME.com. Copyright © 2007 Time Inc. Reprinted by permission. **Fig. 19.6, p. 544:** Reprinted by permission of Jim Foster, Editor, www.diet-blog.com. **Fig. 19.7, p. 545:** http://en.wikipedia.org/wiki/Textbook **p. 546:** Blurb about authors Duffy and Gillig from the Greenwood Press online catalog is reproduced with permission of Greenwood Publishing Group, Inc., Westport, CT. **Fig. 19.8, p. 547:** Reprinted by permission of Alex Alonso, Editor, www.streetgangs.com.

CHAPTER 20

pp. 564, 565: Excerpt from movie review of *Harry Potter and the Sorcerer's Stone* by Roger Ebert, from the Roger Ebert column © 2001. Universal Press Syndicate. Used with permission. **Fig. 20.2, pp. 575, 576:** Title and copyright pages from *Unpaid Professionals* by Andrew Zimbalist are reprinted by permission of Princeton University Press. **Fig. 20.3, p. 579:** Journal table of contents is reprinted by permission of Council of Writing Program Administrators. **Fig. 20.4, p. 583:** Copyright © EBSCO Publishing, Inc. Reprinted with permission. All rights reserved. **Fig. 20.6, pp. 598, 599:** Title and copyright pages from *Teen Gangs* by Maureen P. Duffy and Scott Edward Gillig. Copyright © 2004 by Maureen P. Duffy and Scott Edward Gillig. Reproduced with permission of Greenwood Publishing Group, Inc., Westport, CT. **Fig. 20.7, p. 602:** Journal table of contents page for *Child Development*, Nov/Dec 2005, Vol. 76, n. 6, published by Blackwell Publishing. Used with permission. **Fig. 20.8, p. 606:** Image published with permission of ProQuest LLC. Further reproduction is prohibited without permission. CSA Illumina is produced by ProQuest LLC. Inquiries may be made to: ProQuest LLC, [7200 Wisconsin Avenue, Suite 601, Bethesda, MD 20814 USA. Telephone (301) 961-6700; Email: info@csa.com; web-page: www.csa.com.]

PHOTO CREDITS

Page xxv, xxvii, xxx: © Rubberball Productions; **xxvi**: Getty Images/Digital Vision; **xxxi**: Fancy Photography/Veer

CHAPTER 1

Page 1: Getty Images/Digital Vision, (inset) © Digital Vision/Alamy; **7**: (left) © PhotoAlto/PunchStock, (right) © JGI/Jamie Grill/Getty Images

CHAPTER 2

Page 15: Getty Images/Digital Vision, (inset) Ken Karp for MMH; **21**: Courtesy of BBH, Singapore

CHAPTER 3

Page 33: © Fancy Photography/Veer, (inset) PhotoSpin, Inc./Alamy; **38**: © SuperStock, Inc.

CHAPTER 4

Page 47: (top) Photo courtesy of Felipe Morales, (bottom) © Anton J. Geisser/agefotostock; **51**: © PunchStock; **57**: David Cruz/Newscom Photos; **62**: Ruth Fremson/The New York Times/Redux; **66**: Jeffrey MacMillan for WGBH/Masterpiece Theatre; **74**: Courtesy of the author

CHAPTER 5

Page 90: (A) Courtesy of NASA, (inset B) Courtesy of NSAA Jet Propulsion Laboratory; **91**: (inset C) Courtesy of NASA and STScl; **97**: © Bob Daemmrich/PhotoEdit; **101**: Image courtesy of Kenneth Chang and The New York Times; **107**: Courtesy of John Lurz; **111**: (inset) Photograph by Cecil Stoughton, White House, in the John F. Kennedy Presidential Library and Museum, Boston; **121**: Quarter-dollar coin image from the United States Mint

CHAPTER 6

Page 133: (top inset) © Photodisc/PunchStock, (bottom inset) Courtesy of NASA; **140**: © Bob Daemmrich/PhotoEdit; **143**: Photo courtesy of Carol Ezzell Webb; **147**: © The New York Times/Redux Pictures; **154**: Courtesy of Pamela Brandes

CHAPTER 7

Page 180: © Stockbyte/PunchStock; **181**: (top inset) Centers for Disease Control/Harold G. Scott, (bottom) © Rick Gomez/Corbis; **187**: © The McGraw-Hill Companies/Lars Niki, photographer; **191**: Courtesy of James Lang; **195**: Courtesy Demos: A Network for Ideas & Action, www.demos.org; **199**: Courtesy of The Partnership For A Drug-Free America

CHAPTER 8

Page 222: Courtesy of Mexico Tourism Board; **223**: (top inset) © The McGraw-Hill Companies/Lars Niki, photographer, (bottom inset) © Michelangelo Gratton/Getty Images; **229**: © AP Photos; **233**: Fred R. Conrad/The New York Times/Redux; **235**: Courtesy of Dr. Brian Pereira; **237**: Courtesy Allsup, Inc.; **240**: (top inset) Courtesy Liz Emrich, (bottom) © Darren Green Photography/Alamy

CHAPTER 9

Page 266: © RF/Corbis; **267**: (top inset) © John Eder/Stone/Getty Images, (bottom inset) RKO Radio Pictures Inc./Photofest; **273**: © Luke Stettner/Getty Images; **277**: © 2009, All Rights Reserved, www.albertmohler.com; **282**: Courtesy of Ty Burr; **285**: (top inset) Linda Nylind/Guardian News, (bottom) © Everett Collection, Inc.; **298**: © Jules Frazier/Getty Images

CHAPTER 10

Page 310: Courtesy Lauri Kangas; **311**: (top inset) © ERIK ISAKSON/Getty Images, (bottom inset) © Fancy Photography/Veer; **317**: MM Design; **321**: PRNewsFoto/SeniorNet/Newscom; **327**: © Ed Quinn/CORBIS; **330**: U.S. Food & Drug Administration

CHAPTER 11

Page 359: (top inset) © Sonda Dawes/The Image Works, (bottom inset) © Scott Olson/Getty Images; **365**: © Najlah Feanny/Corbis; **369**: Courtesy of Michelle Mise Pollard; **375**: © Peg Skorpinski; **379**: (top) Courtesy Amy Baskin, Jack Kesselman, photographer, (bottom) Courtesy Heather Fawcett; **390**: Courtesy SkySong, The ASU Scottsdale Innovation Center, rendering by Todd & Associates Architects

CHAPTER 12

Page 407: JP Beato III Photography, (bottom inset) Burke/Triolo/Brand X Pictures/Jupiterimages; **413**: © Lawrence Lucier/Getty Images; **420** (top inset): Photograph by Betsy Rhodes, (right) From Wabi-Sabi by Mark Reibstein and illustrated by Ed Young. Copyright © 2009 by Mark Reibstein and Ed Young. By permission of Little, Brown and Company; **421**: From Wabi-Sabi by Mark Reibstein and illustrated by Ed Young. Copyright © 2009 by Mark Reibstein and Ed Young. By permission of Little, Brown and Company; **426**: Twentieth Century Fox/Photofest; **427**: © Marvel Entertainment, Inc.

CHAPTER 13

Page 429: BananaStock/JupiterImages, (bottom inset) BananaStock/PictureQuest; **443**: © Paramount Pictures/Bureau L.A. Collection/Corbis; **447**: © Jim Wehtje/Getty Images

CHAPTER 14

Page 457: (top) © Mike Segar/Reuters/Corbis, (bottom inset) MacNeil/Lehrer Productions; **461**: © SuperStock, Inc.; **465**: Brett Patterson; **467**: © Sijmen Hendriks; **469**: Courtesy of Stanley Fish; **471**: © Roger Ressmeyer/Corbis; **473**: Courtesy Sports Illustrated; **475**: Copyright © 2007 American Civil Liberties Union

CHAPTER 15

Page 479: (top) BananaStock/JupiterImages, (bottom inset) © Holger Hill/Getty Images

CHAPTER 16

Page 485: © Michael Doolittle/Alamy, (bottom inset) © PhotoSpin, Inc./Alamy; **488**: © Kent Mathews/Riser/Getty Images

CHAPTER 17

Page 493: © images-of-france/Alamy; **493**: (bottom inset) © The Metropolitan Museum of Art; **502**: (top) © Ken Light, (bottom left) © Ken Light/Corbis, (bottom right) © Owen Franken/Corbis

CHAPTER 18

Page 505: (top) United Nations Graphic Design Unity. Outreach Division/DPI, (bottom inset) ABCD Parker Hill/Fenway Neighborhood Service; **508**: (left) USDA Forest Service, (right) Department of Environmental Sciences and

Energy Research/Weizmann Institute of Science; **517**: Courtesy of FUHR Industrial, www.furhindustrial.com; **519**: © Bettmann/Corbis; **520**: Library of Congress, Prints and Photographs Division [LC-DIG-cwpb-04326]; **524**: New Line/Saul Zaentz/Wing Nut/ The Kobal Collection; **528**: Courtesy of Feed the Children, Inc.

CHAPTER 19

Page 533: (top) BananaStock/JupiterImages, (bottom inset) © Stockbyte/Punchstock; **540**: (top) Reprinted with permission of Cambridge University Press, (bottom) American Psychiatric Publishing, Inc.; **541**: PRNewsFoto/Newsweek/AP Photos; **542**: (top to bottom) PRNewsFoto/Business Traveler magazine, Nathan Jalani/AP Photos, Courtesy of Foreign Affairs, Courtesy Arizona Highways; **546**: Maureen Duffy, Teen Gangs. Copyright © 2004 by Greenwood Press. Reproduced with permission of Greenwood Publishing Group, Inc. Westport, CT

CHAPTER 20

Page 559: (top) © The McGraw-Hill Companies, Inc./Christopher Kerrigan, photographer, (bottom inset) Pixland/AGE Fotostock

Index

D

E

M

N

O

Z